Thinking About Texts

Related titles from the same publisher:

A History of English Literature	*Michael Alexander*
The Practice of Reading	*D. Alsop & C. Walsh*
The Novel	*André Brink*
Literary Theory from Plato to Barthes	*Richard Harland*
How to Begin Studying English Literature	*Nicholas Marsh*
The Bedford Glossary of Critical & Literary Terms	*R. Murfin & S. Ray*
Twentieth-Century Literary Theory	*K. M. Newton*
Literary Theories	*J. Wolfreys & W. Baker*

Thinking About Texts

AN INTRODUCTION TO ENGLISH STUDIES

Chris Hopkins

palgrave

First published 2001 by
PALGRAVE
Houndmills, Basingstoke, Hampshire RG21 6XS and
175 Fifth Avenue, New York, N. Y. 10010
Companies and representatives throughout the world

PALGRAVE is the new global academic imprint of
St. Martin's Press LLC Scholarly and Reference Division and
Palgrave Publishers Ltd (formerly Macmillan Press Ltd).

ISBN 0–333–67607–6 hardback
ISBN 0–333–67608–4 paperback

This book is printed on paper suitable for recycling and
made from fully managed and sustained forest sources.

A catalogue record for this book is available
from the British Library.

Library of Congress Cataloging-in-Publication Data
Hopkins, Chris, 1960–
    Thinking about texts : an introduction to English studies / Chris Hopkins.
        p. cm.
    Includes bibliographical references and index.
    ISBN 0–333–67607–6 — ISBN 0–333–67608–4 (pbk.)
     1. English literature—History and criticism—Theory, etc. I. Title.
    PR21 .H66 2000
    820.9'0001—dc21
                                              00–059122

10   9   8   7   6   5   4   3   2   1
10   09   08   07   06   05   04   03   02   01

Printed in China

To Lisa and Sam Hopkins

(who will be glad to hear there's only about another week's work left to do)

Contents

As I reread these texts, I am struck by one feature about which the reader may well have some reservations: their 'intermediate' character. I am not interested in speculation pure and simple, or in the description of facts as such; I continue to move between the two extremes. The entire field of literary theory has this intermediate status: it is challenged by a wholly general reflection on the one hand, and by the study of concrete texts on the other. The same ambiguity persists in my writing style. I try to avoid both impressionistic writing – which I judge irresponsible, not because it is devoid of theory, but because it refuses to acknowledge theory – and terroristic formalism, where the author's sole object is to discover a more precise notation for an observation that is often quite imprecise in itself. I should like my discourse to remain permeable without becoming formless. Clearly, in trying to have it both ways, one risks losing on both counts: an unenviable fate, to which I shall nevertheless adhere.

Prefatory Note to Todorov's *Discourses of Genre* (1978, 1990), p. vii

Acknowledgements

I would like to acknowledge the support given to me (in the way of funding study leave between 1995 and 1999) by the Cultural Research Institute and the Centre for Humanities Research at Sheffield Hallam. My thanks to the heads of those Research Centres, Professor Mick Worboys and Professor Robert Miles – for moral as well as financial support.

My thanks also to the many colleagues in English Studies and in History at Sheffield Hallam who have shown interest, given support and made contributions to this textbook. In particular, I would like to thank Dr Philip Cox (who first had the idea of such a book), Professor Archie Markham (for a lunchtime conversation which developed into a section of the book, and for the more formal interview which he afterwards kindly gave me as E. A. Markham), Professor Peter Cain in History (for casting a professional historical eye over some of the book, as well as for many other literary/historical conversations), Dr Dave Hurry and Ian Baker (for reading my attempts at a description of the book) and Dr Lisa Hopkins (for reading the early drafts).

I would also like to thank all the English students at Sheffield Hallam from 1990 to 1999 who have, in various forms, tested the kind of thinking on which this book is based, as well as those who test drove *Thinking About Texts* more specifically during the past four years. In particular, I would like to thank Alison Wagstaff (1993–6) and Karen Morton (1994–7) for their critical reading of early drafts, and the Level 1 BA English and History cohort of 1998–9 for their pilot use of almost-finished drafts. Needless to say, I probably did not always take the good advice I was offered by colleagues and students; equally needless to say, the imperfections remain my own.

I would also like to thank Margaret Bartley and Beverley Tarquini at the publishers for their exceptional patience with me and my book, and Gabriella Stiles for chasing the large number of permissions needed for *Thinking About Texts*.

Chris Hopkins

Jean Baudrillard, 'The Reality Gulf' from the *Guardian* 11.1.91. Copyright © the *Guardian*. By permission of the *Guardian*.

Anton Chekhov, from 'The Cherry Orchard' in *Plays by Anton Chekhov*, trans. Elizaveta Fen (Penguin Classics, 1954). Copyright © Elizaveta Fen, 1954. By permission of Penguin Books Ltd.

Hélène Cixous, from 'Sorties' reprinted by permission of the University of Massachusetts Press from Elaine Marks and Isabelle de Courtivron (eds), *New French Feminisms: An Anthology*. (Amherst: University of Massachusetts Press, 1980). Copyright © 1980 by the University of Massachusetts Press.

David Dabydeen, 'On Not being Milton: Nigger Talk in England Today' by kind permission of the author.

Mons Daveson, from *Desert Interlude*, permission granted by Harlequin Books S.A. First published by Mills and Boon® in Great Britain in 1990. Copyright © Mons Daveson 1990.

Terry Eagleton, from *Literary Theory: An Introduction* Second Edition. Copyright © 1996. By permission of Blackwell Publishers Ltd.

Anthony Easthope, from *Literary into Cultural Studies* published by Routledge (1991). By permission of Taylor and Francis Books Ltd.

Henry Louis Gates, Jr, from *Figures in Black: Words, Signs and the 'Racial Self'*. Reproduced by kind permission of the author.

Sandra Gilbert & Susan Gubar from *The Madwoman in the Attic: The Woman Writer and the Nineteenth Century Literary Imagination* (1979). Copyright © 1979 by Sandra Gilbert and Susan Gubar. By permission of Yale University Press.

Sally Goodman, 'Against the Revolution', Paul St Vincent, 'Lambchop has Black Thoughts', E. A. Markham, 'Sojourn in a Second Language', from *Living in Disguise* by E. A. Markham, 1986. By permission of Anvil Press Poetry Ltd.

Walter Greenwood, from *Love on the Dole* (1933). Reproduced by permission of the copyright holders.

The *Guardian* 'What is Britishness?' from the *Guardian* 20.1.99. Copyright © the *Guardian*. By permission of the *Guardian*.

Radclyffe Hall, from *The Well of Loneliness*. Published by Weidenfeld and Nicolson. Copyright © 1928 by Radclyffe Hall. Copyright renewed © 1956 by Una Lady Troubridge. Reprinted by permission of Brandt and Brandt Literary Agents, Inc. and Orion Publishing Group Ltd.

Ivan Hannaford, from *Race: The History of an Idea in the West*, pp. 164–7. By permission of Johns Hopkins University Press.

Tony Harrison, 'A Cold Coming', from *A Cold Coming: Gulf War Poems* (Bloodaxe, 1991). Copyright © Tony Harrison 1991. By permission of Gordon Dickerson on behalf of the author.

Rudyard Kipling, 'Puck's Song' by permission of A. P. Watt Ltd on behalf of The National Trust for Places of Historic Interest or Natural Beauty.

D. H. Lawrence, from *Women in Love*. Copyright © 1920, 1922 by D. H. Lawrence, renewed 1948, 1950 by Frieda Lawrence. By permission of Laurence Pollinger Ltd, and Viking Penguin, a division of Penguin Putnam, Inc. and the Estate of Frieda Lawrence Ravagli.

Liz Lochhead, from *Dracula* in *Mary Queen of Scots got her Head Chopped Off and Dracula* (Penguin Books, 1989). Copyright © Liz Lochhead, 1988. By permission of Penguin Books Ltd and the Rod Hall Agency Limited.

John Mole, 'The Advancement of Learning' from *Feeding the Lake*, Secker and Warburg (1981). By kind permission of the author.

Marianne Moore, 'Poetry' by permission of Faber and Faber Ltd and Scribner, a division of Simon and Schuster Inc. from *The Collected Poems of Marianne Moore*. Copyright © 1935 by Marianne Moore; copyright renewed © 1963 by Marianne Moore and T. S. Eliot.

Edwin Morgan, 'Spacepoem 3: Off Course' from *Selected Poems* (1985), reproduced by permission of Carcanet Press Ltd.

Sean O'Casey, from 'Juno and the Paycock' from *Plays One* by permission of Faber and Faber Ltd.

George Orwell, from *Coming up for Air*. Copyright © 1939, George Orwell, reproduced by permission of A. M. Heath & Co. Ltd. on behalf of Mark Hamilton as the Literary Executor of the Estate of the late Sonia Brownell Orwell, and Martin Secker and Warburg Ltd and Harcourt, Inc.

George Orwell, from *Notes on Nationalism*. Copyright © George Orwell, 1945. By permission of Bill Hamilton as the Literary Executor of the Estate of Sonia Brownell Orwell, Martin Secker and Warburg Ltd.

Definitions from the *Oxford English Dictionary* second edition (1989). By permission of Oxford University Press.

Ezra Pound, 'In A Station of the Metro' from *Personae*. Copyright © 1926 by Ezra Pound. By permission of Faber and Faber and New Directions Publishing Corp.

Ernest Renan, 'What is a Nation?' from *Nation and Narration* ed. Homi K. Bhabha, published by Routledge (1990). By permission of Taylor and Francis Books Ltd.

Theodore Roethke, 'Child on top of a Greenhouse' from *The Collected Poems of Theodore Roethke*. Copyright © 1946 by Editorial Publications, Inc. By permission of Faber and Faber and Doubleday, a division of Random House, Inc.

Edward W. Said, from *Orientalism*. Copyright © 1978 by Edward W. Said. Reprinted by permission of Pantheon Books, a division of Random House, Inc.

Gertrude Stein, from *The Autobiography of Alice B. Toklas* (1977) published by Penguin Books Ltd. Reproduced by permission of David Higham Associates.

Tom Stoppard, from *Rosencrantz and Guildenstern Are Dead*. Copyright © 1967. By permission of Faber and Faber and Grove/Atlantic, Inc.

R. S. Thomas, 'IagoPrytherch' by permission of Macmillan Publishers.

Hayden White, from *The Content of Form: Narrative Discourse and Historical Representation*, pp. 24–5, 4, 45, 20–1, ix–xi. By permission of Johns Hopkins University Press.

William Carlos Williams, 'This is Just to Say' from *Collected Poems: 1909–1939, Volume 1*. Copyright © 1938 by New Directions Publishing Corp. By permission of Carcanet Press and New Directions Publishing Corp.

Virginia Woolf, 'The Captain's Deathbed' from 'Mr. Bennett and Mrs. Brown'. By permission of the Society of Authors as the literary representative of the Estate of Virginia Woolf.

Every effort has been made to trace the copyright holders but if any have been inadvertently overlooked the publishers will be pleased to make the necessary arrangement at the first opportunity.

Introduction

1 *Thinking About Texts* – How and Why?

Like all books, this one, *Thinking About Texts: An Introduction to English Studies* was written for certain purposes and with certain assumptions in mind. The aim of this introduction is to explain some of my reasons for writing this book, and for writing it in this particular form. By providing some of the history of the book's production, I would like to do two things for its intended readers. Firstly, since the book itself aims at making ideas about literature clearer and more explicit, it seems right that it should be explicit about how it is approaching this task. Secondly, an account of the intentions of the book provides an overview of how it is meant to be used, and what I hope its readers may get from it.

The idea of the book came from my own teaching at Sheffield Hallam University, particularly on a first-year course called 'Skills for English'. The course aimed to introduce all English students to degree-level study in English. Some of the topics were to do with immediately practical matters (what kind of referencing and bibliography should be used, etc.), but more theoretical matters also needed to be addressed. It was felt that students doing English should have some space provided not just to 'do' English, but also to think about what doing English might mean, and indeed what English was. This is not a task that English or English Literature degrees have always felt to be necessary. On the contrary, generations of English students have spent their three years reading literature, without necessarily being asked to think about what exactly they were doing, or what (or if) literature was. The feeling that there was a need for this kind of thinking arose not (just) from my thoughts about the matter, but because of changes in ways of thinking about English throughout many of the institutions of English Literature.

In particular, this was a response to the rise of theory as a concern of university English departments. During the nineteen eighties, theory, from being a subject of debate, became a central part of English as a university subject. It was not so much that every lecturer wished to discuss theory, or that every student did. But a degree course in English which did not include any discussion of theory no longer represented the norm. However, this was very much a matter for higher education. 'A' level teaching of English did not (and has not) incorporated theory as a necessary part of English. This is not necessarily a bad thing – 'A' level students may well need to concentrate on learning to read and interpret texts, since this is a skill which, up to a certain level, is taken for granted by university courses. The taking for granted part of this is, in fact, itself problematic, partly because while 'A' level syllabuses and access courses tend still to concentrate on the careful reading of set texts, there is less emphasis than at one time on the 'close reading' or 'practical criticism' of a variety of other texts. In one way, students coming to study English at university are very skilled at reading texts, but in other ways they are not necessarily equipped to read the variety and rapid sequence of texts with which degree courses present them (these could, even within a first-year course, range from, say, Andrew Marvell to Baudrillard). Moreover, 'A' level syllabuses tend to be about the interpretation of particular texts, rather than about how we (might) read texts in general. There is usually little explicit exploration of method or theory or the contexts of interpretation. The development of advanced skills in reading texts (any text, any texts, I hope) is as central to the purposes of this book as its other purposes (it is designed to enhance such skills). But to really learn the critical practices needed to interpret texts, I think that one needs to have a sense of method and theory – of how we might read, in short. However, the textual orientation of 'A' level does mean that theory is something which is completely new at university. A sudden initiation into theory may not necessarily be the solution to a lack of theory – partly because theories (e.g. the major works of theorists) are themselves complex texts of a kind very unfamiliar to most English students, partly because such theoretical knowledge needs to be applied to the reading of texts and textual issues of which students may have as yet little clear understanding.

What I wanted to do in my first year Skills teaching was to introduce students not so much to theory as to ways of thinking about English which were new to them, and which would help them with reading English in all its forms, including theory when they came to it. I wanted to do this by using the skills that students brought with them (certain skills in reading certain kinds of texts) but in such a way that the thinking around, behind, preceding the reading of texts became clearer to its users. This would be in contrast to a more direct teaching of theory itself.

Theory itself is, like English, many different things, and there is no single way of teaching it or using it. In some forms though, theory has often seemed unapproachable and inaccessible for students. Some theory courses, for example, have tried to introduce students to a range of important theoretical schools of thought. Such a course might have a lecture programme which looked something like this:

New Criticism
Russian Formalism
Marxism
Psychoanalysis
Structuralism
Deconstruction
New Historicism
Feminist Approaches

It is not that such courses cannot possibly work (it depends how they are taught, at what stage of a course, and what is expected), but I did not want to teach a course like this to first-year students. The main problem with such a course seems to be that it attempts to do too many things at once. Firstly, it tries to give a history of (modern) literary theory. Secondly, it tries to get students to think theoretically about these theories (discussing the problems of each, discriminating between their different attitudes and so on). Thirdly, it asks students to apply these theories to their own study of texts.

I think that students often have difficulty reading theoretical writing to begin with (they have been trained in reading literary writing, which seems to them to be something very different). And theoretical ways of thinking are also not something which students have been prepared for. Instead of this kind of experience I wanted to offer an interesting but more accessible entry point to three of these tasks: learning to reflect on one's own reading practices, learning to read complex texts (theoretical and other) and learning to think conceptually about texts, theories and the relationships between them. This book is definitely not, then, in the usual sense, a theory book, nor even an introduction to theory. It might more justly be called a 'pre-theory' book – since I hope it will make study of theory later on more approachable and more productive. I would best of all like it to be, however, more than this alone: I hope it will introduce students to the whole range of skills needed for studying English as it is now defined: the ability to read a range of texts, literary and critical, and an ability to reflect on how this reading takes place. The kinds of solution which arose on my first-year course, 'Skills For English Studies' – solutions based on what I think is still the dominant English activity, the interpretation of texts – are what lie behind the strategies adopted in this book.

The book is organised around topics which have become central in the study of English. Instead of approaching these problems wholly through the unmediated writings of accomplished theoreticians, I have tried to provide ways of proceeding from the skills and knowledge which first-year students already have towards an understanding of the need for and possibilities of theoretical or conceptual thinking about English. The skills which I assume students bring with them to university include a developed (but developable) skill in reading and interpreting texts. I also assume that far from being totally unaware of theory, all readers are, in a way, conscious of many theoretical questions already, though they may never have read any theorists. For example, my experience of discussing whether literature exists, or whether popular culture is really a completely different kind of thing from 'literature' suggests a great concern with and ability to argue about such 'theoretical' issues. When you have worked your way through this book, you will not have had an introductory explanation of what (for example) Structuralism or Deconstruction are,[1] but you will, I think, be better placed to understand the ideas in those approaches when you do meet them.[2]

The book's structure, then, is to have chapters (subdivided into sections) focusing on important topics which are approached through a great variety of texts and through commentaries – yours and mine – upon questions and issues raised by those texts. It is not only that this seems a good way to approach the book's task, but also that it seems to work through a way of thinking which is essential to both 'theoretical' and 'practical' criticism. That is, the testing of detailed readings against larger readings. A poem or a novel or a piece of theoretical writing is not understood as a whole, but is understood and interpreted by locating the details in terms of the whole, and then the whole in terms of the detail (which feeds back into the reading of further detail). Discussing the passages or texts is meant to help discuss larger ideas, discussing larger ideas is meant to help discuss the texts. Between the texts and the larger theories there is meant to be a cycle of hypothesising and checking, checking and hypothesising.

The title of the book is intended to bring out this approach. It indicates the dual approach through a focus on texts and through a focus on thinking about or around texts. You are invited both to:

(a)   think about *texts* and
(b)   *think about* texts

(i.e. there is as much emphasis on *thinking about* as on *texts*, as much emphasis on *texts* as on *thinking about* – the two are handled in tandem).

All texts are already, in fact, surrounded by thoughts before you ever begin to think about their detail. They are already classified by type, by why and where and when you are reading them, by how you read, by who you are, by your image of the author, by what you expect of literature, by what you expect of history and so on. This book attempts to help you to think through some of those ideas which are in and around texts.

The book does not guarantee neat answers to all (or indeed any) of the questions and enquiries it raises. It tries to provide a way of exploring and clarifying problems, not ways of disposing of them for ever. Above all, it tries to be a book which is useful for the reader, whether using the book alone or as part of a taught course. To this end, it explicitly and frequently provides places in the text where you are invited to think through specific problems about texts, and it follows these tasks with discussion of some possible answers. At the end of each section are tasks which I leave you to discuss on your own. As the book goes on, the proportion of discussion left to you to work through increases. My sample discussions do not exhaust the possible answers, and you are more than welcome to disagree with my ways of approaching the questions. This, after all, is another text surrounded by thinking, and it too can be thought through in many different ways.

II   What Do We Mean by Literature?

Meaning is the key issue of this book. For much of the time its discussions circle round questions of meaning: what do words – and other signifying systems – mean? How do we find out what words mean, and how they came to mean this? To what extent do we agree that we are all using words to mean the same things? Even trying to establish the meaning of 'meaning' soon suggests how complex the concept of meaning is. The words 'mean' and 'meaning' have several senses. The *Oxford English Dictionary* gives the following for the sense we mean here:

> Mean – 'to have in mind as signification', 'to intend, to purpose', 'to destine, design', 'to signify'
> Meaning – 'that which is in the mind or thoughts', 'the sense intended', 'purpose'

Clearly, all these senses are connected, and probably derive from an Old English verb *Maenan* = to think (related to the word 'mind'). The range of meanings given above derives from this root sense of thinking, and there is an interesting oscillation between more and less purposeful definitions. For example, 'purpose' seems much stronger than 'intend', and both 'purpose' and 'intend' seem stronger than 'that which is in the mind or thoughts'. Sometimes 'mean' seems to convey that a purpose has been carried out, sometimes it seems to mean that a purpose has been thought of. In fact, there seem to be two different models of communication suggested by the word 'mean'. In one model a thought originates in the mind, is communicated and put into 'action' ('to purpose'). In the other there is a sense that thought which originates in the mind may not simply be projected into other minds and into the world itself ('the sense intended'). In the second model there is a split between mind and world, in the other meaning seems to be less of a problem.

This rather philosophical approach to the word is present in everyday uses, where there is often a sense that meaning is both clear and something which frequently slips from the grasp:

'I meant to wash the car this afternoon (... but I didn't)'
'I didn't mean to upset him (... but I did)'
'That wasn't what I meant (... the meaning I had in my mind was different from the one understood)'
'But I thought you meant (... the meaning I thought was in your mind was in fact a different one from the meaning you thought you had in your mind)'

This sense of meaning as something both present (clear and indisputable) and always potentially absent (not fulfilled, not properly understood) depends on a notion of a world where messages have to be sent, but can be sent out wrongly, are not always received, or are misunderstood on arrival. The possibility for misunderstanding (or different understandings) comes from the nature of communication, and the questions of ownership and interpretation which it inevitably involves. The Czech linguist Roman Jakobson suggested that all communication contained three fundamental ingredients: an addresser, an addressee and a message. Each of these elements of communication can generate ambiguities about what is meant. The message itself may be readable in different ways because of the very nature of language. Words do not have single meanings, grammatical structures may be ambiguous, the context of a message may alter its meaning and so on.

Given this inherent instability in language, both addresser and addressee are not simply senders and receivers of clear messages, but also have to be interpreters. The addresser has to attempt to construct a meaning which will serve the desired purpose. But as anyone who has ever written more than one draft of a letter, an essay or even a simple note (or a book) knows, there is no one obvious way of communicating a meaning. On the contrary, every act of writing is a complex matter of interpretation, of attempting to formulate what is required in terms of a communication which the intended audience will be able rightly to understand. The situation of the reader is similar. S/he must interpret the message to exclude unintended or improbable meanings, and arrive at a range of useful meaning. The notion of a 'useful' 'intended' or 'probable' interpretation raises the question of ownership. A useful reading from the point of view of the addressee may not be a useful one from the addresser's viewpoint. Intentional misreadings of texts (or speech) are familiar, for example comic or ironic (mis)readings of official notices. In some contexts, we even expect there to be debate about the meanings of texts. For example, though legal writing sets out to be as unambiguous as possible, legal cases often turn on different readings of the Law. But even where we might assume a simpler context and 'good faith', addressers and addressees do not always understand the 'message' in the same way. Messages have to be constructed by both readers and writers, and this can never be an entirely simple act.

The question of where meaning resides or how it can be found is an important one for literary study, since much literary criticism involves arguments about what a literary work means. At various times literary critics have seen meaning as residing (principally) in the author, the text or the reader. Each of these models produces different attitudes to the location of meaning and its interpretation:

Meaning is to be found in:

The Author = the author has total control over the message which s/he sends out, the critic has merely to understand the author's intention

The Text = the text is autonomous; its meaning can be found inside it, independent of author or reader

The Reader = what the reader – or any reader? – understands by a text is its meaning

Each version privileges one part of Jakobson's model over another. If the author is the true origin of meaning, then the role of the message and addressee becomes subordinate:

ADDRESSER > message + addressee

If the text is where meaning lies, then addresser and addressee become less important:

MESSAGE > addresser + addressee

If the reader is where meaning finally comes from, then addresser and message are less privileged:

ADDRESSEE > message + addresser

Each of these approaches has its problems. How do we know what the author intended? What if s/he does not in fact seem to have succeeded in meaning what they apparently intended to mean? Can the reader avoid having to interpret the author through their understanding of the text? Can a text really speak for itself, and thus be the same text for every reader? Can any reading be accepted, or do you have to exclude incompetent readings? Actually, it seems clear that concentration simply on one element is unlikely to explain how meanings are really arrived at. In practice, no critic has ever really wanted to argue that the author or the text or the reader can be completely omitted from consideration. Moreover, there are many contextual conditions which govern the ways in which these three elements are interpreted. These include large and complex cultural contexts such as gender, history, nationality, race, which are discussed later in the book.

Important as these issues are for reading individual literary texts, the problem of meaning also applies to literature in an even more fundamental way. If literature is a kind of communication, then how are we to understand it? Where are we to find the meaning of this term or kind of communication? We are all quite used to the problems of discussing the meanings of individual literary texts, but behind those familiar enquiries lies a larger question about the meaning of literature itself. Until relatively recently, this larger question has often remained unasked, partly because it is quite possible to pursue detailed questions about particular texts without explicitly asking what kind of communicative activity they are part of. The discussion above of why meaning is inherently a complicated notion and activity was introduced first in specific terms, because it is then easier to see why it is a vital question in general for everyone involved in studying literature.

If we need to discuss the meaning of particular texts, do we not also need to discuss the meaning of a term which defines a huge body of texts and ways of reading them? Is the meaning of 'literature' fixed (and if so, where and how)? Can we determine the meaning of literature from the 'message' itself (from all the texts constituting literature)? or should we study the nature of the addresser (the literary author) or the addressee (the reader/s)? Who owns the message of literature, and who controls its meaning?

The title of this introduction itself deliberately contains a complex of ambiguities focused on the word 'mean'. 'What Do We Mean by Literature?' may mean:

1. 'What does the word or notion of literature mean or signify?'
2. 'What kinds of things are literature?'
3. 'What do we intend – to accomplish? – by literature?'
4. 'What does each of us mean when we use the term?'

This book is intended to explore what we mean by literature by working through the major ways in which literary study is, has been, or could be defined. Each of the five chapters which follows approaches literary study through a key issue. Each topic has at some stage, by some people, been seen as a defining (or redefining) one for literature. Though these sections cannot provide single, simple answers, they may help to clarify how we mean, what we think, how we come to think, and how we may command the means to think further about literature.

A Note About Further Reading

Suggestions for further reading on section topics will be found at the end of each chapter. I can also suggest four books which you might find generally helpful as you work through *Thinking About Texts*: two provide concise definitions of critical terms, one provides approachable overviews of topics in literary theory, and the fourth offers a lucid and modern literary history:

Fowler, Roger (ed.), *A Dictionary of Modern Critical Terms*, revised edn (Routledge, London, 1987).

Hawthorn, Jeremy, *A Concise Glossary of Contemporary Literary Theory* (Edward Arnold, London, 1992).

Webster, Roger, *Studying Literary Theory – An Introduction*, 2nd edn (Edward Arnold, London, 1990).

Sanders, Andrew, *The Short Oxford History of English Literature*, revised edn (Clarendon Press, Oxford, 1996).

The Study of Literature

1.1 How Do We Define Literature?

The question 'What is Literature?' might seem the most basic possible question that could be asked about the nature of literary studies. But in fact the question is basic not so much in the sense that it can quickly be answered and so form a stable starting point for discussing literary issues as in the more complex sense that definitions of literature in themselves generate many of the major and fundamental enquiries and problems of literary study. The question then is not necessarily one which can be simply responded to once and for all, but is an essential question to which other critical enquiries constantly return.

Ways of defining the question themselves seem to promise simplicity rather than complexity: 'What is Literature?' and 'How Do We Define Literature?' seem to demand finite answers (literature is a certain kind of writing, a certain set of writings, it has particular qualities which can be defined as follows and so on). But answers to such questions do not seem to be simple ones. Do all readers agree on what is and is not literature? Is there consensus on the function of literature or the features which it must contain? Is literature 'good writing' or a certain kind of writing? Does it remain literature if it gives you personally no pleasure? In short it seems unlikely that a simple listing of liter ary works and literary qualities could be simply drawn up (even by readers of a single shared culture and period). Literature does not seem to be easily definable as an objective category or finite set of writings.

On the other hand, the word and concept of literature does seem to work (it is used and appears to communicate a certain set of notions and refer to some things rather than others). It seems unlikely therefore that the term can be completely free-floating and subjective (few people argue that sculpture is literature, for example). There thus seems to be some kind of systematic shared meaning which governs what the word literature indicates, and yet a clear and universal definition would be hard to agree on.

To ask the question 'What is Literature?' is perhaps partly then to enter into the question of how words mean, and how the meaning of words is established and defined. An answer to the first part of this would involve a lengthy discussion drawing on disciplines such as philosophy and linguistics, but a more immediate, more practical way of investigating the second part at least seems to present itself. There is, of course, a specific genre of book, the dictionary, which sets out to define the usage and meaning of words. A first move in investigating the meaning of a term might be to consult one.

A dictionary establishes the meaning of words by *defining* them, a procedure which involves explaining a word by using other words to paraphrase its meaning. It is worth noting that the word also has the connected but slightly different meaning of 'setting limits to' (from its Latin root *de fine* = of ends, boundaries, limits). Thus a user can look up a word to check the meaning, and/or to establish points at which its meaning reaches a boundary (for example, a boundary point between the meanings of the words 'book' and 'novel' or 'verse' and 'poetry' could be searched for).

In British culture, the *Oxford English Dictionary* (*OED*) is regarded as having an authority for establishing the sense of words in the fullest way. The entry for literature is reproduced below. The entry follows the *OED*'s standard format, which gives an origin or *etymology*, and then makes a distinction between variations or gradations in the meanings of a word. Thus a word is assigned a number of relatively distinct meanings, indicated by typographical layout in distinct and numbered blocks. Within those blocks relatively closer or subtler distinctions are listed by letters. A number of brief quotations of different uses of the word in question are also given, with sources. This gives a range of meanings and variations in usage and meaning over time.

> ◆ Read the entry: Which definition[s] do you find most helpful, or most like your own sense of 'literature'? Is the definition adequate?

literature ('lɪtərətjuə(r)). Forms: 4 *Sc.* lateratour, 5–6 litt-, lytterature, 6 *Sc.* literatur, -uir, 6– literature. [ad. (either directly or through F. *littérature*) L. *litterātūra* (whence Sp. *literatura*, It. *letteratura*, G. *litteratur*), f. *littera* a letter. Cf. LETTRURE.]

1. Acquaintance with 'letters' or books; polite or humane learning; literary culture. Now *rare* and *obsolescent*. (The only sense in Johnson and in Todd 1818.)

c **1375** *Sc. Leg. Saints* xxxi. (*Eugenia*) 53 Scho had leyryte .. of þe sewine sciens .. & part had of al lateratour. c **1425** WYNTOUN *Cron.* ix. xxiii. 2227 Cunnand in to litterature, A seymly persone in stature [etc.]. **1432–50** tr. *Higden* (Rolls) VI. 359 Seynte Grimbalde the monke, nobly instructe in litterature and in musyke. **1513** BRADSHAW *St. Werburge* II. 4 The comyn people .. Whiche without lytterature and good informacyon Ben lyke to Brute beestes. *a* **1529** SKELTON *Bowge of Courte* 449, I know your vertu and your lytterature. **1581** N. BURNE *Disput.* xxv. 109 b, Ane pure man, quha .. hes nocht sufficient literatur to vndirstand the scripture. **1605** BACON *Adv. Learn.* I. To the King §2. 2 There hath not beene .. any King .. so learned in all literature and erudition, diuine and humane. c **1645** HOWELL *Lett.* (1650) I. 346 In comparison of your spacious literature, I have held all the while but a candle to the sun. **1693** J. EDWARDS *Author. O. & N. Test.* 239 Another person of infinite literature [Selden]. **1727** SWIFT *Let. Eng. Tongue* Wks. 1755 II. I. 187 Till better care be taken in the education of our young nobility, that they may set out into the world with some foundation of literature. **1779–81** JOHNSON *L.P., Milton* (1868) 37 He had probably more than common literature, as his son addresses him in one of his most elaborate Latin poems. *Ibid.* 62 His literature was unquestionably great. He read all the languages which are considered either as learned or polite. **1802** MAR. EDGEWORTH *Moral T.* (1816) I. 206 A woman of considerable information and literature. **1862** BORROW *Wild Wales* II. x. 104 The boots [is] a fellow without either wit or literature. **1880** HOWELLS *Undisc. Country* xix. 290 In many things he was grotesquely ignorant; he was a man of very small literature.

2. Literary work or production; the activity or profession of a man of letters; the realm of letters.

1779 JOHNSON *L.P., Cowley* ℙ 1 An author whose pregnancy of imagination and elegance of language have deservedly set him high in the ranks of literature. **1791–1823** D'ISRAELI *Cur. Lit.* (1859) II. 407 Literature, with us, exists independent of patronage or association. **1830** SCOTT *Introd. to Lay Last Minstr.* Poet. Wks. 1833–4 VI. 17, I determined that literature should be my staff, but not my crutch, and that the profits of my literary labour .. should not .. become necessary to my ordinary expenses. **1853** LYTTON *My Novel* VII. viii, Ah, you make literature your calling, sir? **1879** MORLEY *Burke* 9 Literature, the most seductive, the most deceiving, the most dangerous of professions.

3. a. Literary productions as a whole; the body of writings produced in a particular country or period, or in the world in general. Now also in a more restricted sense, applied to writing which has claim to consideration on the ground of beauty of form or emotional effect. *light literature*: see LIGHT *a.*[1] 19.

This sense is of very recent emergence both in Eng. and Fr.

1812 SIR H. DAVY *Chem. Philos.* 6 Their literature, their works of art offer models that have never been excelled. **1838** ARNOLD *Hist. Rome* I. 21 Many common words, which no nation ever derives from the literature of another, are the same in Greek and Latin. **1845** M. PATTISON *Ess.* (1889) I. 1 Such history, almost more than any other branch of literature, varies with the age that produces it. **1856** EMERSON *Eng. Traits, Ability* Wks. (Bohn) II. 41 There is no department of literature, of science, or of useful art, in which they have not produced a first rate book. **1857** BUCKLE *Civiliz.* I. v. 244 Literature, when it is in a healthy and unforced state, is simply the form in which the knowledge of a country is registered. **1874** GREEN *Short Hist.* vii. §7. 413 The full glory of the new literature broke on England with Edmund Spenser. **1879** SEELEY in *Macm. Mag.* XLI. 24 Those who cannot have recourse to foreign literatures are forced to put up with their ignorance.

b. The body of books and writings that treat of a particular subject.

1860 TYNDALL *Glac.* 1. vi. 44, I was well acquainted with the literature of the subject. **1879** HARLAN *Eyesight* i. 9 It .. has accumulated a literature of its own which an ordinary lifetime is hardly long enough to master. **1939** [see NORMALIZABLE *a.*]. **1969** [see DÉCOLLEMENT 2]. **1971** *Nature* 25 June 499/1 We have searched the literature for reliable radiometric ages for Late Pre-Cambrian glaciogenic rocks, but they seem to be rare. **1973** *Sci. Amer.* June 55/3 A voluminous scientific literature accumulates each year on the normal vibrational modes of molecules in liquids and on optical phonons in crystals.

c. *colloq.* Printed matter of any kind.

1895 *Daily News* 20 Nov. 5/2 In canvassing, in posters, and in the distribution of what, by a profane perversion of language, is called 'literature'. **1900** *Westm. Gaz.* 12 Oct. 2/1 A more judicious distribution of posters, and what is termed 'literature'. **1938** WODEHOUSE *Code of Woosters* i. 8 It is some literature from the Travel Bureau. **1962** *Observer* 4 Mar. 37/1 (Advt.), Full details and literature from: Yugoslav National Tourist Office. **1973** D. FRANCIS *Slay-Ride* vii. 78, I talked my throat dry, gave away sheaves of persuasive literature.

literary ('lrtərəri), *a.* [ad. L. *litterāri-us*, f. *littera* letter. Cf. F. *littéraire*.] (Not in Johnson 1755–1775.)

†**1.** Pertaining to the letters of the alphabet. *Obs.*

1646 S<small>IR</small> T. B<small>ROWNE</small> *Pseud. Ep.* I. ix. 37 Our first and literary apprehensions being commonly instructed in Authors which handle nothing else [but idle fictions]. **1769** *Middlesex Jrnl.* 8–11 July 4/2 A complete set of Literary Cards, for teaching children to read, spell, count. **1793** S<small>MEATON</small> *Edystone L.* §334 *note*, The literary references to Plates Nos. 19, and 20.

†2. Carried on by letters; epistolary. *Obs.*

1757–8 S<small>MOLLETT</small> *Hist. Eng.* (1800) II. 252 A literary correspondence was maintained between the English General and the Mareschal de Villars. [**1818** T<small>ODD</small> s.v., *Literary* is not properly used of missive letters.]

3. Of or pertaining to, or of the nature of, literature. **a.** Pertaining to letters or polite learning. **b.** Pertaining to books and written compositions; also, in a narrower sense, pertaining to, or having the characteristics of that kind of written composition which has value on account of its qualities of form. *literary dinner*, *lunch(eon)*, *party*, *prize*; also *literary adviser*: one who gives advice or information on literary matters; *literary agent* (see quot. 1960); also *literary agency*; *literary circle* (see C<small>IRCLE</small> *sb.* 21); *literary criticism* = C<small>RITICISM</small> 2 (of works of literature); so *literary critic*, *literary-critical* adj.; *literary editor*: (*a*) the editor of the literary section of a newspaper; (*b*) the editor of a book of collected writings; so *literary-edit* vb., *-editorship*; *literary executor* (see E<small>XECUTOR</small> 3); *literary history* (e.g. of a legend, a historical personage or event, etc.): the history of the treatment of, and references to, the subject in literature; *literary property*: (*a*) property which consists in written or printed compositions; (*b*) the exclusive right of publication as recognized and limited by law; *literary world* (see W<small>ORLD</small> *sb.* 16b).

1749 L. E<small>VANS</small> *Middle Brit. Col.* (1755) 3 The Seats of some Half a Dozen Gentlemen, noted in the literary Way. **1758** J. G. C<small>OOPER</small> *Retreat Aristippus* Epist. i. 198 With these, and some a-kin to these, .. I live in literary ease. **1759** G<small>OLDSM</small>. *Pol. Learn.* vi. Wks. (Globe) 430/1 A man of literary merit is sure of being caressed by the great, though seldom enriched. **1773** J<small>OHNSON</small> in *Boswell* 29 Apr., Mallet had talents enough to keep his literary reputation alive as long as he himself lived. **1779** — L.P., *Cowley* ℙ₂ His mother .. struggling earnestly to procure him a literary education. **1831** M. E<small>DGEWORTH</small> *Let.* 6 Jan. (1971) 469 He .. criticises so well – not as a mere literary critic appealing to authorities. **1840** M<small>ACAULAY</small> in *Edin. Rev.* Jan. 520 In 1698, Collier published his 'Short View ..', a book which threw the whole literary world into commotion. **1845** G<small>RAVES</small>

From *Oxford English Dictionary* (1989 edn).

 ## Discussion

Some of the definitions seem to me more relevant, and more helpful, than others. Some, as the dictionary points out, are senses which are no longer current. For example, sense **1**, for '**literary**' = 'Pertaining to letters of the alphabet', is not a sense ever used by a contemporary speaker (or by anyone since the eighteenth century). It cannot therefore help us, except as part of the history of the term.[1] Equally, sense **3c** for '**literature**' = 'Printed matter of any kind' (colloquial) seems to me to be too broad to be helpful. It is a perfectly acceptable sense of the word, but it seems to have little to do with an enquiry into what 'literature' is for those studying literature or English.

However, while the first case seems unarguable, the second is perhaps not quite so clear cut. I have certainly taught students who have argued that they do want to define literature as all written texts, in order to exclude nothing. If you have selected this meaning as a helpful one, you might like to formulate what you find helpful about it. My rejection is based on the argument that if everything is 'literature', then there is nothing special about a 'literary' text, and therefore really no need for the term 'literature' as opposed to writing. If we are really interested in all writing, then why not study 'writing'? (or even better Communications, since this includes all kinds of communication). In fact, of course, many people do precisely study for degrees in Communication Studies. They have solved the problem of defining literature by defining a larger field as their area of study. This seems very logical, but it is an awkward strategy for an English or literature student to subscribe to, unless they wish to change degree route. If there is no distinctive field called literature, then why enrol on a degree in it?[2] Admittedly, some other of the dictionary definitions seem to reinforce a general sense of the word. For example, **3a**, 'the body of writings produced in a particular country or period' does not distinguish literature as a special kind of writing. However, the first part of this definition shows an interesting variation when it says, '*Literary* productions as a whole'. A curious circularity begins to appear here. What is literature? Answer: literary productions. What are literary productions? Answer: literature. The shift between a general sense of literature as 'writing' and literature as 'literary writing' is discernible in the *OED*, but is not distinguished by being assigned different numbered senses or typographical blocks. The two senses occur side by side as if seamless. In fact, though, there seems to be a crucial difference. ☐

It is not that I necessarily believe that there is a special kind of writing called literature (that still needs to be discussed). Rather I am arguing that saying all texts are literature sidesteps the question. If we were all thinking about 'literature' in a context where the word really did mean any texts, then that would be different. But at present, the term literature does not seem to me to suggest anything of the sort. On the contrary, literature does not equate to 'writing', but strongly implies a special kind of writing. When people choose to do an English Literature 'A' level or an English degree, I do not believe that in the main they expect to study all kinds of writing. I would think that most have a sense of what literature is in a more restricted sense (if you don't feel this is true for you, feel free to argue against my reasoning!). The kind of more closely defined sense that I would expect to be invoked would be more like the latter part of definition **3a**: 'writing which has claim to consideration on the ground of beauty of form or emotional effect'. The claim for the special nature of literary writing is clear here. Indeed, the definition's wording makes it sound a factual matter: writing with this quality has 'claim to consideration'. The consideration is of a particular kind, involving aesthetic values. We might at this point turn to the question about whether the *OED* definition was adequate. Having narrowed down the dictionary definition to its most relevant area, we can think more specifically through our sense of the adequacy of the *OED*'s treatment:

> ◆ Do you think that 'beauty of form or emotional effect' is at all useful as a definition?
> ◆ Do you want to add further definitions or refinements to the *OED*'s entry?

▶ Discussion 1

My immediate reaction to the first question here is a feeling that 'beauty of form' has a rather old-fashioned sound to it (though this is taken from the 1989 revision of the *OED*, the definition is, in fact, unaltered from the first edition of the volume containing L, dating substantially from 1885, revised before publication in 1903). I cannot imagine many lecturers, teachers or students readily using these words to define literature in the latter half of the twentieth century. 'Emotional effect' seems less obviously old-fashioned, though it too might not seem exactly current. However, both phrases do seem still to point towards qualities which are part of many people's sense of the 'literary', even if they might not want to name them in this way. Thus, both phrases point away from the practical, away from the communicating of messages, and towards the personal or pleasurable or aesthetic. They imply that literature is not to do with the immediately useful or with imparting a particular kind of information or knowledge.

It is, though, a very general kind of definition. Could any kind of writing be literature if it had 'beauty of form'? For example, could a very well designed graph be called literature by this criterion? I suspect that that is not really what the definition has in mind. Rather than giving a criterion, it is really suggesting that literariness is a matter of style, not content. It is, in fact, emphasising a value, rather than defining a feature which can be applied to any writing to gauge its membership of 'literature'. □

▶ Discussion 2

There are many things which could be added to this definition. My first thought is that the general willingness of the *OED* definition to accept any writing as potentially literary may be a weakness. That is, my own sense of what 'literature' is suggests to me that, in fact, literature does seem to consist largely of certain kinds of text. From school onwards, literature seems to be made up not just of 'books' but rather of poetry, plays, novels and short stories. If only certain kinds of text can be literature, then there are generic criteria which a definition could use. I think the addition of a phrase to the dictionary definition indicating that literature is mostly considered to be made up of texts such as poetry, novels and so on would be an improvement. It would remove the wide sense that any kind of writing could be considered literature if it had beauty of form and emotional effect (after all, an advert could have those qualities but would that make it what is usually meant by 'literature'?). It would also correspond to a widely held impression that literature does refer to these types of books or texts. □

This does not, though, solve all the problems. If all novels (for instance) were literature simply because they were novels, then we would have a very straightforward definition of literature in terms of genre type. However, most people do not really think that all novels are literature. Most literature students would be surprised if a course on the twentieth-century novel actually included a wide selection of the kinds of novels (or books?) to be found in, say, an airport bookshop.

We could try to refine the generic definition further to exclude 'non-literary' novels (I am assuming for the moment rather than as a given that we are prepared to exclude some kinds of writing in this way). Thus we could exclude certain subgenres, felt to be inherently non-literary. Such an exclusion list might include science-fiction, fantasy, thrillers and romance, for example. Apart from the question of whether this is an elitist strategy, some immediate problems arise with this instance. Isn't this a rather crude way of classifying? In the right hands, could not a popular genre be transformed into literature? And in fact, examples of these subgenres which are widely accepted as literary (i.e. studied, classed by bookshops as literature and so on) can readily be thought of. H. G. Wells is accepted as a literary author, and his works of science-fiction are (probably?) accepted as literature. Many of Graham Greene's novels are recognisably of a thriller type and they are often classed as literature. And even if these two examples are arguable ones, surely Joseph Conrad's *The Secret Agent* could be said to be a clear example of a literary thriller? But, then, what about the thrillers of an author like John Le Carré, who is clearly much influenced by Conrad and Greene? Most people would automatically say that Mills and Boon type romances were not literature, but it has often been pointed out that the established literary novel *Jane Eyre* (by Charlotte Brontë) has a romance plot of a very similar kind.

It might be possible to resolve some of these cases by introducing further refinements in addition to the generic definition. One could define literature as texts of particular generic kinds of a high quality and seriousness, for example. However, this seems more an evaluative than a descriptive criteria. To say that genre might identify literary works (novels are literature, history books are not: but see section 4.3 below) is to apply an objective description, but it is less obviously an objective matter to say what makes a thriller a literary thriller rather than just a good thriller. To use an example which students (not every student, but a number of students) often raise: why is J. R. R. Tolkien's *The Lord of the Rings* not literature? Clearly, this particular case can be argued about in various ways (and so can other similar cases), but how can this kind of argument about quality or membership be taken account of by a brief dictionary definition?

Arguments of these kinds can be added to with further examples and further kinds of definition (you will probably have raised some different examples, definitions or issues). But however long we spend arguing for a definition, I am not convinced that one could be formulated which objectively and finally made complete sense of the boundary between literary and non-literary. This might seem awkward for me, since I argued earlier that allowing all writing to be included in the term 'literature' did not face up to the fact that the word was not really used in that way. Now I seem equally unhappy with attempts to define the boundary between literature and other kinds of writing. However, my difficulty in the two cases is of a different kind. In the first case, I was unhappy because the all-inclusive definition did not acknowledge the actual definitions made in using the word and concept of literature. In the second case, accepting that literature suggested a restricted area of writing seemed more in accord with the reality of how the term is used. But the actual definition of the boundary of literature and non-literature seemed hard to specify accurately. (In neither case have I argued for my own view about whether I want to use the word 'literature'; rather, for the present,

I have tried to clarify the actual situation, beyond my personal views on the matter, in which literature is a word used to make decisions and distinctions.)

Finally (in the sense that I will move on to another topic, rather than in the sense that everything is neatly resolved...) there is the question of whether the *OED* definition is objective. Much of the discussion above might seem to pre-empt this. If an objective definition of literature is hard to achieve, then how can the *OED* be expected to achieve objectivity? However, the question of how objective the dictionary definition might be, is not quite answered by saying that objectivity is impossible fully to achieve. On the contrary, if the definition is a difficult one for our culture, then it seems all the more important to enquire whether this authoritative reference work takes any particular approach to it.

You may well have identified certain preferences within the *OED*'s definition. These may not be a matter of deliberate bias, of course. Just as I have not argued for my own views about literature, but given some of my views of the problems, so the *OED* may represent dominant cultural definitions as part of an attempt to be objective. If literature is, for instance, generally used with an elitist aura in our culture, then dictionaries would be fair in representing this. It seems to me that the *OED*'s definitions do, in fact, reproduce certain dominant ideas about literature. Even when a wide definition is given, it is clear that 'literature' is always a word with class status. Whether literature is a certain kind of writing or, in an earlier dominant sense, any kind of writing, it is always associated with high social status. Even the quotations confirm this sense that literature is what distinguishes the 'civilised' from the 'uncivilised': 'In many things he was grotesquely ignorant; he was a man of very small literature'. The first quotation for the colloquial sense interestingly confirms that this is a 'low' use of a high-status term: 'In canvassing, in posters, and in the distribution of what, by a profane perversion of language, is called "literature"'. The only reference to literature with a wider social function is that to 'light literature' ('see LIGHT *a*.[1] 19'). The fact that no definition is given at all may suggest that this sense of literature as entertainment is not one felt to be dominant or even worthy. This may seem a simple point: literature is a term with social status. But it is an important one, if we are interested in how and what literature means. Its status is not, perhaps, merely a question about writing, but is linked to wider social concerns.[3]

If the *OED* asserts the dominance of some meanings over others, it does not explicitly engage in arguments about, or analysis of, meanings and changes in meaning. Some other kinds of dictionary, however, may enter into this kind of discussion of the complexity of terms such as 'literature'. A dictionary of literary terms or poetics, while not necessarily partisan, will give a more complex account of variations in meaning and of some of the possible reasons for these (you might like to consult this kind of dictionary to see what it says about how literature may be defined). The next exercise is from Raymond Williams's *Keywords*, a dictionary of this type, though with a wider project than many. Instead of being a dictionary of words, or even of words within a specific academic discipline, it is a dictionary of cultural definition itself. As the title suggests, it picks out a relatively small number of words to define as 'key'. Clearly such an act of selection needs some principal or central topic for deciding what words are key words. Williams's selection procedure is to define and analyse words which encode key concepts of modern culture.

Raymond Williams was a Marxist critic, who therefore believed that all culture (though through a series of complex relationships) was related to economic and social organisation.[4] Thus literature for him was not simply a matter, for instance, of an individual mind expressing its creative urge. On the contrary, literature (one among many cultural products) was a part of a larger social and economic system, and therefore inevitably functions within the politics of that social organisation. Literature (and other similar terms like 'culture') could not then be seen as an abstract universal label for an activity or experience which was always the same in every culture and age. If literature is inevitably defined in actuality by wider social forces, then historical or cultural changes in those forces must alter the ways in which literature is perceived, experienced, defined and produced.

Keywords is motivated, like much of Williams's other work, by these concerns. It attempts to analyse the definitions which are produced by social and economic organisation, including the production of language and meaning, and which helps to reproduce some meanings as more dominant than others. Unlike the *OED* which simply states different senses for a word and indicates changes of meaning over time, *Keywords* gives an account of the reasons for change and of the relation between the term under discussion and related terms. Williams's entry for literature picks up many of the problems we have met in discussion of the *OED*'s definition, as well as raising some other associated difficulties. The entry contains much material not to be found in an ordinary dictionary, and it is worth pausing to clarify how this material can contribute to understanding the term 'literature'.

> Find a copy of Raymond Williams, *Keywords: A Vocabulary of Culture and Society* (nearly all university libraries hold multiple copies; either the first edition of 1976 or the revised edition of 1983 can be used). Read the entry for LITERATURE; how many separate senses of 'literature' are suggested (try listing them)?
> What historical developments are seen as affecting the meaning of the word?

▶ Discussion 1

I can see the following separate senses for 'literature':

- polite learning acquired from reading.
  - being well-read
  - ability to read
  - professional authorship
  - writing classifiable as polite learning
  - well written
  - well-written books of an imaginative kind
  - poems and plays and novels
  - substantial or important writing
  - not speech?
  - fiction
  - books written a long time ago …
  - impressionistic, not factual □

Discussion 2

The changes in meaning discussed by Williams correspond to historical changes which the passage suggests rather than makes entirely explicit. Most of these seem to be connected with the history of reading, of the book, and its availability. From the first emergence of the word in English in the fourteenth century, the passage seems to suggest that there is an association between literature and reading by lay-people rather than clergy. In this sense, literature only comes into being when there are secular (=non-religious) books available (hence the word 'clerk', connected with 'cleric', suggesting precisely an occupational skill in reading formerly possessed mainly by clergy). Even in this sense, then, literature has some connection with leisure or individual self-improvement or amusement. The equivalence between 'literature' and 'literate' presumably occurs because it is assumed that to be able to read is to read works of 'polite learning'. The implication is that there is nothing but this to read (i.e. there is no popular or low matter to read). Every book at this stage does (in Williams's account) contain learned matter.

Later, a distinction grows up between 'good' reading and writing and less good kinds of 'literature'. Thus the churchman and humanist educator John Colet (founder of St Paul's School in London) makes a distinction between 'literature' and 'blotterature'. This implies a wider knowledge of reading and writing than earlier on, so that it is possible to be literate, but not learned or 'polite'. This suggests a wider distribution of books and of learning, and perhaps also the possibility of using writing for activities of lesser social status. In the eighteenth century a new sense of 'literature' emerges. It is still a general term for 'writing', but it seems clear that it refers only to writing of a high quality. Indeed, in Dr Johnson's use of this new sense he begins to name what might be thought of as modern 'literary' qualities: 'Imagination' and 'elegance of language'. This confirms that wider literacy and uses for writing form part of the background for the emergence of literature as a distinctive kind of writing. In particular, Williams associates the development of this meaning with the growth of professional writing.

The next stage of specialisation is towards a meaning of 'imaginative' writing. The sense of 'imaginative' here is presumably opposed to factual or practical writing, the kind of writing used in everyday life for specific purposes. Literature therefore becomes reserved for writing which is in some sense not immediately useful or functional in this ordinary way. This change is not linked by Williams to a historical development of quite the same kind as the earlier shifts in meaning. They were seen as partly a response to the availability of books and the distribution of literacy, as well as to a wide complex of 'social and cultural history'. In this case, though, the main change is specifically attributed to a specialisation of the term within 'the basic assumptions of Romanticism'. It is not that a new kind of thought is solely responsible, but that this is a kind of shorthand way of indicating that a new set of social conditions had led to a shift in ways of thinking about writing. Williams does not explain the assumptions of Romanticism, either because he relies on a knowledge of the term's meaning, or because to do so would swamp this definition by another. Since 'Romanticism' is itself a widely used literary and artistic term, and a problematic one, both explanations probably play a part.

The last cluster of meanings discussed are linked to recent developments in writing, or more accurately, communications. Literature has become so specialised in the sense of written texts rather than spoken, that it cannot obviously be applied to speech or to kinds of writing designed to be spoken. Yet the development of mass media broadcasting has created an enormous amount of textual production of this type. This is connected to the last two negative or unfavourable senses, which see literature as inevitably distant from modern life. In this final sense, literature is over, a dead category. It is not a word indicating creative writing, but a word indicating a finite set of books written in the past. Such books may have cultural status, but they are part of a museum not an ongoing process. □

This analysis of changes in the meaning of literature does not, of course, bring any simple answer. It is a way of systematically investigating the variations of meaning over time, and of suggesting reasons for shifts and developments. The exploration of changes, however, takes us back to the major question of this section rather than supplying an answer. Given that we accept Williams's account, we still need to decide how to define 'literature' for now, or for ourselves, and/or decide what to do about the notion of 'literature'. We will come back to this question at the end of the section.

First, though, we could try a slightly different approach to defining literature. If, instead of discussing a shifting mass of observations about literature, we examine a particular text, perhaps this will approach the issue more practically and clearly. If everyone is more or less agreed that a text is (or is not) literature, might this not suggest that there is some consensus? In that case, problems of definition might be terminological frameworks *surrounding* literature, rather than actually *in* it. This would confirm a traditional view that it is pointless to try to define literature since it will always evade definition, but that we do all recognise the experience of literature when we meet it.

In fact, though, this line of argument seems to run into problems already suggested by some of the discussion above. Can we really judge whether qualities inside a text are literary ones, without some pre-existing model of what literariness is outside that particular text? In this sense any attempt to react to the possible literary qualities or status of a specific text is already enmeshed in the question of systematic definition.

Nevertheless, reading *a* text rather than texts which attempt to define literature does represent a different kind of experience. It might be one we should expect to reveal more (or different things?) about how we define literary texts in practice. A specific text can act as a test case for whatever definitions or codes of literariness we are deploying, and can thus invite us to make explicit our own assumptions. The example chosen – John Mole's 'The Advancement of Learning' – is deliberately a case with some room to argue about whether criteria for a literary text are fulfilled. You might like to take particular note of the bracketed note under the title, and of the attached passages from the *Guardian* referred to by that note.

Read the poem: Is this literature? Why?/Why not?

Do the note and the newspaper articles affect your thinking?

John Mole, 'The Advancement of Learning'

(Taken from the *Guardian* of 26.5.1979 and with acknowledgement to Leon Edel[5])

Maynard Keynes read messages
in hands. They could express
as eyes express, be elegant
or brutal, clasp, unclasp
in nervous fidget, drumming
on an arm-rest or a table,
fussing, reaching, gesturing –
a lexicon of hands.

In Florida, John Spenkelink
was buckled to the chair. A jolt
surged through his body, then his left fist
clenched. His hands
began to curl and blacken.

Extracts from two articles in the *Guardian*, Saturday 26 May 1979

Countdown to death in the chair

From AP in Starke, Florida

The convicted murderer John Spenkelink was executed in Florida's electric chair yesterday, becoming the first prisoner executed unwillingly in the United States for more than 18 years ... Spenkelink was pronounced dead at 10.18 a.m. at the Florida State Prison. He received the first jolt of 2.250 volts at 10.13 a.m. After the first surge which singed the skin on his right calf, sending smoke into the death chamber, Spenkelink received another jolt.

A doctor was then called to check his heart at 10.14 a.m. The doctor looked at the prison superintendent, stepped back and waited two more minutes, when he again checked Spenkelink's heart with a stethoscope and again stepped back. Finally at 10.18 a.m. he made a third check, lifted the death hood and looked at Spenkelink's eyes and checked his pulse. Spenkelink was dead.

The execution which was to have begun promptly at 10 a.m. was inexplicably delayed until 10.11 a.m. when the venetian blinds separating official and media witnesses from the electric chair were opened, showing Spenkelink already strapped in the huge oaken death chair.

He was wearing a white gown rolled up at the sleeves and blue trousers ... A leather harness was placed around his head, over his chin and his arms. Legs and ankles were secured to the chair, with wide leather straps. Spenkelink was not allowed a traditional last statement – contrary to promises from prison officials ...

Spenkelink was fastened so securely in the head harness that he could not open his mouth and stared impassively at the 32 people who witnessed the execution…

Membership of Cambridge's secret elite had a profound impact on John Maynard Keynes. In these extracts from his forthcoming book on Bloomsbury's key figures, LEON EDEL shows how the society [the Apostles] influenced his conduct during the First World War and at the ensuing peace talks.

They were Apostles in a special sense of the word and G. E. Moore was their Christ; he gave them their religion.

Keynes spoke [at Apostles meetings] on probability, logic, mathematics. In eight years he read twenty papers. He would say that with the aid of Moore they had repudiated all versions of the doctrine of original sin. 'We accepted Moore's religion and discarded his morals.'

When Maynard Keynes found himself in a world of dullards, he often took refuge in silence and observation. He looked into faces. He satisfied his own eyes and his senses. He listened. He looked in particular at hands. From his earliest days he had learned that no hands are alike. They can resemble a claw or a paw, they can be elegant, they can be brutal, they can make one shudder at their brutality. They clasp and unclasp in nervous fidget; fingers drum on a table or the arm of a chair; they can be fussy, reaching, gesturing – a whole nervous system. They *express*, as eyes express, as the straightness or droop of a back express, as the way a person sits expresses. Maynard Keynes instinctively learnt to read messages in hands.

 ## Discussion

If I were to argue that this is not a literary text, it would presumably be on the grounds that it is not wholly original. The poet has merely taken sentences from the newspaper articles and arranged them as if they were in a poem. Even the title of the poem is a quotation (it is the title of a seventeenth-century book by Francis Bacon, which argues for the beneficial effects of scientific knowledge). If I were disillusioned by this discovery of lack of imaginative invention, I might also claim that the text lacked any clear meaning. My criteria for these decisions would be based on:

(a)   originality and imagination as a literary requirement;
(b)   a notion that literature should have a message.

I feel much more able to argue, though, that this text is literature. Though the writer has not invented every phrase, I would argue that he has taken them from one context and put them to a new and original use. In fact, I might well feel that the imagination required to see this potential for creativity is a distinct marker of literary authorship. Moreover, the experience of reading this text is radically altered by its recasting in the form or shape of a poem. The act of dividing the original prose into lines of poetry emphasises patterns of sound and meaning which are less apparent in the articles. For example, line division seems to place emphasis on the word 'hands' which occurs in prominent positions at the ends and beginnings of lines. And the participle endings (fussing, reaching...), with their suggestion of constant ongoing movement, seem to be emphasised by their repeated occurrence in one line, reinforced by the rhyme with a similar verb-form two lines before: drumming/fussing, reaching, gesturing. Above all, the writer has placed the two sets of sentences against each other so as to construct a new meaning. While the originals merely gave separate accounts of an event and a famous economist's ideas about hands, the poem establishes a means for a complex set of comparisons. Hands are a sign of the constant activity of life itself, and particularly of a central human activity, the desire to express meaning and emotion in outward signs. Hands are what the executed Spenkelink and the thinker Maynard Keynes have (had) in common, but they are also a way of measuring a contrast between them. Participles are appropriate for Keynes's ability to express subtle ideas about hands, but Spenkelink can express only one last range of emotions. His 'clenched' hand may express anger and rebellion against his fate, but whatever he means, it is his last meaning. Or perhaps, even those movements were no longer his voluntary meanings, but an inescapable physical reaction to the fate to which he is condemned. The curling and blackening of his hands is certainly no longer his expression, but may express for us something of the brutality of capital punishment. Note how the past participle ('buckled', 'clenched') replaces the ongoing present participle used for the living Keynes.

If one reason for denying the text literary status is an accusation that it lacks 'meaning', it could equally be said that a certain resistance to easy understanding can also be said to be a literary quality. Thus we are left to work out the text's principles of coherence and meaning, rather than having them presented explicitly. One could argue that this is rhetorically superior to a more obvious display of meaning, and that the resistance to reading which it creates is also readily identifiable as a literary quality. The superiority can be seen as arising from the greater attention and personal engagement needed to understand the less explicit message. It could also be said that this difficulty makes the construction of meaning a process carried out in a way beyond ordinary, routine signification. If originality is a literary criterion, then a new way of understanding a topic is likely to be valued. This also confirms the likelihood that the original newspaper articles are part of an ordinary way of writing, while this text displays special literary modes of writing. □

This does not exhaust the possible arguments for the text's literary status, or the possible criteria of literariness which could be applied to this piece (you may well have made further points). One further way of using the text occurs to me. It could be that it is not so much what is in the text which makes us read it as literature, but our classification of it. That is, once you have classified this text as probably a literary text (specifically a poem), you may be much more ready to read it in literary ways. If you devote more energy and more flexible reading methods to a text, then it is not surprising that you begin to generate satisfying and complicated meanings from it. It is notable that rejection of this text as literary produces much less discussion than acceptance. This is because lack of meaning – a distrust in the possibility of meaning – is in itself a criteria for rejection. We could shift this kind of emphasis on reading back to the original newspaper articles, however. Are they really completely routine in their messages and ways of expressing them? Or, if we had faith could we in fact produce 'Literary' readings? Do they really lack creativity, the ability to invite us to look afresh at something? Are their ideas about their topics actually of less value than the meaning of the poem? It may well be that you are already reading every text from definitions of *either* literary *or* other kinds of writing which have been made for you. To operate with such definitions does not necessarily prove that they are the right or only possible definitions.

Finally on the question of how literature can be defined, you might like to try to define your own position in the light of this discussion and your reactions to it. I will not provide any of my own responses here – you need to work out what you think and, indeed, how important the question of definition is. As a starting point for your thoughts, read the following extract from Tzvetzan Todorov's essay 'The Notion of Literature'. The passage picks up in its own way a number of the ideas met with so far in this section.

> We need to begin by casting doubt on the legitimacy of the notion of literature. The mere fact that the word exists, or that an academic institution has been built around it, does not mean that the thing itself is self-evident.
>
> Reasons – perfectly empirical ones, to begin with – are not hard to find. The full history of the word *literature* and its equivalents in all languages and all eras has yet to be written, but even a perfunctory look at the question makes it clear that the term has not been around forever. In the European languages, the word *literature* in its current sense is quite recent: it dates back – just barely – to the nineteenth century. Might we be dealing with a historical phenomenon rather than an 'eternal' one? Moreover, many languages (many African languages, for example) have no generic term covering all literary productions... To these initial observations we may add the fragmentation characteristic of literature today. Who dares specify what is literature and what is not, given the irreducible variety of the writing that tends to be attached to it, from vastly differing perspectives?
>
> The argument is not conclusive: a notion may legitimately exist even if there is no specific term in the lexicon for it. But we have been led to cast the first shadow of doubt over the 'naturalness' of literature. A theoretical examination of the problem proves no more reassuring. Where do we come by the conviction that there is indeed such a thing as literature? From experience. We study 'literary' works in school, then in college; we find the 'literary' type of book in specialised stores; we are in the habit of referring to 'literary' authors in everyday conversation. An entity called 'literature' functions at the level of intersubjective [=subjective responses apparently also experienced by others] and social relations; this much seems beyond question. Fine. But what have we proved? That in the broader system of a given society or culture, an identifiable element exists that is known by the label *literature*. Have we thereby demonstrated that all the particular products that take on the function of 'literature' possess common characteristics, which we can identify with legitimacy? Not at all.
>
> From *Genres in Discourse* (published in French 1978; first published in English, 1990), pp. 1–2.

> ◆ Do you believe that there is a special kind of writing called literature? What are the reasons for your yes or no?
>
> ◆ How much difference would it make to you – or to life in general – if the term 'literature' was erased from our culture, and replaced by words like 'writing' or 'books', 'media' or 'communications' or some other terms?

1.2   Literature versus Popular Fiction?

I begin this section with an exercise involving two texts which are deliberately left unidentified at first. Though obviously artificial (you normally can't help noticing various *external* indicators of what you are about to read), this will give us a way of approaching questions about how we think about literature and popular kinds of fiction. Most readers would and will, I imagine, begin to make guesses and even judgements about what kind of text each of these mystery passages might be while reading. In fact, such a process of speculative categorisation seems to me inevitable and not merely something which is added onto a reader's reaction. On the contrary, I would expect decisions about the kind of text being read to be a fundamental part of how that writing is reacted to (as suggested above in section 1.1). This is, of course, exactly the kind of question which this section needs to work through: how do readers deal with categorisations of writing, and how does categorisation come about? 'Literature versus Popular Culture' thus revisits some of the issues raised by the literature/not literature material, but in a more specific way, by focusing on questions of value in texts which we may (perhaps?) be initially inclined to classify in quite clear-cut ways.

Though both of these texts come from books which most people would probably be willing to classify as novels, one of the passages comes from a book which is more likely to be called 'popular' than the other (and, indeed, is an example of a *kind* of book likely to be classed as 'popular'). While reading through the passages, think about the following questions:

> ◆ Which of the two would you class as more 'popular'?
>
> ◆ Why? (quite general or very specific reasons may be equally useful).
>
> ◆ Could you attempt to put any kind of label on each text? (i.e. what kind of book each might be from?).

A.

Chapter 9

COAL-DUST

Going home from school in the afternoon, the Brangwen girls descended the hill between the picturesque cottages of Willey Green till they came to the railway crossing. There they found the gate shut, because the colliery train was rumbling nearer. They could hear the small locomotive panting hoarsely as it advanced with caution between the embankments. The one-legged man in the little signal-hut by the road stared out from his security, like a crab from a snail-shell.

Whilst the two girls waited, Gerald Crich trotted up on a red Arab mare. He rode well and softly, pleased with the delicate quivering of the creature between his knees. And he was very picturesque, at least in Gudrun's eyes, sitting soft and close on the slender red mare, whose long tail flowed on the air. He saluted the two girls, and drew up at the crossing to wait for the gate, looking down the railway for the approaching train. In spite of her ironic smile at his picturesqueness, Gudrun liked to look at him. He was well set and easy, his face with its warm tan showed up his whitish, coarse moustache, and his blue eyes were full of sharp light as he watched the distance.

The locomotive chuffed slowly between the banks, hidden. The mare did not like it. She began to wince away, as if hurt by the unknown noise. But Gerald pulled her back and held her head to the gate. The sharp blasts of the chuffing engine broke with more and more force on her. The repeated sharp blows of unknown, terrifying noise struck through her till she was rocking with terror. She recoiled like a spring let go. But a glistening, half-smiling look came into Gerald's face. He brought her back again, inevitably.

The noise was released, the little locomotive with her clanking steel connecting-rod emerged on the highroad, clanking sharply. The mare rebounded like a drop of water from hot iron. Ursula and Gudrun pressed back into the hedge, in fear. But Gerald was heavy on the mare, and forced her back. It seemed as if he sank into her magnetically, and could thrust her back against herself.

'The fool!' cried Ursula loudly. 'Why doesn't he ride away till it's gone by?'

Gudrun was looking at him with black-dilated, spellbound eyes. But he sat glistening and obstinate, forcing the wheeling mare, which spun and swerved like a wind, and yet could not get out of the grasp of his will, nor escape from the mad clamour of terror that resounded through her, as the trucks thumped slowly, heavily, horrifying, one after the other, one pursuing the other, over the rails of the crossing.

The locomotive, as if wanting to see what could be done, put on the brakes, and back came the trucks rebounding on the iron buffers, striking like horrible cymbals, clashing nearer and nearer in frightful strident concussions. The mare opened her mouth and rose slowly, as if lifted up on a wind of terror. Then suddenly her fore-feet struck out, as she convulsed herself utterly away from the horror. Back she went, and the two girls clung to each other, feeling she must fall backwards on top of him. But he leaned forward, his face shining with fixed amusement, and at last he brought her down, sank her down, and was bearing her back to the mark. But as strong as the pressure of his compulsion was the repulsion of her utter terror, throwing her back away from the railway, so that she spun round and round on two legs, as if she were in the centre of some whirlwind. It made Gudrun faint with poignant dizziness, which seemed to penetrate to her heart.

'No – ! No – ! Let her go! Let her go, you fool, you *fool* – !' cried Ursula at the top of her voice, completely outside herself. And Gudrun hated her bitterly for being outside herself. It was unendurable that Ursula's voice was so powerful and naked.

A sharpened look came on Gerald's face. He bit himself down on the mare like a keen edge biting home, and *forced* her round. She roared as she breathed, her nostrils were two wide, hot holes, her mouth was apart, her eyes frenzied. It was a repulsive sight. But he held on her unrelaxed, with an almost mechanical relentlessness, keen as a sword pressing into her. Both man and horse were sweating with violence. Yet he seemed calm as a ray of cold sunshine.

Meanwhile the eternal trucks were rumbling on, very slowly, treading one after the other, one after the other, like a disgusting dream that has no end. The connecting chains were grinding and squeaking as the tension varied, the mare pawed and struck away mechanically now, her terror fulfilled in her, for now the man encompassed her; her paws were blind and pathetic as she beat the air, the man closed round her, and brought her down, almost as if she were part of his own physique.

'And she's bleeding! She's bleeding!' cried Ursula, frantic with opposition and hatred of Gerald. She alone understood him perfectly, in pure opposition.

Gudrun looked and saw the trickles of blood on the sides of the mare, and she turned white. And then on the very wound the bright spurs came down, pressing relentlessly. The world reeled and passed into nothingness for Gudrun, she could not know any more.

When she recovered, her soul was calm and cold, without feeling. The trucks were still rumbling by, and the man and the mare were still fighting. But she herself was cold and separate, she had no more feeling for them. She was quite hard and cold and indifferent.

They could see the top of the hooded guard's-van approaching, the sound of the trucks was diminishing, there was hope of relief from the intolerable noise. The heavy panting of the half-stunned mare sounded automatically, the man seemed to be relaxing confidently, his will bright and unstained. The guard's-van came up, and passed slowly, the guard staring out in his transition on the spectacle in the road. And, through the man in the closed wagon Gudrun could see the whole scene spectacularly, isolated and momentary, like a vision isolated in eternity.

Lovely, grateful silence seemed to trail behind the receding train. How sweet the silence is! Ursula looked with hatred on the buffers of the diminishing wagon. The gate-keeper stood ready at the door of his hut, to proceed to open the gate. But Gudrun sprang suddenly forward, in front of the struggling horse, threw off the latch and flung the gates asunder, throwing one-half to the keeper, and running with the other half forwards. Gerald suddenly let go the horse and leaped forwards, almost on to Gudrun. She was not afraid. As he jerked aside the mare's head, Gudrun cried, in a strange, high voice, like a gull, or like a witch screaming out from the side of the road:

'I should think you're proud.'

B.

CHAPTER FIVE

Sitting beside the wide river, which wasn't blue at this time of the day, but stained scarlet and crimson, Leonie sighed, knowing she should be going, but lingering for just a few more minutes as the sun sank even lower towards the edge of the world.

Patting the muscled shoulder beneath her knee, she smiled wickedly. This was Mrs Hailstrom's horse she was riding, despite her words to the contrary. But it was an Arab, lighter and more delicate than the heavier, larger animals which were bred in the West.

Irritated, she turned away to her right. The riverbank was empty; there was no need for another rider to come crowding so close.

'There was a time,' said a soft voice in English, 'when you didn't try to move away from me!'

Startled, she turned violently, her horse sidling restlessly as her hands holding the reins tightened. A man was there – an almost stranger, dressed in fawn whipcord breeches, highly polished riding boots, and a white shirt opening on a strong brown throat. Oh, of course, she thought acidly, the shirt that moulded the form it clad would be of silk!

They gazed at one another; the tall, dark, classically handsome man, and the young fair girl, both sitting their horses on the bank of a famous river. He didn't look Arab, thought Leonie. He *did* look Greek. And then her thoughts added, But like a Greek from ancient times.

As he remained silent after those first words, just allowing his glance to slide over her, over all of her, she said carefully, 'He's beautiful!'

A low chuckle escaped the man – the very first time she had heard him laugh normally. She decided astringently that he wouldn't have laughed like that if she had actually said what she had been thinking. That they were both beautiful.

Then Ahmed was answering her. 'Yes, he is, isn't he?' as he patted the shining black satin coat beneath him. 'This beauty is one of the reasons that the Prince was over here, to look over a colt he has just sired … and who is as beautiful as his father.'

'Oh, do you breed horses? I mean, more than one or two to ride?'

Again a low laugh echoed, but this time Ahmed's whole body shook. 'Oh, yes, I think you could say that we breed horses. We are, after all, the Wallifa.'

'Do your …' What was she to call them? 'Do your people breed them?'

'Of course, Leonie. I thought you would know … What's the matter?' The last words were uttered sharply.

They passed over Leonie. She sat there, and it was her eyelids which had fallen shut this time. Ahmed said again, just as curtly, 'What is it?'

It was the way he had spoken her name, of course, the naturalness of it sending tremors rippling through her entire body. She straightened in the saddle, saying, 'No, I didn't know! How would I?'

'I would have expected you to have asked questions. Mrs Hailstrom could have told you.'

'As far as you're concerned, Ahmed, I don't ask questions. How could I let anyone be aware that I know you? You gave me no incentive to do that. Every time … the few times I've met you, been with you, you've always been in such a hurry – and gone.'

'Yes, well, I was escorting the Prince, and I'm afraid everything concerning that time was a formal occasion.'

'It looked like it … and so did you! But now you look very different.'

'I expect I do. However, allow me to inform you that these also are dressing-up clothes, as were those others I was wearing in Cairo. My … my uncle expects the prestige of the Wallifa to be upheld at all times. But you should see me when I'm in my working clothes, filthy and caked with dust.'

'Truly, Ahmed,' warmth coloured her words, 'seeing you as I've done, I simply couldn't imagine you'd get one dirty mark on you! What work do you do?'

'We breed horses … and camels. And believe me, we work while doing it.'

'Was that why …?' Leonie stopped speaking, then made herself continue, 'Was that why you asked me if I could ride? Those words passed over me at the time, but I've thought of them since.'

'You probably had other concerns taking up your attention at that particular time,' said Ahmed with amusement threaded through his voice.

Her glance went across to look directly at him, and she felt a burning wash of heat colour her cheeks. Oh, yes, she *had* had other concerns taking up her attention at that particular time!

Then, as if not seeing her reaction to his words, Ahmed was saying, 'I'm expected at the house; we'd better go.'

'Yes.' Leonie glanced round for Mohammed. He always rode with her when exercising the horses. He was there – a little apart from three other riders. Somehow, not even expecting it, she saw that they were wearing the black and white striped burnous she had seen once before across a crowded restaurant, with a black and silver cord to bind their headdress. That piece of attire she had seen on more than one occasion, even if it had been a trifle more elaborate.

'Three attendants,' she said with a raised eyebrow.

From his greater height Ahmed glanced down at her and grinned. She would never have expected to see such an expression on that austere, proud countenance. Unconsciously, she sent the same kind of smile back.

'Yes, well …' Ahmed said the same two words he had uttered once before this evening, 'the prestige of the Wallifa, you understand.'

'And how many attendants would that other young man have, the one they called "His Highness"?' Unconsciously, Leonie's voice had adopted more than a touch of irony. It *was* too much to have what amounted to a bodyguard.

'Oh, Hassan would have the same number.'

If he had heard that nuance in her tone, it was clear Ahmed didn't care. It made her say crossly, 'But you're not in the desert now. Surely you wouldn't be frightened that there was any danger here?'

Those strong brown hands must have given directions; the beautiful black stallion broke its easy gait as Ahmed swung round, facing her. She thought, apprehensive suddenly, that his face carried the same expression it had held when he first spoke to her on the launch – scowling, hard, contemptuous.

'Frightened …' he said. 'Don't be stupid, Leonie! No one would dare lay a hand on anyone belonging to the Wallifa … not even on any of their possessions! I've told you, it's merely a matter of prestige!' This time – also from directions those hands must have given – his mount lengthened its stride.

They rode now in silence away from a river that showed only the mundane colour of pewter as the water flowed on its way, but remembering Ahmed saying that he was expected at a house, Leonie wondered. Apart from the palatial tourist hotels, and a village, there were not many large houses in Aswan.

'You said,' she remarked carefully, breaking the silence between them, 'that you were expected. Would it be at Mrs Hailstrom's?'

'Where else? Don't tell me you weren't aware that she knows us?'

'I *am* telling you that! How could I be aware of such a thing?'

'I would have imagined you might have been told. Our acquaintanceship is a well-known story.'

'Oh, would you! Well, allow me to inform you that I wasn't told. I don't expect it would occur to my employer to tell me. As far as she's concerned, I met you once at an Embassy reception. She probably wouldn't even remember.'

For once Leonie was angry with him, for once she didn't feel like collapsing into his arms, and tartness showed clearly in her voice.

'Well, that will have to be remedied, won't it? But for now there are more important things to occupy our attention – one of them being…' The words broke off for a moment before he resumed, 'I have been away for ten days; have I been in your thoughts at all during that time?'

What a question to ask! What was she to say? She did say, 'I expect – after that time we were together – that yes, you could say you were in my thoughts some of the time.'

Sharp words in Arabic came to her as he turned, his mount again breaking its easy stride. Then he spoke one word softly in English. 'Leonie…'

That one word, the way he spoke her name, sent her heart plummeting, and she capitulated completely. 'Of course I thought about you – all the time,' she told him.

She saw the white silk of his shirt rise and fall abruptly, then he was saying, 'Thank Allah for that! A man needs to have some self-respect. Because, even when discussing business, even when among the horses, and most of all when being entertained, your face was before me when it shouldn't have been – and allow *me* to inform you, I didn't like it. I like being always in control of everything remotely concerning me.'

'Did it come even between you and the dancing girls?' she couldn't resist asking.

Ahmed laughed, naturally and out loud. 'Even between me and the dancing girls,' he replied. 'But then I have had to learn my lessons in diplomacy.'

Leonie couldn't answer, she could only remember. Did those words imply what she hoped they did? However, she wasn't to know immediately. They were home, riding through the gates, and their escort had closed up with them as they sent their mounts along the cobbled path to the stables.

Then before she could manage to speak, one of the outriders had dropped to the ground and Hussein was past her and holding Ahmed's stirrup.

'Some more of that prestige,' she muttered, preparing to dismount by herself. Because anyone less likely than Ahmed to need help in anything to do with horses, she couldn't imagine. Then she found, in her turn, some-one waiting to help. She gazed down into the dark, handsome face; she put her own hand into the one held out for her, and kicking a foot free, jumped.

Ahmed allowed that hand to drop immediately, and indicated that she go before him. She sent a smile Hussein's way, and got back the smallest bow in return. Then, with a sharp sentence in Arabic to the elderly, bearded man still remaining so straight in the saddle, Ahmed indicated that Leonie precede him.

She asked, her mind still on the horses, 'What do you call him, Ahmed?'

He knew instantly what was the question she was asking. His face slanted down at her carried a wicked grin. 'I had no say in his name. He was called Shaitan before he was ever broken in. And that name was appropriate. He *was* a devil.'

'Oh!' was all she could find to answer. But she could well imagine that breaking in. She did say, 'I suppose it's senseless to ask if it was you who did the breaking in?'

'I should imagine it is. No one else has ever ridden him. Shaitan belongs only to me.'

Dusk was now taking over and before long it would be full dark. Casting a brief glance at the man walking so silently beside her, Leonie thought unhappily that, dressed as he was, incredibly handsome as he was, he belonged to those pictures one saw gazing out from the Sunday supplements, while she ... unconsciously she sighed.

Thinking such thoughts, she put up a hand to pull off the hat Mrs Hailstrom had insisted she wore up here, pushing back the fair dishevelled hair from her forehead.

'What is the matter, Leonie? What is worrying you?'

Startled, for the second time she heard those words from him, and made herself answer. 'Nothing's the matter. Why should you think that?'

'I think it because it is so. And with you, it is not only a matter of catching your expression; it comes also from the feeling that lies between us.'

Leonie ignored his last words for a moment, deciding to put them away until she could examine them more properly, and told him a trifle acidly, 'If you must know, I was thinking that if it had been now that you'd met me for the first time, ungroomed, with a shiny face innocent of make-up, this attraction between us – because it's there, as you say – might not have taken place. Oh, of course it would have with me. But with you ...'

Swung round a corner of the house, out of sight of both stables and the wide arched veranda used as a gathering place before meals, Ahmed reached out a hand to grip her forearm. Unconsciously, Leonie's own hand went up to cover it as she felt the tremor that clasp sent to her every nerve-end.

But that emotion didn't seem to extend to her companion. His head came down towards her and she saw in the dimness that he was smiling; a natural smile with no undercurrents at all shadowing it.

'It wouldn't have mattered what you looked like,' that soft English voice was telling her. 'Either looking like a proper young lady ready for a day's work walking on a river footpath ... or so exquisite in a blue evening dress that I stole time from a business I could ill afford just to come to you. But all that was irrelevant; the damage was already done. *That* happened across a crowded room full of people in a busy airport ...'

 # Discussion

I would expect most responses to the questions to identify B as the more 'popular' of the two extracts (if you have responded differently, test your reasons against mine to see if our assumptions have anything in common). Reasons for this classification might include decisions about the style and type of narrative and perhaps also about its intended function and even readership. Thus one could pick out distinctive stylistic features such as the frequent use in B of explicit adverbial or equivalent commentaries on verbs of saying or thinking:

she smiled *wickedly*	she thought *acidly*
she said *carefully*	she decided *astringently*
the last words were uttered *sharply*	Ahmed said again, just as *curtly*

(there are many other examples throughout). Previous reading experience may suggest that this usage is famously frequent in a particular kind of narrative known as 'romance', and particularly associated with the publishers Mills and Boon. The initial hypothesis may be confirmed by other features, including the emphasis on the woman's awareness of her own emotional/sexual responses, and the general focus on a female pro-tagonist involved in a ritual courtship with a slightly distant and exotic male lead.

Identification of these features does not alone, though, result in the classification of the text as 'popular'. Extract B is likely to be popular or not by virtue of how these features are regarded in some wider view. This wider view could include a number of different elements. For example, the book may be called popular because it is published by a company known to specialise in books which are regarded as popular and which also sell in large quantities. Alternatively, it could be called 'popular' because it is not 'serious' or 'literature' or a 'proper novel'. Decisions on your part about B might have included all of these inferences drawn from stylistic features, or may only have included some of them. It certainly seems to be the case that 'popular' texts do not have to fulfil all of these criteria – *Jane Eyre* could be called popular because it is fairly widely read, but many people would call it 'literature' too. Calling a text 'popular' may mean several dif-ferent things, depending on the user's assumptions about 'popularity'. It could be used to indicate a book which simply has a different function from 'serious' fiction, but it can be used to indicate lack of real achieve-ment, originality or quality.

If stylistic features are a way of helping to make a decision about whether a text is 'popular' or not, then these features have to be related to popularity in some way. The easiest move in this case would be to say that the style is characteristic of a Mills and Boon romance, and that as these are popular kinds of book, this writing is an example of popular fiction. This is not, though, a very probing answer – it leaves untouched any ques-tions about why these books are considered popular, or why this style is typical of this popular genre. It would be more productive to argue for a link between the style and a specific popular function for the book. The emphasis on explicit interpretation in the verbs of saying and thinking could, for example, be said to arise from a desire to focus the reader's attention above all else on emotional/sexual exchanges underneath the surface. There seems, though, a contradiction between the desire to work through things beneath the surface (subtexts) and the desire to concentrate the reader's attention so unswervingly on these. Do subtexts which are so clearly interpreted really remain subtexts?

One explanation for this feature is to see it as incompetence: these romances wish to deal with emotions, but can only do so by making characters express emotions obviously. Thus the inner world of the mind is expressed at every turn by ready made descriptions of little complexity (e.g. 'Leonie sighed'). The reader cannot be left alone to interpret even the simplest exchange. Alternatively it could be said that this very emphasis produces a specific and desirable effect – a sense of the constant emotional intensity openly felt by the protagonist in this context, but which nevertheless remains an inner experience rather than one shared with the other character. Perhaps these alternatives are not merely based on different stylistic judgements, but result from differing degrees of tolerance towards this kind of writing. The more sympathetic explanation finds a way of accounting for the stylistic feature which sees it as successfully achieving a particular kind of fictional effect. The less sympathetic reading sees a failure to achieve the novelistic subtlety which it assumes is aimed at. I will come back again to questions of how we treat 'popular' fiction, but first we should look at extract A and reflect on some possibly different responses.

I assume (though I might be wrong!) that most readers will regard this text as less obviously popular than B. Here, though, I cannot identify any single stylistic feature as a clear 'sign' of 'literariness' or 'seriousness'. Instead, I would (if pushed) argue that the text as a whole seems more complex than B, partly because it does not clearly identify itself with any obvious ('popular') subgenre. If I could pick out a feature, my argument runs, which showed me what kind of writing this is, then I would be able to classify it. That classification would not necessarily be into a 'popular' subgenre (for instance, a text could be obviously a satire, but that would not always make it 'popular'), but the more a simple classification served to identify the type and function of a text, the more inclined I might be to see it as 'popular' fiction. Using these kinds of reasoning (which though unconvincing in many ways seem to be the kind of reasoning which is usually deployed to make this type of decision), I could argue that A is difficult to reduce to any simple formula, and that the experience of reading and interpreting it is not a simple one. This argument draws on a well-established sense that difficulty, complexity and, indeed, an ability to resist easy classification are precisely distinguishing features of 'literature'.[6]

A number of kinds of complexity could be picked out from extract A. Where B could be said to maintain predominantly one viewpoint and one focus (Leonie's view of herself and Ahmed), 'Coal-Dust' moves rapidly between several viewpoints and several focuses for them (variously Gudrun's, Ursula's, and Gerald's views of the locomotive, the mare, and each other). This is not strictly a blow-by-blow analysis of the narration, since in both passages there are in fact considerable complexities in the ways in which the narrator is used to communicate the viewpoints of the characters (where Ahmed speaks, for instance, we could assume that the narrator is observing him, or, as I have above, that we are observing him from Leonie's viewpoint). Rather it is a summary of what I feel the effects of the two passages are: one feels as if it is concentrated on one character (Leonie) with a single interest (Ahmed), where the other seems much more to cover a range of events and viewpoints in a way which is less predictable and even, at times, hard to follow.

It is not always clear whose viewpoint is being seen through in extract A. Who, for example, is the implied viewer of the scene beginning with the sentences: 'A sharpened look came on Gerald's face. He bit himself down on the mare like a keen edge biting home, and *forced* her round'? This could be a narrator reporting the event in their own persona, or it could represent Gerald's experience of his actions. Equally, it could represent Ursula's or Gudrun's or their shared witnessing and reaction to the event. There may be further layers of complexity. When Gerald's actions are described, this could be Ursula's or Gudrun's *interpretation* of what he is doing, rather than a direct insight into what he feels. If it is taken to be a shared perception between the two women, we could never-theless feel that they have different reactions to their imagining of Gerald's actions. Thus, drawing on previous and subsequent characterisation of Ursula and Gudrun, we could argue that this one description of Gerald could represent repulsion for one observer (Ursula?) and sexual attraction for the other (Gudrun?). Any of these solutions are plausible – and they do not exhaust the possibilities. Perhaps even to adopt one rather than another is to falsify the effect of the passage and give it too stable an inter-pretation. Perhaps part of the point is to suggest the complexity of the experience, which does not simply exist as a set of facts, but is rather a set of rapidly shifting viewpoints, some of which are viewpoints of view-points (e.g. Ursula imagining Gerald imagining himself).

Such complexity needs some justification. I have already referred above to a general argument that literature is distinguished from popular fiction by its greater complexity. However, literary complexity cannot pre-sumably merely mean unmotivated complication. For complication or dif-ficulty to become complexity, it needs to be justified or motivated by some effect or result which is worth the greater effort of reading and interpreta-tion demanded of the reader. After all, as in the case of extract B, an unsympathetic reader could accuse this passage of straightforward narra-tive incompetence. It is certainly possible to locate viewpoints more firmly than this passage does, giving a firmer sense of which characters are react-ing to what, and how they respond. To argue that this writing is not just incompetent, you need to suggest ways in which its difficulties take you further than a clearer or simpler text might.

I can certainly make such suggestions. The incident at the centre of this text must occupy a position of significance – it is surely to be regarded as more than merely an interesting thing which happened one day. This assumption is, I suppose, a critic's assumption: 'events' in literary texts are not just events, but must always form networks of meaning. However, in this text that central event is a complex one, which may be viewed from a variety of positions. There are uncertainties about who is viewing, how they respond, and how a reader might respond. These effects suggest a conception of the novel – and the world – which is not a familiar one. Instead of inviting readers to place events and characters, the text presents an unresolved fluidity of boundaries between one person and another. This may ask us to question our own sense of how clear we are about our own viewpoints. Perhaps our own identities are not contained in clear boundaries[7] from which we react only directly to events, but are made up of shifting viewing points and imaginations of others' viewing positions. □

I have presented these two passages as if we could perform a practical experiment with them – a test for 'literariness' or 'popularity'. According to the readings of them I have worked through above, this seems to have been achieved. One had features which I could connect with a popular kind of writing, the other had features which I was able to link with ideas of the 'literary'. However, in my case, unlike for the imagined reader of this book, the passages were not, of course, unseen. I picked them as examples likely to produce the kind of answer which I have given (I could have tried to pick passages which had less clear distinctions between them, but this would not have brought out the common assumptions we need to explore). But I am likely to have been predisposed in all sorts of ways to react as I have done. It is unlikely that I can really react only to the texts themselves in an unbiased way.

On the first page of this section, I commented that the comparison of the two passages was an artificial exercise, since readers could not normally help but notice 'external indicators' about what kind of text they were about to read. These indicators could include all sorts of things outside the actual writing of the texts, but one very obvious set of indicators are literally on, or signalled by, the cover of a book and its title page. For the two passages above, the covers of the books give much information. There is first the presentation of the covers – the use of artwork – and, equally immediately, the titles, names of the authors and the publishers. Very brief inspection tells me the following about the two novels from which the two passages were selected. Extract A comes from D. H. Lawrence's *Women in Love*, first published in Britain by Secker in 1921. My edition is, however, a later edition first published by Penguin in 1960, last reprinted 1993 (and reprinted by Penguin some 25 times between those dates). It has a reproduction of a painting and the Penguin logo is very clearly displayed above the author's name and the title. D. H. Lawrence seems slightly more prominent than the title of the novel, since it is in block capitals, while the title is in lower case italics. The background colour of the cover is the light green of the Penguin Twentieth Century Classics series – and those words are printed in a white box at the top of the back cover. Extract B is from *Desert Interlude* by Mons Daveson, first published by Mills and Boon in 1990, reprinted in 1991. It too has a painting on the front cover, but it looks as if it is an illustration done specially for this book, rather than a recognised painting from a museum collection. The cover displays the title of the novel prominently, but the author's name a little less prominently. As with *Women in Love*, the book's publishers and its membership of a series is made clear by the cover, which displays the words 'Mills and Boon', and that the book is number 3403 in the current 'Romance' series (which have purple covers). The endpage advertises 'Next Month's Romances' (of which there are 16).

◆ Given this rough summary of the outward appearance of these novels' covers, could you compare the ways in which the books are being marketed?

▶ Discussion

The cultural implications of this sparse 'external' information on the two books are probably fairly clear to most readers likely to consider themselves as having 'literary' or 'cultural' interests (though not only to readers who imagine themselves in this way). The fact that Lawrence has frequently been reprinted by Penguin suggests that he is an author with a certain cultural status, probably that of a well-accepted classic. The cover itself only tells us that Penguin publish the book, but we bring knowledge we already possess to bear, and this tells us that Penguin have a reputation for selling 'quality books' (though, interestingly, in large quantities at reasonably cheap prices). The mere fact that the other novel is published by Mills and Boon suggests even more precise interpretations to readers (whether they have ever read a Mills and Boon or not). The book is almost certainly of a type called a 'romance'. Though that term has a long and complex literary history,[8] it has come to mean a narrative of low status (or strong popularity?), centring on amorous adventure and seen as appealing mainly to (a certain class of?) women readers.

The cover artwork has similar messages. The painting on the Lawrence cover is applied to the narrative within (it represents Ursula, presumably?), but because it was not actually painted specifically for that purpose, we are perhaps invited to see it rather as 'Art' than as illustration. The painting's own 'originality' (it was produced not simply to be an eye-catching book cover) and its stylistic membership of the world of 'sophisticated' Art gives it a status above that of a specially drawn cover. That high cultural status is linked by the reader with that of the novel, reinforcing its membership of the class 'literature' or 'classic fiction'. The Mills and Boon cover has a different effect. Its drawing is clearly intended to show the protagonists of *Desert Interlude* specifically, and therefore must have been specially commissioned by the publishers for that book.

In other circumstances, we might expect that a specially commissioned painting would be more original, more closely suited to its purpose, and of greater value than a painting which has been used for a purpose it was not designed for (in terms of subject, but also in terms of colour range, size, technique and so on). However, that is not how the comparison works here. The lower status of the specific 'illustration' stems partly from its less 'artistic' style (one now becoming old-fashioned, perhaps, but which has a clear sense of belonging to a world of magazines and romances). But it also, ironically, stems from its specificity. The function of the illustration is to show the reader the main excitements of this book, giving them an immediate sense that it will provide the kind of pleasure they seek, or allowing them to choose the book most likely to satisfy. This suggests that the book is viewed as a fundamentally commercial product. It offers certain pleasures which are clearly advertised. If the buyer wants that quality of excitement, then this book will (or so it promises) immediately supply it. This implies an aesthetic of easy pleasures and an economy of simple supply and demand, as does the enormous quantity of publication in the 'Romance' series.

The Penguin Lawrence cover seems to constitute a different attitude to the way books are consumed. The 'artistic' status of the cover, with its lack of completely specific reference to the story within the book, may suggest a more indirect approach to the pleasures inside. The painting signals not the exact narrative of *Women in Love*, so much as the kind of more complex artistic value of which it is part. Indeed, the connection between the painting and narrative may not become apparent until the book has been read. The cover is thus not an advertisement of easy satisfaction, but a promise of deferred, but valuable pleasure.

Many distinctions between 'popular fiction' and 'literature' have been founded on notions of originality, a notion itself drawing on a class-based idea that *popular* equals less intelligent, *elite* equals more discriminating. These ideas are certainly involved in the ways these two books are presented. Lawrence's life is described on the inside cover of the Penguin in terms which make it clear that he is seen as a prophet or genius rejected in his own lifetime, but one whose worth is now acknowledged (at least by those discriminating enough to be reading this kind of book…). Thus in the last paragraph of this brief biography, his wife Frieda Lawrence's words are quoted as a form of epitaph in that vein: 'What he had seen and felt and known he gave in his writing to his fellow men, the splendour of living, the hope of more and more life … a heroic and immeasurable gift.'

Mons Daveson has a very different presentation: the book tells us no more than her (?) name. There is no author biography at all. The reasons for this are very clear, and apparently simple: Mons Daveson has no particular reputation – or if she has, that is still not the main appeal of the book. Here it is not the author who is 'sold', but the publisher and the series (though this is also at least partly true of Penguin Twentieth Century Classics). In several ways, far from trying to conceal the appearance of a production line, Mills and Boon seem positively to display the quantity of their production. Thus there is the numbering of books, and the clear advertisement of the 16 titles published *every* month. They even sell a book and tape pack which seems to invite the label 'formula writing': *And Then He Kissed Her … a Mills and Boon Guide to Writing Romantic Fiction* (with sections on characterisation, dialogue, plot and background). □

These differences in presentation and marketing suggest an opposition between individual genius and mass production. It is an opposition which runs through most versions of a distinction between 'popular' and 'literary'. But can we simply accept the assumptions in that opposition? Is the difference really as solid as it appears?

Though I chose not to bring this out in my earlier close readings of the passages, there are, in fact, some similarities as well as differences between them. I immediately picked out Daveson's frequent use of glossed verbs of saying as a distinctive feature of extract B, and then as an identifying feature of the popular 'romance'. In fact, though, the Lawrence passage also tends to use a related kind of commentary almost every time a character speaks:

> 'The fool,' *cried* Ursula *loudly*. 'Why doesn't he ride away till it's gone by?'

> 'No – ! No – ! Let her go! Let her go, you fool, you *fool* – !' *cried* Ursula *at the top of her voice*, completely outside herself.

> 'And she's bleeding! She's bleeding!' *cried* Ursula, *frantic with opposition and hatred* of Gerald.

There is not very much speech in this particular passage, which reduces the frequency of the device. In other parts of *Women in Love* where there is more dialogue there is very frequent use of explicit adverbial commentary, for example on the first page:

> 'Well,' she said, *ironically*, 'it usually means one thing! But don't you think, anyhow, you'd be – ' she *darkened slightly* – 'in a better position than you are now?'
> Again Gudrun paused, *slightly irritated*.
> 'Bound to be, in some way or other,' said Gudrun, *coolly*.

Nevertheless, I think that there is a noticeable tendency even within the original extracted passages for both Lawrence and Daveson to give very firm commentaries, 'stage directions' or interpretations of speeches by characters of a comparable kind.

The extent of the similarity could, I can see, be queried. Do the 'simple' adverbs in the Mills and Boon novel really have the same effect as Lawrence's more complex glosses? Actually, many of Lawrence's glosses are very similar, often involving single adverbs suggesting barely suppressed vexation. However, perhaps it is a forced analogy to say that the following are comparable?

> 'Truly, Ahmed,' warmth coloured her words, 'seeing you as I've done, I simply couldn't imagine you'd get one dirty mark on you!'

> 'No – ! No – ! Let her go! Let her go, you fool, you *fool* – !' cried Ursula at the top of her voice, completely outside herself.

It could be argued that the first uses a simple device for indicating a raised emotional temperature (because it cannot do this through the spoken words directly?), while the second comments on Ursula's speech in a way which is not easy to interpret, but which is suitable to the obviously heightened nature of the event, her reaction to it, and the novel's complex sense of how individual consciousnesses do react to events. But it is equally possible to argue that the first is far from simple or inappropriate. The gloss does not match the spoken words very closely, precisely because the – perhaps still inchoate – emotions to which it refers are not wholly motivated or explained by those words alone. Indeed, it is clear from the context of this quotation, that these spoken comments on clothes are part of a deeper and unresolved concern on Leonie's part with Ahmed's cultural and social position and his behaviour towards her. Nor is the gloss 'warmth coloured her words' simply dismissable as a cliché; it is not a familiar or ready-made phrase, and if it is vague in its application to the situation, that may be part of the point. This is, I think, directly comparable with Lawrence's use of the gloss, which is simultaneously explicit and suggestive of subtexts which are not fully formulated or formulatable.

You may or may not be entirely convinced by this comparison, but it might at any rate serve to suggest that there is not an absolute boundary between the two texts (and you may well notice other similarities). The comparison does not, on the other hand, automatically prove that both texts belong in a single cultural category. They could, for example, both share certain romance features, while remaining in the different spheres of the 'popular' and the 'literary'. But even the possibility of shifting the two texts towards each other may suggest that we should at least be cautious about accepting definitions – for example the definitions made by publishers or critics – of what it is we read and how we read it.

We might also notice that this kind of categorisation is itself not stable and unchanging. Though Lawrence is now published by Penguin in its Twentieth Century Classics series, his novels have in the past been published in their more general 'Fiction' category, along with novels which might or might not be readily classed as 'literature' (for example, Keith Waterhouse's *Billy Liar*, 1959). Some first editions of Lawrence novels were published with cover illustrations which look much more like our sense of those suitable for 'romance' than for 'serious literature'[9] – though, of course, the meaning of those pictorial conventions too may have altered over time. Many other books originally published as entertaining fiction rather than obviously as 'literature' are now marketed as texts with enduring worth. Many of the novels republished by Virago (and as a result available to be taught on university syllabuses) would not have been thought worthy of criticism or study until quite recently. Both Penguin and Oxford University Press have recently launched series with titles which attempt a bridge across a literature/popular divide: Penguin Popular Classics and Oxford Popular Classics.

These last developments may be part of a shift in ideas about what counts as *serious* writing in our culture (partly arising from debates in academic institutions about the status of 'literature' as a special kind of writing). Some critics (including Anthony Easthope in his book *Literary into Cultural Studies*, 1990; see section 1.3 below) have argued that the idea of 'literature' needs to be abandoned for something more inclusive. This idea is addressed concisely by Catherine Belsey in an essay called 'Towards a Cultural History – in Theory and Practice':

> The relegation of certain authors, of particular texts, and, above all, of specific textual practices helps to police the boundaries of truth. Texts which are most obviously difficult to recuperate, which most obviously challenge conservative assumptions ... have been systematically marginalised as 'flawed', or banished from view (and in consequence from print) as inadequate, not *literature*. They are, of course, flawed and inadequate according to literary standards invoked precisely to marginalise them – standards which have denied their own relativity, and indeed the cultural and historical specificity of imposing 'literary standards' at all.

> The cultural history I would like to see us produce would refuse nothing. While of course any specific investigation would find a specific focus, both chronologically and textually, no moment, no epoch, no genre and no form of signifying practice would be excluded from the field of enquiry. Cultural history would have no place for a canon, and no interest in ranking works in order of merit.[10]

Belsey then cites examples of criticism published in 1970 which approached this inclusiveness:

> Kate Millet, Germaine Greer and Eva Figes…all discussed literature, and all three refused to isolate it from the culture of which it formed a part. The writings of Freud and Barbara Cartland, for example…were treated neither as explanatory metalanguage in the first case, nor as cultural context in the second, but in both instances as texts alongside Shakespeare, D. H. Lawrence, and Norman Mailer.[11]

As it happens, some of these examples of texts to be included in a single practice of criticism resemble the two texts which this section has mainly worked with. Clearly, there are ways of arguing that distinctions between 'literature' and 'popular writing' are unnecessary and restrictive. We might broaden this much further by suggesting that distinctions between not only popular fiction and literature can be dissolved, but more generally between 'literature' and many other forms of popular culture. Are films, TV or radio soaps and so on really fundamentally different from literary novels and plays? Is it self-evidently rational to class H. G. Wells as a literary writer but not other science-fiction writers, such as Isaac Asimov or the various scriptwriters of Star Trek?

But it is also possible to argue for 'literature' as something distinct from 'entertainment' writing. Having worked through the material in this section, you might like finally to think about your answers to the following:

> ◆ Where do you stand on this issue?
> ◆ How much difference does your answer make to the kind of 'English course' you would like to do?

1.3   Literature in the Institution

Previous sections have suggested that even the existence of literature is far from self-evident or free from dispute, and that the drawing of boundaries around what is and is not literary is particularly difficult to do. Yet students and teachers in schools, colleges, and universities have read, studied and apparently experienced literature as a specific academic subject since at least the end of the nineteenth century (when the first English degrees were constructed).

Clearly then, whatever the philosophic or practical difficulties of definition, literature does exist within institutions and, indeed, *as* an institution. To take the notion of English as an institution in itself implies certain attitudes. Literature is not natural or self-defining, if it needs institutions; to be interested in the institutions of English suggests that it is not an area which is autonomous, but one which must be studied in terms of wider issues of social organisation. The word 'institution' suggests a material and organisational rather than entirely abstract focus, since its meaning can cover both an actual building made for a particular purpose, and an established and well accepted social system. Indeed, the word's history, and particularly its nineteenth-century flavour, is carried within these two senses.

To be interested in the institution(s) of English, then, is to be concerned with its social practice, with what is actually done with or through that area called 'English' or 'Literature'. This raises a number of questions, particularly of a kind which expand considerably the scope of some of the questions previously asked in this book.

1. What is literature (or the notion of literature) meant to do?
2. Is it addressed to individuals to do as they wish with it, or is there some larger social design which the institutions – wittingly or unwittingly – ensure is carried out?
3. How do institutions pass on or reproduce their sense of what literature is and is for? Do institutions merely reproduce?
4. To what extent do institutions construct the ways in which literature (or books in general?) is read and experienced?
5. How systematic is the institution? How much room for manoeuvre is there? Can the institution be differently formed (or reformed)?

The two passages below address these issues in two complementary ways. Terry Eagleton gives a critical account of the history of English as an institution, while Anthony Easthope argues for the differences between the old institutions of literary study, and the possibilities of a new institution (or new paradigm) of cultural studies which could and should replace it.

The purpose of the passage by Eagleton, was (and is) to 'provide a reasonably comprehensive account of modern literary theory for those with little or no previous knowledge of the topic'. This project is significant in terms of the date of publication, since it is around this period that literary theory begins to become a central aspect of literary study. Eagleton's book marks a turning point – and deliberately seeks to mark that point – in the history of the institution of English in Britain.

◆ Read the passage: How much of a departure is this from conventional 'literary criticism'?
◆ Try to summarise briefly how the two main phases of the 'institutionalisation' of English are characterised by the passage.

Fortunately, however, another, remarkably similar discourse lay to hand: English literature. George Gordon, early Professor of English Literature at Oxford, commented in his inaugural lecture that 'England is sick, and... English literature must save it. The Churches (as I understand) having failed, and social remedies being slow, English literature has now a triple function: still, I suppose, to delight and instruct us, but also, and above all, to save our souls and heal the State.' Gordon's words were spoken in our own century, but they find a resonance everywhere in Victorian England. It is a striking thought that had it not been for this dramatic crisis in mid-nineteenth-century ideology, we might not today have such a plentiful supply of Jane Austen casebooks and bluffer's guides to Pound. As religion progressively ceases to provide the social 'cement', affective values and basic mythologies by which a socially turbulent class-society can be welded together, 'English' is constructed as a subject to carry this ideological burden from the Victorian period onwards. The key figure here is Matthew Arnold, always preternaturally sensitive to the needs of his social class, and engagingly candid about being so. The urgent social need, as Arnold recognizes, is to 'Hellenize' or cultivate the philistine middle class, who have proved unable to underpin their political and economic power with a suitably rich and subtle ideology. This can be done by transfusing into them something of the traditional style of the aristocracy, who as Arnold shrewdly perceives are ceasing to be the dominant class in England, but who have something of the ideological wherewithal to lend a hand to their middle-class masters. State-established schools, by linking the middle class to 'the best culture of their nation', will confer on them 'a greatness and a noble spirit, which the tone of these classes is not of itself at present adequate to impart'.

The true beauty of this manoeuvre, however, lies in the effect it will have in controlling and incorporating the working class. ... Arnold is refreshingly unhypocritical: there is no feeble pretence that the education of the working class is to be conducted chiefly for their own benefit, or that his concern with their spiritual condition is, in one of his own most cherished terms, in the least 'disinterested'. In the even more disarmingly candid words of a twentieth-century proponent of this view: 'Deny to working-class children any common share in the immaterial, and presently they will grow into the men who demand with menaces a communism of the material.' If the masses are not thrown a few novels, they may react by throwing up a few barricades.

Literature was in several ways a suitable candidate for this ideological enterprise. As a liberal, 'humanizing' pursuit, it could provide a potent antidote to political bigotry and ideological extremism. Since literature, as we know, deals in universal human values rather than in such historical trivia as civil wars, the oppression of women or the dispossession of the English peasantry, it could serve to place in cosmic perspective the petty demands of working people for decent living conditions or greater control over their own lives, and might even with luck come to render them oblivious of such issues in their high-minded contemplation of eternal truths and beauties. English, as a Victorian handbook for English teachers put it, helps to 'promote sympathy and fellow feeling among all classes'; another Victorian writer speaks of literature as opening a 'serene and luminous region of truth where all may meet and expatiate in common', above 'the smoke and stir, the din and turmoil of man's lower life of care and business and debate'. Literature would rehearse the masses in the habits of pluralistic thought and feeling, persuading them to acknowledge that more than one viewpoint than theirs existed – namely, that of their masters. It would communicate to them the moral riches of bourgeois civilization, impress upon them a reverence for middle-class achievements, and, since reading is an essentially solitary, contemplative activity, curb in them any disruptive tendency to collective political action. It would give them a pride in their national language and literature: if scanty education and extensive hours of labour prevented them personally from producing a literary masterpiece, they could take pleasure in the thought that others of their own kind – English people – had done so. The people, according to a study of English literature written in 1891, 'need political culture, instruction, that is to say, in what pertains to their relation to the State, to their duties as citizens; and they need also to be impressed sentimentally by having the presentation in legend and history of heroic and patriotic examples brought vividly and attractively before them'. All of this, moreover, could be achieved without the cost and labour of teaching them the Classics: English literature was written in their own language, and so was conveniently available to them.

Like religion, literature works primarily by emotion and experience, and so was admirably well-fitted to carry through the ideological task which religion left off. Indeed by our own time literature has become effectively identical with the opposite of analytical thought and conceptual enquiry: whereas scientists, philosophers and political theorists are saddled with these drably discursive pursuits, students of literature occupy the more prized territory of feeling and experience. Whose experience, and what kinds of feeling, is a different question. Literature from Arnold onwards is the enemy of 'ideological dogma', an attitude which might have come as a surprise to Dante, Milton and Pope; the truth or falsity of beliefs such as that blacks are inferior to whites is less important than what it feels like to experience them. Arnold himself had beliefs, of course, though like everybody else he regarded his own beliefs as reasoned positions rather than ideological dogmas. Even so, it was not the business of literature to communicate such beliefs directly – to argue openly, for example, that private property is the bulwark of liberty. Instead, literature should convey *timeless* truths, thus distracting the masses from their immediate commitments, nurturing in them a spirit of tolerance and generosity, and so ensuring the survival of private property. Just as Arnold attempted in *Literature and Dogma* and *God and the Bible* to dissolve away the embarrassingly doctrinal bits of Christianity into poetically suggestive sonorities, so the pill of middle-class ideology was to be sweetened by the sugar of literature.

There was another sense in which the 'experiential' nature of literature was ideologically convenient. For 'experience' is not only the homeland of ideology, the place where it takes root most effectively; it is also in its literary form a kind of vicarious self-fulfilment. If you do not have the money and leisure to visit the Far East, except perhaps as a soldier in the pay of British imperialism, then you can always 'experience' it at second hand by reading Conrad or Kipling. Indeed according to some literary theories this is even more real than strolling round Bangkok. The actually impoverished experience of the mass of people, an impoverishment bred by their social conditions, can be supplemented by literature: instead of working to change such conditions (which Arnold, to his credit, did more thoroughly than almost any of those who sought to inherit his mantle), you can vicariously fulfil someone's desire for a fuller life by handing them *Pride and Prejudice*.

It is significant, then, that 'English' as an academic subject was first institutionalized not in the Universities, but in the Mechanics' Institutes, working men's colleges and extension lecturing circuits. English was literally the poor man's Classics – a way of providing a cheapish 'liberal' education for those beyond the charmed circles of public school and Oxbridge. From the outset, in the work of 'English' pioneers like F. D. Maurice and Charles Kingsley, the emphasis was on solidarity between the social classes, the cultivation of 'larger sympathies', the instillation of national pride and the transmission of 'moral' values. This last concern – still the distinctive hallmark of literary studies in England, and a frequent source of bemusement to intellectuals from other cultures – was an essential part of the ideological project; indeed the rise of 'English' is more or less concomitant with an historic shift in the very meaning of the term 'moral', of which Arnold, Henry James and F. R. Leavis are the major critical exponents. Morality is no longer to be grasped as a formulated code or explicit ethical system: it is rather a sensitive preoccupation with the whole quality of life itself, with the oblique, nuanced particulars of human experience. Somewhat rephrased, this can be taken as meaning that the old religious ideologies have lost their force, and that a more subtle communication of moral values, one which works by 'dramatic enactment' rather than rebarbative abstraction, is thus in order. Since such values are nowhere more vividly dramatized than in literature, brought home to 'felt experience' with all the unquestionable reality of a blow on the head, literature becomes more than just a handmaiden of moral ideology: it *is* moral ideology for the modern age, as the work of F. R. Leavis was most graphically to evince.

The working class was not the only oppressed layer of Victorian society at whom 'English' was specifically beamed. English literature, reflected a Royal Commission witness in 1877, might be considered a suitable subject for 'women...and the second- and third-rate men who...become schoolmasters.' The 'softening' and 'humanizing' effects of English, terms recurrently used by its early proponents, are within the existing ideological stereotypes of gender clearly feminine. The rise of English in England ran parallel to the gradual, grudging admission of women to the institutions of higher education; and since English was an untaxing sort of affair, concerned with the finer feelings rather than with the more virile topics of *bona fide* academic 'disciplines', it seemed a convenient sort of non-subject to palm off on the ladies, who were in any case excluded from science and the professions. Sir Arthur Quiller Couch, first Professor of English at Cambridge University, would open with the word 'Gentlemen' lectures addressed to a hall filled largely with women. Though modern male lecturers may have changed their manners, the ideological conditions which make English a popular University subject for women to read have not.

If English had its feminine aspect, however, it also acquired a masculine one as the century drew on. The era of the academic establishment of English is also the era of high imperialism in England. As British capitalism became threatened and progressively outstripped by its younger German and American rivals, the squalid, undignified scramble of too much capital chasing too few overseas territories, which was to culminate in 1914 in the first imperialist world war, created the urgent need for a sense of national mission and identity. What was at stake in English studies was less English *literature* than *English* literature: our great 'national poets' Shakespeare and Milton, the sense of an 'organic' national tradition and identity to which new recruits could be admitted by the study of humane letters. The reports of educational bodies and official enquiries into the teaching of English, in this period and in the early twentieth century, are strewn with nostalgic back-references to the 'organic' community of Elizabethan England in which nobles and groundlings found a common meeting-place in the Shakespearian theatre, and which might still be reinvented today. It is no accident that the author of one of the most influential Government reports in this area, *The Teaching of English in England* (1921), was none other than Sir Henry Newbolt, minor jingoist poet and perpetrator of the immortal line 'Play up! play up! and play the game!' Chris Baldick has pointed to the importance of the admission of English literature to the Civil Service examinations in the Victorian period: armed with this conveniently packaged version of their own cultural treasures, the servants of British imperialism could sally forth overseas secure in a sense of their national identity, and able to display that cultural superiority to their envying colonial peoples.

It took rather longer for English, a subject fit for women, workers and those wishing to impress the natives, to penetrate the bastions of ruling-class power in Oxford and Cambridge. English was an upstart, amateurish affair as academic subjects went, hardly able to compete on equal terms with the rigours of Greats or philology; since every English gentleman read his own literature in his spare time anyway, what was the point of submitting it to systematic study? Fierce rearguard actions were fought by both ancient Universities against this distressingly dilettante subject: the definition of an academic subject was what could be examined, and since English was no more than idle gossip about literary taste it was difficult to know how to make it unpleasant enough to qualify as a proper academic pursuit. This, it might be said, is one of the few problems associated with the study of English which have since been effectively resolved. The frivolous contempt for his subject displayed by the first really 'literary' Oxford professor, Sir Walter Raleigh, has to be read to be believed. Raleigh held his post in the years leading up to the First World War; and his relief at the outbreak of the war, an event which allowed him to abandon the feminine vagaries of literature and put his pen to something more manly – war propaganda – is palpable in his writing. The only way in which English seemed likely to justify its existence in the ancient Universities was by systematically mistaking itself for the Classics; but the classicists were hardly keen to have this pathetic parody of themselves around.

If the first imperialist world war more or less put paid to Sir Walter Raleigh, providing him with an heroic identity more comfortingly in line with that of his Elizabethan namesake, it also signalled the final victory of English studies at Oxford and Cambridge. One of the most strenuous antagonists of English – philology – was closely bound up with Germanic influence; and since England happened to be passing through a major war with Germany, it was possible to smear classical philology as a form of ponderous Teutonic nonsense with which no self-respecting Englishman should be caught associating. England's victory over Germany meant a renewal of national pride, an upsurge of patriotism which could only aid English's cause; but at the same time the deep trauma of the war, its almost intolerable questioning of every previously held cultural assumption, gave rise to a 'spiritual hungering', as one contemporary commentator described it, for which poetry seemed to provide an answer. It is a chastening thought that we owe the University study of English, in part at least, to a meaningless massacre. The Great War, with its carnage of ruling-class rhetoric, put paid to some of the more strident forms of chauvinism on which English had previously thrived: there could be few more Walter Raleighs after Wilfred Owen. English Literature rode to power on the back of wartime nationalism; but it also represented a search for spiritual solutions on the part of an English ruling class whose sense of identity had been profoundly shaken, whose psyche was ineradicably scarred by the horrors it had endured. Literature would be at once solace and reaffirmation, a familiar ground on which Englishmen could regroup both to explore, and to find some alternative to, the nightmare of history.

The architects of the new subject at Cambridge were on the whole individuals who could be absolved from the crime and guilt of having led working-class Englishmen over the top. F. R. Leavis had served as a medical orderly at the front; Queenie Dorothy Roth, later Q. D. Leavis, was as a woman exempt from such involvements, and was in any case still a child at the outbreak of war. I. A. Richards entered the army after graduation; the renowned pupils of these pioneers, William Empson and L. C. Knights, were also still children in 1914. The champions of English, moreover, stemmed on the whole from an alternative social class to that which had led Britain into war. F. R. Leavis was the son of a musical instruments dealer, Q. D. Roth the daughter of a draper and hosier, I. A. Richards the son of a works manager in Cheshire. English was to be fashioned not by the patrician dilettantes who occupied the early Chairs of Literature at the ancient universities, but by the offspring of the provincial petty bourgeoisie. They were members of a social class entering the traditional Universities for the first time, able to identify and challenge the social assumptions which informed its literary judgements in a way that the devotees of Sir Arthur Quiller-Couch were not. None of them had suffered the crippling disadvantages of a purely literary education of the Quiller-Couch kind: F. R. Leavis had migrated to English from history, his pupil Q. D. Roth drew in her work on psychology and cultural anthropology. I. A. Richards had been trained in mental and moral sciences.

In fashioning English into a serious discipline, these men and women blasted apart the assumptions of the pre-war upper-class generation. No subsequent movement within English studies has come near to recapturing the courage and radicalism of their stand. In the early 1920s it was desperately unclear why English was worth studying at all; by the early 1930s it had become a question of why it was worth wasting your time on anything else. English was not only a subject worth studying, but *the* supremely civilizing pursuit, the spiritual essence of the social formation. Far from constituting some amateur or impressionistic enterprise, English was an arena in which the most fundamental questions of human existence – what it meant to be a person, to engage in significant relationship with others, to live from the vital centre of the most essential values – were thrown into vivid relief and made the object of the most intensive scrutiny. *Scrutiny* was the title of the critical journal launched in 1932 by the Leavises, which has yet to be surpassed in its tenacious devotion to the moral centrality of English studies, their crucial relevance to the quality of social life as a whole. Whatever the 'failure' or 'success' of *Scrutiny*, however, one might argue the toss between the anti-Leavisian prejudice of the literary establishment and the waspishness of the *Scrutiny* movement itself, the fact remains that English students in England today are 'Leavisites' whether they know it or not, irremediably altered by that historic intervention. There is no more need to be a card-carrying Leavisite today than there is to be a card-carrying Copernican: that current has entered the bloodstream of English studies in England as Copernicus reshaped our astronomical beliefs, has become a form of spontaneous critical wisdom as deep-seated as our conviction that the earth moves round the sun. That the 'Leavis debate' is effectively dead is perhaps the major sign of *Scrutiny's* victory.

What the Leavises saw was that if the Sir Arthur Quiller-Couches were allowed to win out, literary criticism would be shunted into an historical siding of no more inherent significance than the question of whether one preferred potatoes to tomatoes. In the face of such whimsical 'taste', they stressed the centrality of rigorous critical analysis, a disciplined attention to the 'words on the page'. They urged this not simply for technical or aesthetic reasons, but because it had the closest relevance to the spiritual crisis of modern civilization. Literature was important not only in itself, but because it encapsulated creative energies which were everywhere on the defensive in modern 'commercial' society. In literature, and perhaps in literature alone, a vital feel for the creative uses of language was still manifest, in contrast to the philistine devaluing of language and traditional culture blatantly apparent in 'mass society'. The quality of a society's language was the most telling index of the quality of its personal and social life: a society which had ceased to value literature was one lethally closed to the impulses which had created and sustained the best of human civilization. In the civilized manners of eighteenth-century England, or in the 'natural', 'organic' agrarian society of the seventeenth century, one could discern a form of living sensibility without which modern industrial society would atrophy and die. ...

Dismissive of mere 'literary' values, *Scrutiny* insisted that how one evaluated literary works was deeply bound up with deeper judgements about the nature of history and society as a whole. Confronted with critical approaches which saw the dissection of literary texts as somehow discourteous, an equivalent in the literary realm to grievous bodily harm, it promoted the most scrupulous analysis of such sacrosanct objects. Appalled by the complacent assumption that any work written in elegant English was more or less as good as any other, it insisted on the most rigorous discrimination between different literary qualities: some works 'made for life', while others most assuredly did not. Restless with the cloistered aestheticism of conventional criticism, Leavis in his early years saw the need to address social and political questions: he even at one point guardedly entertained a form of economic communism. *Scrutiny* was not just a journal, but the focus of a moral and cultural crusade: its adherents would go out to the schools and universities to do battle there, nurturing through the study of literature the kind of rich, complex, mature, discriminating, morally serious responses (all key *Scrutiny* terms) which would equip individuals to survive in a mechanized society of trashy romances, alienated labour, banal advertisements and vulgarizing mass media.

I say 'survive', because apart from Leavis's brief toying with 'some form of economic communism', there was never any serious consideration of actually trying to *change* such a society. ...

From Terry Eagleton, 'The Rise of English', in *Literary Theory: An Introduction* (Oxford, 1983, 1996), pp. 20–9.

 ## Discussion 1

This kind of writing does not obviously identify itself as literary criticism, and probably looks more like historical rather than literary writing. If this is so, it may support the case that Eagleton makes in the book as a whole: that the institution of English has (except at specific periods of change) remained relatively unable to reflect on its own nature. If we see this passage as non-literary, then it may be because we are categorising it in terms of the institution of English which Eagleton's book is trying to change. Perhaps this kind of writing seems more 'factual' than we expect 'literary criticism' to be. However, most historians would agree that history is far from simply factual, and that every historical account is a construction or interpretation of evidence which might also be assembled into a different account (see sections 4.1 and 4.3 below). This means that, as a matter of principle, there may be other explanations of the rise of English than those offered by Eagleton. Different explanations would, however, be difficult for us to offer without further research (though we can be alert for any moves in the argument that do not convince, or which could be differently weighted).

At any rate, this kind of writing has little in common with literary criticism as it is most commonly conceived: there is no focus on texts at all, no mention of what texts were read in these two institutional phases, and no obvious interest in 'literature itself'. The reasons for these marked differences from normal literary interests are, of course, precisely the point: the institutional contexts which surround and give particular meaning to the study of literature are what is under investigation. □

▶ Discussion 2

For Eagleton the single most important factor in the institutionalisation of English is the decline of the power of religious belief and institutions in late nineteenth-century Britain. He sees the 'Victorian ruling class'[12] in a state of great anxiety over the decline of religion because it was 'an extremely effective ideological control'. Literature could be an effective replacement since it too promoted social unity – by blurring specific class identities into a generalised 'human' and 'English' identity, and by providing an arena for thought and feeling which could be defined as apolitical. Eagleton notes, indeed, that a vision of organic national unity runs through the history of the institutionalisation of English literature:

> The reports of educational bodies and official enquiries into the teaching of English in this period and in the early twentieth century are strewn with nostalgic back-references to the 'organic' community of Elizabethan England in which nobles and groundlings found a common meeting-place in the Shakespearian theatre, and which might still be re-invented today.

The second phase of the institutionalisation of English takes place after the First World War, partly because of a consequent distrust of the established rival to English, philology, which had German associations, and partly because 'English' provided a haven from the horrors of the mechanised, impersonal world revealed by the first modern war. In this respect, the first phase's emphasis on harmony and withdrawal from the world of everyday strife is recycled. It is, however, transformed, at least in the early years of the *Scrutiny* movement, from an urge for quiet and rest into an urge *actually* to transform 'man's lower life of cares' in the real world of 'a mechanised society of trashy romances, alienated labour, banal advertisements and vulgarising mass media'. However, this radical edge is blunted by a rooted individualism which saw transformation as achievable only through personal transmission of 'sensibility', rather than through transformation of actual social conditions through any more politicised discourse. Here, too, it could be said that the first phase emphasis on the generalised personal identity against any specific identity lived on with some force. □

The second passage in this section is from a book by Anthony Easthope. The book has in many ways a similar project to Eagleton's of nearly a decade earlier (indeed, it refers frequently to Eagleton's book as a kind of pioneer of itself). It too discusses the logical flaws and ideological motivations of the institution called English, but spends much more time than Eagleton does (as well as refining and disputing some of his arguments) on what will/can replace it. It is thus another critical history and inquiry into institutions. The chapter from which this passage is taken is particularly interested in that curious double sense which the word institution has, noted earlier in this section. It starts, indeed, with a discussion of the relation of a building to two (apparently?) different kinds of institution which it has housed during its history.

A few of the ideas used may first need some explanation. Just as there is an interest here in the two senses of 'institution', so there is also a focus on the double meanings of the word 'subject' (see section 5.1 below), as it is used in the chapter title. The most familiar usage is that of the educational curriculum: knowledge is divided up into certain subjects (for example, Maths, Chemistry, English). However, a newer meaning for the word is played upon by Easthope: the linguistic/critical notion of the 'subject'. According to this theory, meaning does not originate from an essential autonomous being called the individual. On the contrary, any actual person is constituted (as a 'subject') by the language systems (or discourses) which they use/which use them. Thus meaning does not originate from some inner core, but is given to a person by the language systems they use: meaning is therefore not original, but is always deeply involved with already existing definitions, related to the social organisation of a culture (what Easthope calls 'social formations'). The 'subject', then, is the being subject to language and thence to culture and society.

> ◆ Read the passage: How different is this to 'conventional' literary criticism? How different are its methods from Eagleton's?
> ◆ What in the passage's terms are the 'subject positions' which literary studies produce? How much continuity is there between these and Eagleton's account of the institutions of English?
> ◆ What are the 'subject positions' offered by Cultural Studies in Easthope's view? How do these positions differ from those offered by Eagleton's Victorian or Leavisite English?

The Subject of Literary Studies and the Subject of Cultural Studies

Is it surprising that prisons resemble factories, schools, barracks, hospitals, which all resemble prisons?

Michel Foucault

The building I teach in was built in 1881. Named after an Irish peer, the Duke of Ormond, it was put up to house the Poor Law Commission of Manchester and its Guardians. They distributed money from property taxes to the poor, discriminating individual members of this class between the categories of 'deserving' and 'undeserving' traditional in England since the 1590s. The poor queued outside while doubtful cases were arbitrated by the Guardians. Those refused aid – whose 'destitution had been caused by intemperance or their own improvidence' had to walk the three miles to Withington workhouse. Those accepted were given handouts ('outdoor relief') though some were housed within the edifice itself. The Ormond building therefore has some enormous, formal chambers decorated in neo-Classic style, domes and pilasters, where the Guardians sat to decide cases, and, upstairs and off corridors, much smaller wards for vagrants, these styled with the characteristic mark of Victorian cost effectiveness – the brickwork is painted but not plastered. Added in 1920, the largest hall, where the Board met in private, has four large stained-glass windows each representing the Guardians as they wished to see themselves: the figure of Caritas with a cornucopia. The cellar once housed a morgue for paupers who did not last the night. It is said the building is still visited by the ghost of a man who was refused Poor Law relief, died, and returned to haunt those responsible for his death.

In 1894 the founder of the suffragettes, Emmeline Pankhurst, was appointed a member of the Commission by Labour members of the Manchester Corporation. One November Sunday in 1926 a crowd of several thousand gathered in the square facing the Ormond building to demonstrate against what was felt to be the manifest inscription of their oppression. Later the building was used as the Register Office compiling an official record of all births, marriages and deaths for Chorlton district, then in 1960 transferred to Manchester Polytechnic, where it has come to house the Department of English. The large, neo-Classic halls are used for lectures (on topics including ideology and hegemony), the smaller rooms for seminars.

ONLY PRISONS?

What is a Department of English doing in this building? For the architectural text can be read as posing a question about social institutions and ideology, historical continuities and difference. What Michel Foucault names as the 'disciplinary society' came to be established in the West in the half century after 1770, pervading private and state institutions – factories, schools, barracks, hospitals, prisons. For Foucault the disciplinary society maintains itself by constructing subjectivities according to five regimes: individualisation; compulsory work; the timetable; isolation; examination. Continuity and difference: unlike Eton College in the nineteenth century, the smooth functioning of my Department of English does not rely upon corporal punishment; unlike prisoners students are free to leave.

Yet while they stay their cases are individualised and recorded so that each participant in the department, staff, administration and students, is under personal surveillance with individual details recorded no longer in files and a card index but on disc. Work is obligatory and organised, the penalty for failure to work being dismissal or expulsion from the course (wages or grants discontinued). A timetable designed to run itself and those subject to it operates on a rigid programme – daily, weekly, termly, annually. Isolation? Well, no, but lectures perpetuate in form the chapel lectures of the prison reformers' vision, and, though the social interaction of seminars and free association outside the timetable does not conform to the disciplinary society, the library has of course a 'silent system' where individuals sit alone for work at carols or carrels (a term recalling the monastic origins of the disciplinary timetable). Examination? Oh yes; for the students 'continuous assessment' of essays, termly assessment committees, annually the formal written examinations and an Examination Board; and for the teachers there are files and secret records.

Read against the architectural text – the Poor Law Commission compared to the Department of English – the present organisation seems to differ in only one feature out of five (social interaction is permitted in seminars and leisure time). Through institutions and discursive practices the disciplinary society persists in its aim of constituting concrete individuals as subjects which in Althusser's phrase 'work by themselves'. A humanities department teaching a degree in higher or tertiary education operates to construct subjects in terms of knowledges.

It has been my argument throughout that textuality and discourse has its own specific temporality, autonomous but not independent of social institutions and the rest of the social formation. Since there is not an even correspondence between social practices (in this case, individualisation, oblig- atory work, the timetable, examination) and the reproduction of knowledges within them, there is room for manoeuvre. Even without radical institutional change it is possible to reshape a particular knowledge and the kind of sub- ject position it provides. You can introduce the study of signifying practice on the terrain traditionally occupied by literary studies and the teaching of the canonical works of a national literature. I have been arguing for ways that transition must be made and it follows one should ask what a shift of paradigm would hope to do for students and teachers.

Nothing is ever pure, being at one with itself, and paradigms are no excep- tion. Between the literary studies paradigm as defined and the cultural stud- ies paradigm advocated there are a range of empirical positions. A number of theoretical inputs have already altered 'classic' literary criticism – semiological, Marxist, feminist, psychoanalytic. Practitioners such as Norman Holland or David Lodge occur at positions between old and new, while others, such as Harold Bloom or perhaps Frank Kermode, started in the older paradigm and have moved to the new. Nevertheless, in order to focus on the paradigm shift and to keep my argument clear I have ignored some differences and treated literary and cultural studies as abstract and ideal types.

OBJECT AND SUBJECT IN A DISCOURSE OF KNOWLEDGE

A discourse of knowledge works with an object, a subject, and a means of representation which reproduces the object for that subject. [Earlier I] argued that the paradigm of literary study could be understood as structured around five interlocking terms:

1   a traditionally *empiricist* epistemology;
2   a specific pedagogic practice, the '*modernist*' reading;
3   a *field* for study discriminating the canon from popular culture;

4 an *object* of study, the canonical text;

5 the assumption that the canonical text is *unified*.

If (1), the empiricist epistemology, is singled out, literary studies can be challenged on the grounds established by Althusser when he asserts of scientific and philosophic empiricism that:

> The whole empiricist process of knowledge lies in fact in an operation of the subject called *abstraction*. To know is to abstract from the real object its essence, the possession of which by the subject is called knowledge.

Though not an uncontroversial account of empiricism, this would show that the procedure of empiricism is to construct knowledge through a theoretical process (dependence on a paradigm, tests for evidence, etc.) while denying that construction. In analogous fashion – though in the name of experience as much as knowledge – literary study assumes a paradigm to construct its account of literary texts while disavowing that it does so. It is therefore liable to Althusser's critique: that it casts its characters in an 'ideological scenario' in which the Absolute Subject confronts 'the transcendental or absolute Object' in a relation of immediacy or transparency (since the means of representation appears transparent – unproduced – then subject and object correspondingly appear unproduced, simply there).

A discourse of knowledge, then, always performs with a scenario consisting of an object, a subject and a means of representation by which the former becomes represented for the latter. And though it also entails cognitive as well as experiential consequences (more so in the case of traditional literary than in cultural studies) we can contrast literary and cultural studies by asking what form of identification and positioning each would inscribe for its pedagogic subject, whether students or teachers. This does not mean that actual individuals necessarily occupy their assigned positions – individuals never do – but it does highlight the different possibilities of each paradigm (real individuals in part do become what they study, answering questions by saying things like, 'I'm an American studies major', 'I'm Comp. Lit.').

A good critique of literary study was sketched out in the 1960s and I shall draw on this while supplementing it. In testing for positionality in each case we may consider: (1) *identifications* offered by the particular nature and quality of the object to the subject (the subject's I, writes Lacan, is that 'which is reflected of his (*sic*) form in his objects'); (2) the *position* accorded to the pedagogic subject by the means with which the object is to be represented for that subject.

IDENTIFICATIONS WITH THE OBJECT

Art versus production

The object of literary study presumes an equation between the aesthetic and the experiential in which the complexity of life is synthesised with the unity of art, the 'objective' and transcendent domain of the canon with the most intimately and inwardly 'subjective' response of the reader, thus silently discarding materiality. Cultural studies promises to step aside from this whole Kantian project. By including the texts of everyday life in its object of study it can challenge if not circumvent entirely the privileged self-enclosure of the aesthetic.

Whether choosing its texts from popular culture or the canon, its object is not transcendent but immanent, not art but artifacts, not creation but production.

Authored versus collective texts

In its object literary study discovers the 'presence' of an individual author: so many works, so many great authors, each envisaged as self-created, self-acting, undetermined, owing final allegiance only to *himself* and *his* imagination. Accordingly the material, institutional conditions for literary production – sales of the novels of Dickens, the contemporary reception of *Jude the Obscure*, the price of entry to Shakespeare's theatre – are treated as an accidental outside to the object of interest ('background') while the creative works become the essential inside ('foreground').

Cultural studies can assume no such foundation. A film is manifestly a collective production, involving (in no particular order), producers, director, stars, camera operators, script writers, sound and lighting engineers, set mechanics, 'front office', promoters, advertisers, distributors, theatre managers, and so on (for prestige purposes present-day Hollywood increasingly names the seventy or so individuals who have worked on a production). More importantly, at least in the example of Hollywood, film production is an institution within multinational capitalist production, subject to economic laws governing the production, distribution and exchange of a commodity. The object of cultural studies exhibits a shift from the author towards a decentred account of social production, displacing identification in the transcendent authority of self-creation with a necessarily more dispersed identification. A discourse of knowledge begins to develop which can make no such claims to authority and power but rather installs its subject as relative rather than transcendent, determined rather than sovereign.

The canon and its other: (*a*) synchronically

In literary study the individual work rejoins the canon of the high cultural tradition, finding its own place there as monument within the greater unity of the intersubjective canon.

There can be no such canonical unity in cultural studies if texts from the high and popular traditions are read alongside each other within a common theoretical framework, if for example the concept of gender allows Virginia Woolf's officially high cultural novel, *To the Lighthouse*, to be read alongside a soap opera such as 'Dynasty' as possible versions of a form of representation addressed to women. It is here that we may retrieve positively the implication of the argument put forward negatively in the chapter on literary value. That discussion claimed there was nothing wrong with study of the 'existing monuments' (so long as they were not read as monuments but more neutrally as texts which transhistorically gave rise to different meanings), but here we should go beyond a *nihil obstat* and recognise a necessity to read high and popular together. For the alternative is to circumscribe a kind of counter-cultural enclave – 'the study of popular culture' – implicitly predicated on the superiority of the canon. Put otherwise: the repressed always returns, so if the texts of the canonical tradition are not explicitly confronted and demystified in the way I'm proposing they will remain securely in place as the other of a merely oppositional cultural studies which concedes *de facto* the hegemonic superiority of high culture.

The canon and its other: (*b*) diachronically

Synchronically literary study constitutes its canonical object in disavowed relation to the collective texts of popular culture; diachronically it proceeds as far as possible on the basis of '*the frozen syllabus*', a representation of the historical past as an ideal order, always already completed. Symptomatic of this is the degree to which literary study ignores the contemporary, Beckett except for *Waiting for Godot*, $L=A=N=G=U=A=G=E$ poets, the postmodern novels of Pynchon and Westlake. It is almost unbelievable that the poetry of Pound and Eliot, poetry of seventy years ago, is still widely taught by literary study as though it *were* contemporary. Cultural studies must take the contemporary as its point of departure – this morning's issue of the *Sun* newspaper, this month's television programme, this year's Hollywood blockbuster – in studying an object which is always changing. It thus necessarily confronts the history of popular culture as always in process as construction, innovation, reconstruction. This is not of course to say that popular cultural texts of other historical periods should be ignored but it does mean that it is not sufficient to give a merely historicist account of these (in the manner of New Historicism). They must be read (cultural materialism is right on this) as contemporary as well as being historicised. The present must be at the top of the agenda, for reasons I shall defend further on.

Gender

The two objects of literary and cultural studies do not simply offer identifications in the general sense already described but indeed quite specific identities. The gender identity of literary study remains silently yet overwhelmingly masculine. Despite the licensed enclave of the Victorian and twentieth-century novel, the huge majority of authors, from Chaucer to Pound, are men, and since the discipline aims to position readers in identification with authors, all subjects of literary study are asked to see themselves as masculine. In flat opposition to this, cultural studies is able to put in question gender and gender identity by showing how masculine and feminine are constructed within institutions and discourses, semiotic, social and unconscious. The gender identity of the pedagogic subject is problematised, rendered as provisional rather than natural.

The national culture and its others

As John Spriggs wrote in some earlier work in this area, 'the moment you define literature within any boundaries then you start to present a value-system: a national picture, a class picture, a certain kind of historic convention and so on'. All but invisibly founding itself on the canon of a national high cultural tradition (White Anglo-Saxon Protestant) literary study both in England and the United States offers us an identity by privileging itself as an inside over an outside, home versus alien, us against a rarely acknowledged them. As Said showed, literary study conforms to a larger matrix construing its others as racially and culturally homogeneous, external, subordinate, exotic, mysterious, barbaric, always both feared and desired. A case in illustration would be the way that in England Englit. has dealt with Irish writers; depending on how politically radical they are they have been either incorporated (Yeats) or marginalised (Joyce).

By confronting its subject explicitly with the concept of the other, cultural studies is able to interrogate the conventional strategy of tacit national and racial denigration (one extending well beyond the academy). In addition, by working over particular texts within this framework of analysis (a racist report in a popular newspaper, stereotypes used on British television for Royalty's visit to a developing country) it promises to reinstate the subject of its pedagogy in a more 'lived' relation to his or her self and the cultural other. For these reasons cultural studies must take care to problematise questions of national identity and national culture (the Open University course, so progressive in many ways, hardly touched on national identity). I would foresee the national question being breached on both sides, in a cultural studies concerned on the one hand with regional and sub-cultural groupings, on the other with European and international forms of culture (in England especially it is absurd that students swallowing the national canon should take in George Herbert and bypass Dante).

Class identity

It would be neat if one could say that literary study is founded in a ruling-class definition, cultural studies in a working-class definition of identity, but while the first may be the case, the second is not, or only problematically so. Though older versions of cultural studies turned to popular texts as expressions of working-class culture, subsequent accounts have recognised how far popular culture is produced within the institutions and ideological matrix of corporate capitalism ('The Framework-knitters Lamentation' was a case in point). Particular histories are at issue here, such that the dominant culture in North America is a version of popular culture (the media star as aristocrat) while differences in the British and European cultural traditions still continue to reproduce the opposition between high and popular culture as proximate equivalents to that between ruling and working class. The debate itself continues, remaining an integral aspect of cultural studies, and its effect is again to problematise the pedagogic identity of the subject as available between conflicting class identities while literary study imperceptibly subsumes that identity to a ruling-class tradition (Sir Philip Sidney, Lord Byron, and me).

POSITION AS EFFECT OF THE SUBJECT/OBJECT RELATION

Because of its empiricist (empirico-experiential) method literary study – diagrammed [earlier] as

$$\text{Reader} \longrightarrow \text{Text} (= \text{Author})$$

– is able to hide a number of elisions it performs in constructing its object as something simply *there* ('this is so, isn't it?', as Leavis was wont to say). Not so far explored, these now need to flushed from cover, for they effect a slide between object and subject, the social and the individual, specifically:

1 between the aesthetic domain and the literary canon;
2 between the canon and the text;

3 between the text and the author;

4 and so, between author and reader.

Each individually and certainly the ensemble when laminated together tends to offer the pedagogic subject of literary study a position which is fixed, unified and centred in contrast to that of the subject of cultural studies which is relative, dispersed and decentred. The effect is brought about by the paradigms in each case but also by the way that each either aims to unify a bundle of discourses or, on the contrary, brings them into juxtaposition.

Centred and decentred paradigms

Through its four superimpositions – aesthetic/canon/text/author/reader – literary study establishes its subject in relation to a *centre* to which he or she has access apparently without mediation. Cultural studies can presume no such homogeneity of experience-as-knowledge and no such centring but rather must work across a *non-correspondent* series of conceptualisations. As has been argued, to understand a magazine advertisement requires methods and terms of analysis brought together *unevenly* from semiology (the visual text as operating through denotation and connotation), sociology (the institution of advertising in relation to readers and audience groups), historical materialism (the advertisement as ideological intervention), psychoanalysis (the text as offering distinct positions to masculine and feminine readers through mechanisms of identification and desire), philosophy (the text as structured through binary oppositions). Eschewing a foundational matrix, cultural studies must proceed with imbricated terms – sign system, institution, ideology, gender, subject position, the other. It will therefore position its subject accordingly not in relation to presence and a centre but as effect of a decentred problematic.

Discipline and interdisciplinarity

Beneath the overarching schema of the aesthetic and by claiming a connection with art over against the utilitarianism of science, literary study abrogates for itself a place as a coherent, unified and *separated* discipline. No such strategy is possible for cultural studies, which draws on a range of knowledges conventionally discriminated into disciplines: semiotics, structuralism, narratology, art history, sociology, historical materialism, conventional historiography, post-structuralism, psychoanalysis, deconstruction. It therefore threatens the fixity and homogeneity of subject position proffered in the conventional separation of autonomous and fragmentary knowledges within the human sciences, each constituted by their separated objects and procedures.

From Anthony Easthope, *Literary into Cultural Studies* (London, 1991), pp. 162–72.

▶ Discussion 1

Clearly, this is not a kind of criticism which focuses on particular literary texts. It draws attention to its interest in the institution of English in the initial discussion of the material conditions – the building – in which a particular institution of English exists, and under which an apparently very different type of institution was once organised. This differs from Eagleton's approach to the institutions of English. Where Eagleton attempts to give a national picture, an account of how English arose in general and through particular institutions (e.g. the Oxford English School) from nineteenth-century concerns, Easthope gives a seemingly more anecdotal, more particular account of the history of the nineteenth-century buildings in which the English Department of Manchester Metropolitan University was later housed.

Easthope then, however, makes a move in his argument which might be said to bring back his interests to more traditional 'literary' ones: he looks at how literary texts are read in the institution of English. Though Eagleton gave an overview of the effects of late Victorian and Leavisite ideas of literature, he did not, as we noted, pay very specific attention to literature or texts as such. Easthope does deal with how the institution reproduced itself in and through the individuals who engage with its texts. Thus in the subsection of the passage headed 'Object and Subject in a Discourse of Knowledge' he isolates five assumptions which underpin 'the paradigm of literary study'. Though more theoretical in requiring engagement with ideas about the 'subject of English' in both senses, it could be said that overall this approach gives a less abstract idea of 'English' than Eagleton's historical account – since it can tell us how the way English students read texts is connected to how the whole institution functions, what it does and does not seek to do.[13] □

▶️ Discussion 2

Again, clearly, the passage argues that the subject constructed by 'literary studies' is in many ways a constrained one. According to this view, the literary studies paradigm involves in several ways a process of 'abstraction' from 'the real conditions of existence', which does, indeed, imprison the subject of English. Thus, to summarise:

1. The object of literary study is made to appear to speak directly to its reader – circumventing study of how it was/is actually produced and consumed.
2. Literature thus appears to be about one individual talking to another ('Reader → Text [= Author]').
3. This obscures and collapses a number of links and roles which actually underpin the reading and interpretation of literary texts.
4. The canon lends an illusion of unity and completeness – as if the past and present of culture were unalterable, as if what and how English can function had a large degree of fixity, as if literature is 'simply there' as an empirical object of study.
5. Literary study is not value free – but on the contrary presents a certain 'national picture, a class picture', certain views of history, and specific gender identities.

To take just one of these identity positions as an example, since 'the huge majority of authors … are men, and since the discipline aims to position readers in identification with authors, all subjects of literary study are asked to see themselves as masculine'.

There does seem to be considerable continuity between this description of the 'subject of English' and between Eagleton's English subjects. Easthope's subject does look as if it has indeed descended from those earlier institutions of English. This he (sic?) is still constructed as being involved in a highly individualistic, personal experience, one that is practical and actual rather than theoretical or conceptual. As in Eagleton's Victorian English which is superior and separate from the cares of ordinary life, so here English is abstracted from and more ideal than the 'everyday'. And, like Leavisite English, English in Easthope's account does construct an intense engagement, a sense that literature and literary study offer access to something which really matters and which has an absolute value. All of these Englishes can be seen to be 'quietistic' – to encourage political and social passivity and acceptance, to focus on individual reading and pleasure.[14] □

▶ Discussion 3

Cultural Studies, as you would expect from the discussion above, offers a freer if inherently problematised subject position – or rather range of problematised subject positions, since one of its aims is to liberate from the fixity of the 'literary studies subject'. Indeed, Cultural Studies does not seek to offer a unified subject. It will thus make its object and subject of study authentic, partly by exposing the illusory 'experience' of literary study, and, indeed, the illusory nature of other constructions of social wholeness and unproblematic identity through this kind of critique. Though Cultural Studies cannot entirely escape from the institutions (presumably not only of English but of the university more generally) in which it has developed, it can analyse the everyday alongside the 'academic' texts, making clear the constructedness of both kinds of text in terms of a chain of discourse which is not bounded by the borders of the canon or of the 'academic'. Overall, it will therefore 'position its subject ... not in relation to presence and a centre but as effect of a decentred problematic'. For Cultural Studies thus imagined, there can be no fixed identity which is 'there', but instead meanings and identities which are only always partially there, in process, being constructed to produce subject positions in our society.[15] In comparison with late Victorian and Leavisite English, such a paradigm offers something which is not 'quietistic', nor passive or abstracted, but which actively seeks to understand how social meaning is constructed in texts, and indeed, through texts, and, in fact, *textually*. The paradigm will, of course, produce new subject positions for the student and the lecturer. □

Finally in this section, there is a chance to consider your view of the nature and identity of the institution of English as you experience it. This is important not only because you have not yet been asked directly to consider your own position, but also because some time has passed since Eagleton and Easthope wrote their accounts – perhaps contemporary English has shifted its identity/ies?

◆ What relation do Eagleton's late Victorian and post-First World War versions of 'English' and Easthope's version of literary study bear to 'English' now in your experience?

◆ Easthope's book was written at a point when it seemed possible that 'cultural studies' might replace 'English' in the university; this has not, in fact, happened – English is still a thriving institution which recruits students in large numbers; why do you think that English persists?

◆ What do you think is the purpose or function of the institution/s of contemporary English?

1.4   Literary Canons

Until relatively recently the word 'Canon' had a range of meanings primarily to do with a number of religious matters in the Christian churches. A canon was (and is) a rule or law relating to ecclesiastical matters; canon law is the law of the Church, a record of all decisions of the Church regarding doctrine and discipline. Most relevantly for literary study, the word canon also indicates the books of the Bible accepted as genuine by the Church, a matter determined by much dispute and debate in the Early Church. A literary meaning deriving from this has been used in traditional literary scholarship whereby the word canon meant the works accepted as genuinely by a particular author (for example, the Shakespearian canon can be argued to contain a differing number of plays – usually between 37 and 41 – depending on which plays are considered to be genuinely by Shakespeare). However, the latest meaning of canon for literary studies is closest to the usage indicating the genuine books of the Bible. The literary canon is the set of books and authors accepted as literary, and thus studied in the subject of English.

Generally, the word has, in fact, been used in a way, and in a context, critical to its own assumptions. That is, the word 'canon' is used more by critics who wish to deny that there is a straightforwardly consensual set of sacred 'great works', than by critics who believe there is. The general context of this usage is that of the explosion of literary theory in the late 1970s and the 80s, and more specifically the efforts and impact of feminism on literary study in that period. The canon immediately became an issue for feminist critics because it was all too obvious that it seemed to include very few women authors. For feminist critics it was not enough to assume that the canon preserved those writers best deserving of survival, since they argued that the literary institution responsible for the selection was a male-dominated, patriarchal and sometimes misogynist one. Many feminist literary projects since then have sought to address this basic issue of the denial of recognition to female authors. Thus there has recently been much work put into publishing new editions of neglected works by women (such as the plays of Aphra Behn or the poems in the anthology *Women Romantic Poets 1785–1832*). Other ventures have widened the scope of this opening up of the canon beyond the 'academic'. Most notably, for example, the extremely successful Virago Press has established a wider readership for neglected women writers. Virago specifically saw itself as offering an alternative to the canon, as every Virago book explains:

> The first Virago Modern Classic … launched a list dedicated to the celebration of women writers and to the rediscovery and reprinting of their works. Its aim was, and is, to demonstrate the existence of a female tradition in fiction which is both enriching and enjoyable. The Leavisite notion of the 'Great Tradition', and the narrow academic definition of a 'classic', has meant the neglect of a large number of interesting secondary works of fiction. In calling the series 'Modern Classics' we do not necessarily mean 'great' – although this often is the case. Books are chosen for many reasons: sometimes for their importance in literary history; sometimes because they illuminate particular aspects of women's lives, both personal and public. They may be classics of comedy or storytelling; their interest can be historical, feminist, political or literary.

The denial here of the necessity of a hierarchy of literary value based on only one kind of reading or pleasure is notable: the expansion of the canon, or an attack on the notion of the canon, does not merely transform the set of books being read, but may alter the ways in which they are valued. Indeed, feminist critics have sought to transform not only the set of books read, but the ways in which female writers have been critically discussed, and the ways in which literary criticism itself functions.

The canon could not only be criticised from a feminist viewpoint: it also could be said largely to have excluded black writing, gay and lesbian writing and (as Marxist critics had pointed out from a slightly earlier period) working-class writing.[16] For critics beginning to work with a cultural studies approach,[17] the lack of interest in popular writing, and, more widely, popular culture in general was also a striking canonical exclusion. All of these canonical exclusions not only led particular groups of critics to attack the literary critical establishment, and to attempt to redress the exclusions, but also led to reflection on the notion of the canon itself. Was it merely an historical accident that certain authors rather than others were kept in the canon? Or was there some kind of consistency to the choice? Did the choice betray the ideological preferences and needs of the literary critical establishment?

We will look first at a passage that discusses a specific canonical problem, the exclusion of women from literariness, before moving on to the question of what the canon is for, and whether it needs to exist at all. The first passage is from a seminal (or ovum-like? see passage below) feminist work by Sandra M. Gilbert and Susan Gubar. It addresses the exclusion of women writers from the canon by looking at the gendering of writing which it argues was a major factor in that exclusion.

◆ Read the passage: In its view what aspects of literature are controlled by the 'metaphor of literary paternity'?
◆ The passage focuses on *metaphors*, but does refer briefly to more directly material and social exclusions of women from literature; working from the passage's hints and from any ideas of your own, what kinds of mechanism might keep women out of the canon?

The Queen's Looking Glass: Female Creativity, Male Images of Women, and the Metaphor of Literary Paternity

Is a pen a metaphorical penis? Gerard Manley Hopkins seems to have thought so. In a letter to his friend R. W. Dixon in 1886 he confided a crucial feature of his theory of poetry. The artist's 'most essential quality,' he declared, is 'masterly execution, which is a kind of male gift, and especially marks off men from women, the begetting of one's thought on paper, on verse, or whatever the matter is.' In addition, he noted that 'on better consideration it strikes me that the mastery I speak of is not so much in the mind as a puberty in the life of that quality. The male quality is the creative gift.' Male sexuality, in other words, is not just analogically but actually the essence of literary power. The poet's pen is in some sense (even more than figuratively) a penis....

In medieval philosophy, the network of connections among sexual, literary, and theological metaphors is equally complex: God the Father both engenders the cosmos and, as Ernst Robert Curtius notes, writes the Book of Nature: both tropes describe a single act of creation. In addition, the Heavenly Author's ultimate eschatological power is made manifest when, as the *Liber Scriptus* of the traditional requiem mass indicates, He writes the Book of Judgment. More recently, male artists like the Earl of Rochester in the seventeenth century and Auguste Renoir in the nineteenth, have frankly defined aesthetics based on male sexual delight. 'I...never Rhym'd, but for my Pintle's [penis's] sake,' declares Rochester's witty Timon, and (according to the painter Bridget Riley) Renoir 'is supposed to have said that he painted his paintings with his prick.' Clearly, both these artists believe, with Norman O. Brown, that 'the penis is the head of the body,' and they might both agree, too, with John Irwin's suggestion that the relationship 'of the masculine self with the feminine-masculine work is also an autoerotic act...a kind of creative onanism in which through the use of the phallic pen on the "pure space" of the virgin page...the self is continually spent and wasted....' No doubt it is for all these reasons, moreover, that poets have traditionally used a vocabulary derived from the patriarchal 'family romance' to describe their relations with each other. As Harold Bloom has pointed out, 'from the sons of Homer to the sons of Ben Jonson, poetic influence [has] been described as a filial relationship,' a relationship of '*sonship*.' The fierce struggle at the heart of literary history, says Bloom, is a 'battle between strong equals, father and son as mighty opposites, Laius and Oedipus at the crossroads.'...

Where does such an implicitly or explicitly patriarchal theory of literature leave literary women? If the pen is a metaphorical penis, with what organ can females generate texts? The question may seem frivolous, but both the patriarchal etiology that defines a solitary Father God as the only creator of all things, and the male metaphors of literary creation that depend upon such an etiology, have long 'confused' literary women, readers and writers alike. For what if such a proudly masculine cosmic Author is the sole legitimate model for all earthly authors? Or worse, what if the male generative power is not just the only legitimate power but the only power there is? That literary theoreticians from Aristotle to Hopkins seemed to believe this was so no doubt prevented many women from ever 'attempting the pen' – to use Anne Finch's phrase – and caused enormous anxiety in generations of those women who were 'presumptuous' enough to dare such an attempt. Jane Austen's Anne Elliot understates the case when she decorously observes, toward the end of *Persuasion*, that 'men have had every advantage of us in telling their story. Education has been theirs in so much higher a degree; the pen has been in their hands.' For, as Anne Finch's complaint suggests, the pen has been defined as not just accidentally but essentially a male 'tool,' and therefore not only inappropriate but actually alien to women. Lacking Austen's demure irony, Finch's passionate protest goes almost as far toward the center of the metaphor of literary paternity as Hopkins's letter to Canon Dixon. Not only is 'a woman that attempts the pen' an intrusive and 'presumptuous Creature,' she is absolutely unredeemable: no virtue can outweigh the 'fault' of her presumption because she has grotesquely crossed boundaries dictated by Nature:

> They tell us, we mistake our sex and way;
> Good breeding, fassion, dancing, dressing, play
> Are the accomplishments we shou'd desire;
> To write, or read, or think, or to enquire
> Wou'd cloud our beauty, and exaust our time,
> And interrupt the conquests of our prime;
> Whilst the dull mannage, of a servile house
> Is held by some, our outmost art and use.

Because they are by definition male activities, this passage implies, writing, reading, and thinking are not only alien but also inimical to 'female' characteristics. One hundred years later, in a famous letter to Charlotte Brontë, Robert Southey rephrased the same notion: 'Literature is not the business of a woman's life, and it cannot be.' It cannot be, the metaphor of literary paternity implies, because it is physiologically as well as sociologically impossible. If male sexuality is integrally associated with the assertive presence of literary power, female sexuality is associated with the absence of such power, with the idea – expressed by the nineteenth-century thinker Otto Weininger – that 'woman has no share in ontological reality.' As we shall see, a further implication of the paternity/creativity metaphor is the notion (implicit both in Weininger and in Southey's letter) that women exist only to be acted on by men, both as literary and as sensual objects. Again one of Anne Finch's poems explores the assumptions submerged in so many literary theories. Addressing three male poets, she exclaims:

> Happy you three! happy the Race of Men!
> Born to inform or to correct the Pen
> To proffitts pleasures freedom and command
> Whilst we beside you but as Cyphers stand
> T' increase your Numbers and to swell th' account
> Of your delights which from our charms amount
> And sadly are by this distinction taught
> That since the Fall (by our seducement wrought)
> Our is the greater losse as ours the greater fault.

Since Eve's daughters have fallen so much lower than Adam's sons, this passage says, *all* females are 'Cyphers' – nullities, vacancies – existing merely and punningly to increase male 'Numbers' (either poems or persons) by pleasuring either men's bodies or their minds, their penises or their pens.

In that case, however, devoid of what Richard Chase once called 'the masculine *élan*,' and implicitly rejecting even the slavish consolations of her 'femininity,' a literary woman is doubly a 'Cypher,' for she is really a 'eunuch,' to use the striking figure Germaine Greer applied to all women in patriarchal society. Thus Anthony Burgess recently declared that Jane Austen's novels fail because her writing 'lacks a strong male thrust,' and William Gass lamented that literary women 'lack that blood congested genital drive which energizes every great style.' The assumptions that underlie their statements were articulated more than a century ago by the nineteenth-century editor-critic Rufus Griswold. Introducing an anthology entitled *The Female Poets of America*, Griswold outlined a theory of literary sex roles which builds upon, and clarifies, these grim implications of the metaphor of literary paternity.

> It is less easy to be assured of the genuineness of literary ability in women than in men. The moral nature of women, in its finest and richest development, partakes of some of the qualities of genius; it assumes, at least, the similitude of that which in men is the characteristic or accompaniment of the highest grade of mental inspiration. We are in danger, therefore, of mistaking for the efflorescent energy of creative intelligence, that which is only the exuberance of personal 'feelings unemployed.' ... The most exquisite susceptibility of the spirit, and the capacity to mirror in dazzling variety the effects which circumstances or surrounding minds work upon it, may be accompanied by *no power to originate, nor even, in any proper sense, to reproduce*. [Italics ours]

Since Griswold has actually compiled a collection of poems by women, he plainly does not believe that all women lack reproductive or generative literary power all the time. His gender-definitions imply, however, that when such creative energy appears in a woman it may be anomalous, freakish, because as a 'male' characteristic it is essentially 'unfeminine.'

The converse of these explicit and implicit definitions of 'femininity' may also be true for those who develop literary theories based upon the 'mystical estate' of fatherhood: if a woman lacks generative literary power, then a man who loses or abuses such power becomes like a eunuch – or like a woman. When the imprisoned Marquis de Sade was denied 'any use of pencil, ink, pen, and paper,' declares Roland Barthes, he was figuratively emasculated, for 'the scriptural sperm' could flow no longer, and 'without exercise, without a pen, Sade [became] *bloated*, [became] a eunuch.' Similarly, when Hopkins wanted to explain to R. W. Dixon the aesthetic consequences of a *lack* of male mastery, he seized upon an explanation which developed the implicit parallel between women and eunuchs, declaring that 'if the life' is not 'conveyed into the work and ... displayed there ... the product is one of those *hens' eggs* that are good to eat and look just like live ones but never hatch' (italics ours). And when, late in his life, he tried to define his own sense of sterility, his thickening writer's block, he described himself (in the sonnet 'The Fine Delight That Fathers Thought') both as a eunuch and *as a woman*, specifically a woman deserted by male power: 'the widow of an insight lost,' surviving in a diminished 'winter world' that entirely lacks 'the roll, the rise, the carol, the creation' of male generative power, whose 'strong / Spur' is phallically 'live and lancing like the blow pipe flame.' And once again some lines from one of Anne Finch's plaintive protests against male literary hegemony seem to support Hopkins's image of the powerless and sterile woman artist. Remarking in the conclusion of her 'Introduction' to her *Poems* that women are 'to be dull / Expected and designed' she does not repudiate such expectations, but on the contrary admonishes herself, with bitter irony, to *be* dull:

> Be caution'd then my Muse, and still retir'd;
> Nor be dispis'd, aiming to be admir'd;
> Conscious of wants, still with contracted wing,
> To some few friends, and to thy sorrows sing;
> For groves of Lawrell, thou wert never meant;
> Be dark enough thy shades, and be thou there content.

Cut off from generative energy, in a dark and wintry world, Finch seems to be defining herself here not only as a 'Cypher' but as 'the widow of an insight lost.'

From Sandra M. Gilbert and Susan Gubar, *The Madwoman in the Attic: the Woman Writer and the Nineteenth-Century Literary Imagination* (New Haven, CT, 1979), pp. 3–17.

▶ Discussion 1

The network of metaphors associated with the idea of 'literary paternity' is seen here as an extremely powerful one, which covers every aspect of literary production and reception. Literature and the creation of texts are constructed by the metaphor as uniquely masculine acts, deriving from biological, social and theological analogies, including ideas of masturbation, procreation, fatherhood, divine creation and authority. The metaphor thus gives support to the properly masculine nature of 'writing', its authentic virility, and reinforces the idea that only men can write. Since the literary springs so clearly from men, even the more passive aspects of literature, reading it, thinking about it, enquiring into it, are beyond women. Further, the metaphor is seen as so dominant that women who do 'attempt the pen' have to struggle with a metaphor of authorship which inherently excludes them, constructs them as second-class citizens, or even sees them as impostors, improper women or 'failed' men – eunuchs. Even if all these cultural definitions can be overcome, women writers find that the images of women, of themselves, available in the masculine controlled literary canon are also infected by the same set of assumptions. Thus writing and reading literature is constrained by the metaphor, as is what is written and what can readily be written. One factor – and institution – which seems clearly implicated in the passage is that of literary criticism itself. As examples cited by Gilbert and Gubar suggest, masculine control of the Word does not cease at the moment when women produce writing, but is still powerful in interpreting and controlling it. In other words, even when a woman writer 'has expressed herself' (a difficult concept given the masculine frame described above), a masculine establishment may substantially reproduce their own version of what it was she meant and what 'herself' is or should be. ☐

▶ Discussion 2

The passage refers briefly to a number of matters of social organisation that help to reproduce the power of the literary paternity metaphor. It quotes Jane Austen's character Anne Elliot's observation that 'men have had every advantage of us in telling their story. Education has been theirs in so much higher a degree; the pen has been in their hands'. Men have traditionally had better access to learning and hence to the full resources of literacy, and also have had better access to the means by which books are produced. The phrase 'the pen is in their hands' suggests that there is only one pen – that the better access of men is directly part of the complementary denial of access for women.

The control which men can have over women's writing – over its distribution and reception through publication – is also suggested by the discussion of the nineteenth-century editor and critic Rufus Griswold. While being willing to write an introduction to a book which seems from its proud title (*The Female Poets of America*) to challenge the male control of literature, he openly casts doubt on whether women's writing can show authentic genius. His introduction seems all the more underhand in its use of the argument that the mere *appearance* of 'creative intelligence' in women's writing might well be deceptive:

> We are in danger, therefore, of mistaking for the efflorescent energy of creative intelligence, that which is only the exuberance of personal 'feelings unemployed' ... the most exquisite susceptibility of the spirit, and the capacity to mirror in dazzling variety the effects which circumstances or surrounding minds work upon it, may be accompanied by no power to originate, nor even in any proper sense, to reproduce.

Women cannot win: if they do produce something which looks like great writing, there is, it seems, a strong possibility that it will in fact be disqualified because it *originates* incorrectly. Literature should spring fully formed from the autonomous 'efflorescent energy' of the mind, but for women a similar effect can be produced because they have an excess of emotion which is 'unemployed' (i.e. presumably in the real world). Indeed, what looks like good women's writing is often for Griswold actually a mere mirroring of their surroundings or of surrounding (male?) minds. It is thus not 'original', even when its effect is 'dazzling', because it has not truly been originated. It is an act of reflection, not an act of creation. Thus women are not only found wanting, but also blamed for living women's lives (for having 'feelings unemployed'), as if they had a choice in the matter of where they belonged in nineteenth-century public life. Finally, what might be thought at least a female role – the 'power to reproduce' – is also denied them, because *reflection* is distinguished from *reproduction* by its 'passivity' and essential mindlessness. Women, in short, do not 'author' their material, and are therefore only fake writers.

Whether men or women bought and read *The Female Poets of America*, the poetry within it had to survive this introduction, this assertion that it was only a second-order kind of writing. Of course, it is quite possible that the poems themselves offer different perspectives on women's writing, but the strength of the obstacles to women's writing being seriously received may be suggested by the deviousness and obstinacy of Griswold's argument.

The passage does not explicitly discuss how twentieth-century critics might have tried similarly to control what women's writing did get through the outer defences – but its quotation of Harold Bloom, Norman O. Brown and William Gass suggests that there has at times been continuity with nineteenth-century traditions. This suggests a further set of material conditions which might control women's writing – including domination of the academy by men, and construction of critical discourse in patriarchal ways. □

This exclusion and (mis)representation of women has, presumably, been addressed with considerable energy since Sandra M. Gilbert and Susan Gubar wrote *The Madwoman in the Attic* in 1979. However, while this discussion of the condition of the (nineteenth-century) woman writer looks as if it is a particular and important example of the way in which the institution of the canon can control what and how we write and read, it also points towards larger questions about the canon. Its explorations of metaphors of writing are to do with authority and control, concepts which are themselves at the heart of the notion of the canon. The canon controls that which is and is not literary, that which is and is not seriously read, and ultimately what is or is not kept in print (or in performance). The pen–penis metaphor, though partly, in the critics and writers cited, celebrating masculine creation also seems fixated on a need to control and a fear of loss of control. In attacking the results of this kind of metaphor and the control it exerts, it could be said that Gilbert and Gubar are not just attacking this canon, but are questioning the idea of a canon at all, since the canon – control over what can be written and read – is here associated with a species of sick and phallocentric masculinity.

Frank Kermode picks up the question of what the canon is for, what its function is, and whether we need it, in 'Canon and Period' below. He starts his discussion first with reference to a defender of the canon, and then with an argument about a feminist/Afro-American view of the canon.

◆ Read the passage. Why does Kermode not regard the programme suggested by the Professor of Literature and Human Relations at the University of Pennsylvania as an overturning of everything that is canonical?

◆ Do you agree with Kermode's reading of the manifesto's attitude towards canonicity?

◆ What does Kermode see as the positive value of canons?

I can best start this section on canon by reading an item from the US *Chronicle of Higher Education* dated 4 September 1985. This journal is widely circulated in American institutions of higher education. On this occasion, at the beginning of a new academic year, it ran a symposium in which twenty-two authorities in various fields told readers what developments to expect over the next few years. This is the forecast for literary studies:

> The dominant concern of literary studies during the rest of the nineteenth-eighties will be literary theory. Especially important will be the use of theory informed by the work of the French philosopher Jacques Derrida to gain insights into the cultures of blacks and women.
>
> In fact the convergence of feminist and Afro-American theoretical formulations offers the most challenging nexus for scholarship in the coming years. Specifically the most exciting and insightful accounts of expressive culture in general and creative writing in particular will derive from efforts that employ feminist and Afro-American approaches to the study of texts by Afro-American writers such as Zora Neale Hurston, Sonia Sanchez, Gloria Naylor and Toni Morrison.
>
> Among the promising areas for analysis is the examination of the concerns and metaphorical patterns that are common to past and present black women writers.
>
> Such theoretical accounts of the cultural products of race and gender will help to undermine the half-truths that white males have established as constituting American culture as a whole. One aspect of that development will be the continued reshaping of the literary canon as forgotten, neglected or suppressed texts are re-discovered.
>
> Literary theory is also full of disruptive and deeply political potential, which Afro-American and feminist critics will labor to release in coming years.

This manifesto, for such it appears to be, was written by the Professor 'of English and of Human Relations' at the University of Pennsylvania. It proposes what could well be called a radical deconstruction of the canon, putting in the place of the false elements foisted into it by white males a list of black females. These will be studied by methods specifically Afro-American. The writer points out the political implications of these developments, for he knows that the changes he prophesies will not come to pass without alterations in more than the syllabus. He assumes that the literary canon is a load-bearing element of the existing power structure, and believes that by imposing radical change on the canon you can help to dismantle the power structure. ...

So canons are complicit with power; and canons are useful in that they enable us to handle otherwise unmanageable historical deposits. They do this by affirming that some works are more valuable than others, more worthy of minute attention. Whether their value is wholly dependent on their being singled out in this way is a contested issue. There is in any case a quite unmistakable difference of status between canonical and uncanonical books, however they got into the canon. But once they are in certain changes come over them. First, they are completely locked into their times, their texts as near frozen as devout scholarship can make them, their very language more and more remote. Secondly, they are, paradoxically, by this fact, set free of time. Thirdly, the separate constituents become not only books in their own right but part of a larger whole – a whole because it is so treated. Fourthly, that whole, with all its interrelated parts, can be thought to have an inexhaustible potential of meaning, so that what happens in the course of time – as the original context and language of the collection grows more and more distant – is that new meanings accure. ...

It has been said that 'periodization is colonial politics', which makes 'period' as wicked an idea as 'canon'. It is certainly true of both that they are used to serve our interests, which may be colonialist or political. As Karl Popper remarks, 'Although history has no meaning, we can give it a meaning.' He believes that we should choose such meanings, as we should choose our ends in life, which also has no meanings other than those we give it, by an exercise of conscientious reason. This, no doubt, would always be the claim of the chooser. The meanings chosen will necessarily vary. But most agree that it is a benefit to secure access – by '(re)construction', as Jameson might say – to something in the past that can be made new, made valuable for the present. ...

All the same, we do accept change, in the ways we conceive as open to us. But so long as we seek value in works of the past we shall be forced to submit the show of history to the desires of the mind – whoever 'we' may be. And in order to do that we shall invent new grids and impose them on the past – rewrite the past to suit our modern wishes, as the past has always been rewritten. Yet valuations are handed on, and constantly redefined; so that in the end the question is not whether they are unfairly selective, but whether we want to break the only strong link we have with the past – our ability to identify with the interests of our predecessors, to qualify their judgements without necessarily overthrowing them, to converse with them in a transhistorical dimension.

From Frank Kermode, 'Canon and Period', in *History and Value* (Oxford, 1989), pp. 108–27.

Discussion 1

Kermode argues that the programme would certainly alter the canon – by replacing one set of 'authorised' books by another. But that would be a substitution, not a destruction. The concept of a canon would still continue – in fact, the professor's plans depend on there being an acceptance of an authorised set of books which best represent American culture, which are more valuable, more authentic than the 'half-truths that white males have established as constituting American culture as a whole'. ☐

Discussion 2

I am not quite convinced that the writer of the programme did intend to replace one canon with another, as Kermode suggests. The following sentence implies a different idea of what will happen to the canon: 'One aspect of that development will be the continued reshaping of the literary canon as forgotten, neglected or suppressed texts are re-discovered'. I think that what the professor has in mind is not the replacement of one canon, but the *expansion* of the canon. The sentence just quoted suggests that the new canon will be a fuller one, and in that sense a truer one – one which will reflect the true history of writing in America, including the contribution of black and women writers, as well, I take it, as the present 'great names'. The reshaping of the canon in this model is not so much a single event as a continual process of addition. This is not simply a tacit admission that there ought to be such a thing as a canon, but a different conception of a canon. What one might ask is whether, in fact, a vastly larger canon is possible. Some of Kermode's arguments (see under Discussion 3) suggest that part of the function of the canon is to select; if there are no boundaries to a canon, then it may cease to function in that way, perhaps cease to function at all. □

▶️ Discussion 3

Kermode argues that the (or *a*) canon is undoubtedly an instrument of control, but absolutely necessary. He extends the argument to the use of literary 'periods', which are seen to work in a similar way to the canon in structuring how and what we read. Kermode concludes that the canon does indeed equal power, but that we do all need to be able to control and manipulate the texts which we read within some species of structure allowing selection from the mass of existing writing. Moreover, he does not see the canon as entirely static and conservative – it can and does develop, as other kinds of historical interpretation change through time and social alteration:

> All the same we do accept change, in the ways we conceive as open to us. But so long as we seek value in the works of the past we shall be forced to submit the show of history to the desires of the mind – whoever 'we' may be. And in order to do that we shall invent new grids and impose them on the past – rewrite the past to suit our modern wishes, as the past has always been rewritten.

In particular, ideas of canon do preserve the possibility of 'converse' with the past, with texts and traditions different from those we ourselves produce, even if we can only perceive those differences through inevitably modern interpretations. □

There surely has been a period of change in the canon, and perhaps even the ways we think about canons since the nineteen eighties. Indeed, the plural form *canons* is now used as much as the monolithic singular of *the canon*. For example, it is much more common to study contemporary texts on degree courses than it was (texts are being written and studied within a single decade!), there is more attention paid to women's writing and black writing and writing in English from outside Britain and the USA. There has been some revision of how traditional literary periods are conceived. Thus Romantic poetry once had an entirely male canon, made up of its big six: Blake, Wordsworth, Coleridge, Keats, Shelley and Byron. It is now increasingly common to study women poets alongside them (though I suspect that the male poets here still maintain a certain canonical aura). These revisions do not necessarily dispose of all problems and questions about canons, though. Even if there is revision, how much has the conception of what constitutes literature or the central texts of a given period really altered? We will approach these issues through two final exercises, where, as usual, I will leave you to develop your own responses to the exercises and to the questions raised in the whole section. The first exercise focuses on two particular texts viewed in the light of canonical issues. The second asks you to think about what you study and the current situation in university English.

The two texts are both poems from the Romantic period: Samuel Taylor Coleridge's well-known and firmly canonical 'Kubla Khan' and Anna Barbauld's less well known and until recently at least un-canonical poem, 'To Mr. [S.T.] C[oleridge]'.

◆ Read both poems. Do you think these two poems are of equal value? Why/why not?
◆ To what extent can you ignore the long-established canonical status of 'Kubla Khan' in comparing the two poems?
◆ Does reading the Anna Barbauld poem alter or add to your understanding of the Coleridge poem or of Romanticism more generally?
◆ How readily can Anna Barbauld's 'To Mr. [S.T.] C[oleridge]' be accommodated in the canons of undergraduate English?

KUBLA KHAN

OR, A VISION IN A DREAM

A FRAGMENT

In Xanadu did Kubla Khan
A stately pleasure-dome decree:
Where Alph, the sacred river, ran
Through caverns measureless to man
  Down to a sunless sea.   5
So twice five miles of fertile ground
With walls and towers were girdled round:
And here were gardens bright with sinuous rills,
Where blossomed many an incense-bearing tree;
And here were forests ancient as the hills,   10
Enfolding sunny spots of greenery.

But oh! that deep romantic chasm which slanted
Down the green hill athwart a cedarn cover!

A savage place! as holy and enchanted
As e'er beneath a waning moon was haunted   15
By woman wailing for her demon-lover!
And from this chasm, with ceaseless turmoil seething,
As if this earth in fast thick pants were breathing,
A mighty fountain momently was forced:
Amid whose swift half-intermitted burst   20
Huge fragments vaulted like rebounding hail,
Or chaffy grain beneath the thresher's flail:
And 'mid these dancing rocks at once and ever
It flung up momently the sacred river.
Five miles meandering with a mazy motion   25
Through wood and dale the sacred river ran,
Then reached the caverns measureless to man,
And sank in tumult to a lifeless ocean:
And 'mid this tumult Kubla heard from far
Ancestral voices prophesying war!   30

   The shadow of the dome of pleasure
   Floated midway on the waves;
   Where was heard the mingled measure
   From the fountain and the caves.
It was a miracle of rare device,   35
A sunny pleasure-dome with caves of ice!

   A damsel with a dulcimer
   In a vision once I saw:
   It was an Abyssinian maid,
   And on her dulcimer she played,   40
   Singing of Mount Abora.

   Could I revive within me
   Her symphony and song,
   To such a deep delight 'twould win me,
That with music loud and long,   45
I would build that dome in air,
That sunny dome! those caves of ice!
And all who heard should see them there,
And all should cry, Beware! Beware!
His flashing eyes, his floating hair!
Weave a circle round him thrice,   50
And close your eyes with holy dread,
For he on honey-dew hath fed,
And drunk the milk of Paradise.

(Autumn 1797 or Spring 1798.)

Samuel Taylor Coleridge, 'Kubla Khan' (published 1816). From *S.T. Coleridge –
Selected Poems*, ed. John Beer (London, 1981), pp.167–8.

To Mr. [S.T.] C[oleridge]

Midway the hill of science, after steep
And rugged paths that tire the unpractised feet,
A grove extends; in tangled mazes wrought,
And filled with strange enchantment: dubious shapes
Flit through dim glades, and lure the eager foot
Of youthful ardour to eternal chase.
Dreams hang on every leaf: unearthly forms
Glide through the gloom; and mystic visions swim
Before the cheated sense. Athwart the mists,
Far into vacant space, huge shadows stretch   10
And seem realities; while things of life,
Obvious to sight and touch, all glowing round,
Fade to the hue of shadows. Scruples here,
With filmy net, most like the autumnal webs
Of floating gossamer, arrest the foot
Of generous enterprise; and palsy hope
And fair ambition with the chilling touch
Of sickly hesitation and blank fear.
Nor seldom Indolence these lawns among
Fixes her turf-built seat; and wears the garb   20
Of deep philosophy, and museful sits
In dreamy twilight of the vacant mind,
Soothed by the whispering shade; for soothing soft
The shades; and vistas lengthening into air,
With moonbeam rainbows tinted. Here each mind
Of finer mould, acute and delicate,
In its high progress to eternal truth
Rests for a space, in fairy bowers entranced;
And loves the softened light and tender gloom;
And, pampered with most unsubstantial food,   30
Looks down indignant on the grosser world,
And matter's cumbrous shapings. Youth beloved
Of Science – of the Muse beloved, – not here,
Not in the maze of metaphysic lore,
Build thou thy place of resting! Lightly tread
The dangerous ground, on noble aims intent;
And be this Circe of the studious cell
Enjoyed, but still subservient. Active scenes
Shall soon with healthful spirit brace thy mind;
And fair exertion, for bright fame sustained,   40
For friends, for country, chase each spleen-fed fog
That blots the wide creation –
Now heaven conduct thee with a parent's love!

Anna Barbauld, 'To Mr. [S.T.] C[oleridge]' (1797, published 1799 and 1825).
From *Women Romantic Poets 1785–1832*, ed. Jennifer Breen (London, 1992),
pp. 84–5.

◆ What is the 'canonical' situation now? (Do you think that there is a single canon in the institution of English; do publishers, universities and colleges, 'A' level boards, students and teachers and the 'general reader' all agree on what is canonical? Is there an orthodoxy – or a degree of orthodoxy – with particular values behind it? Are there still important exclusions? Do you think there has to be a canon?)
◆ What kind of canon or canons does your own university or institution teach?
◆ To what extent do you think you should study the kind of literature in the pre-nineteen eighties canon (the great names, presumably)?

Further Reading

Belsey, Catherine, *Critical Practice* (London, Routledge, 1980).

Bennet, Tony (ed.), *Popular Fiction: Technology, Ideology, Production, Reading* (London, Routledge, 1989).

Eagleton, Terry, *Literary Theory – An Introduction* (Oxford, Blackwell, 1983).

Easthope, Anthony, *Literary into Cultural Studies* (London, Routledge, 1991).

Gilbert, Sandra, and Susan Gubar, *The Madwoman in the Attic: the Woman Writer and the Nineteenth Century Literary Imagination* (New Haven, CT, Yale University Press, 1979).

——, *The Norton Anthology of Literature by Women: the Traditions in English* (New York and London, Norton, 1996).

Humm, Peter, Paul Stigant and Peter Widdowson (eds), *Popular Fictions: Essays in Literature and History* (London, Methuen, 1986).

Kermode, Frank, *The Classic* (London, Faber, 1975).

——, *History and Value* (Oxford, Clarendon, 1988).

Storey, John (ed.), *What is Cultural Studies? – A Reader* (London, Routledge, 1996).

Todorov, Tzvetzan, 'The Notion of Literature', in *Genres in Discourse* (Cambridge, Cambridge University Press, 1978, 1990).

Widdowson, Peter, *Literature* (New Critical Idiom series) (London, Routledge, 1998).

Williams, Raymond, *Keywords – a Vocabulary of Culture and Society* (London, Fontana, 1983).

——, *Culture and Society 1780–1950* (Harmondsworth, Penguin, 1963).

Texts, Authors, Critics

2.1 What is a Text?

The question 'What is a text?' may seem even more ridiculously simple than some of the earlier questions in this book may initially have seemed. As is becoming apparent, though, there is often a large HOWEVER attached to simplicity. The idea of a text is no exception and will take some space to explore.

The word text is not a common one in ordinary language, but it is used very frequently among students and teachers of English. It is thus clearly a technical term. Readers more generally do not use the word. This is clear if we make up a sentence, placing 'text' in a less specialised context. For example, a sentence such as 'the new *text* I bought from the station bookstall was a bit disappointing' suggests that the term is not at home in ordinary speech, even about reading (whereas more general words like 'book' or more specific generic ones such as 'novel' and 'thriller' would be fine). For people involved with the subject of English, however, the word 'text' is in common currency: 'Should we use any particular text of *As You Like It?*', 'What text are we doing next week?', 'perhaps closer attention to the text would help you in this answer'. Though a technical term, 'text' often seems to be used quite straightforwardly, as if it were indeed a specialist term, but not one which caused anyone any problems. In the 'academic' examples above, the word has two or three distinct senses, suggesting this combination of apparent obviousness and specialised vocabulary. Thus in these example sentences, the meanings are:

1. text = which edition? (Penguin? Oxford? New Arden? Dover Thrift? …)
2. text = what book? (have we reached *Jude the Obscure* yet? Or are we doing another week on *Middlemarch*? …)
3. text = the actual writing of the book being studied (as opposed to comments about its historical or social context, perhaps; the detail of the text, in particular)

In each of these cases, 'the text' seems to have an obviously physical existence (the book or writing you are studying), together with meanings which are bound up with more precise ideas of literary study. The first question may be an eminently practical one about quality (is one edition better?) and/or cost (will a cheap edition do?), but it can only be asked by someone who knows that a Shakespeare play does not just come in one shape. The second question seems less technical, using text to mean *any* book (the question could reasonably be asked of a tutor teaching poetry, drama, the novel or a mixture of genres). In fact, though, this generality conceals a quite specific assumption: a text is a special kind of writing which you study in its own right if you are 'doing' English. A text is not just a book, a piece of writing. It is rather the essential building block at the foundation of the subject of 'English', something distinctive enough to require seminars, tutors and so on to understand it in its full complexity. To use the word text in this general sense implies not a lack of precision, but a claim to knowledge of how the discipline of English selects as its objects of study particular writings which it subjects to specific and intensive kinds of reading practice. The third sentence again draws on this range of technical assumptions, for the tutor is suggesting to the student the advantage of a particular critical procedure, which the mere words 'close attention to the text' are enough to indicate. It is the assumptions behind, and the meanings in, this common yet specialised word 'text' which this section will investigate. As with previous questions, the answer to 'What is a text?' may well not be 'it is the following', but rather 'if we accept that or this meaning, where does it take us?'.

As so often, the origins of the word 'text' help to provide an approach to its range of current meanings, and to suggest some of the ways in which these meanings are not simple ones. The word comes from the Latin noun *textus* = the style or 'tissue of a literary work'. Even in this form, it is clearly a technical term, and the exact sense is not that easy to grasp. In fact, to explain this earliest meaning, the *OED* has to use the metaphor of a 'tissue' = something woven, the basic material from which a literary work is constructed. Interestingly, this metaphoric explanation itself points backwards to the Latin word which lies behind *textus*: the verb *texere* = to weave.

This verb is also the root of two other modern English words: *textile* and *texture*. These words can help us to see something of the basic meaning of the word text, while also reinforcing its complexity. *Textile* is close to the root word's meaning, indicating woven cloth. *Texture* is a broadening of this basic idea, to signify the feel of a woven material (wool feels different from cotton), the quality of having depth or discernibly separate parts within a whole (e.g. textured wallpaper contains woodchips to give decorative variety to the surface). The original application to cloth has been expanded to other materials. Thus wood or stone can have a texture, that is, a quality of touch produced by the ways the basic materials of the substance are combined. Finally, even events which lack obvious materiality can be said to have texture – the word is used of music: 'the rapidly altering combinations of strings, brass, woodwind, electric bass and didgeridoo give the piece a dense but ever shifting texture' and of the quality of experience: 'it is difficult to imagine the texture of life for most Victorian women of this class. ... '

The literary *text* has meanings very much connected to those in textile and texture. It is usually regarded as something woven out of smaller and identifiable parts, together with a clear unity, a quality given by its organisation of smaller details, but also an overall effect and meaning. The modern English text has shifted its meaning a little from the Latin *textus*, from a focus mainly on the threads (the individual quality of the smaller parts) to an emphasis on the whole piece of material (the finished piece). Thus, we can talk about the *style of a text*, an idea which would be merely repetitive if our 'text' fully retained the smaller focus of the Latin term. At the same time, the phrase used above, 'closer attention to the text', implying rigorous examination of the detail, suggests that we have retained a sense of the word's variable focus on the whole or the part.

In making sense of the modern word text, the relationship between smaller and larger focuses, parts and wholes, remains a vital issue.

> ◆ Read the following extracts from the *OED*'s definition of text.
> ◆ Then briefly list (a) those meanings which focus on parts ('close ups')
> and (b) those meanings which focus on wholes ('whole views').

Though the entries are, of course, already divided up into differing senses, these divisions may in this case not simply match themselves to your (a) and (b) lists.

1.a. The wording of anything written or printed; the structure formed by the words in their order; the very words, phrases, and sentences as written.

…

1.d. The wording adopted by an editor as (in his opinion) most nearly representing the author's original work; a book or edition containing this; also, with qualification, any form in which a writing exists or is current, as a *good, bad, corrupt, critical, received text.*

…

2. The very words and sentences as originally written: (a) in the original language, as opposed to a translation or rendering; (b) in the original form or order, as distinguished from a commentary, marginal or other, or from annotations. Hence … the body of any treatise, the authoritative or formal part as distinguished from notes, appendices, introduction, and other explanatory or supplementary matter.

…

3.a. The very words and sentences of Holy Scripture; hence the Scriptures themselves; also, any single book of the Scriptures.

…

4.a. A short passage from the Scriptures, especially one quoted as authoritative, or illustrative of a point of belief or doctrine … to point a moral, or … as the subject of an exposition or sermon.

From *Oxford English Dictionary* (1989 edn).

It seems to me that all the senses listed do express attitudes towards this issue of 'close up' OR 'whole view.' I would produce lists as follows:

(a) Close-ups
1.a. The wording of anything written or printed
    the very words, phrases, and sentences as written
1.d. The wording adopted by an editor as (in his opinion) most nearly representing the author's original work

2.   The very words and sentences as originally written

3.a. The very words and sentences of Holy Scripture

4.a. A short passage from the Scriptures, especially one quoted as authoritative, or illustrative of a point … the subject of an exposition or sermon.

(b) Whole views

1.a. the structure formed by the words in their order

1.d. a book or edition containing this

      any form in which a writing exists or is current

2. The body of any treatise

3. The Scriptures themselves

I think that my list separates out the differing focuses of the various definitions reasonably clearly. However, you may well have found a number of instances where definitions could be included in both lists, or where perhaps they could be said to fit some middle ground – smaller than a whole work, larger than a few words or sentences. For example, 'the structure formed by the words in their order' certainly could refer either to a segment or a whole. Perhaps, indeed, the separation into two lists artificially obscures a tendency for there to be a continuity between smaller and larger focuses. Many of the definitions could be said to have a range which includes some sense of both part and whole. Sense **3.a** (Scripture) illustrates this very clearly – here 'text' can mean a short passage, a large internal segment, or the whole Bible.

It seems clear enough, then, that the word 'text' is intimately connected with issues of authenticity and of the size of a piece of writing, but also that its usage is strangely ambivalent on a close-up/whole view axis. This is, I think, more than merely a pedantic curiosity. It has several implications for the ways in which the term is used in the discipline of English.

Firstly, we might note that the advice 'pay more attention to *the* text' perhaps conflates the two meanings by suggesting that close focus on the details (the text) will bring better understanding of the whole work (also 'the text'). This seems obvious, but the relationship of complete unity it assumes between the parts and the whole may not be as self-evident as all that. It is possible at times to suggest that some parts of texts are, in fact, contradictory to the general meaning of a text. It may be partially that some of the original senses of *textus* (woven, texture, textile) have suggested an analogy between 'language' texts and woven cloth/textures which is not entirely true. If the individual threads in a cloth are more or less identical and give the whole its texture, that does not mean that the individual sentences or larger segments in a text are necessarily so uniform. Words carry meanings in ways which threads do not. And though the experience of the parts of a text must contribute to its overall meaning, the relationship between parts and whole seems likely to be complex where language is concerned. In Introduction I, I suggested that 'thinking about texts' required a process of 'testing detailed readings against larger readings', and vice versa. It is this kind of process with which the technical term 'text' is identified, referring both to the sense of reading in close detail and the sense of understanding a complete and self-contained work. The relationship between these two kinds of reading is, in fact, extremely complex, as I shall go on to show.

Secondly, there is a related set of ideas about the wholeness of texts, at what point they are *complete, original* and *authentic*. These ideas raise issues about where the boundaries of a text are, and some crucial questions about authority. In several of the *OED* definitions, a distinction is made between the authentic body of a text and associated writing with a different status, often a lesser originality or authority ('the body of any treatise' versus 'notes, appendices, introduction, and other explanatory or supplementary matter'). This builds on a basic sense of text as 'the very words', the original matter itself. Clearly there is a concern here with accuracy and the preservation of the proper meaning of a written communication. The definitions imply that text (or a text) is by its nature self-contained: it has clear boundaries, separating it from other texts and from writing which is not properly part of itself. These boundaries give it a stability by keeping its wording and meaning separate from other meanings in other writings.

One usage of 'text' – referring to the Scriptures – contains this complex of ideas in a specially strong way. From Middle English on, the word 'text' indicates not just writing, but in particular the truest kind of writing of all, the properly transmitted authority of the Bible, often believed to be the record of the Word of God himself. Such words must be preserved from any corruption or addition, because any incursions into the boundaries of this text render it less than the authentic Divine word which governs all belief and behaviour in Christendom. The *OED* gives a number of uses of text of this kind: 'Iesus Crist appeared to Patrik, and took him a staf, and the texte of the gospel' (1387), 'the tixt of Holy Writ' (1430), 'the vast importance of preserving a pure text of the sacred writers' (1875). Each of these examples emphasises the link between stability and authority. Christ himself gives his text to St Patrick (and the sentence goes on to say that this very text – the book itself – is still 'in the erchebishops warde', in the keeping of the Archbishop). The Gospel is the text of 'Holy Writ' (a phrase used to assert the indisputably true nature of this text) and the 'pure' text must be preserved.

There is a noticeable concern in these instances (and in the usage in general) that this Text which is so clearly demarcated is nevertheless threatened by matter from beyond its proper boundaries. Part of this anxiety arises from the (traditionally) central position of the Bible in the Christian world order. If its central authority is disputable, then so are other kinds of authority which it underwrites. But the concern also stems from the fact that in the Middle Ages, the Text itself, being in Latin, could generally *only* be read by its professional interpreters, the clergy. Part of their function was to interpret the Text to the laity, and they did this largely by quoting the 'very words' in Latin, and by then giving an explanation, or expanded commentary, on the meaning of those original words. The lack of direct access to the Text for the laity is partly a consequence of the split between the learned language, Latin, and the vernacular one, but is also supported by religious/social beliefs about the role of the clergy and the sacred status of the Gospel.

This leads to some odd results. The Text which is to be preserved whole and pure is precisely the one to which other writings are routinely and incessantly attached. Very frequently in medieval English usage, the word 'text' is closely accompanied by the word 'gloss' (or 'glose'). This is related to the modern English 'glossary', and means 'an explanation, a commentary'. The *OED* again gives examples:

This was the texte trewely … the glose was gloriousely writen (1377)

This symple creature hadde myche travaile … to studie it [the Latin Bible] … the texte with the glose (1388)

> The tixte of holy writ... hit sleep, but glose be among [= the text sleeps, but is surrounded by glosses] (1430)

These uses give a strong sense of the centrality of the 'text', but are also very aware that it cannot explain itself, and that the gap between it and the explanation may betray the boundaries of that text as much as reinforce them. Thus, in the third example, the glosses 'speak', while the true text is silent (medieval writers such as the poet Langland sometimes use 'glose' ironically precisely to suggest that commentary on the Bible is not a true account of what is really inside that text). It is evident that the Holy Text has the central authority here, but that there is no easy access to that primary meaning.

This problem might be seen as one unique to a culture where knowledge is dominated by Latin, a language known only to an elite group of interpreters. However, looking further down the *OED* examples of usage, there seems to be an enduring problem with the relation between authoritative 'texts' and the means by which they are explained. So the novelist Henry Fielding in 1749 can observe that a recent commentary on a standard law book (Littleton) ranks itself as the equal of the text it glosses: 'Coke upon Littleton, where the comment is of equal authority with the text'. These problems of interpretation are very much bound up with the questions of where a text's boundaries lie, and what makes it whole. Paradoxically, the text, the writing which contains a meaning whose stability is agreed to be of central importance, cannot explain itself. Additionally, it has a unity made up of a complex of small parts, whose individual authenticity is supposed to be as closely guarded by the idea of the text, as the whole meaning to which they allegedly contribute.

These problems are undoubtedly complex, even though they stem from a simple ambivalence about whether a 'text' is a lengthy or short piece of writing, and from the need to define the boundaries of a text. These types of problem have not stood in the way of generations of students (and lecturers) using the word and idea of the text without undue difficulty. However, both in recent criticism and traditional scholarship, there has been a good deal of attention paid to the vital impact of questions about texts on literary meaning. The remainder of this section will explore some of the major issues by focusing on a single text: Shakespeare's *Hamlet*.

Despite all the above discussion, it may still appear, in practice, that knowing where a text ends and begins, and distinguishing between whether the word is intended to mean a whole or small piece of text, is relatively straightforward. Thus students know that if Shakespeare's *Hamlet* is a set text, then they are meant to find an edition and read the play. They may, also, choose to read the introduction, footnotes, other critics, and so on, but their text is clearly, above all, the play itself. The primary meaning they are studying is in that text. When they can think, speak and write independently about the play, they will have done what is expected of them.[1] However, the clarity of the boundaries in this model may be somewhat illusory.

I have picked *Hamlet* as the text for this section both because it is well known and because it allows us to explore a number of ideas about texts. The first thing to say is that for professional Shakespearian critics, it is a piece of very basic knowledge that *Hamlet* has survived in three different but complete texts (the only Shakespearian play in this situation). That is, it has been transmitted to us via three different editions printed in the sixteenth and seventeenth centuries, which differ in a number of ways. These three editions are known partly by the size of paper on which they were printed, partly by their date order. There are thus three editions or 'texts' regarded as stemming (at one remove or other) from the author: First Quarto (Q1, printed 1603), second Quarto (Q2, printed 1604) and First Folio (F, printed 1623). Immediately, then, the notion of the text as that which guarantees boundaries must give a little, for here we have a central work of English literature which exists in more than one form.

The actual form in which *Hamlet* has been read has differed over the years, though there has been considerable consensus since John Dover Wilson examined the texts in his edition of 1934.[2] The Arden Shakespeare *Hamlet* (1982), a widely respected and used edition, does not, exactly, reproduce Q1, Q2 or F. It is based mainly on Q2, but the editor, Harold Jenkins, draws in a range of ways on F and, at times, makes decisions based on Q1, though, in general, he regards this as an unreliable text. These kinds of matter have tended to be left to 'experts', trained in the rigorous procedures of 'textual history' (a discipline originally developed in its modern form for reconstructing the best possible text for the Bible). Students may note in passing that editions of Shakespeare have introductory sections called things like 'The Text' or 'Textual History'. Not surprisingly, though, many students (and perhaps some tutors?) would tend to regard these as in the main falling outside the boundary of 'the text' of *Hamlet* for the purposes of undergraduate study. These sections are in practice treated as, in the *OED* definition of texts, 'additional or supplementary matter'. Strangely, though, these matters apparently outside the text are the editors' accounts of how they have made the text of *Hamlet* whole and consistent. As we shall see, the impact of 'textual history' on meaning can be more than merely trivial.

Below are printed two different texts of the opening scene of *Hamlet*. Read both and then:

> ◆ Decide if you prefer one text to the other.
> ◆ If so, list the reasons for your preference.

A. The Tragicall Historie of *Hamlet* Prince of Denmarke

Enter two Centinels.
1. Stand: who is that?
2. Tis I.
1. O you come most carefully upon your watch,
2. And if you meete *Marcellus* and *Horatio*,
    The partners of my watch, bid them make haste.
1. I will. See who goes there.

Enter Horatio and Marcellus.

Hor.   Friends to this ground.
Mar.   And leegemen to the Dane,
          O farewell honest souldier, who hath relieved you?
1.   *Barnado* hath my place, give you good night.
Mar.   Holla, *Barnado.*
2.   Say, is *Horatio* there?
Hor.   A peece of him.
2.   Welcome *Horatio*, welcome good *Marcellus.*
Mar.   What hath this thing appear'd againe to night.
2.   I have seen nothing.
Mar.   *Horatio* sayes tis but our fantasie,
          And will not let our beliefe take hold of him,
          Touching this dreaded sight twice seen by us,
          Therefore I have intreated him along with us
          To watch the minutes of this night,
          That if again this apparition come,
          He may approove our eyes, and speake to it.
Hor.   Tut, t'will not appeare.
2.   Sit downe I pray, and let us once againe
          Assaile your eares that are so fortified,
          What we have two nights seene.
Hor.   Wel, sit we downe, and let us heare *Bernardo* speake of this.
2.   Last night of al, when yonder starre that's west-ward
          from the pole, had made his course to
          Illumine that part of heaven. Where now it burnes,
          The bell then towling one.

Enter Ghost.
Mar.   Breake off your talke, see where it comes againe.

в. The Tragedy of Hamlet, Prince of Denmark

ACT I
SCENE I

Enter BARNADO *and* FRANCISCO, *two Sentinels.*

Bar.   Who's there?
Fran.   Nay, answer me. Stand and unfold yourself.
Bar.   Long live the King!
Fran.   Barnado?
Bar.   He.
Fran.   You come most carefully upon your hour.

Bar.   'Tis now struck twelve. Get thee to bed, Francisco.

Fran.   For this relief much thanks. 'Tis bitter cold,
           And I am sick at heart.

Bar.   Have you had quiet guard?

Fran.   Not a mouse stirring.

Bar.   Well, good night.
           If you do meet Horatio and Marcellus,
           The rivals of my watch, bid them make haste.

Fran.   I think I hear them.

Enter HORATIO and MARCELLUS.

                        Stand, ho! Who is there?

Hor.   Friends to this ground.

Mar.   And liegemen to the Dane.

Fran.   Give you good night.

Mar.   O, farewell honest soldier, who hath reliev'd you?

Fran.   Barnardo hath my place. Give you good night.

Mar.   Holla, Barnardo!

Bar.   Say, what, is Horatio there?

Hor.   A piece of him.

Bar.   Welcome, Horatio. Welcome good Marcellus.

Hor.   What, has this thing appear'd again tonight?

Bar.   I have seen nothing.

Mar.   Horatio says 'tis nothing but our fantasy,
           And will not let belief take hold of him,
           Touching this dreaded sight twice seen of us.
           Therefore I have entreated him along
           With us to watch the minutes of this night,
           That if again this apparition come,
           He may approve our eyes and speak to it.

Hor.   Tush, tush, 'twill not appear.

Bar.   Sit down awhile,
           And let us once again assail your ears,
           That are so fortified against our story,
           What we have two nights seen.

Hor.   Well, sit we down.
           And let us hear Barnardo speak of this.

Bar.   Last night of all,
           When yond same star that's westward from the pole,
           Had made his course t'illumine that part of heaven
           Where now it burns, Marcellus and myself,
           The bell then beating one –

Enter GHOST.

Mar. Peace, break thee off. Look where it comes again.

Discussion

I think that most readers are likely to identify Text B as being preferable, though that is not inevitable (you may have chosen differently). I assume this, because in a number of ways, B seems to me to be a better text. The phrase 'better text' has a technical meaning for textual scholars and editors – it indicates a version of a text which is clearly preferable on various grounds (for example, one which has fewer printing errors, or that is known to have been corrected by the author). My use of it here is less technical. I am using the phrase to indicate that text B seems to me more plausible as I read through it (though I have not investigated the publishing history in any detailed way).

My reasoning here is that B generally seems more accomplished, more consistent, and to make better sense throughout at every level. Thus, speeches by different characters seem closely integrated in B, while the flow of dialogue in A is often rather jerky and abrupt. For example, in A (lines 6–7), there seems to be a problem. Centinel 1's line, 'I will. See who goes there' is succeeded by a line which does not obviously follow, Horatio's 'Friends to this ground'. In B the equivalent line is clearly Horatio's answer to Francisco's challenge: 'Who is there?' There are other instances in A of lines which do not obviously answer each other (line 4 'And if you meete *Marcellus* and *Horatio*, / The partners of my watch, bid them make haste' seems to appear in A as if from nowhere, whereas it is carefully led up to in B.

The most obvious explanation of these differences between A and B would seem to be that A is a slightly confused version of B. Thus where B has the challenge 'Who is there?' followed by an answer, A reproduces the answer, 'Friends to this ground', but somehow misses out the question which motivated it: 'Who is there?' In fact, looking at the line in A which precedes the answer, we can see that it contains something close to these words, but in a form which is no longer interrogative: 'See who goes there'. It could be that this statement is really a mistake for the question. Equally, it seems quite likely that in A some lines have been missed out before 'And if you meete *Marcellus* and *Horatio*'.

The superiority of B in terms of these quite mundane matters of coherence is also, I think, to be seen in more complex dramatic effects. Thus there is often a much more rapid acceptance of facts by characters in A than in B, where it frequently seems more difficult to establish things clearly. In A, it takes only two lines for the first Centinel to recognise the second. But in B, it takes 5 lines before Francisco and Barnardo are sure of each other's identity. I prefer B's treatment because it seems to me to suggest a tenser atmosphere on the battlements of Elsinore, as well as some satisfying thematic points. Instead of guards who immediately recognise each other, as in A, there are here guards who even when they are acquaintances, cannot quickly be sure who is who at dead of night. Instead of straightforward question and answer sequences, where the role of questioner and respondent are clear ('*1.* Stand: who is that? / *2.* Tis I'), B instead shows Barnardo and Francisco as both equally unwilling to relinquish the more authoritative role of questioner (*Bar.* Who's there? / *Fran.* Nay, answer me. Stand and unfold yourself). Francisco avoids declaring his identity positively in his first line by counter-challenging, while Barnardo in his response again delays saying who he is in personal terms through identifying a general identity (as one loyal to the King). In fact, personal identity is only revealed when Francisco feels confident enough to hazard a guess at the other's name. This lack of trust on the watchtowers of Elsinore suggests at once that there are uncertainties in the state of Denmark, and that one cannot immediately be sure that all is as it seems. Thematically, the suggestion that it is not easy to know who is who can be linked to other concerns in the play: 'To thine own self be true' says Polonius to Laertes (Act I, scene iii), but the self may not be easy to establish in a kingdom where it is not clear who is the real king, who is sane, who is a hawk and who a handsaw, and so on.

In this case, I take the uncertainty in B to be superior to the certainty of A, because I can account for B's handling of the lines as being more dramatically complex and involving (which gives better support than A to my expectations of *Hamlet* as a good play ...). I am, in effect, assuming that B is more authentic than A, because it better accords with my sense of the play *Hamlet* and the playwright Shakespeare. As so often, decisions about the details of a text depend on assumptions about the whole text. Similar kinds of argument can be made about many of the detailed differences between A and B, and you may well have used quite different examples and constructed somewhat different justifications of a preference for B. ☐

So far, this discussion has been uncharacteristically certain of its ground. I have claimed that B is a better text, and that this can be clearly demonstrated from its detail ('the very words and phrases'). Yet above, I said that the boundaries of texts were far from clear or simple. Is this an exception? Is B's superiority and authenticity really that evident? Is B the authentic *Hamlet*, while A is a text whose integrity has been corrupted by extraneous matter? Traditionally, the answer to this is that B has indeed been accepted as an undoubtedly better text of *Hamlet*, for it is taken from The Arden Shakespeare, and thus substantially is the version of *Hamlet* contained in the 1604–5 Second Quarto and established as the best text since 1934 (though there are some editorial additions from the 1623 Folio). A is taken from the 1603 Quarto, often called *The Bad Quarto*, usually regarded as a pirated publication, printed without Shakespeare's cooperation, compiled from an actor's memorial reconstruction of the whole play. This explanation has largely been accepted since the nineteen thirties, and my sense that text A is less satisfying, less good, is the conventional one taken by editors of *Hamlet* and by Shakespeare critics (I couldn't help starting the exercise with that knowledge, so the empirical test I appear to have performed is not simply an objective one).

However, this consensus is not quite a universally accepted fact. Indeed, one should note the oddity that the 'authoritative' text is not that of the 1623 Folio, which could be considered as something like a collected edition of Shakespeare's work, possibly incorporating the author's final revisions. Moreover, even when it comes to the distinction between the 'Bad' Quarto and the 'Good' Quarto, the objectively better quality of the second is not quite wholly agreed upon. If you preferred text A to B, or found virtues in both, you may not simply have made 'an error', and you are not the only person ever to have argued for the force of this version of *Hamlet*. In 1992, two editors, Graham

Holderness and Bryan Loughrey, published this Q1 text of *Hamlet* in their Shakespearian Originals: First Editions series (though that claim of *originality* for the 'Bad Quarto' was, and remains, controversial). They argued that it was not merely a poor version of the more commonly accepted text, but a genuinely different text and one of great value, unfairly neglected.

> ◆　**Read the following extract from the Introduction to their edition of Q1 *Hamlet*: What do they see as valuable in this text of *Hamlet*?**

'Enormous dramatic economy and force' …

'a brisk, exciting play that lacks only the best qualities of subtlety and poetry in the second, authentic quarto' …

'Great lines may be missing from this version but the vitality … means that we never feel the loss' …

'the most entirely satisfactory piece of tragic acting of the year'

These phrases of positive celebration were ironically responses to a performance (at the Orange Tree Theatre, Richmond, in 1985) of a text then, as now, still routinely designated the 'Bad Quarto' of Shakespeare's *Hamlet* … Though often still anxious to preserve for this text … the status of derivative or second rate, reviewers of that landmark 1985 production were none the less forcibly surprised by the theatrical potentialities of the 'bad' text in performance …

It is generally conjectured that the First Quarto was pirated … and published without permission of the author or his company. The Second Quarto (some copies of which are dated 1604, some 1605), which bears on its title page the description 'Newly imprinted and enlarged to almost as much againe as it was, according to the true and perfect coppie', would then have been a publication by dramatist and company of an authorised text. If that were the case, it would be reasonable to assume that the Second Quarto represents both Shakespeare's intended text and the version the company used for performances.

But this received account brings in its wake a host of problems. We do not know how the 1603 and 1604–5 texts found their way into print; but we do know that the same publisher, Nicholas Ling, printed both texts. We do not know what the Second Quarto claims to be a true and perfect copy of – the author's manuscript? the transcript prepared and submitted to the censor? the prompt book? What we do know is that neither the Second Quarto nor the Folio texts … are likely to have represented acting versions: they are both, and especially Q2, inconveniently long. It would take some four hours to play the Second Quarto, even at high speed. … Jacobean open-air performances took place approximately between two and four in the afternoon. … It is generally accepted that *The Tragicall Historie of Hamlet Prince of Denmark* (1603) represents an acting version of the play. Whether it was a first, hastily prepared script, or a cut-down touring version; whether it was taken down from an actual performance, or hurriedly assembled from an uncompleted author's draft, it is scarcely possible to know with any certainty. What we can assume with reasonable confidence is that this text comes closer than the other texts to actual Jacobean stage practice.

From Graham Holderness and Bryan Loughrey, Q1 text of *Hamlet Prince of Denmark*, Shakespearian Originals: First Editions, *Hamlet* (London, 1992), pp. 13–14.

▶ Discussion

Clearly, there is a stress in this account on the play as theatre, rather than as written text – I note the opening collection of quotations from reviews, the reference to the actual conditions of performance, and the final declaration that this version does, indeed, have a greater claim to originality than the longer printed versions, since it is (they say) closer to what could actually have been staged. In performance, it is argued, this play does work well. This has been obscured because these performance virtues have been inappropriately compared to qualities of consistency which are essentially those to be expected of a printed rather than performed text.

They are more interested in this version of the text *as it exists*, than in judging it against another version of *Hamlet* produced for a different purpose (you might like to look back at your own arguments about texts A and B, and at mine, to see whether you agree that this is what was going on in these discussions).[3] Indeed, they suggest that the criteria for judging which might be the better text of *Hamlet* have been distorted by anachronistic assumptions about written texts and the primacy of the author in their production. Thus, they go on to argue:

> Since we have no means of knowing the extent to which authorial influence (as distinct from the influences of actors, theatre entrepreneurs, scribes, printers, pirates) uniquely determined the shape and content of the printed texts, we are stuck with a self-evidently and irredeemably collaborative cultural production. … In practice, however, this general acceptance of the 'Shakespearian' drama as a collective rather than an individual form has not been permitted to dislodge the rigid hierarchy of functions implicitly assumed by traditional editorial practices: what the writer writes, others (actors, theatre entrepreneurs, scribes, printers, pirates) corrupt, mangle, and pervert to illegitimate uses. (p. 16)

They would want us to accept the equal (at least) validity of different texts of *Hamlet*, and the idea that, anyway, any actual realisation of *Hamlet* was for a particular purpose and was therefore the result of various complex collaborations *on that specific occasion*. This leads to a very different idea of a text from that which looks for the 'best text' in an abstract way (i.e. the best text of *Hamlet* for all occasions!). In stressing collaboration instead of an originating author, Holderness and Loughrey produce a definition of a text which has a focus on the 'weaving together of many small parts', rather than on the 'unified whole resulting from the perfect combination of smaller parts'. Indeed, they are willing to accept that the smaller components of a text may be recombined in a number of different ways to produce different versions of a text. □

If we accept that there are different but equally valid texts for *Hamlet*, then this means that there are different possible *Hamlets*, and perhaps, even, by implication, different Shakespeares. We can begin to look at this effect by comparing the Hamlets of Q1 and Q2 in a particular speech.

> ◆ Look at the following two speeches by Hamlet (the first is from Q1, the second from Q2). Give a critical account of the characterisation of Hamlet suggested by the two different speeches.

(DO NOT – this time – argue about which text you prefer, or think better. Instead, try to treat the texts as equals, and discuss how different the two Hamlets produced by the texts are.)

Q1

Ham. To be or not to be, I there's the point,
     To Die, to sleep, is that all? I all:
     No to sleepe, to dreame, I marry there it goes,
     For in that dreame of death, when wee awake,
     And borne before an everlasting Judge,
     From whence no passenger ever return'd,
     The undiscovered country, at whose sight
     The happy smile, and the accursed damn'd.
     But for this, the joyfull hope of this,
     Who'ld beare the scornes and flattery of the world,
     Scorned by the right rich, the rich curssed of the poor?
     The widow being oppressed, the orphan wrong'd,
     The taste of hunger, or a tirants raigne,
     And thousand more calamities besides,
     To grunt and sweate under this weary life,
     When that he may his full *Quietus* make,
     With a bare bodkin, who would this indure,
     But for a hope of something after death?
     Which pusles the braine, and doth confound the sence,
     Which makes us rather beare those eviles we have,
     Than flie to others that we know not of.

I that, O this conscience makes cowardes of us all,
Lady in thy orizons, be all my sins remembred.

From Shakespearian Originals: First Editions, *Hamlet Prince of Denmark*, ed. Graham Holderness and Bryan Loughrey (London, 1992), pp. 60–1. There are no Act or Scene divisions nor line numbers in this edition as a matter of editorial policy.

Q2

Ham. To be, or not to be, that is the question:
　Whether 'tis nobler in the mind to suffer
　The slings and arrows of outrageous fortune,
　Or to take arms against a sea of troubles
　And by opposing end them. To die – to sleep,
　No more; and by a sleep to say we end
　The heart-ache and the thousand natural shocks
　That flesh is heir to: 'tis a consummation
　Devoutly to be wish'd. To die, to sleep;
　To sleep, perchance to dream – ay there's the rub:
　For in that sleep of death what dreams may come,
　When we have shuffled off this mortal coil,
　Must give us pause – there's the respect
　That makes calamity of so long life.
　For who would bear the whips and scorns of time,
　Th'oppressor's wrong, the proud man's contumely,
　The pangs of dispriz'd love, the law's delay,
　The insolence of office, and the spurns
　That patient merit of th' unworthy takes,
　When he himself might his quietus make
　With a bare bodkin? Who would fardels bear,
　To grunt and sweat under a weary life,
　But that the dread of something after death,
　The undiscover'd country, from whose bourn
　No traveller returns, puzzles the will,
　And makes us rather bear those ills we have
　Than fly to others that we know not of?
　Thus conscience doth make cowards of us all,
　And thus the native hue of resolution
　Is sicklied o'er with the pale cast of thought,
　And enterprises of great pitch and moment
　With this regard their currents turn awry
　And lose the name of action. Soft you now,
　The fair Ophelia! Nymph, in thy orisons
　Be all my sins remember'd.

From The Arden Shakespeare, *Hamlet*, ed. Harold Jenkins (London, 1982), Act III, Sc. i, ll. 56–89.

The first thing which strikes me about Q1's Hamlet is that his speech is much shorter, and, indeed, very differently paced from that of the Q2 Hamlet. Thus Q1 Hamlet takes 12 fewer lines to make his speech. At several points there is much less elaboration, notably in the opening lines where the first rhetorical question comes to a much more rapid climax or point of pause in 'I there's the point' than Q2's Hamlet, who glosses that first question with two further alternative formulations ('Whether ... Or ...). Just as Q1's Centinels are more certain of things than Q2's watchers, so Q1 Hamlet is more certain than Q2 Hamlet. At several points here he at least appears to make definite responses to his own questions, however philosophically difficult they may seem. Thus we have:

I, there's the point	(compared to)	'that is the question'
I, all	(compared to)	'ay, there's the rub'
I, that	(no equivalent in Q2).	

Q2 Hamlet asks more questions, but can provide no answers, and has difficulty stemming the stream of questions, which are often expansion of the previous questions, even with the mere form of an answer or definite statement.

We might want to characterise Q1 Hamlet as a more decisive figure than Q2's. Q1 notably lacks not only the actual delay caused by Q2's greater elaboration of the question, but also Hamlet's explicit commentary on how thought, consciousness, moral reflection ('conscience') lead to indecision, delay and lack of action. Thus Q1 Hamlet has simply 'I that, O this conscience does make cowardes of us all', where Q2 Hamlet meditates at length:

> Thus conscience does make cowards of us all,
> And thus the native hue of resolution
> Is sicklied o'er with the pale cast of thought,
> And enterprises of great pitch and moment
> With this regard their currents turn awry
> And lose the name of action. (ll. 83–9)

If we are prepared to accept Q1 as a valid text of *Hamlet*, then we may well be able to produce readings which are markedly different from those which have been produced from Q2. If this reading based on close reading of part of the text can be sustained by a reading of the whole text, then it could be said that Q1 Hamlet is a different figure from Q2 Hamlet. Classic critical questions about *Hamlet* and Hamlet, including the question of whether he delays in carrying out vengeance, and all the implications this can have for interpreting the play, will presumably have different answers for the different texts. Indeed, the different texts will themselves raise different questions.

Clearly, these issues about texts are extremely important for early modern texts – since the conditions of their production, printing and distribution lead to the kinds of complication which we have explored in a single case. But how common is this degree of textual uncertainty and complication? There are other instances in the Shakespeare canon – *King Lear* exists in two versions (Q1 1608 and F 1623) which are both 'good texts' (i.e. are internally consistent and convincing), but which are substantially different. It is now usually thought that F represents a later revision by Shakespeare.[4] But both seem to stem from the author in ways which may not so evidently be true for Q1 of *Hamlet*. More generally, textual uncertainty is common in many texts printed before the eighteenth century. It is probably true that conditions of publication and authorship have made modern texts more stable in some respects, but there are examples of recent texts which have specific complexities. The poet Auden revised his own work of the nineteen thirties for later editions, altering words and lines in many texts, and in some cases even suppressing poems entirely. These revisions are often concerned with Auden's attitude to his own work and political attitudes in the thirties and with his post-war conversion to Anglican belief. Which Auden texts should be read? The Thirties 'originals'? or the poet's final thoughts on them? The answers to these questions depend on what ideas about editing texts are adopted, or, perhaps, what is being looked for. For a critic who is studying writing between the two world wars, it may be the texts printed in the thirties which are authoritative. For a critic writing about Auden's whole career, the choice is not so simple. However, that is still a particular difficult case. Surely we don't have to worry about textual instability in every piece of literature we read?

Perhaps not, in terms of distinguishing what it is that constitutes the 'very words and phrases' of a particular work. There is, as far as I know, little dispute about, say, the bulk of the wording of the texts of Graham Greene's novels. But does even agreement about what words are in a text quite make it evident what its boundaries are, about where it ends and some other kind of writing begins?

When discussing the ways in which the very word text seemed centrally concerned with issues of size and authenticity, I suggested that ideas about *boundaries* give a text stability by 'keeping its wording and meaning separate from other meanings in other writings'. We might seem to be on safe ground in asserting that a text does keep its *words* at least separate from those in another text or kind of writing. This seems to be true – the sequence of words and phrases in *Hamlet* is different from that in, say, *King Lear* or *Twelfth Night* or Graham Greene's *Our Man in Havana* to the point where it is difficult to confuse one of these texts with another. However, this does not quite exclude the possibility that particular groups of words can be found in common in two (or more) texts. The Fool in *King Lear* does, in fact, sing a song, 'When that I was but a little tiny boy', which occurs in exactly the same words in *Twelfth Night*, sung by that play's fool, Feste. For that matter, an early novel by Graham Greene, *The Name of Action* (1930) has, in its title, words identical to some occurring towards the end of the soliloquy in *Hamlet* Q2, 'To be or not to be' (see line 87 of the speech, 'And lose the name of action', quoted above). And *Hamlet* Q1 also seems to share some words with *Twelfth Night*. Its equivalent to Polonius, Corambis, ends a speech: 'such men often prove, / Great in their wordes, but little in their love' (p. 48). This has been said to be derived from Viola's 'we men … prove / Much in our vows, but little in our love'.[5] These examples suggest that though we can be reasonably sure that in many cases texts are separate from other texts in terms of their overall sequence of words and phrases, we cannot be so sure what belongs to one text or another when we look at smaller pieces of text. Quotation, allusion and reference are common features of literary texts (and other kinds of texts as well, for that matter). At times, it may be difficult to say which text first uses an identifiable phrase. Thus Q1 can be said (as it is by the Arden editor of *Hamlet*) to have in this instance *plagiarised*

Twelfth Night: Harold Jenkins thinks that the memorial reconstruction of the play filled in some of its lines by drawing on other plays in which the actor concerned had appeared.[6] But it may be that both Q1 and *Twelfth Night* are not original in their use of this phrase. Holderness and Loughrey argue that it was already a proverbial phrase, since in Q1 it is bracketed, like many other of Corambis's wise *quotations* of various texts. If meant to be taken as quotation, it presumably gives the line a rather different effect in both plays.

We might also wonder to what extent first (*recorded*) use of a phrase gives eternal ownership of it. If a text quotes a previously existing text, but in such a way that it changes its original meaning, is that merely copying? Or is it also a creation of new meaning? Perhaps, indeed, any quotation inevitably introduces some alteration to the meaning of the quoted portion in a different text? We might ask if any text is wholly original or if it can ever be possible to avoid a certain amount of quotation or reference to a previous text or texts. Many critics think that originality in that pure sense of sharing no phrases or influences is extremely unlikely in even the most startling piece of literary genius. The French critic Julia Kristeva invented a new word in the 1960s to describe the tendency of texts constantly to refer to other texts: the term *intertextuality*. She suggested that 'no text is "free" of other texts'.[7]

This seems a powerful argument. If accepted, it follows that there is no absolute point at which the meaning of a text can be entirely isolated from the meanings of other texts with which it is, has been, or might be connected. Thus, to stay with *Hamlet* – focusing on the more familiar Q2 version this time – we might say its meaning is partly produced not only by what is in its 'own' text, but also by any other texts it touches.

> ◆ Make a list of ANY texts (i.e. either specific texts or *kinds* of writing) which might have any impact on *your understanding* of the meaning of *Hamlet*.

(*My list*):

Saxo Grammaticus's *Life of Hamlet* (circa 1200), translated, with a history and commentary by William F. Hansen (1983).

The Spanish Tragedy (Play by Thomas Kyd, 1587?).

Julius Caesar (Play by Shakespeare, 1599).

The Revengers' Tragedy (1600? Published 1607).

Editions of *Hamlet* (including Introduction, Textual History, explanatory notes, etc.) (various publication dates, e.g. The Arden *Hamlet*, edited Harold Jenkins, 1982; The Oxford Shakespeare *Hamlet*, edited G. R. Hibbard, 1987).

Hamlet Q1! (Play by Shakespeare? Memorially reconstructed? published 1603; edited and introduced by Graham Holderness and Bryan Loughrey, 1992).

Films of *Hamlet* (various dates).

Performances of the play *Hamlet* (various dates).

Critical works (e.g. *Shakespearean Tragedy: Lectures on Hamlet, Othello, King Lear, Macbeth*, by A. C. Bradley (1905); *New Essays on Hamlet* edited by Mark Thornton Burnett and John Manning (1994).

Lectures on Shakespearian tragedy (attended when I was a student, 1980–3).

Cartoons (e.g. in newspapers such as the *Guardian* and *The Times Literary Supplement*).

'The Love Song of J. Alfred Prufrock' (Poem by T. S. Eliot, 1917, lines 111–19).

'Lapis Lazuli' (Poem by W. B. Yeats, 1938, lines 9–24).

Hamlet, Revenge! (Thriller by Michael Innes, 1938).

Rosencrantz and Guildernstern Are Dead (Play by Tom Stoppard, 1967).

Dogg's Hamlet, Cahoot's Macbeth (Play by Tom Stoppard, 1980).

The Conscience of the King (episode 13 of *Star Trek*, produced September 1966).

My list is made up of as many texts as I can think of which refer to *Hamlet*, and that seem to be associated in my mind with the play in one way or another. In some ways my list is individual to myself, and indeed needs some further explanation (the same is presumably true of yours). Thus my inclusion of *Julius Caesar* is not self-evident. It is there because I happen to know that there is a strong association between it and *Hamlet* (Polonius refers repeatedly to Julius Caesar in ways specifically suggesting references to the play – the same actor may have played Caesar and Polonius, and the two plays may have been performed on subsequent days on one occasion). Your list may well not include a *Star Trek* episode – but that is one of the texts that came into my mind in connection with *Hamlet*. In other ways, it has some predictable contents (I might expect other people to mention critical writings on *Hamlet*, or particular performances they had seen, as having an effect on their understanding of the play). But whether idiosyncratic or more obvious, it seems reasonable to think that these kinds of texts play an undoubted part in my understanding of the text which generated the list.

This leads me to various curious speculations about the idea of the text guaranteeing stability and identity. Firstly, if any text is partly explained by a whole series of other texts, then its meaning clearly does not reside wholly inside it, but is also produced by its relation with other texts. In turn the other texts which this 'first' text draws on presumably also draw on other texts … and so on … and so on. Additionally, perhaps the texts which any reader/viewer brings to bear on a particular text may alter their understanding of that text. In that case, every reader may have differing understanding of 'the central matter' they are reading, depending on the 'marginal matter' they associate with it (though I assume that some textual connections would be commoner than others). If I read something new on *Hamlet* – a new critical essay, most obviously – then presumably this might also give me a new text associated with the play. In that case, then, the texts with which *Hamlet* (or any other text) is intertextual can alter over time for an individual – and even for a culture – as new points of contact between texts are made. This leads to an idea of texts as having texture, being woven, in an even more complex way than when that metaphor is applied to something described as a 'self-contained' text. Katie Wales points this out in *A Dictionary of Stylistics*:

> **Text** and **textuality** in recent literary theory … come close to ideas of *intertextuality*. The etymological meanings of weaving are revived in notions

that all understanding is textual in the sense that words interlink with each other in their associations in an endless 'deferral'; and in the sense also that the process of *interpretation* involves our reading of a text interacting with the design of the text itself, and with our readings of other texts, which themselves call forth other texts, and so on. The traditional autonomy of the text is thus undermined.[8]

(You may recall the discussion of how a dictionary defines meaning in section 1.1 above – there is a similarity in the way in which one meaning is based on other meanings and so on and so on.)

When discussing *Hamlet* Q1 earlier in this section, I referred to one of Graham Holderness and Bryan Loughrey's arguments about the distortion of responses to the textual history of the play caused by (in their view) anachronistic assumptions about literary authorship as the act of a single person. They argued that it would be more appropriate to approach an Elizabethan play as a collaborative work, and accept that its meaning was inevitably constructed by many hands (they list actors, theatre entrepreneurs, scribes, printers, 'pirates' as possible contributors). This is a specific argument about the conditions of play production in the Elizabethan theatre. However, one might go on to say that, in fact, all texts are to some degree defined as much by collaboration as by authorial origin in the ways they produce meaning. I would like to end this section by briefly introducing three related issues bearing on the idea of the text: collaboration, performance and interpretation. We will be returning to related issues in more detail in the second two parts of this chapter, 'What is an Author?' and 'What do Critics do?'

In *Hamlet* Q2,[9] Hamlet expresses to the Players his views on some issues of performance, interpretation and authorial ownership:

> *Ham.*   Speak the speech, I pray you, as I pronounced it to you …
> And let those that play your clowns speak no more than is set down for them – for there be of them that will themselves laugh, to set on some quantity of barren spectators to laugh too, though in the meantime some necessary question of the play be then to be considered. That's villainous, and shows a most pitiful ambition in the fool that uses it.[10]

Hamlet's concern here is for the speech which he has written to add to the play *The Murder of Gonzago*. He does not want any addition of extraneous material to his text (though one might see the irony that *he* has added this extra speech to a pre-existing play specifically for reasons of his own). The kind of additions he criticises are partly those involving 'words and phrases' not in the 'original', but he also, in an earlier part of the scene, criticises additions which are to do with *performance*: 'Nor do not saw the air too much with your hand …' (l. 25). Despite what Holderness and Loughrey say about an anachronistic idea of the author as originator, Hamlet here seems to have strong feelings on precisely that issue – while also suggesting that actual performance practices did not always accept the priority of that authorial model.

One observation we might make about this scene in terms of our discussion of the stability of texts is that for any play, how it is performed can have an enormous effect on meaning. If Hamlet objects to some performance practices, there must nevertheless be performance of some kind if drama is to be played rather than merely read. His advice that the purpose of acting is 'to hold as 'twere the mirror up to nature' (l. 22) is all very well, but does it actually tell actors what they must do to achieve this 'natural' style of performance? Perhaps, in some way, we should feed this discussion by Hamlet of his aesthetic assumptions back into our interpretation of Hamlet himself and the whole play? Is it so easy to 'act' actuality naturally in a play, when, in the reality of Elsinore, it is not clear who is what, and what it means to be what? (see the comment on identity above in the discussion of the opening scene). At any rate, it seems clear that if we are to see a play performed, then, in some sense we are bound to experience some 'additions' to the 'pure text'. How can directors, producers, costume designers and actors avoid adding something? (indeed, isn't it their job to add something? Otherwise why not simply advise the audience to visit a bookshop and read the play?).

The decisions which performers such as these make, and the skills which they bring to performance, are sometimes, indeed, called 'interpretation' – a word very familiar to literary critics. We might see some similarities between the two uses of the word. A critical discussion of *Hamlet* explores, discusses, argues for or brings out a particular meaning. So too does a production. Any individual performance or piece of criticism is likely to stress some aspects of the play rather than others, to engage with some previous readings (intertexts?) rather than others, and some contexts in preference to others. Both performance and critical readings certainly add things to the 'text' in the sense of connecting to it groups of words, gestures, symbols – *meanings*, in short – which are not simply 'in' the text. If they were not to add anything, how could they happen at all?

Moreover, if plays inevitably need intermediaries who interpret the text, can this not also be said of written texts too? In my Introduction II is a version of Jakobson's diagram of how language works using the three terms: the addresser, the addressee and the message. Though we might wish to start with the idea that a text is a message sent from addresser (author) to addressee (reader/viewer), it seems obvious that the message has no meaning until the addressee reads it and makes sense of it. As we have just been discussing, the reader cannot but help relate the text to other texts and to use whatever ways of reading are useful, customary and available. To understand a text could be said to give it a 'performance' which must be an interpretation in one way or another. The meaning of a text is presumably not produced solely by an author, but is surely a complex collaboration between author, text and reader. There seems no guarantee in this process that the sender of the message, the conventions of the message itself, and the reading conventions of the reader are necessarily identical in any simple way. On the contrary, it seems that while a text certainly does give *a sense* of where borders are, and of what the 'central matter' is, there can be no complete distinction between 'the text itself' as distinguished from 'a commentary, marginal or other, or from annotations… appendices, introduction, and other explanatory or supplementary matter' (*OED*). For, as we have seen, the text itself depends in a range of ways on the words and contexts which surround it. Even when there can be complete agreement about the words which should be in a text, the meaning could be said to be *woven* not only from the interrelation of smaller and larger portions of the text itself, but also from an almost infinite and various set of other texts. There is, in a fundamental sense, always a continuous web of complex thinking *about* texts.

Finally, in this section, there is an exercise which I will leave you to work on alone as a way of thinking through some of the ideas about texts discussed here.

Below is an extract from Tom Stoppard's play *Rosencrantz and Guildenstern Are Dead*. Read through it and then think about the following:

> ◆ To what extent would you say this was an *original* text?
> ◆ How does this play, judging from this scene, use the text of Shakespeare's *Hamlet*? (You might like to check the scene against the equivalent in *Hamlet*, Act II, Scene ii, [ll. 365–79, 385–9 in the Arden edition].)
> ◆ Would you accept the idea that *all texts* in fact work in a similar way to this one (i.e. in inhabiting other texts)?

Act Two

HAMLET, ROS *and* GUIL *talking, the continuation of the previous scene. Their conversation on the move, is indecipherable at first. The first intelligible line is* HAMLET*'s, coming at the end of a short speech – See Shakespeare Act II, scene ii.*

HAMLET: S'blood, there is something in this more than natural, if philosophy could find it out.

(*A flourish from the tragedians' band*)

GUIL: There are the players.

HAMLET: Gentlemen, you are welcome to Elsinore. Your hands, come then. (*He takes their hands.*) The appurtenance of welcome is fashion and cere-mony. Let me comply with you in this garb, lest my extent to the players (which I tell you must show fairly outwards) should more appear like entertainment than yours. You are welcome. (*About to leave.*) But my uncle-father and aunt-mother are deceived.

GUIL: In what, my dear lord?

HAMLET: I am but mad north north-west; when the wind is southerly I know a hawk from a handsaw.

(POLONIUS *enters as* GUIL *turns away.*)

POLONIUS: Well be with you gentlemen.

HAMLET (*to* ROS): Mark you, Guildenstern (*uncertainly to* GUIL) and you too; at each ear a hearer. That great baby you see there is not yet out of his swaddling clouts … (*He takes* ROS *upstage with him, talking together.*)

POLONIUS: My Lord! I have news to tell you.

HAMLET (*releasing* ROS *and mimicking*): My lord, I have news to tell you…
       When Roscius was an actor in Rome…
(ROS *comes downstage to re-join* GUIL)
POLONIUS (*as he follows* HAMLET *out*): The actors are coming hither my lord.
HAMLET: Buzz, buzz.
(*Exeunt* HAMLET *and* POLONIUS.)
(ROS *and* GUIL *ponder. Each reluctant to speak first.*)
GUIL: Hm?
ROS: Yes?
GUIL: What?
ROS: I thought you…
GUIL: No.
ROS: Ah.
       (*Pause.*)
GUIL: I think we can say we made some headway.
ROS: You think so?
GUIL: I think we can say that.
ROS: I think we can say he made us look ridiculous.
GUIL: We played it close to the chest of course.
ROS (*derisively*):   'Question and answer. Old ways are the best ways'! He was
       scoring off us all the way down the line.
GUIL: He caught us on the wrong foot once or twice, perhaps, but I thought
       we gained some ground.
ROS (*simply*):   He murdered us.
GUIL: He might have had the edge.
ROS (*roused*):   Twenty-seven – three, and you think he might have had the
       edge?! He *murdered* us.
GUIL: What about our evasions?
ROS: Oh, our evasions were lovely. 'Were you sent for?' he says. 'My lord, we
       were sent for' … I didn't know where to put myself.
GUIL: He had six rheticals –
ROS: It was question and answer all right. Twenty-seven questions he got out
       in ten minutes, and answered three. I was waiting for you to *delve*.
       'When is he going to start *delving?*' I asked myself.
GUIL: – And two repetitions.
ROS: Hardly a leading question between us.
GUIL: We got his *symptoms*, didn't we?
ROS: Half of what he said meant something else, and the other half didn't
       mean anything at all.
GUIL: Thwarted ambition – a sense of grievance, that's my diagnosis.
ROS: Six rhetorical and two repetition, leaving nineteen of which we
       answered fifteen. And what did we get in return? He's depressed! …
       Denmark's a prison and he'd rather live in a nutshell; some shadow-play
       about the nature of ambition, which never got down to cases, and
       finally one direct question which might have led somewhere, and led in
       fact to his illuminating claim to tell a hawk from a handsaw.
       (*Pause.*)
GUIL: When the wind is southerly.
ROS: And the weather's clear.
GUIL: And when it isn't he can't.

ROS: He's at the mercy of the elements. (*Licks his finger and holds it up –
        facing audience.*) Is that southerly?
        (*They stare at audience*).

From Tom Stoppard, *Rosencrantz and Guildenstern Are Dead* (London, 1967),
pp. 40–2.[11]

2.2   What is an Author?

Originality has often been seen as a key quality in literature – and, indeed, in modern Western Art in general. Thus, in section 1.2 it was an obvious starting point to contrast the originality of the 'literary' Lawrence with the 'formulaic' narrative of Mills and Boon. However, our discussion in the last section of the complexities of distinguishing original text from a plethora of surrounding texts may suggest that the concept of originality needs to be, at the least, thought upon further. In fact, our discussion was focused so single-mindedly on texts, that it did not consider at all another area of thought closely linked to the idea of the text. For, if our conceptions of text depend on notions of autonomous and original wholes, so too to an enormous degree do our ideas of the *author*. This section will be mainly concerned with how the wholeness – or otherwise – of authors has been variously defined and debated.

We can start, as so often, by turning for guidance to the dictionary definitions of the *OED*. An *author*, we are told, has five distinct definitions. Three of these are unusual or obsolete. The two dominant senses are given as follows:

> **1.a.** The person who originates or gives existence to anything: … an inventor, constructor or founder … **b.** The Creator …
> **3.a.** One who sets forth written statements; the composer or writer of a treatise or book. … **b.** *elliptically* put for: an author's writings

A number of the less usual senses suggest close links in meaning between the words *author* and *authority*:

> **4.** The person on whose authority a statement is made; an authority, an informant
> **5.** One who has authority over others; a director, ruler, commander

In fact, all of these senses centre on ideas of *origination*, or the power to originate. Though authority and author are generally regarded as distinct words, they both have shared roots in the Latin *auctor*, a noun deriving from the verb *augere* = to increase, to produce. 'Author' is derived directly from the Latin noun, while authority comes from a more abstract Latin noun itself stemming from *auctor*: *auctoritas* = the power or quality of being able to initiate or determine. The most usual modern sense of author as a writer has clearly specialised the central concept of origination so that it applies specifically to the activity of writing.

Some of the issues raised by this connection between *power* and *originality* are closely related to ideas about textual stability. Just as in the Middle Ages 'textes' could be cited as clear reference points of established meaning, so too could 'authors' be referred to as authoritative proofs of authenticity. Thus Chaucer can write in *The Legend of Good Women*: 'of manye a geste / As autouris seyn' (= of many a deed, as authors say). This kind of authenticating reference to previous authors is common in Chaucer and in medieval writers in general. Clearly, when 'authors' are cited in this way, they are being called upon as 'authorities' or sources which have the power to ground statements in a truth beyond mere individual opinion or casual storytelling. The link between true texts and truthful creators is made particularly strongly in a comment by Wycliff about the Bible cited by *OED*: 'if holy writte be fals, certis god author ther-of is fals' (if the Bible is untrue, then God as its author must certainly also be untrue). Wycliff's usage here probably also specifically invokes sense **1.b** (The Creator) – God is author of the Bible and author of the universe itself. In this case, at least, the power of authorship is clear.

In fact, the idea of authorship as a godlike activity can be found applied to mortals too, and long after the medieval period. This is no doubt connected to traditions of imaging the author as father or patriarchal creator, a metaphor discussed by Gilbert and Gubar (see section 1.4). The author as God is the ultimate version of this image.

> ◆ Read the following poem, 'Sonnet I Am', by John Clare (1793–1864).[12]
> How can it be seen to make use of ideas about the author as God, or
> god-like?

Sonnet I Am

I feel I am, I only know I am
And plod upon the earth as dull and void
Earth's prison chilled my body with its dram
Of dullness, and my soaring thoughts destroyed.
I fled to solitudes from passions dream   5
But strife pursued – I only know I am.
I was a being created in the race
Of men disdaining bounds of place and time –
A spirit that could travel o'er the space
Of earth and heaven – like a thought sublime,   10
Tracing creation, like my maker, free –
A soul unshackled like eternity,
Spurning earth's vain and soul debasing thrall
But now I only know I am – that's all.

▶▷ Discussion

The poem seems to me to depend on a basic opposition between formerly godlike powers and present dullness. This 'dullness' is associated with earth (= soil) and being earth-bound (= confined to this material world). Hence in his present state the speaker can only 'plod' upon the earth, where once he spurned its 'thrall' – that is its condition of slavery. Against this dullness, the poem places an original state in which the speaker was 'a being', 'a spirit', 'a soul' who was unbounded and who could travel freely through earth and heaven, space and time. This former freedom is specifically linked to creativity – he was 'created', was able to trace 'Creation', was, indeed, a creator like his own Creator. There are various touches which suggest that this opposition is specifically one to do with authorship, and with a grand conception of it. Thus, 'men disdaining bounds of place and time' are perhaps best identified not only as 'free spirits', but particularly as authors, whose imaginations can soar above the merely given. The spirit of such a one is like a 'thought sublime' – that is a thought of the most exalted, original kind. There is, I suspect, moreover, a concern with the power of authorship in two intertexts with authors admired by Clare. The author who actually attempted to trace creation is Milton, in his Christian epic, *Paradise Lost* (1674), which represents the Divine creation of the world and attempts to 'justify the ways of God to man'. The other term in the opposition, dullness, was a key word in Alexander Pope's satiric epic, *The Dunciad* (1728), which, also based partly on *Paradise Lost*, mocked the dullness, the utter lack of divine spark, in contemporary hack authors (the dunces of the title). It is possible, too, to attach biographical details of Clare's life to the conceptions of the poem[13] – his feelings that his capacity for inspiration had faded, his anguish at being confined in the asylum, his loss of public recognition as a poet. □

The idea of authorship as an originating power analogous to that of God's seems very clear in this poem, and was perhaps particularly strong in the Romantic period to which Clare is usually more or less assigned. Weaker versions of the idea seem still to be with us, and, indeed, still form a dominant way of talking about authors. Reviews and book jackets quite frequently refer to creation, distinctive worlds, and genius. However, though this idea of authorship, which we have briefly traced from the Middle Ages, via the early nineteenth century, up to now, is an important one, it is not the only way of looking at authors. Indeed, some of the examples and definitions with which this section began suggest that though authors produce new tellings of stories, they do so as much through knowledge and reassembly of a previous set of originals or authorities as through spontaneous creation from nothing. Thus Chaucer seems keen to show his command of original authors. In Chaucer's case this is no doubt partly a version of the practice of glossing biblical and other church texts (see section 2.1 above), but it is also related to an ancient function for the composer of narratives, the preservation and transmission of traditional knowledge. Thus the Old English poem known as *Widsith*[14] implies somewhat different functions for the 'teller' than those suggested by 'Sonnet I Am' for the author.

> Read the extracts from the poem and list the implied responsibilities
> and functions of the 'teller' (known in Old English as a *scop*=shaper,
> poet, singer). The extracts include the opening of the poem and its
> conclusion. The speaker, Widsith, clearly speaks as a *scop*.

WIDSITH

Widsith spoke forth, and unlocked the treasury of his words, he who had travelled through most of the peoples, nations and tribes upon the earth; many a
time on the floor of the hall he had received some commemorative treasure.
His family were sprung from the Myrgingas, and he had in the first instance
gone with Ealhild, the beloved weaver of peace, from the east out of Anglen
to the home of the king of the glorious Goths, Eormanric, the cruel
troth-breaker. He began then to say many things. (ll. 1–8)

I have heard tell about many men ruling over nations. Every prince ought to
live ethically … who presumes to receive its princely throne. Hwala was at one
time the noblest of these, and Alexander the most powerful of all mankind
and he prospered most of those of whom I have heard tell throughout the
earth. (ll. 9–17)

Attila ruled the Huns, Eormanric the Goths, Becca the Baningas, Gifica the
Burgundians. Caesar ruled the Greeks and Caelic the Finns, Hagena the
Holmrygas, and Heoden the Glommas. Witta ruled the Swabians, Wade the
Haelsingas, Meaca the Myrgingas … (ll. 18–21)
…
I have been with the Saracens and with the Seringas. I have been with the
Greeks and with the Finns and with Caesar who held sway over festive cities,
over riches and desirable things and over the empire of the Romans. (ll. 75–8)
…
So the people's entertainers go wandering fatedly through many lands; they
declare their need and speak words of thanks. Always whether south or
north, they will meet someone discerning of songs and unniggardly of gifts
who desires to exalt his repute and sustain his heroic standing until everything passses away, light and life together. This man deserves glory; he will
keep his lofty and secure renown here below the heavens. (ll. 135–end)

From *Anglo-Saxon Poetry*, ed. and trans. S. A. J. Bradley (London, 1982).

▶ Discussion

There seem here to be a whole range of qualities attributed to the poet
which differ from those suggested by 'I Am', and, I suspect, are less familiar to us than Clare's representation of the author as a semi-divine creator.
Firstly, I notice that Widsith claims to be in a literal sense a witness to the
events, people and lands which he names. One of his claims to poetic
authority seems to be that he has 'travelled through most of the peoples,

nations and tribes upon the earth' (l. 1). It is true that Clare's poetic persona is also a traveller, 'tracing creation', but where he is precisely free of the bounds of time and space, able presumably to travel wherever his imagination allows, Widsith needs to claim an actual presence. Though both poems are about being a poet, it is notable that where 'I Am' refers to the ability and inability to achieve the journeys of the imagination, *Widsith* actually recounts the geographical knowledge which Widsith has, as if it guarantees his status as *scop*. Hence the middle part of this extract from *Widsith* is in the main a list of nations and their rulers (much of the material which is omitted is also of this kind, so that the listing is, indeed, encyclopaedic).

It seems likely that one of the roles of the Old English poet that this poem is both speaking about and actually performing is that of remembering *knowledge*. That function was mentioned in talking earlier about medieval texts, but this seems a particularly striking use of poetry to remember – almost as if this poem performs a function now taken over by other definitively 'non-poetic' and 'non-literary' genres such as encyclopaedias and atlases. It is clear that this ability to remember is not a trivial one, however. In the last verse Widsith speaks of those who understand that the poet can 'sustain his [the patron's] heroic standing until everything passes away' (l. 135). It is not only knowledge of facts which is passed down through poetry – though this poem certainly does catalogue the rulers and peoples of the Anglo-Saxon world – but also remembrance of reputations. Poetry is able to preserve this knowledge until the end of the world itself, so that until Doomsday, the deserving 'will keep his lofty and secure renown here below the heavens' (last line).

I also notice what may seem a surprisingly explicit interest in 'desirable things' (l. 77) – one notes the phrases: 'commemorative treasure' (l. 3), 'festive cities', 'riches' and 'unniggardly of gifts' (in a verse I have omitted, the poet remembers how Eormanric, King of the Goths, 'gave me a collar in which there was six hundred coins' worth of pure gold', ll. 88 and after). The receipt of gifts of gold is clearly expected by poets in this culture (Clare does not mention the lack thereof as a cause for the earth-bound poet's dejection ...). Careful following-through of these references to 'gifts' seems to suggest that they refer to a system of patronage with its own implicit understandings. The poet has to 'declare their need' (l. 135), and the deserving patron has to give gifts freely to him; in return, the poet will 'exalt his repute', by speaking 'words of thanks'. One might note that the first line of the poem refers to the '*treasury* of his words' – perhaps there is a system of exchange here whereby golden treasure rewards poetic treasure?

This seems at first a rather crude exchange – as if the poet is merely hired to praise. However, there may well be a further understanding behind this in which the rewarding of poetry with gifts is a sign not merely of a wealthy lord, but of one who understands and fulfils the correct relationships between people. It is not so much that a bad patron could buy praise, but that a good lord would naturally express his goodness by ensuring the well-being of poets, just as he would ensure the correct social relations with all in his care ('every prince ought to live ethically', l. 9). It is noticeable that the poet is clearly associated with rulers in *Widsith* – as if the poet's main function is to praise kings. Perhaps this is what unites the catalogue of rulers with the poet's quite explicit commentary about the function of the poet – the poet can and will remember kings, both bad and good, so that every king's deeds will be remembered and rightly judged through the poet. Thus in *Widsith* (and we might want to conclude in Anglo-Saxon tradition) the poet had a vital social function in recording and regulating the proper behaviour of kings.

Compared to Clare's sense of the poet as 'A soul unshackled like eternity', the function of the Anglo-Saxon poet may seem somewhat 'earth-bound', or less romantically and more positively, much more closely linked to the central material concerns of his society. A passage in the final verse, though, suggests a slightly more 'inspired' role for the *scop*: 'So the people's entertainers go wandering fatedly through many lands'. The phrase 'the people's entertainers' implies a possible role in representing communal interests, while the 'fatedly' suggests the impersonal, magical function of the poet. Indeed, though it is not immediately obvious, there is the suggestion of an ability to wander through time and space, and across all boundaries which is analogous to the poet's freedom in 'I Am'. In fact, greater knowledge of some of the many references in the poem could reinforce this magical and less literal sense of the poet. For actually, Widsith, though he appears to claim actual presence at all these sites, cannot as an ordinary mortal have been an eye-witness at all these places and to all of these rulers, as the translator of the poem, S. A. J. Bradley, comments: 'the speaker is … a symbolic poet who has travelled all the known world and the near and far reaches of history as no real man could have done in one lifetime'.[15]

Perhaps then, there are some likenesses between the two conceptions of the 'author' or 'poet' in these two poems, since both do have attributes of freedom and even magical resonances. But the stresses in one case on the author as *god-like creator*, and in the other on the author as *remembrancer to an earthly ruler* also suggest some of the range of possible difference in the ways that tellers of narratives can be conceived. Where in *Widsith* there is little emphasis on artistic creativity (though one might pick out 'unlocked the treasury of his words' and 'someone discerning of songs'), this is central to the speaker of 'I Am'. *Widsith* sees the greatest power of the teller as being the ability to preserve, and implicitly to judge rightly, while 'I Am' sees originality as the essence of the poetic. Both of these functions are possibilities in the root meanings of author (*auctoritas* – the power or quality of being able to *initiate or determine*), but the differences – and the network of different cultural meanings which these two texts draw on – are clearly great.

It is, of course, not surprising that there are enormous differences between these two versions of authorship,[16] separated by at least 800 years: like other concepts the author changes through history, allowing different aspects of the role to be recognised, prioritised and, indeed, invented at different times. If, as seems likely, we base decisions about what texts mean on, among many other things, ideas about authors, we should keep in mind that current conceptions of authorship may not be identical to those dominant at the time of writing. We might also think about the question of whether, even in a single time period or culture, the author is always represented in a way which is absolute and indivisible. We can investigate this by looking at different ways in which texts can represent authors not only from period to period, but even within more-or-less the same period. ☐

> Read the following three extracts. What part does the author appear to play in each of these texts?

A. Fielding, *Tom Jones*

BOOK I

CONTAINING AS MUCH OF THE BIRTH OF THE FOUNDLING AS IS NECESSARY OR PROPER TO ACQUAINT THE READER WITH IN THE BEGINNING OF THIS HISTORY

Chapter I

The Introduction to the Work, or Bill of Fare to the Feast

An author ought to consider himself, not as a gentleman who gives a private or eleemosynary treat, but rather as one who keeps a public ordinary, at which all persons are welcome for their money. In the former case, it is well-known, that the entertainer provides what fare he pleases; and tho' this should be very indifferent, and utterly disagreeable to the taste of his company, they must not find any fault; nay, on the contrary, good breeding forces them outwardly to approve and to commend whatever is set before them. Now the contrary happens to the master of an ordinary. Men who pay for what they eat, will insist on gratifying their palates, however nice and even whimsical these may prove; and if every thing is not agreeable to their taste, will challenge a right to censure, to abuse, and to d—n their dinner without controul.

To prevent therefore giving offence to their customers by any such disappointment, it hath been usual, with the honest and well-meaning host, to provide a bill of fare, which all persons may peruse at their first entrance into the house; and, having thence acquainted themselves with the entertainment which they may expect, may either stay and regale with what is provided for them, or may depart to some other ordinary better accommodated to their taste.

As we do not disdain to borrow wit or wisdom from any man who is capable of lending us either, we have condescended to take a hint from those honest victuallers, and shall prefix not only a general bill of fare to our whole entertainment, but shall likewise give the reader particular bills to every course which is to be served up in this and the ensuing volumes.

The provision then which we have here made is not other than HUMAN NATURE. Nor do I fear that my sensible reader, though most luxurious in his taste, will start, cavil, or be offended because I have named but one article... Nor can the learned reader be ignorant, that in *Human Nature*, tho' here collected under one general name is such prodigious variety, that a cook will have sooner gone through all the several species of animal and vegetable food in the world, than an author will be able to exhaust so extensive a subject.

From Henry Fielding, *Tom Jones* (1749), Book I, ch. 1. Extract from Penguin edn (1981), pp. 51–3.

B. Austen, *Persuasion*

Chapter 1

Sir Walter Elliot, of Kelynch-hall, in Somersetshire, was a man who, for his own amusement, never took up any book but the Baronetage; there he found occupation for an idle hour, and consolation in a distressed one; there his faculties were roused into admiration and respect, by contemplating the limited remnant of the earliest patents; there any unwelcome sensations, arising from domestic affairs, changed naturally into pity and contempt, as he turned over the almost endless creations of the last century – and there, if every other leaf were powerless, he could read his own history with an interest which never failed – this was the page at which the favourite volume always opened.
…

Vanity was the beginning and the end of Sir Walter Elliot's character; vanity of person and of situation. He had been remarkably handsome in his youth; and, at fifty-four, was still a very fine man. Few women could think more of their personal appearance than he did; nor could the valet of any new made lord be more delighted with the place he held in society. He considered the blessing of beauty as inferior only to the blessing of a baronetcy; and the Sir Walter Elliot, who united these gifts, was the constant object of his warmest respect and devotion.

From Jane Austen, *Persuasion* (1818), ch. 1. Extract from Penguin edn (1984), pp. 35–6.

C. Richardson, *Pamela*

Letter I

Dear Father and Mother,

I have great trouble, and some comfort, to acquaint you with. The trouble is that my good lady died of the illness I mentioned to you, and left us all much grieved for the loss of her: she was a dear good lady, and kind to all us her servants. Much I feared, that as I was taken by her ladyship to wait upon her person, I should be quite destitute again, and forced to return to you and my poor mother, who have enough to do to maintain yourselves; and, as my lady's goodness had put me to write and to cast accounts, and made me a little expert at my needle, and otherwise qualified above my degree, it was not every family that could have found a place that your poor Pamela was fit for: but God, whose graciousness to us we have so often experienced, put it into my good lady's heart, just an hour before she expired, to recommend to my young master all her servants one by one; and when it came to my turn to be recommended (for I was sobbing and crying at her pillow), she could only say – 'My dear son!' and so broke off a little; and then recovering, 'Remember my poor Pamela.' – And these were some of her last words. O how my eyes run! Don't wonder to see the paper so blotted.

From Samuel Richardson, *Pamela* (1740), Letter 1. Extract from Penguin (1985), pp. 43–4.

▶ Discussion

It seems fairly clear that the author appears with varying degrees of obviousness in each of these three passages. To deal first with the most obvious, the Fielding passage surely has the most apparent author.[17] The passage starts with a generalisation about authors, which makes explicit the fact that authors are the main topic of this text: 'An author ought ...' Moreover, this general discussion of authors is specifically linked to the author of this very book, who turns to his own case, and directly addresses us (the reader) in person: 'nor do *I* fear that *my* sensible reader ...'. The most obvious communication model seems to be in place here, with the addresser (apparently = author in this case) sending a message to the addressee (= the reader). In fact, as the chapter heading makes clear, this chapter contains material which is, in a sense, not part of the book proper at all. It is, instead, a preamble where the author can clear up some points before he starts on the main matter of narrating the events arising from a set of characters. These fictional persons are not mentioned at all in this chapter, which deals *only* with the actual persons involved in the novel: author and reader.

The author seems, at the least, to play a much less extrovert part in the opening of *Persuasion*. Where in the Fielding passage, the author identifies himself and speaks through a pronoun ('I' and the more rhetorical 'we'), here there is no such explicit identification of the author. Though there is a voice speaking, telling the story, it does not refer to itself. Instead there is a concentration on describing the character Sir Walter Elliot without any obvious attempt to assign this description to a *person*. Readers, however, seem to have no problem in coping with this unidentified voice – largely because, in fact, novel readers are very familiar with the conventions which govern its use. We usually assume that this narrative voice is, indeed, one possessing authority, at least, and often that it is an authorial narrator. That is to say, unless there is contrary evidence (i.e. irony suggesting an unreliable narrator), we tend to read this voice as providing reliable guidance to characters and events in a novel. Behind this convention there is evidently a sense that there is a voice which ranks above that of characters' voices, which articulates a central viewpoint, and which speaks to the reader. Though readers who have progressed through a critical education in English literature have usually been trained to be wary of calling this voice 'the author', there are some ways at least in which the voice plays a comparable role to that of Fielding's author in the first passage. Thus the voice does talk apparently intimately to the reader, it does provide guidance, and it is separate from the actual events and persons of the narrative itself.

However, the voice's non-referral to itself does suggest a different effect from the author-in-person of *Tom Jones*. Firstly, this lack of emphasis on the identity of the speaker tends to suggest that the viewpoint is not a personal one grounded in a particular experience of the characters and events, but is rather an impersonal view – what anyone with a clear view would say. Thus authorial narration tends to be accepted by readers in the first instance as natural and neutral. Where the Fieldingesque author plays an obviously eccentric and whimsical role, expressing opinions and idiosyncrasies at every opportunity, this voice seems to avoid speaking egotistically – it suppresses any bodily existence from which the voice issues.

Though I think my analysis of the part played by the author at the opening of *Persuasion* is correct, it is also far from complete. So far, I have suggested a superficially straightforward kind of narration, where the impersonal voice influences our responses by *telling us about characters*, while itself remaining very much in the background. However, the 'telling us about' part of this, though true up to a point, obscures the fact that this voice, far from remaining neutral, distanced and reassuringly static, actually frequently moves between two different points of origin. Thus the following two clauses do not speak of Sir Walter from exactly the same position:

Vanity was the beginning and the end of Sir Walter Elliot's character
...

...and the Sir Walter Elliot, who united these gifts, was the constant object of his warmest respect and devotion.

Though both remarks are similar enough to be read as part of a single continuous utterance, one is a simple statement of opinion *by* the narrative voice *about* the character; the other is more complex, since it appears to express a contrary view. In the first remark, vanity is roundly condemned, in the second we are invited to see from the *inside* Sir Walter's self-love. Thus, instead of being asked to identify with a disapproving narrator, we are now asked to identify with Sir Walter's pleasure in his own self-regard. Being trained novel readers, we are most likely to eliminate the apparent disparity of viewpoint by regarding the second statement as ironic: it is read as a piece of unreliable (self) narration precisely bearing out the 'dominant' other voice's view that Sir Walter can see nothing beyond himself.

In the third passage, there is similarly a kind of mimicry of a character's voice – but here the effect is much more sustained: Pamela appears to speak – write – for herself throughout the extract. In this sense the author appears to play no part at all in the narrating of these words. Where in the Fielding there was an obvious author present, and where in the Austen there was the implication of an authorial narrator carefully guiding the reader, here there seems to be no author present in the text: the character speaks her own lines. The novel proceeds, in other words, as if these were real letters, needing no author, beyond that of the actual authors of the letters (Pamela *is* the author of this letter, we are invited to believe). In this kind of narration, the reader is invited to assume – for the purposes of the fiction – that the character is elevated to the status of author, while the author becomes merely an editor, who arranges the letters in date order.

Clearly, each of the passages represents, with its own particular idiosyncrasies, a different kind of authorial appearance, which we might *provisionally* (see below!) call explicit, inexplicit and absent. The communicative situation in each differs in ways which we could represent diagrammatically by adapting Jakobson's model (represented in its most basic form in Introduction II above):

A: FIELDING
(explicit authorial appearance)

Addresser →→→ (Message) →→→ Addressee

Author →→ (Direct address – discussion of novels) →→→ Reader

B: AUSTEN
(inexplicit authorial appearance)

Addresser →→→ (Message) →→→ Addressee

Narrator (authorial?)→ (Description of Sir Walter/mimicry of his viewpoint)→ Reader

C: RICHARDSON
(absent author)

Addresser →→→ (Message) →→→ Addressee

Character →→→ (letter to parents) →→→ Mr and Mrs Andrews

    → →Reader

I stress the *provisional* nature of these diagrams because, though I think they are helpful, I can see fairly quickly that there are factors they do not really take into account. ☐

◆ Examine each of the three diagrams and see if you can add anything, or have any queries about the way they represent the communicative situation in the three passages.

(You might like to photocopy or copy out the diagrams and try adding in elements or comments).

 **Discussion**

It strikes me that a number of elements in the diagrams imply excessive certainty – and simplification – of the situation and the roles within it. I will add my queries and expansions to each of the diagrams below, and then see if there are general conclusions to be drawn about notions of the author. You may well have picked out similar problems – though there are several ways of describing them (and I may not have seen some possibilities, of course). □

A. DIAGRAM

> Addresser →→→ (Message) →→→ Addressee
>
> Author →→ (Direct address – discussion of novels) →→→ Reader

Really Fielding himself exactly?	Strictly, more an *illusion* of direct address to You a specific reader? – not actually a one-to-one address, since not really tied to any specific reader?	Is the reader You as a biographical person? Or is it rather a function the novel needs to build up (see second comment under author)?

'The author' – 'I', 'we' – is more something the novel needs than a direct expression of the biographical, historical person called Henry Fielding (1707–54)?

Better seen as a character called 'the author'?

B. DIAGRAM

> Addresser →→→ (Message) →→→ Addressee
>
> Narrator (authorial?) → (Description of Sir Walter / mimicry of his viewpoint)→Reader

The narrator here makes no direct claim to be the author – though that doesn't inhibit our feeling that the narrator is an authoritative (hence authorial?) voice.

Perhaps the mimicry almost makes Sir Walter an addresser? (i.e. we seem to hear his voice speaking?).

But, as with Passage A, this may not necessarily correspond to the person, Jane Austen, who wrote the novel?

Perhaps we really need a diagram which shows the passage as having *two* models of communication:

Again, better seen as a character called 'the narrator'?

> Narrator → Reader
> +
> Narrator mimics/represents Sir Walter → Reader, OR Sir Walter → Himself (→ Reader)

C. DIAGRAM

> Addresser →→→ (Message)→→→ Addressee
> Character →→→ (letter to parents) →→→ Mr and Mrs Andrews
> ↘
> →→ Reader

Models the *novel's illusion* of communication rather than the actual situation?

The diagram only represents what is happening in *one* letter – really the novel is made up of a whole series of letters.

Surely an author is at some level an addresser?

Reader is implicitly the addressee, but has to read *through* the explicit addressee?

OR does the reader feel they are 'eavesdropping', reading letters not really meant for their eyes?

Letters deliberately allow for two different readerships? (who may read different things into the letters from their differing positions?)

Do we really need a diagram more like the following?

> Addresser→→→→→→→ (Message) →→→→→ Addressee
> Author →→→ Novel in epistolary form →→→ Reader
> i.e.
> ↘
> (fictional addressers → (set of letters) → fictional addressees)

Even this diagram does not resolve all the complexities, of course. The exact relationship or relationships between Reader and fictional addressees could be seen in several different ways – as my comments on the first Passage C Diagram suggested. □

Most of my doubts about my first-attempt diagrams arise from an idea that these roles of addresser and addressee/author and reader do not precisely or necessarily represent simple, let alone actual, identities. The 'Author' who 'speaks' to us in the Fielding may be given their identity as much by the rhetorical structure and needs of the novel as by the actual Fielding's need to tell us what he thinks about novels (though we cannot necessarily be certain that there *isn't* an autobiographical element). The narrative voice in the Austen passage does not always simply speak from one viewpoint, but represents a shifting set of different relationships between the different communicative roles. In the Richardson passage the function of the narrator appears to have disappeared – leaving the character to speak directly (though not directly to us!). Nevertheless, we might well suspect that there is an organising presence which does work across all the apparently free-standing letters, so that they are not, for example, in random order, so that there is a development during the whole length of the novel and so that common themes arise from the correspondence. We do not have to call this presence an author, or even an (absent) narrator, though: we could instead argue that it is itself a rhetorical function arising from the sequence of fictional letters, and being at least partly constructed by the reader's need to make sense of the material.

The theatrical metaphor beneath the surface of my earlier question: 'What *part* does the author appear to *play* in each of these texts?' seems now to be a helpful one in the light of this discussion. In a text the appearance of an author is, indeed, an acted part as much as a real presence. Though 'the author' may undoubtedly suggest a strong sense of presence in a whole variety of kinds for the reader, the author (from this point of view at least) is perhaps part of the text, rather than? as much as? above the text as a clear point of origin or controller.

These different possibilities for the author's appearance in a text might best be called rhetorical variation, as opposed to the historical variation which we have worked through in the first part of the section. The two are separate in that rhetorical variation presumably exists in any one period, while variation in the conceptions and manifestations of the author occurs across history. However, the two types of variation are also intertwined in that different rhetorical possibilities for the author have histories (new techniques of narrative can/have been invented), and may be part of historical variation (for example, perhaps one kind of use of authorial voice is particularly prevalent at a certain historical period, perhaps for general or specific cultural reasons that can be analysed).

Indeed, even the trend of the argument above towards the idea that the author is not so much a person sending out a text, as either a biographical distraction or a function in a text is, in itself, part of an identifiable historical tendency to interpret or represent the author thus. This tendency has only become dominant in the Anglo-American literary critical establishment since the 1940s, and has been reinforced by developments in French critical traditions. The tendency to downplay the prime role of the author as originating person was perhaps first strongly established by an essay about poetry published in 1946, called 'The Intentional Fallacy' by two American academics, W. K. Wimsatt and Monroe C. Beardsley. They ended the essay with a forceful argument that the author as a person who sent out a message was not a relevant subject for concern when interpreting a literary text.

◆ Read the passage: Why, in Beardsley and Wimsatt's view, is the author not 'an oracle'?

• • • • • • • • • •

As a poetic practice allusiveness would appear to be in some recent poems an extreme corollary of the romantic intentionalist assumption, and as a critical issue it challenges and brings to light in a special way the basic premise of intentionalism. The following instance from the poetry of Eliot may serve to epitomise the practical implications of what we have been saying. In Eliot's 'Love Song of J. Alfred Prufrock', towards the end, occurs the line: 'I have heard the mermaids singing, each to each', and this bears a certain resemblance to a line in a Song by John Donne, 'Teach me to heare Mermaides singing', so that for the reader acquainted to a certain degree with Donne's poetry, the critical question arises: Is Eliot's line an allusion to Donne's? Is Prufrock thinking about Donne? Is Eliot thinking about Donne? We suggest that there are two radically different ways of looking for an answer to this question.

There is (1) the way of poetic analysis and exegesis, which inquires if it makes any sense if Eliot–Prufrock *is* thinking about Donne ... The exegetical observer may wonder whether mermaids considered as strange sights (to hear them in Donne's poem is analogous to getting with child a mandrake root) have much to do with Prufrock's mermaids, which seem to be symbols of romance and dynamism ... This method of inquiry may lead to the conclusion that the given resemblance between Eliot and Donne is without significance, and is better not thought of, or the method may have the disadvantage of providing no certain conclusion. Nevertheless, we submit that this is the true and objective way of criticism, as contrasted to what the very uncertainty of exegesis might tempt a second kind of critic to undertake: (2) the way of biographical or genetic inquiry, in which taking advantage of the fact that Eliot is still alive, and in the spirit of a man who would settle a bet, the critic writes to Eliot and asks what he meant, or if he had Donne in mind. We shall not here weigh the probabilities – whether Eliot would answer that he meant nothing at all; had nothing at all in mind – a sufficiently good answer to such a question – or in an unguarded moment might furnish a clear and, within its limit, irrefutable answer. Our point is that such an answer to such an inquiry would have nothing to do with the poem 'Prufrock'; it would not be a critical inquiry. Critical inquiries, unlike bets, are not settled in this way. Critical inquiries are not settled by consulting the oracle.

From W. K. Wimsatt and Monroe C. Beardsley, 'The Intentional Fallacy', reprinted in *The Verbal Icon – Studies in the Meaning of Poetry* (1954; British

• edn, 1970), pp. 17–18. Originally published in *Sewanee Review*, LIV (Summer,
• 1946).

• • • • • • • • • • •

▶ Discussion

For Wimsatt and Beardsley (or should we say, for the passage?), the author
both as biographical person and as a point of origin for a poem is irrelevant to critical enquiry because once the text has been created it takes on
an autonomous life of its own. The only valid critical questions are ones
which can be asked of the text and which it can answer. The author may
well have had personal psychological reasons for writing a particular line
or phrase, may well have had an intention – but only reasons which are
in the text itself matter now it is written. They are in agreement with
D. H. Lawrence's maxim: 'Believe the tale, not the teller'. □

The culmination of this tradition of pushing the figure of the author to the mar-
gins of literary study – and even literary or textual production – is Roland
Barthes' 1968 essay, 'The Death of the Author'. Many of its points pick up ideas
about authors which this section has discussed earlier in its own fashion (and,
indeed, ideas about meaning and texts also discussed above), but it pushes them
towards a point where the very category *author* is argued to have become defunct.

◆ Read the extract from this essay. How close is the argument about the
author to that in Wimsatt and Beardsley?
◆ What kind of author does Barthes/the essay argue has died? (the
author as biographical person? the rhetorical author in a text? the
author as an idea believed in by readers? a certain historical idea of
the author?)
◆ Are you completely convinced by the argument of Barthes' essay?
Whether you are or not, can you suggest any ways of arguing against
the thesis that the author is 'dead'?

• • • • • • • • • • •

In his story *Sarrasine*, Balzac, describing a castrato disguised as a woman,
writes the following sentence: '*This was woman herself, with her sudden
fears, her irrational whims, her instinctive worries, her impetuous boldness,
her fussings, and her delicious sensibility.*' Who is speaking thus? Is it the hero
of the story bent on remaining ignorant of the castrato hidden beneath
the woman? Is it Balzac the individual, furnished by his personal experience
with a philosophy of Woman? Is it Balzac the author professing 'literary' ideas
on femininity? Is it universal wisdom? Romantic psychology? We shall never
know, for the good reason that writing is the destruction of every voice,
of every point of origin. Writing is that neutral, composite space where our

subject slips away, the negative where all identity is lost, starting with the very identity of the body writing.

No doubt it has always been that way. As soon as a fact is *narrated* no longer with a view to acting directly on reality but intransitively, that is to say finally outside of any function other than that of the very practice of the symbol itself, this disconnection occurs, the voice loses its origin, the author enters into his own death, writing begins. The sense of this phenomenon, however, has varied; in ethnographic [= pre-modern] societies the responsibility for a narrative is never assumed by a person but by a mediator, shaman or relator whose 'performance' – the mastery of the narrative code – may possibly be admired but never his genius.[18] The author is a modern figure, a product of our society insofar as ... it discovered the prestige of the individual, of, as it is more nobly put, the 'human person' ... the *author* still reigns in histories of literature, biographies of writers, interviews, magazines, as in the very consciousness of men of letters anxious to unite their person and their work through diaries and memoirs. The image of literature to be found in ordinary culture is tyrannically centred on the author ... The *explanation* of a work is always sought in the man or woman who produced it, as if it were always in the end, through the more or less transparent allegory of the fiction, the voice of a single person, the *author* confiding in us.

...

Leaving aside literature itself ... linguistics has recently provided the destruction of the Author with a valuable analytical tool by showing that the whole of the enunciation is an empty process, functioning perfectly without there being any need for it to be filled with the person of the interlocutors. Linguistically, the author is never more than the instance writing, just as *I* is nothing other than the instance saying *I*: language knows a 'subject', not a 'person', and this subject, empty outside of the very enunciation which defines it, suffices to make language 'hold together'. ...

The removal of the Author ... is not merely an historical fact or an act of writing; it utterly transforms the modern text (or – which is the same thing – the text is henceforth made and read in such a way that at all its levels the author is absent) ... We now know that a text is not a line of words releasing a single 'theological' meaning (the 'message of the Author-God'), but a multidimensional space in which a variety of writings, none of them original, blend and clash. The text is a tissue of quotations drawn from the innumerable centres of culture ... [The writer's] only power is to mix writings, to counter the ones with the others, in such a way as never to rest on any one of them. Did he wish to *express himself*, he ought at least to know that the inner 'thing' he thinks to 'translate' is itself only a ready-formed dictionary, its words only explainable through other words, and so on indefinitely. ...

Once the Author is removed, the claim to decipher a text becomes quite futile. To give a text an Author is to impose a limit on that text, to furnish it with a single signified, to close the writing. Such a conception suits criticism very well, the latter then allotting himself the important task of discovering the Author (or its hypostases [= stand-ins]: society, history, psyche, liberty), beneath the work: when the Author has been found, the text is 'explained' – victory to the critic. Hence there is no surprise that the reign of the Author has also been that of the Critic, nor in the fact that criticism ... is today undermined along with the Author. In the multiplicity of writing, everything is to be *disentangled*, nothing *deciphered*...Writing ceaselessly posits meaning ceaselessly to evaporate it, carrying out a systematic exemption of meaning. In precisely this way literature (it would be better from now on to say *writing*), by refusing to assign a 'secret', an ultimate meaning, to the text (and to the world as text), liberates what may be called an anti-theological activity, an activity that is truly revolutionary since to refuse to fix meaning is, in the end, to refuse God and his hypostases – reason, science, law.

Let us come back to the Balzac sentence. No-one, no 'person' says it: its source, its voice, is not the true place of the writing, which is reading...a text is made of multiple meanings, drawn from many cultures and entering into mutual relations of dialogue, parody and contestation, but there is one place where this multiplicity is focused and that place is the reader, not, as was hitherto said, the author. The reader is the space on which all the quotations that make up a writing are inscribed without any of them being lost; a text's unity lies not in its origin but in its destination. Yet this destination cannot any longer be personal: the reader is without history, biography, psychology; he is simply that *someone* who holds together in a single field all the traces by which the written text is constituted...Classic criticism has never paid any attention to the reader; for it, the writer is the only person in literature...We know that to give writing its future, it is necessary to overthrow the myth: the birth of the reader must be at the cost of the death of the Author.

From Roland Barthes, 'The Death of the Author', in *Image–Music–Text*, ed. and trans. Stephen Heath (London, 1977), pp. 142–8. Essay first published in French as 'Le mort de l'auteur', in *Manteia*, V (1968).

Discussion 1

There clearly are some affinities between Wimsatt/Beardsley and Barthes. In both essays, biographical authors are seen as absent from the text, as completely disconnected from what they have written once it has been written. In both, the idea of authorial intention is seen as an empty idea – no traces of authorial intent can be seen in the text itself. Wimsatt/Beardsley and Barthes seem to coincide in their description of a communicative relation which we can draw as:

$$(\text{Message} \longrightarrow \text{Addressee})$$
$$\text{Text} \longrightarrow \text{Reader}$$

In this model, if an author does appear to be speaking to us from/through a text, this is, in fact, an illusion, an effect of the text itself, which we could represent thus:

```
(Message  →→  Addressee)

       ↓

        ([Addresser is illusion created by message])
Text→→Reader

↓

[Author is device created in text]
```

Moreover, Wimsatt/Beardsley and Barthes each draw attention to the way in which it is often difficult to be sure who exactly the addresser is (is it author or character? Eliot or Prufrock? Balzac or his character-as-narrator?).

However, there is, I think, a difference in emphasis, when it comes to the text itself. Both passages agree in seeing the text as the replacement for the author as addresser. It is, therefore, the text which sends messages out to readers, or, anyway, provides a space in which readers can find meanings. Both passages also agree in regarding the text's message as inherently far from single or simple – Wimsatt/Beardsley write of 'the very uncertainty of exegesis', while Barthes speaks of our knowledge that:

> a text is not a line of words releasing a single 'theological' meaning (the 'message' of the Author-God) but a multi-dimensional space in which a variety of writings … blend and clash.

Indeed, we can see this kind of idea of intertextuality at work in the example of allusiveness which Wimsatt and Beardsley lead us through. However, the Wimsatt/Beardsley passage is not, I think, entirely in accord with the Barthes' notion that 'in the multiplicity of writing, everything is to be *disentangled*, nothing *deciphered* … the space of writing is to be ranged over, not pierced'. Though Wimsatt and Beardsley suggest the complexity of the text, they do not see critical explanation ('analysis and exegesis') – rational preference for one reading over another – as a 'hypostasis'. They object to the use of the figure of the author as a way of *avoiding* reading and interpreting the text itself, rather than to interpretation as a displaced version of the tyrannical myth of the Author. □

▶◁ Discussion 2

Barthes does not explicitly distinguish between different kinds of author. Thus at the beginning of the extract, there is the phrase 'Balzac the author'. This could refer to a biographical author (=the man Balzac who originally 'sent out' the 'message'), but equally the phrase could indicate the author Balzac who is created or implied by the text. In the next paragraph, there is firstly a striking metaphorical representation of the rhetorical position of the author, who cannot, it is asserted, be present in his/her own work: 'the voice loses its origin, the author enters into his own death, writing begins'.

This is rapidly followed by discussion of the author as a historical identity – 'the author is a modern figure' – which has changed (Shaman to author, *scop* to Romantic poet), and which can change further. This historical formation of the identity of the figure of the author is then seen as a concept which various literary parties use: literary historians, critics, interviewers, journalists, and, indeed, even actual biographical authors, who deploy that identity to think about themselves: 'as in the very consciousness of men of letters anxious to unite their person and their work'. This last case is perhaps an indicator of *why* the passage does not separate out different kinds of author for discussion – because there is a continuity between biographical, rhetorical and historical authors, between readers' authors and writers' authors. The rhetorical devices by which texts represent authors are also the devices by which authors represent themselves to their public and to themselves. Thus biographical, historical and rhetorical categories overlap. Oddly, this almost takes us back to the most traditional seeming, apparently common-sense model of the author as a unified being linked to the texts produced by them, the life lived by them, the history and culture which produced them and so forth. There is, however, a striking difference: the links between these distinct roles are not given, but are supplied by various kinds of reading functions: the author reads himself, the public read the author, the critic reads the author as a construction of the text, a historical construction, a (spurious?) biographical persona. There is thus no longer any clear connection between a person as author (the human whose hand writes or types the text) and any of the ways in which anyone (including that human her/himself) might understand that author.

For Barthes, then, it seems that all these kinds of author, being conjoined, are equally dead. Once, since culture and history have moved on from this unscientific fantasy, you no longer believe in the author as a sender of messages, you can no longer credit any authorial function. The author as guarantor of authority, of a point of origin, is now replaced by writing, which is precisely a special space where there is, and can be, no authority: 'the destruction … of every point of origin'. Hence meaning now emanates not from the sender of a message, but in the receiver of it. Every reader is, in short, their own author – writing the text they read as they read it, unifying it or not as they wish or are able (though the reader who does attempt to unify a text might be said to be haunted by the ghost of the 'Author' …). Perhaps the only kind of author which the essay does not imagine dying is the biographical person who actually writes – it is not envisaged that writers will stop writing, that the production of texts will be seen as fruitless, so much as that they – and we – will stop regarding them as 'Authors'. □

▶ Discussion 3

The title of Barthes' essay was and is – of course – partly an invitation to an argument. How can such a counter-intuitive idea be right? How can an idea/figure with which literature students (at least) are so familiar be pronounced dead? How could writers, readers, reviewers, journalists, biographers, publishers, bookshops and critics survive without the 'Author'? Doesn't the author self-evidently exist, even if you can argue about what their image/function should be? However, the essay itself seems from the beginning to be intent not on controversy but on persuasion. Starting with a clear example, the essay picks out a question the force of which is hard to deny: 'who is speaking thus?' From that first piece of 'close reading', clearly-stated arguments, linguistic, narratorial and historical follow step by step. In short, the essay does not seem that easy to argue against!

But we should presumably not be overawed by the tyranny of the author or text, since we are liberated readers in the post-authorial age … One argument which occurs to me is to argue against the basic premise that we have all (post-1968), in fact, lost faith in *every* aspect of traditional ideas of the author. Even if I do not believe that an author is sending out a message in any simple way, does it follow that the author is not therefore still a point of origin? Is it merely a polite fiction that there is something identifiably Austenesque in the writings of Jane Austen, or characteristically Morrisonian in the novels of Toni Morrison? And if that is so, then is there not some kind of presence which at least appears to be a point of origin? I do not say that Austen's or Morrison's novels are simply messages sent out by the people bearing those names, but that for many readers, the persona at least of the author is alive and well. Most readers seem still, in fact, to deal with an author who is constructed in the text as part of its method for transacting meaning. Moreover, it seems unlikely that this is the same author in every text – different texts/different kinds of texts imply different authors. Thus, I could say that the kind of *implied author*, at least, created by Austen's writing is limited or determined by certain factors in ways which recur across Austen texts. Limitations imply a point or points of origin – since the rhetorical author possible in a text by Jane Austen (or another author at a particular period) *can only* be some things, and *cannot* be other things. This might not seem to get us very far (and certainly not as far as saying that the biographical author is THE point of origin for a text). But it does appear to counter Barthes' notion that 'writing is the destruction of every voice … the negative where all identity is lost, starting with the very identity of the body writing'. Barthes argues that any apparent unity always reveals itself as an illusion, but do we have to accept that? Far from dissolving all identities, one might argue that, in fact, a good deal of writing establishes an identity or identities as vital parts of its method.

This may only suggest that the rhetorical illusion of the author is a useful one for many readers, making the author a matter of faith. If you believe, the author exists; if you lose faith, the author dies (like Tinkerbell?). This is true not only of the rhetorical author in the text, but of any more bodily author, whose existence as a person might be considered as an origin for a text.

Many readers (and, perhaps in varying ways, authors?) may well still wish to exercise this act of faith. One could attempt to go further and argue that authorship is, not indeed, merely a rhetorical effect. One might want then to argue that, in fact, the people called Jane Austen and Toni Morrison really are points of origin (amongst others) for the texts which bear their names. This does not necessarily mean a return to a naïve idea of the author, nor to a sense of the author as in control of all the meanings in a text. But I could argue (and actually many recent critics do implicitly assume this in their work) that texts really do have some origination in an actual person in a way which can be rationally discussed, by referring to factors playing on an entity that is quite well explained by the term 'author'. The French philosopher and critic Michel Foucault in his essay on the author 'What is an Author?' lists the kinds of unity which faith in the author can produce:

> the author provides the basis for explaining not only the presence of certain events in a work, but also their transformations, distortions, and diverse modifications (through his biography, the determination of his individual perspective, the analysis of his social position, and the revelation of his basic design). The author is ... the principle of a certain unity of writing – all differences having to be resolved, at least in part, by the principles of evolution, maturation or influence. The author also serves to neutralise the contradictions that may emerge in a series of texts: there must be – at a certain level of his thought or desire, of his consciousness or unconscious – a point where contradictions are resolved, where incompatible elements are at last tied together or organised around a fundamental or originating contradiction. Finally, the author is a particular source of expression that, in more or less completed forms, is manifested equally well, and with similar validity, in works, sketches, letters, fragments, and so on.[19]

Actually, this essay is very much a successor to Barthes' 'The Death of the Author', and is convinced that the author is not in any substantial sense a point of origin for a text. In this particular paragraph, Foucault summarises the functions which authors have served for believers (who for him still include the body of literary critics). But one could even regard these functions as authentically fulfilled by the author (though the very power of the figure of the 'author' as a unifier also suggests a potential weakening of its credibility – since as Foucault's listing makes clear, this point of origin can routinely be deployed as a catch-all to answer *every* question, to resolve contradictions of whatever kind and severity). □

You may have found other objections to acceptance of 'the death of the author', or having argued the case, you may feel it is unarguable. You may or may not be convinced by this attempt to argue against the death of the author. The purpose of the discussion is not, of course, to convince you either way, but to point out the complexity of a term/idea which has a long history and which is (surely?) still heavily relied upon in much critical writing. Understanding of this complexity is, presumably, a necessary step on the way towards better defining your own views of 'the author', and better understanding of what you do – or would like to do – when you talk about an author.

I want to bring this section towards a conclusion with three more activities:

1. An exercise based on critical interpretation of three poems.
2. An interview with the author of one of those poems focusing on his views of 'authorship'.
3. A final exercise asking you to test your view of 'the author' against proposals arguing for a different focus for the study of texts.

The following three poems (all published in Britain in the 1970s) are by the poets Sally Goodman, Paul St Vincent, and E. A. Markham.

> ◆ Read each poem and make brief notes for a critical interpretation of each; do you need or wish to make any use of ideas of 'the author' in your critical responses?

Sally Goodman, Against the Revolution

For it would happen on a day, like today
when I caught myself in the street,
my blouse buttoned the wrong way
('cute' at home and in peacetime,
like the bread-machine in a friend's kitchen)...
This is the wrong day
even though heroes seek to reassure me
as the hint of ache
comes to disturb the base of my tooth
and spreads unease
to the unfinished book, interrupted conversation:
but I could be ready given time.
The shriek of a child which grips the spine, burns the neck
comes from the playground, is followed by laughter; a reprieve
(This is the wrong day to come to the aid of the people...)

Till I learn to dress without thinking,
and to cut the loaf without threat of a white jacket,
and be sure that revolutions leave dentists undisturbed
and I come to distinguish the child at play
and what curdles my dreams;
and the leader promises to wear a skirt
and put toilet facilities in her jails –
until then I am unready.

Paul St Vincent, *Lambchops Has Black Thoughts*

for the university is here
and here tonight and most nights

after midnight at this vandalized
bus-stop, this gutted telephone –

box; the trail of black thoughts
singe and tear a path for him

flattening enemy barricades, old
white elephants that obstruct.

Yet, forerunners failed
in everything but to predict

him, trapped like this, a hurricane
with due warning. Next morning

he traces a black thread
(was there fire too?) backwards

from murder, from suicide; he tries
to bully the black mood into

comedy; he rinses the black film
from his countenance and looking

towards the light, becomes a negative.
The storm has been eliminated.

New buildings to contain his thought,
emerge. A Brother redecorating

his house in a good part of town
passes down his advice, the ladder

to advancement.
Burn it. Burn it.

E. A. Markham, *Sojourn in a Second Language*

He wants to write in English
to make these tourist attractions
part of our dreaming, familiar
as the dull streets of grandparents

grown ragged with life, resisting
new urges. The Language, he knows,
has been alive before God,
its monuments more solid than mountains

which separate family from family.
Like stone palaces your words
withstand tribal shifts, local wars,
becoming grander as invaders add to them.

And is this where he comes in,
a guest deposited by chance, armed
with dictionaries? He brings the usual gift:
a family history in translation

cribbed from an ancient text.
Only the bold survive this tongue,

and we know it. So he grasps
an impossible word, risking, hoping

the *coup* will turn messenger into seer
a handful of arrows into a trick called History.
I edge from definition sensing
something fetid, throbbing, murky.

I recall (among the Presidents or among
the dead) another convert from student
days, whom the language did not fit,
describing Dickens as *voluminous*.

Now I dredge images of heartbeat
not from a fairy-tale '60s
more a Jane Austen lady in fancy dress
and parasol, running into the suitor of a friend;

and I look up the offending word:
we are journeymen in the master's building.
Now the Highland village *pullulates*
with arrows arching down; with the thoughts

of a growing boy overwhelming its adult;
and the bare breasts and clean sheets
of mid-Atlantic fragrance, merge,
teem with the bare-arsed, the ragged –

till we compromise by citing the Arms Race.
And here I pause
not liking the sound of contrived voices,
not knowing which of us is wearing

this second language, cast off by aliens.

▶ Discussion

The speaker of 'Against the Revolution' is evidently to be identified as female from the range of specific references, many of them domestic ('my blouse', 'the bread-machine in a friend's kitchen' and so on). She seems to be a comfortably-off, middle-class speaker, with leisure for books and conversation. Though seeming to welcome 'the Revolution', her private concerns dominate, and (as the long run of 'ands' in the second stanza suggest), make it easy to find excuses. I note that the complacency is most disturbed by 'The shriek of a child', which is linked with the unnameable terror that 'curdles my dreams'.

I apparently found little need to use the idea of the author at all in this brief reading. However, I suspect that there is a concealed quasi-identification of the poem's speaker with the poem's author, Sally Goodman (that is, in the absence of any contradictory evidence, it is easy not to draw much distinction between the author behind the persona, and the persona itself). At any rate, the poem's speaker – and our acceptance of a certain unity and individuality represented thereby – contributes a great deal to the meaning of the poem.

In 'Lambchops Has Black Thoughts', the narration is third person, but nevertheless, since it represents the thoughts of Lambchops, the effect is not wholly unlike a first person narration. There is, though, a certain distancing effect produced by the third person voice – an implication that Lambchops's thoughts can be reproduced by an external narrator, that they are the thoughts of a type, perhaps. A key feature of the poem is a play on the meanings of the word 'black'. Lambchops's 'black thoughts' are both melancholic ones, and characteristic thoughts of a black man in Britain in the 1970s. These two senses of 'black' are merged by the poem – what other thoughts but black ones, could Lambchops have in this environment? A further play on 'black' ('he rinses the black film / ... becomes a negative') suggests that trying to hope is for him as much the abandonment as the positive adoption of an identity. He would thus become a 'negative' – a white image.[20] However, this is a temptation: as 'new buildings emerge', there is the possibility of 'the ladder to advancement'. The poem ends with negation and the rejection of this optimism – 'Burn it. Burn it'.

Again, there seems little need explicitly to invoke an author, but as with 'Against the Revolution' there is a temptation to see the narrator as an authorial voice – perhaps even more so in this case, since the narrator and character are separated through the third person narration.

E. A. Markham's 'Sojourn in a Second Language' seems the most difficult of the three poems to interpret. The central narrative is much less clear – largely because it is not focused on one character, and because the relation between characters and narrator is less obvious. We may well have some initial difficulty in identifying the 'He' in the first line, and subsequent 'he's. And it is not self-evident who is referred to by 'our' in line 3, 'your' in line 10 and 'us' in the penultimate stanza. Until we have some sense of how these references work, it may be difficult to know where the 'I' introduced in stanza 6 stands.

The interrelation of the pronouns can, though, be clarified. The initial 'He' who wants to write in English (and who therefore cannot be originally, wholly, anglophone?) and the 'I' must be members of the group identified by the plural pronouns 'our' and 'we'. Some part of the kinship between the two is thus presumably that neither has English as a first language. This points to the poem's strong focus on language and definition: 'The Language', 'your words', 'dictionaries', 'an impossible word', 'definition', 'the offending word'. The poem seems very much concerned with belonging – with a need to belong to a group, to a landscape, to use a language which you fully possess. But for the 'he' and 'I' personas of the poem there is little confidence that they do belong in this language. They feel the very act of trying to make English their own language betrays outsider status. Thus, knowing that 'only the bold survive this tongue', 'he grasps an impossible word' (stanza 5). The italicised *coup* which describes the effect aimed for, also acts as a perfect example of the impossible word that betrays, particularly because, while unarguably adopted into English, *coup* remains a deeply un-English word. Other case-studies of this 'impossible word' syndrome follow: *'voluminous'*, *'pullulates'*, *'teem'* – the italicisation now acting as shorthand to show us that the words are precisely not natural, are in quotation marks. Not every case is the same, though. While *coup* cannot escape its

French origins, *teem* is odd for the opposite reasons – it is so Anglo-Saxon, so old that it has died out of 'natural' English. *Voluminous* is cited as the effort of 'another conver t … / … whom the language did not fit'. This is the word of an apparently less skilled user, with a hint of comic inappropriateness, perhaps, in describing Dickens so literally (and indisputably) as the author of *many volumes*. *Pullulate* on the other hand, is all too learned – a dictionary word, not a word in use.

The poem has a central interest in a language which 'did not fit'; clothing metaphors are several times used of language: 'wearing', 'cast off by aliens' (perhaps there is a connection with the 'bare-arsed' theme of the pre-penultimate stanza). It seems important, though, that this language can be, at least, put on – for, as the conclusion suggests, linguistic belonging is not a clear-cut state. The speaker pauses, not liking an unnatural, contrived voice, but not quite able to distinguish 'which of us' wears 'this second language'. The final phrase further complicates the situation, for the apparently natural possessors of the language, also now described using the imagery of clothing, have cast off English as if it were a second language to them, too. The distinction between alien and natural has blurred – perhaps to the point where all parties 'Sojourn in a Second Language'.

I have, again, felt little need to use the word 'author', but the 'I' could easily be regarded as assimilable to the poet. However, there are moments of irony in the poem suggesting a possible presence beyond either the 'he' or the 'I'. The line 'we are journeymen in the master's building' has an air of mock humility – as if someone knows that the master himself has little mastery of the language being learnt, and that the journeymen (=craftsmen hired by the day) are actually experts. Indeed, despite the attention drawn to the unnatural use of the 'impossible words', they are ironically used with precision, originality and brilliance. If they are odd, they are nevertheless exactly the right word in the right place – each actually is a *coup*, if not for the speaker, then for the poem itself. This sense of irony could belong to the 'I' persona, but might suggest an authorial perspective on the poem as a whole. In this perspective, maybe there is a great strength in sojourning in a second language, a deliberate sense of language which is far raised above the casual. □

If we apply Barthes' question, 'Who speaks thus?' to these poems, there are certainly complexities. But I have little sense of the concepts of identity and origination dissolving – on the contrary the specification of points of origin for the voices is vital. This does not necessarily assert that the author is alive, or a unified function or voice; only that the device is still credible. Moreover, this device is commonly carried beyond the boundaries of texts themselves. In the case of these three poems, this can be seen in the signs of congruence between implied and actual authors in the biographical notes provided for Sally Goodman, Paul St Vincent and E. A. Markham in various volumes in which their work has appeared:

SALLY GOODMAN is Welsh, an Embassy child educated all over Europe. She is now 29, fully recovered from marriage, and bringing up a child. She's had poems in *Poetry Wales*, *The Little Word Machine*, *Titmouse Review*, and other magazines. Her first pamphlet will be published in 1978.[21]

PAUL ST VINCENT. Born in Antigua, 1944, spent early youth in St Vincent, and came to England when he was 8. Since then, has had many schools and more jobs. Experienced sheet-metal worker. Parts of Lambchops have appeared in Omens, Matrix, Orbis ... and the L. W. M. Carribean Anthology. A pamphlet *LAMBCHOPS* will be brought out by Omens in 1976.[22]

E. A. MARKHAM. Born in Montserrat, educated in the Westindies and at various universities in Britain. Is based in London. He has toured the Caribbean and the Continent with poetry and theatre groups. Has worked as English lecturer and theatre critic in London, and as a truck driver in Sweden. Has lived as a member of the Cooperative Ouvrière du Batiment in the south of France. He contributes to Westindian and literary journals and little magazines in Britain and East Africa. His small book of poems, *Cross-Fire*, was published by Outposts Publications; *A Black Eye* by Bettiscome Press; *MAD* by Aquila Publishing. He has co-edited the Uganda Asian Anthology, *Merely a Matter of Colour*.[23]

There seem, at the least, few surprises here – no signs of radical disjunction between author and poetic persona. Thus, if 'Against the Revolution' has little reference to Wales or an European education, its speaker and the person described in the Contributors Note do not obviously differ. A temptation to continue an identity across from author to persona has even greater warrant in the cases of St Vincent and Markham. St Vincent's self-description ('many schools and many jobs') contributes easily to a sense that his own experience might inform Lambchops's Black Thoughts (though his marking out of an identity as a black poet through his listing of published work might seem alien to Lambchops's totally 'black mood'). Equally, E. A. Markham's Author's Note does seem to match well with the 'I' persona of 'Sojourn in a Second Language'. Markham's cosmopolitan experience – across a geographical, occupational and class range, truck driving as well as university education – might well inform the sophisticated 'I' of the poem, with its capacity for observing others with sympathy, and with its complex sense of unease.

It may be that all these matches between identities can prove – each filtered through interpretation by the reader – is the persistence of the idea (rather than any *fact*) of authorship. Bizarrely, the particular examples provided by these three poems may show the continuing usefulness of the idea in a specially powerful way – since, I must now confess, two of the authors whom we have spent time discussing are, beyond doubt, mere fictions.[24] This is best explained by *their* author, E. A. Markham.

Interview with E. A. Markham (Sheffield, 14 July 1998)

CH: My first question is about the Goodman/St Vincent/Markham case.

EAM: Yes.

CH: At one stage in your writing career you simultaneously published under three different names. Can you just tell me why you did it? How it came about?

EAM: I mean I suppose most of my notions of why are retrospective, so it's... I'm old-fashioned as a writer, in that I have notions that – I respect the text, but somehow what fascinates me always is the subtext, where I think that's where you begin to find things that are of – that are of value. Things that go – well, by its own definition, beneath the surface, and reveal, not necessarily with the author's collusion, or conscious intention, reveal things that are valuable. Anyway, my persona – obviously, I started out as Markham – well, it's not obvious, but I started out as Markham – and there were difficulties at the start with what I realised later were questions of identity. My first book, pamphlet really, of poetry, which was published in 19 – I think – 73, was held up because we had a dispute about my name. The publisher properly thought that 'Archie Markham' made sense. I've never liked the name Archie. My first name is Edward, as it happens, but because it's an official name, a name on official documentation and that sort of thing, it's not a name that I respond to in an intimate sort of context. Therefore, I suppose because I have notions about the book, I was unhappy to go into print under a name which I was uncomfortable about, uncomfortable with, but at the same time I couldn't go into print as Edward Markham because that actually didn't *feel* right, it didn't feel as if it was me. In the end we compromised with 'E. A. Markham'. Now during that time – the early 70s – I didn't of course have much of a reputation, but those few people who knew me, knew my work, were all agreed that the work was difficult. The work was difficult because one, in their view, had a middle-class upbringing in the West Indies. It was difficult because I went to university, and not many West Indians – well not many West Indians who lived in England – went to university in those days, and that I was perhaps cut off from the experience of other West Indians in this country, and of what they called working-class people in this country. And it was then that I began to think that there might well be areas of experience that were natural to me, areas of experience that really I *should* have got into, but that because of my background and my luck to have, if you like, had this ladder of education, that I had perhaps been avoiding those areas of experience which were characterised as 'black boys dealing with the police in Brixton', that sort of thing. And I then felt that it was important to begin to investigate this, to see if one was quite simply driven by certain social forces, by certain ways of trying to separate oneself from the crowd and by trying to sort of erase one's West Indianness and that sort of thing. That was how Paul St Vincent came about. I – it was a dual challenge, initially to inhabit those spaces – I later called Paul St Vincent's enterprise sort of dramatising those footnotes to our social history that the sociologists and perhaps even the historians were beginning to talk about. It was partly that and partly to investigate whether the verse style, the form, the type of imagery, the type of language that I had been using, whether that was natural for me to use or whether it was just that I used it because everyone else I knew used it. So Paul St Vincent then, instead of being imagistic, in the way that Markham to a certain extent tended to be, cerebral in some ways, Paul St Vincent was anecdotal, it was narrative, it was meandering, it located itself squarely

within the boundaries of categories set down by other disciplines like sociology and history and politics. If it said that this was a poem about mugging, it *was* a poem about mugging, whereas a Markham poem about
mugging would not have been about mugging, it would probably be about
plagiarism or something of that kind. I decided that one should try and
inhabit the skin of this new person, so that I found an address for him in a
part of London where it seemed right – in Battersea as it happens – I lived
in those days in North London: I think I must have been living in Finchley or
somewhere like that, or Highgate, in those days. I tried to see Paul as a
character with his own integrity, speaking his own language, so outside the
poetry he developed a way of writing letters that were very different from
mine – he used Nation Language, he used dialect. He had a sort of, if you
like, aggressiveness, or let's say a directness, which I didn't have, in his
letter-writing. The result was that – the poems were built round three main
characters, which again would be very different from mine, because they
were almost characters in a narrative, a long-running one. The main character was called Lambchops, the second character was called Philpott, which
was Lambchops twenty years on, and there was a woman who was called
Maureen who was – whose identity, whose position was always in doubt.
The result was that because the poems were easier to understand, because
they located themselves so firmly within categories that people were comfortable with, people who were not particularly into contemporary poetry
were comfortable with, the poems then became enormously popular, and
there came a point – I remember in 1976 three pamphlets came out, three
Paul St Vincent pamphlets came out – and it was at that point that I
thought, well, this is actually too easy, because really one was just testing
whether certain areas of experience were not just available to me but natural to me, and really how they would help me reposition myself as a
writer. And because they began to be automatic-seeming – the poems – I
discontinued. But the quest was still on, I think, to avoid being typecast,
which in a way carries over from, if you like, what I like to think of my other
areas of living, and I see writing as one of those areas of living, and I
thought, 'I need to continue this project, this search, this investigation in a
more challenging way'. Well this was an age when certain notions of feminism were very much in the air, with a force and vitality that perhaps we've
lost now, and I thought: how to extend the Paul St Vincent-type challenge?
Paul was another West Indian, younger than me, but born in the West
Indies; it just so happened that he had a different life-experience in this
country. Too easy. So I thought: how about someone who was not a West
Indian, and then that meant, perhaps, someone who was not black, someone who was not male. And that's how Sally Goodman came about, where
one tried to – as I defined it later – to extend the range, the base of my
sympathies as a writer, hoping that this would have a knock-on effect on
me as a person, and thinking that certain structural or certain organisational ways of doing this might (a) be more interesting to do, because I
believe in *process*, and (b) might result in something more identifiably different, create a perceptible sort of shift. So Sally Goodman was born. Now,
again this was not a theoretical thing. Because it's like any bit of writing,
you need at least two forces to collide. Any form of art – there needn't be
forces, but just two things, two notions. During the tail-end of Paul St

Vincent, then, the Sally Goodman poems began to be written. Then I found myself in Germany, with a group of people, mainly foreigners to Germany, French, American, English, New Zealand, Portuguese people, all teaching English in and around Cologne, and we were, as I mentioned earlier to you outside this context, we were interested in the idea of gender and how, if you like, ruled we were by this. And we tried to explore, we tried to identify, in our own writing, the maleness of it or the femaleness of it. But what was interesting, when you're an artist, when you're doing things rather than thinking about them, events take over, and gradually, in the group, in Cologne, all the men fell away, lost interest, except me. We found ourselves with performing spaces, very small spaces in basements and in lofts, and as the experiment was that we wouldn't put our names to what we had written, and I wasn't performing at all, so it was perceived as a women's group, and of course inevitably as a feminist group. And you just contributed to this. And there were times when you were in the audience and you listened to your own lines and you thought 'That's an interesting way in which an American – that's an interesting American interpretation', because an American woman was reading my lines. And it wasn't till much later you thought, well, but maybe this is the way to do it. So I actually learned, much later, when I reclaimed Sally Goodman, I learned to interpret the poems from these women who first performed Sally Goodman. And of course the idea was the same – the project, you know, good New Labour word – was the same as – was the same as Paul St Vincent's: to extend the base of one's sympathies and to effect a shift, a shift from the Markham thing, because one was never quite sure, going back to the naming and what goes behind the naming and – one wasn't quite sure just how to locate Markham – West Indian, someone from Africa who really has never been to Africa and who at that time had if you like fairly minimal interest in Africa, part of the New World, part of the Third World, part of, you know … One is part of the Third World where one grew up in a household which was in some ways very splendid, very comfortable, very privileged. One came to England and immediately had a lifestyle that was actually very, very, very different from that, you know, so it was actually very confusing to know where the Third World – where Third-Worldness was.

CH: It sounds as if you're saying that E. A. Markham is a persona just as –

EAM: Yes.

CH: Goodman and Paul St Vincent are personas –

EAM: Yes –

CH: But do you feel in the end the Markham persona is a more authentic one, one that's closer to some real you?

EAM: Yes. And I think that Paul St Vincent and Sally Goodman have helped me to discover this, because I now no longer feel there are identities and selves out there that I, Markham, might inhabit. I think now I have, if you like, tried on those clothes, lived in those countries, and they have helped me to put the whole, the Markham thing in context, so when I go back to early Markham I find it partial. You know, as I said earlier, I'm really very conventional in these matters in that I believe the, you know, all the old prejudices – Eliot's notion of tradition and the individual talent, that, you know, until you get the tension between the two, until you bring the two into some sort of creative tension, you are dishonouring both, or you are not – that's perhaps too strong a term, but you are failing to realise, you know, what's possible for you as a writer. And so I think all the time, I have notions of a writer as someone who having chosen to focus on the art of writing has a responsibility (a) both to affirm the connection between writing and speech, you know, that wonderfully democratic thing, speech, that most of us have access to, and that very privileged, violin-playing, whatever, specialised training, specialised activity which is writing. Both to do this and (b) – this is the second point – to make a mark, to leave one's impression, to create through the idiom of language a special sense of being alive. So how do you sort of maintain the link between speech and writing, but at the same time show that it is taken to a higher plane, or it is a richer experience, or it is an experience that is able to repackage those things that everyone might want to say but not quite in this way, but your having the ability to say them in this way meaning finding the right rhythm and finding the right everything else, you somehow bring all of those people into that experience, you enable them to recognise their own experience, you begin to make people who think their life-experiences are different to understand what they have in common, even if it's recognising in a new and sympathetic way someone's difference. So, you know, you feel that all the time, I suppose you're mediating between the expert and I suppose the consumer and the rest. So you know you – I mean I suppose you believe that the writer has a responsibility for himself, herself, for making sure that the art-form, that the art is not devalued in his or her hands, you know, the old business again, Eliot, of purifying the language of the tribe on one hand, extending the language of the tribe on the other. You know there's – it seems to me that if you are not doing either you are actually reneging on your responsibility as a writer. Anyway, I won't go on.

CH: Do you think – You've begun to talk about what, as it were, you think poetry should do, what writing must do. Is there something in your three personas, is there something in Markham, in Goodman, and in St Vincent that actually is a kind of signature of yours, a common quality, or are they – how different are they?

EAM: Yes, I think – Well, again on the surface they're different but I think under the surface they're perhaps not *so* different, because I think my project is to avoid typecasting, and in order to do that as a writer – well, you're fortunate as a writer in being able to inhabit other people's clothes, and I think that that gives you an opportunity to avoid stereotyping. And I think the fact that one wanted to move across class and gender was part of my way of investigating, keeping in check my own maleness. And I didn't want to do this in a purely theoretical way, because of course every man is against chauvinist behaviour, except those particular chauvinist acts that he is in fact perpetrating. And I thought that in a way it would be more genuine, and more fun – and of course one is a writer, so of course why, if you want to investigate something like this, why say, 'All right, I won't do it in my major area of activity, which is writing poems, I will do it in writing essays, or giving lectures?' So it seems to me that one should take – it was a way of taking one's own art seriously, and using that as a corrective to the progress of one's art so far, and there is no – I find *no* need now to use persona, because I think the gains of Paul St Vincent, in directness, that sort of thing, the gains of Sally Goodman, in terms of not assuming the other gender to be 'other', and not assuming that things must be viewed and located in one of my male voices, until something happens when then I realise, 'Ah, I need that other voice – I need to investigate, or to tune in to that other type of sensibility'. I think one tries to, if you like, make sure that all those types of approaches are located within what one would call Markham, and I know in my later books people have said that they felt there is a difference in tone, a difference in – what's the phrase people use – that there is a generosity of feeling which perhaps isn't present in the earlier work. Now if this is true, that there's a new generosity of feeling, that I think has something to do with inhabiting those persons' lives.

CH: Presumably, did publishers and editors – they thought these personas were three separate people –

EAM: Yes.

CH: – presumably treated them as three people in various ways, would that be –

EAM: Absolutely. Often Paul and Markham appeared in the same anthology, or the same magazine, and, let's say, the financial arrangements were never the same for both. You know, they would lie, they would say, sometimes, to Paul, we don't pay, you know. They would treat them differently, try to match their tone. Paul's covering letters were usually in Nation Language, mine were in more standard forms of English, and often they would respond, certainly if they were Caribbean, to Paul in Nation Language. But they would also patronise Paul. They would assume with me a knowingness about the literary world, and they would assume that Paul didn't know. So it was mildly interesting from a social point of view. Some of the letters are in my archives at the University of Hull. What was perhaps interesting – well, perhaps not so interesting, but funnier – were some of the letters to Sally Goodman, where the sexual play came into, well, was evident. There were middle-aged men who were editors of magazines, who thought 'This is a nice young girl whom we can take under our wing'. And I – obviously I can't deny that a lot of Sally Goodman poems got published because she was thought to be a young girl from Wales. A lot of Paul St Vincent poems got published because here was a West Indian, writing often in dialect, not directly competing with the main fare of poetry in England, whereas I was always seen to be competing with the main stream, and sometimes was given a very hard time as a result, because my – a lot of my earlier reviews said well why is he, why is this West Indian trying to write like a middle-class Englishman? Why has he abandoned the tradition of West Indian writing, you know. And they still say it from time to time. Whereas with Paul, fresh – and Paul had sort of a rapport with readers – you know, you would open a letter from Barbados or Washington DC, and a five-dollar note would fall out, and they'd say 'I've just read your wonderful poems', etcetera etcetera. Well of course no-one felt able to be that free and easy with me, you see. So with Sally there was the sexual thing, with Paul there was 'Yes, yes, show them, tell them', you know – and in fact often, 'Tell people like Markham', you know. So it was fun, it was fun to do.

CH: If I could generalise the conversation a bit, and talk more generally about authors, some modern critics, particularly modern French critics, Barthes, Foucault, have begun to argue that really the author is a defunct historical category, that if we could forget about authors, we could find new ways of talking about writing. They argue often that all sorts of other factors are much more important: genre, the marketplace, class, that the creative individual isn't at the centre of it. How do you feel about that, how much sympathy do you have for the idea of the author as 'the creative individual'?

EAM: Well, you know – you see, I think things go in cycles, and of course when you say an author is dead, *the* author is dead, the novel is dead, – all that stuff – I mean basically you're just saying, well, we've come to the end of this cycle, this way of making poems, of writing novels, and of trying to interpret poetry, so let's see if we can do it differently. So I'm not particularly challenged by those notions, because I think they are notions that writers have always had. I mean, you know, – look at this really rather fun book of Calvino's, *If on a Summer's Night*, you know, where the readers are writing the novel. It's fun, but it's not – I think it works brilliantly – but it's not a particular notion that any writer would actually find strange or bizarre. A writer would just say, 'Ah yes, that's really an interesting way of doing it today'. It's just a way of redefining the author. The author, you see, has always been a character in his or her own book. And every sophisticated reader has understood that, so in a way I think that these are things that – you know, death of the author, death of the book – death of the book probably a bit more problematic than death of the author – problematic in the sense that there might be more to it because of the new technology – but I think these are just ways of saying, 'Well, we're bored writing about books in a certain way, let's write about books in another way'. And I can't see that it goes further than that, because it's not a million miles away from saying, 'Let's talk about the unreliable narrator', when everyone is talking about the unreliable narrator. OK, it's taking it one stage further. Barthes, whom you mention, wants to romanticise the reader rather than the writer: he is wrong when he says the reader is without history, biography, psychology. Now we all assume – you know, the most unsophisticated reader now knows the narrator to be unreliable. You see, so I don't see these notions as challenging anything other than the way in which we choose to write about the author.

CH: I think that's something which most critics are very clear about, that the author is a character, that almost in any text there is a character of the author who appears, but I think some modern critics have begun to say there is no connection between the character of the author who can appear and any actual living person – they want to cut off the text entirely from the author.

EAM: I disagree with this strongly, in that it is obvious to me that there are certain psychological drives, one of which is just to complete a text, that have to do with self-definition, just the idea of continuity. I know there are some novels now where the characters change names, but even that is built into a structure where, if the novels are successful, the text doesn't fall apart. So under all this there is a form of continuity, and that has something to do with the sensibility of the writer. It is nonsense to say that Chekhov's sensibility and Gogol's sensibility and Dostoyevsky's sensibility are the same thing, and it's all got something to do with Russianness, or nineteenth centuriness – you know. Because what is interesting is not really the social history of Russia, it's not really the literary history of Russia, it's not even that such magnificent characters are brought fully alive, it's the fact that there is a certain peculiar, human, humane way of seeing people looking at life, relating to people, etcetera etcetera, that Chekhov has, that is, that isn't actually shared by any of his contemporaries. They have other qualities. Now, so, it seems to me that if you have any sensibility at all, if you have any respect, for human psychology, human relating, ways of perceiving, and dealing with your own and other people's vulnerabilities, that you cannot actually say that one big Russian equals another big Russian, because they all do it in such extraordinarily different ways. This is true of people in our own time. It's very interesting that at one time people reviewing, let's say, my work used to review me with other Caribbean writers, and that they used to think there was a sameness. Now what they're actually doing is sort of teasing out the difference. I think that's because they know the work better now, but also because they realise, 'My God, you know, that was a racist project that I was involved in, you know'. Again, one isn't, one is part of the tradition, and one is honoured to be part of the tradition, but at the same time it is one's point of entry into that tradition, both historically and from the point of view of the mix of personality, ambition, talent, whatever, that make one interesting, and indeed, it seems to me, that make one able to renew that tradition, because in fact unless you have that individual thing you, if you like, you're parasitic on the tradition. I don't think it's – I know people criticise this business at Cambridge, and indeed at Oxford, where, you know, you have to identify bits of *Henry VI* as Shakespeare, but it seems to me that that is necessary, because part of the writer's responsibility is not merely to be fed by the tradition – it's not free water, it's not free food. And if you're honourable and if you're talented and if you take your responsibilities seriously, you somehow have to contribute to that tradition, you have to modify it. Well you cannot do it by reneging on your responsibilities as author.

CH: Thank you.

I will not discuss this interview at length, since I assume that the issues (if not the resolutions) are reasonably clearly established by now. However, I hope that you will find that it – and the Goodman/St Vincent/Markham case in general – contributes some further views of the author (these may be particularly relevant to the next exercise). You might think that these views support some of the critical views already discussed – or you might feel that the ideas emerging from the interview are essentially opposed to some recent critical scepticism about 'the author'.

Finally in this section, you might find it useful to see if you can come to any sense of definition or conclusion about how you do – or would like to – use the critical term 'author'. As usual with the final exercises in a section, I will not provide any discussion, but leave you to your own responses.

Below is a brief extract from the end of Michel Foucault's essay 'What is an Author?' In these paragraphs, Foucault outlines his sense of the undesirable function of the 'Author', and presents another approach to reading texts.

> Having worked through the varying definitions of the author in this section, how sympathetic do you feel to Foucault's suggestion? Do you feel we still need to talk about authors at all? *Does* it matter who is speaking?

The question then becomes: How can one reduce the great peril, the great danger with which fiction threatens our world? The answer is: one can reduce it with the author. The author allows a limitation of the cancerous and dangerous proliferation of significations within a world where one is thrifty not only with one's resources and riches, but also with one's discourses and their significations. The author is the principle of thrift in the proliferation of meaning. As a result, we must entirely reverse the traditional idea of the author. We are accustomed ... to saying that the author is the genial creator of a work in which he deposits, with infinite wealth and generosity, an inexhaustible world of significations. We are used to thinking that the author is so different from all other men, and so transcendent with regard to all languages that, as soon as he speaks, meaning begins to proliferate, to proliferate indefinitely.

The truth is quite the contrary: the author is not an indefinite source of significations which fill a work; the author does not precede the works; he is a certain functional principle by which, in our culture, one limits, excludes, and chooses; in short, by which one impedes the free circulation, the free manipulation, the free composition, decomposition, and recomposition of fiction. In fact, if we are accustomed to presenting the author as a genius, as a perpetual surging of invention, it is because, in reality, we make him function in exactly the opposite fashion ... The author is ... the ideological figure by which one marks the manner in which we fear the proliferation of meaning.

In saying this, I seem to call for a form of culture in which fiction would not be limited by the figure of the author ...

All discourse, whatever their status, form, value, and whatever the treatment to which they will be subjected, would then develop in the anonymity of a murmur. We would no longer hear the questions that have been rehashed for so long: who really spoke? Is it really he and not someone else? With what authenticity or originality? And what part of his deepest self did he express in his discourse? Instead, there would be other questions, like these: What are the modes of existence of this discourse? Where has it been used, how can it circulate, and who can appropriate it for himself? What are the places in it where there is room for possible subjects? Who can assume these various subject functions? And behind all these questions, we would hear hardly anything but the stirring of an indifference: What difference does it make who is speaking?

From Michel Foucault, 'What is an Author?' in *The Foucault Reader*, ed. Paul Rabinow (London, 1990), pp. 118–20.

2.3   What Do Critics Do?

If you are reading this you are most probably someone who knows something of what is meant in English Studies circles by the terms 'critic', 'criticism' and 'critical'. You will know this, because (if you correspond at all to the reader I and the publisher imagine for this book) you are already to some degree part of these 'circles'. As with all the other basic terms we have applied ourselves to so far, our apparent understandings need to be made more explicit in order to understand what common assumptions we share or dispute, and what the range of possibilities for definition might be.

The word critic comes from the Ancient Greek noun *kritikos* = a judge, which derived from the verb form *krinein* = to judge, to discriminate. It is related to the Greek word *kriterion* = criterion – a standard for judging against. Given that I have already assumed a degree of knowledge about what a critic is, the section will open with a chance to establish an initial sense of what modern literary critics do.

> If you had to describe what critics do in one brief phrase, what would you say?

▶ Discussion

There is, of course, more than one possible answer – though I imagine that most people would see some answers as less current than others. Possibilities might include:

- Critics make judgements about texts (in line with the word's origins).
- Critics interpret texts.

- Critics spread knowledge about texts.
- Critics appreciate texts.

Each of these has, or has had, some validity, and we will return to them all in the course of this section. But if I had to answer the question posed in this way, I would say that the main current role of critics in the academy is to interpret texts (and, as teachers, to teach students how to interpret texts). Unfortunately, this term 'interpretation' does not magically make it clear what a critic does – because its sense is, I suspect, only really clear to those who already know what 'literary criticism' is. Part of the problem in a straightforward definition of what critics do, is that, in fact, criticism covers quite a range of functions, which we do not always separate out. However, I will make a start towards clarifying the functions of critics by starting from the definition: 'Critics interpret texts', since that seems to me the most mainstream definition. If you suggested a different answer – either prioritising judgement or disseminating knowledge or some other function – I hope that these issues will be picked up in the discussion that follows. If they are not, you might want to test your sense of what a critic primarily does, or should do, against my working out of a range of answers. ☐

The role of *interpreters of texts* does seem to distinguish between critical and other literary roles. Thus *a critic* is generally considered to be different from *an author*, because while the critic needs texts to discuss, the author creates texts.[25] Equally, *a critic* is generally, I presume, distinguished from *a reader*. The distinction between author and critic seems (on the face of it) clear: one produces, the other consumes, or to put this in terms of communication, one has the role of addresser, the other, therefore, the role of addressee. In fact, though, this last description gives me pause. The most obvious addresser and consumer of an author's text is surely the reader, rather than the critic? Pursuing this may help us to refine what distinguishes a critic's role.

> ◆ What makes *a critic* different from *a reader?*

▶ Discussion

There are several distinctions to be drawn out – mainly arising from inter-connected ideas about function and status. Put against 'reader' the term 'critic' at once suggests a more specialised role, placing the reader as the performer of an ordinary function. Hence my doubt about the critic as consumer. It is more in line with the ways in which we normally think about these two roles, to say that the reader is the ordinary consumer, while the critic does more than 'merely' consume, more than simply complete the process of communication by receiving the text. There is overlap between the roles – but only in one direction, it seems. All critics must also be readers, but not all readers are critics. Critics can talk about the whole process of communication involved in reading – including the effect of the text on the reader – but we would not expect the (apparently necessarily) ordinary reader to take it as part of their role to discuss the effect of the text on the critic.

The critic's role is therefore extra to the act of communication:

Addresser →→ Message →→ Addressee
Author →→→ Text →→→ Reader

↑

[Critic interprets text? – but that may involve consideration of the whole process, including functions of the Author and the Reader? – and possibly other kinds of inquiry?]

This bears out the distinction between the reader as performer of an ordinary function, and the critic as performer of a specialised, additional function. Later on I will come back to the question of the *status* of the critic, but first I would like to refine what we might mean by 'the interpretation of texts', given that this is (if you accept that premise) what critics mainly do. ☐

◆ Read the following text, and produce notes for a brief critical interpretation.
◆ Try to analyse exactly what you did in order to produce your interpretation.
◆ What *kind* of interpretation do your notes give? (i.e. what *type* of understanding do they give you of the poem?)

Marianne Moore, *Poetry*

I, too, dislike it: there are things that are important beyond all this
        fiddle.
    Reading it, however, with a perfect contempt for it, one discovers in
    it after all, a place for the genuine.
        Hands that can grasp, eyes
        that can dilate, hair that can rise
            if it must, these things are important not because a

high-sounding interpretation can be put upon them but because they are
    useful. When they become so derivative as to become unintelligible,
    the same thing may be said for all of us, that we
        do not admire what
        we cannot understand: the bat
            holding on upside down or in quest of something to

eat, elephants pushing, a wild horse taking a roll, a tireless wolf under
    a tree, the immovable critic twitching his skin like a horse that feels
        a flea, the base –

ball fan, the statistician –
  nor is it valid
     to discriminate against 'business documents and

school-books';[26] all these phenomena are important. One must make a
  distinction
   however: when dragged into prominence by half-poets, the result is not
     poetry,
   nor till the poets among us can be
   'literalists of
   the imagination'[27] – above
     insolence and triviality and can present

for inspection, 'imaginary gardens with real toads in them', shall we have
  it. In the meantime, if you demand on the one hand,
   the raw material of poetry in
     all its rawness and
     that which is on the other hand
        genuine, you are interested in poetry.

From *The Norton Anthology of Poetry*, 3rd edn, ed. Alexander Allison et al.
(New York and London, 1983), p. 986. First published in 1921.

▶ Discussion 1

An immediately unusual feature of the poem is that it is about poetry
itself – an effect strikingly brought to the reader's attention by the title
which runs into the first line of the poem itself via the rather blunt reference 'I, too, dislike *it*'. The use of reference through such pronouns is itself
a noticeable feature of the poem; in the first stanzas, for example, we have:
'dislike it', 'reading it', 'contempt for it', 'discovers in it', 'these things'. It
seems odd to use 'it' so frequently to refer to poetry in preference to
repeating the noun 'poetry' itself. The effect is to strip the word of its dignity – making it a basic literal object, contemptuously regarded, perhaps,
rather than an abstraction, a personification or an activity – all of which are
possible alternatives.

   This literalism which reduces poetry to object can be linked to the
statement in stanza 4, which gives strongly positive value to the literal: 'till
the poets among us can be / "literalists of / the imagination"'. The point is
that poetry is, in fact, valuable when it is, in some sense, literal. The
abstraction and cultural aura of poetry is the target of the contempt. The
problem lies in the 'fiddle', the 'high-sounding interpretation'. When
poetry is an 'it' or makes 'it' real, then it is true poetry, which can do something 'useful': 'Hands that can grasp'. But the literal does not seem to be
easy for poetry to grasp – the depiction of something too easily becomes
distant from the thing itself: 'so derivative as to become unintelligible'.

   I notice that at this point of the poem, there seems to be a curious contradiction. While literal reference has been raised from a position of apparent 'contempt' to a prime value, some of the use of reference is now far

from precise. Thus the following lines in stanza 2 have some odd uses of reference:

> When they become so derivative as to become unintelligible,
> the same thing may be said for all of us, that we
>   do not admire what
>   we cannot understand: the bat
> …

There is an oddity about what 'they' refers to, even though there is only one set of preceding nouns: 'Hands that can grasp, eyes / that can dilate'. Though grammatically clear, it is strange to say that these hands and eyes have become 'derivative' – normally a word applied only to *representation* (one could not normally say 'that horse is derivative', unless the horse in question were in a painting). There is also a puzzling ambiguity about what 'we cannot understand' refers to – are the things we cannot understand the things in the list beginning 'the bat', *or* are the bat, the elephant, the immovable critic and so on referred to by the 'we'? In one reading, the bat (etc.) is the agent doing the understanding; in the other, the bat (etc.) is the object which is not admired because we cannot understand it.

If for this poem the role of true poetry is to *point at actual things*, then how desirable is this ambiguity or vagueness? Perhaps the point of the mixture of markedly anti-abstract reference ('it' rather than 'poetry') with ambiguous or semantically odd reference is that though the literal is the aim of poetry, it cannot in fact be achieved without effort. Describing 'the genuine' is not a matter of restricting yourself only to what can easily be described, to what your language can already formulate unthinkingly. On the contrary, the genuine is not simply available in reality – poetry must make it real. Hence the style of this poem itself which grounds itself in the basic, but represents the basic in ways which disrupt ready-made ways of describing and seeing. I take it that this is what the difficult last sentence of the poem reveals in a way which is appropriately resistant to simple interpretation: that 'the genuine' has to be produced by a complex interaction between what is simply there – 'all its rawness' – the raw (not derivative) materials of poetry, and the test of the genuine itself. □

▶ Discussion 2

I think the steps by which I produced this critical interpretation are fairly clear, and usual. Having read through the poem as a whole, I began to identify odd features of language use and/or meaning which stood out. This is a very practical approach, in that it enables the critic rapidly to isolate features on which to comment. I next tried to work out significant meanings and explanations for these linguistically odd details and then to link these local explanations to the development of an understanding of the meaning of the poem as a whole. Halfway through, in checking specific details against the overall interpretation which was emerging from my explanations of particular features, I realised that some details in the poem seemed not to fit my general understanding. Thus, the hypothesis that the poem condemned abstraction and the consciously 'poetic' and celebrated the literalness of true poetry ran into the problem that this poem was not itself evidently 'literal' throughout. It might have been appropriate at this stage to conclude that the initial idea was a misreading – but instead I argued that this apparent contradiction in fact confirmed (while complicating) that initial interpretation. I could then say that the poem did, indeed, assert the value of literal poetry, but that to do so it complicated the very idea of the literal. The poem, therefore, in this interpretation, is in favour of the literal, the graspable – but against any idea that the literal readily exists: it is the job of real poetry to make things literal. You may have produced interpretations of the poem which differ in detail, in general conclusion, or perhaps in kind (a possibility picked up in the next paragraph of discussion). □

▶ Discussion 3

I imagine that the kind of reading I have worked through for the poem is probably the response to be expected from most readers who are already 'critics'.[28] It is a kind of interpretation which seems to follow these procedures:

1. It works solely from the text itself.
2. It concentrates initially on detailed explanation of small parts of the text.
3. It looks first for oddness, unusual usages – things which need to be explained and hence generate material for 2.
4. It builds up general hypotheses about the meaning of the whole poem from these small-scale investigations, taking oddities to be characteristic 'devices'.
5. It then integrates these small-scale explanations into larger-scale explanations of the poem, and finally into an account which explains the meaning of the text as a whole.
6. There is an underlying assumption that local oddities can be explained in terms of a general, unified meaning, and that the local and large-scale effects reinforce each other.

In short, this kind of interpretation is one which pays attention to language, particularly language deviating from norms, and by understanding those deviations constructs a meaning which justifies departures from some of those language rules (you may notice that this is very much what this particular poem is about as well – at least according to this method of reading it ...). This type of reading is very much a *formalist* one – that is, it concentrates on formal features and devices in the text itself.

Such reading has become a usual type of critical response, particularly to this genre, the short modern lyric. However, your notes may have suggested some additional or other approaches; in general, it seems unlikely that this critical response to this particular text has exhausted all the critical possibilities. □

> ◆ Try to think of other/additional ways in which a critic might approach a text (you do not have to think only in terms of the previous exercise – you might want to think about other kinds of text, and other kinds of enquiry).

▶ Discussion

There are a number of things that critics do, which the sample reading of 'Poetry' did not attempt. A critic *might* do some of the following to a text:

1.   Discuss it in historical terms.
2.   Discuss textual variations – such as whether this is the only or best text of the work (see section 2.1!).
3.   Discuss its relationship to other texts by the same author.
4.   Discuss the poem's relationship to the life of the author.
5.   Discuss its relationship to other similar texts.
6.   Discuss whether a text successfully carries out what it attempts.

The first five of these would, in fact, have been difficult to carry out for 'Poetry' in the terms set up by the exercise, since you were unlikely to have had the necessary contextual information (information which is not directly part of the text under examination). However, given the right situation and access to information, it would clearly be possible to produce criticism of the poem not wholly covered by the formalist approach. Thus we could expand the headings above to give a more detailed sense of what further lines of enquiry each might generate.

1. HISTORICAL TERMS

What historical knowledge would help to understand the origins of this view of poetry? (Perhaps knowledge of ideas about poetry and everyday language in 1920s America? Knowledge of where these ideas in turn might have arisen? – e.g. a post-First World War sense that neither 'high' culture nor everyday language were any longer true guarantors of real meaning?)

What might this poem tell us about the culture which produced it? (A different question from the 'historical knowledge' one, focusing on understanding of the culture rather than on understanding of the poem as an end product – but drawing on a similar kind of historical knowledge: American ideas in the twenties about the relevance or otherwise of poetry, or art in general, to actual life; attitude of other twenties poets.)

2. DISCUSS TEXTUAL VARIATIONS

This discussion might not arise with the same force for every text, but is a fundamental enquiry. In this case, there is in fact, a major textual variant. Moore later revised the poem, so that it read as follows:

> I, too, dislike it: there are things that are important beyond all this
> fiddle.
> Reading it, however, with a perfect contempt for it, one discovers in
> it after all, a place for the genuine.

(i.e. she cut all the lines after line 3!). Clearly, it matters considerably, which of these two texts of 'Poetry' you read and base your criticism on. The radical cutting of the first text may suggest that Moore concluded that the remainder of the poem was itself 'all this fiddle', rather than true poetry (but would we be able to see so clearly that meaning for the poem if we only had the shorter version to read?). A textual critic would need to pursue a number of questions about the effect of the cuts on the possible meanings of the poem, what they tell us about Moore's poetry, if one text is to be preferred and so on.[29]

3. RELATIONSHIP TO OTHER TEXTS BY MARIANNE MOORE

How characteristic is this poem of her work? In particular, is her poetry best discussed in the terms set up in her poem on 'Poetry'? (Clearly such a question could not be answered from a single text – but the approach resembles the formalist one in relating smaller-scale units of meaning to larger ones; William Carlos Williams, a contemporary of Moore's, 'likened "the edge to edge contact of things" in her poetry to Picasso's cubist portraits'[30] – so the focus on things, on the hard-edged, does sound characteristic.)

4. RELATIONSHIP TO THE LIFE OF THE AUTHOR

How does the poem stem from the author's life? What might it tell us about her? (A distinctly unfashionable approach to reading texts since the 1940s at least – see section 2.2 – however, works of literary biography do, by definition, approach authors and their texts in this way, and by no means inherently simplisticly; equally critics focusing on the whole output of an author are likely to make some use of connections between biography and text.)

5. DISCUSS ITS RELATIONSHIP TO OTHER SIMILAR TEXTS

Do other poems from the nineteen twenties discuss poetry in similar terms? Do poems from other periods make poetry itself their subject matter in comparable ways? Do other American poems from that period have a comparable style and aesthetic? (If you know any poetry from the same period by the American poet William Carlos Williams, you will be able to see that the interest in the literal, in a poetry which is stripped of decoration, is not unique to Moore; both are in fact associated with a distinctive American modernist poetic which does reject many of the conventions of poetry, in order to produce what they regard as a 'real poetry'; this aesthetic might be linked to the modernist movement which was very active in high culture in the first two decades of the century, and might also be seen as having specifically American impulses – especially a desire to break free from the accumulated weight of outworn European conventions.)

Equally there certainly are many other poems directly concerned with poetry from other periods – they would provide alternative conceptions of poetry presumably.

6. DISCUSS WHETHER A TEXT SUCCESSFULLY CARRIES OUT WHAT IT ATTEMPTS

Is this a good poem? Is it a productive discussion of poetry? Is it both of these – that is a genuinely good discussion which also gains from being a poem? (This approach is often called evaluation; it is a function implied by the original meaning of *kritikos* = a judge, and, indeed, judges of Greek drama did literally rank plays in order, since they had the task of awarding a prize; however, it has not been a fashionable critical approach since the nineteen sixties at least; university English students are not now encouraged to discuss explicitly how good a text is; perhaps because it is implied to be good by definition if they are studying it? – though reviewers of new fiction and poetry, even by established 'literary' authors, do comment on the worth of works; perhaps too some kinds of historical, cultural or political criticism are making evaluative moves in seeing texts as oppositional or complicit in cultural struggles?) □

These approaches are not, of course, necessarily used in isolation, and individual critics may well combine critical approaches in complex ways. It may be useful next to look at some actual examples of criticism, to perform criticism on criticism, and see what kinds of critical acts are being undertaken. We should presumably expect to see evidence of criticism in the kinds of category discussed above – but it is possible, of course, that some alternatives, or at least significant variations, will be revealed.

◆ Read the following four critics, and then make brief notes about what their criticism aims to achieve in this example of their work.

. . . .

F. R. Leavis on D. H. Lawrence's novel *Women in Love* (1921)

To suggest the range and flexibility of Lawrence's art one may set over against 'The Industrial Magnate' the earlier chapter (IX), 'Coal-dust'[31] in which Gerald forces his terror-stricken Arab mare to stand while the colliery train passing the level-crossing does its worst with wheels, brakes, buffers, chains, and whistle. The whole thing is rendered with shattering immediacy; with Ursula and Gudrun we stand, tortured by hideous noise and clenched in violent protest, while the rider compels the frantic mare back against herself and into the assaulting terrors. The significance of the episode needs no eliciting or developing by anything in the nature of comment from the novelist. The little drama – the image of Gerald, 'a glistening and half-smiling look on his face', as he 'bites down' on the mare, and strikes his spurs into her bleeding sides – crystallizes our sense of Gerald and gives it a new sharp edge. It picks up and brings to a focus of significance a multitude of intimations…We now realise the energy of will in Gerald as something more cruelly and dangerously ruthless…

Where Gerald's 'go' goes to is ultimately self-destruction: the novel shows the process, in all its aspects with inexorable convincingness. To analyse step by step the process of art by which this is done would take inordinate space. And it is unnecessary; for once the reader has grasped the general nature of Gerald's case he should find that the subtleties of the art tell sufficiently at a first current reading to make the development of the themes, and the ways in which they are organised, clear.

From F. R. Leavis, *D. H. Lawrence: Novelist* (1955). Here quoted from the Pelican edn (1973), p.185.

Helen Gardner, on Eliot's *The Waste Land* (1922)

While in *Ulysses* the three main persons become more and more solid against the background of the crowded city, in the *Waste Land*, though it is thronged with people and we hear many and varied voices, there are no characters in the strict sense, no persons, and in the end the city itself dissolves. In a note Mr Eliot said that the most important personage in the poem, although 'a mere spectator and not indeed a "character"' was Tiresias: 'Just as the one-eyed merchant…melts into the Phoenician Sailor, and the latter is not wholly distinct from Ferdinand Prince of Naples, so all the women are one woman, and the two women meet in Tiresias'. In the same way the time is all time and no time. Though we are plainly at times in modern London, it is an 'unreal city' and in the last section the city has vanished. It is all humanity that seems to be waiting then…Great crowds swarm from ruined cities, the refugees from every empire which has ever fallen. Although *The Waste Land* may begin with the 'dilemma of the modern mind', it discovers that the modern dilemma is the historic dilemma; and to limit the poem's meaning to being primarily the expression of modern lack of faith is to mistake its form and scope. Its true subject is ageless; it discovers a radical defect in human life and makes clear 'the insufficiency of human enjoyments'.

From Helen Gardner, 'The Dry Season', in *The Art of T. S. Eliot* (1949). This extract is from the Faber edn (London, 1968), p. 88.

Leah S. Marcus on Shakespeare's
The Tempest

In Act 1, scene 2 of *The Tempest*, Prospero describes Caliban's mother Sycorax as a 'damn'd Witch' condemned to death in 'Argier' ... Because of 'one thing' Sycorax 'did / They wold not take her life' but banished her instead: 'This blew-ey'd hag, was hither brought with child' – her child being Caliban, born somewhat later on the island where he, Prospero, Miranda, and others presently reside.

...

Let us return to Sycorax's blue eyes – blew in the First Folio, but regularly modernised to 'blue' in recent editions. Why has so little been made of their colour in recent critical studies of the play? The mention of eye colour in Shakespeare is rare, and blue eyes are particularly rare. Why are the witches eyes blue? Much of the interpretive energy surrounding *The Tempest* in the late twentieth century has gone towards the deconstruction of the play's apparent opposition between the properly European (Prospero, Miranda, Ferdinand) and the colonial or otherwise alien stranger (Caliban, Sycorax). We might have supposed that Sycorax's eye colour would be a prominent piece of evidence in such critical revisionism, since blue eyes, in our culture at least, are associated with the Anglo-American imperialist and with the 'self', rather than with the colonised peoples and with the 'other'. As a blue-eyed Algerian, Sycorax would fail to fit our racial stereotypes in a number of interesting ways. We tend not to think of Africans as blue eyed, even though North Africans of 'Argier' and elsewhere sometimes are. But the witch's blue eyes scarcely surface in the critical discussions I have read: the critics have dutifully read the explanatory notes to the play in the editions they have used, and modern editions overwhelmingly reject the possibility that 'blue-eyed' in this instance can possibly mean blue-eyed.

From Leah S. Marcus, 'The Blue-Eyed Witch', in *Unediting the Renaissance* (1996), pp. 5–7.

Jonathan Culler, 'Literary Competence'

We also tend to think of meaning and structure as properties of literary works, and from one point of view this is perfectly correct: when the sequence of words is treated *as a literary work* it has these properties ... The work has structure and meaning because it is read in a particular way, because these potential properties, latent in the object itself, are actualised by the theory of discourse applied in the act of reading. 'How can one discover structure without the help of a methodological model?' asks Barthes (*Critique et Verité*, p. 19). To read a text as literature is not to make one's mind a *tabula rasa* [a blank page] and approach it without preconceptions; one must bring to it an implicit understanding of the operations of literary discourse which tells one what to look for.

Anyone lacking this knowledge, anyone wholly unacquainted with the conventions by which fictions are read, would, for example, be quite baffled if presented with a poem. His knowledge of the language would enable him to understand phrases and sentences, but he would not know, quite literally, what to *make* of this strange concatenation of phrases. He would be unable to read it *as* literature ... because he lacks the complex 'literary competence' which enables others to proceed, he has not internalised the 'grammar' of literature which would permit him to convert linguistic sequences into literary structures and meanings.

From Jonathan Culler, *Structuralist Poetics* (London, 1975), pp. 113–14.

Discussion

LEAVIS

The Leavis passage seems to me mainly concerned to bring out the meaning of *Women in Love*, as revealed in the chapter cited. However, oddly, though there is much reference to the meaning ('a multitude of intimations'), there is little actual statement of that meaning *or* of how it is achieved. Instead, there is an interest in doing two things: (1) to assert that Lawrence is (despite his detractors) a great novelist and (2) to communicate to the reader a sense of the excitement and atmosphere of the original text. This carries out critical action 5 (evaluation), and adds a critical function which I did not list in my answer to the exercise: that of recreating something of the atmosphere which the critic thinks the reader will have felt on reading the original text. This technique of describing the effect of the text might best be seen as belonging to the critical function of appreciation, which I suggested above was not obviously dominant in current understandings of what critics do. The passage does not carry out many of the other critical functions suggested above, and is not primarily a formalist reading, since there is no real discussion of techniques or devices or deviations from the norm. The piece does refer to interpretation, but tends to assume that all readers will agree on what the effect of the text is anyway ('he should find ...'). To an extent, and contrary to the distinction suggested above between critics and readers, this critical piece does assume that to read a Lawrence novel is – almost instinctively – to interpret it.

HELEN GARDNER

This passage does offer an interpretation of its text, and is probably a more conventional example of what has been accepted as criticism over the last few decades. The reading is a formalist one: it picks out devices/specific features ('many and varied voices'; 'there are no characters') and proceeds from these details to a reading of the whole text. Thus, the treatment of the 'persons', who are not distinct and who melt into one another and into the city background is seen as being reproduced also in the treatment of time ('in the same way the time is all time and no time'). From these two analogous features, the text's general meaning, 'a radical defect in human life' is derived. The passage also carries out some other functions suggested earlier as critical possibilities. It compares *The Waste Land* with another text, Joyce's *Ulysses*, mainly to reinforce its sense of the different features peculiar to the poem (*Ulysses* is picked as a relevant comparison since it is also a modernist work which represents a modern city). The passage also looks as if it will interpret not only the text, but modern culture too ('the dilemma of the modern mind'), thus performing a historical critical move. In fact, though, it rapidly contradicts that specific kind of historicising reading, by arguing that it would be a 'mistake'. The best interpretation gives the poem a universal meaning: 'All humanity … seems to be waiting … Its true subject is ageless … [it] makes clear "the insufficiency of human enjoyments".' This critical move is now deeply unfashionable, but has a long pedigree: it sees the interpretation of the text as leading to a piece of wisdom which has universal validity. This is in its own way an evaluative move too (with some resemblances to Leavis's assertions of Lawrence's meaning) – since the wisdom of the poem is universal, it is, and always will be, great literature.

LEAH S. MARCUS

This passage focuses on a very specific detail, the description of Caliban's mother Sycorax in one line of *The Tempest* as 'blew-ey'd'. It picks the detail out as important because it could contribute to recent critical discussions of the play's representations of early colonialism. But Marcus notes that though the description is noted as a problem by the notes in editions of the play, there is a curious unwillingness to accept that Sycorax can have blue eyes, presumably because the detail has not been seen as consistent with a dominant reading of Sycorax as 'alien'. Marcus goes on to discuss what the phrase might alternatively be read as (should it really be blear eyed?) or whether blue eyes had a different range of meanings in the seventeenth century (there are instances where the phrase seems to refer to blue circles *round* the eyes, rather than to the colour of the iris). There are a series of critical functions here. Firstly, there is a classic formalist move, with the selection of a curious detail as a focus for investigation. This is then linked to a critical tradition (colonial readings) which makes clear the potential importance of the detail. Finally, there is a move back to the detail of the text as seen through the attempts of generations of editors to dispose of the problematic phrase either by altering it (emendation) or by explaining it. The passage thus uses a combination of formalist readings of the text, testing of textual detail against recent and older critical traditions, and testing of editorial glosses. Beyond these specific enquiries in this passage is a project, as the title *Unediting the Renaissance* suggests, which has three aspects: it is textual (it investigates what the 'original matter' of the text might mean); it is historicising (what are the range of meanings possible in the seventeenth century for any specific textual variation and for the larger readings constructed from such details?); and it is formalist (it is interested in the differences made to interpretation by relationships between details, hypotheses and whole texts).

JONATHAN CULLER

This passage shows an immediate difference from each of the other examples of critics at work. It is not a discussion of a text. It is thus unlike the basic model of criticism we have worked with so far in this section, where criticism is a commentary motivated by a particular text (a model with a long history going back at least as far as medieval biblical commentaries and glosses – see section 2.1). Instead, this passage is about how we read literary texts *in general*, though it does refer to poetry (but not *a* poem) as a particular example of a genre. Instead of interpreting a text, this passage aims to clarify the rules by which we read texts and interpret them. It argues that meaning in literary texts depends on conventions which are not those of 'ordinary language usage' (an idea which I undoubtedly depended on in my interpretation of Marianne Moore's 'Poetry'). To read literature, therefore, one needs to have internalised an understanding of these conventions and thus have gained 'literary competence'. It is noticeable that in this model, the roles of the reader and the critic are not as distinct as in a model which assumes that readers 'just read', while critics interpret. Here, the very act of reading a literary text requires interpretation according to conventions and skills which are learnt. This implies an active and skilled reader, rather than a passive consumer. The role of the critic would still presumably be to make these interpretative strategies more explicit – and, indeed, as here, to formulate ways of understanding the underlying rules for reading. □

These examples of critics at work are not able (and not intended) to cover anything like the whole range of critical possibilities. They are intended, instead, to introduce the practice of criticising critics, of making their meanings and assumptions clear, while giving some indication of the possible variations. It seems reasonable to assume that there are a finite number of things critics can do (and there are various attempts to categorise these more fully than has been done here), but also reasonable to assume that there is room for significant variation in practice and room to debate what critics should do. Even a similar critical act (i.e. focusing on the text alone) will not, of course, necessarily produce even the same kind of criticism, let alone the same interpretation. The starting point of this discussion was based on discussion of critics as 'interpreters of texts', and most of the examples have been of critics interpreting particular literary works. This is, indeed, still the dominant feature of literary study in universities, though increasingly there is a strong sense of texts as parts of a literary/historical system, rather than on seeing them as 'autonomous'. However, it should certainly be noted that there are kinds of modern criticism which do not start from the study-of-texts basis. Jonathan Culler (not surprisingly given the approach in the extract above) discusses this alternative in *Structuralist Poetics*:

Structuralism effects an important reversal of perspective, granting precedence to the task of formulating a comprehensive theory of literary discourse and assigning a secondary place to the interpretation of individual texts. Whatever the benefits of interpretation to those who engage in it, within the contexts of poetics it becomes an ancillary activity ... as opposed to the study of literature itself as an institution. To say that is in no way to condemn interpretation ... [but] a structuralist poetics would claim that the study of literature involves only indirectly the critical act of placing a work in a situation, reading it as a gesture of a particular kind, and thus giving it a meaning. ... This would not need to be said if interpretative criticism had not tried to persuade us that the study of literature means the elucidation of individual works. (pp. 118–19)

There will be opportunities later in this section for you to think through what your critical preferences are, but it seems worth pausing at this point to bring out some issues about interpreting texts, since these bear directly on the very book you are working through now. *Thinking About Texts* clearly does start all of its discussions from the basis of individual texts.

One response to Culler might be to say that the study of a system of communication does not render irrelevant the study of particular utterances within it (learning French grammar does not necessarily make speaking it, or trying to work out the exact sense of a particular phrase, or reading Balzac, a secondary activity). Interpretation without any study of the system of conventions which make it possible does seem less than methodical, but perhaps what we need is a mode of literary study which includes both a poetics and the investigation of particular realisations of meaning? Culler does carefully try to avoid condemning interpretation, but despite this the relegation of interpretation to an 'ancillary activity' is clear. One could argue that there is no system without individual instances, just as there are no individual instances without an underlying system. I think that *Thinking About Texts* attempts both a poetics (an analysis of how the general system works) *and* an investigation of particular instances. The system and the individual instances seem to me to be in a highly dynamic interrelationship: the system both underpins individual texts, and is derived from their realisation of its general codes. My response is presumably not surprising given that the project of this book is, indeed, to develop interpretative skills in reading specific texts and to develop further understanding of what makes interpretation possible.

Having established some sense of what critics can do in the relatively literal sense (what acts can they perform on texts – or on the codes underlying texts ...), we can move on to ask, 'What do Critics do?' in a slightly different sense: what do critics achieve, what is their function?

◆ Read the following three passages about criticism: What are their visions of the function of the critic?

• • • • • • • • • •

Alexander Pope, *An Essay on Criticism*

> You then whose judgement the right course would steer,
> Know well each ancient's proper character;
> His fable, subject, scope in every page;
> Religion, country, genius of his age:
> Without all these at once before your eyes,

Cavil you may, but never criticise.
Be Homer's works your study and delight,
Read them by day, and meditate by night;
Thence form your judgement, thence your maxims bring,
And trace the Muses upwards to their spring.

…

Some beauties yet no precepts can declare,
For there's a happiness as well as care.
Music resembles poetry, in each
Are nameless graces which no methods teach,
And which a master hand alone can reach.
If, where the rules not far enough extend
(Since rules were made but to promote their end)
Some lucky license answers to the full
The intent proposed, that license is a rule.

…

Great wits sometimes may gloriously offend,
And rise to faults true critics dare not mend;
But though the antients thus their rules invade
(As kings dispense with rules themselves have made)
Moderns, beware! or if you must offend
Against the precept, ne'er transgress its end;
Let it be seldom, and compelled by need;
And have at least their precedent to plead.
The critic else proceeds without remorse,
Seizes your fame, and puts his laws in force.

From Alexander Pope, *An Essay on Criticism*, Part I (1709, 1711), ll. 119–27, 141–50, 159–68.

T. S. Eliot, 'The Necessity of Criticism'

The important moment for the appearance of criticism seems to be the time when poetry ceases to be the expression of the mind of a whole people. The drama of Dryden, which furnishes the chief occasion for his critical writing, is formed by Dryden's perception that the possibilities of writing in the mode of Shakespeare were exhausted … But Dryden was not writing plays for the whole people; he was writing in a form which had not grown out of popular tradition or popular requirements, a form the acceptance of which had therefore to come by diffusion through a small society … But the part of society to which Dryden's work, and that of the Restoration comedians, could immediately appeal constituted something like an intellectual aristocracy; when the poet finds himself in an age in which there is no intellectual aristocracy, when power is in the hands of a class so democratised that whilst still a class it represents itself to be the whole nation; when the only alternatives seem to be to talk to a coterie or to soliloquise, the difficulties of the poet and the necessity of criticism become greater …

From T. S. Eliot, *The Use of Poetry and the Use of Criticism* (1933), in *Selected Prose of T. S. Eliot*, ed. Frank Kesmode (1975), p. 79.

Terry Eagleton, 'The Function of Criticism'

Perhaps I could best describe the impulse behind this book by imagining the moment in which a critic, sitting down to begin a study of some theme or author, is suddenly arrested by a set of disturbing questions. What is the *point* of such a study? Who is it intended to reach, influence, impress? What functions are ascribed to such a critical act by society as a whole? A critic may write with assurance as long as the critical institution itself is thought to be unproblematical.

Once that institution is thrown into radical question, then one would expect individual acts of criticism to become troubled and self-doubting. The fact that such acts continue today, apparently in all their traditional confidence, is doubtless a sign that the crisis of the critical institution has either not been deeply enough registered, or is being actively evaded.

The argument of this book is that criticism today lacks all substantive social function. It is either part of the public relations branch of the literary industry, or a matter wholly internal to the academies. That this has not always been the case, and that it need not even today be the case, I try to show by a drastically selective history of the institution of criticism in England since the early eighteenth century … I examine this history as a way of raising the question of what substantive social functions criticism might once again fulfil in our own time, beyond its crucial role of maintaining from within the academies a critique of ruling-class culture.

From Terry Eagleton, Preface to *The Function of Criticism – from 'The Spectator' to Poststructuralism* (London, 1984), pp. 8–9.

Discussion

POPE

In the essay by Alexander Pope, the reader is instructed in the knowledge which will enable someone properly to perform the role of critic. The critic needs to form 'judgement' and to develop a set of 'maxims' (=rules, summaries of wisdom). The general function of the critic is to deploy appropriate rules in order to differentiate between great and indifferent poetry and poetic practices. Indeed, the passage is dominated by ideas about 'rules'. It is noticeable how often synonyms for 'rules' are used: 'maxims', 'precepts' (twice), 'rules' (5 times), 'precedent', 'laws'; and how many words in the poem are linked to ideas of containment within/trespass over proper boundaries: 'the right course', 'proper character', 'license', faults', 'invade', transgress'. Though these words are drawn from a variety of spheres (steering a ship, monarchical rule, invasion), there is distinct concentration on legal terms, leading to the conclusion of the passage where the critic confiscates poetic law breakers' goods as he 'proceeds without remorse, / Seizes your fame, / and puts his laws in force'. This kind of critical function has, in fact, sometimes been called 'legislative criticism', a criticism which lays down general rules on how literature should be written, what produces good literature, and what produces bad literature. Pope is not, though, wholly rule bound. Some 'beauties' have no precedent – but are still 'graces', because in fact they fulfil the *aim* of the rules, if not any pre-existent rule. The critic's task here is to learn a certain set of knowledge (classical literature), to derive the best rules from this knowledge and to discriminate between good and bad on this basis. There is no function which resembles 'interpretation' of the text. The only commentary required is one which classes the work as good or bad, and no explanatory or analytical discussion is seen as necessary.

T. S. ELIOT

Though discussing the poet and dramatist Dryden (who flourished a generation before Pope), Eliot has a quite different sense of the function of the critic. Here, the task of the critic seems to be to explain and diffuse ideas about literature to an audience which has no immediate understanding of its (present) forms. Indeed, he only sees the need for criticism when literature does become cut off from the general experience, and from popular traditions and requirements. Those from the 'intellectual aristocracy' have no need for criticism, since they already understand literature. This sounds a very different function for the critic than that envisaged by Pope. Where in *An Essay in Criticism*, the critic has to learn and apply rules, here, in Eliot's view anyway, the critic had to explain to and educate an untutored audience. Indeed, as the concluding part of the passage makes clear, Eliot sees that educative role as the function of the critic in the 1930s too. For Pope, a lack of proper critics may lead to an increase in bad poetry; for Dryden as-seen-by-Eliot it may lead to the loss of any audience.

TERRY EAGLETON

Eagleton starts by trying to imagine what the link is between the individual critic sitting down to write and the wider impact of the critic's work. Eagleton is not convinced that criticism in the 1980s actually has any real point, and is puzzled that critics continue to write at all given the lack of any clear *end* in doing so. He starts from the position that 'the critical institution' has patently lost any consensus it might have once had about its role in society (I am not entirely certain what the phrase 'critical institution' means here – is it the institutional practice of criticism or is it the social organisation through which criticism is carried out – presumably the academy?). Individual acts of criticism, therefore, lacking any defining purpose beyond the immediate, are merely fossils of a time when criticism actually had an active role to play in the public sphere. Critics continue either because they have not understood the severity of this crisis, or because they are not willing to acknowledge it (easier to go on writing criticism …). Instead of playing a part in important public processes, criticism in this view becomes a relatively superficial matter, of marginal concern only to the publishing companies and certain newspapers and other kinds of media, or an entirely internal matter for English departments, in which critical specialists speak only to other specialists. Eagleton is not wholly despairing. He intends to trace in his history a time when criticism meant something to a wider public and to suggest how criticism might once again recover some real function (there seems to be a contradiction at the end of the passage, where a vital function *is* ascribed to the allegedly empty activity of present-day criticism: 'its crucial role of maintaining from within the academy a critique of ruling-class culture'). □

These passages cover a range of possible answers to the question: 'What do critics do?' In these examples, critics can judge and discriminate, they can disseminate knowledge, they can be fossils with no function, they can be a vital point of reflection on (or resistance to?) the dominant culture. These positions do not exhaust the possibilities, presumably, and nor do they pursue all the complexities of where or what the end of different critical activities might be. As with the analysis earlier of what a critic can do to a text, and what critical acts different critics perform, what it is important to note is that these differences are neither straightforward, nor beyond analysis. If we can learn to see precisely what critics are doing in every instance, then we can see better what we ourselves are doing as critics, and what we might do alternatively/additionally. Moreover, by thinking through critical acts, we can ask large questions of the kind that Eagleton poses: 'what is the *point* of such a study?'

This section started with the assumption that the most likely reader of this book was already likely to be a critic – to be living out some of the problems raised through their own experience. What we have not so far considered is whether criticism is, in fact, necessary at all. Eliot suggests that there was little need for criticism before Dryden; Eagleton suggests that current criticism does not succeed in fulfilling a need. The section will end with a text which argues against interpretative criticism, and with a chance to test against this your own sense of what criticism is for, of what you do or could do when you act as a critic. As usual, I will leave you at this stage to work through your answers yourselves.

> ◆ Read the following passages taken from Susan Sontag's *Against Interpretation*, and then consider what your responses to the following questions are.
> ◆ How much sympathy do you feel for her argument?
> ◆ If you feel that criticism is useful, how would you justify it as an activity?
> ◆ What kind of critic are you? What do you try to achieve through criticism?

• • • • • • • • • •

Susan Sontag, 'Against Interpretation'

III

The old style of interpretation [e.g. allegorical interpretation of biblical narratives] was insistent but respectful; it erected another meaning on top of the literal one. The modern style of interpretation excavates, and as it excavates destroys; it digs 'behind' the text, to find a sub-text which is the true one. The most celebrated and influential modern doctrines, those of Marx and Freud, actually amount to... aggressive and impious theories of interpretation... To understand is to interpret. And to interpret is to restate the phenomenon, in effect to find an equivalent for it.

Thus interpretation is not... an absolute value, a gesture of mind situated in some timeless realm of capabilities. Interpretation must itself be evaluated, within a historical view of human consciousness. In some cultural contexts, interpretation is a liberating act. It is a means of revising, of transvaluing, of escaping the dead past. In other cultural contexts, it is reactionary, impertinent, cowardly, stifling.

IV

Today is such a time... Like the fumes of the automobile and of heavy industry which befoul the urban atmosphere, the effusion of interpretations of art poisons our sensibilities. In a culture whose already classical dilemma is the hypertrophy of the intellect at the expense of energy and sensual capability, interpretation is the revenge of the intellect upon art.

Even more. It is the revenge of the intellect upon the world. To interpret is to impoverish, to deplete the world – in order to set up a shallow world of 'meanings'... The world, our world, is depleted, impoverished enough. Away with all duplicates of it, until we again experience more immediately what we have.

...

VIII

What kind of criticism, of commentary on the arts, is desirable today?... What would criticism look like that would serve the work of art, not usurp its place?... Valuable would be acts of criticism which would supply a really accurate sharp, loving description of the appearance of a work of art...

IX

Transparence is the highest, most liberating value in art – and in criticism – today. Transparence means experiencing the luminousness of the thing itself, of things being what they are... What is important now is to recover our senses. We must learn to *see* more, to *hear* more, to *feel* more ... The function of criticism should be to show *how it is what it is*, even *that it is what it is*, rather than to show *what it means*.

X

In place of a hermeneutics [a systematic mode of discovering meaning] we need an erotics of art.

From Susan Sontag, *Against Interpretation and Other Essays* (1965), pp. 3–14; these extracts are from the essay's sections III, IV, VIII, IX, X, pp. 6, 7, 13–14.

Further Reading

Barthes, Roland, 'The Death of the Author' in *Image–Music–Text: Roland Barthes Essays*, selected and trans. Stephen Heath (London, Fontana, 1977).

Belsey, Catherine, *Critical Practice* (London, Routledge, 1980).

Burke, Sean, *Authorship: From Plato to the Postmodern – A Reader* (Edinburgh, Edinburgh University Press, 1995).

——, *The Death and Return of the Author: Criticism and Subjectivity in Barthes, Foucault and Derrida* (Edinburgh, Edinburgh University Press, 1998).

Culler, Jonathan, *Structuralist Poetics: Structuralism, Linguistics and the Study of Literature* (London, Routledge, 1994).

Eagleton, Terry, *The Function of Criticism – from 'The Spectator' to Poststructuralism* (London, Verso, 1984).

Eliot, T. S., *T. S. Eliot: Selected Essays* (London, Faber 1932; reprinted many times).

Fish, Stanley, *Is there a Text in this Class? The Authority of Interpretative Communities* (Cambridge, MA, Harvard University Press, 1988).

Foucault, Michel, 'What is an Author?' in *The Foucault Reader,* ed. Paul Rabinow (Harmondsworth, Penguin, 1991).

Freund, Elizabeth, *The Return of the Reader: Reader-Response Criticism* (London, Methuen, 1987).

Gubar, Susan and Jonathan Kamholtz, *English Inside and Out: the Places of Literary Criticism* (London, Routledge, 1993).

Hawkes, Terence, *Structuralism and Semiotics* (London, Methuen, 1977).

Hawthorne, Jeremy, *Unlocking the Text: Fundamental Issues in Literary Theory* (London, Edward Arnold, 1987).

Genre

3.1 Kind, Genre, Subgenre

This book has, so far, debated several kinds of distinction, and the difficulties of making them: Is literature different from non-literature? Where does one text end and another begin? What do authors do? What do critics do? But in one important area centrally concerned with making distinctions about literature the book has not yet made any explicit distinction: that of genre.

The word has a simple derivation from the French *genre* = kind, family, a word related to the Latin *genus* = family or a people. The literary use of the term has not shifted very far from these roots; to ask a question about genre is to enquire about family membership and differences between families.

The first question about genre might be, simply: why? Why do we need or wish to split up literature (or writing, if you prefer) into subgroups of texts? One answer might be that we must, another that it is helpful to do so. Other questions will doubtless follow from our answers to this fundamental question of why:

1. How do genre distinctions work? (for texts/authors/readers/critics)?
2. What difference to meaning does genre make?
3. How fixed/flexible are genres?
4. Do we HAVE to think in terms of genre?

However, before addressing the question of *why*, it would be helpful to gain an initial sense of the categories generally considered to be genres.

> ◆ Make a list of about ten kinds of literature (genre, subgenre or any other *kind*; there is no particular need to order or arrange them at this stage).
> ◆ Write a brief note of what each term indicates.
> ◆ How consistent are the terms in your list (do they all refer clearly to one family, to the same kind of family, the same scales of family differences)?

SAMPLE LIST

Comedy, tragedy, tragi-comedy, pastoral, historical novel, thriller, poetry, mystery play, satire, modern lyric. (Your lists might or might not include any of these terms – there are undoubtedly many other generic labels of various sorts.)

DEFINITIONS

Comedy: anything which is funny, a comic drama with a traditional form (usually ending in marriage); other kinds of literature with this form (e.g. a novel can be described as a 'social comedy').

Tragedy: form of drama first performed in Ancient Greece, ending almost without exception with the violent death of the protagonist, a 'great man'; label not often applied to novels in the way that 'comedy' can be (though its adjective form 'tragic' applied sometimes to other forms than drama, e.g. novels – 'Goethe's *The Sorrows of Werthe* is a tragic novel').

Tragi-comedy: a mixed form, primarily of drama, which combines some features of tragedy, and some of comedy. Thus Shakespeare's *The Winter's Tale* (1611) has a tragic first half (including deaths – which practically never happen in comedies), and a comic second half, in which all is resolved with marriages (and some, though, interestingly, not all, of the dead are resurrected).

Pastoral: not principally a specific form, but rather a set of attitudes and features applied to a range of kinds (short poems, plays or parts of plays, and prose works, including some novels); features include a rustic or otherwise primitive setting and characters, and a sense (often nostalgic) of the special values – profound yet simple – of that milieu.

Historical novel: a type of novel set in a particular period of the past, usually showing considerable attention to historical detail and atmosphere, while telling a fictional story or, at any rate, narrating and expanding on known historical facts in a novelistic manner; at times regarded as a major type of European novel (e.g. Sir Walter Scott's novels), at others as a subgenre with a middle-brow escapist or romantic appeal (e.g. since the First World War, in Britain).

Thriller: type of fiction occurring in various forms: novel, film (two main forms?) and drama; usually centres on a crime, on police-work, or on other areas marginal to 'normal' life (e.g. spying); often regarded as a popular genre (or worse, e.g. pulp novels); sometimes divided into specific subcategories: e.g. detective stories, spy thrillers, crime novels, police procedurals, etc.

Poetry: a major category of literary activity; a kind of production oral in origin (e.g. Homeric epic, Anglo-Saxon poetry), now mainly written, but often preserving a sense of sound and voice as an important feature; writing in a specific form: e.g. metrical, rhymed, with strict alliterative patterns, strict patternings of lines (i.e. sonnets); writing in free form, but stressing that form (so there can be no mistaking it for prose: i.e. free verse, in which, unlike in prose, the exact layout on the page matters and is scrupulously reproduced to match the 'best text' of the work); sometimes also used in the sixteenth to nineteenth centuries to mean literature of the highest value in general (regardless of form).

Mystery play: a medieval play, originally 'mastery' play, since it was performed (and financed) by the *masters* of a particular guild in a particular city between the thirteenth century and the early sixteenth century,[1] when such dramas were discouraged after the Reformation; plays of this type tell the Christian story from the Creation of the world to the Crucifixion, via Noah's Flood, the expulsion of Adam and Eve from Eden and the Nativity; the plays are generally fairly brief;

they are quite varied in type: some are very dignified (the Creation), others are comic (but not necessarily following Graeco-Roman patterns, e.g. Nativity plays such as the First Shepherds Pageant), some include comedy within mainly tragic narratives (e.g. Crucifixion plays, which often show the soldiers who nail Jesus to the Cross in a savagely comic-ironic light).

Satire: a kind of writing which expresses antipathy to and criticism of contemporary ideas and attitudes, usually through slightly indirect means such as irony; sometimes a term applied to a specific verse genre (i.e. Donne's Satires); more frequently used to indicate an attitude in a text, rather than a particular form – thus satires can be novels (e.g. Orwell's *Animal Farm*, 1949), long poems (e.g. Pope's *The Dunciad*, 1742), or shorter poems (e.g. Swift's *The Lady's Dressing Room*); the term satire derives from the ancient Greek *satyr* play, a short drama of a clownish and comic kind, which was performed at the end of a tragedy.

Modern lyric: generally short poems based on a personal persona (most often first person), a form which has dominated poetry since the turn of the century (e.g. William Carlos Williams's 'This is Just To Say' or Sylvia Plath's 'Daddy').

▶ Discussion

There seems no great consistency to these terms, in several ways. Firstly, *what* is indicated by a term is often far from transparent or stable; secondly, the scales of difference implied by terms can be very various. Thus, some generic labels refer principally to formal features (e.g. poetry = non-prose), while others refer as much to an attitude (e.g. satire = works which are satirical in a variety of forms; there are related tendencies in labels like tragedy and comedy). Some terms demarcate vast literary territories (poetry, prose, drama), others very specific forms (e.g. mystery play). Some terms are ambiguous, referring to a specific form in a particular period, but to a more loosely defined form or an attitude in other periods (e.g. pastoral, or satire). Many generic labels show a capacity to be applied to other genre labels in hyphenated or adjectival forms (e.g. tragi-comedy, satirical comedy, tragic history, comic novel, historical novel). Other generic terms can be modified by period terms (e.g. modern lyric, modernist novel). Even family membership is disputable (in one way it seems clear that the thriller is a subgenre of the *novel* genre, but it is equally clear that it is an inferior member of that genre AND that it is therefore not really a *novel* at all!). □

> ◆ Why do you think this complexity in labelling arises?

▶ Discussion

My feeling is that the complexity stems precisely from the fact that genre is not actually a single unified system, though in many respects it is thought of as one. Generic labels convey information of several sorts about texts; formal features, inherent features, probable features, length of lineage, membership of a classic form, hybridity, content, mass culture or high culture, continuities and differences, place in literary history, characteristics at a general level, characteristics at a very specific level. □

This does not necessarily mean that genre is too chaotic a concept to be valid, though. The complexity presumably arises precisely because there are a range of generic descriptions which we find useful or necessary (or, at worst, unavoidable). This brings us back to the question: why?

◆   Why do you think generic distinctions exist?

Discussion

I can suggest a number of possible reasons of a positive kind, and a few more negative explanations:

1.   Because human realities actually correspond to a number of different modes, which genre encodes (i.e. there really are tragic experiences, comic experiences, pastoral experiences and so on).
2.   Because such categories are long established as templates for representing human experience (they may not be real, as 1 above asserts, but their long lineage has given credence and value to their capacity for representation).
3.   Because they help authors and readers to organise material productively (i.e. by providing criteria for achievement of a particular kind, they support both production and consumption within that type).
4.   Because they are hallowed by long usage – and therefore have validity for older literature, at least.
5.   Because they allow critics to exercise their obsessive urge for tidy categories, for rational order.
6.   Because writing and reading and criticism have allowed themselves to become ossified, trapped within outmoded categories which have nothing to do with the real possibilities of contemporary writing or, indeed, of actual life. □

All of these reasons have been given at one time or another. By the end of this section, you will be in a position to see which explanations you find most sympathetic. Next though, we might look at a more extended argument about why genres exist.

◆   Read the following extract: What are its explanations of the existence of literary genres?
◆   How convincing do you find Todorov's argument that modern 'free form' literature is actually just as generic as older 'generic' literature?

Tzvetan Todorov, 'The Origin of Genres'

To persist in paying attention to genres may seem to be a vain if not anachronistic pastime today. We all know that genres used to exist: in the good old days of classicism, there were ballads, odes, sonnets, tragedies, and comedies; but do these exist today? Even the genres of the nineteenth century, poetry or novel … seem to be coming undone … It is even considered a sign of authentic modernity in a writer if he ceases to respect the separation of genres … More forcefully than anyone else, Blanchot has said what others have not dared to think or have not known how to express: today there is no intermediate entity between the unique individual work and literature as a whole, the ultimate genre … [However,] in the very texts where Blanchot announces the disappearance of genres we find categories at work whose resemblance to generic distinctions is hard to deny … Speaking of the same Broch [a prose-writer discussed earlier in the passage] … Blanchot says that he 'indulges in all modes of expression – narrative, lyric, and discursive' … Thus 'genre' as such has not disappeared; the genres-of-the-past have simply been replaced by others …

In the process of arguing the legitimacy of a study of genres, we have come across an answer to the question raised implicitly in the title: the origin of genres. Where do genres come from? Quite simply from other genres. A new genre is always the transformation of an earlier one, or of several: by inversion, by displacement, by combination … There has never been a literature without genres …

The question of origin that I should like to raise, however, is not historical but systematic in nature … Not 'what preceded genre in time?' but 'what presides over the birth of a genre at any time?'. More precisely, is there such a thing in language … as forms which, while they may foreshadow genres, are not yet included within them? And if so, how does the passage from one to the other come about?

…

In a given society, the recurrence of certain discursive properties[2] is institutionalised, and individual texts are produced and perceived in relation to the norm constituted by that codification. A genre whether literary or not, is nothing other than the codification of discursive properties … To put it simply, autobiography [as an example] is defined by two identifications: the author's identification with the narrator, and the narrator's identification with the chief protagonist. This second identification is obvious: it is the one expressed in the prefix *auto-* and the one that makes it possible to differentiate autobiography from biography or memoirs. The first one is more subtle: it distinguishes autobiography … from the novel, even though a given novel may be full of elements drawn from the author's life. In short, this identification separates all the 'referential' or 'historical' genres from all the 'fictional' genres: the reality of the referent is clearly indicated, because we are dealing with the author of the book himself, an individual who has a civil status in his home town.

Thus we are dealing with a speech act that codifies both semantic properties (this is what is implied by the character-narrator identification; one must speak of oneself) and pragmatic properties (by virtue of the author-narrator identification; one claims to be telling the truth and not a fiction). In this form, the speech act is very widely distributed outside literature: it is practiced every time anyone *tells his or her own story* …

> The rapid enumeration I have just proposed … makes it possible to see that there is not an abyss between literature and what is not literature, that the literary genres originate, quite simply, in human discourse.
>
> From Tzvetan Todorov, *Genres in Discourse* (1978); originally published in French, extract from first English translation (Cambridge, 1990), pp. 13–27.

▶ Discussion 1

Todorov starts his discussion by noting that according to many writers/critics since the nineteenth century, genre is, anyway, dead. Thus instead of the exhausted generic categories, we now have, according to a writer like Blanchot, only one megagenre: literature. Within that genre, there is no regulation of form by set names or laws, because the literary is by definition that which escapes from prefabricated forms and conventions.

Todorov, however, disputes the accuracy of this account, arguing that, symptomatically, Blanchot in describing the freedom from generic form of modern texts cannot in fact avoid using generic terms. Therefore when Blanchot argues that the writer Broch's work is without genre, he has to use a combination of genre terms to describe what its characteristics are: '[he] indulges in all modes of expression – narrative, lyric and discursive'. Todorov's point is that if Broch (as a representative modern writer) is not using a long-recognised generic form, he is nevertheless using elements of recognised forms. If this is not writing within a genre, it is not exactly outside genre either.

From this starting point, Todorov argues that genre has not, and does not, disappear: instead it changes and develops into new forms. A new genre 'is always the transformation of an earlier one, or of several'. This gives him a position from which to investigate why genre exists: he suggests that the literary genres with which we are familiar must themselves be transformations of genres which already exist, and that all genres however complex must derive from prototypes which exist not just in *literary* language, but in '*ordinary*' language.

For Todorov the term genre indicates the 'codification of discursive properties', institutionalisation of 'the recurrence of certain discursive properties'. Thus, genre is not a feature special to literature, but is a universal element in human discourse. Human language, in short, always relies on certain sets of rules for governing meaning and form, and literary genres are simply specialised versions of this need. This has various implications – including the idea that generic categories need to be used in analysing 'real' language as well as literary, and that the megagenre 'literature' shares smaller genres with its twin megagenre 'non-literature', dissolving the 'abyss' between those two categories.[3] □

▶ Discussion 2

I am convinced that apparently genreless texts will nevertheless contain generic markers, and that these are very likely to be from several different genres, since generic 'confusion' or contradiction seems a prime way of displaying a text's claim to be 'non-generic' in the sense of belonging clearly to one or other set generic form. On the other hand, this suggests a similarity between *set genres* and *genres-which-mix-genres* that I am not so sure about. Is a text which uses multiple genres a new genre, or does it remain something less stable, less easy to read and interpret, a form of discourse with inherent contradictions of the rules? It may be that Todorov's main point is that all texts are *generic*, rather than that all texts have *a genre*. Some texts may show a clear membership of a single genre, while others may draw on the 'discursive properties' of several. We will return to questions about the differences in the effect of these uses of genre later on in this section and in sections 3.2 and 3.3. □

Next, though, we should look at some of the range of ways in which writers and critics have talked about genre,[4] before moving on to look at how genre *works* in texts.

> ◆ Read the following three passages and make some notes on the attitude of each to genre.

Aristotle, *Poetics*

I

Epic Poetry and Tragedy, and Comedy, Considered In General As Forms Of Imitative Art

In this work, we propose to discuss the nature of the poetic art in general, and to treat of its different species in particular, with regard to the essential quality or function of each species – which is equivalent to the proper and characteristic effect of each upon the trained sensibilities of the judicious...

More particularly, now, Poetry broke up into two varieties, corresponding to a difference of personal character in the authors; for the graver spirits would represent noble actions, while the meaner would represent the doings of the ignoble. And whereas others composed hymns and panegyrics, the latter sort at first produced lampoons...

When Tragedy and Comedy came into existence, however, those poets whose natural bent was toward lower subjects no longer took up lampooning, but became writers of comedy; and the graver spirits no longer became epic poets, but producers of tragedy. And the reason was that these newer forms were grander, and were held in greater esteem.

Tragedy at all events originated in improvisations, as did comedy also; for tragedy goes back to the improvising poet-leaders in the dithyrambic chorus of satyrs; and comedy to the leaders of the Phallic song and dance ... And from this beginning, Tragedy progressed little by little, as the successive authors gradually improved upon what preceded them. Finally the development ceased, when tragedy, through a long series of changes, had attained to its natural form. The principal changes were three.

(1) From the single spokesman of the primitive form, Aeschylus increased the number of actors to two; he diminished the part taken by the Chorus – that is, he reduced the amount of choral chanting; and he made the spoken dialogue the chief element in the play.

(2) Sophocles brought about the innovation of three actors, and was the first to make use of painted scenery.

(3) Furthermore, there was a change in the magnitude of the actions represented; for the little plots of the primitive form were abandoned; and, with its development out of the satyr-dance, Tragedy also discarded the grotesque early diction. Thus, at a late period, however, it assumed its characteristic elevation of tone. At the same time, the trochaic tetrameter gave way to an iambic measure. Indeed, the reason for the early use of the trochaic tetrameter was that Tragedy retained its connection with satyrs, and was more nearly allied to choral dancing than at present. But so soon as the element of spoken discourse entered in, nature herself suggested the appropriate metre – the iambic; for this is the readiest metre in speaking, as may be seen in ordinary conversation, where we are apt to fall into an iambic measure …

As for comedy, this as we have said, is an artistic imitation of men of an inferior moral bent; faulty, however, not in every way, but only so far as their short-comings are ludicrous; for the Ludicrous is a species or part, not all of the Ugly. It may be described as that kind of short-coming or deformity which does not strike us as painful, and causes no harm to others; a ready example is the comic mask, which is ludicrous, being ugly and distorted, without any suggestion of pain.

From Aristotle, *Poetics* (5th century BC), in *Aristotle on the Art of Poetry*, trs. Lane Cooper (1913, 1917), pp. 1–14.

Sir Philip Sidney, *The Defence of Poesie*

It shall not be amisse in a word to cite the speciall kinds, to see what faults may be found in the right use of them.

Is it then the Pastoral Poem which is misliked? (For perchance, where the hedge is lowest they will soonest leape over.) Is the poor pype disdained, which sometime out of Melibeus' mouth can shew the miserie of people under hard Lords or ravening souldiours? And again, by Titrius, what blessednes is derived to them that lye lowest from the goodnesse of them that sit highest? Sometime under the prettie tales of Wolves and Sheepe, can include the whole consideration of wrong dooing and patience; sometimes shew that contention for trifles can get but a trifling victorie …

…

No, perchance it is the Comick, whom naughtie Playmakers and Stage-Keepers have justly made odious. To the argument of abuse I will answer after. Onely thus much now is to be said, that the Comedy is an imitation of the common errors of our life, which he representeth in the most ridiculous and scornefull sort that may be; so it is impossible that any beholder can be content to be such a one.

…

So that the right use of Comedy will (I thinke) by no body be blamed, and much lesse of the highe and excellent Tragedy, that openeth the greatest wounds, and sheweth forth the ulcers that are covered with tissue; that maketh Kinges fear to be Tyrants, and Tyrants manifest their Tyrannical humours.

From Sir Philip Sidney, *The Defence of Poesie* (written 1582; published 1595). Extract from *Defence of Poesie, Astrophil and Stella and other Writings*, ed. Elizabeth Porges Watson (London, 1997), pp. 103–5.

Emile Zola, *Naturalism in the Theatre*

Let us forget Aristotle...

I have said that the naturalist novel is simply an inquiry into nature, beings and things. It therefore no longer directs its ingenuity towards a fable which is well invented and developed according to certain rules. The imagination no longer has a function...I mean that...[the novelist] does not intervene to diminish or add to reality, nor does he construct a fabric out of whole cloth according to the needs of a preconceived idea. We begin with the idea that nature is all we need...she is sufficiently beautiful and great to provide a beginning, a middle and an end. Instead of imaging an adventure...we simply take from life the story of a being or group of beings whose acts we faithfully set down. The work becomes an official record, nothing more ... On occasion, it is not even a whole life, with a beginning and end that is being told; it is only a shred of existence, a few years from the life of a man or a woman, a single page of human history, which has attracted the novelist in the same way that the special study of a body may interest a chemist. The novel, then, no longer has limiting boundaries; it has invaded and dispossessed the other genres. Like science it is master of the world. It attempts all subjects, writes history, treats of physiology and psychology, soars to the highest poetry, studies the most varied questions: politics, the social economy, religion, manners. All of nature is its domain. It moves there freely, adopting the form which pleases it...We are far removed from the novel as our forefathers understood it...In the old rhetorics the novel was placed at the very foot of the scale between the fable and light verse.

From Emile Zola, 'Naturalism in the Theatre'. (Originally published in French as 'Le Naturalisme au Théâtre', in Zola's *Le Roman Experimental* (Paris, 1880); reprinted and translated in *Documents of Modern Literary Realism*, ed. George J. Becker (Princeton, NJ, 1963), pp. 197–229. Extract is from pp. 199 and 207.)

Discussion

ARISTOTLE

Here there is clearly a notion at work that a particular genre achieves an ideal form, in which it attains its 'essential quality or function'. It is said to be evident that a genre has reached its 'proper' form when it has the effect that such a genre should have on 'the trained sensibilities of the judicious'. When a genre has taken up this ideal form, there is no further change. Thus tragedy's development ceased when, after 'a long series of changes' it 'attained to its natural form'.

Nevertheless, Aristotle has a rich sense of generic history and change – indeed, like Todorov, he clearly sees that genres evolve from other genres, rather than being immutable. Genre is defined in terms of author (authors themselves are generic, because their characters incline them towards certain genres), conventions for performance (how many actors, how much emphasis on choral chant or on speech), verse form (trochaic or iambic), material treated (tragedy in its mature form had to treat of events of 'magnitude') and effect on the audience (presenting to them the noble or the ludicrous, for example). There is a clear hierarchy of genre in Aristotle's thinking – with epic poetry and tragedy ranking above satire and comedy, although at a lower level these forms are seen to have their function.

SIR PHILIP SIDNEY

In this passage Sidney responds to contemporary attacks on particular genres in order to argue that each has its proper place and function, though each may also be misused. He lays most emphasis on the social effects of genres – spending very little time on formal definition – their role in making apparent to audiences their correct social roles and faults in the most effective way. Thus, pastoral serves to show to the great the effects of their actions for 'the lowest' – their misery under a hard lord, their happiness derived from goodness high above them. Even if the subject matter of pastoral seems artifical and irrelevant ('prettie tales of Wolves and Sheep'), the genre can, in fact, give a full account of 'wrong dooing' to the great. The low setting of pastoral is not a fault, but a necessary part of how the genre works on its audience. Similarly, tragedy addresses the very highest, kings themselves, and concerns the highest earthly matters, the state of the nation. In tragedy kings and subjects can see the dangers of tyranny, and the health of the state beneath the superficial 'tissue' which may cover concealed ulcers. In this view, tragedy is not about universal suffering, but is potentially a directly political form which warns good kings and provokes the tyrant to show himself.[5] Comedy ought to warn the viewer off ridiculous behaviour – though it sounds as if in the wrong hand of the 'naughtie' the effect may be the opposite one of celebrating anti-social and malicious 'ridicule'.

ZOLA

Here the starting point is clearly a rejection of traditional definitions of genre. Zola wants to look to the present to define genre, not the past and idealised or ossified definitions. Indeed, like the writer Blanchot (quoted above by Todorov), Zola believes that the reality of modern life is essentially a genreless one. Thus the most vital modern form, the novel must inquire into actuality, into the things that are there: 'nature, beings and things'. This actuality must not be cramped into 'fables' or written up in term of the (generic) 'imagination' or preconceived ideas. Instead, reality must have its own shape, its own beginning, middle and end.

However, I note that this initial assertion of freedom from *forms* at the opening of the passage soon runs into an argument which cannot entirely do without generic terms, though these are far from traditionally deployed. Thus, we are told that there is a form which supremely represents the fact that 'genre' is no longer needed: 'the naturalist novel'. The naturalist novel is, in Zola's view, an escape from genre in several ways. Firstly, it is not a 'fictional' form, but is allied to 'factual', naturally occurring forms which merely register what occurs: 'the work become an official record, nothing more'. Secondly, the naturalist novel escapes from genre because it has no boundaries; there is nothing it cannot take as its subject matter, no areas covered by another genre which it cannot move into and record with greater insight than that offered by that territory's original genre. At this point, though, we might notice that not only does the novel 'invade and dispossess' the other genres' empires, but that it also takes possession of several generic *names*. Of these the most traditional is 'poetry', usually as a *kind* a contrary of prose. 'History' too, though, is a kind of writing which one could readily say is defined by generic understandings, by 'the codification of discursive properties'. The other names conquered are not so obviously genres in a literary sense, but are academic disciplines or social areas where it would be easy to identify an association with a particular kind of book, or writing or discourse: physiology, psychology, politics, social economy, and religion at least might seem to be ways of dividing up social reality in terms analogous to the generic divisions of literature. And the 'master' term for Zola, 'like science it is master of the world', is equally a generic name in these terms.

The logic of the argument is that the novel is genreless because it can inhabit any and all other genres as need requires, and is therefore not itself a member of any specific and circumscribed genre, and that in recording actuality accurately it inevitably escapes from genre, since actuality is not generic in form. We are back with Blanchot's argument again: *a text which mixes multiple genres is not itself generic*. And, of course, we can also repeat Todorov's point that even if genre is dead, there seems a curious need to continue thinking about how texts behave through generic terminologies. Nevertheless, we should not underestimate the potentially radical nature of the shift from thinking in terms of one genre or another to that of thinking in terms of a rapid succession of genres switching not according to some 'preconceived idea', but because of the shifting nature of reality itself. Certainly, there is a large gap between Aristotle's sense of genre as finally settling into a form ideally suited to its function, Sidney's sense that, properly used, each genre has a distinct social function, and Zola's notion of a genre offering such explanatory and explorative power that it is no longer confined within any normal generic term. □

Whether or not the modern world or modern text needs genre, there is no disputing that we have had it, and that there is a strong tendency to continue employing the names and concepts of genre. Given that literature is categorised in this way, how does labelling actually affect the meaning of texts?[6]

Though I suggested earlier that genre labelling is not an entirely consistent system, it would be incorrect to see it as simply random. There is a hierarchy of genre terms, so that labels become increasingly specific as we go down the scale:

Kind   →   e.g. Poetry
             ↓
Genre   →   Lyric
             ↓
Subgenre   →   Sonnet

Kind   →   e.g. Prose
             ↓
Genre   →   Novel
             ↓
Subgenre   →   Epistolary novel

Kind   →   e.g. Drama
             ↓
Genre   →   Comedy
             ↓

Subgenre → New Comedy (a kind of Greek and Roman comedy, written by, for example, Terence)

To start at the highest of these levels, how much does it matter if a text is labelled poetry rather than prose, prose rather than drama?

> ◆   Read the following two texts and make brief notes for an
> interpretation of each: How much does knowing the *kind* of each
> text influence or help you?

Poetry: Edwin Morgan, 'Spacepoem 3: Off Course'

the golden flood   the weightless seat
the cabin song   the pitch black
the growing beard   the floating crumb
the shining rendezvous   the orbit wisecrack
the hot spacesuit   the smuggled mouth-organ
the imaginary somersault   the visionary sunrise
the turning continents   the space debris
the golden lifeline   the spacewalk
the crawling deltas   the camera moon

the pitch velvet   the rough sleep
the crackling headphone   the space silence
the turning earth   the lifeline continents
the cabin sunrise   the hot flood
the shining spacesuit   the growing moon
    the crackling somersault   the smuggled orbit
    the rough moon   the visionary rendezvous
    the weightless headphone   the cabin debris
    the floating lifeline   the pitch sleep
    the crawling camera   the turning silence
    the space crumb   the crackling beard
    the orbit mouth-organ   the floating song

From Edwin Morgan, *From Glasgow to Saturn* (Manchester, 1973), p. 65.

Prose: George Orwell, *Coming Up for Air*

PART ONE

I

The idea really came to me the day I got my new false teeth.

I remember the morning well. At about a quarter to eight I'd nipped out of bed and got into the bathroom just in time to shut the kids out. It was a beastly January morning, with a dirty yellowish-grey sky. Down below, out of the little square of bathroom window, I could see the ten yards by five of grass, with a privet hedge round it and a bare patch in the middle, that we call the back garden. There's the same back garden, same privets, and same grass, behind every house in Ellesmere Road. Only difference – where there are no kids there's no bare patch in the middle.

I was trying to shave with a bluntish razor-blade while the water ran into the bath. My face looked back at me out of the mirror, and underneath, in a tumbler of water on the little shelf over the washbasin, the teeth that belonged in the face. It was the temporary set that Warner, my dentist, had given me to wear while the new ones were being made. I haven't such a bad face, really. It's one of those bricky-red faces that go with butter-coloured hair and pale-blue eyes. I've never gone grey or bald, thank God, and when I've got my teeth in I probably don't look my age, which is forty-five.

Making a mental note to buy razor-blades, I got into the bath and started soaping. I soaped my arms (I've got those kind of pudgy arms that are freckled up to the elbow) and then took the back-brush and soaped my shoulder-blades, which in the ordinary way I can't reach. It's a nuisance, but there are several parts of my body that I can't reach nowadays. The truth is that I'm inclined to be a little bit on the fat side. I don't mean that I'm like something in a side-show at a fair. My weight isn't much over fourteen stone, and last time I measured round my waist it was either forty-eight or forty-nine, I forget which. And I'm not what they call 'disgustingly' fat, I haven't got one of those bellies that sag half-way down to the knees. It's merely that I'm a little bit broad in the beam, with a tendency to be barrel-shaped. Do you know the active, hearty kind of fat man, the athletic bouncing type that's nicknamed

Fatty or Tubby and is always the life and soul of the party? I'm that type. 'Fatty' they mostly call me. Fatty Bowling, George Bowling is my real name.

But at that moment I didn't feel like the life and soul of the party. And it struck me that nowadays I nearly always do have a morose kind of feeling in the early mornings, although I sleep well and my digestion's good. I knew what it was, of course – it was those bloody false teeth. The things were magnified by the water in the tumbler, and they were grinning at me like the teeth in a skull. It gives you a rotten feeling to have your gums meet, a sort of pinched-up, withered feeling like when you've bitten into a sour apple. Besides, say what you will, false teeth are a landmark. When your last natural tooth goes, the time when you can kid yourself that you're a Hollywood sheik is definitely at an end. And I was fat as well as forty-five. As I stood up to soap my crutch I had a look at my figure. It's all rot about fat men being unable to see their feet, but it's a fact that when I stand upright I can only see the front halves of mine. No woman, I thought as I worked the soap round my belly, will ever look twice at me again, unless she's paid to. Not that at that moment I particularly wanted any woman to look twice at me.

But it struck me that this morning there were reasons why I ought to have been in a better mood. To begin with I wasn't working today. The old car, in which I 'cover' my district (I ought to tell you that I'm in the insurance business. The Flying Salamander. Life, fire, burglary, twins, shipwreck – everything), was temporarily in dock, and though I'd got to look in at the London office to drop some papers, I was really taking the day off to go and fetch my new false teeth. And besides, there was another business that had been in and out of my mind for some time past. This was that I had seventeen quid which nobody else had heard about – nobody in the family, that is. It had happened this way. A chap in our firm, Mellors by name, had got hold of a book called *Astrology applied to Horse-racing* which proved that it's all a question of the influence of the planets on the colours the jockey is wearing. Well, in some race or other there was a mare called Corsair's Bride, a complete outsider, but her jockey's colour was green, which it seemed was just the colour for the planets that happened to be in the ascendant. Mellors, who was deeply bitten with this astrology business, was putting several quid on the horse and went down on his knees to me to do the same. In the end, chiefly to shut him up, I risked ten bob, though I don't bet as a general rule. Sure enough Corsair's Bride came home in a walk. I forget the exact odds, but my share worked out at seventeen quid. By a kind of instinct – rather queer, and probably indicating another landmark in my life – I just quietly put the money in the bank and said nothing to anybody. I'd never done anything of this kind before. A good husband and father would have spent it on a dress for Hilda (that's my wife) and boots for the kids. But I'd been a good husband and father for fifteen years and I was beginning to get fed up with it. ...

From George Orwell, *Coming Up For Air* (1939). Extract from Penguin edn (1983), pp. 7–8.

▶ Discussion

1. POETRY

I think that the mere visual realisation that this text is set out as a poem has a major impact on how we read it. We can see at a glance that this is a short text which can be seen in its entirety on a single page. This makes it much easier to read repeatedly in a short time and to move around in any order we need to. This is consistent with the kind of reading we might expect to make of poetry – involving a recognition of deviant and unusual language uses and then an attempt to make sense of these departures from the norm in terms of an overall meaning for the poem. The short length of the text makes this possible, and our generic expectation of this *kind* is likely to offer us the faith to puzzle away at the meaning of a text which lacks some usual means of easing communication. In this case, for instance, the lack of a main verb might be more disturbing if it occurred (didn't occur) at the end of a longish paragraph of prose. These kinds of expectation encourage us to produce hypotheses which 'make sense' of the poem.[7]

2. PROSE

I suspect that in the case of prose we see the kind as less obviously helpful or important, because it seems merely to signal membership of the class of 'normal writing', unlike the poetic layout of the previous example. However, this very ordinariness does lead us towards certain expectations. It is immediately clear that this is not the whole text that we have before us, that we could not therefore devote minute attention to every word and line *of the whole text* (as we might in a poem) and that the language is thus unlikely to be as resistant to reading or as densely packed with unusual meaning (there are of course, prose works which would entirely defeat this expectation – but it is still the normative one: prose is the kind for every-day use). We would probably not as readers pay very close attention to the details of the language here because of these expectations and are quite likely to regard them as purveyors of background information rather than anything else. Since the passage in question looks very much as if it concerns a markedly ordinary character in a notably ordinary environment, it may well be that here the ordinariness is in fact being strongly fore-grounded – but our normal expectation would not allow us to see that without reading further into the text.[8] □

It seems clear that conceptions of kind are not merely labels externally imposed on texts, but are an internal element of textual production and consumption, including both reading and interpretation. It seems reasonable to assume that this is also true as we go down the scale to genre and subgenre. We can test the omnipresence of genre in literary works by simply looking at the way in which even fragments of texts show signs of genre.

◆ Guess the likely genre and/or subgenre of the texts to which each of the following unidentified extracts belong.
◆ What clues lead you to your supposition?

A. The arrival of the bus was timed to perfection. Nobody of the slightest importance saw it at all. Traffic was slack, the theatres were only halfway through the evening performances, and no police were due on point duty until the after-the-show crush seventy minutes away.

B. In the great hall of Hygelac, King of the Geats, supper was over and the mead horns going round. It was the time of evening, with the dusk gathering beyond the firelight, when the warriors called for Angelm the King's bard to wake his harp for their amusement; but tonight they had something else to listen to than the half-sung, half-told stories of ancient heroes that they knew by heart. Tonight there were strangers in their midst, seafarers with the salt still in their hair, from the first trading ship to reach them since the ice melted and the wild geese came north again.

C. There was once a woman who wished for a very little child; but she did not know where she should procure one. So she went to an old witch and said, 'I do so very much wish for a little child! Can you not tell me where I can get one?'
     'Oh! That could easily be managed,' said the witch.

 Discussion

EXTRACT A

This looks as if it must come from a thriller, probably of a who-done-it kind. It therefore belongs broadly to the novelistic genre, but has a more precise subgenre identification. Even within four lines this is clear from the marked references to the lack of witnesses and the precision about time and place. These details are being signalled as of future importance. Since other kinds of novel do not usually demand that readers pay much attention to precise details about times and who saw what, the concentration on those matters here has an unmistakable impact as a genre marker.

EXTRACT B

This seems to me to have clear marks of being an historical novel. Though obviously set in a heroic past, there seems to be quite a strong desire to inform the reader about life in that past under the guise of setting atmosphere and describing the scene. Thus the phrase 'half-sung, half-told stories' strikes me as being motivated by a wish to give this information about how heroic tales were performed. The story feels like a reconstruction of that age, rather than a story told at the time. I think there is an urge to tell us everything we need to know to understand the setting, whereas an actual Viking saga or Anglo-Saxon epic would take much of this for granted and would contain things that were obscure to the modern reader. In fact, I recognise one of the characters, Hygelac the Geat, as a king who is mentioned in the actual Old English epic *Beowulf*; nevertheless, I don't think this is a translation of an original.

EXTRACT C

I would say that this is a fairy tale. The formulaic opening phrase, 'there was once ... ', the apparently unspectacular presence of the witch, and the rather ritual narration, where the motif about wishing for a *little* child is repeated in full, rather than being summarised, all seem to point to this identification. □

In these three cases, things are what they seem: each of these extracts does indeed come from a text of the most likely sort. The three extracts come from the following three texts:

A.   Margery Allingham's *Hide My Eyes* (1958; an Albert Campion mystery, the book jacket adds).
B.   Rosemary Sutcliff's *Dragon Slayer* (1961; a children's novel based on *Beowulf*).
C.   'Thumbellina' from Hans Christian Andersen's *Fairy Tales*.

(I, of course, inevitably cheated through already knowing what kinds of texts the extract came from – it is at least conceivable that you will have made different identifications without the extremely useful evidence provided by the three book covers, titles, author's name and so on.)

The examples in both the *kinds* and the genre/subgenre exercises all work fairly straightforwardly. However, it's important to realise that this is not always the case. Texts can (and do) sometimes work against or challenge or develop genre expectations. At times, attribution to a generic category is a markedly interpretative matter (Is it a short story or a novella? Poetic prose or a poem? Drama to be performed or drama to be read?).

◆   Read the following two texts: To what kind and genre would you assign them? How do they challenge or work against generic expectations?

Ezra Pound, *In a Station of the Metro*

> The apparition of these faces in the crowd;
> Petals on a wet black bough.

From *The Norton Anthology of Poetry*, 3rd edn, ed. Alexander Allinson et al. (Norton, New York and London, 1983), p. 963. Poem written in 1916.

Gertrude Stein, *The Autobiography of Alice B. Toklas*

BEFORE I CAME TO PARIS

I was born in San Francisco, California. I have in consequence always preferred living in a temperate climate but it is difficult, on the continent of Europe or even in America, to find a temperate climate and live in it. My mother's father was a pioneer, he came to California in '49, he married my grandmother who was very fond of music. She was a pupil of Clara Schumann's father. My mother was a quiet charming woman named Emilie.

My father came of polish patriotic stock. His grand-uncle raised a regiment for Napoleon and was its colonel. His father left his mother just after their marriage, to fight at the barricades in Paris, but his wife having cut off his supplies, he soon returned and led the life of a conservative well to do land owner.

I myself have had no liking for violence and have always enjoyed the pleasures of needlework and gardening. I am fond of paintings, furniture, tapestry, houses and flowers and even vegetables and fruit-trees. I like a view but I like to sit with my back turned to it.

I led in my childhood and youth the gently bred existence of my class and kind. I had some intellectual adventures at this period but very quiet ones. When I was about nineteen years of age I was a great admirer of Henry James. I felt that The Awkward Age would make a very remarkable play and I wrote to Henry James suggesting that I dramatise it. I had from him a delightful letter on the subject and then, when I felt my inadequacy, rather blushed for myself and did not keep the letter. Perhaps at that time I did not feel that I was justified in preserving it, at any rate it no longer exists.

Up to my twentieth year I was seriously interested in music. I studied and practised assiduously but shortly then it seemed futile, my mother had died and there was no unconquerable sadness, but there was no real interest that led me on. In the story Ada in Geography and Plays Gertrude Stein has given a very good description of me as I was at that time.

From then on for about six years I was well occupied. I led a pleasant life, I had many friends, much amusement, many interests, my life was reasonably full and I enjoyed it but I was not very ardent in it. This brings me to the San Francisco fire which had as a consequence that the elder brother of Gertrude Stein and his wife came back from Paris to San Francisco and this led to a complete change in my life.

I was at this time living with my father and brother. My father was a quiet man who took things quietly, although he felt them deeply. The first terrible morning of the San Francisco fire I woke him and told him, the city has been rocked by an earthquake and is now on fire. That will give us a black eye in the East, he replied turning and going to sleep again. I remember that once when my brother and a comrade had gone horse-back riding, one of the horses returned riderless to the hotel, the mother of the other boy began to make a terrible scene. Be calm madam, said my father, perhaps it is my son who has been killed. One of his axioms I always remember, if you must do a thing do it graciously. He also told me that a hostess should never apologise for any failure in her household arrangements, if there is a hostess there is insofar as there is a hostess no failure.

As I was saying we were all living comfortably together and there had been in my mind no active desire or thought of change. The disturbance of the routine of our lives by the fire followed by the coming of Gertrude Stein's older brother and his wife made the difference.

Mrs. Stein brought with her three little Matisse paintings, the first modern things to cross the Atlantic. I made her acquaintance at this time of general upset and she showed them to me, she also told me many stories of her life in Paris. Gradually I told my father that perhaps I would leave San Francisco. He was not disturbed by this, after all there was at that time a great deal of going and coming and there were many friends of mine going. Within a year

I also had gone and I had come to Paris. There I went to see Mrs. Stein who had in the meantime returned to Paris, and there at her house I met Gertrude Stein. I was impressed by the coral brooch she wore and by her voice. I may say that only three times in my life have I met a genius and each time a bell within me rang and I was not mistaken, and I may say in each case it was before there was any general recognition of the quality of genius in them. The three geniuses of whom I wish to speak are Gertrude Stein, Pablo Picasso and Alfred Whitehead. I have met many important people, I have met several great people but I have only known three first class geniuses and in each case on sight within me something rang. In no one of the three cases have I been mistaken. In this way my new full life began.

From Gertrude Stein, *The Autobiography of Alice B. Toklas* (1933). Extract from Penguin edn (1977), pp. 1–3.

▶ Discussion

1. POUND

I would say this is a poem – but it certainly does challenge normal expectations, primarily through its brevity. Though modern poetry is dominated by the short lyric, this is exceptionally short to the point where the usual 'modernist' reading which we apply to short poems is challenged. There is very little 'whole' against which to test hypotheses about detail, and for that matter very little detail to make it cohere into an overall reading. On the other hand, it is possible to make a modernist reading work, and to feel satisfaction in so doing. The poem lacks a main verb, and the two lines therefore are not grammatically related. We are therefore invited to supply a connection between the 'faces' and the 'petals': perhaps the second line is a simile and we need to supply the word 'like'? However, we could argue that the impact is much stronger for the wordlessness of the comparison, the need to grasp the similarity/the simile in one sudden insight.[9] Thus this text can be read like a poem and does fulfil generic expectation – but somewhat against expectations.

2. STEIN

The title suggests that this will be an autobiography of Alice B. Toklas, but the author's name is Gertrude Stein, not that of the autobiographical subject. The fundamental convention of the autobiography, as described by Todorov, is thus challenged. Therefore, it would be rash to identify it as an autobiography – unless I decided that it was in fact an autobiography of Stein (which in many respects, it is). I could alternatively call it a biography if I felt that it was really focused on Alice B. Toklas, but the opening does not readily confirm this. The effect on the way in which Stein is talked about/talks about herself is notable and does challenge the conventions used in talking about oneself. □

Both of these are Modernist examples, and arise in an aesthetic movement which particularly valued experiment and resistance to convention. However, it is also the case that genre expectations can shift over time, and bring readers up against generic expectations they may not find easy. Students commonly find very long poems somewhat resistant to reading and study. Milton's *Paradise Lost* is the obvious example. Though there may, of course, be specific difficulties arising from this text, there may also be a more general problem with generic expectations. During the twentieth century, poetry as a kind has been dominated by short lyric forms to the point where it has become difficult for the uninitiated to conceive of poetry as anything but brief and concentrated. The very idea of reading a poem of 12 books and thousands of lines is often met with (initial?) disbelief. And, indeed, a long poem does require a very different approach from a short lyric. Instead of requiring concentrated reading and re-reading and interpretation of, say, less than a page of text, a long poem requires long periods of reading and responses partially akin to those required by a long prose narrative (such as a novel). This modern generic expectation has certainly not always been the case – during the eighteenth and nineteenth centuries many readers relatively 'uninitiated' in formal learning read Milton without any difficulty. As we shall see in the next section, genre is far from static, and is concerned with forgetfulness and innovation, as well as with continuity. Finally in this section I will, as usual, leave you to your own arguments about the final exercise – based on a short rather than an epic poetic form.

> ◆ Read the following poem: How much of its meaning is determined by generic conventions (literary or otherwise)?

William Carlos Williams, 'This is Just to Say'

This is Just to Say

I have eaten
the plums
that were in
the icebox

and which
you were probably
saving
for breakfast

Forgive me
they were delicious
so sweet
and so cold

From *The Norton Anthology of Poetry*, 3rd edn, ed. Alexander Allinson et al. (New York and London, 1983), pp. 945–6. Poem first published 1934.

3.2 The Meanings of Genre

The last section introduced a number of ideas and problems arising from the notion of genre as a system of categories. Here we will focus more on the *meanings* of individual genres (though, of course, those meanings presumably take place within – or at least in relation to? – a generic system).

At various points in section 3.1, I mentioned in passing a number of examples of historical changes in the meanings of generic terms:

'Poetry' could refer to all *literature* in the seventeenth century (as in Sir Philip Sidney's *A Defense of Poesie*).

Satire was, before the nineteenth century, a fairly specific verse form; later it referred more to an approach than a form, but was, and is, most found in prose forms, sometimes novelistic.

The novel was a term signifying low and often 'non-literary' genres for much of the eighteenth century; from the mid-nineteenth century on it often signified a serious literary work.

Pastoral was most frequently a verse form with associated specific characteristics in the sixteenth, seventeenth and eighteenth centuries (though with considerable impact in prose works and in drama too), but thereafter a much more general term referring to certain attitudes and subject matter in a range of genres.

Every term we have looked at so far – literature, text, author   has been subject to historical variation, so it is no surprise to find this of genre terms too. However, it is, perhaps, slightly alarming to find that this system for differentiating and relating family members is so affected by change. For, if one of the main functions of genre is to govern and shape meaning and understanding, then constant change threatens to be potentially very disruptive. Indeed, if there is no continuity between seventeenth-century genre categories and the same genre terms (and genres?) over the next three centuries, then to what extent is genre working at all reliably in making distinctions and resemblances readable? One response to this query would be to say that, of course, genre is not a static system, but one which evolves constantly in all its constituent parts, and thus as a whole. This is fine, but makes it all the clearer why we need to gain a better sense of how genre retains continuity and/or changes. This is important in a number of ways:

1. For seeing how individual texts can be related to genre conventions.
2. For understanding 'tradition and the individual talent'.
3. For understanding how changes within genres might happen, and their possible significance.
4. For exploring what kind of membership genre confers.

This section will explore these issues through a case-study of a particular genre, pastoral, as it is realised through a number of English texts over a period of 400 years, but which have their roots in an ancient Greek genre. Pastoral may have its individual peculiarities, but can serve as a model for the kinds of issues which arise in what could be called the *life* of a genre.

Case Study: Some Versions of Pastoral

A brief off-the-cuff definition of Pastoral was given as part of my answer to the first exercise in section 3.1, and a further definition was given in a passage taken from Sidney in a later exercise. Before looking at quite a number of pastoral texts, it might be helpful to return to these definitions and to add a twentieth-century definition. These definitions may not, of course, wholly match the actual examples which follow; the description of genre is never simple and 'definite', whether working with examples of a genre or with 'metadiscursive' discourses about a genre. Indeed, this problem is at the centre of this section: *how much* does a genre label specify, how much continuity is there in discourses of genre? what does genre determine?

DEFINITIONS OF PASTORAL

My note from section 3.1

> Not principally a specific form, but rather a set of attitudes and features applied to a range of kinds (short poems, plays or parts of plays, and prose works, including some novels); features include a rustic or otherwise primitive setting and characters, and a sense (often nostalgic) of the special values – profound yet simple – of that milieu.

Sir Philip Sidney, from The Defense of Poesie *(repeated from section 3.1)*

> Is it then the Pastoral Poem which is misliked? (For perchance, where the hedge is lowest they will soonest leape over.) Is the poor pype disdained, which sometime out of Melibeus' mouth can shew the miserie of people under hard Lords or ravening souldiours? And again, by Titrius, what blessednes is derived to them that lye lowest from the goodnesse of them that sit highest? Sometime under the prettie tales of Wolves and Sheepe, can include the whole consideration of wrong dooing and patience; sometimes shew that contention for trifles can get but a trifling victorie …

William Empson, from 'Proletarian Literature' in Some Versions Of Pastoral *(1935)*

> The essential trick of the old pastoral, which was felt to imply a beautiful relation between rich and poor, was to make simple people express strong feelings (felt as the most universal subject, something fundamentally true about everybody) in learned and fashionable language (so that you wrote about the best subject in the best way). From seeing the two sorts of people

combined like this you thought better of both; the best parts of both were used.

...

The convention was, of course, often absurdly artificial ... so it was much parodied, especially to make the poor man worthy but ridiculous, as often in Shakespeare; nor is this merely snobbish when used in its full form. The simple man becomes a clumsy fool who yet has better 'sense' than his betters and can say things more fundamentally true; 'he is contact with nature' ... he can speak the truth because he has nothing to lose. (pp. 11–13 in the Hogarth edition of 1986.)

> ◆ Now read the following poem, a sixteenth-century English translation
> of a poem by the classical Greek author Theocritus, regarded as the
> founder of 'pastoral'; list any features which you regard as 'pastoral'.
> ◆ How closely does the text correspond to the metadiscursive accounts
> of pastoral above?

Theocritus, *Polyphemus to Galatea*

O Galatea faire, why dost thou shun thy lover true?
More tender than a Lambe, more white than cheese when it is new,
More wanton than a calfe, more sharpe than grapes unripe I finde.
You use to come, when pleasant sleepe my senses all doe binde.
But you are gone againe, when pleasant sleepe dooth leave mine eie,
And as a sheep you run, that on the plaine a Woolf doth spie.
I then began to love thee, Galate, when first of all
You with my mother came, to gather leaves of Crowtoe small
Upon our hill, when I as usher, squirde you all the waie.
Nor when I saw thee first, not afterward, nor at this daie,
Since then I could refraine, but you, by Jove, nought set thereby.
But well I knowe fair Nimphe, the verie cause why you thus flie.
Because upon my front, one onlie brow, with bristles strong
From one eare to the other is stretched all along.
Nethe which one eie, and on my lipps a hugie nose there standes.
Yet I, this such a one, a thousand sheep feed on these lands.
And pleasant milke I drinke, which from the strouting bags is prest
Nor want I cheese in summer, nor in Autumne of the best,
Nore yet in winter time. My cheese-rackes ever laden are,
And better can I pipe than any Cyclops maie compare.

...

Come forth, faire Galate, and once got out, forget thee well
(As I doe sitting on this rocke) home to return againe.
But feede my sheepe with me, and for to milke them take the paine,
And cheese to presse, and in the milke, the rennet sharpe to straine.
My mother only wrongeth me, and her I blame, for shee
Spake never yet to thee, one goode or lovelie word of me,
And that although she daily sees how I awaie do pine.

...

O Cyclops, Cyclops, whither is thy wit and reason flowne?
If thou wouldst baskets make, and cut downe browzing from the tree,
And bring it to thy lambes, a great deal wiser thou shouldst be!
Goe, Coie some present Nimphe, why dost thou follow flying wind?
Perhaps an other Galate, and fairer thou shalt find.
For manie maidens in the evening tide with me will plaie,
And all doe sweetly laugh, when I stand harkning what they saie,
And O some bodie seeme, and in the earth doe beare a swaie.

From *Idyll* xi, ll. 19–79. This translation by an unknown author comes from a manuscript in the Bodleian Library, Oxford, known as the *Sixe Idillia*, dated to 1588; reprinted in *The Oxford Book of Greek Verse in Translation*, ed. T. F. Higham and C. M. Bowra (Oxford, 1938), pp. 557–60.

▶ Discussion 1

Clearly, there is a rustic setting, and specifically one with shepherds. Thus the poem's speaker, Polyphemus (a Cyclops) refers frequently to his sheep, and even when he uses metaphors, these equally refer to his vocation as a shepherd: 'more tender than a lambe, more white than cheese when it is new'. The problematic relationship between shepherd and shepherdess also seems a characteristically pastoral theme. □

▶ Discussion 2

The poem certainly has general features described in the three definitions. There is 'a rustic or otherwise primitive setting and characters', it is a tale of 'sheepe', if not of wolves, and it does seem to make 'simple people express strong feelings' and express 'values profound yet simple'. However, there are many features mentioned in the definitions which are not clearly or at all present, and some features of the poem not alluded to by the definitions. Thus none of the definitions refer to love and its obstacles as a pastoral feature. Neither do any of them mention that a pastoral shepherd may be specific figures from the ancient Greek world, such as Polyphemus, the Cyclops whom Odysseus blinds in *The Odyssey* (they do not exclude the possibility, but their shepherds sound more anonymous, 'generic' figures). Sidney's arguments about the value of pastoral do not seem to apply at all well to this example: thus there is little here of his sense of pastoral as being about the relations of social hierarchies – 'the miserie of people under hard Lords or ravening souldiours? And what … blessednes is derived to them that lye lowest from the goodnesse of them that sit highest?'. I wonder also about Empson's 'strong feelings in fashionable language' and his idea that 'from seeing the two sorts of people combined like this you thought better of both; the best parts of both were used'. It is perhaps difficult to judge how primitive Polpyhemus's language is meant to seem, but lines such as:

> Because upon my front, one onlie brow with bristles strong
> From one eare to the other is stretched all along

do not seem likely to appear obviously sophisticated. Indeed, more generally in the poem one might feel that simplicity is on the verge of passing into
clumsiness as much as into profundity. How profound is Polyphemus' argument that no girl could resist a man who makes so much cheese? ('My
cheese rackes ever laden are'). It may be that the comic possibilities of the
genre which Empson raises at the end of his account are here even from the
beginning, and that part of the effect of this poem is to allow the reader –
presumably not a shepherd – to enjoy the simplicity and laugh at its naïvety.

None of these discrepancies necessarily proves that the poem is not
pastoral or that the definitions are inadequate. But they do suggest that
definition and particular example are not always (or ever?) easily matched.
And that suggests a family resemblance or group with some room for
manoeuvre within it. □

◆ Read the following poem: How similar/different is it to the Theocritus
pastoral?

Christopher Marlowe, *The Passionate Shepherd to His Love*

Come live with me and be my love,
And we will all the pleasures prove
That valleys, groves, hills and fields,
Woods, or steepy mountain yields.

And we will sit upon the rocks,
Seeing the shepherds feed their flocks,
By shallow rivers to whose falls
Melodious birds sing madrigals.

And I will make thee beds of roses
And a thousand fragrant posies,
A cap of flowers and a kyrtle
Embroidered all with leaves of myrtle;

A gown made of the finest wool
Which from our pretty lambs we pull;
Fair lined slippers for the cold,
With buckles of the purest gold;

A belt of straw and ivy buds,
With coral clasps and amber studs:
And if these pleasures may thee move,
Come live with me, and be my love.

The shepherds' swains shall dance and sing
For thy delight each May morning:
If these delights thy mind may move,
Then live with me and be my love.

From *The Norton Anthology of Poetry,* 3rd edn, ed. Alexander Allinson et al. (New York and London, 1983), pp. 813–14. Poem first published 1599, 1600.

Discussion

There certainly are similarities: both poems have as their speakers a shepherd addressing a shepherdess whom they would like to be their 'love'; both share a general rustic setting. However, the rusticity is of a very different sort. Instead of exceptionally high cheese yields, and ewes with 'strouting bags', we have melodious birds who sing madrigals, beds of roses and finest wool (as an alternative sheep product). This is a more idealised view of sheep farming, offering more sophisticated pleasures – though still markedly simple ones. This simple nobility seems more akin to that envisaged by Empson – and here we might hear a fashionable yet simple language. The conclusion of the address too seems somewhat more sophisticated. Where Polyphemus was left blaming his mother and suddenly realising that there are plenty more shepherdesses in the field, Marlowe's speaker leaves his addressee to contemplate whether such pleasures are indeed the most profound that can be imagined. Indeed, one might suspect that the artful or artificial simplicity of this pastoral is acknowledged even within the poem. Perhaps the phrase 'If these delights thy *mind* may move' indicates that these delights are imaginary rather than actual, that they are images performed by the poem as much as anything that could really exist. Perhaps the sophistication required from the shepherdess is similar to that required from the reader – who needs both to appreciate the simplicity and to see that it is a work of art, not nature. □

Now read the following texts; for each note briefly any features which you think might represent departures, additions or omissions from/to 'the pastoral tradition'.

Sir Walter Raleigh, 'The Nymph's Reply to the Shepherd'

If all the world and love were young,
And truth in every shepherd's tongue,
These pretty pleasures might me move
To live with thee and be thy love.

Time drives the flocks from field to fold
When rivers rage and rocks grow cold,
And Philomel becometh dumb;
The rest complains of cares to come.

The flowers do fade, and wanton fields
To wayward winter reckoning yields;
A honey tongue, a heart of gall,
Is fancy's spring, but sorrow's fall.

Thy gowns, thy shoes, thy beds of roses,
Thy cap, thy kirtle, and thy posies
Soon break, soon wither, soon forgotten –
In folly ripe, in reason rotten.

Thy belt of straw and ivy buds,
Thy coral clasps and amber studs,
All these in me no means can move
To come to thee and be thy love.

But could youth last and love still breed,
Had joys no date nor age no need,
Then these delights my mind might move
To live with thee and be thy love.

From *The Norton Anthology of Poetry*, 3rd edn, ed. Alexander Allinson et al.
(New York and London, 1983), pp. 105–6. Poem written in 1600.

Andrew Marvell, 'The Mower Against Gardens'

Luxurious man, to bring his vice in use,
Did after him the world seduce,
And from the fields the flowers and plants allure,
Where Nature most was plain and pure.
He first enclosed within the gardens square
A dead and standing pool of air,
And a more luscious earth for them did kneade,
Which stupefied them while it fed.
The pink grew then as double as his mind;
The nutriment did change the kind.
With strange perfumes he did the roses taint;
And flowers themselves were taught to paint.
The tulip white did for complexion seek,
And learned to interline its cheek;
Its onion root they then so high did hold,
That one was for a meadow sold:
Another world was searched through oceans new,
To find the marvel of Peru;
And yet these rarities might be allowed
To man that sovereign thing and proud,

Had he not dealt between the bark and tree,
Forbidden mixtures there to see.
No plant now knew the stock from which it came;
He grafts upon the wild the tame,
That the uncertain and the adulterate fruit
Might put the palate in dispute.
His green seraglio has its eunuchs too,
Lest any tyrant him outdo;
And in the cherry he does Nature vex,
To procreate without a sex.
'Tis all enforced, the fountain and the grot,
While the sweet fields do lie forgot,
Where willing Nature does to all dispense
A wild and fragrant innocence;
And fauns and fairies do the meadows till
More by their presence than their skill.
Their statues polished by some ancient hand,
May to adorn the gardens stand;
But howsoe'er the figures do excel,
The gods themselves with us do dwell.

From *The Norton Anthology of Poetry*, 3rd edn, ed. Alexander Allinson et al. (New York and London, 1983), pp. 342–3. Published posthumously in 1681; probably written many years earlier.

Earl of Rochester, 'A Song: To Chloris'

Fair Chloris in a Pig-Stye lay,
Her tender Herd lay by her:
She slept, in murmuring gruntlings they,
Complaining of the scorching Day,
Her slumbers thus inspire.

She dreamt, while she with careful pains
Her Snowy Arms employ'd,
In Ivory pails, to fill out Grains,
One of her Love-convicted Swains,
Thus hasting to her cry'd:

Flie, Nymphe, oh! flie, e're 'tis too late,
A dear-lov'd life to save:
Rescue your Bosom Pig from Fate,
Who now expires, hung in the gate
That leads to yonder Cave.

My self had try'd to set him free,
Rather than brought the News:
But I am so abhor'd by thee,
That even thy Darlings life from me,
I know thou wou'dst refuse.

Struck with the News, as quick she flies
As blushes to her Face:
Not the bright lightening from the Skies,
Nor Love, shot from her brighter Eyes,
Moves half so swift a Pace.

This Plot, it seems, the lustful Slave
Has laid against her Honour:
Which not one God took care to save;
For he persues her to the Cave,
And throws himself upon her.

Now pierced is her Virgin Zone,
She feels the Foe within it;
She hears a broken amorous Groan,
The panting Lover's fainting moan,
Just in the happy Minute.

Frighted she wakes, and waking Friggs,
Nature thus kindly eas'd,
In Dreams rais'd by her murmuring piggs,
And her own thumb between her Leggs,
She innocent and pleas'd.

Poem XXIV from *Poems by John Wilmot, Earl of Rochester*, ed. Vivian De Sola Pinto (London, 1953); the final stanza printed in this edition's notes is here included, as it was in versions of the poem published in 1680 and 1685.

R. S. Thomas, 'Iago Prytherch'

Iago Prytherch, forgive my naming you.
You are so far in your small fields
From the world's eye, sharpening your blade
On a cloud's edge, no one will tell you
How I made fun of you, or pitied either
Your long soliloquies, crouched at your slow
And patient surgery under the faint
November rays of the sun's lamp.

Made fun of you? That was their graceless
Accusation, because I took
Your rags for theme, because I showed them
Your thought's bareness; science and art,
The mind's furniture, having no chance
To install themselves, because of the great
Draught of nature sweeping the skull.

Fun? Pity? No word can describe
My true feelings. I passed and saw you

Labouring there, your dark figure
Marring the simple geometry
Of the square fields with its gaunt question.
My poems were made in its long shadow
Falling coldly across the page.

From R. S. Thomas, *Poetry for Supper* (London, 1967).

Ralph Bates, *The Olive Field*

The couple approached the tree which Caro pointed out, and Lucia stood still while he walked round it slowly several times. Then he came to her side, and laying his hand upon the smooth young bark he said: 'We'll make a branch grow out of here. That will balance the tree and make it like a tripod...'

...

Caro did not at once begin work, but remained by Lucia's side regarding the tree gravely. It was a healthy young tree, slender of trunk and delicate of limb, and its bark was smooth and light in hue, having that tender appearance which told him of the sap moving up from the roots to the topmost clusters of leaf... Something in the tree pleased him, and it was a pleasure he could not have described... It seemed that the olives were the very spirit of that land, and, at peace with it and its iron law, stood patiently regarding the dry unnurturing soil from which the sun's fierce round mouth had long ago sucked all the juices, content laboriously to move the little sap it afforded and content also at length to produce their little green and red and purpleblack fruit.

...

He was silent a while, working the knife into the bark with firm and deliberate pressure. The girl did not move or speak, watching him with absorbed interest, though she had seen this shield-grafting done many, many times.

From Ralph Bates, *The Olive Field* (London, 1986), pp. 42–4. First published 1936.

 Discussion

RALEIGH

This particular text shows an obvious continuity with the pastoral tradition as represented by Marlowe's poem, at any rate, but by the same token suggests an addition or room for debate within the genre, since it is an answer to that poem. Raleigh's poem responds to the artificiality of the Marlowe poem – perhaps specifically the imaginary nature of its alluring 'delights' – by creating the reply of a critical 'nymph' (rather than shepherdess). This speaker picks up the images from Marlowe's shepherd, but adds a more 'realistic', less innocent context. Indeed, where Marlowe's poem ends with an 'If', this poem begins with one: 'If all the world and love were young / And truth in every shepherd's tongue'. The point may be to begin by pointing out the artifice, even the deceit, of the Shepherd's vision, rather than leading up to that artifice as the supreme moment of the poem. In the world imagined by this nymph, every delight is matched by a negative which naturally ensues: shepherd's words are not always the exact truth, time passes, winter comes, the flocks must seek shelter, rivers rage, Philomel, having been raped, loses her voice, all have anxieties for things which may yet happen and so on. If the poem does not quite show the life of shepherds under Sidney's hard lords and ravening soldiers, it does at least gesture towards the harshness of a shepherd's life in itself. If the poem does not have Polyphemus's rustic obsession with his cheese stores, it does reintroduce a certain counter-current of reality and loss. In these ways, Raleigh's poem might seem to have anti-pastoral elements in emphasising what such a life might really be like, rather than what it might be imagined as.

On the other hand, the last verse does return to the imaginative 'if' of Marlowe's shepherd: 'But could youth last and love still breed / ... Then these delights my mind might move'. Having pointed to the dangerous artificiality of Marlowe's poem's delights, this poem could itself be said to acknowledge the appeal of that imaginary and timeless pastoral vision. Perhaps Raleigh states more openly what is already there in Marlowe's poem – that this vision can never be literally grasped. Both poems might be said to show considerable continuity with pastoral traditions – picking up and making explicit an inherent artificiality of the tradition, resulting from the gap between the sophisticated reader imagining simplicity from a distance and the inhabitants of that simple world.

MARVELL

Again there are continuities here. The speaker is a rustic figure – though a mower rather than a shepherd, and therefore associated with work on a farm, rather than out in pastures. That apart, though, there is not that much left of the familiar shepherd's world: no sheep, no shepherdesses, no love – though we do return to the fields at the end of the poem. Instead, the poem and its speaker are concerned with articulating a view about something which it takes as the contrary of 'pastoral': gardens. Nevertheless, there is some familiar ground in this topic. The problem with gardens is that they have made nature itself into artifice. Man has brought wild flowers into the garden, has enclosed them and altered even their nature and colours. Despite the lack of love interest in the poem, there is a strong vein of sexual language: the flowers and plants were seduced and allured; the artificially enriched earth of the garden is corruptly luxurious, stupefying the plants and making them false to their kind, causing them to paint and 'interline' their cheeks (i.e. to use make-up). Thus flowers become as untrue as man. Indeed, the garden is an essentially fallen world here – the association between the garden and sexual depravity links it to the garden of Eden and the forbidden fruit (note the poem's 'Forbidden mixtures' and 'the adulterate fruit'). In the end this licence to make plants into anything even unsexes them entirely, producing 'eunuchs' – but ones who paradoxically can reproduce. But this profusion is 'all enforced', a result of loss not gain. The poem ends by referring to a more authentic pastoral nature which carries on without artifice, where 'a wild and fragrant innocence' is produced uncontrolledly by 'presence' rather than 'skill'. It is not the images of the gods, but where the gods dwell which matters.

This seems the greatest departure so far from 'pastoral tradition', but nevertheless, the oppositions between artifice and nature are familiar, as is the sense of regrettable loss which arises in Raleigh's poem. It could even be said that, as in Marlowe's poem, there is actually a strong sense within the poem of the artificiality of the imagined world of innocence, which helps to construct the appeal of what is precisely not immediately available. For this mower is hardly an average seventeenth-century farmworker, presumably. His language is elaborate and sophisticated, and he is highly knowledgeable about the latest devices of seventeenth-century horticulture. He, and his world where English mowers believe in classical gods and fauns (I'm more prepared to accept fairies as indigenous), may be as much an artifice designed to allow the sophisticated to imagine an enjoyment of nature as is the garden.

ROCHESTER

Here we again have the basic rusticity of pastoral, though this is the first time we have met a pig-keeper. In fact, the pigs seems more than incidental – they suggest a more mundane reality than the usual 'lambs', and the poem stresses their physicality, with their gruntlings and murmurings. There are signs of deliberately bathetic effects (i.e. comic switches in level). Thus in the first verse 'fair Chloris in a pig-stye lay' suggests a clash of styles and worlds, a contrast also sustained with the poetic register of 'complaining' and 'inspire' (especially applied to pigs). These two worlds are made even more explicit by the poem's use of Chloris's inset dream. In the dream, she uses a more obviously pastoral poetic language than the narrator uses of her in the opening and closing verses (though there are bathetic effects here too as in the casual 'And throws himself upon her'). This bathos is not entirely new – Polyphemus comes close to a descent into the ridiculous, as we noted – but the sexual content of the poem is something we have not met before. In the examples in this case study, there is usually a stress on innocent love (which in pastoral probably includes a notion of 'sex' as essentially natural and innocent). Here, there is (presumably) a rape within the dream (portrayed without comment as Chloris's fantasy), and in the last verse Chloris masturbates (friggs rhyming with piggs suggesting a certain basic rusticity, I assume).

This would seem to be a departure – and could be seen as a leaving behind of anything like our normal expectations of pastoral. However, it could be suggested that even this explicit sexual content arises from a sense of the genre. Perhaps, Chloris in enjoying her pastoral sexual fantasy is to be seen as like the reader of pastoral in general – who knows very well that there is a gap between the imagined and the reality. And Chloris, like the pastoral reader, is at the end of the poem both 'innocent and pleas'd'. She has not interacted with reality in her fantasy, but she is safe and happy. Perhaps this poem, unlike Raleigh's reply to Marlowe, is a defence, in its own (Rochesteresque) way, of the delights of the imagination?[10]

R. S. THOMAS

In this twentieth-century poem we seem to have come quite a distance from the conventional scenery and personae of pastoral. Gone are the classical setting and arcadian shepherds and shepherdesses. However, Iago Prytherch is certainly a farmer (and probably keeps sheep). Moreover, I think the poem has a strong consciousness of the pastoral tradition OR, at least, creates unconsciously a situation where many of the features of pastoral are reproduced. Thus though the poem does not draw attention to the artificial or imaginary nature of its vision – on the contrary – it does show a great interest in the gap between poet (and reader) and the 'simple man' who is the poem's subject. In fact, this gap is the poem's central concern. It starts by addressing the subject, Iago Prytherch, asking forgiveness for 'naming' him, for making him the subject of poetry. But as the second stanza suggests, it is unlikely that Iago Prytherch has heard of the poem, and the direct address of poet to farmer seems likely to be a fiction too, a palpable device of the poem, not an attempt at bridging the gap. Nevertheless, the poem is acutely aware that the poet has been representing the farmer for his own purposes or has been seen as so doing: 'How I made fun of you, or pitied ...'. But the second stanza goes on to argue that this 'graceless / Accusation' is actually the misunderstanding of the pseudo-sophisticated, who can imagine only these two attitudes of superiority to the 'simple man'. The poet did, indeed, show Iago Prytherch's utter simplicity, his lack of any culture, 'your thought's bareness'. There are, though, other ways of looking at this bareness, though 'culture' has no ready-made language for it: 'No word can describe / my true feelings'. Prytherch's simplicity is not one that can be mastered and made to perform a simple function for the articulate; it asks a profound yet unarticulable question (the 'gaunt question' that the poem never asks, but can only refer to). There is no means to bridge the gap between Iago Prythrch and 'us', but for this poem that is the point. There is no explanation of such bareness – it really is a simplicity which is profoundly alternative. The poem thus engages a critical sense of the artificiality of pastoral by arguing for the reality of this kind of vision. One could, of course, say that ascribing such a point of view to Iago Prytherch is patently an act of imagination on the poet's part – but actually the poet does no such thing. The vision is inspired in the poet *by* Iago Prytherch – the gap between articulate and inarticulate produces it (though that does require Iago to be completely inarticulate ...). I would say there is a deep continuity between pastoral traditions and this poem, though it is more interested in talking *about* imagining the 'simple man', than in actually imagining him.

BATES

This extract from a novel is clearly different in not being a poem, but then there certainly are prose-works from the seventeenth century onwards which can be called pastoral. It does have a clearly rural setting and does have a pair of lovers, whose tending of the olive trees is obviously central to the effect of the passage (the novel's title suggests the olive trees are central to the whole text). The passage dwells on the skills of grafting olive trees in a way which makes it a ritual, suggesting communion with nature in an unartificial, direct way, through a working relationship. The harshness of this natural world is referred to – 'the dry unnurturing soil', the 'iron law' of the land – but Caro and Lucia both take great satisfaction in the work. They are close to the land and the trees and to each other; the closeness and pleasure are beyond language (fashionable or otherwise):[11] 'Something in the tree pleased him and it was a pleasure he could not have described'.

So far, my reading here seems to suggest an authentic pastoral; I haven't used the word artificial that has figured in so many of my answers to this exercise. And, indeed, I do not think this passage does draw any attention to artificiality or an imagined world of nature. Instead, it actually tries to evoke a sense of closeness to the natural world (perhaps the generally realist *kind* of the novel plays a part in this?). I think this might constitute a major difference between this passage and all the others (and depending how you define pastoral, perhaps it disqualifies this text from membership?). However, if one turns to the probable reader of the novel at the time of publication or since, this may reintroduce an element of reconstruction at least. I assume that the book was and is in general more likely to be read by city-dwellers than olive growers. This does not render its attempted authentic evocation of a pastoral mood artificial, but it does suggest that contact with this agricultural world is inevitably imaginative rather than actual for most readers. Moreover, if I can cheat by introducing information from outside this extract, the whole novel concerns the abandonment of this way of life in Spain, as the main characters are variously forced from their traditional occupation by political conflict with the landowning classes. Some characters move to the mining area of Asturias, where, eventually, political commitment to political struggle makes some restitution of the organic unity they felt as workers in the olive fields. In the context of the leftist politics of the nineteen thirties it might be that the pastoral feeling evoked by the passage, the sense of meaningful work and social relations arising from it, could be seen as an image of the kind of social relations which might again exist under communism. Empson at any rate saw this kind of 'proletarian writing' as a modern form of pastoral, though he did stress its artificiality. □

Finally in this section read the following extract from an essay by T. S. Eliot. Bearing its ideas in mind, consider the following more general questions which stem from the case study on pastoral.

1. Judging from the case study, how much room for innovation or variation is there in a particular genre?
2. How much of the meaning of an individual text do you think is determined by genre?
3. Could we manage (better?) without attempting to classify texts by genre, by responding to their individuality, not to their (quasi?) membership of a 'class'?

T. S. Eliot, 'Tradition and the Individual Talent'

One of the facts that might come to light in this process [of criticism] is our tendency to insist. When we praise a poet upon those aspects of his work in which he least resembles anyone else, in these aspects or parts of his work we pretend to find what is individual, what is the peculiar essence of the man. We dwell with satisfaction upon the poet's difference from his predecessors, especially his immediate predecessors; we endeavor to find something that can be isolated in order to be enjoyed. Whereas if we approach a poet without this prejudice we shall often find that not only the best, but the most individual parts of his work may be those in which the dead poets, his ancestors, assert their immortality most vigorously. And I do not mean the impressionable period of adolescence, but the period of full maturity.

Yet if the only form of tradition, of handing down, consisted in following the ways of the immediate generation before us in a blind or timid adherence to its successes, 'tradition' should be positively discouraged. . . .

No poet, no artist of any art, has his complete meaning alone. His significance, his appreciation is the appreciation of his relation to the dead poets and artists. You cannot value him alone; you must see him, for contrast and comparison, among the dead. I mean this as a principle of aesthetic, not merely historical, criticism. The necessity that he shall conform, that he shall cohere, is not one-sided; what happens when a new work of art is created is something that happens simultaneously to all the works of art which preceded it. The existing monuments form an ideal order among themselves, which is modified by the introduction of the new (the really new) work of art among them. The existing order is complete before the new work arrives; for order to persist after the supervention of novelty, the *whole* existing order must be, if ever so slightly, altered; and so the relations, proportions, values of each work of art towards the whole are readjusted; and this is conformity between the old and the new. Whoever has approved this order, of the form of European, of English literature will not find it preposterous that the past should be altered by the present as much as the present is directed by the past.

From *T. S. Eliot: Selected Essays* (London, 1932), pp. 13–22; extract is from pp. 14–15. Essay first published in 1919.

3.3 Switching Genres

So far, genre has been discussed as a system and in terms of meaning within an individual genre. However, we should return to a curious but important tendency in genre briefly introduced above in section 3.1. There it was noted that genre had a tendency not only to historical change, but also to hybridisation, such as modification by another generic term. Additionally, it should be noticed that a single text does not always remain fully, or clearly, within a single genre throughout. And, indeed, a text can be *adapted* from one kind or genre to another (for example, a novel can be adapted as a play or a play can be made into a novel). Hence the term taken for the title of this section, 'genre switching'. The section will explore what these three broadly related effects – hybridisation, genre switching, adaptation – can tell us about genre, its functions and significance.

In *Hamlet* the character Polonius notoriously outlines the genres and hybrids in which the Players are expert:

> The best actors in the world, either for tragedy, comedy, history, pastoral, pastoral-comical, historical-pastoral, tragical-historical, tragical-comical-historical-pastoral, scene individable, or poem unlimited: Seneca cannot be too heavy, nor Plautus too light. For the law of writ and the liberty, these are the only men. (Act II, scene ii.2)

◆ What do you take the point of this speech to be?

▶ Discussion

I assume that there is a comic or satirical edge here, with Polonius's pedantry – and the lore of generic distinction in general – as its target. He starts with just four terms and then more or less exhausts the possibilities for hybridising them (though he misses out a possible comical-historical hybrid). Clearly, by the time Polonius has named his ultimate four-term hybrid 'tragical-comical-historical-pastoral', one might be led to wonder how much such catch-all genre labels can tell you. This is reinforced by the last two forms at which the actors are expert – since these are generically indescribable, presumably containing even more multiplicity than the four-term hybrid, or being even more fundamentally outside generic systems.

One recent critic has argued that, in fact, genre, every genre, is from its very beginning, in the very nature of its system, beyond any clear systematisation, inherently mixed. Though we will come back to Polonius and particular hybrid forms, we should look at this radical conception of genre switching or mixing. The critic in question is the French thinker Jaques Derrida, who argues both for the omnipresence of genre and its lack of presence in actual texts of any particular genre. □

◆ Read the following passage: What are the arguments against the 'purity' of any genre?
◆ How convinced are you by these arguments?

Jacques Derrida, 'The Law of Genre'

Genres are not to be mixed.

...

'Genres are not to be mixed' could strike you as a sharp order. You might have heard it resound the elliptical but all the more authoritarian summons to a law of 'do' or 'do not' which, as everyone knows, occupies the concept or constitutes the value of genre. As soon as the word *genre* is sounded, as soon as it is heard, as soon as one attempts to conceive it, a limit is drawn. And when a limit is established, norms and interdictions are not far behind…

Thus, as soon as genre announces itself, one must respect a norm, one must not cross a line of demarcation, one must not risk impurity, anomaly or monstrosity…If a genre is what it is…one should not mix genre…or, more rigorously, genres should not intermix. And if it should happen that they do intermix, by accident or through transgression…then this should confirm, since, after all, we are speaking of 'mixing', the essential purity of their identity. This purity belongs to the typical axiom: it is a law of the law of genre…

And suppose for a moment that it were impossible not to mix genres. What if there were, lodged within the heart of the law itself, a law of impurity or a principle of contamination?…It is precisely a principle of contamination, a law of impurity, a parasitical economy. In the code of set theories, if I may use it at least figuratively, I would speak of a sort of participation without belonging – a taking part in without being part of, without having membership in a set. The trait that marks membership inevitably divides, the boundary of the set comes to form…an internal pocket larger than the whole…

The trait common to [all genres of genre] is precisely the identifiable recurrence of a common trait by which one recognises, or should recognise a membership in a class. There should be a trait upon which one could rely in order to decide that a textual event, a given 'work', corresponds to a given class (genre, type, mode, form, etc.). And there should be a code enabling one to decide questions of class membership on the basis of this trait.…It is always possible that a [text] re-marks on this distinctive trait within itself.…I submit this axiomatic question for your consideration: can one identify a work of art…but especially of discursive art, if it does not bear the mark of genre, if it does not signal or mention it or make it remarkable in any way?…If I am not mistaken in saying that such a trait is remarkable in every aesthetic, poetic or literary corpus, then consider this paradox, consider the irony…: this supplementary and distinctive trait, a mark of belonging or inclusion, does not properly pertain to any genre or class. The re-mark of belonging does not belong. It belongs without belonging…To formulate it in the scantiest manner… – I submit for your consideration the following hypothesis: a text would not *belong* to any genre. Every text *participates* in one or several genres, there is no genreless text, there is always a genre and genres, yet such participation never amounts to belonging. And not because of an abundant overflowing or a free, anarchic and unclassifiable productivity, but because of the *trait* of participation itself…In marking itself generically, a text unmarks itself…if remarks of belonging belong without belonging, then *genre designations cannot be simply part of the corpus.* Let us take the designation 'novel' as an example. This should be marked in one way or another, even if it does not appear in the explicit form of a sub-titled designation, and even if it proves deceptive or ironic. This designation is not novelistic; it does not, in whole or in part, take part in the corpus whose denomination it nevertheless imparts. Nor is it simply extraneous to the corpus. But this singular *topos* places within and without the work, along its boundary, an inclusion and exclusion with regard to genre in general…It gathers together the corpus and, at the same time…keeps it from closing, from identifying itself with itself.

•   From Jacques Derrida, 'The Law of Genre', first given as a lecture in French in
•   1979, trans. Avital Ronnell in 1980; reprinted with some modification in *Acts*
•   *of Literature,* ed. Derek Attridge (London, 1992), pp. 223–31.[12]

▶️ Discussion 1

Derrida starts his argument with the idea that by definition concepts of
genre are concerned with limitation and demarcation. The function of
genre is to divide up one kind of text, one kind of genre from other kinds.
It is true that genre can, in practice, be mixed (e.g. tragi-comedy and so on
as discussed above), but even so, the constituent elements of the genres
concerned must be separable, otherwise generic distinction has collapsed.
The maintenance of categories is the supreme 'law of the law of genre'.

The next move in the argument is to ask what happens to genre's
essential role if the law requiring 'purity' is, in fact, impossible to observe.
This would mean that, paradoxically, no genre or discourse of genre can
actually carry out its generic function – genres are *not to be* mixed, but genres *must* be mixed. The next step in Derrida's argument is to say that this
contradictory law within the generic law is precisely unavoidable because
the marking of generic membership within texts is itself an impurity. He
illustrates why this is so using the idea of sets and an imagined Venn diagram (ideas you may have met in maths – if not, this, at least, will become
clear below). He explains that if generic markers indicate membership of a
set, they cannot by virtue of their role as an indicator of membership themselves be part of the set the boundaries of which they demarcate. Thus the
'boundary of the set comes to form … an internal pocket larger than the
whole'. The boundary is not within the set, yet it marks where that set
begins and ends. This can (I think) be represented in an actual Venn diagram in the form below.[13]

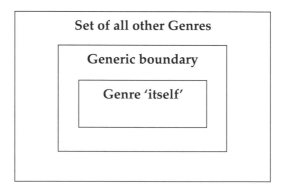

Thus, for Derrida, all genres are mixed *because* 'genres are not to be
mixed'. A novelistic text is designated as such by generic markers which
are not themselves novelistic. Presumably a subtitle such as ' – A Novel'
would illustrate this by being a genre marker, but *not* itself being a feature

found *within* a novel. Therefore, it is argued, genre or a genre is never a finite set – it always contains the impurity of its own generic markers. This may (I suspect...) seem somewhat abstract and philosophical, but the implication is presumably radical for the ways in which we think about genre and, indeed, texts. Since genre markers are neither inside nor outside texts but in a blurred boundary set participating in the 'genre "itself"', but not belonging to it, this means that no text is ever straightforwardly describable in generic terms. Yet, neither can genre terms be simply discarded as unreliable, since they do describe some line of demarcation, they do play a part in how we read and interpret. Genre is thus an inherently necessary but unstable system, a system with a systematic flaw. It is no wonder, if this is so, that generic descriptions and the continuity of features across members of a genre are complex: both are attempts to describe something which does not have a clear existence. Thus, presumably, no genre can ever be fully described and no text can ever fully be accounted for in terms of genre: 'from identifying itself with itself'. Indeed, my term for what is in the central set of my Venn diagram is itself a paradoxical one; for what is it that is *in* the 'genre "itself"' once we have excluded the 'genre markers' from this group? *Is* the real meaning, the real originality of a text that which is not a genre marker? But can we really say that there is anything in a text which is not in some way a genre marker? (for example, what part of a poem is not also an indicator of the membership of this text in the class 'poem'?). □

▶ Discussion 2

The steps in the argument are at first difficult to grasp because they seem to run counter to ingrained generic thinking in which genres are thought of as self-contained classes. However, the logic of the argument is carefully followed through, and it is not enough to reject it, unless we can find a fault in the argument. One objection I can think of might be to say that Derrida conceives of all generic markers as metadiscursive, as 'designations', terms which *name* a genre. We could argue that Todorov's distinction between metadiscursive 'discourses of genre' and the internal discursive rules of generic discourses themselves[14] allows us to dispute Derrida's conclusions. For, if genre can be thought of in this way, then the category 'the genre "itself"' begins to have a more clearly defined existence. A genre, we could say, is best described not by metadiscursive 'designations', but by the rules about it contained within itself. Thus what makes a novel novelistic are all the features which cause it to conduct meaning in one set of ways rather than another, rather than 'outside' terms like 'novel', and 'novelistic'. These *discursive* rules are not outside the text, but the very features which give it its being.

There are possible objections to this line of argument, though. The term 'discursive properties' was one coined by Todorov to indicate the features or rules specific to a particular discourse concerning what is to be included and excluded: 'we find that any aspect of discourse can be made obligatory'. Here we are back with Derrida's starting point about the demarcating role of genre, but also at this finishing point about the generic markers which are neither within nor outside a text. For if we can argue that there is something which can reasonably be called 'the genre itself' made up of the rules which produce it, we would surely have to note that these discursive properties cannot really be seen as entirely inside a genre. As Todorov's use of the terms 'included and excluded' suggests, these properties must be produced within a system which is never fully present in any example. In this sense, all generic features could be said to be 'metadiscursive', in that they point towards a system of partly exterior demarcating rules in the very process of constituting particular meanings within their own genre or text. Perhaps this effect does help to explain why we feel that we can describe genres quite well, yet can never actually provide an exhaustive account which will cover all examples. It may also allow the kind of simultaneous alteration and continuity which we have observed in the case of pastoral.[15]

Returning to Polonius's more specific hybridisation, one might note that this comic classification may have its connections to Derrida's pleasure in finding genres inherently hybrid and unfixable. Polonius's generic terminologies may well be involved with the play's general sense of the difficulty of knowing things precisely, its, or Hamlet's, sense of incredulity about the capacity of language to pin things down. Nevertheless, generic labels did, of course, have great currency in this period, and there were debates about the validity and value of hybrid genres. One of the most famous contributions to these was by the playwright John Fletcher who defended not only the hybrid genre *tragi-comedy* from accusations of being an improper mixture, but made a further Polonius-like step in defending his play *The Faithful Shepherdess* (probably 1609) as a 'pastoral tragi-comedy'. □

> Read the passage: What, for Fletcher, seem to be (a) the disadvantages and (b) the advantages of this kind of hybrid?

John Fletcher, 'To The Reader' [of *The Faithful Shepherdess*]

To the Reader

If you be not reasonably assured of your knowledge in this kind of poem, lay down the book, or read this, which I would wish had been the prologue. It is a pastoral tragi-comedy, which the people seeing when it was played, having ever had a singular gift in defining, concluded to be a play of country hired shepherds in gray cloaks, with curtailed dogs in strings, sometimes laughing together, and sometimes killing one another; and missing Whitsun-ales, cream, wassail, and morris-dances, began to be angry. In their error I would not have you fall, lest you incur their censure. Understand therefore a pastoral to be a representation of shepherds and shepherdesses with their actions and their passions, which must be such as may agree with their natures, at least not exceeding former fictions and vulgar traditions; they are not to be adorned with any art, but such improper ones as nature may be said to bestow, as singing and poetry; or such as experience may teach them, as the vertues of herbs and fountains, the ordinary course of the sun, moon, and stars and such like. But you are ever to remember shepherds to be such as all the ancient poets, and modern, of understanding, have received them; that is, the owners of flocks, and not hirelings. A tragi-comedy is not so called in respect of mirth and killing, but in respect it wants deaths, which is enough to make it no tragedy, yet brings some near it, which is enough to make it no comedy, which must be a representation of familiar people, with such kind of trouble as no life be questioned; so that a gods as lawful in this as in a tragedy, and mean people as in a comedy. Thus much I hope will serve to jus- tify my poem, and make you understand it; to teach you more for nothing, I do not know that I am in conscience bound.

From the first edition of Fletcher's plays, the 1647 folio. Reprinted in *Beaumont and Fletcher's Plays*, ed. G. P. Baker (London, 1911, 1953), p. 242.

▶ Discussion

The most significant problem Fletcher comments on is that of the compre- hension and reaction of the audience. Clearly, the play was a flop at its first performance. Fletcher is certain this arose from a generic misunderstanding. He claims that the audience appreciated that the play was a hybrid 'pastoral tragi-comedy', but due to their 'singular gift in defining' created entirely false expectations which were quickly disappointed. The audience expected the play to contain what they took to be the defining elements of comedy and tragedy (mirth and killing) within what they equally took to be the essentials of a pastoral setting: 'country hired shepherds in gray cloaks', 'cur- tailed dogs in strings', 'Whitsun-ales,[16] cream, wassail, and morris-dances'. Their mistake was a two-fold one in wrongly defining pastoral and in mis- understanding the outcome of the hybridisation of tragedy and comedy.

If the audience's understanding of genre had been less eccentric, says Fletcher, they would have had a more refined sense of what is truly pas- toral and truly tragi-comic. True pastoral must contain true shepherds, not clownish antics. True shepherds must, as Empson was later to imply, com- bine an utter simplicity with an absolute dignity. They are simple and thus unadorned by any artificial art;[17] the only arts they can practise are ones that natural, dignified shepherds of their type really could command. These simple yet dignified arts are even called 'improper' to stress their lack of premeditation. Nevertheless, they turn out to make up a consider- able list, which includes the 'improper' art of poetry. A key distinction is that the proper shepherds with their suitably improper arts are owners of sheep, whereas the audience expected clownish 'hireling shepherds'. A sophisticated audience would never have made this mistake, and, indeed, Fletcher seems to hope that surely no one in the reading classes could be so

misled. However, his confidence in the mainstream nature of his definitions of pastoral may seem to be a little undermined by his address to the
reader which rehearses and corrects the first audience's mistake.

That audience made the crude mistake of thinking that tragi-comedy
mixed two characteristics of its constituent genres: laughing and kill-
ings (which Fletcher represents as an absurd combination by implying
that they are equal and randomly alternating entertainments for the shepherds and the mistaken audience). In fact, the combination of the two
produces something much more interactive, which is partly about the
not-quite fulfilment of their separate generic patterns. Thus, a tragi-
comedy contains no deaths, since that would make it tragic, but brings
some near to death, which precludes it from being comic. On the other
hand, the form is near enough to comedy to include 'mean' (ordinary
rather than base) people, and near enough to tragedy in that lives are in
the balance to justify the appearance of gods and intervention beyond the
natural order.

The possibilities of these quite new patternings of plot and experience
in the hybrid presumably constitute its advantages. Instead of being
restricted to either 'mirth' or 'killing', the tragi-comedy can explore closeness to death rather than actual death and the experiences of ordinary people who are not merely comic or perpetually merry. Though the passage
does not relate very closely what the 'pastoral' modification adds further
to this already transformed hybrid, it could be suggested that its dignified
but simple shepherds add characters who are neither too mean to come
near to the tragic, not too grand to lose contact with the comic (as long as it
remains somewhat refined ...).

The questions raised in these two Renaissance discussions of hybrid
genres are principally three:

1. What limits are there to such mixtures?
2. What is legitimate in a particular hybrid?
3. How are we to select which combination of features from two genres
    make sense?

Thus, one might feel that despite Fletcher's feelings about that first audience of *The Faithful Shepherdess*, the wrongness of their tragi-comic mixture
and the rightness of his is not so self-evident. How are we to judge what
the hierarchy of generic features is in any hybrid genre? Indeed, behind
each of these questions lies a more general one about the credibility and
use of hybrid genres. Presumably the anxiety is that hybridity undermines
the very idea of genre (of family membership and distinction), while at the
same time claiming it. Thus a tragi-comedy claims that tragic and comic
generic patterns are valid, yet also asserts that they can be combined in
one story or text – which must, one would expect, undermine those two
distinct patterns of plot, personae, subject matter, conclusion and other
conventions. In some works, such as Shakespeare's *The Winter's Tale* – a
play which like others of the 'last plays' may have been partly a response
to Fletcher's new romances with their generic mixtures – the overall patterns of both genres may be retained. Thus in *The Winter's Tale* there is a

tragic (seeming) first half and a comic second half which restores some, but not all, of the dead to life. Other, and particularly modern, examples of genre mixing are often less predictable in retaining long narrative patterns associated with their generic ingredients. Critics, particularly champions of naturalism, from the nineteenth century on began to argue in a variety of ways that genre was an outmoded imposition on literature (e.g. Zola, and Blanchot, cited by Todorov; see section 3.1), and that to represent actuality, a work should either be genreless, or should be multiply hybrid to accommodate the constantly shifting, multigeneric nature of life itself.[18] This idea was often elaborated by reviewers and critics of modern drama, such as that of Chekhov. Thus the critic George Calderon wrote in 1912 of Chekhov's escape from obvious generic forms:

> Having no villains, it goes without saying that Chekhov has no heroes. His drama is not a drama of conflicting wills. He does not invite you to stake your sympathies on this side or that. All his characters are ranged together against the common enemy, Life, whether they are drawn up in two battalions or in one … If the Russians are realists, it is not because they go to real life for their matter … [Chekhov] endeavours to restore to it [life] the flavour of reality. He endeavours to manifest the very texture and illusion of life itself.
>
> Chekhov had that fine comedic spirit which relishes the incongruity between the actual disorder of the world and the underlying order. Seeking as he did to throw our eyes outwards from the individual destiny, to discover its relation to surrounding life, he habitually mingled tragedy (which is life seen close at hand) with comedy (which is life seen from a distance). His plays are tragedies with the texture of comedy.[19] □

> Read the following three extracts, two from plays and one from a novel; each has been selected as displaying some form of genre switching or generic uncertainty. How would you describe the effect of the genre switching in each?

Anton Chekhov, *The Cherry Orchard*

LIUBOV ANDRYEEVNA. Well, we can go now. I'm leaving with two worries on my mind. One is Feers – he's sick, you know. [*Glances at her watch.*] We have another five minutes or so. …

ANIA. Mamma, Feers has been taken to hospital already. Yasha sent him this morning.

LIUBOV ANDRYEEVNA. The other is Varia. She's been accustomed to getting up early and working, and now, without work, she's like a fish out of water. She's got so thin and pale, and she cries a lot, poor thing. [*A pause.*] You know very well, Yermolai Aleksyeevich, that I'd been hoping to get her married to you...and everything seemed to show that you meant to marry her, too. [*Whispers to* ANIA, *who nods to* CHARLOTTA, *and they both go out.*] She loves you, and you must be fond of her, too...and I just don't know, I just don't know why you seem to keep away from each other. I don't understand it.

LOPAKHIN. Neither do I myself, I must confess. It's all so strange somehow....If there's still time, I'm ready even now....Let's settle it at once and get it over! Without you here, I don't feel I shall ever propose to her.

LIUBOV ANDRYEEVNA. That's an excellent idea! You'll hardly need more than a minute, that's all. I'll call her at once.

LOPAKHIN. There's champagne here, too, quite suitable for the occasion. [*Takes a look at the glasses.*] But they're empty, someone's drunk it up. [YASHA *coughs.*] I should have said lapped it up.

LIUBOV ANDRYEEVNA [*with animation*]. I'm so glad. We'll go outside. Yasha, allez! I'll call her....[*Through the door.*] Varia, come here a moment, leave what you're doing for a minute! Varia! [*Goes out with* YASHA.]

LOPAKHIN [*glancing at his watch*]. Yes....[*A pause.*] [*Suppressed laughter and whispering is heard from behind the door, and finally* VARIA *comes in and starts examining the luggage. After some time she says*:]

VARIA. It's strange, I just can't find...

LOPAKHIN. What are you looking for?

VARIA. I packed the things myself, yet I can't remember....

[*A pause.*]

LOPAKHIN. Where are you going to now, Varvara Mihailovna?

VARIA. I? To the Rogulins. I've agreed to look after the house for them...to be their housekeeper, or something.

LOPAKHIN. That's at Yashnevo, isn't it? About seventy miles from here. [*A pause.*] So this is the end of life in this house....

VARIA [*examining the lugggage*]. But where could it be? Or perhaps I've packed it in the trunk?... Yes, life in this house has come to an end...there won't be any more....

LOPAKHIN. And I'm going to Kharkov presently....On the next train. I've got a lot to do there. And I'm leaving Yepihodov here....I've engaged him.

VARIA. Well! ...

LOPAKHIN. Do you remember, last year about this time it was snowing already, but now it's quite still and sunny. It's rather cold, though....About three degrees of frost.

VARIA. I haven't looked. [*A pause.*] Besides, our thermometer's broken....[*A pause.*]

[*A voice is heard from outside the door: 'Yermolai Aleksyeevich!'*]

LOPAKHIN [*as if he had long been expecting it*]. Coming this moment! [*Goes out quickly.*]

[VARIA, *sitting on the floor, with her head on the bundle of clothes, sobs softly. The door opens,* LIUBOV ANDRYEEVANA *enters quietly.*]

LIUBOV ANDRYEEVNA. Well? [*A pause.*] We must go.

VARIA [*stops crying and wipes her eyes*]. Yes, it's time, Mamma dear. I'll just be able to get to the Rogulins today, if only we don't miss the train.

LIUBOV ANDRYEEVNA [*calls through the door*]. Ania, put your coat on.

[*Enter* ANIA, *followed by* GAYEV *and* CHARLOTTA IVANOVNA. GAYEV *wears a heavy overcoat with a hood. Servants and coachmen come into the room.* YEPIHODOV *fusses with the luggage.*]

Now we can start on our journey!

ANIA [*joyfully*]. Yes, our journey!

GAYEV. My friends, my dear, kind friends! Now as I leave this house for ever, how can I remain silent, how can I refrain from expressing to you, as a last farewell, the feelings which now overwhelm me. ...

ANIA [*imploringly*]. Uncle!

VARIA. Uncle, dear, please don't!

GAYEV [*downcast*]. I pot the red and follow through. ... I'll keep quiet.

[*Enter* TROFIMOV, *then* LOPAKHIN.]

TROFIMOV. Well, ladies and gentlemen, it's time to go.

LOPAKHIN. Yepihodov, my coat!

LIUBOV ANDRYEEVNA. I'll just sit down for one little minute more. I feel as if I'd never seen the walls and ceilings of this house before, and now I look at them with such longing and affection. ...

GAYEV. I remember when I was six years old – it was Holy Trinity day – I was sitting on this window-still, looking at Father – he was just going to church. ...

LIUBOV ANDRYEEVNA. Have they taken out all the luggage?

LOPAKHIN. It looks as if they have. [*To* YEPIHODOV, *as he puts on his coat.*] See that everything's all right, Yepihodov.

YEPIHODOV [*in a husky voice*]. Don't worry, Yermolai Aleksyeevich!

LOPAKHIN. What are you talking like that for?

YEPIHODOV. I've just had a drink of water, I must have swallowed something.

YASHA [*with contempt*]. What ignorance!

LIUBOV ANDRYEEVNA. When we leave here there won't be a soul in the place. ...

LOPAKHIN. Until the spring.

VARIA [*pulls an umbrella from a bundle of clothes;* LOPAKHIN *pretends to be frightened that she is going to strike him*]. Now, why ... why are you doing that? ... I never thought of ...

TROFIMOV. Ladies and gentlemen, come, let's get into the carriage. It's high time. The train will be in soon.

VARIA. Pyetia, here they are, your goloshes, beside the suitcase. [*Tearfully.*] And how dirty and worn-out they are! ...

TROFIMOV [*puts them on*]. Come along, ladies and gentlemen!

GAYEV [*greatly embarrassed, afraid of breaking into tears*]. The train, the station. ... In off into the middle pocket. ...

LIUBOV ANDRYEEVNA. Let us go!

LOPAKHIN. Is everyone here? No one left behind? [*Locks the door on the left.*] There are some things put away there, it had better be locked up. Come along!

ANIA. Good-bye, old house! Good-bye, old life!

TROFIMOV. Greetings to the new life! ... [*Goes out with* ANIA.]

[VARIA *glances round the room and goes out slowly.* YASHA *and* CHARLOTTA, *with her little dog, follow.*]

LOPAKHIN. And so, until the spring. Come along, ladies and gentlemen. ... Au revoir! [*Goes out.*]

[LIUBOV ANDRYEEVNA *and* GAYEV *are left alone. They seem to have been waiting for this moment, and now they embrace each other and sob quietly, with restraint, so as not to be heard.*]

GAYEV [*with despair in his voice*]. Sister, my sister. ...

LIUBOV ANDRYEEVNA. Oh my darling, my precious, my beautiful orchard! My life, my youth, my happiness ... good-bye! ... Good-bye!

ANIA'S VOICE [*gaily*]. Mamma! ...

TROFIMOV'S VOICE [*gaily and excitedly*]. Ah-oo! ...

LIUBOV ANDRYEEVNA. For the last time – to look at these walls, these windows. ... Mother used to love walking up and down this room. ...

GAYEV. Sister, my sister! ...

ANIA'S VOICE. Mamma!

TROFIMOV'S VOICE. Ah-oo!

LIUBOV ANDRYEEVNA. We're coming. ... [*Both go out.*]

[*The stage is empty. The sound of doors being locked is heard, then of carriages driving off. It grows quiet. The stillness is broken by the dull thuds of an axe on a tree. They sound forlorn and sad.*

There is a sound of footsteps and from the door on the right FEERS *appears. He is dressed, as usual, in a coat and white waistcoat, and is wearing slippers. He looks ill*].

FEERS [*walks up to the middle door and tries the handle*]. Locked. They've gone. ... [*Sits down on a sofa.*] They forgot about me. Never mind. ... I'll sit here for a bit. I don't suppose Leonid Andryeevich put on his fur coat, I expect he's gone in his light one. ... [*Sighs, preoccupied.*] I didn't see to it. ... These youngsters! ... [*Mutters something unintelligible.*] My life's gone as if I'd never lived. ... [*Lies down.*] I'll lie down a bit. You haven't got any strength left, nothing's left, nothing. ... Oh, you ... you're daft! ... [*Lies motionless.*]

[*A distant sound is heard, coming as if out of the sky, like the sound of a string snapping, slowly and sadly dying away. Silence ensues, broken only by the sound of an axe striking a tree in the orchard far away.*]

CURTAIN

From *Chekhov, Plays* (Penguin edn, 1954, 1979), *The Cherry Orchard*, Act 4, pp. 394–8. Play written in 1904.

Sean O'Casey, *Juno and the Paycock*

Mrs Madigan. Oh, Mrs Boyle, God an' his blessed mother be with you this night!

Mrs Boyle. [*Calmly.*] What is it, Mrs Madigan? It's Johnny – something about Johnny.

Mrs Madigan. God send it's not, God send it's not Johnny!

Mrs Boyle. Don't keep me waitin', Mrs Madigan; I've gone through so much lately that I feel able for any thing.

Mrs Madigan. Two polismen below wantin' you ... Some poor fella's been found, an' they think it's, it's ...

Mrs Boyle. Johnny, Johnny!

...

Mrs Boyle. We'll go. Come Mary, an we'll never come back here agen. Let your father furrage for himself now; I've done all I could an' it was all no use – he'll be hopeless till the end of his days. I've got a little room in me sisther's where we'll stop till your trouble is over, an' then we'll work together for the sake of the baby.

Mary. My poor little child that'll have no father!

Mrs Boyle. It'll have what's far better – it'll have two mothers ... maybe I didn't feel sorry enough for poor Mrs Tancred when her poor son was found as Johnny's been found now – because he was a Diehard! Ah, why didn't I remember that then he wasn't a Diehard or a Stater, but only a poor dead son! ... Mother o'God, Mother o' God, have pity on us all! Blessed Virgin where was you when me darlin' son was riddled with bullets, when me darlin' son was riddled with bullets? Sacred Heart o'Jesus, take away our hearts o'stone, and give us hearts o' flesh! Take away this murderin' hate, and give us Thine own especial love! [*They all go out slowly.*]

[*There is a pause; then a sound of shuffling steps on the stairs outside. The door opens and Boyle and Joxer, both of them very drunk, enter.*]

Boyle. I'm able to go no farther ... Two polis, ey ... what ere they doin' here, I wondher? ... Up to no good, anyhow ... an' Juno and that lovely daughter of mine with them [*taking a sixpence from his pocket and looking at it*]. Wan single, solitary tanner left out of all I borreyed ... [*he lets it fall*]. The last of the Mohicans ... The blinds is down, Joxer, the blinds is down!

Joxer. [*Walking unsteadily across the room, and anchoring at the bed.*] Put all ... your throubles ... in your ol' kit-bag ... an' smile ... smile ... smile!

Boyle. The country'll have to steady itself ... It's goin' to hell ... where'r all the chairs ... gone to ... steady itself, Joxer ... Chairs'll ... have to ... steady themselves ... No matther ... what any one may ... say ... Irelan' sober ... is Irelan' ... free.

Joxer. [*stretching himself on the bed.*] Chains ... an' ... slaveree ... that's a darling motto ... a daarlin' motto!

Boyle. If th' worst comes ... to th' worse ... I can join a ... flyin' ... column ... I done ... me bit ... in Easther Week ... had no business ... to ... be ... there ... but Captain Boyle's Captain Boyle!

Joxer. Breathes there a man with a soul ... so ... de ... ad ... this ... me ... o ... wn, me nat ... ive .l... an'!

Boyle. [*Subsiding into a sitting posture on the floor.*] Commandant Kelly died ... in them ... arms ... Joxer ... tell me Volunteer Butties ... says he ... that ... I died for ... Irelan'!

Joxer. D'jever rade Willie ... Reilly ... an' his own ... Colleen ... Bawn? It'sa darlin' story, a daarlin' story!

Boyle. I'm telling you ... Joxer ... th' whole worl's ... in a terr ... ible state o' ... chassis!

CURTAIN.

From *Sean O'Casey: Three Plays* (London, 1980), *Juno and the Paycock*, Act III, pp. 70–3. Play written in 1925.

Margaret Atwood, *The Handmaid's Tale*

I reach the top of the stairs, knock on the door there. He opens it himself, who else was I expecting? There's a lamp on, only one but enough light to make me blink. I look past him, not wanting to meet his eyes. It's a single room, with a fold-out bed, made up, and a kitchenette counter at the far end, and another door that must lead to the bathroom. This room is stripped down, military, minimal. No pictures on the walls, no plants. He's camping out. The blanket on the bed is grey and says U.S.

He steps back and aside to let me past. He's in his shirt sleeves, and is holding a cigarette, lit. I smell the smoke on him, in the warm air of the room, all over. I'd like to take off my clothes, bathe in it, rub it over my skin.

No preliminaries; he knows why I'm here. He doesn't even say anything, why fool around, it's an assignment. He moves away from me, turns off the lamp. Outside, like punctuation, there's a flash of lightning; almost no pause and then the thunder. He's undoing my dress, a man made of darkness, I can't see his face, and I can hardly breathe, hardly stand, and I'm not standing. His mouth is on me, his hands, I can't wait and he's moving, already, love, it's been so long, I'm alive in my skin, again, arms around him, falling and water softly everywhere, never-ending. I knew it might only be once.

I made that up. It didn't happen that way. Here is what happened.

I reach the top of the stairs, knock on the door. He opens it himself. There's a lamp on; I blink. I look past his eyes, it's a single room, the bed's made up, stripped down, military. No pictures but the blanket says U.S. He's in his shirt sleeves, he's holding a cigarette.

'Here,' he says to me, 'have a drag.' No preliminaries, he knows why I'm here. To get knocked up, to get in trouble, up the pole, those were all names for it once. I take the cigarette from him, draw deeply in, hand it back. Our fingers hardly touch. Even that much smoke makes me dizzy.

He says nothing, just looks at me, unsmiling. It would be better, more friendly, if he would touch me. I feel stupid and ugly, although I know I am not either. Still, what does he think, why doesn't he say something? Maybe he thinks I've been slutting around, at Jezebel's, with the Commander or more. It annoys me that I'm even worrying about what he thinks. Let's be practical.

'I don't have much time,' I say. This is awkward and clumsy, it isn't what I mean.

'I could just squirt it into a bottle and you could pour it in,' he says. He doesn't smile.

'There's no need to be brutal,' I say. Possibly he feels used. Possibly he wants something from me, some emotion, some acknowledgement that he too is human, is more than just a seedpod. 'I know it's hard for you,' I try.

He shrugs. 'I get paid,' he says, punk surliness. But still makes no move.

I get paid, you get laid, I rhyme in my head. So that's how we're going to do it. He didn't like the makeup, the spangles. We're going to be tough.

'You come here often?'

'And what's a nice girl like me doing in a spot like this,' I reply. We both smile: this is better. This is an acknowledgement that we are acting, for what else can we do in such a setup?

'Abstinence makes the heart grow fonder.' We're quoting from late movies, from the time before. And the movies then were from a time before that: this sort of talk dates back to an era well before our own. Not even my mother talked like that, not when I knew her. Possibly nobody ever talked like that in real life, it was all a fabrication from the beginning. Still, it's amazing how easily it comes back to mind, this corny and falsely gay sexual banter. I can see now what it's for, what it was always for: to keep the core of yourself out of reach, enclosed, protected.

I'm sad now, the way we're talking is infinitely sad: faded music, faded paper flowers, worn satin, an echo of an echo. All gone away, no longer possible. Without warning I begin to cry.

At last he moves forward, puts his arms around me, strokes my back, holds me that way, for comfort.

'Come on,' he says. 'We haven't got much time.' With his arm around my shoulders he leads me over to the fold-out bed, lies me down. He even turns down the blanket first. He begins to unbutton, then to stroke, kisses beside my ear. 'No romance,' he says. 'Okay?'

That would have meant something else, once. Once it would have meant: *no strings*. Now it means: *no heroics*. It means: don't risk yourself for me, if it should come to that.

And so it goes. And so.

I knew it might only be once. Goodbye, I thought, even at the time, goodbye.

There wasn't any thunder though, I added that in. To cover up the sounds, which I am ashamed of making.

It didn't happen that way either. I'm not sure how it happened; not exactly. All I can hope for is a reconstruction: the way love feels is always only approximate.

Partway through, I thought about Serena Joy, sitting down there in the kitchen. Thinking: cheap. They'll spread their legs for anyone. All you need to give them is a cigarette.

And I thought afterwards: this is a betrayal. Not the thing itself but my own response. If I knew for certain he was dead, would that make a difference?

I would like to be without shame. I would like to be shameless. I would like to be ignorant. Then I would not know how ignorant I was.

From Margaret Atwood, *The Handmaid's Tale* (Virago edn, 1987), pp. 272–5.

Discussion

CHEKHOV

Chekhov's plays are, as the critical paragraph above suggests, famously indeterminate in genre, and hence tone and meaning. Here, though the scene is clearly from the end of the play it has a strong sense of inconclusiveness, to the point where one might feel that no generic pattern is being worked through to an end. There are though, as Todorov remarks of Blanchot (in section 3.1) nevertheless many signs – or at least promises – of genre. Thus there is much stress laid by characters on the moment as one of exceptional and momentous sadness, the ending of their lives as they have known them: 'So this is the end of life in this house'. Though not tragic in a classical sense (there are no deaths), we might feel that this is a modern equivalent, the passing of characters who are flawed yet noble, who have lived through things that ordinary people will not see. On the other hand, there are numerous trivial, comic and inapposite contradictions of this sense of momentous closure. 'When we leave here,' says Liubov Andryeevna, 'there won't be a soul in the place ...'. 'Until the spring' responds Lophakin.

Indeed, Lopakhin promises a closure of a different genre in announcing his long-delayed intention to ask Varia to marry him:

> LIUBOV ANDRYEEVNA. She loves you, and you must be fond of her too ... and I just don't know, I just don't know why you seem to keep away from each other. I don't understand it.
> LOPAKHIN. Neither do I myself, I must confess. It's all so strange somehow ... If there's still time, I'm even ready now ... Let's settle it at once – and get it over! Without you here, I don't feel I shall ever propose to her.

It is almost as if the characters themselves know that the genre could be turned at any moment into that of romantic comedy, with all obstacles to the family staying in the house removed by Varia's marriage to its new, rich owner, Lopakhin. But none of them is generically settled enough to be able to shape the genre they are in by any definite course of action. Lopakhin, instead of asking Varia to marry him, asks her where she is going next. It might be that their speeches, with the various hints of generic patterns, are cast out in the hope that saying the right kind of thing will make the situation become clearer, become one genre or another. But it never does. At the end Feers may be a tragic figure or a comic one. The scene is very much affected by genre switching to the point where its genre does seem indeterminate – but not, I think, genre free. Perhaps specifically in this case the scene, and the play, and indeed, the characters *participate* in genre, but do not *belong* to any. A shape for life is ever being promised, but never realised.

O'CASEY

The genre switching here is differently organised. The first part of the scene with Mrs Boyle and Mary seems obviously tragic (again in a modern rather than classical sense, though there is a death in this case), while the second part might most easily be called comic, with its versions of the ancient comic figure of the *miles gloriosus* (the braggart soldier) and its clownish drunkenness. The two generic worlds are thus quite distinct, having no characters in common and no sharing of attitudes. Thus while Mrs Boyle laments the political hatred of the Irish civil war, Boyle and Joxer celebrate their version of patriotism. The tragic world is one in which women live, the comic world is for men.

As in the case of the Chekhov passage, this is the end of the play, and the two generic worlds give it a dual closure. However, it seems clear that there is a hierarchy of genres here: one is meant to see the tragic closure as more authentic than the comic one, and as containing it. Thus the comic ending in no sense offers an alternative point of view or opposition to the tragic closure, but is seen instead within the terms laid down by the tragedy. The comedy of the two drunken nationalists is therefore to be read as a sign of just how remote they are from the realities of the situation (the two 'polismen' up to no good have brought news of the death of the Boyle's son, Johnny), and how their irresponsible fantasies fuel the cycle of hatred. The comedy then is actually not 'comic', but a reinforcement of the tragedy. While the women have insight, the men still know nothing. This effect differs from that in the Chekhov in being much more clearly readable in terms of quite traditional genre distinctions, though these are manipulated in an innovative way.

ATWOOD

The genre switching in this part of *The Handmaid's Tale* is distinctive in consisting not of a sequence of elements in which there are variations of genre, but rather in re-running the *same* scene several times *as* different genres. Thus there are three genres of love scene, drawing particularly on cinematic ways of dealing with love scenes, rather than literary genres. First comes the sexual-romantic version: 'I'm alive in my skin, again, arms around him, falling and water softly everywhere, never-ending. I knew it might only be once.' Second is the brutalised-transaction version: ' "I get paid," he says, punk surliness.' Then, inset within the second version is a third genre which they invoke by quotation from 'late movies' (the quotation is, I think, itself generic – referring to a kind of film from the nineteen forties, rather than to any specific movie). This third performance could be called a wise-cracking version.

The woman who is the first person speaker acknowledges at the end of each of these versions that none of them is authentic: 'It didn't happen that way either'. Here the very concentration on genre opposes generic membership to authenticity – but also acknowledges that any description is generic. The woman has to tell her story somehow, and that somehow always involves generic choices. Those genres do not match actuality, but there is no other way to represent the actual. In fact, experience itself cannot be told as it happened, it can only be accounted for in the ways which genre enables, not as a uniquely appropriate account which really refers to what happened: 'All I can hope for is a reconstruction.' The primacy of genre is particularly made clear through the use of the inset movie-quotation version of the scene, where the gap between the artificiality of genre and reality is drawn attention to:

> We're quoting from late movies, from the time before. And the movies then were from a time before that: this sort of talk dates back to an era well before our own. Not even my mother talked like that, not when I knew her. Possibly nobody ever talked like that in real life, it was all a fabrication from the beginning. Still it's amazing how easily it comes back to mind ... I can see now what it's for, what it was always for: to keep the core of yourself out of reach, enclosed, protected.

Perhaps this commentary on genre is to be applied to language in general – there is no natural match between language and situation, language and experience. The effect of the genre switching here is more like that in the Chekhov passage than that of the O'Casey passage. In both these cases, there is a sense of the inauthenticity of genre and of its inevitability. There are things that cannot be said generically, but there are no kinds of speech that are not generic. □

Interestingly, the genre switching in the passage from *The Handmaid's Tale* involves reference to a different *kind* – cinema. The invention of cinema, radio and television created new kinds and genres, but these new media have often been interested in adaptation – a particular species of genre switching – of literary genres. Thus, from its very beginnings film adapted Shakespeare plays; they were a very popular topic for silent film makers, despite the fact that they could use little of the spoken part of stage drama (i.e. only in brief captions). Shakespeare and other 'classics' continue to be popular candidates for adaptation in both cinema and television versions. Such adaptation is not wholly new. In fact, there were even contemporary adaptations of Shakespeare's plays and those of his contemporaries, into short ballad forms (for example, there are surviving ballads adapted from Shakespeare's *Titus Andronicus* and from John Ford's *The Broken Heart*).[20] As you can imagine, there are some major changes involved in this kind of adaptation. It is presumably more or less possible to adapt any genre into any other genre – something we will investigate further at the end of this section.

Sometimes adaptation has been performed without any overt rewriting, as in the case of Shakespeare's plays during the Romantic and Victorian periods, when there grew up a belief that the full richness of such texts was better realised by individual reading than by public theatrical performance. This tradition is said to have started in the eighteenth century with Samuel Johnson's comment that 'many of Shakespeare's plays are the worse for being acted' and continued into the twentieth century with T. S. Eliot's argument that Shakespeare was a playwright 'to be read rather than seen, because it is precisely in that drama which depends on an actor of genius, that we ought to be on guard against the actor'.[21] The argument is most famously stated by a figure from the romantic period, the essayist Charles Lamb.

> ◆ Read the extract below from an essay by Lamb. How does he justify his arguments?

On the Tragedies of Shakspeare, considered with reference to their fitness for Stage Representation

(First printed in *The Reflector*, Oct.–Dec. 1811.)

Taking a turn the other day in the Abbey, I was struck with the affected attitude of a figure, which I do not remember to have seen before, and which upon examination proved to be a whole-length of the celebrated Mr. Garrick. Though I would not go so far with some good catholics abroad as to shut players altogether out of consecrated ground, yet I own I was not a little scandalized at the introduction of theatrical airs and gestures into a place set apart to remind us of the saddest realities. Going nearer, I found inscribed under this harlequin figure the following lines:

To paint fair Nature by divine command,
Her magic pencil in his glowing hand,
A Shakspeare rose: then, to expand his fame
Wide o'er this breathing world, a Garrick came.
Though sunk in death the forms the Poet drew,
The Actor's genius bade them breathe anew;
Though, like the bard himself, in night they lay,
Immortal Garrick call'd them back to day:
And till Eternity with power sublime
Shall mark the mortal hour of hoary Time,
Shakspeare and Garrick like twin-stars shall shine,
And earth irradiate with a beam divine.

It would be an insult to my readers' understandings to attempt any thing like a criticism on this farrago of false thoughts and nonsense. But the reflection it led me into was a kind of wonder, how, from the day of the actor here celebrated to our own, it should have been the fashion to compliment every performer in his turn that has had the luck to please the town in any of the great characters of Shakspeare, with the notion of possessing a *mind congenial with the poet's*: how people should come thus unaccountably to confound the power of originating poetical images and conceptions with the faculty of being able to read or recite the same when put into words;[1] or what connection that absolute mastery over the heart and soul of man, which a great dramatic poet possesses, has with those low tricks upon the eye and ear, which a player by observing a few general effects, which some common passion, as grief, anger, &c. usually has upon the gestures and exterior, can so easily compass. To know the internal workings and movements of a great mind, of an Othello or a Hamlet for instance, the *when* and the *why* and the *how far* they should be moved; to what pitch a passion is becoming; to give the reins and to pull in the curb exactly at the moment when the drawing in or the slackening is most graceful; seems to demand a reach of intellect of a vastly different extent from that which is employed upon the bare imitation of the signs of these passions in the countenance or gesture, which signs are usually observed to be most lively and emphatic in the weaker sort of minds, and which signs can after all but indicate some passion, as I said before, anger, or grief, generally; but of the motives and grounds of the passion, wherein it differs from the same passion in low and vulgar natures, of these the actor can give no more idea by his face or

[1] It is observable that we fall into this confusion only in *dramatic* recitations. We never dream that the gentleman who reads Lucretius in public with great applause, is therefore a great poet and philosopher; nor do we find that Tom Davies, the bookseller, who is recorded to have recited the Paradise Lost better than any man in England in his day (though I cannot help thinking there must be some mistake in this tradition), was therefore, by his intimate friends, set upon a level with Milton.

gesture than the eye (without a metaphor) can speak, or the muscles utter intelligible sounds. But such is the instantaneous nature of the impressions which we take in at the eye and ear at a playhouse, compared with the slow apprehension oftentimes of the understanding in reading, that we are apt not only to sink the play-writer in the consideration which we pay to the actor, but even to identify in our mind in a perverse manner, the actor with the character which he represents. It is difficult for a frequent playgoer to dis-embarrass the idea of Hamlet from the person and voice of Mr. K. We speak of Lady Macbeth, while we are in reality thinking of Mrs. S. Nor is this confu-sion incidental alone to unlettered persons who, not possessing the advan-tage of reading, are necessarily dependent upon the stage-player for all the pleasure which they can receive from the drama, and to whom the very idea of *what an author is* cannot be made comprehensible without some pain and perplexity of mind: the error is one from which persons otherwise not meanly lettered, find it almost impossible to extricate themselves.

Never let me be so ungrateful as to forget the very high degree of satisfac-tion which I received some years back from seeing for the first time a tragedy of Shakspeare performed, in which these two great performers sustained the principal parts. It seemed to embody and realize conceptions which had hith-erto assumed no distinct shape. But dearly do we pay all our life after for this juvenile pleasure, this sense of distinctness. When the novelty is past, we find to our cost that instead of realizing an idea, we have only materialized and brought down a fine vision to the standard of flesh and blood. We have let go a dream, in quest of an unattainable substance.

How cruelly this operates upon the mind, to have its free conceptions thus crampt and pressed down to the measure of a strait-lacing actuality, may be judged from that delightful sensation of freshness, with which we turn to those plays of Shakspeare which have escaped being performed, and to those passages in the acting plays of the same writer which have happily been left out in performance. How far the very custom of hearing any thing *spouted*, withers and blows upon a fine passage, may be seen in those speeches from Henry the Fifth, &c. which are current in the mouths of school-boys from their being to be found in *Enfield Speakers*, and such kind of books. I confess myself utterly unable to appreciate that celebrated soliloquy in Hamlet, beginning 'To be or not to be', or to tell whether it be good, bad, or indiffer-ent, it has been so handled and pawed about by declamatory boys and men, and torn so inhumanely from its living place and principle of continuity in the play, till it is become to me a perfect dead member.

It may seem a paradox, but I cannot help being of opinion that the plays of Shakspeare are less calculated for performance on a stage, than those of almost any other dramatist whatever. Their distinguished excellence is a reason that they should be so. There is so much in them, which comes not under the province of acting, with which eye, and tone, and gesture, have nothing to do. . . .

The character of Hamlet is perhaps that by which, since the days of Betterton, a succession of popular performers have had the greatest ambition to distinguish themselves. The length of the part may be one of their reasons. But for the character itself, we find it in a play, and therefore we judge it a fit subject of dramatic representation. The play itself abounds in maxims and reflexions beyond any other, and therefore we consider it as a proper vehicle for conveying moral instruction. But Hamlet himself – what does he suffer meanwhile by being dragged forth as a public schoolmaster, to give lectures to the crowd! Why, nine parts in ten of what Hamlet does, are transactions between himself and his moral sense, they are the effusions of his solitary musings, which he retires to holes and corners and the most sequestered parts of the palace to pour forth; or rather, they are the silent meditations with which his bosom is bursting, reduced to *words* for the sake of the reader, who must else remain ignorant of what is passing there. These profound sorrows, these light-and-noise-abhorring ruminations, which the tongue scarce dares utter to deaf walls and chambers, how can they be represented by a gesticulating actor, who comes and mouths them out before an audience, making four hundred people his confidants at once? I say not that it is the fault of the actor so to do; he must pronounce them *ore rotundo*, he must accompany them with his eye, he must insinuate them into his auditory by some trick of eye, tone, or gesture, or he fails. *He must be thinking all the while of his appearance, because he knows that all the while the spectators are judging of it.* And this is the way to represent the shy, negligent, retiring Hamlet.

It is true that there is no other mode of conveying a vast quantity of thought and feeling to a great portion of the audience, who otherwise would never earn it for themselves by reading, and the intellectual acquisition gained this way may, for aught I know, be inestimable; but I am not arguing that Hamlet should not be acted, but how much Hamlet is made another thing by being acted....

So to see Lear acted, – to see an old man tottering about the stage with a walking-stick, turned out of doors by his daughters in a rainy night, has nothing in it but what is painful and disgusting. We want to take him into shelter and relieve him. That is all the feeling which the acting of Lear ever produced in me. But the Lear of Shakspeare cannot be acted. The contemptible machinery by which they mimic the storm which he goes out in, is not more inadequate to represent the horrors of the real elements, than any actor can be to represent Lear: they might more easily propose to personate the Satan of Milton upon a stage, or one of Michael Angelo's terrible figures. The greatness of Lear is not in corporal dimension, but in intellectual: the explosions of his passion are terrible as a volcano: they are storms turning up and disclosing to the bottom that sea, his mind, with all its vast riches. It is his mind which is laid bare. This case of flesh and blood seems too insignificant to be thought on; even as he himself neglects it. On the stage we see nothing but corporal infirmities and weakness, the impotence of rage; while we read it, we see not Lear, but we are Lear, – we are in his mind, we are sustained by a grandeur which baffles the malice of daughters and storms; in the aberrations of his reason, we discover a mighty irregular power of reasoning, immethodized from the ordinary purposes of life, but exerting its powers, as the wind blows where it listeth, at will upon the corruptions and abuses of mankind. What have looks, or tones, to do with that sublime identification of his age with that of the *heavens themselves*, when in his reproaches to them for conniving at the injustice of his children, he reminds them that 'they themselves are old'. What gesture shall we appropriate to this? What has the voice or the eye to do with such things? But the play is beyond all art, as the tamperings with it shew: it is too hard and stony; it must have love-scenes, and a happy ending. It is not enough that Cordelia is a daughter, she must shine as a lover too. Tate has put his hook in the nostrils of this Leviathan, for Garrick and his followers, the showmen of the scene, to draw the mighty beast about more easily. A happy ending! – as if the living martyrdom that Lear had gone through, – the flaying of his feelings alive, did not make a fair dismissal from the stage of life the only decorous thing for him. If he is to live and be happy after, if he could sustain this world's burden after, why all this pudder and preparation, – why torment us with all this unnecessary sympathy? As if the childish pleasure of getting his gilt robes and sceptre again could tempt him to act over again his misused station, – as if at his years, and with his experience, any thing was left but to die.

Lear is essentially impossible to be represented on a stage.

From *Charles Lamb: Prose and Poetry*, with an Introduction and Notes by George Gordon (Oxford, 1921), pp. 83–9. Extract is from pp. 83–8.

▶ Discussion

Lamb justifies his view by arguing that there are two essentially different ways of experiencing a Shakespearean play: via performance and via solitary reading. It is no coincidence that the essay opens with Lamb's meditations being started up by the memorial statue of the eighteenth-century actor David Garrick in Westminster Abbey. This at once associates acting with superficial qualities: 'I was struck with the affected attitude of a figure', 'the introduction of theatrical airs and gestures into a place set apart to remind us of the saddest realities', 'this farrago of false thoughts and nonsense'. The epitaph to Garrick so clearly linked to this merely surface level (dismissed as not really poetry in any real sense) expresses, of course, a view of acting Shakespeare very much opposed to Lamb's. Thus it sees the performance of the actor as akin to the creation of the author – and, indeed, essential to the continued life of the dramatist's creation. Without the genius of the actor, Shakespeare's divinely inspired paintings share the oblivion of their author. Together, Shakespeare and Garrick will resist death till the end of the world, first by their respective revitalisings of the world, and then by their combined geniuses that continue to shine on the earth even after their deaths (I do not mind attempting criticism on the piece).

Lamb wants to establish a different relationship between author and actor, in which there is a gulf between the achievement of the two. He argues that audiences make a gross error in regarding a great actor or great performance as giving insight into the greatness of the author's creation through displaying an affinity with its vision. For him, the actor performs merely physical 'gestures'; while the greatness of Shakespeare is a mental activity. What connection is there between the author's 'absolute mastery over the heart and soul of man ... with those low tricks upon the eye and ear, which a player ... can so easily compass'. Even the language of the plays is seen as an exterior characteristic, reproduced merely mechanically by the actor. Greatness lays in 'the power of originating poetical images and conceptions'. An actor is simply 'able to read or recite the *same when put into words*'. This statement seems particularly extraordinary to a modern reader, because Shakespeare's language is normally seen as a supreme achievement. Here, though, the 'words' are merely superficial gestures recording an originating power which is presumably not verbal, but 'visionary'.

To gain genuine insight into Shakespeare's creations – creations distinguished by an authentic autonomy – a different mode of realisation is needed. Othello or Hamlet are not only created by Shakespeare's mind, but are themselves supremely mental characters. To think that their mental activities can be acted is to accept a crude performance at third hand: 'the bare imitation of the signs of these passions in the countenance or gesture'. Lamb sees the specific realisations of the actor as closing down the freer possibilities that a mental vision derived from reading can achieve: 'How cruelly this operates upon the mind, to have its free conceptions thus crampt and pressed down to the measure of a strait-lacing actuality'. It seems clear that for Lamb what is great in a Shakespearean play is a meaning which cannot directly or easily be expressed or made public. Anything which can be performed through bodily gesture is seen as inferior ('brought down a fine vision to the standard of flesh and blood'). Moreover, anything which can be put into speech is likewise seen as inferior due to physical realisation, its embodiedness. There is a moment when this categorisation of language as physical rather than mental seems to threaten Lamb's distinction between performance and reading, since both are clearly mediated through words, even if only one involves performed words: 'nine parts in ten of what Hamlet[22] does … are the silent meditations with which his bosom is bursting, reduced to *words* for the sake of the reader, who must else remain ignorant of what is passing there'. The argument overall, however, is clear: though written as drama Shakespeare's plays cannot be contained within that *kind*, they transcend what Lamb sees as the inherent limitations of theatre for imagination of this scope and intensity. Therefore the best reading of Shakespeare's plays is achieved through regarding them as a non-theatrical genre, or at least as a kind of drama which is best acted privately in the individual mind. This is a striking reaction for twentieth-century critics, when it has become axiomatic that the written text of a play is only a script which is fully (and infinitely variably) realised through performance, when a whole range of meanings and effects impossible in a written text are realised.[23]

Clearly, adaptation raises many questions about the meaning of a text:

1. Is the adaptation 'true' to the original?
2. Does an essential meaning remain in a work *whatever* genre it is adapted into?
3. Is the meaning of a text determined more by the genre than by anything else?
4. Is an 'original' always clearly superior to an adaptation?
5. How significant is any chronological gap between production of an original and an adaptation?
6. Does an adaptation only have meaning by virtue of its relationship to an original?

7. Is there a kind which is essentially the true and only genre of a text so that any adaptation is inherently inferior? ☐

Finally in this section, I will leave you to explore some of these issues in two exercises concerned with adaptation.

First,

◆ Adapt the short lyric poem printed below into the following genres:
1. diary entry;
2. dramatic version (brief);
3. *short* story version (no more than a page).

◆ What kinds of changes had to be made to the poem in each case?

Theodore Roethke, 'Child on Top of A Greenhouse'

The wind billowing out of the seat of my britches,
My feet crackling splinters of glass and dried putty,
The half-grown chrysanthemums staring up like accusers,
Up through the streaked glass, flashing with sunlight,
A few white clouds all rushing eastward,
A line of elms plunging and tossing like horses,
And everyone, everyone pointing up and shouting!

From *The Lost Son and Other Poems* (1948), reprinted in *The Collected Poems of Theodore Roethke* (London, 1968), p. 43.

Second,

◆ Now read the following extracts from Bram Stoker's *Dracula* (1897 novel), his own stage adaptation (1897 play) and Liz Lochhead's *Dracula* (1987 play). Which of the two adaptations do you prefer? Why?

◆ Judging from these extracts, to what extent do the 'meanings' of *Dracula* remain constant across these three versions?

Bram Stoker, *Dracula*

DRACULA

This then was the Un-Dead home of the King-Vampire, to whom so many more were due. Its emptiness spoke eloquent to make certain what I knew.

Before I began to restore these women to their dead selves through my awful work, I laid in Dracula's tomb some of the Wafer, and so banished him from it, Un-Dead, for ever.

Then began my terrible task, and, I dreaded it. Had it been but one, it had been easy, comparative. But three! To begin twice more after I had been through a deed of horror; for if it was terrible with the sweet Miss Lucy, what would it not be with these strange ones who had survived through centuries, and who had been strengthened by the passing of the years; who would, if they could, have fought for their foul lives ...

Oh, my friend John, but it was butcher work; had I not been nerved by thoughts of other dead, and of the living over whom hung such a pall of fear, I could not have gone on. I tremble and tremble even yet, though till all was over, God be thanked, my nerve did stand. Had I not seen the repose in the first face, and the gladness that stole over it just ere the final dissolution came, as realization that the soul had been won, I could not have gone further with my butchery. I could not have endured the horrid screeching as the stake drove home; the plunging of writhing form, and lips of bloody foam. I should have fled in terror and left my work undone. But it is over! And the poor souls, I can pity them now and weep, as I think of them placid each in her full sleep of death, for a short moment ere fading. For, friend John, hardly had my knife severed the head of each, before the whole body began to melt away and crumble into its native dust, as though the death that should have come centuries agone had at last assert himself and say at once and loud 'I am here!'

Before I left the castle I so fixed its entrances that never more can the Count enter there Un-Dead.

When I stepped into the circle where Madam Mina slept; she woke from her sleep, and, seeing me, cried out in pain that I had endured too much.

'Come!' she said, 'Come away from this awful place! Let us go to meet my husband who is, I know, coming towards us.' She was looking thin and pale and weak; but her eyes were pure and glowed with fervour. I was glad to see her paleness and her illness, for my mind was full of the fresh horror of that ruddy vampire sleep.

And so with trust and hope, and yet full of fear, we go eastward to meet our friends – and *him* – whom Madam Mina tell me that she *know* are coming to meet us.

Mina Harker's Journal

6 *November*. – It was late in the afternoon when the Professor and I took our way towards the east whence I knew Jonathan was coming. We did not go fast, though the way was steeply downhill, for we had to take heavy rugs and wraps with us; we dared not face the possibility of being left without warmth in the cold and the snow. We had to take some of our provisions too, for we were in a perfect desolation, and, so far as we could see through the snow-fall, there was not even the sign of a habitation. When we had gone about a mile, I was tired with the heavy walking and sat down to rest. Then we looked back and saw where the clear line of Dracula's castle cut the sky; for we were so deep under the hill whereon it was set that the angle of perspective of the Carpathian mountains was far below it. We saw it in all its grandeur, perched a thousand feet on the summit of a sheer precipice, and with seemingly a great gap between it and the steep of the adjacent mountain

on any side. There was something wild and uncanny about the place. We could hear the distant howling of wolves. They were far off, but the sound, even though coming muffled through the deadening snowfall, was full of terror. I knew from the way Dr Van Helsing was searching about that he was trying to seek some strategic point, where we would be less exposed in case of attack. The rough roadway still led downwards; we could trace it through the drifted snow.

In a little while the Professor signalled to me, so I got up and joined him. He had found a wonderful spot, a sort of natural hollow in a rock, with an entrance like a doorway between two boulders. He took me by the hand and drew me in: 'See!' he said, 'here you will be in shelter; and if the wolves do come I can meet them one by one.' He brought in our furs, and made a snug nest for me, and got out some provisions and forced them upon me. But I could not eat; to even try to do so was repulsive to me, and, much as I would have liked to please him, I could not bring myself to the attempt. He looked very sad, but did not reproach me. Taking his field-glasses from the case, he stood on the top of the rock, and began to search the horizon. Suddenly he called out: –

'Look! Madam Mina, look! look!' I sprang up and stood beside him on the rock; he handed me his glasses and pointed. The snow was now falling more heavily, and swirled about fiercely, for a high wind was beginning to blow. However there were times when there were pauses between the snow flurries and I could see a long way round. From the height where we were it was possible to see a great distance; and far off, beyond the white waste of snow, I could see the river lying like a black ribbon in kinks and curls as it wound its way. Straight in front of us and not far off – in fact so near that I wondered we had not noticed before – came a group of mounted men hurrying along. In the midst of them was a cart, a long leiter-wagon which swept from side to side, like a dog's tail wagging, with each stern inequality of the road. Outlined against the snow as they were, I could see from the men's clothes that they were peasants or gypsies of some kind.

On the cart was a great square chest. My heart leaped as I saw it, for I felt that the end was coming. The evening was now drawing close, and well I knew that at sunset the Thing, which was till then imprisoned there, would take new freedom and could in any of many forms elude all pursuit. In fear I turned to the Professor; to my consternation, however, he was not there. An instant later, I saw him below me. Round the rock he had drawn a circle, such as we had found shelter in last night. When he had completed it he stood beside me again, saying: –

'At least you shall be safe here from *him*!' He took the glasses from me, and at the next lull of the snow swept the whole space below us. 'See,' he said, 'they come quickly; they are flogging the horses, and galloping as hard as they can.' He paused and went on in a hollow voice:–

'They are racing for the sunset. We may be too late. God's will be done!' Down came another blinding rush of driving snow, and the whole landscape was blotted out. It soon passed, however, and once more his glasses were fixed on the plain. Then came a sudden cry: –

'Look! Look! Look! See, two horsemen follow fast, coming up from the south. It must be Quincey and John. Take the glass. Look, before the snow blots it all out!' I took it and looked. The two men might be Dr Seward and Mr Morris. I knew at all events that neither of them was Jonathan. At the same time I *knew* that Jonathan was not far off; looking around I saw on the north side of the coming party two other men, riding at break-neck speed. One of them I knew was Jonathan, and the other I took, of course, to be Lord Godalming. They, too, were pursuing the party with the cart. When I told the Professor he shouted in glee like a schoolboy, and, after looking intently till a snowfall made sight impossible, he laid his Winchester rifle ready for use against the boulder at the opening of our shelter. 'They are all converging,' he said. 'When the time comes we shall have the gypsies on all sides.' I got out my revolver ready to hand, for whilst we were speaking the howling of wolves came louder and closer. When the snowstorm abated a moment we looked again. It was strange to see the snow falling in such heavy flakes close to us, and beyond, the sun shining more and more brightly as it sank down towards the far mountain tops. Sweeping the glass all around us I could see here and there dots moving singly and in twos and threes and larger numbers – the wolves were gathering for their prey.

Every instant seemed an age whilst we waited. The wind came now in fierce bursts, and the snow was driven with fury as it swept upon us in circling eddies. At times we could not see an arm's length before us; but at others as the hollow-sounding wind swept by us, it seemed to clear the air-space around us so that we could see afar off. We had of late been so accustomed to watch for sunrise and sunset, that we knew with fair accuracy when it would be; and we knew that before long the sun would set.

It was hard to believe that by our watches it was less than an hour that we waited in that rocky shelter before the various bodies began to converge close upon us. The wind came now with fiercer and more bitter sweeps, and more steadily from the north. It seemingly had driven the snow clouds from us, for, with only occasional bursts, the snow fell. We could distinguish clearly the individuals of each party, the pursued and the pursuers. Strangely enough those pursued did not seem to realize, or at least to care, that they were pursued; they seemed, however, to hasten with redoubled speed as the sun dropped lower and lower on the mountain tops.

Closer and closer they drew. The Professor and I crouched down behind our rock, and held our weapons ready; I could see that he was determined that they should not pass. One and all were quite unaware of our presence.

All at once two voices shouted out to: 'Halt!' One was my Jonathan's, raised in a high key of passion; the other Mr Morris's strong resolute tone of quiet command. The gypsies may not have known the language, but there was no mistaking the tone, in whatever tongue the words were spoken. Instinctively they reined in, and at the instant Lord Godalming and Jonathan dashed up at one side and Dr Seward and Mr Morris on the other. The leader of the gypsies, a splendid looking fellow who sat his horse like a centaur, waved them back, and in a fierce voice gave to his companions some word to proceed. They lashed the horses which sprang forward; but the four men raised their Winchester rifles, and in an unmistakeable way commanded them to stop. At the same moment Dr Van Helsing and I rose behind the rock and pointed our weapons at them. Seeing that they were surrounded the men tightened their reins and drew up. The leader turned to them and gave a word at which every man of the gipsy party drew what weapon he carried, knife or pistol, and held himself in readiness to attack. Issue was joined in an instant.

The leader, with a quick movement of his rein, threw his horse out in front, and pointing first to the sun – now close down on the hill tops – and then to the castle, said something which I did not understand. For answer, all four men of our party threw themselves from their horses and dashed towards the cart. I should have felt terrible fear at seeing Jonathan in such danger, but that the ardour of battle must have been upon me as well as the rest of them; I felt no fear, but only a wild, surging desire to do something. Seeing the quick movement of our parties, the leader of the gypsies gave a command; his men instantly formed round the cart in a sort of undisciplined endeavour, each one shouldering and pushing the other in his eagerness to carry out the order.

In the midst of this I could see that Jonathan on one side of the ring of men, and Quincey on the other, were forcing a way to the cart; it was evident that they were bent on finishing their task before the sun should set. Nothing seemed to stop or even to hinder them. Neither the levelled weapons or the flashing knives of the gypsies in front, or the howling of the wolves behind, appeared to even attract their attention. Jonathan's impetuosity, and the manifest singleness of his purpose, seemed to overawe those in front of him; instinctively they cowered aside and let him pass. In an instant he had jumped upon the cart, and, with a strength which seemed incredible, raised the great box, and flung it over the wheel to the ground. In the meantime, Mr Morris had had to use force to pass through his side of the ring of Szgany. All the time I had been breathlessly watching Jonathan I had, with the tail of my eye, seen him pressing desperately forward, and had seen the knives of the gypsies flash as he won a way through them, and they cut at him. He had parried with his great bowie knife, and at first I thought that he too had come through in safety; but as he sprang beside Jonathan, who had by now jumped from the cart, I could see that with his left hand he was clutching at his side, and that the blood was spurting through his fingers. He did not delay notwithstanding this, for as Jonathan, with desperate energy, attacked one end of the chest, attempting to prize off the lid with his great kukri knife, he attacked the other frantically with his bowie. Under the efforts of both men the lid began to yield; the nails drew with a quick screeching sound, and the top of the box was thrown back.

By this time the gypsies, seeing themselves covered by the Winchesters, and at the mercy of Lord Godalming and Dr Seward, had given in and made no further resistance. The sun was almost down on the mountain tops, and the shadows of the whole group fell long upon the snow. I saw the Count lying within the box upon the earth, some of which the rude falling from the cart had scattered over him. He was deathly pale, just like a waxen image, and the red eyes glared with the horrible vindictive look which I knew too well.

As I looked, the eyes saw the sinking sun, and the look of hate in them turned to triumph.

But, on the instant, came the sweep and flash of Jonathan's great knife. I shrieked as I saw it shear through the throat; whilst at the same moment Mr Morris's bowie knife plunged into the heart.

It was like a miracle; but before our very eyes, and almost in the drawing of a breath, the whole body crumbled into dust and passed from our sight.

I shall be glad as long as I live that even in that moment of final dissolution, there was in the face a look of peace, such as I never could have imagined might have rested there.

The Castle of Dracula now stood out against the red sky, and every stone of its broken battlements was articulated against the light of the setting sun.

The gypsies, taking us as in some way the cause of the extraordinary disappearance of the dead man, turned, without a word, and rode away as if for their lives. Those who were unmounted jumped upon the leiter-wagon and shouted to the horsemen not to desert them. The wolves, which had withdrawn to a safe distance, followed in their wake, leaving us alone.

Mr Morris, who had sunk to the ground, leaned on his elbow, holding his hand pressed to his side; the blood still gushed through his fingers. I flew to him, for the Holy circle did not now keep me back; so did the two doctors. Jonathan knelt behind him and the wounded man laid back his head on his shoulder. With a sigh he took, with a feeble effort, my hand in that of his own which was unstained. He must have seen the anguish of my heart in my face, for he smiled at me and said: –

'I am only too happy to have been of any service! Oh, God!' he cried suddenly, struggling up to a sitting posture and pointing to me, 'It was worth this to die! Look! look!'

The sun was now right down upon the mountain top, and the red gleams fell upon my face, so that it was bathed in rosy light. With one impulse the men sank on their knees and a deep and earnest 'Amen' broke from all as their eyes followed the pointing of his finger as the dying man spoke: –

'Now God be thanked that all has not been in vain! See! the snow is not more stainless than her forehead! The curse has passed away!'

And, to our bitter grief, with a smile and in silence, he died, a gallant gentleman.

Note

Seven years ago we all went through the flames; and the happiness of some of us since then is, we think, well worth the pain we endured. It is an added joy to Mina and to me that our boy's birthday is the same day as that on which Quincey Morris died. His mother holds, I know, the secret belief that some of our brave friend's spirit has passed into him. His bundle of names links all our little band of men together; but we call him Quincey.

In the summer of this year we made a journey to Transylvania, and went over the old ground which was, and is, to us so full of vivid and terrible memories. It was almost impossible to believe that the things which we had seen with our own eyes and heard with our own ears were living truths. Every trace of all that had been was blotted out. The castle stood as before, reared high above a waste of desolation.

When we got home we got to talking of the old time – which we could all look back on without despair, for Godalming and Seward are both happily married. I took the papers from the safe where they have been ever since our return so long ago. We were struck with the fact, that in all the mass of material of which the record is composed, there is hardly one authentic document; nothing but a mass of type-writing, except the later notebooks of Mina and Seward and myself, and Van Helsing's memorandum. We could hardly ask anyone, even did we wish to, to accept these as proofs of so wild a story. Van Helsing summed it all up as he said, with our boy on his knee: –

'We want no proofs; we ask none to believe us! This boy will some day know what a brave and gallant woman his mother is. Already he knows her sweetness and loving care; later on he will understand how some men so loved her, that they did dare much for her sake.'

JONATHAN HARKER

From *Dracula*, Norton Critical Edition, ed. Nina Auerbach and David J. Skal (New York and London, 1997), pp. 320–7.

Bram Stoker, *Dracula or The Undead*

[Scene 5] – {The Same, Evening}

[Van Helsing, Seward, Godalming,
Morris, Mina and Harker]

MINA: {Here is a memorandum which I should like you all to consider.}
{*Reads*} "*Ground of inquiry*. – Count Dracula's problem is to get back to his own place.

(a) He must be *brought back* by some one. This is evident; for had he power to move himself as he wished he could go either as man, or wolf, or bat, or in some other way. He evidently fears discovery or interference, in the state of helplessness in which he must be – confined as he is between dawn and sunset in his wooden box.

(b) *How is he to be taken?*: – Here a process of exclusions may help us. By road, by rail, by water?

   1 *By Road*. – There are endless difficulties, especially in leaving a city.

   (x) There are people, and people are curious and investigate. A hint, a surmise, a doubt as to what might be in the box would destroy him.

   (y) There are, or there might be, customs and octroi officers to pass.

   (z) His pursuers might follow. This is his greatest fear; and in order to prevent his being betrayed he has repelled, so far as he can even his victim – me!

   2 *By Rail*. – There is no one in charge of the box. It would have to take its chance of being delayed; and delay would be fatal with enemies on the track. True, he might escape at night, but what would he be, if left in a strange place with no refuge that he could fly to. This is not what he intends; and he does not mean to risk it.

   3 *By Water*. – Here is the safest way, in one respect, but with most danger in another. On the water he is powerless except at night, and even then he can only call fog and storm and snow and his wolves. But were he wrecked, the living water would engulf him, helpless; and he would indeed be lost. He could have the vessel drive to land; but if it were unfriendly land wherein he was not free to move, his position would still be desperate.

We know from the record that he was on the water; so what we have to do is to ascertain what water.

The first thing is to realise exactly what he has done as yet; we may, then, get a light on what his later task is to be.

Firstly, – We must differentiate between what he did in London as part of his general plan of action, when he was pressed for moments and had to arrange as best he could.

Secondly we must see, as well as we can surmise it from the facts we know of, what he has done here.

As to the first, he evidently intended to arrive at Galatz, and sent invoice to Varna to deceive us lest we should ascertain his means of exit from England! his immediate and sole purpose then was to escape. The proof of this, is the letter of instructions sent to Immanuel Hildesheim to clear and take away the box before sunrise. There is also the instructions to Petrof Skinski. These we must only guess at; but there must have been some letter or message, since Skinski came to Hildesheim.

That, so far, his plans were successful we know. The *Czarina Catherine* made a phenomenally quick journey – so much so that Captain Donaldson's suspicions were aroused; but his superstition united with his canniness played the Count's game for him, and he ran with his favouring wind through fogs and all till he brought up blindfold at Galatz. That the Count's arrangements were well made, has been proved. Hildesheim cleared the box, took it off and gave it to Skinski. Skinski took it – and here we lose the trail. We only know that the box is somewhere on the water, moving along. The customs and the octroi, if there be any, have been avoided.

Now we come to what the Count must have done after his arrival – on land, at Galatz.

The box was given to Skinski before sunrise. At sunrise the Count could appear in his own form. Here, we ask why Skinski was chosen at all to aid in the work? In my husband's diary, Skinski is mentioned as dealing with the Slovaks who trade down the river to the port; and the man's remark, that the murder was the work of a Slovak, showed the general feeling against his class.

My surmise is, this: that in London the Count decided to get back to his Castle by water, as the most safe and secret way. He was brought from the Castle by Szagany, and probably they delivered their cargo to Slovaks who took the boxes to Varna, for there they were shipped to London. Thus the Count had knowledge of the persons who could arrange this service. When the box was on land, before sunrise, or after sunset, he came out from his box, met Skinski and instructed him what to do as to arranging the carriage of the box up some river. When this was done and he knew that all was in train, he blotted out his traces, as he thought, by murdering his agent.

I have examined the map and find that the river most suitable for the Slovaks to have ascended is either the Pruth or the Sereth, I read in the typescript that in my trance I heard cows low and water swirling level with my ears and the creaking of wood. The Count in his box, then, was on a river in an open boat – propelled probably either by oars or poles, for the banks are near and it is working against stream. There would be no such sound if floating down stream.

Of course it may not be either the Sereth or the Pruth, but we may possibly investigate further. Now of these two, the Pruth is the more easily navigated, but the Sereth is, at Tundu, joined by the Bistritza which runs up round the Borgo Pass. The loop it makes is manifestly as close to Dracula's Castle as can be got by water."

VAN H.: Our Madam Mina is once more our teacher. Her eyes have seen where we were blinded. Now we are on the track once again, and this timewe may succeed. Our enemy is at his most helpless; and if we can come on him by day, on the water our task will be over. He has a start, but he is powerless to hasten, as he may not leave his box lest those who carry him may suspect; for them to suspect would be to prompt them to throw him in the stream where he perish. This he knows, and will not. Now men to our Council of War; for, here and now, we must plan what each and all shall do.

GODALMING: I shall get a steam launch and follow him.

MORRIS: And I, horses to follow on the bank lest by chance he land.

VAN H.: Good! both good. But neither must go alone. There must be force to overcome force if need be; the Slovak is strong and rough, and he carries rude arms.

MORRIS: I have brought some Winchesters; they are pretty handy in a crowd, and there may be wolves. The Count, if you remember, took some other precautions! he made some requisitions on others that Mrs. Harker could not quite hear or understand. We must be ready at all points.

SEWARD: I think I had better go with Quincey. We have been accustomed to hunt together, and we two, well armed, will be a match for whatever may come along. You must not be alone Art. It may be necessary to fight the Slovaks, and a chance thrust – for I don't suppose these fellows carry guns – would undo all our plans. There must be no chances, this time; we shall not rest until the Count's head and body have been separated, and we are sure that he cannot reincarnate.

VAN H.: Friend Jonathan, {you must go with my Lord Godalming}, this is to you for twice reasons. First, because you are young and brave and can fight, and all energies may be needed at the last; and again that is your right to destroy him – that – which has wrought such woe to you and yours. Be not afraid for Madam Mina; she will be my care, if I may. I am old. My legs are not so quick to run as once; and I am not used to ride so long or to pursue as need be, or to fight with lethal weapons. But I can be of other service; I can fight in other way, and I can die if need be, as well as younger men. Now let me say that what I would is this; while you, my Lord Godalming, and friend Jonathan go in your so swift little steamboat up the river, and whilst John and Quincey guard the bank where perchance he might be landed, I will take Madam Mina right into the heart of the enemy's country. Whilst the old fox is tied in his box, floating on the running stream whence he cannot escape to land – where he dares not raise the lid of his coffin-box lest his Slovak carriers should in fear leave him to perish – we shall go in the track where Jonathan went, from Bistritz over the Borgo, and find our way to the Castle of Dracula. Here, Madam Mina's hypnotic power will surely help, and we shall find our way – all dark and unknown otherwise – after the first sunrise when we are near that fateful place. There is much to be done, and other places to be made sanctify, so that that nest of viper be obliterated.

HARKER: Do you mean to say, Professor Van Helsing, that you would bring Mina, in her sad case and tainted as she is with that devil's illness, right into the jaws of his deathtrap? Not for the world! Not for Heaven or Hell! Do you know what the place is? Have you seen that awful den of hellish infamy – with the very moonlight alive with gristly shapes, and every speck of dust that whirls in the wind a devouring monster in embryo? Have you felt the Vampire's lips upon your throat? Oh my God what have we done to have this terror upon us!

VAN H.: Oh my friend, it is because I would save Madam Mina from that awful place that I would go. God forbid that I should take her into that place. There is work – wild work – to be done there, that her eyes may not see. We men here, all save Jonathan, have seen with their own eyes what is to be done before that place can be purify. Remember that we are in terrible straits. If the Count escape us this time, and he is strong and subtle

and cunning, he may choose to sleep him for a century; and then in time
our dear one –

> (*He took my hand*) [*Mina's.*]

– would come to him to keep him company, and would be as those others
that you, Jonathan, saw. You have told us of their gloating lips; you heard
their ribald laugh as they clutched the moving bag that the Count threw
to them. You shudder; and well may it be. Forgive me that I make you
so much pain, but it is necessary. My friend, is it not a dire need for
the which I am giving, if need me, my life? If it were that anyone went
into that place to stay it is I who would have to go, to keep them
company.

HARKER: Do as you will. We are in the hands of God!

Scene [5] – {Outside Castle Dracula, Night}

> {*Professor Van Helsing makes a ring round Mina.*}

MINA: No! No! Do not go without. Here you are safe!

VAN H.: But you? It is for you that I fear!

MINA: Fear for me! Why fear for me? None is safer in all the world from them
than I am.

> {*Rising up the three women float round the ring.*}

WOMAN: Come, sister. Come to us. Come! Come!

{*Dawn.*}

Scene [6] – {The Same, Towards Sunset}

VAN H.: {And now I have made safe the Castle and destroyed those poor
Un-Deads. We must only wait till He and our friends arrive.} Look!
Madam Mina, look! look!

MINA: {I see a far off party of gypsies surrounding a cart wherein is a great
box.}

VAN H.: {Keep within the ring.} At least you shall be safe here from him!

MINA: See, they come quickly; they are flogging the horses, and galloping as
hard as they can.

VAN H.: They are racing for the sunset. We may be too late. God's will be
done.
{But see, two horsemen from far off in the north.} Look! Look! See, two
{other} horsemen follow fast, coming up from the south. It must be
Quincey and John. Take the glass. Look, before the snow blots it all out!

MINA: They are all converging, when the time comes we shall have the
gypsies on all sides.

> {*Gypsies and horsemen draw near.*}

MORRIS: Halt!

> {*Horsemen fight with Gypsies and Morris and Harker throw box from cart and prise it open. Count seen. Fades away as knives cut off his*}

head. Sunset falls on group. Morris is wounded and Harker holds up his head.}

MORRIS: I am only too happy to have been of any service! Oh, God! It was worth for this to die! Look! look!

{The sunset falls on Mina and they see her forehead stainless.}

[MORRIS:] Now God be thanked that all has not been in vain! See! the snow is not more stainless than her forehead! The curse has passed away.

CURTAIN

From Stoker's own stage version of *Dracula*, ed. Sylvia Starshine (Nottingham, 1997), pp. 186–93.

Liz Lochhead, *Dracula*

SCENE 15

SEWARD *performs the ritual of staking* LUCY. *Steels himself. Crosses himself. Does it with deliberation. Just a single stroke. Perhaps a single gasp or deep sigh or a sort of shudder of* LUCY's *voice. Certainly nothing violent, not a scream, a consummation.* SEWARD *sobs with a couple of dry, racking shudders.*

SEWARD: Lucy, my darling, forgive me … I failed you.

SCENE 16

'NISBETT' *and* 'GRICE', *during the laying out of* RENFIELD, *stripping him naked, washing him down, putting cottonwool in ears and nostrils, keep up a schizophrenic switch back and forward between their two modes,* her *two modes? Both 'sides' of the character are, 'good' and 'bad', reconciling themselves – by* RENFIELD's *redemption – sacrifice? He certainly ought to look like a pietà.* FLORRIE *brings on basin and* 'NURSES' *and frozen, shocked* FLORRIE *work together.* 'NURSES' *prattle matter-of-factly at first – of course they always were one single person.*

GRICE: Dead, eh? Would you credit it. Just on my way off duty and Seward nabs us. White as this sheet here, he was. Nurse! Nurse! there's been a terrible accident. Some bloody accident!
NISBETT: Sewage pipes. Who'd have thought old Renfield'd commit sewage pipes? I'd've thought 'e'd of been the last, I always says to Drinkwater, such a lust for life he had in him, old Renfield, even at his maddest and most miserable.
GRICE: Must've went beserk and chucked himself down the well of the stair and with one hell of a force to stove his head in and make a mulch of himself like that –

NISBETT: – Tragedy really. (*Pause.*) You get attached. Funny how they've all got their own personalities –

GRICE: In some cases several.

(*Pause.*)

NISBETT: Some of 'em, though, when they're gone, so dead you'd think they'd never been alive, others, eh, pinker 'n' realer than ever, 'cept they've not the breath in them to mist the mirror.

GRICE: (*To* FLORRIE) Feel sick, girlie? Go on, then, I'll manage. Never seen no one what's croaked before? Get to my age you seen it all –

NISBETT: It's all one to me.

(*From now on the* NISBETT/GRICE *split disappears till we have a single grieving whole. Bad and good. Accepting each other at this point the simple two-women-laying-out-a-corpse picture is broken by every extra on and cleaning up and clearing the stage of everything except* RENFIELD'*s body, on a sheet, on a trolley which can be wheeled out.* FLORRIE *and* NURSE *continue their rituals.*)

GRICE: Poor old Renfield! One minute it's professors and doctors queuing up for you wiv pennies-for-your-thoughts, now it's pennies-for-your-eyes, eh?

NISBETT: What you do it now for, though, eh? Me day off. Goin' to a wedding. Would choose the time I'd been invited to a bit of a knees-up. Could've been singin' and 'uggin' and kissin' and rollin' out the barrel stead of layin' out a stiff under a windin' sheet.

GRICE: Hey, but we'll miss you, eh, Renfield? Poor mad bugger.

NISBETT: Heigh ho!

(*She embraces Florrie. Then she breaks down and sobs,* FLORRIE *comforting her and helping her. In a sort of cortège,* FLORRIE, *her weeping released, wheels off the covered-over* RENFIELD. *The stage is bare and clear empty, except for Dracula's cloak. Black velvet on the bare stage.*)

SCENE 17

Everything is cleared away and, in the mist and darkness, appear the heavy gates of Dracula's castle. Three great thumps at them from behind and they bulge and strain, but hold. Silence after the third battery, and MINA'*s voice is heard ringing out clearly, from behind these gates at the back of the stage.*

MINA: Stand aside, you men!

(*The gates fly open wide (or fall down). The mist clears and we see* MINA, *wrapped in furs and deathly pale, blindfolded, reaching out straight ahead of her. Quite far back, held behind* VAN HELSING'*s outstretched arm, are the amazed-looking* JONATHAN *and* SEWARD. *There are flurries of snow outside and on all their clothes.*)

SEWARD: She only had to touch!

MINA: We are home now at the black heart of him. I knew it. (JONATHAN *runs to* MINA, *leaving their bags and stake.*)

JONATHAN: Mina, my own wife, my brave one.

MINA: Untie my eyes and let me see.

(*He does so. Even more obvious now is the red mark left by the Communion Host.* MINA *holds the blindfold, her eyes still shut. Then opens them, blinking. The others look around, afraid, alert all during* MINA*'s next speech.)*

All these weeks in the dark with those I loved, travelling blind. My other senses told me I was on a railway train – the smell of smoke, the sound and vibration of the iron wheels – but behind my eyes I was on the open seas. You fed me oranges; I smelt the peel, spat out the pips, but all the time I tasted blood. Then all around me the noise and bustle of an English port, whilst already in the darkness of my own head I was landed on a European shore. You comforted me in my cabin while all along I sped in a black coach behind a dark driver who whipped six black horses faster than the wind and the wheels hardly bumped on rutted roads. When you crowded me round, protecting me from the gasps and fear and hatred of the inn girls who saw my mark, and you spoonfed me with stew and rye bread among the babble of foreign tongues, I was already here alone on the high crag of my castle and when you, my husband, held me tight and tethered to the earth in strange bed after strange bed, while you slept I flew wild and free in the night.

JONATHAN: We will kill him and set you free. And … if we fail I'll come with you, I won't let you go into the dark alone.

VAN HELSING: Thus this devil can make true married love into something which can swell his ranks. It is very very dark but, thank God, the dawn will soon be here.

(DRACULA *bursts out of his tomb high up above the gates of the castle.*)

DRACULA: So, old enemy, you have pursued me till I have caught you. You are standing corn for me to reap.

(VAN HELSING *and* JONATHAN *whip out crucifixes, hold them aloft,* JONATHAN *holding his in front of* MINA, *who is straining to get free and snarling like a dog, with her eyes flickering horridly.* DRACULA *coos like a dove.*)

Pretty one, pretty one … (*Coos.*)

MINA: Yes!

(*She moans and strains towards him.*)

SEWARD: Lucy, my love, I'll kill him! Mina!

(*And* SEWARD *runs towards* DRACULA *with a knife but* DRACULA *grabs his hand by the wrist and holds it at arm's length, easily.*)

VAN HELSING: Arthur, wait, the light!

DRACULA: All my darlings, I knew that you would come.

SEWARD: Lucy!

(DRACULA *reaches out the other hand and snaps* SEWARD*'s neck bone deftly. He falls.* DRACULA *laughs.* MINA *screams in anguish, and sobs Arthur's name.*)

DRACULA: Hush, darling one, later you can feast on his sweet flesh.

(*And he has waited too long, been too distracted … light, rosy light, floods in.*)

Help me!

(*He sinks to his knees.* VAN HELSING *swiftly grabs the equipment and* JONATHAN *and* VAN HELSING *rush to him and despatch him with the stake.* JONATHAN *hammers it home.* MINA *is sunk to her knees sobbing. For* ARTHUR? *No – probably for* DRACULA. *Anyway, very ambiguously …*)

MINA: Oh, my love!

(VAN HELSING *goes to her, taking a silver mirror out of his bag.*)

VAN HELSING: Look at yourself!

(*She stops crying and does so.*)

The mark! It has gone for ever.

MINA: I am cursed no more!

(VAN HELSING *touches her with the Host. She laughs out loud in relief.*)

I'm clean.

VAN HELSING: At last!

(VAN HELSING *takes* JONATHAN *and joins them, hand to hand, together.*)

Love each other and live.

(*They kiss. Then* JONATHAN *pulls apart.*)

JONATHAN: You wanted him.

MINA: Yes. (*Pause.*) You wanted her.

JONATHAN: That bride …? Oh yes, I did. I wanted them all.

VAN HELSING: In the name of him who gave his all for you, the best and truest friend any of us will ever know, I tell you to forgive!

(*He takes them over to* SEWARD*'s body and they all look down at it, weeping.*)

Sons should bury fathers. You should have taken me! (*Sobbing, he crosses* SEWARD*'s hands, then goes to* DRACULA. *Looks down.*) God be our witness, when we killed him True Dead it was an act of mercy and not of hate.

JONATHAN: I hate him yet. I hate him. If I could send his soul to burning hell ten times over, then I would and would again.

VAN HELSING: Who wrought all this misery, he is the saddest case of all. Whose victim was he, he made us suffer so? Remember, husband, until today's sweet release she was likely to some day need such pity. Would you have had her denied it by someone with reason for a heart as full of terror and revenge as yours?

Forgive!

Dracula is dead, long live Mina and Jonathan. May God forgive all his poor creatures, the living and the dead.

(JONATHAN *crosses* DRACULA*'s hands just as* VAN HELSING *did his friend* SEWARD*'s, something sacred and final.* MINA *kisses* JONATHAN, *gently, in gratitude for his mercy.* VAN HELSING *picks up the hammer and the three stakes, touches the crucifix to his own forehead, then touches it to the hammer and stakes.*)

(*Quietly, as if to himself*) And now his three vile brides. One final, hellish bit of butchery and God's iciest winds will sear through these ruins and cauterize them clean.

(VAN HELSING *exits through the open gates.* MINA *and* JONATHAN *go to* SEWARD *and look down.* MINA, *on her knees behind his head, bends down and kisses his dead face. As she straightens up the first screaming screech from the first vampire bride and* MINA *shudders with each echoing blow from the hammer as if it was through her.* JONATHAN *pulls her to her feet, kisses her as second scream and set of blows ring out. As it stops they fall back and look at each other breathing.* JONATHAN *grasps Dracula's cloak of darkness and spreads it out at their feet. They sink down on it, kissing. Third and final set of shriek and hammer blows. As it dies away with our lovers entwined on Dracula's cloak, white snow begins to fall, then blush-pink petals like apple blossom and confetti, darker pink and finally red, red petals as the curtain falls.*)

From *Dracula* and *Mary Queen of Scots Got her Head Chopped Off* (Harmondsworth, 1989), pp. 142–7.

Further Reading

Cartmell, Deborah (and others), *Pulping Fictions: Consuming Culture Across the Literature/ Media Divide* (Pluto Press, 1996).

——, and Imelda Whelan (eds), *Adaptations: From Text to Screen, Screen to Text* (London, Routledge, 1999).

Derrida, Jacques, 'The Law of Genres' in *Acts of Literature*, ed. Derek Attridge (London, Routledge, 1992).

Duff, David, *Modern Genre Theory* (London, Longman, 2000).

Dubrow, Heather, *Genre* (Critical Idiom Series) (London, Methuen, 1982).

Fowler, Alistair, *Kinds of Literature: An Introduction to the Theory of Genre and Modes* (Oxford, Clarendon Press, 1982).

Furst, Lilian R. and Peter N. Skrine, *Naturalism* (Critical Idiom Series) (London, Methuen, 1971).

Griffiths, James, *Adaptations as Imitations: Films from Novels* (London, Associated University Presses, 1997).

Todorov, Tzvetan, *Genres of Discourse* (Cambridge, Cambridge University Press, 1978, 1990).

History

4.1 History, Literature, Texts

In some cultures there has been no sharp distinction between literature and history: your stories were your record of the past. We have already looked at the Anglo-Saxon poem *Widsith*, which is both poem and history (and geography ...). Similarly, for Greeks in classical times, Homer's epic poem of the Trojan war, the *Iliad* (written down circa eighth century BC) was both the supreme work of literature and a work of history.

However, history and literature, though regarded as having kinship, are equally often seen as distinct, and, in some respects, opposed spheres in modern Western cultures. In the sixteenth century, Sir Philip Sidney famously suggests some of the distinctions and resemblances between the two (and between some other areas) in an essay which argues for the supreme value of literature (= poesie) above all other verbal arts.

> ◆ Read the two paragraphs below from Sidney's *Defense of Poesie*. How does he characterise history and 'poesie'?

And even Historiographers (although theyr lippes sounde of things doone, and veryty be written in theyr fore-heads) have been glad to borrow both fashion and perchance weight of Poets ... either [stealing or usurping] of Poetrie their passionate describing of passions, the many particularities of battailes, which no man could affirme, or ... long Orations put in the mouthes of great Kings and Captaines, which it is certain they never pronounced. So that, truely, neyther Phylosopher nor Historiographer coulde at the first have entred into the gates of popular judgement, if they had not taken a great pasport of Poetry ...

The Lawyer sayth what men have determined. The Historian what men have done. The Grammarian speaketh only of the rules of speech; and the Rhethoritian and Logitian, considering what in nature will soonest prove and perswade ... Only the Poet, disdayning to be tied to any such subjection, lifted up with the vigor of his own intention, doothe growe in effect into another nature, in making things either better than Nature bringeth forth, or, quite newe forms such as never were in nature … freely ranging onley within the Zodiack of his owne wit.

Written c. 1582; published 1595. Extract from *Defense of Poesie, Astrophil and Stella and other Writings*, ed. Elizabeth Watson (1997), p. 85, ll. 23–35; p. 89, ll. 8–27.

▶ Discussion

Sidney's basic opposition here is between History as being based in *fact* ('veryty', 'things doone') and Poesie as springing from *imagination and invention* ('newe formes such as never were'). He does, however, suggest a similarity between History and Poesie in the first paragraph, when he argues that History is not entirely factual, but uses a range of poetic (or literary devices) in order to enhance its narratives of 'what men have done'. Sidney is specifically referring to early history writing here – arguing his view that history was only accepted as a relatively popular form (= a pleasurable, profitable kind of reading in this case?) because it borrowed interesting devices from literature (the description of emotion, the specific details given in narratives, the use of dramatic speeches). This literary element in history has been discussed by some modern thinkers too, as we shall see later in the section.

The distinction between fact and fiction is still though the most obvious way of distinguishing the two areas (the two terms will recur). Yet there remains a close association between literary study and historical study – usually in the opposite direction to that suggested by Sir Philip Sidney. Where he sees history borrowing from Literature,[1] it is probably more common now to see literary criticism as having a firm base in history for certain of its usual elements. □

> ◆ Read the following introductory passage by Arthur Pollard. What does the Introduction aim to do? How does it link history and literature?

It is difficult to characterise in a brief compass a span of time as long as that in which Queen Victoria reigned over England and her realms beyond the seas. Not only did it cover so many years, but those years also witnessed political, economic, intellectual and scientific change previously unparalleled in British history … W. E. Houghton cites many who felt themselves to be living in an age of transition … 'an awful age of transition' was Tennyson's phrase …

In the 1840s the half had not been told. By the end of the century Britain exercised 'dominion over palm and pine' … the Navy imposed a *pax Britannica* on many parts of the world. Trade and Christianity followed the flag. At home successive Reform Acts made democracy more and more a reality … Science and technology together testified to man's adventure and achievement. Darwin and his associates gave man an entirely new view of himself and his place on earth, whilst technical advances extended and completed the revolution in industry that had begun in the previous century. These technical advances were themselves accompanied and in some ways made possible by the changes which brought into being the necessary commercial and financial structure of modern capitalism ...

If progress is one Victorian watchword, freedom is the other ... the middle classes were supreme. They were immensely self-confident, commercially successful, scornful of the old establishments of aristocracy and Church, but though they often showed a fine sense of social responsibility (... Mrs Gaskell is a fine literary example of their conscience in this respect), most of them failed to see the relevance of culture ...

Hope was not fulfilled, confidence ebbed, and the last years of the century were marked by reaction, resignation and disillusion ... It all amounted to what Mark Pattison described as 'the present mood of depression and despondency' ... Tennyson was discouraged, Hardy gloomy, Shaw devastatingly critical, Wilde scintillatingly cynical. Arnold had lamented the age's 'sick hurry, its divided aims'; at the end it came to worse than this. It appeared to have lost all sense of purpose ... A period in which so many contrary forces interacted so intricately and energetically cannot fail to be interesting. Its writers, expressing the spirit of the age with all the resources of imagination, feeling and thought, abundantly reveal their response to their time ...

From Arthur Pollard, *Sphere History of Literature in the English Language.* Extract from Introduction to vol. 6: *The Victorians* (1970), pp. 9–11.

Discussion

The introduction plainly aims to give a sense of the entire Victorian period as a unit, though it also stresses that the period was various and needs to be further subdivided. Nevertheless, it is seen as possible to characterise periods and subperiods through describing what are said to be their dominant characteristics:

1840s – a distinctive Victorianism not yet achieved
1850s–1880s – a period of great change, and of optimism about progress
1890s – loss of direction and confidence; a pessimistic end to the period

This ability to characterise the period and its subdivisions provides the link to the passage's references to literature generally and specifically. Thus writers are seen to share (and express) the most characteristic features of the period and its smaller segments. Tennyson's phrase about transition sums up the feelings of many, and serves to label the whole period; the novelist Mrs Gaskell is an example of the middle-class optimism of the middle period; Tennyson, Hardy, Shaw and Wilde all share (thus proving its characterising force) the gloom of the final decade. The use of these writers as examples shows the passage's urge to see writers and literature moving in step with the general history of the time. Indeed, it is this close relationship which motivates the whole Introduction. It concentrates on the mood of the period in general on the understanding that the reader will apply this to literature both as a background and as a guide to the character of Victorian literary texts. It could be said that this gives the great range of Victorian literary texts at least the appearance of a shared origin in a 'factual' history. □

Though the particular example brings out this 'in-step' approach to literature and history especially clearly, it is not peculiar in moving back and forth between mutually supporting literary examples and general characterisations of an age. The broad assumptions that the passage makes – that literary/historical periods can be similarly characterised, that knowledge of history and of literature is mutually supporting – are found widely in literary study. It is, for example, common to teach university English in a historical sequence, and to organise syllabuses in terms governed by historical periods. Thus an archetypal university English degree might have a structure something like the following:[2]

Year 1
Middle English Literature
Poetry 1540–1770
Drama – Elizabethan, Jacobean,
          Caroline, Restoration
The Eighteenth-century Novel

Year 2
Romantic Poetry
Victorian Poetry
European Drama 1880–1960
The Nineteenth-century Novel

Year 3
The Novel – Modernism to Postmodernism
Modern Poetry – 1922–1990
Contemporary Drama – 1960 to the Present
Postcolonial Literatures – 1948–1990

Organisation of degree courses in this way is so usual as to seem natural. In fact, though, it assumes certain relationships between literature and history which can be thought through.

 Why are literary texts (so often) grouped in historical periods?

 ## Discussion

The grouping of texts presumably partly arises from the need to organise literary study and knowledge (e.g. as courses with reading lists and exams…). In order to group texts, some principles of difference and similarity are needed. Though not the only possible criterion,[3] the period of a text's first appearance is clearly a way of readily assigning any text to a group. However, this alone would not necessarily suggest anything more significant than a neat filing system. Presumably we suggest rather more than this by grouping texts historically. We expect that historically grouped sets of texts will show real kinship in ways which are worth studying, and which actually explain features of those texts. □

In this sense, literary study often *is* seen as historical: period of origin is regarded as making a major contribution to meaning, and is therefore an essential basis for interpretation. Thus, if we did not know when a text was written, this would presumably make a considerable difference to our ability to interpret it (or, rather to how we interpreted it?). We could imagine, to take a slightly absurd example, a slightly misinformed student who wrote about the novels of Jane Austen (who died in 1817) in the belief that she was a Victorian writer (i.e. active in the period between 1837 and 1901). In terms of facts, the student would be wrong by between 20 and 85 years (!), but, even more importantly, widely held assumptions about Victorian culture (e.g. ideas about prudishness, industrialised society, and religion) might shape the interpretation of the text very considerably. For many critics, any such interpretations assuming the wrong historical origins for Jane Austen's work would be invalid, since they start from a false premise (it would not be impossible for the student to say valid things about the text – but anything drawing on the context would be suspect). Mistakes are not, of course, confined to students; professional critics have been known to get their dates wrong (I recall a professional medievalist in a momentary lapse describing a group of peasants round a fire in a fifteenth-century manuscript illustration as 'roasting potatoes'[4]). Errors apart, a number of canonical literary texts, especially from earlier periods, cannot be precisely dated. For example, Marlowe's play *Dr Faustus* has been dated to either 1589 or 1592; and there has been some discussion of how early (and how pagan?) or how late (and how Christian?) an Anglo-Saxon poem like *Beowulf* is.[5] It is noticeable that critical discussions of such works frequently do discuss the date, because different points of origin (sometimes a matter of centuries, sometimes a matter of a few years or even months) can make substantial differences to the interpretations which are possible or plausible. For *Beowulf*, different points of origin assign it literally to different cultures (pagan/Christian) or to different phases of development between those two cultures; for Marlowe's *Dr Faustus*, a date of 1589 puts the play as an early work, a date of 1592 makes it his last play, written after all his other works. Study of literature by period also allows other operations to be performed. Critics can look for repeated patterns (as well as variation and development) across different texts, including those from different genres, grouped within a period. The use of literary periods can equally, for some critics, allow a move away from a focus on texts to a focus on culture and cultural history. *Periodisation* itself often appears to be an unproblematic and straightforward device for grouping literary texts (and, indeed, for categorising historical study, too) in terms of specific divisions of chronology. However, there are reasons for thinking that it is not simply an objective set of categories, and that periodisation, different kinds of period label, and the ways these are used are themselves highly interpretative (as you may have begun to see in the case of the passage by Arthur Pollard). Before we look at the relationships between historical and literary (-historical) periodisation specifically, we should explore more closely the relationship between literary and historical studies in general.

So far, this section has established a (variably intimate) relationship between literature and history, but without giving any definition of what might distinguish the two. If history and literature, historical study and literary study, are linked yet distinct, we should perhaps get a better sense of what each does, and of how these activities interrelate.

> ◆ Complete the chart below, as concisely as possible (the questions are all, of course, impossible to answer exhaustively – but try to give an initial sense of where the two subjects might differ/resemble each other).

	Literature	History
Studies What?		
Studies How?		
Purpose of Study?		

▶ Discussion

	Literature	History
Studies What?	Literary texts (novels, poems, plays, etc.); stories, fictions, narratives	History (i.e. the past in all its manifestations); 'what actually happened'
Studies How?	Interprets texts, analysing how and what they mean, how they work, how they relate to other texts of a comparable kind	Gathers all available evidence (including texts) about a particular topic/period, analyses it and gives an account which aims to describe what happened, why and how
Purpose of Study?	To understand literature or/and the culture from which it originates, including its language structures	To understand exactly what happened in the past, how a past state/people/culture functioned

☐

Perhaps surprisingly, given some of the links the section has been making, the chart as completed with my sample answers (yours may differ) does not suggest anything like a closeness of interests at all points. Where literary studies has a clearly defined and relatively narrow field of study (literary texts), history is markedly broad (it studies *everything* in the past). Where the criterion for inclusion in one is the practice of a particular kind of activity/evidence (literature, or, anyway, writing), the criterion for inclusion in the other is simply pastness in general. History seems interested mainly in facts, whereas literary study focuses on fiction. One could add that historians are interested in many things which are not facts in any simple sense, including beliefs, motivations, ideologies, national myths and so on, and that literature does not exclude some factual narratives, such as travel-writing, documentaries, and autobiographies. Nevertheless, the distinction between stories and actuality does seem to retain its force.[6] This inclusiveness/selectivity contrast characterises not only What and How, but also Purpose. History aims to study more than just one activity. However, where literature claims to study culture and language, this, clearly, does approach closer to the ambitions of history's aims.

Why, then, the associations between the subjects which were pointed to earlier? The answer to this arises in (a) much literature is from 'the past' and (b) that 'interpreting texts', while sounding a self-contained activity, often draws on or grounds itself in useful contexts – and history provides a major context for any past text.[7] Moreover, there are aspects of the chart's comparison which could be drawn closer together by looking in more detail at the practices described (and the words used to describe them).

Thus, though modern history does, indeed, study 'the past in all its manifestations', history has traditionally been (and still is) dominated by evidence gathered from written sources. Indeed, pre-history is usually defined as 'the past before writing' and the term 'proto-history' is used to indicate the period when writing had only just been invented, and where there are relatively few surviving records for historians to work on. Traditionally, the historian picked up where the archaeologist left off – implying that material remains were the prime concern of one discipline, written texts the main concern of the other. Some modern historians might also make the point that even artefacts which are not books still form a kind of text which the historian reads (for example, a Greek vase can be read in various ways, as can a building: what did this design, in this place, at that time, signify?). And even if the historian's field is the whole of past actuality, it could be said that their main contact with that reality is nevertheless gained through writing, through texts or representations read in an analogous way. This then would suggest a closer kinship between literary and historical study.

Though I answered the question 'History Studies How?' using the words 'analyses' and 'evidence', deploying different terms can suggest further grounds for seeing history and literary criticism as akin. If 'analyse' is replaced with 'interpret', and 'evidence' with 'primary sources', then (some of) the activities carried out by historians and critics may move closer together:

Literary Critics	Interpret Texts	producing Criticism
Historians	Interpret Primary Sources	producing History

The term 'primary sources', which I have introduced, deserves some explanation, especially as I have not felt readily able to substitute without further comment the more literary word 'text' for it. 'Primary sources' is the terminology which historians would normally use to refer to the most immediate evidence on which historical study depends. A primary source is any evidence which was produced in the period of study, relevant to the enquiry being undertaken. Thus a historical study of how united Victorian society was in the period between

1850 and 1880 might draw its primary evidence from documents such as written versions of speeches by politicians, records of speeches by trade unionists, personal diaries of people of different rank and occupation and so on. What makes these sources primary is that they come from the period and represent evidence from the period itself, rather than a historical interpretation produced at a later date (whether by a historian working in 1900 or one working in 1990). These later historical interpretations (essentially the 'history' which historians are aiming to produce from primary evidence) are also used by historians in writing history, but are referred to as secondary sources. Thus a historian writing on this topic of Victorian social consensus in the year 2000 should discuss any relevant historian's accounts from the 1900s to 1990s, but must still go back to evidence from the period 1850–80 as her/his central evidence.

The terms 'primary' and 'secondary' have been adopted in literary study (and in other disciplines) from history where they, and the kinds of rigorous methodology in which they originate, were first invented. Thus literary bibliographies contain 'primary' and 'secondary' sections, which differentiate between 'texts' and 'critical writings' about them. Working practices in the two disciplines seem broadly comparable from this account of their shared focus on primary material, especially if we accept that most historical evidence is based on texts.[8] Interpretation, at any rate, seems so far to be a key activity for both disciplines. Though the imagined reader of this book is presumably not principally an historian,[9] we should next look in more detail at *how* both historians and critics respectively interpret texts. Once we have established a sense of how literary critics and historians work in their own spheres, we can better return to how the one makes use of the other.

◆ Read the following two passages, both from the period 1850–80. One is clearly suitable for use as a 'primary source', but not as a literary text; the other is a literary text (though that does not prevent a historian from using it as a primary source).
◆ For the primary source, produce an historical interpretation of the document in the light of the question supplied.
◆ For the literary text, produce a critical interpretation (no further question is supplied, because I am assuming that one is not needed; we will come back to this peculiarity).

PRIMARY SOURCE

Question: What might this document tell us about social consensus and unity between 1850 and 1880?

Notes by the Chief Constable of Staffordshire of a Meeting of Colliers held at Horsely Heath, Staffordshire (30 Aug. 1858)

Present in the open-air 800 Colliers; with Colonel Hogg, Chief Constable of Staffordshire, with a strong body of police assisted by Capt. Seagrave, Chief

Constable of Wolverhampton, and a detachment of men under him. – Time, from 10 a.m. till 1.20.

Joseph Linney was called to the chair. He gave out a Hymn. When it had been sung he said that their employers compelled them to strike. Before the strike the work they had would not support their wives and their children, and now their masters wanted to reduce one shilling. He had looked at it in all its various shapes and forms, and a more barbarous action never could be acted, than was now attempted by the masters. From Xmas last to the time that the strike took place, the average wages of the miners was not more than 15/- a week. (Voices: It was not so much as that.) Out of the 15/- they had to pay 1s for drink and 6d for 'sick' money before they left the 'field' ...

He did not wish to injure their employers, but it was the duty of their master to give them a fair day's wages for a fair day's work; and he thought they would all agree with him when he said with the auctioneer – 'we ask no more and we will take no less'. (*Ld app.*) The speaker said he was a teetotaller and a Sunday School teacher. Because he would not drink he had been turned out of a pit ... When the policemen saw the dangers that the miners worked in they said – 'why we would not work in such places for a pound a day'. (*Ap.*) And the colliers might get a pound a day if they liked – for the coal was the spring of all commerce and industry, and a pound of it was worth more than a pound of gold. They had to sell their labour, and it was their duty to sell it at the highest price. If all the colliers in the Kingdom were to lay down their tools and demand a high price for their labour they could get it. It was because of the extravagance of their masters in a time of prosperity that they now that trade was bad wanted to reduce their wages. They wanted even now to spend on themselves what they got out of the wages of their workmen. But should they reduce their wages? (*Cries of No!!*) ...

Job Radford, a brickmaker, of Oldbury, then spoke at some length encouraging the miners to form a trade association, similar to that of the brickmakers of Manchester – in consequence of which association the brickmaker now got twice the wages that he used to get ...

Job Radford again spoke inculcating temperance; after which it was determined that a meeting should be held at Brierley Hill on that day week at 11 o'clock ... after which the proceedings terminated.

LITERARY TEXT

George Eliot, *Felix Holt the Radical*

In the evening ... Mr Lyon was expecting the knock at the door that would announce Felix Holt ...

''Tis the quality of the page you care about' ... said Felix ... 'you're thinking that you have a roughly-written page before you now' ...

'I abstain from judging by the outward appearance only,' he answered, with his usual simplicity ... 'You will not, I trust, object to open yourself fully to me, as to an aged pastor ...'

'… For a young man so well furnished as you, who can questionless write a good hand and keep books, were it not well to seek some higher situation as a clerk or assistant? … There are ranks and degrees – and those who can serve in the higher must not unadvisedly change what seems to be a providential appointment …'

'Excuse me, Mr Lyon; I've had all that out with my mother, and I may as well save you any trouble by telling you that my mind has been made up about that a long while ago. I'll take no employment that obliges me to prop up my chin with a high cravat, and wear straps, and pass the live-long day with a set of fellows who spend their spare money on shirt pins. That sort of work is really lower than many handicrafts; it only happens to be paid out of proportion. That's why I set myself to learn the watchmaking trade … I mean to stick to the class I belong to – people who don't follow the fashions.'

Mr Lyon was silent a few moments. His dialogue was far from plain sailing; he was not certain of his latitude and longitude. If the despiser of Glasgow preachers had been arguing in favour of gin and Sabbath-breaking, Mr Lyon's course would have been clearer. 'Well, well,' he said deliberately, 'it is true that St Paul exercised the trade of tent-making, though he was learned in all the wisdom of the Rabbis.'

'St Paul was a wise man,' said Felix. 'Why should I want to get into the middle class because I have some learning? The most of the middle class are as ignorant as the working people about everything that doesn't belong to their own Brummagem life. That's how the working men are left to foolish devices and keep worsening themselves: the best heads among them forsake their born comrades, and go in for a house with a high door-step and a brass knocker.'

From George Eliot, *Felix Holt the Radical* (1866), ch. 5. Extract from Penguin edn, ed. Peter Coveney (1972), pp. 139–40, 144–5.

▶ Discussion 1

In a number of ways the document is evidence of at least some lack of unity and consensus (though before going any further it should be noted that the document can only contribute a partial answer to the question posed, however we interpret it, since it can only tell us something about 1858, and cannot alone give us evidence about the whole period specified). That there is a meeting in the first place suggests dissatisfaction, and a willingness to make it public, as do the more detailed complaints made about 'the masters'' attempts to reduce wages. The presence of the police at the meeting in large numbers equally suggests a fear on their part that dissatisfaction may become public disorder, the most open demonstration of a breakdown in social cohesion. There are other more detailed indications that employers and workers do not always share a joint set of values and purposes. Thus, there is a sense of grievance on the miners' part about being compelled to spend a shilling of their pay on 'drink' – something felt particularly strongly by the speaker Joseph Linney, since he is a teetotaller and has been sacked by one mine-employer for refusing to conform to this 'custom'. The men's leaders also feel that the employers are treating themselves and their workers very differently; in bad times they ask the workers to accept lower pay, but continue to spend on themselves at the same rate.

However, there are also signs of a degree of unity and consensus across different social groups (if often somewhat complex ones). Thus, though there is clearly conflict between employers and men, this is not without some restraint. Indeed, even the use of the term 'masters' does suggest a degree of acceptance of a traditional system of rank, with mutual obligations on either side ('he did not wish to injure their employers, but it was the *duty* of the masters to give them a fair day's pay for a fair day's work') – unless this is seen as purely customary, a fossilised and merely verbal remnant of an earlier social relationship. There does seem to be uncertainty about the relationship between masters and men; at one point there are mutual duties based on fair exchange of pay/work, at another the miners' duty becomes a more competitive one: 'to sell it [their labour] at the highest price'. Thus though there is some tendency to defer to their 'betters', there is also a strongly independent stance.

Other signs of cohesion are perhaps stronger than this muted element of deference to the employers. The religious affiliations of the miners – presumably a set of values they would be likely to share with a range of other social groups – are made plain. The meeting opens with a Hymn in which all join; Joseph Linney makes reference to his status as a teetotaller and a Sunday School teacher; Job Radford speaks 'inculcating temperance' (a word presumably referring to restraint in general here, rather than solely to avoidance of alcohol, but which anyway has a clear religious resonance). So too is their associated general respectability made clear: they are family men, compelled, if anything, to drink by their masters' sharp practices, who conduct their meetings with great order and dignity (with a presiding chair who calls speakers in turn and terminates the meeting). These, again, are values we may regard as likely to be shared with the middle and upper classes of the period, although there is also an association with religious nonconformity,[10] which was often linked to political radicalism of varying degrees. Indeed, we might note that there is evidence here of social unity across working-class communities, with links between brickmakers in Manchester and miners in Staffordshire, especially through their leaders, who appear to have a number of shared values.

Surprisingly, there is also evidence of consensus and unity between the police and the miners: 'When the police saw the dangers that the miners worked in they said – "why we would not work in such places for a pound a day"'. It is not quite clear whether this is Joseph Linney referring to the police present at this meeting, or whether he refers to a previous occasion when policemen actually came to a mine and saw the dangers faced by miners. In one case, Linney would be claiming consensus between miners and police; in the other, the police would be expressing it spontaneously. In either case, the Chief Constable of Staffordshire seems to record the instance of (unlikely?) consensus without any adverse comment (there is no indication that he thinks that Linney is fabricating the policemen's remarks, for example). Indeed, the willingness of the Chief Constable to make his notes in a way which represents the striking miners so favourably itself suggests that he does not regard them as anything like wholly outside the range of consensual values of which he is in one way and another an official upholder.

In conclusion, the document can tell us that there were particular pressures on social unity in that year in a particular part of England, but it can also suggest that there might be a good deal of common ground in terms of social values of respectability and fairness between miners and other (skilled) workers and between other figures whom we might expect to represent establishment values. Interpretation of this single primary source would have to be put together with interpretations of a range of other documents bearing on social consensus between 1850 and 1880 in order to contribute to any historical enquiry into the topic. □

▶◁ Discussion 2

In this passage from George Eliot's novel the working man Felix Holt calls on the nonconformist minister, Mr Lyons. The passage consists almost wholly of dialogue between the two. The conversation does not, however, proceed quite as we might expect it to: instead of the socially superior Mr Lyons being in command of the discussion, he soon finds himself puzzled how to go on: 'his dialogue was far from plain sailing; he was not certain of his latitude and longitude'. Instead of Mr Lyons passing on the benefits of his wisdom to Felix Holt, Felix is soon questioning Lyon's ideas and asserting his own beliefs and the chains of thought and experience which have led to them.

There is, indeed, an ironic reversal after the first two speeches quoted. In the first of these, Felix apparently acknowledges his inferior social position by admitting to being a 'roughly-written page', and Lyons gracefully accepts *and* denies this self-valuation by asserting that outer appearances are not the only basis for judgement. He is surprised to be taken at his word, as Holt does 'open fully' 'the roughly-written page'. In fact, although Lyons claims this insight into qualities beneath the surface, there is a tendency for him to be quite concerned with surfaces and to be thrown by the unaccustomed. Thus, despite Holt's own metaphor of the 'roughly-written page', Lyons is quickly thinking of Felix's marketable qualities: 'for a young man so well *furnished* as you, who can questionless write *a good hand* ...' Lyons is in a sense right that Felix Holt does have these qualities of 'polish', but the transition from his alleged focus on depth to matters of surfaces is rapid. Mr Lyons is not given to questioning too deeply the apparent order of the world, or, at least, would as soon rely on unexamined appearances as on strongly asserted conviction: 'those who can serve in the higher must not inadvisedly change what seems to be a providential appointment'.

The styles of speech of the two characters are contrasted in a way which picks up on this interest in surfaces and depths. While Lyons shows his membership of polite society by being, indeed, polite, there is a good deal of concealment of his real views, carried out through his good manners. Felix Holt certainly lacks – or has no time for – this kind of social polish, and bluntly challenges anything which does not match his beliefs. Throughout the whole passage the expected hierarchy is challenged and inverted as Holt pronounces his views forthrightly and Mr Lyons mutes his. Mr Lyons' underlying belief that social hierarchies, even if not really valuable, should nevertheless be observed is denied by Holt. He plainly states at the end that the 'upward' status of the middle classes is illusory, and the thing which prevents working-class achievers from making real (as opposed to shallow) progress: 'the most of the middle class are as ignorant as the working people ... That's how the working men ... keep worsening themselves'. □

I have tried (without cramping my own style) to give sample answers to both exercises which are *characteristic* of the probable approaches of a historian and a literary critic to their task. Your own answers may (as usual) vary considerably in content, but I would hope that they have some similarity in terms of approaches to carrying out a historical interpretation of a primary source and a critical interpretation of a text. The next step is to think through how these two approaches to texts might differ.

◆ Compare and contrast the methods and assumptions of the two interpretations.

▶ Discussion

Both interpretations rely on close attention to the text/source, but seek different kinds of information and have different starting points. Since the primary source has a specific question attached to it,[11] this question is likely to govern fairly strictly the way in which the task is approached. The question directs the historian (in this case you) to search for information about social unity and consensus. The information which the passage contains is certainly not all 'facts' exactly, though some evidence seems indisputable (e.g. that there were union meetings where dissatisfaction was expressed with the attitude of the employers). Much of the interpretation consists of picking out evidence of various kinds and weighing how much and how it can bear on the enquiry in hand. Thus the word 'masters' is discussed as a possible sign of agreement about the social hierarchy, but then balanced against the willingness to defy their employers shown elsewhere in the speeches reported. Other kinds of consensus are also considered, including the possible continuity of values between classes suggested by the interest in religion and respectability (but this has to be judged against the idea that this may be a sign of class independence and self-sufficiency as much as of cohesion).

These uses of evidence are undoubtedly interpretative ones (they need complex decisions about the value of different factors), but it would still be true to say that they assume there are events/views which existed in reality and which we can come to a rational knowledge of. There is thus a focus on the question: 'What does this evidence tell us about what people actually felt?' (this being the relevant version of 'What actually happened?' for a question about values).

The literary text exercise does not start with a specific question – I assume that the reason it does not need one is because the literary critic has 'default' questions always in mind through which interpretation of texts takes place: 'What does this text mean?'/'How does it mean?' As in the reading of the poem 'Poetry' in section 2.3, the method is to look for anomalies and try to form them into a pattern which adds up to a significant and characteristic overall interpretation. Thus, here, the expected social relationship is taken as an absent norm, against which deviations are read. The focus of enquiry is very much: 'How does this text work to construct a meaning for the reader?'

There are several contrasts in approach, therefore. The primary source reading assumes:

1. That the evidence in the source refers back to events/views which actually existed.
2. That they are part of a larger picture – rather than autonomous or self-contained.
3. That there is a content (in this case evidence of social views recorded in the document).

The literary text reading assumes:

1. That meaning is constructed by the text (i.e. it is a fiction: it does not refer, directly at any rate, back to an actuality).
2. That the text has boundaries which make it possible to read it as a source of meaning in its own right and terms.
3. That HOW the text constructs its meaning is the major matter for enquiry (i.e. that textual devices construct the meaning). □

It is possible to apply these methods *uncharacteristically* by switching the enquiries: treating the primary source as a literary text, and the literary text as a primary source.

Primary source *as* literary text	Literary text *as* primary source
Colliers' Meeting	*Felix Holt (social consensus and unity?)*
expectations reversed	expectation of hierarchical deferential relationship not fulfilled
antagonism between police and miners expected	open dissent by Felix from conventional views of class (i.e. that knowledge and comfort increase with upward mobility)
Respectability and orderliness established: not a mob	
solidarity of miners established	*but* an acknowledgement within this by Felix that working and middle classes do generally share upward aspirations
(through stage directions: *Ld app*, etc.)	
sympathy of police established	*and* shared religious knowledge – though some dispute about values within that between Lyons and Felix Holt
sympathy of narrator – the Chief Constable – established throughout	
Reader inclined to believe in reasonableness of the miners – against initial expectations, given the narrator	some fellow feeling between them
	Reader inclined to question apparent shape of class structure

This unusual procedure brings out the distinctions in accepted literary critical/historical methods very clearly, throwing attention in the primary source towards its status as a text, and in the literary text towards its potential status as a primary source referring back to a Victorian reality. The first interpretation would, I think, be an unusual thing to undertake. It would imply that the main interest of this document comes from the way in which its narrator – an authorial one – has constructed his text, and might therefore transfer attention to why the Chief Constable constructs such a surprisingly positive view of the miners. This seems quite a productive reading, but shifts the focus away from the source as primary (in terms of it being about the miners), and makes it much more about the Chief Constable's textual strategies.[12]

The second reading – of *Felix Holt* as primary source – is less unusual, partly because historians do include literary works amongst the range of possible sources, and partly because literary critics do quite commonly use historical context as part of their interpretative strategy. Indeed, putting the two texts together suggests that they can both contribute interestingly to an answer to the historical enquiry: 'What might these documents tell us about social consensus and unity between 1850 and 1880?' We could note several interesting parallels between the two documents, including a certain shared feeling of the self-respect of the working men in each, with their willingness to argue against their 'betters' and to challenge the status quo where it seems unjustly conceived. Felix Holt is less obviously 'respectable' than Joseph Linney and Job Radford (it is stressed that he is a 'rough page', and he is more willing here to challenge social conventions openly), but even Felix shows considerable knowledge of religion, so that we can be sure there was considerable consensus about the centrality of religion. The *possibility at least* of open class antagonism can be seen in both documents, with Felix's blunt contempt for middle-class values, and the presence of the police at the meeting. However, we could also note that the Chief Constable and Mr Lyons, though of higher class status, seem to show considerable respect for the self-respect of the miners/Felix Holt, in spite of a potential for conflict between this independence and the dominant class structure. This might even arise from a shared valuation of qualities of respectability, manliness and independence. We might, though, wish to make a distinction between the Chief Constable (a person who actually existed) and Mr Lyons (a character in a novel). Mr Lyons, after all, exists only in a text, and is thus not a real viewpoint in the same way as the Chief Constable. This does not entirely invalidate the novel as a 'primary source' – it is still evidence of Victorian views of the question – but its fictionality needs to be taken into account. In particular, some historians might wish to consider the social status of the novel's author as the origin – or, at least, constructor – of the views articulated through Lyons and Felix Holt.[13]

There are clearly some resemblances in the ways in which historians and critics read textual evidence, but also some fairly sharp distinctions. It should also be said that the interpretation of a single text – though a common pedagogic exercise in both disciplines – does not represent either subject's total set of procedures. However, there is a difference even here. While professional critics and historians will both construct longer arguments from a series of readings of single texts, there is little doubt that for literary critics an in-depth interpretation of a single text *can* constitute 'literary criticism' (e.g. a whole book about *Felix Holt*), while a historian must refer to a range of documents if attempting anything beyond an exercise in method. This stems from the different field of study in each: in literary study a text is (or has often been) regarded as the central object of study, and as having a degree of autonomy; in historical study, texts are evidence for something else: for an actuality which happened and of which 'primary sources' are a partial record.

Having made some broad distinctions between the usual practices of history and literary criticism, we can return to questions about how literature uses history. If we return also to the passage from Arthur Pollard's 'Introduction' to the *Sphere History of Literature in the English Language, Vol. 6: The Victorians*, we should now be able to approach it with something a little closer to a professional historian's eye.

> ◆ The passage is reprinted below; how happy do you think an historian would be with its use of history?

It is difficult to characterise in a brief compass a span of time as long as that in which Queen Victoria reigned over England and her realms beyond the seas. Not only did it cover so many years, but those years also witnessed political, economic, intellectual and scientific change previously unparalleled in British history ... W. E. Houghton cites many who felt themselves to be living in an age of transition ... 'an awful age of transition' was Tennyson's phrase ...

In the 1840s the half had not been told. By the end of the century Britain exercised 'dominion over palm and pine' ... the Navy imposed a *pax Britannica* on many parts of the world. Trade and Christianity followed the flag. At home successive Reform Acts made democracy more and more a reality ... Science and technology together testified to man's adventure and achievement. Darwin and his associates gave man an entirely new view of himself and his place on earth, whilst technical advances extended and completed the revolution in industry that had begun in the previous century. These technical advances were themselves accompanied and in some ways made possible by the changes which brought into being the necessary commercial and financial structure of modern capitalism ...

If progress is one Victorian watchword, freedom is the other ... the middle classes were supreme. They were immensely self-confident, commercially successful, scornful of the old establishments of aristocracy and Church, but though they often showed a fine sense of social responsibility (... Mrs Gaskell is a fine literary example of their conscience in this respect), most of them failed to see the relevance of culture ...

Hope was not fulfilled, confidence ebbed, and the last years of the century were marked by reaction, resignation and disillusion ... It all amounted to what Mark Pattison described as 'the present mood of depression and despondency' ... Tennyson was discouraged, Hardy gloomy, Shaw devastatingly critical, Wilde scintillatingly cynical. Arnold had lamented the age's 'sick hurry, its divided aims'; at the end it came to worse than this. It appeared to have lost all sense of purpose ... A period in which so many contrary forces interacted so intricately and energetically cannot fail to be interesting. Its writers, expressing the spirit of the age with all the resources of imagination, feeling and thought, abundantly reveal their response to their time ... (pp. 9–11)

Discussion

I don't think that most historians would find this piece totally lacking in historical understanding. In particular, the passage shows a strong sense of the caution which historians tend to prize, with its unwillingness to generalise about the whole Victorian period (1837–1901), and its repeated view that the period needs to be subdivided into phases. It also does draw on primary evidence, citing documents from the time (albeit in a very brief form suitable to its introductory function).

However, I suspect a historian might wish to query whether there is a very wide range of evidence drawn on. All the evidence refers to writers, who might not be widely representative (those cited here do not obviously include any writers from the industrial working classes, or any writers who might speak for agricultural as opposed to urban viewpoints). The passage is aware of the need for caution in periodising, but less aware of the need to draw evidence from a social and, indeed, geographical/regional range. One might specifically query whether the third phase of *fin-de-siècle* depression for which Pollard cites several sources was widely felt by all classes (did 'despondency' clearly characterise most middle-class or working-class Britons in those years? Or were ideas of technological and social progress perhaps still at least as powerful as they had been at mid-century?). Perhaps Pollard gives the textual evidence he cites, and thence the period itself, a uniformity which he has not properly established in historical terms (much of Tennyson's poetry, even in the period 1850–80, is not self-evidently buoyant in the manner suggested as characteristic, so his despondency in the 1890s[14] may not be so obviously a result of historical change, let alone representative). There is also a general tendency to regard sources of evidence as having a *single* import; the middle classes were en bloc confident, commercially successful, responsible but uncultured. As we have seen from more detailed interpretation of Victorian primary sources, evidence is not always so clear-cut.

Of course, the introduction is operating under certain rules and has certain functions which govern what it can do – it does not have space to enter into detailed analysis of primary sources/texts at length. And, above all, it has a generalising function, because it wishes to give a unity to the period, to the book, and to literary and other activities. Nevertheless, it may suggest a more general desire on the part of (some) literary critics to stabilise history in order to make it a factual background against which the (allegedly) more nuanced art of literary interpretation takes place. □

History itself does produce more generalised views from detailed analysis (it is part of interpretation that detail is used to formulate broader, more general understandings and conclusions). But perhaps because literary study has to get on with its own business, there is (or has been) a tendency to place history as relatively stable, as factual, rather than interpretative.

This may be part of the function of literary periodisation – it groups texts in ways which define them and the contexts in which they can be read, so that the range of possibilities is not open-ended. This is not unique to literary study; history too needs to define areas of study and set up boundaries to investigations, as well as to make significant interpretative groupings of events. But where historians tend to argue explicitly about periodisation, there has been a certain tradition in literary studies of proceeding as if literary-historical periods were inherently established and reliable. If this is not so true as it used to be, the organisation of undergraduate curricula does, at any rate, give the impression that the dividing line between (say) Romantic Poetry and Victorian Poetry or Jacobean and Caroline drama is a historical fact – as if these periods can be periodised symmetrically in terms of historical phases and the kinds of texts produced in them.

It could be said that the deployment of boundaries is, indeed, essential to enable study of a discipline to take place (just as a sense that texts have boundaries enables literary studies to focus its attentions[15]). Given what was said earlier about these groupings implying significant kinship, it would be no surprise if literary periodisation contributes to how we read particular texts (and groups of texts) and what we see in them.

> ◆ Read the following passage from *History and Value* by Frank Kermode, and its quotation of the art historian Jean Rousset.
> ◆ What is Rousset's view of periodisation? Are you convinced by it?
> ◆ What is Kermode's view?

It appears, then, that concepts of period not only make history manageable but inevitably involve valuation; so that the characteristics thought to confer value (or its opposite) can be sought … with the object of making further valuations based upon a period archetype. Nevertheless that archetype remains in place, and what is said about a period style is deeply involved with one's apprehension of the period itself, more generally considered.

...

Most of us believe in the Renaissance, though we have been taught to be cautious: … And, as Panofsky remarks, even those who profess not to believe in it behave as if they do …

Once a period has got itself established we can not only argue about whether it ever existed in the way we habitually say it did, but use it very freely to scan history and make judgements of particular styles, and in particular, works of art. This goes on despite all the judicious qualifications made by the scholars. The Renaissance was only one aspect of sixteenth-century culture, says Huizinga; we should be careful about the way we use such terms as 'Baroque', says Jean Rousset:

> We must of course remember that it is a kind of grid constructed by us, the twentieth-century historians, and not by seventeenth-century artists. One must avoid confusing the grid and the artists, the interpretative schema and the works undergoing interpretation. The categories are only means of investigating these facts, the works; and one should think of them as working hypotheses, instruments of research, scaffoldings which lose their utility once the building is finished.

But it is very difficult to remember all this when actually using the period words … The last thing you can say about them in actual use is that they are 'value-free'; they not only impose valuations on particular works and particular periods, but they all tend more or less silently to place uniquely high value on our own period, since it is on behalf of that period that the valuations are made. We want to select from the past what is modern about it and assume that we have a very privileged view of the past that enables us to do so...

From Frank Kermode, *History and Value* (Oxford, 1988), pp. 121–3.

Discussion 1

Rousset argues that periodisation (the use of terms such as Renaissance, Baroque and so on) is a method of investigation into the evidence presented by works of art (or in our case, literary texts), rather than a substantive conclusion. The term baroque has been invented by modern critics as a way of explaining and grouping particular works, but the term does not directly come from the period it seeks to explain and is not directly connected to the evidence. Thus the term 'baroque' is a working hypothesis, a piece of scaffolding. Once the building (the critical commentary, presumably) is complete, this scaffolding is no longer needed. □

Discussion 2

I am not very convinced by his conclusions. The point that these period terms are (often) invented after the period under study in order to study it seems right, as does the argument that such terms are inherently interpretative, since they are ways of ordering the evidence in order to understand it. But I do not feel persuaded by the scaffolding/building analogy. I cannot see how the building can have a shape independent of the constraints placed on it from the outset by the scaffolding. Even if the critical commentary detects qualities and characteristics not present in the initial framework, these departures will surely inevitably be measured against the framework which has revealed them. The framework is thus still a prime determinant of the meaning of the individual work. The term Baroque raises a set of expectations and issues, the work is explored in terms of these, and its conformity or otherwise to the basic criteria remains central to the interpretation. One definition of Baroque will interpret the work differently from an alternative definition, so that a work which reveals its own true nature whatever framework you start from seems unlikely. □

Discussion 3

Kermode argues that periodisation always involves valuation too. To assign a work to a period, or to describe a general set of characteristics for a period is in his view always carried out within a framework of values, which either esteem or disesteem those values and that period. In particular, since he sees periodisation as interpretative in this way, we always measure different periods against our conception of our own period. Thus what we say about other periods always comes from what we want to say about our own in one way or another. It is not so much that we interpret other periods, as that other periods are ways of interpreting what we are or would like to be. (This is a long way from any view of history and historical methodologies as factual ....) The next section will study further why literary critics might be drawn to historicise literature. □

Finally in this section, you might like to consider the extent to which ideas about history inform your own reading of literary texts (as usual I will leave you to develop your own ideas at this point).

> ◆ Read the following text and produce a critical reading of it.
> ◆ Do historical knowledge or historical ideas contribute to your reading? If so, what kind of historical knowledge/ideas?
> ◆ How much does either literary or historical periodisation contribute to your reading?
> ◆ Might there be further historical knowledge which might extend or alter your reading? (List any questions about the text which historical ideas or knowledge might help you to answer.)

Elizabeth Barrett Browning, *Aurora Leigh*

The critics say that epics have died out
With Agamemnon and the goat-nurse gods;
I'll not believe it. I could never deem
As Payne Knight did, (the mythic mountaineer
Who travelled higher than he was born to live,
And showed sometimes the goitre in his throat
Discoursing of an image seen through fog,)
That Homer's heroes measured twelve feet high.
They were but men: his Helen's hair turned gray
Like any plain Miss Smith's who wears a front;
And Hector's infant whimpered at a plume
As yours last Friday at a turkey-cock,
All actual heroes are essential men,
And all men possible heroes: every age,
Heroic in proportions, double-faced,
Looks backward and before expects a morn
And claims an epos.
                        Ay, but every age
Appears to souls who live in't (ask Carlyle)
Most unheroic. Ours, for instance, ours:
The thinkers scout it, and the poets abound
Who scorn to touch it with a finger-tip:
A pewter age, – mixed metal, silver-washed;

An age of scum, spooned off the richer past,
An age of patches for old gabardines,
An age of mere transition. …

…

                              Every age,
Through being beheld too close, is ill-discerned
By those who have not lived past it…

…

                         But poets should
Exert a double vision; should have eyes
To see near things as comprehensively
As if afar they took their point of sight.

…

I do distrust the poet who discerns
No character or glory in his times,
And trundles back his soul five-hundred years,
Past moat and drawbridge, into a castle court,
To sing – o, not of lizard or of toad
Alive in the ditch there, – 't were excusable,
But of some black chief, half-knight, half sheep-lifter,
Some beauteous dame, half chattel and half queen,
As dead as must be, for the greater part,
The poems made on their chivalric bones

…

Nay, if there's room for poets in this world
A little overgrown, (I think there is)
Their sole work is to represent the age,
Their age, not Charlemagne's, – this live, throbbing age
That brawls, cheats, maddens, calculates, aspires,
And spends more passion, more heroic heat,
Betwixt the mirrors of his drawing-rooms,
Than Roland with his knights at Roncesvalles.

From *Aurora Leigh* (1857), ed. Margaret Reynolds (Athens, GA, 1992), Book V,
ll. 139–63, 183–207.

4.2 Why Historicise?

In the last section, we worked through some of the relationships between literature and history, mainly in terms of the two disciplines themselves. Though
some suggestions were made about history's grounding function in literary
study (giving literary interpretation a starting point, or – useful? – possibilities
of delimitation), we did not look in any great depth at what the range of actual
practices were for the use of history in literary studies. This section will investigate the variety and motivations of a range of uses of history, in traditional and
more recent forms of literary study. Where section 4.1 focused on establishing a
sense of history in its own right, and then on the relationship between this discipline and literature, here we focus mainly on history as it is handled within
literary study. However, we should briefly start by asking what might motivate

the study of history itself, to provide a control against which to measure literary historicising.

> ◆ List some motivations for the study of history (i.e. why is there a desire to study the past?)
> ◆ Comment on any which you think are less 'legitimate' reasons.

SAMPLE LIST (key words underlined)

1. <u>Curiosity</u> about the past.
2. An urge to <u>preserve</u> knowledge of the past.
3. Offers temporary <u>escape</u> from the present.
4. Gives a sense of <u>useful alternatives</u> to the assumptions of the present.
5. A desire to know <u>what changes</u> have happened in human life.
6. A desire to investigate the <u>processes</u> by which human life changes.
7. A desire to know how we <u>became</u> what we now are.
8. A desire <u>to cope</u> with the present through knowing about the past.
9. A desire <u>to predict</u> the future through establishing patterns in the past.
10. A love of <u>debate</u> about things which can never be conclusively proved (since only scientific subjects involve proof – and history is not a science).
11. A love of the <u>processes of studying history</u>: seeking evidence, weighing it, interpreting it, coming to some conclusion about it.

▶ Discussion

It is possible that all of these are valid motivations for studying history (and there may be other valid reasons I have not thought of). Most would, I think, be reasonably acceptable to professional historians, though one or two might be looked at with suspicion. I suspect that few historians would be convinced that it is a mainstream function of history to *predict* the future, and perhaps 'escape from the present' might be regarded as more of a psychological explanation than a professional motivation for the discipline's existence. There is undoubtedly more we could do to refine these motivations – we could argue about which are most central, which are more characteristic of rigorous, modern history, which more characteristic of popular forms of history, and so on. However, it is sufficient for the moment to leave them as a rough definition of the motivations of history – to place against the motivations of history in literary study.

Presumably some of these motivations are present in literary study too – though we might not all necessarily list them as primary motivations – and, presumably, the more interested literary criticism is in historicising, the closer it comes to these (purely) historical motivations. However, though some kinds of literary study and historical study may have moved closer together, there are still (clearly) boundaries between the disciplines, perhaps mainly stemming from the definition of their fields of study. For critics who prioritise reading particular texts, it may be that history is mainly something which can be deployed to help read those texts; for critics who see their role as being that of a historian of cultures, it may be that they would claim actually to be a historian of a specific kind (e.g. a cultural historian might be part of historical enquiry in the same way that an economic historian or a political historian might be). Thus there are probably a number of positions in literary critical practice for where the focus of study lies between the literary and the historical. At one end of this range, the boundaries between literary and historical study remain distinct, while, at the other, literary study as a separate practice might (almost) disappear into historical study. The two diagrams try to give a sense of the two end positions in the range.

```
┌─────────────────────────────────────────┐
│          Historical background           │
│   ┌───────────────────────────────────┐  │
│   │                                   │  │
│   │         Literary Text –           │  │
│   │         Foregrounded              │  │
│   │                                   │  │
│   │                                   │  │
│   └───────────────────────────────────┘  │
│                                           │
└─────────────────────────────────────────┘
```

```
┌─────────────────────────────────────────┐
│                                           │
│   ┌───────────────────────────────────┐  │
│   │     Literary and other texts –    │  │
│   │        a source for history       │  │
│   └───────────────────────────────────┘  │
│                                           │
│           (Cultural?) History             │
│              Foregrounded                 │
│                                           │
└─────────────────────────────────────────┘
```

Between these possibilities are presumably a range of other, perhaps more nuanced, relationships between literature and history. The next exercise aims to look at actual examples of literary critics using history in order to explore these possibilities.[16] □

◆ The following five extracts are drawn from a variety of critical works about English literature from the Anglo-Saxon period to the twentieth century. Read each of the passages.

◆ Assign each passage to a position on the following line which best represents its interests (by using the letter identifying each; more than one passage may occupy a particular position if desired).

```
┌─────────────────────────────────────────────────────────┐
│  Foregrounds Literary Texts ──────────── Foregrounds History  │
└─────────────────────────────────────────────────────────┘
```

◆ Make a brief note about what you think the attitude of each passage is to literature, history and the relationship between them.

A. George Saintsbury, 'The Earliest Anglo-Saxon Poetry'

The oldest document which has a possibly authentic claim to be English Literature, if but English Literature in the making and far off completion, is the poem commonly called *Widsith*, from its opening word, which some take to be a proper name. Others simply see in it the designation of a 'far travelled' singer, who here recounts his journeyings in 143 lines of no great literary beauty, and only interesting as sketching the gainful and varied life of a minstrel in the Dark Ages, were it not for the proper names which bestrew the piece. Not a few of these occur, or seem to occur, in other early verse, and have the interest of the 'parallel passage'. But three are, or seem to be, those of persons well known to history – Eormanric or Hermanric, King of the Goths; Aelta or Attila, the Scourge of God and the King of the Huns; and lastly a certain Aelfwine, whom some think identical with Alboin or Albovine, King of the Lombards, the husband, the insulter, and the victim of Rosmunda. It is, of course, obvious at once that though it is not impossible for the same man to have been contemporary with Hermanric, who died in 375, and Attila, who died in 453, no contemporary of either could have seen the days of Alboin, who felt his wife's revenge in 572. Therefore either Aelfwine must be somebody else or the poem is doubtful. Into such discussions this book will never enter, unless there is the strongest reason of a purely literary character, and there is none such here...

[The] language...is arranged, or can be arranged, in lines of not strictly regular length, and obeying no law of rhythm that apparently resembles those of modern or classical prosody...as for the purely literary characteristics, the nature of the piece, which...is little more than a catalogue of names, gives very small scope. Imaginative critics have, however, discovered in it that specially English delight in roving which has distinguished many of our race – as well as, for instance, such hardly English persons as Ulysses and Sindbad.

From George Saintsbury, *A Short History of English Literature* (1898), ch. 1, pp. 1–3.

B. C. S. Lewis, 'The Earth and her Inhabitants'

Physically considered, the Earth is a globe; all the authors of the high Middle Ages are agreed on this. In the earlier 'Dark' Ages, as indeed in the nineteenth century, we can find Flat-earthers...

The implications of a spherical Earth were fully grasped. What we call gravitation – for the medievals 'kindly enclyning' – was a matter of common knowledge. Vincent of Beauvais expounds it by asking what would happen if there were a hole bored through the globe of Earth so that there was free passage from the one sky to the other, and someone dropped a stone down it. He answers that it would come to rest at the centre. Temperature and momentum, I understand, would lead to a different result in fact, but Vincent is clearly right in principle. Mandeville in his *Voiage and Travaile* teaches the same truth more ingenuously: 'from what part of the earth that men dwell, either above or beneath, it seemeth always to them that dwell that they go more right than any other folk. And right as it seemeth to us that they be under us, right so it seemeth to them that we be under them' (XX). The most vivid presentation is by Dante, in a passage which shows that intense realising power which in the medieval imagination oddly co-exists with its feebleness in matters of scale. In *Inferno*, XXXIV, the two travellers find the shaggy and gigantic Lucifer at the absolute centre of the Earth, embedded up to his waist in ice. The only way they can continue their journey is by climbing down his sides – there is plenty of hair to hold on by – and squeezing through the hole in the ice and so coming to his feet. But they find that though it is *down* to his waist, it is *up* to his feet. As Virgil tells Dante, they have passed the point towards which all heavy objects move (70–111). It is the first 'science-fiction effect' in literature.

The erroneous notion that the medievals were Flat-earthers was common enough till recently. It might have two sources. One is that medieval maps, such as the great thirteenth century *mappemounde* [= mappa munda, map of the world] in Hereford cathedral, represent the earth as a circle, which is what men would do if they believed it to be a disc. But what would men do if, knowing it was a globe and wishing to represent it in two dimensions, they had not yet mastered the late and difficult art of projection? Fortunately, we need not answer this question. There is no reason to suppose that the *mappemounde* represents the whole surface of the Earth. The theory of the Four Zones taught that the equatorial region was too hot for life. The other hemisphere of the Earth was to us inaccessible. You could write science-fiction about it, but not geography.

From C. S. Lewis, *The Discarded Image. An Introduction to Medieval and Renaissance Literature* (1964), pp. 140–2.

c. Stephen Greenblatt, 'Invisible Bullets: Renaissance Authority and its Subversion, *Henry IV* and *Henry V*'

To understand Shakespeare's whole conception of Hal, from rakehell to monarch, we need in effect a poetics of Elizabethan power, and this in turn will prove inseparable, in crucial respects, from a poetics of the theatre. Testing, recording and explaining are elements in this poetics that is inseparably bound up with the figure of Queen Elizabeth, a ruler without a standing army, without a highly developed bureaucracy, without an extensive police force, a ruler whose power is constituted in theatrical celebrations of royal glory and theatrical violence visited upon enemies of that glory. Power that relies upon a massive police apparatus, a strong middle-class nuclear family, an elaborate school system, power that dreams of a panopticon in which the most intimate secrets are open to the view of an invisible authority, such power will have as its appropriate aesthetic form the realist novel; Elizabethan power, by contrast, depends upon its privileged visibility. As in a theatre, the audience must be powerfully engaged by this visible presence while at the same time held at a certain respectful distance from it. 'We princes', Elizabeth told a deputation of Lords and Commons in 1586, 'are set on stages in the sight and view of all the world.'

Royal power is manifested to its subjects as in a theatre, and the subjects are at once absorbed by the instructive, delightful, or terrible spectacles, and forbidden intervention or deep intimacy. The play of authority depends upon spectators – 'for 'tis your thoughts that now must deck our kings' – but the performance is made to appear entirely beyond the control of those whose 'imaginary forces' actually confer upon it its significance and force. These matters, Thomas Moore imagines the common people saying of one such spectacle, 'be king's games, as it were stage plays, and for the more part played upon scaffolds. In which poor men be but the lookers-on. And they that wise be will meddle no further.' Within this theatrical setting, there is a remarkable insistence upon the paradoxes, ambiguities, and tensions of authority, but this apparent production of subversion is, as we have already seen, the very condition of power. I should add that this condition is not a theoretical necessity of theatrical power in general but an historical phenomenon, the particular mode of this particular culture …

It is precisely because of the English form of absolutist theatricality that Shakespeare's drama, written for a theatre subject to State censorship, can be so relentlessly subversive: the form itself, as a primary expression of a Renaissance power, contains the radical doubts it continually provokes … And we are free to locate and pay homage to the plays' doubts only because they no longer threaten us. There is subversion, no end of subversion, only not for us.

From *Political Shakespeare. New Essays in Cultural Materialism*, ed. Jonathan Dollimore and Alan Sinfield (Manchester, 1985), pp. 44–5.

D. F. R. Leavis, 'Ezra Pound'

Even when, as in *Lustra* and after, he finds his themes in the contemporary world and writes consciously modern poems –

Here they stand without quaint devices
Here they stand with nothing archaic about them

– his modern interests, one feels, are for him mainly opportunities, taken or made, for verse practice: his partiality for the epigram has its significance … However, there are some memorable pieces, and we have to recognise a growing subtlety in his verse. His dropping of archaisms and poeticisms, and his use of modern speech-idiom are particularly interesting. But however remarkable the achievement in verse may be, it is not such that one could have foreseen *Mauberley* in it …

In *Mauberley* we feel a pressure of experience, an impulsion from deep within. The verse is extraordinarily subtle, and its subtlety is the subtlety of the sensibility that it expresses. No one would think here of distinguishing the way of saying from the thing said. It is significant that the pressure seems to derive (we are reminded of Mr Yeats) from a recognition of bankruptcy, of a devoted life summed up in futility. A study of the earlier work, then, does at least help the commentary on *Mauberley*: it helps to bring out the significance of the poem for the inquiry in hand.

Mauberley is in the first place … the summing up of an individual life. It also has a representative value, reflecting as it does the miscellaneousness of modern culture, the absence of direction, of an alphabet of forms, or of any one predominant idiom; the uncongeniality of the world to the artist; and his dubious status there. It offers, more particularly, a representative experience of the phase of English poetry in which it became plain that the Romantic tradition was exhausted. One might … call it quintessential autobiography, taking care, however, to add that it has the impersonality of great poetry: its technical perfection means a complete detachment and control.

From F. R. Leavis, *New Bearings in English Poetry. A Study of the Contemporary Situation* (Oxford, 1932), pp. 104–5.

E. Alison Light, 'Introduction' to *Forever England*

In the outline of women's history this century, the inter-war years have so far been sketched in as primarily one of feminism's deepest troughs, the era as a whole assumed as having an 'anti-progressive and reactionary character'.

Yet it is hard to reconcile this sombre and depressing depiction of the inter-war years as a slough of feminine despond with the buoyant sense of excitement and release which animates so many of the broadly cultural activities which different groups of women enjoyed in the period. What new kinds of social and personal opportunity, for example, were offered by the changing cultures of sport and entertainment, from tennis clubs to cinema-going, by new forms of spending which hire-purchase and accessible mortgages made possible, by new patterns of domestic life which included the introduction of the daily servant rather than the live-in maid, new forms of household appliance, new attitudes to housework? How can we write about the idea of female freedom without considering the changing relationship to the female body which surely dominates the post-war years: perhaps the disposable sanitary napkin was in its own way as powerful an event as increasing female education or shifts in the employment market? In other words, we still have much to learn about the modernisation of women's lives, the realignment of public and private behaviours and values … and we need a history which can encompass this kind of narrative as well as the more conventional and self-consciously political forms of emancipation …

One of my aims in this book is to suggest the need to review these years as marking for many women their entry into modernity, a modernity which was felt and lived in the most interior and private of places … And even if a new commercial culture of 'home-making' was conservative in its assumptions in assuming this to be a female sphere, it nevertheless put woman and the home, and a whole panoply of connected issues, at the centre of modern life.

- Indeed, the more I read of writing by women in these post-war years the
- more I was struck by the sense of something radically other to, and rebelling
- against the domestic world pre-1918 which at the same time was quite com-
- patible with deeply defensive urges ... Even those who would by no means call
- themselves feminists (and this is true of all the authors I discuss) were linked
- by a resistance to 'the feminine' as it had been thought of in late Victorian or
- Edwardian times. In other words, by exploring the writing of middle-class
- women at home in the period (a far from stable category in itself) we can go
- straight to the centre of a contradictory and determining tension in English
- social life in the period which I have called a conservative modernity: janus-
- faced, it could simultaneously look backwards and forwards; it could accom-
- modate the past in the new forms of the present; it was a deferral of
- modernity and yet it also demanded a different sort of conservatism from that
- which had gone before. It is the women of an expanding middle class between
- the wars who were best able to represent Englishness in both its most modern
- and reactionary forms.

- From Alison Light, *Forever England*: *Femininity*, *Literature and Conservatism*
- *Between the Wars* (1991), pp. 9–11.

SAMPLE CHART

> Passage
>
> **Foregrounds Literary Texts** | --A--D---C-E-B---- | **Foregrounds History**

(My sample completion of the chart is by no means unarguable. My decisions should be explained by the discussion which follows; you should feel free to argue for your own decisions if they place the passages in other positions.)

▶ Discussion

A. SAINTSBURY ON *WIDSITH*

Although Saintsbury certainly uses historical knowledge (such as information about the death dates of historical figures), his interest is in a primarily *literary history,* which focuses from the opening on a specific literary
text. This emphasis continues throughout as he several times expresses an
intention not to pursue questions which are non-literary ones, suggests
that this particular text is of more historical than genuine literary interest,
and judges its literary qualities as low-level ones. His definition of the literary takes in quality of achievement, beauty, 'parallel passages' (a form of
what we might now call intertexuality – though he seems to rate this as of
only minor literary interest), use of regular metre and conventions, and
membership of a specific tradition, 'English Literature'. His literary history
is concerned with the order in which texts were written, their relation to
each other in a sequence and the kinds of formal devices each uses. He is
not interested in what such an early text might tell us about Anglo-Saxon

culture or history, relegating its sketch of a 'minstrel's' life to the category of the incidental and factual, rather than the literary. He is also content to leave oddities of fact alone and unresolved – presumably because for him the text does have an autonomous life of its own in which facts are not important. Thus, Saintsbury passes on quickly from the curious span of *Widsith*'s historical reference (where more recent critics might see this as precisely a question of a 'literary character'[17]). In short, history here is very much a background for literature; historical knowledge is needed as part of a general knowledge which gives a context to literary works, but the literary text is very much in the foreground. I have therefore placed the passage closest to the literary end of the chart's line.

B. C. S. LEWIS ON MEDIEVAL GEOGRAPHY

Unlike the Saintsbury passage, this piece does not start with a focus on a particular literary text, but with the investigation of a historical topic: 'what shape did medieval people envisage the Earth having?' In referring to a historical reality outside texts,[18] Lewis seems to be acting as much as a historian as a literary critic. One might note, however, that his evidence is markedly textual: 'as all authors … are agreed', and his evidence is here largely drawn from narratives which could be called 'literary' (Dante's *Inferno*, Mandeville's *Travels*). Still, most historical evidence is derived from texts, and it is true that two of Lewis's sources in this passage are not what would normally be considered literary ones: Vincent of Beauvais and the Hereford Cathedral *Mappa Mundi*. These are surely 'primary sources' rather than 'texts', to use the distinction deployed in section 4.1. Moreover, in his use of the term 'authors' Lewis is most probably invoking the medieval range of meaning for that word, in which an 'author' is a source of authority, knowledge on any topic, rather than a specifically literary kind of writer (see section 2.1). On the other hand, medievalists and Anglo-Saxonists have generally and traditionally been interested in a wider range of kinds of text than critics working in later periods – almost as if critics often work in tandem with the changing definition of the category 'literary' as it applies in their period (see section 1.1). And, if the passage has a certain inclusive historicising urge, it is also true that there is an interest in matters 'of a literary character': the medieval imagination, medieval humour and irony (Mandeville on relative viewpoints), the 'first "science-fiction effect" in literature'. Overall, though, I would place this passage as closest to the foregrounding history end of the line.

C. GREENBLATT ON *HENRY IV* AND *HENRY V*

This passage does start with a particular author and a particular play or plays, and states as its main aim what seems a clearly literary objective – an *understanding* of 'Shakespeare's conception of Hal' (i.e. Henry V before he becomes King). However, the interests of the passage thereafter do not look very literary at all – there is no reference to a text in any detail[19] – and instead there is a concern with a wide sense of how Elizabethan power worked. This looks much more like what we might expect of a historical than a literary enquiry (a key quotation is from an actual speech by the Queen rather than from a play). However, the investigation, though of actuality, rather than textuality, turns out in fact to have a markedly literary frame of reference. Thus, Elizabethan power is said to have a 'poetics', it relies on 'theatrical celebrations of royal glory', on 'theatrical violence', and the subjects who are controlled through this power are called 'the audience', 'spectators'. There is a marked desire in the passage to resist foregrounding either the literary text *or* the historical actuality. Indeed, the boundaries between these are blurred by its suggestion that the (literary) *form* of the theatre is not only one form of actual Elizabethan power, but that there is a continuity between actual/textual – so that textual (or, anyway, play-textual) relationships characterise the actual exercise of power. The literary is not considered here to be a separate sphere from the political or historical, but to be in continuous contact. Thus, reality itself is organised through formal literary features, and fictions, 'stage-plays', are as much part of reality as anything else (perhaps more so, if they are a privileged model for power relations). I therefore placed the passage at a mid-point on the literary/history foregrounding line, since it seeks to avoid *layering* literature and history at all.

D. LEAVIS ON POUND

The passage has a clear focus on a particular author, and, indeed, on a specific poem, which it regards as his greatest achievement. It shows a marked interest in formal literary features, noting Pound's invention of a modern poetic idiom which moves on from the 'poeticism' of an exhausted tradition, and praising his 'growing subtlety' of verse technique. In the last paragraph there is also a stress laid on formal matters: the terminal fatigue of Romanticism, the lack of a distinctive contemporary style, 'technical perfection', 'detachment and control', 'the impersonality of great poetry'. If we know anything of Leavis's position as the chief of English 'New Critics', this emphasis on the form of the text should come as no surprise, since New Criticism was usually said to accord the text priority and, indeed, autonomy. However, we might also notice that the book's subtitle, 'A Study of the Contemporary Situation', suggests an interest in the context of modern poetry. This is borne out by a closer look at the way in which the passage actually uses its interest in formal matters. For, in fact, the discussion of all these features takes place within an idea of relevance to contemporary culture. Thus there is a hint of critical distance in the comment 'his modern interests ... are for him mainly opportunities ... for verse practice' – implying that there may be something lacking in Pound's engagement with the contemporary. A related detachment of poet from society is, curiously enough, seen as part of the meaning of *Mauberley* itself in the third paragraph of the piece. This shifts considerably the focus on textual features towards a focus on contemporary history, by suggesting that formal concerns are not a concern for poetry only. Contemporary life itself has 'an absence of direction, of an alphabet of forms'. This is reminiscent of the shifting of textuality into actuality in the Greenblatt passage, and produces an analogous effect, in which foreground and background are run together. Having said that, I would argue that there is not here quite the same emphasis on equality between the literary and the actual as in the 'Invisible Bullets' passage. The possibility is present, but there is still in the main a foregrounding of the textual – of questions about poetry. I would place this passage therefore further toward the literary end of the line, though closer to the centre point than I might have expected.

E. ALISON LIGHT ON BRITISH WOMEN, CONSERVATISM AND WRITING BETWEEN THE WARS

This passage clearly has wide-ranging historical interests, showing a detailed awareness of 'the past in all its manifestations'.[20] It opens by focusing on what seems a specific historical enquiry – what were the values of (conservative) women in the period between 1919 and 1940? It refers to a whole range of detailed facets of women's lives where great changes were occurring – from new sporting opportunities to new ways of organising domestic work to new attitudes to menstruation – before suggesting the more general hypothesis that all these changes can be studied in terms of the complexities of women's entry into modernity after the First World War. These complexities can be studied particularly in the 'most private' places, in the domestic environment, where they have their centre. In the first three paragraphs of the passage there is virtually no reference to texts or the literary at all; the topic of middle-class women's writing and reading is only raised in the final paragraph as the main focus of the book's investigation of its themes. The justification for this focus is that these critically neglected (or, worse, scorned) kinds of writing will take us to the heart of the cultural history with which the book is concerned. I would place the passage quite near to the history end of the line, therefore, but only a little beyond the mid-way point to show its still considerable focus on literary texts (or texts, anyway). ☐

These particular possibilities do not, of course, exhaust the positions between the 'textual' and the 'historical', but may suggest some of the ways in which literary study can use history. No definitive answer has been provided to the question 'Why historicise?' (though you might not expect one by this stage of *this* book), but instead a range of practices have been explored. At one end of the line, these examples perhaps come quite close to sharing exactly the motivations of history at least in as far as history itself is foregrounded. At the other end of the line, there is one example which shows very little concern with historical motivations, though it does not shake off all connections. Most of the examples, though, show a close relationship with history which never quite becomes identical to historical study (I suspect this is characteristic, but as some even of this small sample of critical writings might suggest, the blurring of borders between disciplines is far from impossible). In the final exercises in this section, there will be opportunities to think through your own attitude to what motivates your use of history in criticism (as usual you will be left to your own thoughts at this stage).

> Go back to the suggested motivations for historical study at the opening of this section; to what extent do these motivations cover your own reasons for pursuing literary studies?
>
> Would you regard yourself as essentially a specific kind of historian when you study English? If so, why? If not, why not?
>
> Read the following extract by J. A. Cuddon from the final paragraph of a definition of 'historicism'. How sympathetic are you to the writer's reservations about using history in literary study?

It has been argued, for instance, that a modern reconstruction of the cultural or ideological identity of a past age must still be essentially modern in its point of view. Historicism cannot transform a twentieth-century mind; it may only be transferring modern preconceptions from the critical to the historical plane of thought. Moreover, historicism must inevitably be selective and interpretative in treating what evidence there is concerning standards and habits of mind that differ from our own; it may tend to impose a falsifying uniformity and immobility upon its conception of a literary 'period', and its findings are themselves demonstrably subject to change from generation to generation. Much of the historicism of thirty years ago is now as obsolete as other kinds of literary interpretation which were merely of their age. In addition, there is a tendency in historicism to interpret and measure the work of great and original imagination by the commonplaces of its time, reducing the uniqueness and subtlety of genius to the lowest common denominator of a reconstructed idea of 'period'. If, for instance, a knowledge of Elizabethan ideas about kingship, or of their dramatic conventions, helps us to understand Shakespeare's history plays, we must still remember that Shakespeare is hardly to be circumscribed by an abstraction of the average mentality of his contemporaries. Conventions that have been obliterated by time may be recovered for us by historicism, but the great writers of the past are more than conventional.

Historicism, therefore, cannot provide us with an absolute or objective measure of literary meaning or value. It is not a substitute for the act of intelligent imagination which we call criticism; but it is, properly used, one of the critic's most valuable tools. Provided its limitations are recognised, it can extend and refine our understanding of the literature we most admire. The validity of historicism rests not upon antiquarian curiosity about how a writer was influenced or interpreted by the world he lived in, but upon the endeavour to enrich modern sensibilities by comprehending and transmitting those ideas and values which preserve the values of our civilisation.

From J. A. Cuddon, *Dictionary of Literary Terms* (London, 1977), p. 116.

4.3   The End of History?

Throughout this book, I have always to imagine what the general practices of literary critics are in order to discuss what I take to be something like a shared experience of, or set of conventions for, studying literature (I could not discuss how we read texts, if I had no idea at all about how you are likely to have studied

English). This undoubtedly has its dangers, and there may well be occasions on which you have needed to contrast your experience or assumptions with my suppositions. It is probably even more dangerous for me to imagine what the general practice of historians is, as I have done in sections 4.1 and 4.2 (as for English, there is more than one version of History) – since I am not even a historian by trade. Nevertheless, we needed definitions of history to work with in this chapter, if we were to make any progress in discussing relations between history and literature.[21] I have tried to use what I take to be mainstream definitions. However, there are some modern historiographers and other cultural theorists who have suggested rather different ways of looking at history from the models so far referred to here. These different ways of thinking of history have links with some recent traditions of thought in philosophical and literary study which may make us reconsider what the relationship of history and literature is. These developments include a number of kinds of thought which, though they are not a neat and coherent package, do have connections. Thus this part of the book will look at some texts and thoughts about texts stemming from recent historiography, New Historicism, and Postmodernism. The section is called 'The End of History?'[22] to suggest just how radically these ideas might undermine some of the conventional ideas of history which literary and historical study have shared/been divided by.

Section 4.1 began by looking at both the closeness and separation of history and literature. In passing, I commented on Sir Philip Sidney's observation that history at first used the devices of poesy to produce its accounts, and that these devices were what made history a palatable genre. We then developed through section 4.1 a general idea that History did, despite its complexity, retain a certain emphasis on fact, or at least actuality, while literary study tended to stress the text as a representation, a narrative constructed out of language. We should now revisit this fact/fiction opposition.

◆ Read the following passages from an essay by the historian Hayden White. What is his view of the relationship between narrative and history?

◆ To what extent does this kind of approach blur the boundaries between historical and literary study?

Historiography is an especially good ground on which to consider the nature of narration and narrativity because it is here that our desire for the imaginary, the possible, must contest with the imperatives of the real, the actual. If we view narrative and narrativity as the instruments with which the conflicting claims of the imaginary and the real are mediated, arbitrated, or resolved in a discourse, we begin to comprehend both the appeal of narrative and the grounds for refusing it. If putatively real events are represented in a nonnarrative form, what kind of reality is it that offers itself, or is conceived to offer itself, to perception in this form? What would a nonnarrative representation of history look like? In answering this question, we do not necessarily arrive at a solution to the problem of the nature of narrative, but we do begin to catch a glimpse of the basis for the appeal of narrativity as a form for the representation of events construed to be real rather than imaginary.

[Hayden White discusses two forms of history – annals and chronicles[23] – generally considered by modern historians to be inferior forms of history because, he argues, they precisely do not 'attain to full narrativity'.]

…

I do not offer these reflections on the relation between historiography and narrative as aspiring to anything other than an attempt to illuminate the distinction between story elements and plot elements in the historical discourse. Common opinion has it that the plot of a narrative imposes a meaning on the events that make up its story level by revealing at the end a structure that was immanent [= inherently present] in the events all along. What I am trying to establish is the nature of this immanence in any narrative account of real events, events that are offered as the proper content of historical discourse. These events are real not because they occurred but because, first, they were remembered and, second, they are capable of finding a place in a chronologically ordered sequence. In order however, for an account of them to be considered an historical account, it is not enough that they can be recorded in the order of their original occurrence. It is the fact that they can be recorded otherwise, in an order of narrative, that makes them, at one and the same time, questionable as to their authenticity and susceptible to being considered as tokens of reality. In order to qualify as historical, an event must be susceptible to at least two narrations of its occurrence. Unless at least two versions of the same set of events can be imagined, there is no reason for the historian to take upon himself the authority of giving the true account of what really happened. The authority of the historical narrative is the authority of reality itself; the historical account endows this reality with form and thereby makes it desirable by the imposition on its processes of the formal coherency that only stories possess.

The history then belongs to the category of what might be called 'the discourse of the real', as against the 'discourse of the imaginary' or 'the discourse of desire' … I … wish to suggest that we can comprehend the appeal of historical discourse by recognising the extent to which it makes the real desirable, makes the real into an object of desire, and does so by its imposition, upon events that are represented as real, of the formal coherency that stories possess. Unlike that of the annals, the reality represented in the historical narrative … displays to us a formal coherency to which we ourselves aspire. The historical narrative, as against the chronicle, reveals to us a world that is putatively 'finished', done with, over, and yet not dissolved, not falling apart. In this world reality wears the mask of meaning, the fullness and completeness of which we can only imagine, never experience. Insofar as historical stories can be completed, can be given narrative closure, can be shown to have had a plot all along, they give to reality the odor of the ideal. This is why the plot of an historical narrative is always an embarrassment and has to be presented as 'found' in the events rather than put there by narrative techniques.

From Hayden White, 'The Value of Narrativity in the Representation of Reality', *The Content of Form: Narrative Discourse and Historical Representation* (Baltimore, MD, 1990), pp. 4–5, 14, 20–1.

 Discussion 1

He argues that there is a close link between narrative and history. Indeed, by looking at 'nonnarrative' forms of history, which are not categorised as history proper by modern historians, he argues that there has to be a narrative in order for an account to be regarded as history. He is not, of course, arguing that *any* narrative is history, but that narrative constructed under particular conditions is essential for a text to be recognised as historical writing. In arguing for the centrality of narrative, White is opposing some mainstream traditions of historical writing which have been, at the least, 'embarrassed' by the detection of narrative and plot structure, where these are seen as anything more than a form for presenting the actual historical content – the patterns formed by the events themselves at the time.

In fact, White implies, if (hypothetically) a set of events formed themselves into an indisputable pattern at the time, and no further commentary on this could be made, then that set of events would not be capable of representation *as* history. A sequence of events only becomes history when it is tellable, when it needs telling, when it can be told in alternative ways. If such narration (which has a relation to what we called historical interpretation in section 4.1), a particular form requiring a narrator, is not needed, then the set of events would become inherently 'annalistic' rather than a subject for history.[24]

This need for narrative is described by White as a source of uncertainty in that narrativity acts within historical discourse as both a guarantor of the reality of the explanation (a better explanation of the ways in which events fit together, a better narrative *is* better history, all other things being equal), and as an intervention in the 'inherent' factuality and actuality of historical evidence. □

▶ Discussion 2

If narrative is a central feature of historical study, and also a central interest of literary study, then there would seem to be strong common ground between the two – a common ground which may remove some of the boundaries that seemed to distinguish the two disciplines in section 4.1. Thus, the differing focus of literary study on texts and of historical study on a field of study which is actual rather than textual would be impacted by a version of history which admitted that it was always, in fact, constructed through the devices of narrative and plot. It is important to note, however, that Hayden White is not simply undermining the value of history by arguing that it is not authentic in the way it should be, but is suggesting that the traditional claim for authenticity is wrongly formulated, partly as a result of history's desire for 'the discourse of the real'. Thus a fundamental element of history is to give to 'reality the odor of the ideal'. In collapsing the boundaries between real and ideal (reality only feels real in the idealised form provided by ordering narrative), White might certainly be said to be approaching close to literary territory – where fiction has traditionally been seen as having its own kinds of truth, revealed through its capacity to order at a level higher than that of which ordinary life is naturally capable.[25]

A dissolution of the borders between the literary and the historical and other fields is further clarified in his Preface to *The Content of Form*, where Hayden White makes it clear that it is not only history which is affected by these ideas about narrativity and reality. Indeed, he sees it as a characteristic of a specific phase of history, that all things turn to narrative:

Many modern historians hold that narrative discourse ... is the very stuff of a mythical view of reality, a conceptual or pseudoconceptual 'content' which, when used to represent real events, endows them with an illusory coherence and charges them with the kinds of meanings more characteristic of oneiric [= dreaming] than of waking thought.

This critique of narrative discourse by recent proponents of scientific historiography is of a piece with the rejection of narrativity in literary modernism, and with the perception, general in our time, that real life can never be truthfully represented as having the kind of formal coherency met with in the conventional, well-made or fabulistic [= fable-like] story. Since its invention by Herodotus, traditional historiography has featured predominantly the belief that history itself consists of a congeries of lived stories, individual and collective, and that the principal task of historians is to uncover these stories and to retell them in narrative, the truth of which would reside in the correspondence of the story told to the story lived by real people in the past ...

According to this view, it was possible to believe that whereas writers of fictions invented everything in their narratives – characters, events, plots, motifs, themes, atmosphere, and so on – historians invented nothing but certain rhetorical flourishes or poetic effects to the end of engaging their reader's attention and sustaining their interest in the true story they had to tell. Recent theories of discourse, however, dissolve the distinction between realistic and fictional discourses based on the presumption of an ontological difference [= difference in the nature of their existence] between their respective referents, real and imaginary, in favour of stressing their common aspect as semiological apparatuses that produce meanings by the systematic substitutions of signifieds (conceptual contents) for the extra-discursive [= existing outside discourse, i.e. 'in reality'] entities that serve as their referents. In these semiological theories of discourse, narrative is revealed to be a particularly effective system of discursive meaning production by which individuals can be taught to live a distinctively 'imaginary relation to their real conditions of existence,' that is to say, an unreal but meaningful relation to the social formations in which they are indentured to live out their lives and realise their destinies as social subjects.

To conceive of narrative discourse in this way permits us to account for universality as a cultural fact and for the interest that dominant social groups have in controlling what will pass for the authoritative myths of a given cultural formation ... Myths and ideologies based on them presuppose the adequacy of stories to the reality whose meaning they purport to reveal. When belief in this adequacy begins to wane, the entire cultural edifice of a society enters into crisis, because not only is a specific system of beliefs undermined but the very condition of the possibility of socially significant belief is eroded. This is why, I think, we have witnessed across the whole spectrum of human sciences over the course of the last two decades a pervasive interest in the nature of narrative, its epistemic authority [= authorisation of knowledge], its cultural function, and its general social significance.

Lately, many historians have called for a return to narrative representation in historiography. Philosophers have sought to justify narrative as a mode of explanation different from, but not less important than, the nomological-deductive mode [= based on the deduction of general laws] favoured in the physical sciences. Theologians and moralists have recognised the relation between a specifically narratavistic view of reality and the social vitality of any ethical system … And cultural critics, Marxists and non-Marxists alike, have commented on the death of the 'great master narratives' that formerly provided precognitive bases of belief … and sustained … utopistic impulses to social transformation. And, indeed, a whole cultural movement in the arts, generally gathered under the name postmodernism, is informed by a programmatic, if ironic, commitment to the return to narrative as one of its enabling presuppositions.

From Hayden White, Preface to *The Contact of Form*, pp. ix–xi.

Here narrative becomes the central intellectual concern of the postmodern age, and the tools for understanding narrative are drawn from the literary-linguistic fields in which they were (variously) developed into the ambits and concerns of many other disciplines. Even more fundamentally, narrative becomes, according to this view, the central anxiety for postmodern society as a whole, particularly because there is apparently both a collapse of faith in narratives *and* a conviction that all (?[26]) values and knowledge can only be represented narratively. Hence White's references to various disciplines seeking a return to narrative, to cultural critics noting the death of 'master narratives', and to postmodern art, which having it both ways, is said to return to narrative, but with irony. □

Hayden White's work may not quite seem to justify being called 'the end of history' (though perhaps some historians would call it that?), but it certainly suggests a distinctive kind of history. And, indeed, its interest in narrative can be connected to postmodern ideas which do, indeed, variously proclaim or imply the end of history (or history as we have known it) and the reign of narrative. A focus on narrative in itself tends towards the idea that any account (except those in a nonnarrative mode, if there is such a thing) is as much a work of construction as of transcription. That is, an account of what has happened will always be more a story told *about* something *by someone afterwards* than a story which arises in the form it takes because that is the form of the events themselves. In this view of narrative, the present always dominates the past – because the present tells about the past as it wishes.[27] This might be seen as particularly problematic for a history which sees authenticity as vital, for a history which sees itself as different from fictional discourses (though the idea that the past must be 'constructed', 'interpreted' is by no means news to historians).

Paradoxically, for many thinkers in this vein, the collapse of the 'master narratives' is what has drawn attention to the omnipresence of narratives. For, once the underpinning narratives which give a common range of starting points to all explanations are seen to be bankrupt, a more local authority has to be derived for explanation, and this is the narrative authority not of a widely shared narrative, but of a narrative which derives its status from being local, that is, from not being a 'master' narrative. For some, this is a liberation – being freed from the generalising narratives which seek to control all the more various stories which might be told. For others, it is a symptom of a culture adrift, one which has lost one system of authentication and, failing to develop any coherent replacement, is left with a collection of fragments which are all equally valid and unvalidatable.

These kinds of ideas clearly have wide-ranging consequences for the whole spectrum of human knowledge, to the extent where questions about 'literature' might seem trivial and old-fashioned. At the same time, there is a curious restoration of literature to the centre-stage of human experience in this engagement with narrative, which implies that all experience is, in fact, based in textual devices. Thus the distinctions of section 4.1 between 'primary source' (evidence of a reality pre-existing that source and continuing after it has been written) and 'text' (where meaning is constructed as one reads from the language itself without any precise reference to actuality) perhaps disappears. In terms of conventional distinctions between history/literature, fact/fiction, this makes all experience second order: narration rather than occurrence, since there are no occurrences which are not part of one narration or other.

For literary study this concentration on narrative and textuality and the demise of any 'universal history' impacts on all sorts of issues: is any systematic literary history possible; is any grounding of literary texts in 'history' possible? Is legitimation of interpretation any longer possible? More fundamentally, the question is raised of whether literature or representation in general can any longer be about anything other than its own narration. Finally in this section, are two responses to a (now) historical, then real (one might presume ...) event which might give a sense, at least, of how controversial, how important, ideas about narration and history, the end of history, the focus on the present, postmodernity, might be.

> ◆ Read the following passage by Jean Baudrillard, from 'The Reality
> Gulf', printed in the *Guardian*. Where does its focus on narration and
> representation lead it?

From the start it was clear that this war would not exist. After the 'hot' war, and then after the cold war, we now have the dead war. The thawing of the cold war has left us in the embrace of a corpse of war, needing to handle this decomposing cadaver which no one within the confines of the Gulf has managed to revive. What the United States, President Saddam Hussein and the local powers are fighting over in the Gulf is in fact the corpse of war. War itself has entered a definitive crisis. It is too late for a hot third world war. The moment has passed.

It has been distilled in the course of time into the cold war and there will be no other. Some may have thought that the end of the eastern block, by taking the wraps off deterrence, might open up new 'areas of freedom' for war.

That hasn't happened. The deterrent has not been taken to its intended conclusion. In fact, quite the reverse. The reciprocal deterrent between the two blocks worked because of what might be termed the excess of the means of destruction. Today, though, it works even better as a total self-deterrent, which has gone so far as to create the self-dissolution of the eastern block. Yet it is also a profound self-deterrent for US might and for western power in general. This power has also been cowed and paralysed by its own strength. It is incapable of using its position within the balance of power. That is why the Gulf War will not happen. This phenomenon – the marginalisation of war into interminable suspense (rather like a form of psychoanalysis) – is neither reassuring nor comforting. Looked at like this, the non-event of the Gulf is at least as serious as the possibility of war. It is the equivalent of that destructive period in which a corpse rots, a period which causes nausea and impotent lethargy. In both cases, our rituals and symbolic defences are very weak. We are incapable of even putting an end to war, and so we live through the experience with the self-same shameful indifference as with the hostages.

The manipulation and negotiation over hostages is a degenerate form of war which perfectly embodies this 'non-war'. Hostage-taking and blackmail are the purest products of the era of deterrence. The hostage has replaced the warrior. Even by pure inactivity he takes the limelight as the main protagonist in this simulated non-war. The warriors can be buried in the desert, while the hostages occupy centre-stage. Today's hostage is a phantom player, a walk-on who fills the impotent vacuum of modern war.

[...]

It affects us all. We are all hostages to media intoxication. We are all manipulated in the general indifference, induced to believe in the coming war as we were once induced to believe in revolution in Romania, under house arrest to the pretend war. We are all in place as strategic hostages. Our strategic site is the television screen, from which we are daily bombarded, and in front of which we also serve as a bargaining counter. In this sense, President Saddam's grotesque charade is performed as a diversion – both from war and from active international terrorism. At least such 'soft' terrorism enables President Saddam to put an end to 'hard' terrorism (whether Palestinian or some other). In this guise he reveals himself, as in many other ways, as the perfect accomplice of the west.

The difficulties of the path to war have led to the triumph of blackmail as a strategy. It is the triumph of blackmail and the end of true threats. In the case of Iran, there was an element of true threat; with President Saddam there is nothing but blackmail. What makes President Saddam so despicable is his vulgarisation of everything. He has debased the challenge of religion into a false holy war. He has made the sacrificial hostage into the commercial hostage. He has made war itself into an impossible farce.

Of course the West did a lot to help, by encouraging him to believe he had won the war against Iran, and so fostering the illusion of further victory, this time against the West. The only enjoyable aspect of this whole story is the sight of this chicken coming home to roost.

We are experiencing neither the logic of war nor the logic of peace. We are experiencing the logic of deterrence, inexorably pursuing its course for the last 40 years. It is working itself out as a logic of weakness, through events that are becoming ever weaker, whether in eastern Europe or the Gulf or as exemplified by the vaguaries of our French politicians. The United Nations has given the green light to a diluted kind of war – the right to war. It is a green light for all kinds of precautions and concessions, making it a kind of extended contraceptive against the act of war. First safe sex, now safe war. A Gulf War would not even register two or three on the Richter scale this way. It is unreal, war without the symptoms of war, a form of war which means never needing to face up to war, which enables war to be 'perceived' from deep within a darkroom. WE OUGHT to have been on our guard because of the disappearance of the declaration of war. There can be no real war without a declaration – it is the moment of passing from word to deed. Once that disappears, then the operations of war disappear, too (French soldiers were even armed at one time with fake bullets!). Then the ending of the war disappears, too. The distinction between victors and vanquished ceases. War becomes interminable because it never began. We dreamed of a pure war – a strategic orbital war purged of all local and political details. Now we have fallen into its feeble alternative – a derisory fantasy in which the adversaries outdo each other in de-escalation, as if the outbreak of war, the true event of war, had become intolerable. Thus everything transfers itself into a "virtual" form and so we are confronted with a 'virtual' apocalypse. That is much more dangerous in the long term than a genuine apocalypse.

[…]

An accumulation of troops in the desert of Saudi Arabia can only lead to a violent solution. But this is a realist Aristotelian logic to which we no longer subscribe. We must now be satisfied with virtual reality which, contrary to the Aristotelian perception, deters from passage to the deed. In our fear of the real, of anything that is too real, we have created a gigantic simulator. We prefer the virtual to the catastrophe of the real, of which television is the universal mirror. Indeed it is more than a mirror: today television and news have become the ground itself, television plays the same role as the card which is substituted for territory in the Borges fable. War has not escaped this process. Even soldiers have not been able to retain for themselves the privilege of real war. Arms have not kept the privilege of the value of their use. Deterrence has passed this way and it spares nothing. Arms have mislaid their real function, their function of death and destruction. They are hooked by the lure of war just as others are hooked by power's lure.

PS: It is perhaps rash to demonstrate the reasons for the impossibility of a war just at the very moment when it is supposed to happen and when the signs of its outbreak are accumulating. But wouldn't it have been even more stupid not to seize the opportunity?

From the *Guardian*, 11 January 1991, EUR page 25. 'The Reality Gulf,' Jean Baudrillard.

> Then read the following poem by Tony Harrison. Where does its focus on narration and representation lead it?

Tony Harrison, *A Cold Coming*

'A cold coming we had of it.'
T. S. Eliot: JOURNEY OF THE MAGI

I saw the charred Iraqi lean
towards me from bomb-blasted screen

his windscreen wiper like a pen
ready to write down thoughts for men,

his windscreen wiper like a quill
he's reaching for to make his will.

I saw the charred Iraqi lean
like someone made of Plasticine

as though he'd stopped to ask the way
and this is what I heard him say:

'Don't be afraid I've picked on you
for this exclusive interview.

Isn't it your sort of poet's task
to find words for this frightening mask?

If that gadget that you've got records
words from such scorched vocal chords,

press RECORD before some dog
devours me mid-monologue.'

So I held the shaking microphone
closer to the crumbling bone:

'I read the news of three wise men
who left their sperm in nitrogen,

three foes of ours, three wise Marines
with sample flasks and magazines,

three wise soldiers from Seattle
who banked their sperm before the battle.

Did No. 1 say God be thanked
I've got my precious semen banked.

And No. 2: O praise the Lord
my last best shot is safely stored.

And No. 3: Praise be to God
I left my wife my frozen wad?

So if their fate was to be gassed
at least they thought their name would last,

and though cold corpses in Kuwait
they could by proxy procreate.

Excuse a skull half roast, half bone
for using such a scornful tone.

It may seem out of all proportion
but I wish I'd taken their precaution.

They seemed the masters of their fate
with wisely jarred ejaculate.

Was it a propaganda coup
to make us think they'd cracked death too,

disinformation to defeat us
with no post-mortem millilitres?

Symbolic millions in reserve
made me, for one, lose heart and nerve.

On Saddam's pay we can't afford
to go and get our semen stored.

Sad to say that such high tech's
uncommon here. We're stuck with sex.

If you can conjure up and stretch
your imagination (and not retch)

the image of me beside my wife
closely clasped creating life …'

(I let the unfleshed skull unfold
a story I'd been already told,

and idly tried to calculate
the content of ejaculate:

the sperm in one ejaculation
equals the whole Iraqi nation

times, roughly, let's say, 12.5
though that .5s not now alive.

Let's say the sperms were an amount
so many times the body count,

2,500 times at least
(but let's wait till the toll's released!).

Whichever way Death seems outflanked
by one cold tube of cold bloblings banked.

Poor bloblings, maybe you've been blessed
with, of all fates possible, the best

according to Sophocles i.e.
'the best of fates is not to be'

a philosophy that's bleak
for any but an ancient Greek

but difficult these days to escape
when spoken to by such a shape.

When you see men brought to such states
who wouldn't want that 'best of fates'

or in the world of Cruise or Scud
not go Kryonic if he could,

spared the normal human doom
of having made it through the womb?)

He heard my thoughts and stopped the spool:
'I never thought life futile, fool!

Though all Hell began to drop
I never wanted life to stop. I was filled with such a yearning
to stay in life as I was burning,

such a longing to be beside
my wife in bed before I died,

and, most, to have engendered there
a child untouched by war's despair.

So press RECORD! I want to reach
the warring nations with my speech.

Don't look away! I know it's hard
to keep regarding one so charred,

so disfigured by unfriendly fire
and think it once burned with desire.

Though fire has flayed off half my features
they once were like my fellow creatures',

till some screen-gazing crop-haired boy
from Iowa or Illinois,

equipped by ingenious technophile
put paid to my paternal smile

and made the face you see today
an armature half-patched with clay,

an icon framed, a looking glass
for devotees of "kicking ass",

a mirror that returns the gaze
of victors on their victory days

and in the end stares out the watcher
who ducks behind his headline: GOTCHA!

or behind the flag-bedecked page 1
of the true-type-setting SUN!

I doubt victorious Greeks let Hector
join their feast as spoiling spectre,

and who'd want to sour the children's joy
in Iowa or Illinois

Or ageing mothers overjoyed
to find their babies weren't destroyed?

But cabs beflagged with SUN front-pages
don't help peace in future ages.

Stars and Stripes in sticky paws
may sow the seeds for future wars.

Each Union Jack the kids now wave
may lead them later to the grave.

But praise the Lord and raise the banner
(excuse a skull's sarcastic manner!)

Desert Rat and Desert Stormer
without scars and (maybe) trauma,

the semen bankers are all back
to sire their children in the sack.

With seed sown straight from the sower
dump second-hand spermatozoa!

Lie that you saw me and I smiled
to see that soldier hug his child.

Lie and pretend that I excuse
my bombing by B52s,

pretend I pardon and forgive
that they still do and I don't live,

pretend they have the burnt man's blessing
and then maybe I'm spared confessing

that only fire burnt out the shame of things I'd done in Saddam's name,

the deaths, the torture and the plunder
the black clouds all of us are under.

Say that I'm smiling and excuse
the Scuds we launched against the Jews.

Pretend I've got the imagination
to see the world beyond one nation.

That's your job, poet, to pretend
I want my foe to be my friend.

It's easier to find such words
for this dumb mask like baked dogturds.

So lie and say the charred man smiled
to see the soldier hug his child.

This gaping rictus once made glad
a few old hearts back in Baghdad,

hearts growing older by the minute
as each truck comes without me in it.

I've met you though, and had my say
which you've got taped. Now go away.'

I gazed at him and he gazed back
stared right through me to Iraq.

Facing the way the charred man faced
I saw the frozen phial of waste,

a test-tube frozen in the dark,
crib and Kaaba, sacred Ark,

a pilgrimage of Cross and Crescent
the chilled suspension of the Present.

Rainbows seven shades of black
curved from Kuwait back to Iraq,

and instead of gold the frozen crock's
crammed with mankind on the rocks,

the congealed genie who won't thaw
until the World renounced War,

cold spunk meticulously jarred
never to be charrer or the charred,

a bottled Bethlehem of this come-
curdling Cruise / Scud-cursed millennium.

I went. I pressed REWIND and PLAY
and I heard the charred man say:

First printed in the *Guardian*, 18 March 1991.

Further Reading

Belsey, Catherine, 'Towards Cultural History – in Theory and Practice', in *New Historicism and Cultural Materialism: A Reader*, ed. Kiernan Ryan (London, Edward Arnold, 1996).

Black, Jeremy and Donald M. MacRaild, *Studying History* (London, Macmillan, 1997).

Brooker, Peter, *Modernism/Postmodernism* (London, Longmans, 1992).

Carr, E. H., *What is History?*, 2nd edn (Harmondsworth, Penguin, 1987).

de J. Jackson, J. R., *Historical Criticism and the Meaning of Texts* (London, Routledge, 1989).

Fukuyama, Frances, *The End of History and the Last Man* (Harmondsworth, Penguin, 1992).

Greenblatt, Stephen, *Renaissance Self-fashioning: from More to Shakespeare* (Chicago University Press, 1984).

Hutcheon, Linda, *Poetics of Postmodernism – History, Theory, Fiction* (London, Routledge, 1988).

Jenkins, Keith, *On 'What is History?' from Carr and Elton to Rorty and White* (London, Routledge, 1995).

Marwick, Arthur, *The Nature of History* (London, Macmillan, 1989).

McGann, Jerome J. (ed.), *Historical Studies and Literary Criticism* (University of Wisconsin Press, 1985).

Ryan, Kiernan (ed.), *New Historicism and Cultural Materialism: A Reader* (London, Edward Arnold, 1996).

Veeser, Aram. H. (ed.), *The New Historicism* (London, Routledge, 1989).

White, Hayden V., *Content of the Form: Narrative Discourse and Historical Representation* (Baltimore, MD, Johns Hopkins University Press, 1990).

Identities

5.1 Reading the Subject

I have frequently referred through this book to Roman Jakobson's model of the communicative situation, with its three functions of Addresser, Addressee and Message. During and after chapter 2, this model has been filled out by various contexts – functional,[1] generic, and historical – which imply that the basic situation of communication is constantly within larger systems which govern its exact behaviour. This has often led us to observe that the roles in the model are indeed functions as much as persons, aspects of a system as much as unique instances.[2] Nevertheless, the 'person', or what appears to be the 'person', the unique human individual with a specific identity, has played an enormously important part in literary studies. What recent critical discussion has often called 'the subject' (the focus or apparent focus of subjectivity, that which might conventionally be seen as the individual or 'person') is, indeed, a vital part of the subject of English. Thus we saw in sections 2.1 and 2.2 how influential the idea of origination and individuation has been – with its associations with notions of the autonomy and originality of texts, and with the idea of the author as creator.[3] Indeed, you may recall Terry Eagleton's sarcastic commentary on 'the Rise of English' in section 1.3, which draws attention to some of the ways in which 'literature' was 'officially' seen in the nineteenth century as a 'personal' matter:

> Literature was in several ways a suitable candidate for this ideological enterprise. As a liberal 'humanizing' pursuit, it could provide a potent antidote to political bigotry and ideological extremism. Since literature, as we know, deals in universal human values rather than in such historical trivia as civil wars, the oppression of women or the dispossession of the English peasantry, it could serve to place in cosmic perspective the petty demands of working people for decent living conditions or greater control over their own lives … English, as a Victorian handbook for English teachers puts it, helps to 'promote sympathy and fellow feeling among all classes'; another Victorian writer speaks of literature as opening a 'serene and luminous region of truth where all may meet and expatiate in common,' above 'the smoke and stir, the din and turmoil of man's lower life of care and business and debate'.

It is notable how (in this account at least) literature worked in both a universalising way (dealing with values shared by all humans) and a specifically personal level (where particular class or political values felt by groups were replaced by interpersonal exchange between individuals). In this model, identity exists most authentically in the individual, and is realised perfectly in a state of harmonious identity between all people.[4] Indeed, larger scale social life is seen to give only a false and crass sense of identity – the identity of 'political bigotry', which seemed to unite, but did so through unexamined assumptions that saw society in terms of groups with mass identities. Against this, literature could offer an area where individual conversations could take place. The ordinary world outside literature suggested by the second writer quoted, is very much, in Victorian terms, a modern one. That world is an industrial one of 'smoke and stir', 'business and debate' – of pollution, of disruptive activity, of competition and the clashes of differing viewpoints. Literature offers an antidote to this world (and one might suspect that this is not only for working-class consumption, in fact), a space where the human can escape from the excessive stress caused by the machinery of modern society.

Such an opposition between individual and mass identity, between the human and the machine, the personal and the system, has played a large part in the ways in which 'English' and literature have been shaped. A similar opposition between 'mass industrial culture' and individual discrimination and higher values was active in the thinking of the New Criticism championed by F. R. Leavis, which dominated literary study in England from after the Second World War until the arrival of theory in the nineteen eighties. Moreover, the association of literature with the personal is far from an exhausted or dead one. 'English' students are still very likely (at least on arrival at university? ...) to say they are motivated by pleasure, by personal interest, by the ways in which studying literature is a matter of personal response and so on (and they – you – may be right to do so: it is no inevitable fact that the particularity of literature is an illusion). Of course, students of Business Studies or Chemistry may say similar things, but I suspect that that these subjects do not so readily or inherently suggest a 'personal' space. It may well be that English students even find literary theory (at least initially) counter to their expectation of literary study precisely because it seems to demand *systematic knowledge and command* of a whole body of secondary material, which may not immediately seem a source of the personal response or pleasure which they feel they get from literary texts.

Modern literature itself has also often seemed particularly concerned with ideas of personal identity as against systematic, general or imposed identity (one might think of George Orwell's *Nineteen Eighty-Four* [1949], or Ken Kesey's *One Flew Over the Cuckoo's Nest* [1962], or Margaret Atwood's *The Handmaid's Tale* [1987], or perhaps even the dominance of the lyric in modern poetry). Modern criticism too has been particularly engaged with identity in a whole range of ways: some negative (exposing the illusions of conventional notions of identity), but some positive (the potential of literature to explore, establish and liberate or express repressed identities, individual or group – particularly-working class, ethnic and sexual identities).

This chapter will explore some of the ways in which ideas of identity are active in literary study. The first section will introduce a number of recent approaches to identity. The following three sections will give you the opportunity to pursue issues in particular areas – those of class, gender and sexuality and, finally, race and nationality.[5] Since this is our final chapter, and since many of the questions about identity are linked to the range of ideas covered earlier, the final three sections will have a relatively strong emphasis on exercises and on your (personal?) responses to them. In each of these sections, there will be an introductory exercise for which there will be a sample discussion, and then, following and expanding the model used at the end of other sections, there will be sequences of exercises which will be mainly left to you to work out. I am assuming, or imagining, that at this stage you will have a considerable command of both the 'thinking' and the 'texts' parts of these exercises, and that you will be able to work through your own (if anything is our own?) senses of literary identity.

The word 'identity' comes from the Latin word *identitas* = being the same, which is derived from the word *idem* = the same. It is related to 'identical' and to 'identify' (identify comes from the Latin *identificare*, from *idem*, the same, and *facere*, to make). The word 'identical' is used in a range of ways to indicate the sameness of two persons or objects, for example:

> *identical twins*, twins developing from one zygote;
> *identic note*, a diplomatic note which two states jointly send to a third nation.

Identity, however, has come to refer not so much to sameness between two different things or persons, but to sameness between one thing and itself. This seems a slightly absurd idea initially (yet we all use the concept) – a feeling perhaps summed up for those who have not studied logic by the logical *law* or *principle of identity*, which states that: 'A is A, that a thing is the same as itself'.[6] This feeling of absurdity and the need for establishing a thing/person as itself presumably arise from a contradiction in the way we think about 'sameness'. The law of identity seems absurd if we assume that the sameness of something is self-evident and unmistakable; on the other hand, the general sense and force of the word 'identity' presumably arises from a strong conception that, actually, sameness is not always so easy to judge or be assured of.

The use of the word identity in official contexts concerned with legal identification makes this point in one specific way. We need (or may be required to need at times) various documents to prove our identity, such as, for example, *an identity card* ('a card … bearing the owner's or wearer's name, etc., used to establish his identity').[7] Clearly such documents are required to control entry to particular areas or kinds of property, to allow access to money, to check that individuals are not breaking some restriction enacted by the state, and so on. The need for such formal identification only arises in modern societies where people live in large communities and where there is a large degree of anonymity, so that membership of that community is not something which its guardians can know purely from personal experience, but for which they must have a coordinated system of proofs. In such a social system (to varying degrees and in varying ways), 'sameness' is proved to others through these specialised kinds of texts – which are signs of who you are, what category of person you are, what your rights are and so on.

Literature in general and specific texts in particular may well be concerned with identity cards and the state regulation of identity in these ways, but identity in literary contexts probably usually points more immediately to questions that are focused on identity to a self:

> 'what or who is A?'   'who is A really?'
> 'how did A become A?'   'how did A become A while B became B?'

'what can A become?'   'can A fully become the true A?'
'How sure can I be that I am actually A?'   'is A A?'

As each of these questions (and there are undoubtedly others along these lines) might suggest, the self-evidence of identity is unlikely to be straightforward in literature. One could name many familiar literary texts which explore these kinds of question: for example, Fielding's *Tom Jones*, Charlotte Brontë's *Jane Eyre*, Joseph Conrad's *Lord Jim*, Alice Walker's *The Color Purple*, and so on. For the first exercise here, we could take as an example an extract from one text which seems very much concerned with the question, 'what or who is A?'

◆ Does the passage encourage you to come to any conclusions about what or who Gatsby is?
◆ What kind of ideas about identity might the passage be exploring?

F. Scott Fitzgerald, *The Great Gatsby*

And then came that disconcerting ride. We hadn't reached West Egg village before Gatsby began leaving his elegant sentences unfinished…

'Look here, old sport,' he broke out surprisingly, 'what's your opinion of me, anyhow?'

A little overwhelmed, I began the generalised evasions which that question deserves.

'Well, I'm going to tell you something about my life,' he interrupted. 'I don't want you to get a wrong idea of me from all these stories you hear… I'll tell you God's truth.' His right hand suddenly ordered divine retribution to stand by. 'I am the son of some wealthy people in the Middle West – all dead now. I was brought up in America but educated at Oxford, because all my ancestors have been educated there for many years. It is a family tradition.'

He looked at me sideways – and I knew why Jordan Baker had believed he was lying. He hurried the phrase 'educated at Oxford', or swallowed it, or choked on it as though it had bothered him before. And with this doubt, his whole statement fell to pieces, and I wondered if there wasn't something a little sinister about him after all.

'What part of the Middle West?' I enquired casually.

'San Francisco.'

'I see.'

'My family all died and I came into a good deal of money.'

His voice was solemn, as if the memory of that sudden extinction of a clan still haunted him. For a moment I suspected that he was pulling my leg, but a glance at him convinced me otherwise.

'After that I lived like a young rajah in all the capitals of Europe – Paris, Venice, Rome – collecting jewels, chiefly rubies, hunting big game, painting a little, things for myself only, and trying to forget something very sad that had happened to me long ago.'

With an effort I managed to restrain my incredulous laughter. The very phrases were worn so threadbare that they evoked no image except that of a turbaned 'character' leaking sawdust at every pore as he pursued a tiger though the Bois de Boulogne.

'Then came the war, old sport. It was a great relief, and I tried very hard to die, but I seemed to bear an enchanted life. I accepted a commission as first lieutenant when it began. In the Argonne Forest I took the remains of my machine-gun battalion so far forward that there was a half-mile gap on either side of us where the infantry couldn't advance. We stayed there two days and two nights, a hundred and thirty men with Lewis guns, and when the infantry came at last they found the insignia of three German divisions among the piles of dead. I was promoted to be a major, and every Allied government gave me a decoration – even Montenegro, little Montenegro down on the Adriatic Sea!'

... My incredulity was submerged in fascination now; it was like skimming hastily through a dozen magazines.

He reached in his pocket, and a piece of metal, slung on a ribbon, fell into my palm. 'That's the one from Montenegro.'

To my astonishment, the thing had an authentic look. 'Orderi di Danilo,' ran the circular legend, 'Montenegro, Nicholas Rex.'

'Turn it.'

'Major Jay Gatsby,' I read, 'For Valour Extraordinary.'

'Here's another thing I always carry. A souvenir of Oxford days. It was taken in Trinity Quad – the man on my left is now the Earl of Doncaster.'

It was a photograph of half a dozen young men in blazers loafing in an archway through which were visible a host of spires. There was Gatsby, looking a little, not much, younger – with a cricket bat in his hand.

Then it was all true. I saw the skins of tigers flaming in his palace on the Grand Canal; I saw him opening a chest of rubies to ease, with their crimson lighted depths, the gnawings of his broken heart.

From F. Scott Fitzgerald, *The Great Gatsby* (1926). Extract from the Penguin edn (1982), pp. 70–3.

 ## Discussion 1

The passage certainly does not seem to try to give Gatsby a clear and unambiguous identity (a consistent unity or sameness). On the contrary, there are many signs in it of the inconsistency and fragility of Gatsby's narrative of himself, so that his solemn intention to tell the monolithic and indisputable 'God's truth' is undermined as soon as stated. Some elements of his story are undoubtedly untrue – cannot be true. Thus, when the narrator, Nick Carraway, probes his claim to 'Middle Western' origins, Gatsby bizarrely names a city which is not in the Mid-West at all, but on the Pacific coast. Similarly, Gatsby despite his apparent conviction cannot have hunted big game in Rome or Venice or Paris!

Other details or elements in the story strike the narrator as unconvincing, but are not necessarily so evidently false. In these cases, it is usually the style, the mode of storytelling, that seems to Nick not to observe the normal rules for convincing an audience, and with these doubts 'his whole statement fell to pieces'. Thus, Nick particularly notes hesitations (as in the case of the phrase 'educated at Oxford') and the deployment of what appear to be, indeed, stories, rather than authentically personal narratives.[8] Nick notes instances of narrative which fail to convince him of their identity with their narrator, including the following:

> 'The very phrases were worn so threadbare that they evoked no image except that of a turbaned "character"'
> 'My incredulity was submerged in fascination now; it was like skimming hastily through a dozen magazines.'

In both these cases, the problem is that Gatsby's story is precisely too obviously a story and therefore untrue. This draws on an assumption that a story is a fiction and that real life will have a unique form and particularity which authenticates it as real in opposition to the codified shapeliness of fictions. In the first quotation, the problem is that the language appears to Nick to refer to nothing except previous uses of language, and therefore has no contact with reality. In the second quotation, Gatsby's ways of narrating his life too evidently seem to draw on all the clichéd tropes of popular fiction ('trying to forget something very sad that had happened to me long ago'; 'I tried very hard to die, but I seemed to bear an enchanted life').

However, it should be said that the fact that Gatsby describes these experiences in clichéd narrative does not in itself prove that he is lying. Like other narrators, he has to choose some form in which to tell his story, and perhaps these are the only forms he knows, or the forms which do, in fact, shape his life. If they are the stuff of popular romance, perhaps this is because Gatsby sees himself as a figure from that world – and sees that world as real rather than patently fictional (on the first page of the novel Nick remarks that 'the intimate revelations of young men, or at least the terms in which they express them, are usually plagiaristic'). The passage draws attention to the difficulties of knowing how to distinguish true and falsified evidence: 'To my astonishment, the thing had an authentic look. "Orderi di Danilo," ran the circular legend, "Montenegro, Nicholas Rex."' The fact that this medal seems to prove Gatsby's story true, can, oddly, count against it, since it might indeed be a sign of authenticity which Gatsby carries round with him *in order to* falsify. His comment 'Here's another thing I always carry' is suspicious because it implies that he deliberately carries round 'things' which may prove his story – as if he is used to being accused of lying and as if even he knows that his story is not convincing without 'concrete' proof. But, of course, these proofs are fabricatable because they are 'things' and so their use as evidence comes back to the factor that they are designed to supplement: faith in Gatsby's narrative. Curiously, at the end of this extract (and the end of this part of the scene in the novel), Nick Carraway does seem, at least for a moment, convinced by Gatsby's story: 'Then it was all true. I saw the skins of tigers flaming in his palace on the Grand Canal; I saw him opening a chest of rubies to ease, with their crimson lighted depths, the gnawings of his broken heart.' This seems a paradoxical recognition of truth, however, since it accepts elements of the story which are still obviously recognised as fantasy; perhaps the recognition is that for Gatsby his stories are true, or that there is a truth behind these ways of telling the story or that truth is not merely a matter of literal fact? □

▶ Discussion 2

The passage seems to be interested in exploring the ways in which identity can be a convincing whole, or can fail to give the appearance of a natural, cohesive whole. Though the easiest explanation is to see Gatsby as a liar (in fact, it is clear that he is in some details), one might also see the passage as exploring how identity is more generally composed of fragments or, anyway, separate elements combined into the appearance of a whole by acts of narrative ('if personality is an unbroken series of successful gestures', Nick observes of Gatsby, 'then there was something gorgeous about him' [p. 8]). Perhaps identity vitally depends on narrative – on an enactment of what is not obvious, the *principle of identity*, that: 'A is A, that a thing is the same as itself.' □

As with all the devices and themes of literary texts, there is doubtless enormous variation, both synchronic and historical, in how identity is treated in different texts or periods or genres. But certainly in much contemporary literature and in recent critical thinking there has been a strong tendency to see identity as far from unified. As the passage from *The Great Gatsby* might suggest, this is not simply a contemporary critical invention, but something which novels, for instance, have themselves variously explored. Some fluidity of identity is, in fact, quite traditionally seen as central to such central literary devices as narrative, plot and character. However, recent critical ideas, particularly those deriving from linguistics, have developed radical critiques of ideas of identity not only in literary texts and in the ways in which we use and read literature, but also in our social conceptions of identity and individualism. This questioning of 'identity' has also developed in other disciplines such as anthropology, sociology and psychology.

> Read the following passage from a psychology book about recent developments in approaching identity in that subject: How relevant to literary study are the concerns it summarises?

Edward E. Sampson, 'Foundations for a Textual Analysis of Selfhood'

Whatever else it may do, psychology's task is to study the individual and to develop the laws of his or her functioning.

Psychology has implicitly assumed that this object of its enquiry is a natural entity with attributes that psychology can empirically study. My aim in this chapter is the critical analysis of that very familiar and taken-for-granted object of enquiry, the individual person that is psychology's subject. In this, I am carrying forward some of my previous work (e.g. Sampson, 1977), in which I described the special quality of the American ideal... as a self-contained individualism. This refers to the firmly bounded, highly individuated conception of personhood, most aptly described by Geertz (1973, 1979) in the following passage:

> The Western conception of the person as a bounded, unique, more or less integrated motivational and cognitive universe, a dynamic center of awareness, emotion, judgement and action, organised into a distinctive whole and set contrastively against other such wholes and against a social and natural background is, however incorrigible it may seem to us, a rather peculiar idea within the context of the world's cultures. (Geertz, 1979, p. 229)

At least six discernible challenges to this commonly assumed subject of psychological inquiry have appeared. (1) Cross-cultural investigation has suggested the peculiarity of the current North American view and has uncovered several significant, less individuated, alternatives... (2) Feminist reconceptualisations of the patriarchal version of social, historical and psychological life have introduced some strikingly different views of personhood... (3) Social constructionism has amplified the earlier ideas of Mead (1934), arguing that selves, persons, psychological traits and so forth, including the very idea of individual psychological traits, are social and historical constructions, not naturally occurring objects. Constructionism casts grave doubts about the inevitability of the currently dominant Western version... (4) Systems theory has presented an epistemological position in which ontological primacy is granted to relations rather than to individual entities... (5) Critical theory, originating in the Frankfurt School tradition, has located the current North American conception in the heartland of advanced capitalist ideology. These theorists... also force us to consider the possibility that psychology's subject is a character designed primarily to serve ideological purposes... (6) Deconstructionism, a relatively recent perspective developed within post-structuralist literary criticism and linguistic analysis, has challenged all notions that involve the primacy of the subject (or author)...

The resistance of North American psychology to modify its assumptions in the light of these devastating challenges is truly amazing. ...

From *Texts of Identity*, ed. John Shotter and Kenneth J. Gergen (1989), pp. 1–3.

Discussion

The passage's concerns are very much relevant to literary study. Indeed, as it makes clear, some of the approaches to identity which are summarised have their roots in modes of thought arising from or variously associated with literary and cultural studies. Moreover, the implicit assumptions which American psychology is said to make about its central object of enquiry might also seem familiar in literary studies. As Terry Eagleton suggests in the material discussed earlier, a sense of the 'personal', the individual, may be seen as central to English. Thus the passage's critique of the notion of the 'firmly bounded, highly individuated conception of personhood' and 'the primacy of the subject (or author)' is related to a similar scepticism about personal identity found in (some) recent literary critical work.[9] ☐

We have, in fact, already met some related ideas to those referred to in this passage in two other sections: 2.2 (What is an Author?) and 4.3 (the End of History?). You may recall that Roland Barthes describes the identity, the unitary being, of the author as a tyrannical illusion, a product of language and culture, which can be overthrown in a new post-authorial age. The essay ends though with the famous statement that 'the birth of the reader must be at the cost of the death of the Author'. This appears to promise liberation from an old and oppressive identity – the Author – for a new and freer identity – the reader. It may also be that this identity promises a model for a modern and liberating conception of identity in general.

> ◆ Re-read this paragraph from 'The Death of the Author'. How is
> the contrast between the identity of the Author and the reader
> constructed? (you may find it helpful to draw up a list of qualities
> for each role).
> ◆ How convinced are you by the description of the role of the reader?

The *explanation* of a work is always sought in the man or woman who produced it, as if it were always in the end, through the more or less transparent allegory of the fiction, the voice of a single person, the *author* confiding in us.

...

Leaving aside literature itself ... linguistics has recently provided the destruction of the Author with a valuable analytical tool by showing that the whole of the enunciation is an empty process, functioning perfectly without there being any need for it to be filled with the person of the interlocutors. Linguistically, the author is never more than the instance writing, just as *I* is nothing other than the instance saying *I*: language knows a 'subject', not a 'person', and this subject, empty outside of the very enunciation which defines it, suffices to make language 'hold together' ...

The removal of the Author ... is not merely an historical fact or an act of writing; it utterly transforms the modern text (or – which is the same thing – the text is henceforth made and read in such a way that at all its levels the author is absent) ... We now know that a text is not a line of words releasing a single 'theological' meaning (the 'message of the Author-God'), but a multidimensional space in which a variety of writings, none of them original, blend and clash. The text is a tissue of quotations drawn from the innumerable centres of culture ... [The writer's] only power is to mix writings, to counter the ones with the others, in such a way as never to rest on any one of them. Did he wish to *express himself*, he ought at least to know that the inner 'thing' he thinks to 'translate' is itself only a ready-formed dictionary, its words only explainable through other words, and so on indefinitely ...

Let us come back to the Balzac sentence. No-one, no 'person' says it: its source, its voice, is not the true place of the writing, which is reading... a text is made of multiple meanings, drawn from many cultures and entering into mutual relations of dialogue, parody and contestation, but there is one place where this multiplicity is focused and that place is the reader, not, as was hitherto said, the author. The reader is the space on which all the quotations that make up a writing are inscribed without any of them being lost; a text's unity lies not in its origin but in its destination. Yet this destination cannot any longer be personal: the reader is without history, biography, psychology; he is simply that *someone* who holds together in a single field all the traces by which the written text is constituted... Classic criticism has never paid any attention to the reader; for it, the writer is the only person in literature... We know that to give writing its future, it is necessary to overthrow the myth: the birth of the reader must be at the cost of the death of the Author.

From Roland Barthes, 'The Death of the Author'.

▶ Discussion

The passage is clearly sceptical about the notion of a literary work expressing a personal voice, and therefore about the authenticity of any sense of an author who expresses him/herself. This sense of a personal voice is not only an illusion, but an assumption which confines us to obeying the 'single "theological" meaning' sent out by the Author-God (the kind of authoritative meaning which medieval writers often refer to in their ideas about 'textes' – see the discussion in section 2.1). In fact, though, Barthes argues, texts are not messages, but always remain true to their etymology: they are indeed texts, 'tissues' woven from quotations. These quotations are from 'the innumerable centres of culture' and thus have no single point of origin, no single meaning or indisputable order.

The Author attempting self-expression should know that the sense of self is an illusion anyway: 'that the inner "thing" he thinks to "translate" is itself only a ready-formed dictionary, its words only explainable through other words, and so on indefinitely'. This last statement perhaps moves its focus from the textual author (the illusory identity created in a text) to the author as person. Even if a person writes a text which they feel expresses something they wish to say, they should be aware that actually there is no unique or authentic 'inner' life. Instead there is a dictionary which gives you a set of words to quote from: the author does not create the language s/he uses; rather the language s/he quotes creates the sense of an author, the sense of an inner identity. The implication is that not only authors are created by texts, but individuals in general. *All* sense of identity – even when expressed through speech instead of writing – must in these terms be an illusion created through quotation of devices of language which do not originate from the self nor truly hold the self together. The quotations lack any identifiable focus which would make it evident that 'A is A, that a thing is the same as itself', that the author/individual has any coherence.

Against the author as a collection of fragments which looks superficially whole, Barthes places a reader whose acknowledged multiplicity makes up a genuine whole. Barthes' reader – only just coming into being after centuries of domination by the Author – is the one place where textual 'multiplicity is focused'. Thus 'a text's unity lies not in its origin but in its destination'. This seems to imply that if a text is not a message sent out as a whole, it can nonetheless be made whole upon receipt by the reader. This might seem slightly odd – if fragments are sent, then surely fragments are received?

Barthes' reader does, indeed, receive only quotations and fragments, but is described as capable of bringing into being a unity which is a free and proper unity, distinct from the illusory and tyrannical imposition of the deceased Author. This unity discards nothing, and imposes no authority: 'the reader is the space on which all the quotations that make up a writing are inscribed without any of them being lost'. All the quotations within a text are able to play freely in the reader, suggesting infinite and infinitely open possibilities for meaning. Barthes immediately, however, forestalls any suggestion that this reader has personality of the kind once ascribed to the dead Author: 'the reader is without history, biography, psychology; he is simply that *someone* who holds together in a single field all the traces by which the written text is constituted'. Thus, the reader refuses to be an Author.[10]

Barthes' portrayal of these two identities, Author and reader, requires that the two be distinct and opposed along the following lines:

Author	reader
traditional	new
God	human
tyrant	liberated subject
single meaning	multiple meanings
illusory whole	unity in multiplicity
rigid identity	'a space', 'a single field'

It is even noticeable that one identity has a capital letter, the other is always lower case – as if the Author is a myth or an abstraction or emphatically a persona, while the more humble reader is an ordinary and real human being. □

▶ Discussion 2

One might perhaps query whether the reader described is, actually, any less of an abstraction or myth than the Author. Do real readers, or anyway, does every reader, perform the role Barthes describes? Might not some readers at least, either implicitly or actively, try to make sense of texts specifically by 'losing' some 'traces' and ranking others as more important? In thus ordering and reducing a text's possible meanings, a reader could be said to be acting quite like an Author, who seems in Barthes' model to impose coherence and continuity. I am also inclined to rebel against the assertion that the reader is 'without history, biography, psychology'. These modes of explanation are, it is true, used by Authors (of both histories and fictions) and could thus be categorised as forms giving illusory coherence to identity, but even so, it seems likely that readers do make use of them, not only to explain 'books', but also to explain themselves and other people. They may be mistaken in thinking that these are good explanations for anything (though we do not have to accept that without pause), but if readers persist, it seems positively Authorial to assert that the reader is inherently a space where a search for signification is suspended. It could be argued at least that readers do, of course, bring their own histories, biographies and psychologies to their reading, as well as their conceptions of those discourses.

It may be, of course, that I am misreading what is meant by the reader, and that really Barthes' reader is more ideal than real – the reader who could attain true readership by throwing off authorial habits. But, since I suspect that, as suggested in the previous discussion, Barthes' ideas about authors are also applied to individual identity more generally, it is hard to see how any actual '*someone*' can do any more than, in their turn, 'translate' from a 'ready-formed dictionary'. Though Barthes' argument needs a reader to have a more authentic identity than an author, it is possible that the reader is inevitably caught in Barthes' own ways of resisting the self-authoring performed by individuals. Perhaps part of the problem is that Barthes' stimulating and forceful case for 'the destruction of the Author' also spills over into the destruction of individual identity more generally, so that identity itself becomes seen as inherently illusory: a trick of authorship. Indeed, the identity he constructs for the reader seems to me a 'sad non-identity',[11] a neutral space; a '*someone* who holds together in a single field all the traces by which a written text is constituted' is not, in any usual sense, an identity. That may, of course, be the point, that Western constructions of firmly bounded, highly determined individuality are dangerous fictions. Yet the passage also seems to bear some traces that its 'reader' is still given qualities derived from more conventional ideas of identity: from the idea of the oppressed human being who resists the tyrannical overlord, who expresses a more authentic human possibility and who can be liberated. □

The ideas of Hayden White about the function of narrative in historical discourse also seem to pick up related issues about the force of concepts of identity, and current incredulity (in some places) about their authenticity.

> ◆ Read the following passage: How might its doubts and ideas be linked to Barthes' ideas about identity?

Hayden White, 'The Value of Narrativity in the Representation of Reality'

(This paragraph was not included in the earlier extract; it comes near the end of the essay in a summary of the general argument and issues raised.)

What I have sought to suggest is that this value attached to narrativity in the representation of real events arises out of a desire to have real events display the coherence, integrity, fullness, and closure of an image of life that is and can only be imaginary. The notion that sequences of real events possess the formal attributes of the stories we tell about imaginary events could only have its origins in wishes, day-dreams, reveries. Does the world really present itself to perception in the form of well-made stories, with central subjects, proper beginnings, middles and ends, and a coherence that permits us to see 'the end' in every beginning? Or does it present itself more in the forms of that the annals and chronicles suggest, either as mere sequence without beginning or end or as sequences of beginnings that only terminate and never conclude? And does the world, even the social world, ever really come to us as already narrativised ...? Or is the fiction of such a world, capable of speaking itself and displaying itself as a form of story, necessary for the establishment of that moral authority without which the notion of a specifically social reality would be unthinkable?

From Hayden White, *The Content of Form* (1987).

 Discussion

A number of ideas here seem to strike familiar chords. Just as Barthes is doubtful that the coherence apparently manifested by the Author can ever be more than an illusion, so Hayden White feels that only fiction could ever display the sense of wholeness which History (and perhaps not only History?) desires. White, like Barthes, doubts the authenticity of experience which is shaped and formed into a whole. His non-narrative forms of History, like Barthes' reader, refuse to shape or interpret or close down their sense of experience. Both thinkers also respectively associate the (originally) literary ideas of narrative and the Author with social authority; White wonders if we crave narrativity because without it, we feel the grounds of all kinds of stability and authority swept away from under us; Barthes positively welcomes the dethronment of such social restriction and closure. ☐

Finally in this section, we turn back to a literary text to see how it conceives of[12] identity or identities.

> Read the following text: How does it use ideas of identity?
> How positive or negative is its conception of identity?
> To what extent does this text, at least, accept the 'firmly bounded, highly individuated conception of personhood'?[13]
> In general, do you think that literature and literary criticism do assume the wholeness described as a fundamental assumption by Clifford Geertz?[14]

Margaret Atwood, 'Happy Endings'

John and Mary meet.
What happens next?
If you want a happy ending, try A.

A. John and Mary fall in love and get married. They both have worthwhile and remunerative jobs which they find stimulating and challenging. They buy a charming house. Real estate values go up. Eventually, when they can afford live-in help, they have two children, to whom they are devoted. The children turn out well. John and Mary have a stimulating and challenging sex life and worthwhile friends. They go on fun vacations together. They retire. They both have hobbies which they find stimulating and challenging. Eventually they die. This is the end of the story.

B. Mary falls in love, with John but John doesn't fall in love with Mary. He merely uses her body for selfish pleasure and ego gratification of a tepid kind. He comes to her apartment twice a week and she cooks him dinner, you'll notice that he doesn't even consider her worth the price of a dinner out, and after he's eaten the dinner he fucks her and after that he falls asleep, while she does the dishes so he won't think she's untidy, having all those dirty dishes lying around, and puts on fresh lipstick so she'll look good when he wakes up, but when he wakes up he doesn't even notice, he puts on his socks and his shorts and his pants and his shirt and his tie and his shoes, the reverse order from the one in which he took them off. He doesn't take off Mary's clothes, she takes them off herself, she acts as if she's dying for it every time, not because she likes sex exactly, she doesn't, but she wants John to think she does because if they do it often enough surely he'll get used to her, he'll come to depend on her and they will get married, but John goes out the door with hardly so much as a goodnight and three days later he turns up at six o'clock and they do the whole thing over again.

Mary gets run down. Crying is bad for your face, everyone knows that and so does Mary but she can't stop. People at work notice. Her friends tell her John is a rat, a pig, a dog, he isn't good enough for her, but she can't believe it. Inside John, she thinks, is another John, who is much nicer. This other John will emerge like a butterfly from a cocoon, a Jack from a box, a pit from a prune, if the first John is only squeezed enough.

One evening John complains about the food. He has never complained about the food before. Mary is hurt.

Her friends tell her they've seen him in a restaurant with another woman, whose name is Madge. It's not even Madge that finally gets to Mary: it's the restaurant. John has never taken Mary to a restaurant. Mary collects all the sleeping pills and aspirins she can find, and takes them and half a bottle of sherry. You can see what kind of a woman she is by the fact that it's not even whiskey. She leaves a note for John. She hopes he'll discover her and get her to the hospital in time and repent and then they can get married, but this fails to happen and she dies.

John marries Madge and everything continues as in A.

C. John, who is an older man, falls in love with Mary, and Mary, who is only twenty-two, feels sorry for him because he's worried about his hair falling out. She sleeps with him even though she's not in love with him. She met him at work. She's in love with someone called James, who is twenty-two also and not yet ready to settle down.

John on the contrary settled down long ago: this is what is bothering him. John has a steady respectable job and is getting ahead in his field, but Mary isn't impressed by him, she's impressed by James, who has a motorcycle and a fabulous record collection. But James is often away on his motorcycle, being free. Freedom isn't the same for girls, so in the meantime Mary spends Thursday evenings with John. Thursdays are the only days John can get away.

John is married to a woman called Madge and they have two children, a charming house which they bought just before the real estate values went up, and hobbies which they find stimulating and challenging, when they have the time. John tells Mary how important she is to him, but of course he can't leave his wife because a commitment is a commitment. He goes on about this more than is necessary and Mary finds it boring, but older men can keep it up longer so on the whole she has a fairly good time.

One day James breezes in on his motorcycle with some top grade California hybrid and James and Mary get higher than you'd believe possible and they climb into bed. Everything becomes very underwater, but along comes John, who has a key to Mary's apartment. He finds them stoned and entwined. He's hardly in any position to be jealous, considering Madge, but nevertheless he's overcome with despair. Finally he's middle-aged, in two years he'll be bald as an egg and he can't stand it. He purchases a handgun, saying he needs it for target practice – this is the thin part of the plot, but it can be dealt with later – and shoots the two of them and himself.

Madge, after a suitable period of mourning, marries an understanding man called Fred and everything continues as in A, but under different names.

D. Fred and Madge have no problems. They get along exceptionally well and are good at working out any little difficulties that may arise. But their charming house is by the seashore and one day a giant tidal wave approaches. Real estate values go down. The rest of the story is about what caused the tidal wave and how they escape from it. They do, though thousands drown. Some of the story is about how the thousands drown, but Fred and Madge are virtuous and lucky. Finally on high ground they clasp each other, wet and dripping and grateful, and continue as in A.

E. Yes, but Fred has a bad heart. The rest of the story is about how kind and understanding they both are until Fred dies. Then Madge devotes herself to charity work until the end of A. If you like, it can be 'Madge', 'cancer', 'guilty and confused', and 'bird watching'.

F. If you think this is all too bourgeois, make John a revolutionary and Mary a counterespionage agent and see how far that gets you. Remember, this is Canada. You'll still end up with A, though in between you may get a lustful brawling saga of passionate involvement, a chronicle of our times, sort of.

You'll have to face it, the endings are the same however you slice it. Don't be deluded by any other endings, they're all fake, either deliberately fake, with malicious intent to deceive, or just motivated by excessive optimism if not by downright sentimentality.
The only authentic ending is the one provided here:
John and Mary die. John and Mary die. John and Mary die.

> So much for endings. Beginnings are always more fun. True connoisseurs, however, are known to favour the stretch in between, since it's the hardest to do anything with.
>
>   That's about all that can be said for plots, which anyway are just one thing after another, a what and a what and a what.
>
>   Now try How and Why.
>
> From *The Secret Self 1: Short Stories by Women*, ed. Hermione Lee (London, 1991), pp. 381–4. Story first published in 1984.

5.2   Class

As we have seen in sections 1.3 and 5.1, Terry Eagleton suggests that one of the prime tasks of 'English' in later Victorian Britain was to damp down an explicit sense of class difference and to promote social cohesiveness, by replacing the cross-class ideology of religion with a cross-class ideology of 'literature'.[15] If this is so,[16] then we might expect criticism from that period to be unlikely to bring class identities to the fore, except perhaps in order to 'resolve them in discourse', as Hayden White might put it. The next phase of Leavisite English which, on the whole, dominated British universities from the nineteen forties until the nineteen eighties, had, as Eagleton points out, a complex relationship to class identities. While the new paradigm for studying English mounted a radical challenge to the Walter Raleigh type[17] of English as an allegedly class-neutral, harmonious space, there was a reluctance to engage with politics directly, especially after the early period: 'The *Scrutiny* case was inescapably elitist: it betrayed a profound ignorance and distrust of the capacities of those not fortunate enough to have read English at Downing College [where F. R. Leavis taught].'[18] Thus here, too, class identities were not a major or explicit focus of critical enquiry. One might have expected this to change with the arrival of a more politicised and reflective approach to English through the critical theory phase of the nineteen eighties. And, certainly, as a book like Eagleton's *Literary Theory – An Introduction* (1983) might suggest, there was a development of interest in the political assumptions of English. But actually much of the energy liberated by theory went into the study of newer fields of (political) enquiry, particularly those concerned with the nature of the discipline of English itself, and those concerned with gender, sexual and racial identities. To a degree, class as a topic for study perhaps suffered from an image problem – that of being old-fashioned, though the topic had never been exactly 'fashionable' in universities, either. In fact, class identities have never been a dominant interest for mainstream university English, though there have been a number of critics, including Raymond Williams (see section 1.1), for whom class has been a major concern. At present, class is probably not a major topic for most undergraduate English courses[19] – there are almost certainly more undergraduate options focused on gender, race or sexuality than on class. At the same time, though, ideas about class still underpin many critical accounts of both individual texts and approaches to particular genres, especially the novel and its origins ('the rise of the novel'). Recent ideas about the collapse of 'master narratives' may tend to reinforce the unfashionability of 'class', which might be regarded as a somewhat generalising category, and is also liable to be seen as part of the exhausted master narratives of Marxism (and perhaps of industrial capitalism too?). Nevertheless, we should certainly pay some attention to class when discussing identities, and to those critical traditions which have pressed for the central importance of class in understanding literature, culture and social experience itself.

Class itself is a complex term, over which sociologists, historians and others have spent much effort. In general, literary critics have not spent so much effort in trying to probe or further systematise the term, but, certainly in earlier criticism, have tended to use class terminologies as ready-made labels, derived either from 'everyday' uses of class concepts, from a received historical sense of class or, more systematically, from Marxist modes of classification. While it is not surprising to find that literary writing relies on the 'everyday' language of class, it is also true that Marxist terminologies of class are not particularly alien to literary writing, because these have passed into widely used discourses of politics. We will look first at a passage from a novel to see how a particular literary text deals with class, before going on to look at some writers on class in general, and then at some groups of literary and critical texts which emphasise class relations.

> ◆ Read the following passage from an autobiographical novel.[20] How does the narrator use class to represent his identity?

Christopher Isherwood, *Lions and Shadows: An Education in the Twenties*

Also, of course, the majority of the men were secretly embarrassed at finding themselves practically naked in the presence of a lot of semi-naked and (presumably to them) attractive girls. And this subconscious embarrassment had the effect of bringing out, in each individual, some characteristic defect in carriage or stance; the scarcely visible limp became accentuated, the sloping shoulders drooped more miserably than ever, while the stiffly muscle-bound torso bulged into a ridiculous caricature of itself and its owner trotted snorting into the water like an absurd little bull. Surprisingly few of them, it seemed, could swim more than a few yards. Many a young man would strike out, with powerful faultless strokes, as if starting for France, and then, as he passed the diving-raft, turn abruptly aside and grab hold of it, gasping violently for breath.

But beneath all my note-taking, my would-be scientific detachment, my hatred, my disgust, there was the old sense of exclusion, the familiar grudging envy. For, however I might sneer, these people *were* evidently enjoying themselves in their own mysterious fashion, and why was it so mysterious to me? Weren't they of my own blood, my own caste? Why couldn't I – the would-be novelist, the professional observer – understand them? Why didn't I know – not coldly from the outside, but intuitively sympathetically, from within – what it was that made them perform their grave ritual of pleasure; putting on blazers and flannels in the morning, plus-fours or white trousers in the afternoon, dinner jackets in the evening; playing tennis, golf, bridge; dancing, without a smile, the fox-trot, the tango, the blues; smoking their pipes, reading the newspapers, organizing a sing-song, distributing prizes after a fancy-dress ball? True, I wasn't alone in my isolation. Chalmers, had he been here, would have felt just as I did. Madame Cheuret would have said: 'Not really very cosy.' Weston, despite his enthusiasm for the English, would have made these bathers the text for a grandly patronizing psycho-analytical lecture. People like my friends and myself, I thought, are to be found in little groups in all the larger towns; we form a proudly self-sufficient, consciously declassed minority. We had our jokes, we amuse each other enormously; we are glad, we say, that we are different. But are we really glad? Does anybody ever feel sincerely pleased at the prospect of remaining in permanent opposition, a social misfit, for the rest of his life? I knew, at any rate, that I myself didn't. I wanted – however much I might try to persuade myself, in moments of arrogance, to the contrary – to find some place, no matter how humble, in the scheme of society. Until I do that, I told myself, my writing will never be any good; no amount of talent or technique will redeem it: it will remain a greenhouse product; something, at best, for the connoisseur and the clique. And I envied Philip, that amazing social amphibian. He alone, of all my friends, could have met the hotel guests in their own element; could have talked their language and observed their customs: could have been accepted by them as one of themselves. It was Philip, not Weston, who truly understood 'the English'; it was Philip, not myself, whom nature had equipped to be their novelist. The most I shall ever achieve, I thought, will be to learn how to spy upon them, unnoticed. Henceforward, my problem is how to perfect a disguise.

I had a disguise, of sorts, already; but it wasn't intended for the hotel guests. Every morning, after bathing, I strolled along the shingle bank, to pay my daily visit to Bruiser and Tim, the fishermen, who looked after old Mr. Straw's boats. Bruiser was a big hearty man, tattooed all over his chest, who worked fifteen or sixteen hours a day, partly at the boats, partly in the quarry, getting up in the middle of the night to row out and attend to his lobster pots. The combined earnings of his various trades were just sufficient to keep himself, his wife and his five-year-old son alive in a tumbledown cottage, on meals of butcher's leavings, margarine and bread. Bruiser, despite his robust appearance, had something the matter with his lungs. He could neither read nor write. His sharp brown eyes twinkled with good-humoured contempt for all summer visitors, white-collar workers and for everybody who stayed in bed after six a.m. 'Good evening,' he would greet me, ironically: 'Lovely day it's been.'

'Why,' Tim would exclaim, looking up from his net-mending: 'If it isn't our Marmaduke! How fwightfully allurin'. Well, Marmaduke, and how's the trahsers?'

This was our stock joke. The truth was (it embarrasses me a little to have to admit this, even now) that, in my eagerness to make myself acceptable to Bruiser and Tim – and, no doubt, to dissociate myself from my class-mates on the bathing beach – I had half-consciously assumed a slight Cockney twang. Tim, whose vowels were from Portsmouth, had, of course, noticed it at once; indeed, he would probably have found my ordinary university accent much less remarkable and comic. But, having started, I couldn't stop; and, after a few days' practice, I found myself slipping quite naturally into my disguise-language whenever the two boatmen or any of the other villagers were present. It was all rather ridiculous, and I'm sure it didn't take in Bruiser for a moment. I never felt really at ease under his bright ironical eye. Tim was less critical. Having accepted me as a casual gossip and drinking companion, he asked no questions of any kind – not even my name.

The companionship of Tim seemed, to my violently inverted snobbery, the peak of my social ambition at the Bay; I had set myself to win it with all the wiles that the most assiduous climber could practise upon a millionaire or a duke. I was never so happy as when squatting beside him outside Mr. Straw's hut, drinking with him at the pub, or accompanying him to the dance-hall in the village. I did my best to acquire that slow insulting stare (so discomforting when directed upon oneself) with which Bruiser and Tim followed the movements of a tripper. I grinned obsequiously at Tim's favourite catch-phrases and jokes: 'How fwightfully allurin'…Many moons ago, when the world was young…The man who killed the Dead Sea whitewashing the Last Post…' The greatest mark of favour ever (apparently) bestowed upon me by Bruiser was his suggestion, one Saturday afternoon when they were short-handed, that I should row some of the hotel guests out to sea for a view of the lighthouse. There was an unpleasant swell that day, and after half an hour in the glaring sunshine without a hat I began to feel distinctly seasick; but the visitors were all excellent sailors and determined to have their money's worth. They asked questions about place names, distances and the heights of the cliffs which I couldn't correctly answer, though I did my best, obstinately maintaining my cockney twang. They disembarked at last, not a moment too soon, without tipping me. Bruiser eyed my greenish face, grinned cynically but said nothing. I had the sensation of having failed yet another test.

It was during the evenings that I finally managed to earn Tim's esteem. Tim was extremely vain of his powers as a lady-killer. 'You see, Marmaduke,' he would explain, 'I've got it.' He was seventeen years old, had a good figure and the face of an attractive monkey. His snub nose was covered with innumerable black freckles, which he was never tired of admiring in the splinter of looking-glass nailed to the wall of the hut: 'Handsome men,' he assured me, 'is slightly sunburnt.' Apparently the girls thought so too. Tim's spare time was a round of assignations – he called it 'spicket-drill.' Together, we visited the local cinema, picked up a couple of girls and cuddled them throughout the performance. I found that I was particularly good at cuddling; especially after three or four 'dog's noses' (gin and beer) at the pub. Indeed, my very inhibitions made me extremely daring – up to a point. Tim, who really meant business, was often curiously shy in the opening stages. Once or twice, having pushed things farther than I had intended, I was scared to find myself committed to a midnight walk over the downs. But, on these occasions, I always discovered an excuse for passing my girl on to Tim. Next morning, he would be grateful and suitably impressed. 'You ought to have seen our Marmaduke last night,' he would tell Bruiser. 'Honest, I was surprised…Our Marmaduke's a dark horse – ain't you Marmaduke?'

From Christopher Isherwood, *Lions and Shadows: An Education in the Twenties* (1938). Extract from Methuen edn (1982), pp. 151–4.

▶ Discussion

The narrator from the very beginning of the passage represents himself as an outsider: he is an observer, not a member of this group of young people from a particular class. It is notable, though, that while this is what he desires – it is part of his education as a writer to observe with detachment – he notes that he is anyway excluded. This exclusion is an important part of his identity, but not a source of security:

> Beneath all my note-taking, my would-be scientific detachment, my hatred, my disgust, there was the old sense of exclusion, the familiar grudging envy. For, however I might sneer, these people were enjoying themselves in their own mysterious fashion, and why was it so mysterious to me? Weren't they of my own blood, my own caste?

Clearly, the narrator is, or should be, a member of this class. Interestingly, the word class itself is not used here,[21] but instead there are terms implying an even more inescapable membership: that of heredity (or race?) and 'caste' membership. However, the fact that he is a member by most 'external' measures (presumably including the kind of education he has received, the kind of English he speaks, the occupations of his parents and so on), does not seem automatically to give him any full sense of belonging: 'Why didn't I know – not coldly from the outside, but intuitively sympathetically from within – what it was that made them perform their grave ritual of pleasure?'

From the narrator's point of view, full membership of a class seems to account thoroughly for all aspects of behaviour. If he felt wholly inside his class, he would act and therefore be as all these anonymous young men he describes. Class confers a mass and indivisible identity – at least for those on the outside. He sees his identity as a would-be writer as originating from this exclusion, since he needs to pursue something which is different from the rituals of his peers, and writing provides space outside social norms. Writers, in his mind, seem to necessarily be outside the received class ethos – and so perhaps do other kinds of intellectuals and 'misfits':

> People like my friends and myself, I thought, are to be found in little groups in all the larger towns; we form a proudly self-sufficient, consciously declassed minority.

This makes 'people like him' sound a little like revolutionary cells (a resonance which seems likely in writing from this period) and asserts the value of their declassed position. However, the following sentences express doubts about this state of 'permanent opposition'. He wishes that he could at least *appear* to be like these people who fit into their own class; as it is, he feels that his exclusion from his class is also an exclusion from the nation: only his friend Philip, 'the social amphibian', understands 'The English'.

Perhaps the problem is that he feels his identity is constructed mainly from exclusion (though he does see himself as a member of an excluded group). In the next part of the passage, he tries to achieve a more positive membership of a social group, though he knows from the outset that this is a 'disguise', a pretence, rather than an actuality: 'in my eagerness to make myself acceptable to Bruiser and Tim – and, no doubt, to disassociate myself from my class-mates[22] ... I had half-unconsciously assumed a slight Cockney twang'. Clearly, he wishes to assume the identity of another class – presumably the working class. This is particularly associated with escaping Bruiser's automatic contempt for outsiders, 'visitors'. The narrator's urge to belong, or his urge not to be excluded, is powerful. At least he is able to attempt belonging with Bruiser and Tim, whereas the rituals of his 'own caste' were beyond performance of any kind.

The overall answer to the question, then, seems to be that the narrator uses a strong sense of exclusion to define himself against class definition (class is something other people inhabit), while also representing the attractions of what he portrays as instinctive, unthinking class membership. He, the troubled, insecure, individual, opposes himself to the group of his peers which is indivisible. Interestingly, though, the class he tries to (pretend to) join is represented not as a group, but as two individuals with differing attitudes. Bruiser and Tim, while clearly 'working class', are seen as less group-oriented and more tolerant of eccentricity than his 'class-mates'.

In this particular case – though perhaps this only enters the interpretation if one knows something of the biography of the author – it may well be that this crisis of class identity is also linked to a particular sexual identity. Isherwood was a gay writer, who was able to be much more outspoken in print in later years than he was during the thirties. Nevertheless, for those who wished to find it his thirties novels had fairly evident – indeed, often central – concerns with sexual identity. The phrase 'people like my friends and myself' (like the title of his later autobiographical book *Christopher and his Kind*) might suggest a group who are excluded by sexuality as well as for other reasons. Indeed, the rituals of his peers for which the narrator feels such distaste and incomprehension are quite specifically acceptable upper-middle-class heterosexual courtship rituals (all that tennis, bridge, dancing ...).

Perhaps, as Derrida argues about genre, one of the problems of class is that there is no such thing as full membership, only a participation which is always partial? Or perhaps ideas of class membership are often opposed and undermined by ideas or ideologies of individuality and personal uniqueness? Perhaps, class is often a way of describing other people, or other social groups, but that never fits 'people like my friends and myself'? As we shall see in passages later in this section, questions of definition, system and description, and questions about how general systems relate to specific instances, frequently arise when discussing ideas of class. The capacity of discourses of class to explain identities and social existence is therefore a key issue, and one which may well raise questions of a kind related to that other classificatory system of genres which you worked on in chapter 3. □

> Read the following three passages taken from discussions of class in general (rather than in specific application to literature). To what extent does each passage think that ideas and terminologies of class explain anything?
>
> Which, if any, of the passages do you find most convincing?

Friedrich Engels and Karl Marx, *The Communist Manifesto*

I   BOURGEOIS AND PROLETARIANS[1]

The history of all hitherto existing society[2] is the history of class struggles.

Freeman and slave, patrician and plebeian, lord and serf, guild master[3] and journeyman, in a word, oppressor and oppressed, stood in constant opposition to one another, carried on an uninterrupted, now hidden, now open fight, a fight that each time ended either in a revolutionary reconstitution of society at large or in the common ruin of the contending classes.

In the earlier epochs of history we find almost everywhere a complicated arrangement of society into various orders, a manifold gradation of social rank. In ancient Rome we have patricians, knights, plebeians, slaves; in the Middle Ages, feudal lords, vassals, guild masters, journeymen, apprentices, serfs; in almost all of these classes, again, subordinate gradations.

The modern bourgeois society that has sprouted from the ruins of feudal society has not done away with class antagonisms. It has but established new classes, new conditions of oppression, new forms of struggle in place of the old ones.

Our epoch, the epoch of the bourgeoisie, possesses, however, this distinctive feature: it has simplified the class antagonisms. Society as a whole is more and more splitting up into two great hostile camps, into two great classes directly facing each other: bourgeoisie and proletariat.

---

[1] By 'bourgeoisie' is meant the class of modern capitalists, owners of the means of social production and employers of wage labour. By proletariat, the class of modern wage labourers who, having no means of production of their own, are reduced to selling their labour power in order to live. [Note by Engels to the English edition of 1888.]

[2] That is, all *written* history. In 1847 the pre-history of society, the social organisation existing previous to recorded history, was all but unknown. Since then Haxthausen discovered common ownership of land in Russia, Maurer proved it to be the social foundation from which all Teutonic races started in history, and by and by village communities were found to be, or to have been, the primitive form of society everywhere from India to Ireland. The inner organisation of this primitive communistic society was laid bare, in its typical form, by Morgan's crowning discovery of the true nature of the *gens* and its relation to the *tribe*. With the dissolution of these primeval communities society begins to be differentiated into separate and finally antagonistic classes. I have attempted to retrace this process of dissolution in *Der Ursprung der Familie, des Privateigenthums und des Staats [The Origin of the Family Private Property and the State*], second edition, Stuttgart, 1886 [Note by Engels to the English edition of 1888.]

[3] Guild master, that is, a full member of a guild, a master within, not a head of a guild. [Note by Engels to the English edition of 1888.]

From the serfs of the Middle Ages sprang the chartered burghers of the earliest towns. From these burgesses the first elements of the bourgeoisie were developed.

The discovery of America, the rounding of the Cape opened up fresh ground for the rising bourgeoisie. The East Indian and Chinese markets, the colonisation of America, trade with the colonies, the increase in the means of exchange and in commodities generally, gave to commerce, to navigation, to industry an impulse never before known, and thereby, to the revolutionary element in the tottering feudal society, a rapid development.

The feudal system of industry, under which industrial production was monopolised by closed guilds, now no longer sufficed for the growing wants of the new markets. The manufacturing system took its place. The guild masters were pushed on one side by the manufacturing middle class; division of labour between the different corporate guilds vanished in the face of division of labour in each single workshop.

Meantime the markets kept ever growing, the demand ever rising. Even manufacture no longer sufficed. Thereupon steam and machinery revolutionised industrial production. The place of manufacture was taken by the giant, modern industry, the place of the industrial middle class by industrial millionaires, the leaders of whole industrial armies, the modern bourgeois.

Modern industry has established the world market, for which the discovery of America paved the way. This market has given an immense development to commerce, to navigation, to communication by land. This development has, in its turn, reacted on the extension of industry; and in proportion as industry, commerce, navigation, railways extended, in the same proportion the bourgeoisie developed, increased its capital, and pushed into the background every class handed down from the Middle Ages.

We see, therefore, how the modern bourgeoisie is itself the product of a long course of development, of a series of revolutions in the modes of production and of exchange.

Each step in the development of the bourgeoisie was accompanied by a corresponding political advance of that class. An oppressed class under the sway of the feudal nobility, an armed and self-governing association in the medieval commune;[4] here independent urban republic (as in Italy and Germany), there taxable 'third estate' of the monarchy (as in France), afterwards, in the period of manufacture proper, serving either the semi-feudal or the absolute monarchy as a counterpoise against the nobility, and, in fact, cornerstone of the great monarchies in general, the bourgeoisie has at last, since the establishment of modern industry and of the world market, conquered for itself, in the modern representative state, exclusive political sway. The executive of the modern state is but a committee for managing the common affairs of the whole bourgeoisie.

The bourgeoisie, historically, has played a most revolutionary part.

The bourgeoisie, wherever it has got the upper hand, has put an end to all feudal, patriarchal, idyllic relations. It has pitilessly torn asunder the motley

---

[4] 'Commune' was the name taken, in France, by the nascent towns even before they had conquered from their feudal lords and masters local self-government and political rights as the "third estate." Generally speaking, for the economic development of the bourgeoisie, England is here taken as the typical country; for its political development, France. [Note by Engels to the English edition of 1888.]

feudal ties that bound man to his 'natural superiors,' and has left remaining no other nexus between man and man than naked self-interest, than callous 'cash payment.' It has drowned the most heavenly ecstasies of religious fervour, of chivalrous enthusiasm, of Philistine sentimentalism in the icy water of egotistical calculation. It has resolved personal worth into exchange value and, in place of the numberless indefeasible chartered freedoms, has set up that single, unconscionable freedom – freetrade. In one word, for exploitation, veiled by religious and political illusions, it has substituted naked, shameless, direct, brutal exploitation.

The bourgeoisie has stripped of its halo every occupation hitherto honoured and looked up to with reverent awe. It has converted the physician, the lawyer, the priest, the poet, the man of science into its paid wage labourers.

The bourgeoisie has torn away from the family its sentimental veil, and has reduced the family relation to a mere money relation.

From *The Manifesto of the Communist Party* (1848). From *Basic Writings on Politics and Philosophy by Karl Marx and Friedrich Engels*, ed. Lewis S. Fuer (London, 1969), pp. 48–51.

Arthur Marwick, *Class: Image and Reality in Britain, France and the USA since 1930*

The problem can be put in a number of ways. We can show that, subjectively, classes exist, and we can prove, objectively, that inequalities exist; but it is not so easy to tie the two together. We can recognize that people do perceive the existence of something they call class, but we cannot be sure that this class has an objective existence; we can perceive that inequality exists, but we cannot be sure that this inequality is due to class. We cannot be sure, that is, unless we equate class with occupation, or unless we have some theory which, we believe, enables us, of itself, to allocate a person or group to a particular class. For example, Marxist sociology declares that a person's social class is determined by his relationship to the mode of production. It is not here contended that Marxist sociology or, indeed, any other theoretical approach to class, is necessarily wrong; simply that, in complex modern societies, determining someone's relationship to the mode of production is not an easy task, and that any such definition of class does not, at first sight, coincide with what I am calling the *colloquial* and *historical* interpretation of class.

This book seeks to explore the subjective aspects of class, to clarify the images of class held by different groups in the different societies, and then to integrate these images with the realities of social inequality. What people write, say and think about class provides the broad categories – 'upper class', 'working class' and so on; once one has broad categories which actually seem to meet the circumstances of a particular society at a particular point in time, one can then organize the detailed quantitative evidence regarding social inequality. It may be that some of the *a priori* theories about the nature of class turn out to be supported by this line of inquiry; but it very firmly starts from the evidence rather than from the theory.

First, however, I should say something about the other approaches which have, very properly, held the field for so long. To many sociologists, 'class' is an abstract concept, vital for the precise analysis of contemporary society but not corresponding directly with any exact social or historical reality. Over and over again, sociologists writing about class, with all the laboured nullity of the reaction shots in an American television soap opera, warn us against the dangers of 'reification', that is, of taking for real something that is only a theoretical construct. I take an exactly opposite view: I believe that class is real – though, of course, I have yet to demonstrate this – but also believe that, in keeping with historical reality, it is messy and not amenable to the sort of precision to which so many social scientists aspire. Disciples of the German sociologist Max Weber insist that one should not confuse a person's class (relating only to his economic position in society), his status (or social prestige) and his 'party' (or position in regard to political power). W. G. Runciman tells us that:

> Much of the trouble is caused by the use of the term 'class' in ordinary language. 'Class' is apt to be used not only as a general term for social stratification but also in a context where it is in fact status which is meant. ...

I prefer the 'ordinary language'. I prefer 'class' to mean what people in everyday life mean by it, rather than what Runciman or Weber tell me I should mean by it. I have never yet heard anyone speak of 'working-status' homes, nor of 'middle-status' education. Sociologists, I fear, often preach in preference to practising. John Raynor, in his excellent book on *The Middle Class*, tells us that really he would prefer to speak of the 'middle stratum' but then proceeds cheerfully to go on talking about the middle class throughout the rest of the book, apart altogether from the fact that he is no more prepared to call his book *The Middle Stratum*, than I am to call my book *Status: Image and Reality*, or *Strata: Image and Reality*. If the Weberians wish to put a very limited meaning on the term class, that, of course, is their business, and good luck to them. But for historians attempting to make a comparative study of different societies and their evolution through a period of time, it does not seem to make a great deal of sense to place the same person in one particular class for one purpose, a different status group for another purpose, and yet a different 'party' for still another purpose. Class, perhaps, is too serious a subject to leave to the social scientists. ...

From Arthur Marwick, *Class: Image and Reality in Britain, France and the USA since 1930* (London, 1980), pp. 13–15.

P. N. Furbank, *Unholy Pleasure: The Idea of Social Class*

Among the most helpful things written on 'class' and 'class'-language are Raymond Williams's articles on 'Class', 'Bourgeois' etc. in his *Keywords* (1976). Williams is strong on the structure of class ideas. However, running through these articles, there is a note almost of lament at the ambiguity, the 'difficulty' and the 'confusion' attending the use of these words. What this shows, I would want to suggest, is that he is looking for the wrong thing. He points out that English 'class'-language exhibits relics of two conflicting conceptions or models. There was the Upper/Middle/Lower model; and on the other hand the Saint-Simonian model, according to which 'both the self-conscious *middle classes* and the quite different people who by the end of the period would describe themselves as the *working classes* adopted the descriptions *useful* or *productive classes*, in distinction from and in opposition to the *privileged* or the *idle*'. And this use as he says, 'sorts oddly with the other model of *lower, middle* and *higher*' and has 'remained both important and confusing'. There were by now two common terms, increasingly used for comparison, distinction or contrast, which had been formed within quite different models:

> On the one hand *middle* implied hierarchy and therefore implied 'lower class': not only theoretically but in repeated practice. On the other hand *working* implied productive or useful activity, which would leave all who were not 'working class' unproductive and useless (easy enough for an aristocracy, but hardly accepted by a productive 'middle class'). To this day this confusion reverberates.

Well, we can admit the *complication* all right. But what one wants to say, somehow, is: if a 'confusion' is purposeful or convenient, can it be properly called a confusion? I will come to my most general and crude point at once. Such terms, and the way they are used, are – as I have said – rhetorical. That is to say, their *raison d'être* is, under a disguise, to further certain purposes or desires. We have to forget any idea that 'classes' 'really' exist. They are not that sort of thing, but rather fictions or imaginary frames that people project upon others, and these will differ of necessity according to who is doing the projecting and why; moreover the same people will construct these frames differently in different contexts and under the pressure of different circumstances.

It follows that the idea that 'classes' can be defined by economic or material *criteria*, or indeed *defined* by criteria at all, is a mistake. Fairly plainly – though there are those, even rather absurdly some sociologists, who seem to assume otherwise – describing people as 'middle class' or 'working class' or 'upper class' is not just a matter of definition. Those who use these phrases do not merely mean that certain people, by fulfilling certain conditions (of form of employment, income, birth, choice of marriage-partners, education, accent, etc.) are *by definition* 'middle class' or 'working class' or 'upper class' (as you might say that somebody who is wholly the property of another is by definition a slave, or somebody who disbelieves in the divinity of Christ is by definition a Socinian). If there were no more to it than that, no one would ever get heated on the subject, or even be much interested by it. What is being asserted by these phrases, rather, is the existence of a group of people possessing something deeply in common – of which similarity of form of employment, or income, or birth, choice of marriage-partners, education, accent, etc. is merely a *sign*. (What kind of thing they are supposed to have in common will of course differ very widely according to the speaker: for a Marxist it is a destiny, for others it is a culture.)

Thus the point is, to assign people to the 'middle class', or the 'working class' or the 'upper class' is a judgement and a speculation, and these will inevitably be coloured by who is doing the judging and the speculating and with what motive. The truth is, users of these terms demand a vast, and quite 'unscientific', freedom of manoeuvre. It may be a very strong card to play, politically speaking, to include, or *not* to include, such-and-such people within a certain 'class' (the class you claim to belong to, or the class whose interests you claim to be defending, or the class you are attacking), and you will not lightly give up the right to be inconsistent on the matter and to delimit the classes differently in different circumstances.

From P. N. Furbank, *Unholy Pleasure: The Idea of Social Class* (1985), pp. 12–13.

Discussion

1. MARX AND ENGELS

Clearly, the idea of class is seen here as having enormous and far-reaching explanatory power: struggle between different classes is the key idea for understanding the whole span of human history throughout the world.[23] Once differentiation of class begins to occur in primitive communist societies, class antagonism becomes the force behind all changes in human social organisation and hence behind all change and development in human history. This competition was made inevitable by differential access to 'the means of social production' (i.e. the means to produce everything needed for survival and other social benefits).

Class antagonism takes on particular forms in different periods of history, not merely randomly, but in ways determined by previous class struggles and by ongoing class antagonisms. While as a general idea Marx and Engels see class as existing from pre-history onwards, they also distinguish in their use of terminology between the modern form of class and the ancient and medieval forms of class distinction. Thus when they refer to the classical and feudal periods they note that 'in the earlier epochs of history we find almost everywhere a complicated arrangement of society into various orders, a manifold gradation of social rank'. This is an important distinction for them, because it enables their argument that the present modern age does represent a new development, a climactic point, in the history of class and therefore of humanity. Thus there was in the ancient and medieval worlds a complex gradation of social order, producing societies based on rank, a class membership usually acquired through being born into it. In the modern nineteenth-century industrial world these gradations have been replaced by only two classes: the bourgeoisie and the proletariat, based (allegedly) on economic status alone.

These two classic Marxist terms are defined here in Engels' footnote of 1888:

the bourgeoisie = 'the class of modern capitalists, owners of the means of social production and employers of wage labour';

the proletariat = 'the class of modern wage labourers who, having no means of production of their own, are reduced to selling their labour power in order to live'.

The distinction between the multiple terminologies of the societies based on rank and the two-term classification of modern society is not merely incidental, but is part of how Marx and Engels see the shape or narrative of history.[24] Human society diversifies from a state of simplicity into complexity and, then, as a result of the forces within this system and represented by the class terminologies, returns towards a new state of simplicity:

primitive communism $\rightarrow\rightarrow$ complex rank gradation $\rightarrow\rightarrow$ two-classes $\rightarrow\rightarrow$ communism

The simplification brings modern society openly back to the central fact of social organisation: class antagonism, expressed in modern capitalism (hence the bourgeoisie 'has left remaining no other nexus between man and man than naked self-interest, than callous "cash payment"').

This modern condition not only explains the shape of history, but implicitly for Marx and Engels has the power to analyse all aspects of past and current social conditions. Thus developments in social and economic organisation led to the conditions for technological change, and these changes in turn result in the conditions for other kinds of cultural change. As well as explaining economic and political changes, class can explain all other social relations, including the familial and interpersonal, and the nature of religious or philosophical belief. In short, class is the key to all social existence and the ultimate analytic category underlying all sociological explanation. Indeed, for Marx and Engels, the power of these kinds of idea was equivalent to the explanatory power of science for the natural world: marxist analysis could not only understand the past and present, but also predict the future.[25]

2. MARWICK

For Marwick, part of the problem is that abstract, large-scale ideas about class do not convincingly coincide with the detail of the evidence. He is clear that social inequality is a fact, but not that class always best describes or explains that inequality. He is clear that sociologists' attempts to refine class terminologies (in some cases, separating out different aspects such as status, economic position and political position) seem to him to construct a different and more abstract terminology than that actually used by real people. However, he does not dispute the explanatory power of ideas of class. Indeed, he is also clear that ideas of class are omnipresent in the period and region he is studying, and that they must be taken into account, even if image outweighs reality (though presumably, the image is part of reality, if not quite the same as 'reality'). At the very least, 'people *believe* that classes exist, and are influenced in their behaviour by that belief'. Where Marx and Engels are certain of the central importance of class to society and history, Marwick can ask the questions: 'How true? How significant?', 'in relation to all the other social phenomena in which people believe or by which they are affected'.

While unhappy with the abstract fragmentation of class terminology and explanation adopted by some sociologists, it is noticeable that Marwick's project does itself break up class into different spheres: 'academic images', official images', 'unofficial and private images' and 'media images'. But the point of this approach is probably precisely the opposite to that of the Weberian sociologists: where they wish to multiply the analytic categories in order to produce a more complete and precise explanation, Marwick accepts that his history of class will always remain partial, an incomplete jigsaw.

In sum, Marwick does have considerable faith that class has explanatory power, and that class terminology is significant, but *not* in any simple sense objective. Where Marx and Engels (in this text at least) give the impression that the terms 'bourgeoisie' and 'proletariat' map a historical reality, Marwick gives a sense of class as partly based in fact, but largely based in 'subjective imagery', which bears on reality rather than describing it directly.

3. P. N. FURBANK

Furbank argues that there is actually a fatal impressionism about all class terms, and that, in fact, we are very often perfectly aware of an act of dishonesty even as we use the words. While the labels seem to point clearly at a kind or group of people and their behaviours, it is actually very unclear what they refer to. Class terms only continue to be used because we do not wish to probe them too closely: 'these are the words that people use ... so it must be proper to use them'. This objection is here applied to 'everyday' uses of class language, but Furbank feels a related objection to more technical uses too: the labels assign people to groups without any real evidence that these groups actually exist or mean anything. When Furbank says class terminology is 'rhetorical' he presumably means that it has substance *only* in language, and never in reality.

Indeed, he is sure that class terminology is deployed not to tell you anything about the people thus described, but to project onto them a meaning which the describer has a need or desire to enact:

> We have to forget any idea that 'classes' 'really' exist. They are not that sort of thing, but rather fictions or imaginary frames that people project on others, and these will differ of necessity according to who is doing the projecting and why; moreover the same people will construct these frames differently in different contexts and under the pressure of different circumstances.

Thus for Furbank, ideas of class account for nothing: they are false and falsifying explanations, signifying a lazy preparedness to accept dubious generalisations as if they indicated something true. □

▶ Discussion 2

I find things to admire in all three passages, but I feel least convinced overall by the Furbank passage, though I note the force of its arguments. I am more convinced by the first two passages, each in their own way. I have two main problems with Furbank's attitude to class. The first is that for all his interesting arguments about why class is merely a set of vague generalisations without basis, I cannot help thinking that such generalisations, however unsatisfactory, do, in fact, at least gesture towards something which is real and which does affect us all. While the definite article in '*the* working class' does seem unwarrantable (something quite commonly recognised perhaps in the variation 'the working classes' and the less definite sounding adjectival form in 'working-class culture'), I am unwilling to believe that terms like 'working class' and 'middle class' do not make some useful distinctions between the social experiences of groups of people. My second doubt arises from a related issue: Furbank's attitude to language. He argues that class terminology is unsatisfactory, because it is never ultimately capable of precision: it remains for ever in the realm of generalisation. But then so do many kinds of language use: is a term necesarily a false friend because an ultimate and indisputable example or instance cannot be cited? Many terms are generalisations – we have already met classificatory terms which are difficult to pin down precisely, for example: literature, the novel, pastoral and so on. But the vagueness of the boundaries of these terms does not mean that there is no such thing as a novel. Indeed, it could be said that such ungroundedness is the normal condition of language – but we still have to proceed in forming ideas of the world through language, there being no alternative it seems (this is true even for thinkers who argue that language lacks any ground other than itself – they must still use language to communicate).

Having said this, it is probably no surprise that I do feel fairly convinced by Marwick's pragmatic approach, his critical construction of a general view from particular instances: the very fact that people do act as if class matters, must mean that it does matter. Of course, this has its weakness; one might suspect that the way in which Marwick uses the words 'image' and 'reality' does not always precisely account for the relationship between how people talk about class and how it actually acts. Perhaps he would say that this, indeed, cannot be precisely mapped. I also worry about whether this way of understanding class does, because of its very flexibility, seem slightly too loose – as if class had no real underlying structure.

The certainty of Marx and Engels about the shape of human history gives me pause for thought – especially since things have not obviously yet worked out as they predicted. I wonder if their two-class model does – or even did – really describe something which actually exists/existed (it could, of course, be argued that even if people talked in terms of a three-term class structure, the reality which they could not readily perceive due to the blinkers of ideology was nevertheless the naked antagonism of proletariat and bourgeoisie). On the other hand, the explanatory potential of their ideas about how historical change happens and about the relationship between economic and social organisation and all aspects of culture still seems to me to be immense.

As usual, these are only my workings through of some of my responses – you may have different views and arguments based on your ways of looking within or without or at language. □

Having looked at some general issues and problems in thinking about class, we can now return to questions of literary study. The following passages are made up of grouped sets of extracts from literary texts and from critical writings about class. They are intended to focus discussion of how general ideas of class can explain particular examples, and to investigate how much consistency and clarity there is in the use of conceptions of class in literary writing.

> ◆ Read the following two groups of passages (one for the nineteenth and one for the twentieth century): How does each passage use ideas about class?
> ◆ How much variety or consistency is there in how critical and literary passages see class within each century – group?

(I will leave you to discuss these passages yourselves.)

NINETEENTH CENTURY

Karl Marx, Speech on the Fourth Anniversary of *The People's Paper*

The so-called revolutions of 1848 were but poor incidents – small fractures and fissures in the dry crust of European society. However, they denounced the abyss. Beneath the apparently solid surface they betrayed oceans of liquid matter, only needing expansion to rend into fragments continents of hard rock. Noisily and confusedly they proclaimed the emancipation of the proletarian, i.e. the secret of the nineteenth century, and of the revolution of that century. That social revolution, it is true, was no novelty invented in 1848. Steam, electricity, and the self-acting mule were revolutionists of a rather more dangerous character than even citizens Barbès, Raspail and Blanqui. But, although the atmosphere in which we live weighs upon every one with a 20,000 lb. force, do you feel it? No more than European society before 1848 felt the revolutionary atmosphere enveloping and pressing it from all sides. There is one great fact, characteristic of this our nineteenth century, a fact which no party dares deny. On the one hand, there have started into life industrial and scientific forces which no epoch of former human history had ever suspected. On the other hand, there exist symptoms of decay, far surpassing the horrors recorded of the latter times of the Roman empire. In our days everything seems pregnant with its contrary. Machinery, gifted with the wonderful power of shortening and fructifying human labour, we behold starving and overworking it. The new-fangled sources of wealth, by some strange weird spell, are turned into sources of want. The victories of art seem bought by the loss of character. At the same pace that mankind masters nature, man seems to become enslaved to other men or to his own infamy. Even the pure light of science seems unable to shine but on the dark background of ignorance. All our invention and progress seem to result in endowing material forces with intellectual life, and in stultifying human life into a material force. This antagonism between modern industry and science on the one hand, modern misery and dissolution on the other hand; this antagonism between the productive powers and the social relations of our epoch is a fact, palpable, overwhelming, and not to be controverted. Some parties may wail over it; others may wish to get rid of modern arts, in order to get rid of modern conflicts. Or they may imagine that so signal a progress in industry wants to be completed by as signal a regress in politics. On our part, we do not mistake the shape of the shrewd spirit that continues to mark all these contradictions. We know that to work well the new-fangled forces of society, they only want to be mastered by new-fangled men – and such are the working men. They are as much the invention of modern time as machinery itself. In the signs that bewilder the middle class, the aristocracy and the poor prophets of regression, we do recognize our brave friend, Robin Goodfellow, the old mole that can work in the earth so fast, that worthy pioneer – the Revolution. The English working men are the first-born sons of modern industry. They will then, certainly, not be the last in aiding the social revolution produced by that industry, a revolution which means the emancipation of their own class all over the world, which is as universal as capital-rule and wages-slavery. I know the heroic struggles the English working class have gone through since the middle of the last century – struggles [no] less glorious because they are shrouded in obscurity, and burked by the middle-class historian. To revenge the misdeeds of the ruling class, there existed in the Middle Ages, in Germany, a secret tribunal called the 'Vehmgericht'. If a red cross was seen marked on a house, people knew that its owner was doomed by the 'Vehm'. All the houses of Europe are now marked with the mysterious red cross. History is the judge – its executioner, the proletarian.

From *Surveys from Exile*, ed. D. Fernbach (1973) vol. 2, pp. 299–300. Speech made in London on 14 April 1856.

Charles Dickens, *Hard Times*

CHAPTER 5

The Key-note

Coketown, to which Messrs Bounderby and Gradgrind now walked, was a triumph of fact; it had no greater taint of fancy in it than Mrs Gradgrind herself. Let us strike the key-note, Coketown, before pursuing our tune.

It was a town of red brick, or of brick that would have been red if the smoke and ashes had allowed it; but, as matters stood it was a town of unnatural red and black like the painted face of a savage. It was a town of machinery and tall chimneys, out of which interminable serpents of smoke trailed themselves for ever and ever, and never got uncoiled. It had a black canal in it, and a river that ran purple with ill-smelling dye, and vast piles of building full of windows where there was a rattling and a trembling all day long, and where the piston of the steam-engine worked monotonously up and down, like the head of an elephant in a state of melancholy madness. It contained several large streets all very like one another, and many small streets still more like one another, inhabited by people equally like one another, who all went in and out at the same hours, with the same sound upon the same pavements, to do the same work, and to whom every day was the same as yesterday and tomorrow, and every year the counterpart of the last and the next.

These attributes of Coketown were in the main inseparable from the work by which it was sustained; against them were to be set off, comforts of life which found their way all over the world, and elegancies of life which made, we will not ask how much of the fine lady, who could scarcely bear to hear the place mentioned. The rest of its features were voluntary, and they were these.

You saw nothing in Coketown but what was severely workful. If the members of a religious persuasion built a chapel there – as the members of eighteen religious persuasions had done – they made it a pious warehouse of red brick, with sometimes (but this only in highly ornamented examples) a bell in a bird-cage on the top of it. The solitary exception was the New Church; a stuccoed edifice with a square steeple over the door, terminating in four short pinnacles like florid wooden legs. All the public inscriptions in the town were painted alike, in severe characters of black and white. The jail might have been the infirmary, the infirmary might have been the jail, the town-hall might have been either, or both, or anything else, for anything that appeared to the contrary in the graces of their construction. Fact, fact, fact, everywhere in the material aspect of the town; fact, fact, fact, everywhere in the immaterial. The M'Choakumchild school was all fact, and the school of design was all fact, and the relations between master and man were all fact, and everything was fact between the lying-in hospital and the cemetery, and what you couldn't state in figures, or show to be purchaseable in the cheapest market and saleable in the dearest, was not, and never should be, world without end, Amen.

A town so sacred to fact, and so triumphant in its assertion, of course got on well? Why no, not quite well. No? Dear me!

No. Coketown did not come out of its own furnaces, in all respects like gold that had stood the fire. First, the perplexing mystery of the place was, Who belonged to the eighteen denominations? Because, whoever did, the labouring people did not. It was very strange to walk through the streets on a Sunday morning, and note how few of *them* the barbarous jangling of bells that was driving the sick and nervous mad, called away from their own quarter, from their own close rooms, from the corners of their own streets, where they lounged listlessly, gazing at all the church and chapel going, as at a thing with which they had no manner of concern. Nor was it merely the stranger who noticed this, because there was a native organization in Coketown Itself, whose members were to be heard of in the House of Commons every session, indignantly petitioning for acts of parliament that should make these people religious by main force. Then, came the Teetotal Society, who complained that these same people *would* get drunk, and showed in tabular statements that they did get drunk, and proved at tea parties that no inducement, human or Divine (except a medal), would induce them to forego their custom of getting drunk. Then, came the chemist and druggist, with other tabular statements, showing that when they didn't get drunk, they took opium. Then, came the experienced chaplain of the jail, with more tabular statements, outdoing all the previous tabular statements, and showing that the same people *would* resort to low haunts, hidden from the public eye, where they heard low singing and saw low dancing, and mayhap joined in it; and where A. B., aged twenty-four next birthday, and committed for eighteen months' solitary, had himself said (not that he had ever shown himself particularly worthy of belief) his ruin began, as he was perfectly sure and confident that otherwise he would have been a tip-top moral specimen. Then, came Mr Gradgrind and Mr Bounderby, the two gentlemen at this present moment walking through Coketown, and both eminently practical, who could, on occasion, furnish more tabular statements derived from their own personal experience, and illustrated by cases they had known and seen, from which it clearly appeared – in short it was the only clear thing in the case – that these same people were a bad lot altogether, gentlemen; that do what you would for them they were never thankful for it, gentlemen; that they were restless, gentlemen; that they never knew what they wanted; that they lived upon the best, and bought fresh butter, and insisted on Mocha coffee, and rejected all but prime parts of meat, and yet were eternally dissatisfied and unmanageable. In short it was the moral of the old nursery fable:

> There was an old woman, and what do you think?
> She lived upon nothing but victuals and drink;
> Victuals and drink were the whole of her diet,
> And yet this old woman would NEVER be quiet.

From *Hard Times* (1854), ch. 5, 'The Key-Note'. Extract from Penguin edn (1985), pp. 65–7.

Elizabeth Gaskell, *North and South*

CHAPTER 17

What Is a Strike?

> 'There are briars besetting every path,
>   Which call for patient care;
> There is a cross in every lot,
>   And an earnest need for prayer.'
>   ANON

Margaret went out heavily and unwillingly enough. But the length of a street – yes, the air of a Milton street – cheered her young blood before she reached her first turning. Her step grew lighter, her lip redder. She began to take notice, instead of having her thoughts turned so exclusively inward. She saw unusual loiterers in the streets: men with their hands in their pockets sauntering along; loud-laughing and loud-spoken girls clustered together, apparently excited to high spirits, and a boisterous independence of temper and behaviour. The more ill-looking of the men – the discreditable minority – hung about on the steps of the beer-houses and gin-shops, smoking, and commenting pretty freely on every passer-by. Margaret disliked the prospect of the long walk through these streets, before she came to the fields which she had planned to reach. Instead, she would go and see Bessy Higgins. It would not be so refreshing as a quiet country walk, but still it would perhaps be doing the kinder thing.

Nicholas Higgins was sitting by the fire smoking, as she went in. Bessy was rocking herself on the other side.

Nicholas took the pipe out of his mouth, and standing up, pushed his chair towards Margaret; he leant against the chimney-piece in a lounging attitude, while she asked Bessy how she was.

'Hoo's rather down i' th' mouth in regard to spirits, but hoo's better in health. Hoo doesn't like this strike. Hoo's a deal too much set on peace and quietness at any price.'

'This is th' third strike I've seen,' said she, sighing, as if that was answer and explanation enough.

'Well, third time pays for all. See if we don't dang th' masters this time. See if they don't come, and beg us to come back at our own price. That's all. We've missed it afore time, I grant yo'; but this time we'n laid our plans desperate deep.'

'Why do you strike?' asked Margaret. 'Striking is leaving off work till you get your own rate of wages, is it not? You must not wonder at my ignorance; where I come from I never heard of a strike.'

'I wish I were there,' said Bessy, wearily. 'But it's not for me to get sick and tired o' strikes. This is the last I'll see. Before it's ended I shall be in the Great City – the Holy Jerusalem.'

'Hoo's so full of th' life to come, hoo cannot think of th' present. Now I, yo' see, am bound to do the best I can here. I think a bird i' th' hand is worth two i' th' bush. So them's the different views we take on th' strike question.'

'But,' said Margaret, 'if the people struck, as you call it, where I come from, as they are mostly all field labourers, the seed would not be sown, the hay got in, the corn reaped.'

'Well?' said he. He had resumed his pipe, and put his 'well' in the form of an interrogation.

'Why,' she went on, 'what would become of the farmers?'

He puffed away. 'I reckon, they'd have either to give up their farms, or to give fair rate of wage.'

'Suppose they could not, or would not do the last; they could not give up their farms all in a minute, however much they might wish to do so; but they would have no hay, nor corn to sell that year; and where would the money come from to pay the labourers' wages the next?'

Still puffing away. At last he said:

'I know nought of your ways down South. I have heerd they're a pack of spiritless, down-trodden men; welly clemmed to death; too much dazed wi' clemming to know when they're put upon. Now, it's not so here. We know when we're put upon; and we'en too much blood in us to stand it. We just take our hands fro' our looms, and say, "Yo' may clem us, but yo'll not put upon us, my masters!" And be danged to 'em, they shan't this time!'

'I wish I lived down South,' said Bessy.

'There's a deal to bear there,' said Margaret. 'There are sorrows to bear everywhere. There is very hard bodily labour to be gone through, with very little food to give strength.'

'But it's out of doors,' said Bessy. 'And away from the endless, endless noise, and sickening heat.'

'It's sometimes in heavy rain, and sometimes in bitter cold. A young person can stand it; but an old man gets racked with rheumatism, and bent and withered before his time; yet he must just work on the same, or else go to the workhouse.'

'I thought yo' were so taken wi' the ways of the South country.'

'So I am,' said Margaret, smiling a little, as she found herself thus caught. 'I only mean, Bessy, there's good and bad in everything in this world; and as you felt the bad up here, I thought it was but fair you should know the bad down there.'

'And yo' say they never strike down there?' asked Nicholas, abruptly.

'No!' said Margaret; 'I think they have too much sense.'

'An' I think,' replied he, dashing the ashes out of his pipe with so much vehemence that it broke, 'it's not that they've too much sense, but that they've too little spirit.'

'Oh, father!' said Bessy, 'what have ye gained by striking? Think of that first strike when mother died – how we all had to clem – you the worst of all; and yet many a one went in every week at the same wage, till all were gone in that there was work for; and some went beggars all their lives at after.'

'Ay,' said he. 'That there strike was badly managed. Folk got into th' management of it, as were either fools or not true men. Yo'll see, it'll be different this time.'

'But all this time you've not told me what you're striking for,' said Margaret, again.

'Why yo' see, there's five or six masters who have set themselves again paying the wages they've been paying these two years past, and flourishing upon, and getting richer upon. And now they come to us, and say we're to take less. And we won't. We'll just clem to death first; and see who'll work for 'em then. They'll have killed the goose that laid 'em the golden eggs, I reckon.'

'And so you plan dying, in order to be revenged upon them!'

'No,' said he, 'I dunnot. I just look forward to the chance of dying at my post sooner than yield. That's what folk call fine and honourable in a soldier, and why not in a poor weaver-chap?'

'But,' said Margaret, 'a soldier dies in the cause of the Nation – in the cause of others.'

He laughed grimly. 'My lass,' said he, 'yo're but a young wench, but don't yo' think I can keep three people – that's Bessy, and Mary, and me – on sixteen shilling a week? Dun yo' think it's for mysel' I'm striking work at this time? It's just as much in the cause of others as yon soldier – only, m'appen, the cause he dies for it's just that of somebody he never clapt eyes on, nor heerd on all this born days, while I take up John Boucher's cause, as lives next door but one, wi' a sickly wife, and eight childer, none on 'em factory age; and I don't take up his cause only, though he's a poor good-for-nought, as can only manage two looms at a time, but I take up th' cause o' justice. Why are we to have less wage now, I ask, than two year ago?'

'Don't ask me,' said Margaret; 'I am very ignorant. Ask some of your masters. Surely they will give you a reason for it. It is not merely an arbitrary decision of theirs, come to without reason.'

'Yo're just a foreigner, and nothing more,' said he, contemptuously. 'Much yo' know about it. Ask th' masters! They'd tell us to mind our own business, and they'd mind theirs. Our business being, yo' understand, to take the bated wage, and be thankful; and their business to bate us down to clemming point, to swell their profits. That's what it is.'

'But,' said Margaret, determined not to give way, although she saw she was irritating him, 'the state of trade may be such as not to enable them to give you the same remuneration.'

'State o' trade! That's just a piece o' masters' humbug. It's rate o' wages I was talking of. Th' masters keep th' state o' trade in their own hands; and just walk it forward like a black bug-a-boo, to frighten naughty children with into being good. ...

From *North and South* (1855), ch. 17, 'What is a Strike?' Extract from Penguin edn (1986), pp. 180–3.

3. TWENTIETH CENTURY

Ralph Fox, *The Novel and the People*

The reaction against the monotony, the baseness of life in capitalist society of the nineteenth century prevented the novelist from understanding and mastering some of the most interesting aspects of human life in the century. That he should, on the whole, have ignored the working class was natural. The novelist had no contact with the worker, looked upon him as the inhabitant of a strange, incomprehensible world, and only later, after the Paris Commune, began seriously the difficult effort of exploring that world. Edmond de Goncourt writes frankly that he feels like a police spy when gathering the materials for a novel of 'low life,' but that he is drawn to it 'perhaps because I am a well-born literary man, and the people, the "canaille," if you like, attract me like an unknown, undiscovered nation, with something of the "exotic" that travellers look for with a thousand sufferings in distant lands.' For most writers the working class have still merely this attraction of the 'exotic,' regardless of the fact that it is impossible to create human personality from such a viewpoint. With one or two rare exceptions (Mark Rutherford, for example) the novelist has never succeeded in drawing convincing men and women of the working class, and, because of this difficulty in breaking down the barrier between 'the two nations,' has rarely even tried the task.

But it is more remarkable that two other types of man should have been excluded from imaginative literature by the bourgeois novelist, two types who really played a decisive part in the history of capitalist society, the scientist and the capitalist 'leader,' the millionaire ruler of our modern life.

Of the world's supreme scientists, Archimedes, Galileo, Newton, Lavoisier, Darwin, Faraday, Pasteur and Clerk Maxwell, four are Englishmen and three of these are Englishmen of the nineteenth century. Humphry Davy, first of the great physical scientists in nineteenth century England, was the intimate friend of Southey, Coleridge, Wordsworth and the novelist Maria Edgeworth. There can have been few more interesting Englishmen than the chemist Dr. Joseph Priestley, yet he has not even had the tribute of a good biography (possibly because he was neither a Jesuit, an eccentric, nor a Tory). You may search in vain through the work of the really good novelists of the nineteenth century for so much as a recognition that the existence of science should mean more to man than the existence of public lavatories, a useful, necessary, but unpleasant convenience. Both are excluded from the field of literature. Even in our own day, when science is fully recognized and the lavatory has its honoured place in literature, it is only a few rather second-hand writers who have recognized the right of the scientist to be placed at least on a par with the prostitute and the actress as a subject for art.

Do not imagine that this is a plea for the scientist to be recognized as 'a subject' as de Goncourt recognized the actress or Zola the slaughterhouse and Arnold Bennett the luxury hotel. The scientist is not a subject, he is a type of man whose creative mind approaches that of the great artist, he is a part of human life and no possible picture of human life in the modern world is complete which ignores him. There are two reasons why this kind of man, one of the really creative forces of our time, has been ignored by the novelist. The first is that the novelist is himself so ignorant of science. ...

From *The Novel and the People* (London, 1937), 'Death of the Hero', pp. 92–3.

Walter Greenwood, *Love on the Dole*

CHAPTER I

HANKY PARK

They call this part 'Hanky Park'.

It is that district opposite the parish church of Pendleton, one of the many industrial townships comprising the Two Cities. In the early nineteenth century Hanky Park was part of the grounds of a wealthy lady's mansion; at least, so say the old maps in the Salford Town Hall. The district takes its name from a sloping street, Hankinson Street, whose pavements, much worn and very narrow, have been polished by the traffic of boots and clogs of many generations. On either side of this are other streets, mazes, jungles of tiny houses cramped and huddled together, two rooms above and two below, in some cases only one room alow and aloft; public houses by the score where forgetfulness lurks in a mug; pawnshops by the dozen where you can raise the wind to buy forgetfulness; churches, chapels and unpretentious mission halls where God is praised; nude, black patches of land, 'crofts', as they are called, waterlogged, sterile, bleak and chill.

The doorsteps and window-sills of the houses are worn hollow. Once a week, sometimes twice, the women clean them with brown or white rubbing stone; the same with portions of the pavement immediately outside their front doors. And they glare at any pedestrians who unavoidably muddy their handiwork in traversing the strip. Some women there are whose lives are dedicated to an everlasting battle with the invincible forces of soot and grime. They are flattered when you refer to them as 'house-proud'. But they are few. The others prefer to have a weekly tilt at the demon dirt and to leave the field to him for the next six days. Of a Friday evening when this portion of the housework is generally done, the pavements have a distant resemblance to a patchwork quilt. Women, girls and children are to be seen kneeling on all fours in the streets, buckets by their sides, cloth and stone daubing it over the flags, then washing it into one even patch of colour.

Families from south of the Trent who take up residence here are astonished at the fashion and say that from whence they came nothing like this is ever seen. The custom persists. The 'sand-bone men' who purvey the lumps of sandstone in exchange for household junk, rags and what-not, can be seen pushing their handcarts and heard calling their trade in rusty, hoarse, sing-song voices: 'San' bo – . Donkey brand brown sto – bo – one,' which, translated, means: 'I will exchange either brown or white rubbing stone for rags, bones or bottles.'

At one time, in the old days, when local men made their millions out of cotton and humanity, when their magnificent equipages trotted along Broad Street past Hanky Park from the local Eccles Old Road – or 'Millionaires' Mile' as it then was called – when large families lived in the Park's one room cellar dwellings and when the excess in population was kept in check by typhus and other fevers, it was the custom of the 'sand-bone men' to sprinkle sand on the newly scoured flag-paved floors of the houses in exchange for bones, which, I suppose, went to the tallow factories to be made into farthing dips. Most of the flag-paved floors are gone, now. The years have brought their changes. Water closets have superseded the earth and tin privies, though not so very long ago; the holes in the tiny backyard walls from which the pestiferous tins were drawn when to be emptied of the ordure are still to be traced, the newer bricks contrasting in colour with those of the original wall. Fever is rarer; large families are no longer permitted to live in cellars; instead, by force of circumstance and in the simplicity of their natures, they pay much more than their grandparents did for the convenience of living in a single room over a cellar.

The identical houses of yesterday remain, still valuable in the estate market even though the cost of their building has been paid for over and over again by successive tenants. The houses remain: streets of them where the blue-grey smoke swirls down like companies of ghosts from a million squat chimneys: Jungles of tiny houses cramped and huddled together, the cradles of generations of the future. Places where men and women are born, live, love and die and pay preposterous rents for the privilege of calling the grimy houses 'home'.

CHAPTER 2

GETTING UP

5.30 A.M.

A drizzle was falling.

The policeman on his beat paused awhile at the corner of North Street halting under a street lamp. Its staring beams lit the million globules of fine rain powdering his cape. A cat sitting on the doorstep of Mr Hulkington's, the grocer's shop, blinked sleepily.

'Tsh-tsh-tsh-tsh-tsh,' said the bobby and stooped to scratch the animal's head. It rose, crooked its back, cocked its tail, pushed its body against his hand and miowed.

The melancholy hoot of a ship's siren sounded from the Salford Docks.

A man wearing clogs and carrying a long pole tipped with a bunch of wires came clattering down Hankinson Street. His back was bent, beard stained and untrimmed, his rusty black bowler hat was tipped over his eyes. Blind Joe he was called, though he never gave wrong change out of a shilling nor had need to ask his way about. Whether or no he actually was blind none could say; he was Blind Joe Riley, that was all.

The bobby straightened himself as Joe approached: 'Mornin', Joe. Heigh, hei, ho. More rain, more rest,' said the copper.

'N' rest f' t' wicked, lad, 'cept them as is bobbies, an' they ne'er do nowt else. Ah don't know how some folks ...'

'Ah know, Joe. ... Ah know,' the bobby interrupted: 'Ah know all about it.'

'Well there's one thing Ah'd like t' know if tha knows all about it ... how thee and thy mates have cheek to hold hand out for wages just f' walkin' about streets. ... N' wonder folks call it a bobby's job.' ...

From *Love on the Dole* (1933), chs 1 and 2. Extract from Penguin edn (1969), pp. 11–13.

Elizabeth Bowen, *The Death of The Heart*

'Yes, if one thing doesn't turn up, it's all the more likely that another will ... The only trouble is, I've got a bit out of touch.'

'Oh yes?'

'Yes, I've stuck out there abroad too long, it rather seems. I'd rather like, now, to be in touch for a bit; I'd rather like to stay for a bit in this country.'

'But in touch with what?' said Thomas. 'What do you think there is, then?'

Some obscure hesitation, some momentary doubt made Major Brutt frown, then look across at Thomas in a more personal manner than he had looked yet. But his look was less clear – the miasma thickening in the study had put a film over him. 'Well,' he said, 'there must be something going on. You know – in a general way, I mean. You know, something you all –'

'We all? We who?'

'Well, you, for instance,' Major Brutt said. 'There must be something – that's why I feel out of touch. I know there must be something all you people get together about.'

'There may be,' said Thomas, 'but I don't think there is. As a matter of fact, I don't think we get together. We none of us seem to feel very well, and I don't think we want each other to know it. I suppose there is nothing so disintegrating as competitiveness and funk, and that's what we all feel.

The ironical thing is that everyone else gets their knives into us bourgeoisie on the assumption we're having a good time. At least, I suppose that's the assumption. They seem to have no idea that we don't much care for ourselves. We weren't nearly so much hated when we gave them more to hate. But it took guts to be even the fools our fathers were. We're just a lousy pack of little Christopher Robins. Oh, we've got to live, but I doubt if we see the necessity. The most we can hope is to go on getting away with it till the others get it away from us.'

'I say, don't you take a rather black view of things?'

'What you mean is, I ought to take more exercise? Or Eno's, or something? No, look here, my only point was that I really can't feel you are missing very much. I don't think much goes on – However, Anna might know – Cigarette?'

'No thanks: not at the moment.'

'What's that?' said Thomas sharply.

Major Brutt, sympathetic, also turned his head. They heard a key in the hall door.

'Anna,' Thomas said, with a show of indifference.

'Look here, I feel I probably ought –'

'Nonsense. She'll be delighted.'

'But she's got people with her.' There certainly were voices, low voices, in the hall.

Repeating 'No, stay, do stay,' with enormous concentration, Thomas heaved himself up and went to the study door. He opened the door sharply, as though to quell a riot. Then he exclaimed with extreme flatness: 'Oh … Hullo, Portia … oh, *hullo*; good afternoon.'

'Good afternoon,' returned Eddie, with the matey deference he now kept for Thomas out of office hours.

'I say, don't let us disturb you: we're just going out again.' Expertly reaching round Portia, he closed Thomas's hall door behind Thomas's sister. His nonchalance showed the good state of his nerves – for since when had old Thomas taken to popping out? Portia said nothing: close beside Eddie she stood smiling inordinately. To Thomas, these two appeared to be dreadful twins – they held up their heads with the same rather fragile pride; they included him in the same confiding smile. Clearly, they had hoped to creep in unheard – their over-responsiveness to Thomas only showed what a blow Thomas had been. They both glowed from having walked very fast.

Thomas showed what a blow they were by looking heavily past them. He explained: 'I thought you were Anna.'

Eddie said nicely: 'I'm so sorry we're not.'

'Isn't she in?' said Portia mechanically.

'But I'll tell you who *is* here,' said Thomas. 'Major Brutt. Portia, you'd better show up, just for a minute.'

'We – we were just going out.'

'Well, a minute won't hurt you, will it?'

…

From *The Death of the Heart* (1938), 'The World'. Extract from Penguin edn (1962, 1981), pp. 94–5.

▶ Your Discussions

☐

> ◆ According to at least one recent critic:
>
> Literature and literary criticism have had an ambivalent relationship towards issues of class in that much literature and criticism would appear to be oblivious to questions of class, representing the literary work as in some way transcending specific social and historical formations.[26]
>
> Bearing in mind all the work in the section, how do you think literary critics might most helpfully use ideas of class? What aspects of literary texts can class explain?

5.3   Gender and Sexuality

Before the nineteen sixties, gender and sexuality hardly existed as explicit topics of critical interest in English. Since then, with the rise of feminist and gay liberation movements (often strong if not uncontested in English departments), the study of gender and sexuality has become a central concern for English. Indeed, these topics to a degree displaced an earlier radical focus on class. At first, the emphasis was on the representation and exclusion of women in literature and in English in various forms; later, there were developments in the study of gay/lesbian writing, in gender issues broadly conceived, and in the construction of sexual and gender identities, including the study of 'masculinities'. This set of concerns arose partly from developments outside the academy, but also through the rise of critical theory, particularly psychoanalysis, and the range of approaches which came to be called feminist critical theory.

The critical possibilities in this kind of work covered – and still cover – an enormous range. Some critical writing about gender draws on relatively conventional ideas of criticism and history, some uses an array of ideas from the most recent developments in critical theory. Rather than attempting exhaustively to distinguish the different strands of approaches to gender and sexuality, this section will, as usual, try to give an introductory sense of some of the issues through particular texts.

> ◆ Read the following two Victorian poems: What part do ideas of gender play in them?
> ◆ How critical do you think the poems are of *Victorian* gender roles?

Christina Rossetti, *In An Artist's Studio* (1856; 1896)

In An Artist's Studio

One face looks out from all his canvases,
One selfsame figure sits or walks or leans:

We find her hidden just behind those screens,
That mirror gave back all her loveliness.
A queen in opal or in ruby dress,
A nameless girl in freshest summer-greens,
A saint an angel – every canvas means
The same one meaning, neither more nor less.
He feeds upon her face by day and night,
And she with true kind eyes looks back on him,
Fair as the moon and joyful as the light:
Not wan with waiting, not with sorrows dim;
Not as she is, but was when hope shone bright;
Not as she is, but as she fills his dream.

Robert Browning, *My Last Duchess* (1842)

My Last Duchess

Ferrara

That's my last duchess painted on the wall, looking as if
   she were alive. I call
That piece a wonder, now: Fra Pandolf's hands
Worked busily a day, and there she stands.
Wil't please you sit and look at her? I said
'Fra Pandolf' by design, for never read
Strangers like you that pictured countenance,
The depth and passion of its earnest glance,
But to myself they turned (since none puts by
The curtain I have drawn for you, but I)
And seemed as they would ask me, if they durst,
How such a glance came there; so, not the first
Are you to turn and ask thus. Sir, 'twas not
Her husband's presence only, called that spot
Of joy into the Duchess' cheek: perhaps
Fra Pandolf chanced to say 'Her mantle laps
Over my lady's wrist too much,' or 'Paint
Must never hope to reproduce the faint
Half-flush that dies along her throat': such stuff
Was courtesy she thought, and cause enough
For calling up that spot of joy. She had
A heart – how shall I say – too soon made glad,
Too easily impressed; she liked whate'er
She looked on, and her looks went everywhere.
Sir, 'twas all one! My favour at her breast,
The dropping of the daylight in the West,
The bough of cherries some officious fool
Broke in the orchard for her, the white mule
She rode with round the terrace – all and each
Would draw from her alike the approving speech,

Or blush at least. She thanked men – good! But thanked
Somehow – I know not how – as if she ranked
My gift of a nine-hundred-years-old name
With anybody's gift. Who'd stoop to blame
This sort of trifling? Even had you skill
In speech – which I have not – to make your will
Quite clear to such an one, and say, 'Just this
Or that in you disgusts me; here you miss,
Or there exceed the mark' – and if she let
Herself be lessoned so, nor plainly set
Her wits to yours, forsooth, and made excuse,
– E'en then would be some stooping; and I choose
Never to stoop. Oh sir, she smiled, no doubt,
Whene'er I passed her; but who passed without
Much the same smile? This grew; I gave commands;
Then all smiles stopped together. There she stands
As if alive. Wil't please you rise? We'll meet
The company below then. I repeat,
The Count your master's known munificence
Is ample warrant that no just pretense
Of mine for dowry will be disallowed;
Though his fair daughter's self, as I avowed
At starting is my object. Nay we'll go
Together down, sir. Notice Neptune, though,
Taming a sea-horse, thought a rarity,
Which Claus of Innsbruck cast in bronze for me!

▶ Discussion 1

Both poems are particularly interested in exploring ideas about art and gender, which in turn point towards more general ways of defining gender in nineteenth-century Britain. Both poems are interested in contrasting images with realities.

Thus in Christina Rossetti's poem, we approach a relationship between the male artist and a woman whom he has painted (perhaps she has acted as a model), not through seeing that relationship develop, but through the static images of it provided by the series of paintings that he has produced. The narrative has therefore to be deduced from these vestiges of it, and from the comments which the narrator makes on contrasts between the paintings and the reality which succeeded them. The story is very much at second hand – about things left over (the images) rather than about living beings acting directly.

Indeed, it is noticeable that neither participant is active at all in any ordinary sense: the male artist 'feeds upon her face by day and night' and his dreams are filled by her image. She is seen mainly in terms of frozen poses and roles in which he has painted her: she with 'true kind eyes looks back on him'; she 'sits or walks or leans', 'a queen', a nameless girl', 'A saint an angel'. Within this world of static fascination, there are differentiated roles for the man and woman, though both are fixated on *looking*. He looks; she is looked at – indeed, seen wholly in terms of appearances, colours and lights.

From this series of appearances, though, we can reconstruct a narrative of a change which the paintings do not record: clearly, the relationship has broken down for reasons which we must deduce. The story is not entirely straightforward, for the man seems still to 'feed' upon her image, while she, now, is 'wan with waiting' and dim with sorrows.[27] One might expect that their desires could, therefore, be fulfilled, since each is still obsessed with the other. But, instead, both are locked into their roles: he looks at images of her; she maintains a single, frozen moment of sorrow, as if she has become in life a painting. There are hints in the poem that she has, indeed, *become* a painting: 'We find *her* hidden just behind those screens' – as if the paintings represent not just images of her, but her essence. Perhaps this is exactly the artist's problem: he regards the image as superior to the actual, and has come to love that image absolutely. The narrator refers to an obsessive repetition in the paintings: 'One face looks out from all his canvases / One selfsame figure sits or walks or leans / ... – every canvas means / The same one meaning, neither more nor less.' This recording of the 'one face' might look like an act of adoration, but it seems also to drain the model of life – fixing her in a single moment, and a single meaning. The curious phrase 'neither more nor less' sounds as if it refers to his unswerving love for her (image), but the limitation of meaning is worrying: there can be no development, no change, no expansion of possibilities. What she was when painted, she must always be. The desire for power and control in this is pathological. The lack of a present and a narrative in the poem is thus highly appropriate: in this relationship there can be no ongoing present, only a fixed past, a single image.

The Robert Browning poem starts from some very similar ideas. Again, there is the static image and the reality of the woman, again an obsession with 'looking'. But in this case, I would say that the inequality of the male–female relationship remains more threatening because the male speaker is not seen as weakened by being trapped – he does not see himself as trapped, even if we might want to. Where in the Rossetti poem both artist and model are trapped by the images and reduced to at least analogous states of unfulfillable desire, here the Duke is still able to act – and monstrously. Like 'In an Artist's Studio', the poem opens with the image rather than the reality: 'That's my last duchess painted on the wall' – and also implies again that the image *is* the Duchess. The clause 'looking as if she were alive' suggests a criterion of excellence for a painting – it is so good that she looks alive, yet ironically, as we shall see, the Duchess's 'liveliness' is the problem that the Duke cannot live with. Indeed, the phrase 'as if she were alive' takes on a further sinister irony once we have read further: 'I gave commands; / then all smiles stopped together'. The image which is praised for its lifelike quality is all that is 'alive' of the Duchess now.

In several respects the painting seems to be an improvement on the original for the Duke. He now has absolute control over who looks at 'her' (his words – we could alternatively say 'it'):

'Wil't please you sit and look at her?'

But to myself they turned (since none puts by
The curtain I have drawn for you, but I).

However, though the Duke controls who looks at the painting, the Duchess' *looks* still provide an image with a certain illusion – or record? – of autonomy. Thus, the artist Fra Pandolfo has painted her distinctive 'glance', its 'depth and passion'. Though the Duke controls access, the effect of the painting is, he says, always the same: the viewer wants to know 'How such a glance came there?'

In answering this question (which, in fact, the Duke has himself raised, since he insists on making public the question he imagines that everyone would ask if they dared), the Duke has to rehearse the problem of his 'last duchess':

… She had
A heart – how shall I say – too soon made glad,
Too easily impressed; she liked whate'er
She looked on, and her looks went everywhere.

The Duke is motivated by jealousy, but this is curiously focused, not so much on ideas of direct sexual 'possession' and exclusiveness, but on anxiety about her lack of discrimination in regard to *status*: 'Sir, 'twas all one!' …/ … As if she ranked / My gift of a nine-hundred-years-old name / With anybody's gift.'

The poem's use of gendered definitions of identity focuses on this opposition between the Duke's love of status and the static, on immobility, and the Duchess' love of movement, exchange and the natural world. The Duke uses numerous words and phrases signifying fixedness, rigidity, and dominance: 'here you miss, / Or there exceed the mark', 'I choose never to stoop'. At the end of the poem, his parting reference to another item in his collection stresses immobility – he points out Neptune '*taming* a sea-horse', 'cast in bronze' (moreover, '*for me*'). As we learn at the end, this speech is made to an ambassador who has come to negotiate on behalf of his master the Duke's marriage to his *next* duchess, and 'his fair daughter's self, as I avowed / At starting is *my object*'. Though 'object' can mean *aim*, we might by this stage of the poem suspect another meaning: he does, indeed, want to have her as a 'thing', another addition to his collection.

I am unsure whether the 'glance' of the (last) Duchess pictured in the painting is a sign of something of hers which continues to disturb the Duke, to resist his dominance, or whether in a perverse way, it lends that quality which the Duke seeks from Art – an illusion of life which never wanders from a set pattern. At any rate, the major gender definitions of the poem seem clear: the masculine is associated with control and rigidity, with the possession (rather than making) of art – and with death, an ultimate kind of control and stasis, and perhaps also the essential quality of art – something opposed to real life? ☐

Discussion 2

I would say that the poem by Christina Rossetti is highly critical of domi-nant Victorian gender roles. It may suggest that the perverse and unequal relationship between this artist and this woman is a model for what is wrong with gender definitions more generally. The masculine role demands that women be fixed, under control, the object of the male gaze – but this powerful viewpoint also traps the masculine viewer into an immo-bility and an inability to live in contact with reality, which the poem sug-gests is characterised by the movement and change which are absent from its narrative.[28] On the other hand, it does not provide any suggestion of any different role for the woman other than as passive victim (she is pas-sive when 'hope shone bright' as equally as when 'wan with waiting'). But since the poem works by only showing what is dead and immobilised, we might be expected to imagine a contrary state.

Similarly, Robert Browning's poem is highly critical of a set of gen-dered identities – though its setting in renaissance Italy may distance it from the contemporary somewhat. It too does not directly move beyond the roles we might expect it (and the culture it comes from) to assign to the masculine and feminine – the woman's association with nature is in many ways traditional, as is the man's with the made, the constructed.[29] But it does imply that the feminine qualities of 'naturalness', flexibility, and unselfconscious pleasure are superior to the masculine desire for posses-sion. Both poems can be said to mount a critique of gender through a cri-tique of art, and thus to give value to the 'feminine' terms which might normally be seen as properly subordinate. □

> ◆ Read the following passages: How does each use definitions of gender? (In each case you might find it useful as a starting point to draw up a comparative list of gendered oppositions.)
> ◆ How much continuity is there with nineteenth-century ideas (at least as represented in the two poems discussed above)?

(NOTE. I will provide discussion of just the first passage and leave you to work through your own responses to the second.)

Virginia Woolf, 'Mr. Bennett and Mrs. Brown'

But we cannot hear her mother's voice, or Hilda's voice; we can only hear Mr. Bennett's voice telling us facts about rents and freeholds and copyholds and fines. What can Mr. Bennett be about? I have formed my own opinion of what Mr. Bennett is about – he is trying to make us imagine for him; he is try-ing to hypnotize us into the belief that, because he has made a house, there must be a person living there. With all his powers of observation, which are marvellous, with all his sympathy and humanity, which are great, Mr. Bennett has never once looked at Mrs. Brown in her corner. There she sits in the corner of the carriage – that carriage which is travelling, not from Richmond to Waterloo, but from one age of English literature to the next, for Mrs. Brown is eternal, Mrs. Brown is human nature, Mrs. Brown changes only on the surface, it is the novelists who get in and out – there she sits and not one of the Edwardian writers has so much as looked at her. They have looked very powerfully, searchingly, and sympathetically out of the window; at factories, at Utopias, even at the decoration and upholstery of the carriage; but never at her, never at life, never at human nature. And so they have developed a technique of novel-writing which suits their purpose; they have made tools and established conventions which do their business. But those tools are not our tools, and that business is not our business. For us those conventions are ruin, those tools are death.

You may well complain of the vagueness of my language. What is a convention, a tool, you may ask, and what do you mean by saying that Mr. Bennett's and Mr. Wells's and Mr. Galsworthy's conventions are the wrong conventions for the Georgians? The question is difficult: I will attempt a short-cut. A convention in writing is not much different from a convention in manners. Both in life and in literature it is necessary to have some means of bridging the gulf between the hostess and her unknown guest on the one hand, the writer and his unknown reader on the other. The hostess bethinks her of the weather, for generations of hostesses have established the fact that this is a subject of universal interest in which we all believe. She begins by saying that we are having a wretched May, and, having thus got into touch with her unknown guest, proceeds to matters of greater interest. So it is in literature. The writer must get into touch with his reader by putting before him something which he recognizes, which therefore stimulates his imagination, and makes him willing to co-operate in the far more difficult business of intimacy. And it is of the highest importance that this common meeting-place should be reached easily, almost instinctively, in the dark, with one's eyes shut. Here is Mr. Bennett making use of this common ground in the passage which I have quoted. The problem before him was to make us believe in the reality of Hilda Lessways. So he began, being an Edwardian, by describing accurately and minutely the sort of house Hilda lived in, and the sort of house she saw from the window. House property was the common ground from which the Edwardians found it easy to proceed to intimacy. Indirect as it seems to us, the convention worked admirably, and thousands of Hilda Lessways were launched upon the world by this means. For that age and generation, the convention was a good one.

But now, if you will allow me to pull my own anecdote to pieces, you will see how keenly I felt the lack of a convention, and how serious a matter it is when the tools of one generation are useless for the next. The incident had made a great impression on me. But how was I to transmit it to you? All I could do was to report as accurately as I could what was said, to describe in detail what was worn, to say, despairingly, that all sorts of scenes rushed into my mind, to proceed to tumble them out pell-mell, and to describe this vivid, this overmastering impression by likening it to a draught or a smell of burning. To tell you the truth, I was also strongly tempted to manufacture a three-volume novel about the old lady's son, and his adventures crossing the Atlantic, and her daughter, and how she kept a milliner's shop in Westminster, the past life of Smith himself, and his house at Sheffield, though such stories seem to me the most dreary, irrelevant, and humbugging affairs in the world.

But if I had done that I should have escaped the appalling effort of saying what I meant.... May I end by venturing to remind you of the duties and responsibilities that are yours as partners in this business of writing books, as companions in the railway carriage, as fellow travellers with Mrs. Brown? For she is just as visible to you who remain silent as to us who tell stories about her. In the course of your daily life this past week you have had far stranger and more interesting experiences than the one I have tried to describe. You have overheard scraps of talk that filled you with amazement. You have gone to bed at night bewildered by the complexity of your feelings. In one day thousands of ideas have coursed through your brains; thousands of emotions have met, collided, and disappeared in astonishing disorder. Nevertheless, you allow the writers to palm off upon you a version of all this, an image of Mrs. Brown, which has no likeness to that surprising apparition whatsoever. In your modesty you seem to consider that writers are of different blood and bone from yourselves; that they know more of Mrs. Brown than you do. Never was there a more fatal mistake. It is this division between reader and writer, this humility on your part, these professional airs and graces on ours, that corrupt and emasculate the books which should be the healthy offspring of a close and equal alliance between us. Hence spring those sleek, smooth novels, those portentous and ridiculous biographies, that milk and watery criticism, those poems melodiously celebrating the innocence of roses and sheep which pass so plausibly for literature at the present time.

Your part is to insist that writers shall come down off their plinths and pedestals, and describe beautifully if possible, truthfully at any rate, our Mrs. Brown. You should insist that she is an old lady of unlimited capacity and infinite variety; capable of appearing in any place; wearing any dress; saying anything and doing heaven knows what. But the things she says and the things she does and her eyes and her nose and her speech and her silence have an overwhelming fascination, for she is, of course, the spirit we live by, life itself.

From 'Mr. Bennett and Mrs. Brown' (1927).[30] Extract from *Collected Essays*, vol. 1 (London, 1966), pp. 330–1, 336–7.

J. Stutfield, 'Tommyrotics'

Hysteria, whether in politics or art, has the same inviolable effect of sapping manliness and making people flabby...

In no previous age has such a torrent of crazy and offensive drivel been poured forth over Europe – drivel which is not only written, but widely read and admired, and which the new woman and her coadjutors are now trying to popularise in England... [Stutfield blusters about the English capacity to withstand this continental drift into degeneracy.] In this country, at any rate, amid much flabbiness and effeminacy, there is plenty of good sense and manliness left... [however, he dwells long and colourfully on the modern disease.] Never was there an age that worked so hard or lived at such high pressure, and it would be strange indeed if the strain upon our nerves were not beginning to tell. In fact, excessive nervous sensibility is regarded by some as a thing to be admired and cultivated. It is a bad sign when people grow proud of their diseases, especially if the disease is one which, if left unchecked, will poison the springs of national life … [As far as Stutfield is concerned, women play a very large part in spreading the 'moral cancer'.] I think it cannot be denied that women are chiefly responsible for the 'booming' of books that are 'close to life' – life, that is to say, as viewed through sex-maniacal glasses. They are greater novel readers than men … and not a few of them regard [the new authors] as champions of their rights …

But let the Philistine take heart of grace. He is not alone in his fight for common-sense and common decency. That a large number of really cultivated people whose instincts are still sound and healthy, who … cling to the old ideals of discipline and duty, of manliness and self-reliance in men, and womanliness in women … who, despising the apes and mountebanks of the new culture, refuse to believe that to be 'modern' and up-to-date is to have attained to the acme of enlightenment, – all these will be on his side.

From 'Tommyrotics', *Blackwood's* (magazine), 157 (1895), pp. 833–45.[31]

Sample Discussion

Mr BENNET AND Mrs BROWN

1. As we might expect from the title of this essay, the argument is fundamentally built up from a gendered contrast: Mr Bennet/Mrs Brown. From this spring a set of contrasts which can be broadly summarised along the following lines:

Mr Bennett	Mrs Brown/Hilda Lessways[32]
masculine	feminine
writer	character/subject
we can hear his voice	but not hers, nor her mother's
external facts	inner nature
surfaces	depths
common ground	interiority
public sphere	private life
properties and possessions	'human nature'
describable	resistant to description
realism	a new kind of representation?
metonymy	metaphor

This list does not by any means wholly explain Woolf's complex argument,[33] but it does provide essential starting points. Though the essay does not explicitly name gender as central, it arises at every point. In her representation of the history of the novel, Woolf gives the generations a gendered aspect – so that all Georgian novelists are male, and can be represented in a shorthand way as a kind of composite male novelist: Bennett–Galworthy–Wells. The now outmoded conventions of this/these representative novelists are those of the previous generation, but are thus also a masculine set of conventions. Moreover, there are suggestions that the issues of representation raised are not only novelistic and artistic matters, but have wider cultural repercussions. When Woolf writes: 'For us those conventions are ruin, those tools are death', we might suspect that those conventions may, now at least, lead not just to poorer novels, but to various ruins and deaths: of the reader, of Mrs Brown's true character, of women perhaps, of 'life itself'.

The kind of novelist depicted here in some ways resembles Barthes' Author – in dominating and suppressing the reader through illusion, in sending messages through texts, in being tyrannical, patriarchal voices. This author cannot, Woolf suggests, represent the true being of Mrs Brown. Where Bennett (et al.) proceed from 'facts' in a deterministic chain (if she owns this type of house, she is this type of person), Woolf argues that we need a more truthful set of conventions. Part of their truth will come from their complexity, which will lead to a need for indirectness, for lack of single-minded certainty:

> All I could do was to report … to say, despairingly, that all sorts of scenes rushed into my mind, to proceed to tumble them out pell-mell, and to describe this vivid, this overmastering impression by likening it to a draught or a smell of burning.

In general, this masculine mode is seen as problematic because of its urge for domination, for categorisation and the solidifying of evident meaning into the rigidity of 'facts'. In its stead, we need ways of writing which liberate the reader and Mrs Brown (as character, as woman, as individual subject) from meanings imposed by the author from without:

> 'you allow the writers to palm off upon you … an image of Mrs Brown'

> 'you seem to consider that they know more of Mrs Brown than you do'

> 'for she is just as visible to you who remain silent as to us who tell stories about her'.

In place of Mr Bennett's Mrs Brown, the writer and the reader need collaboratively to 'insist on an old lady of unlimited capacity and infinite variety'.

2. There does seem considerable continuity between the nineteenth century ideas of masculinity/femininity we met in Christina Rossetti and Browning and some of the oppositions here. All three texts share an emphasis on a masculine desire to freeze humans into categories or facts, things which can be absolutely controlled. Art created in this mode is seen as a false art which kills where it should celebrate life (each of the texts contains a set of debates about life, death and art, in fact). All three also suggest that 'the feminine' is to be associated with the contrasted qualities of flexibility, spontaneity, natural life, and movement. However, we might note that Woolf's assertion of a distinctive feminine aesthetic seems more assertive.

It may well be that dominant ideas of femininity and masculinity – despite many shifts in gender roles in this period of a hundred years – have not changed enough to alter the basic terms of the oppositions. We can bring this discussion further up to date by looking next at some recent work on the oppositions feminine/masculine. □

> ◆ Read the following passage by the French critic Hélène Cixous. What does it add to the ideas about gender we have met so far in this section?
> ◆ How conventional a piece of critical writing is this?

Where is she?
  Activity/passivity,
  Sun/Moon,
  Culture/Nature,
  Day/Night,

  Father/Mother,
  Head/heart,
  Intelligible/sensitive,
  Logos/Pathos.

  Form, convex, step, advance, seed,
  progress.
  Matter, concave, ground – which supports
  the step, receptacle.

  Man
  _____
  Woman

Always the same metaphor: we follow it, it transports us, in all of its forms, wherever a discourse is organized. The same thread, or double tress leads us, whether we are reading or speaking, through literature, philosophy, criticism, centuries of representation, of reflection.

  Thought has always worked by
  opposition,
  Speech/Writing
  High/Low

By dual, *hierarchized* oppositions, Superior/Inferior. Myths, legends, books, Philosophical systems. Wherever an ordering intervenes, a law organizes the thinkable by (dual, irreconcilable; or mitigable, dialectical) oppositions. And all the couples of oppositions are *couples*. Does this mean something? Is the fact that logocentrism subjects thought – all of the concepts, the codes, the values – to a two-term system, related to 'the' couple man / woman?

  Nature/History,
  Nature/Art,
  Nature, Mind,
  Passion/Action.

Theory of culture, theory of society, the ensemble of symbolic systems – art, religion, family, language, – everything elaborates the same systems. And the movement by which each opposition is set up to produce meaning is the movement by which the couple is destroyed. A universal battlefield. Each time a war breaks out. Death is always at work.

Father/son	Relationships of authority, of privilege, of force.
Logos/writing	Relationships: opposition, conflict, relief, reversion.
Master/slave	Violence. Repression.

And we perceive that the 'victory' always amounts to the same thing: it is hierarchized. The hierarchization subjects the entire conceptual organization to man. A male privilege, which can be seen in the opposition by which it sustains itself, between *activity* and *passivity*. Traditionally, the question of sexual difference is coupled with the same opposition: activity / passivity.

That goes a long way. If we examine the history of philosophy – in so far as philosophical discourse orders and reproduces all thought – we perceive that: it is marked by an absolute constant, the orchestrator of values, which is precisely the opposition activity/passivity.

In philosophy, woman is always on the side of passivity. Every time the question comes up; when we examine kinship structures; whenever a family model is brought into play; in fact as soon as the ontological question is raised; as soon as you ask yourself what is meant by the question 'What is it?'; as soon as there is a will to say something. A will: desire, authority, you examine that, and you are led right back – to the father. You can even fail to notice that there's no place at all for women in the operation! In the extreme the world of 'being' can function to the exclusion of the mother. No need for mother – provided that there is something of the maternal: and it is the father then who acts as – is – the mother. Either the woman is passive; or she doesn't exist. What is left is unthinkable, unthought of. She does not enter into the oppositions, she is not coupled with the father (who is coupled with the son).

There is Mallarmé's tragic dream, a father lamenting the mystery of paternity, which mourning tears out of the poet, the mourning of mournings, the death of the beloved son: this dream of a union between the father and the son – and no mother then. Man's dream is the face of death. Which always threatens him differently than it threatens woman.

'an alliance a union, superb	And dream of masculine
– and the life	filiation, dream of God the father
remaining in me	emerging from himself
I shall use it	in his son, – and
to –	no mother then
so no mother then?'	

She does not exist, she may be nonexistent; but there must be something of her. Of woman, upon whom he no longer depends, he retains only this space, always virginal, matter subjected to the desire that he wishes to imprint.

And if you examine literary history, it's the same story. It all refers back to man, to his torment, his desire to be (at) the origin. Back to the father. There is an intrinsic bond between the philosophical and the literary (to the extent that it signifies, literature is commanded by the philosophical) and phallocentrism. The philosophical constructs itself starting with the abasement of woman. Subordination of the feminine to the masculine order which appears to be the condition for the functioning of the machine.

The challenging of this solidarity of logocentrism and phallocentrism has today become insistent enough – the bringing to light of the fate which has been imposed upon woman, of her burial – to threaten the stability of the masculine edifice which passed itself off as eternal-natural; by bringing forth from the world of femininity reflections, hypotheses which are necessarily ruinous for the bastion which still holds the authority. What would become of logocentrism, of the great philosophical systems, of world order in general if the rock upon which they founded their church were to crumble?

If it were to come out in a new day that the logocentric project had always been, undeniably, to found (fund) phallocentrism, to insure for masculine order a rationale equal to history itself?

Then all the stories would have to be told differently, the future would be incalculable, the historical forces would, will, change hands, bodies; another thinking as yet not thinkable will transform the functioning of all society. Well, we are living through this very period when the conceptual foundation of a millenial culture is in process of being undermined by millions of a species of mole as yet not recognized.

When they awaken from among the dead, from among the words, from among the laws. ...

From Hélène Cixous, 'Sorties', trs. in *New French Feminisms*, ed. Elaine Marks and Isabelle de Courtivron (Paris, 1975), pp. 366–71.

Discussion 1

The passage's opening list precisely highlights the familiar idea of opposed pairs as basic to gender distinction. We should, however, also note the question which precedes even the list: *'where is she?'* In one sense the answer to this is evident – the feminine side of each pair can easily be identified: 'Activity/passivity... Head/heart' and so on. In another sense, though, the question may imply that *'she'* cannot really be found in these contraries (here, we might say, are many pairings which seem to define feminine/masculine – but do they really represent a feminine term in *itself*?).

The next part of the argument – the next chart – certainly does move on to add a new idea to ideas of gender as opposed terms. It is not only gender which displays this pattern of representation; so too does 'literature, philosophy, criticism' and the very modes of thought which underpin all areas of (Western?) culture: 'Thought has always worked by/opposition'. Moreover, the two terms are never equal, but always 'hierarchized'. Cixous asks whether this deep structure is not merely shared by gender and other aspects of culture, but actually stems from gendering itself. Thus she suggests that Western culture is founded on a 'two-term system related to "the couple man/woman"'. It is no surprise then that (gendered) oppositions are everywhere, since 'everything elaborates the same systems'.

After some observations of how 'Death is always at work' in these couples (to which I'll return later), Cixous then makes the point that the hierarchy of couples produces the entire realm of ideas as inescapably dominated by the masculine: 'the hierarchization subjects the entire conceptual organization to man'. Hence the whole of philosophy and, indeed, the whole of literature is based on this difference. This does not quite mean, though, that things could never be different. Two sentences in particular suggest that something in the dominated side of the couple may/could escape from domination: 'Either the woman is passive; or she doesn't exist. What is left is unthinkable, unthought of'. The first sentence here describes the logic of the situation seen from that masculine-weighted side:

the feminine is what is opposed to the masculine
the masculine is active
therefore
the feminine is passivity and can be nothing else.

However, what if there were something in the feminine which was not passive? Since through the logic laid out above, this could not exist, it cannot be seen: it is 'left unthinkable, unthought of'. *But* what if, nevertheless, there was a residue of the feminine not thought of in the logic of the couple? Could not this non-possibility come into being?

And, indeed, Cixous argues in the following paragraph that the rule of the logic of the couple is precisely threatened now by the 'bringing forth' of the buried possibilities within the term of feminity. Since the logic of this domination is entirely circular (the masculine term is superior *solely* because the feminine term is inferior and vice versa), any fault in the system will bring collapse. If there is something in the feminine not defined by active/passive, then there is, indeed, such a flaw that 'threatens the stability of the masculine edifice'.

At this point, Cixous uses the terms 'logocentrism' and 'phallo-centrism' to describe the logic of oppositions that she has been discussing. These terms have the following senses:[34]

Logocentrism = centring on the *logos* (Greek for 'word', 'reason')
Phallocentrism = centring on the *phallos* (Greek for the phallus)[35]

These terms reinforce the passage's general sense of the masculine term as one which always desires to dominate, to pin down, to categorise, to limit with set terms (and for Cixous, indeed, logocentric terms are, of course, always set, always the hierachised couple *masculine*/feminine). These phallo-gocentric modes have sought to 'insure for masculine order a rationale equal to history itself' – that is to ensure that no other explanation is possible: masculine order is not one account of what has or can be, but the only account. Thus what has happened, what could happen, what will happen become one: the events of history are not separate from the ways in which they are explained; nothing has existence but the invincible explanation itself.

There is some common ground here with the earlier passages in this section: the association of masculinity with categorisation, fixity and clear classification, the concomitant association of the feminine with flexibility, fluidity and the unclassifable. But to this set of oppositions is added an idea of extraordinary range and power: that such oppositions are not merely what is happening at a particular moment in the sphere of gender, but are the whole foundation of every aspect of (Western?) history thus far. This makes Cixous' ideas about gender analogous to Marx and Engels' about class: in both cases, what seems a particular aspect of culture is revealed as its driving force. It does not seem as clear for Cixous (here, anyway) as it does for marxist thought that this current order will necessarily end through the workings of dynamic internal forces or contradictions. However, the close of this Cixous passage does suggest that there is a process analogous to Marx and Engels' sense of a modern crisis point in class (see section 5.2):

> the historical forces would, will, change hands, bodies; another thinking as yet not thinkable will transform the functioning of all society. Well, we are living through this very period when the conceptual foundation of a millennial culture is in process of being undermined by millions of species of a mole as yet not recognised.[36] □

▶ Discussion 2

Though asked to deal first with Cixous' ideas, you might well have noted some distinctive stylistic features of this piece. While its argument does seem to me clear and rigorous, I am not sure it is entirely conventional as a critical essay.[37] The most striking feature is the use of the inset lists or charts or diagrams (or could they be poems?). It is not unknown for books of literary criticism or theory to use lists or diagrams (*Thinking About Texts* uses them quite frequently), but it does seem unusual to open with such a specialised type of text *before* there has been any introductory *prose*. I think it would be more normal (more logocentric?) to introduce an idea and then clarify it with a diagram. Moreover, though this seems to me an excellent and productive diagram, there are perhaps features which may push at the boundaries of the genre 'academic diagram'. The title (or is it a first unpaired term?) '*Where is she*?' is not really a diagram title or caption – is not the same in function as the much more humdrum 'Paired Gender Attributes, Figure 1'. In fact, as the discussion of this phrase above might suggest, its meaning may be not be the straightforward 'labelling' we might expect: the question may partly cohere with but also partly undermine the apparently inescapable oppositional structure of the diagram/text (where all terms should be either/or). One could say that only imagination – or anyway the skills of interpretation – can make sense of the relation of '*Where is she*?' to the rest of the text.

There are other features too, where the, surely desirable, lucidity of a diagram might be seen to dissolve. Though the oppositional structure of the first four lines and the second four lines (or the first two stanzas?) is regular (.../...), there is variation in the next four lines, and again in the last two lines. If clarity is the main aim, why alter the very clear pattern so far established? Why not have:

Form/Matter
Convex/Concave

and so on? Why is it:

Man

Woman

instead of Man/Woman? But if we were to lay out the contraries in the third paragraph on either side of a stroke (/), we would see that actually the pattern of opposites has broken down or, anyway, complexified here. 'Step' and 'ground' are not really opposites in a literal sense, though one can certainly see a hierarchical relationship – as well perhaps as other possibilities (is a step necessarily superior to the ground?). And anyway, there are too few terms in the second half of this paragraph for any literal one-to-one set of oppositions along the lines of the first half of the diagram (there are six masculine terms, but only five feminine, and one of those is not a term, but a gloss on another term: '– which supports the step'). And 'receptacle' is not a literal opposite to either 'advance' or 'progress'. On the other hand, if clarity is to be sought, the final lines could be nicely interpreted as representing very clearly the hierarchy of gender distinction – woman is below the line, not on the other side of a /.

Overall, I do not feel that most diagrams do work in this way, and I come back to my least likely suggestion of a genre for this text: a poem. We could say that poetry is the best generic description for both the devices and the complexity of this piece. This might easily be said of some of the other diagrammatic parts of 'Sorties' too. Of course, this urge to classification may itself be a (masculine) desire for domination – why distinguish between diagram and poem? Why not allow the text to work as it may work?

Though these inset pieces of text are the most striking examples of ways in which 'Sorties' could be said to push at boundaries, one could also point to some other passages of prose, where the rules of academic argument are not met in the most obvious ways. For example, the sentences which follow: 'the couple is destroyed' are somewhat elliptical, lacking the explicit connections and elaboration through which such a discourse usually proceeds:[38] 'Death is always at work'. These maxims can be made sense of, but interpretation and imagination are needed.[39]

It might well be that part of the point of these departures is to resist the categorisation which 'has passed itself off as natural-eternal', the masculine/feminine hierarchy. Why must every text accept the dominant oppositions of poetry/criticism, rationality/pleasure, logic/imagination? Why not a text which allows buried possibilities to come to light, subverting the 'intelligible/sensitive' alternatives? □

I posed the second of the two questions just discussed to raise the point that texts might not just describe gender relations, but perhaps transform them. Hélène Cixous is well known as the inventor of the discourse she called *écriture féminine* which was precisely meant to transform the gendered hierarchies in texts – distinctions between academic and personal, analytic and narrative and so on – in order to resist them and open up the unthought/unthinkable. Some critics have associated these kinds of ideas with postmodernism:

A narrative has emerged in postmodernist theory that reads something like this. Feminism is the paradigmatic political discourse of postmodernism. Its affirmation of the absence, the periphery, the Other – spaces in which the position of women is structurally and politically inscribed – has more political credibility than Marxism, a patriarchal discourse of 'mastery / transparency / rationalism'.[40]

The radical nature of this move is not, it should be pointed out, accepted by all feminist thinkers. Indeed, this summary is part of a critique of the association by Laura Kipnis.

> ◆ Read the two passages below; the one by Julia Kristeva supports the liberating potential of postmodernism in terms comparable to those of Cixous, the other, by Laura Kipnis, suggests some potential problems with this conception of liberation.
> ◆ What is Kipnis's anxiety about *écriture féminine*?

Julia Kristeva, 'Postmodernism?' and Laura Kipnis, 'Feminism: the Political Conscience of Postmodernism?'

If it is true that the sciences of Man have used language as a lever to breach the protective shield and the neuralgic locus of rationality, it is also true that this epistemological reinvestigation, the hallmark of our century, is accompanied by one of the most formidable attempts to *expand the limits of the signifiable* that is, to expand the boundaries of human experience through the realignment of its most characteristic element, language.

Let us say that postmodernism is that literature which writes itself with the more or less conscious intention of expanding the signifiable and thus human realm. With this in mind, I should call this practice of writing an 'experience of limits', to use Georges Bataille's formulation: limits of language as communicative system, limits of the subjective and naturally the sexual identity, limits of sociality. Compared to the media, whose function it is to collectivise all systems of signs, even those which are unconscious, writing-as-experience-of-limits *individuates*.

(Julia Kristeva)

From these radical insights of continental feminism we move to the practice of *écriture féminine*, which in posing a counterlanguage against the binary patriarchal logic of phallogocentrism, is an attempt to construct a language that enacts liberation rather than merely theorising it. For Cixous, it is the imaginary construction of the female body as the privileged site of writing; for Irigaray, a language of women's laughter in the face of phallocratic discourse; for both, private, precious languages that rely on imaginary spaces held to be outside the reign of the phallus: the pre-Oedipal, the female body, the mystical, women's relation to the voice, fluids.

Here we have, once again, the assertion of a political praxis through essentially modernist textual practices, which relegates the analysis of the symbolic construction of alterity into an aestheticism that closes off referentiality like blinders on a horse: in this notion of literary 'productivity', the text itself comes to operate as a transcendental signified, as an ultimate meaning. The attempt to straitjacket these designated spaces into the text seems an essentially defensive maneuver, safeguarding against their escape beyond the confines of *écriture* into wider social praxis by limiting the dissemination of these forms of knowledge to the consumers of avant-garde culture. A narrative has emerged in postmodernist theory that reads something like this. Feminism is the paradigmatic political discourse of postmodernism. Its affirmation of the absence, the periphery, the Other – spaces in which the position of women is structrually and politically inscribed – has more current political credibility than Marxism, a patriarchal discourse of 'mastery/transparency/rationalism,' a master code issuing from a transcendent point of view, the path that leads from 'totality to totalitarianism, from Hegel to the gulag'.

(Laura Kipnis)

From essays in Peter Brooker (ed.), *Modernism/Postmodernism* (London 1992), pp. 207 and 199–200.

▶ Discussion

Laura Kipnis's concern here is that the expansion of the 'limits of the signifiable' remains a textual game – something from the sphere of aesthetics. Thus, it may be true that certain ways of writing texts and of reading texts can liberate us from the 'neuralgic locus of rationality' through opening up the possibilities of meanings which are buried in the 'protective shield' of hierarchised binary oppositions. But are those new meanings actually liberated for general use?

Kipnis suspects that these new 'spaces' of signification may be themselves confined, by the social systems which restrict access to 'consumers of avant-garde culture'. Liberation thus imagined becomes a purely textual event: 'the text itself comes to operate as a transcendental signifier, as an ultimate meaning'. Will this have any effect on the phallogocentric grip on other forms of culture?[41] It is noticeable that Kristeva seems here to show quite a traditional sense of a divide between literary or art culture and popular culture.[42] Thus we could sketch the implications of the last paragraph of the relevant passage:

literature	media
individuates	collectivises
expands signifiable	already signifiable
experience-of-limits	reinforces limits

One might worry that this aesthetic individuation for an elite remains simply that. Indeed, if it is culturally categorisable in this way, is it really individuation, or might it be better seen as simply giving a comforting illusion of individual autonomy and freedom? We could argue the opposite, that there will only be a genuine shift when the collective system of signs has its signifying possibilities expanded. But then can a mode of representation based on the liberating power of the unsignifiable ever become part of an established signifying system? It might give some pause for thought, if we were to reflect that the terms of *écriture féminine* with its 'private, precious languages' do show considerable continuity with the very binary oppositions it opposes. The private sphere remains its realm, while the public sphere of activity and shared meanings continues outside these 'imaginary spaces'. Perhaps this mode has not really dissolved the founding logocentric couplings?

So far, this section has concentrated on the set of oppositions centred on masculine/feminine, and has traced through some instances of how these oppositions work in particular texts, and how they can be used and, perhaps, resisted. However, this focus on *gender* is only one aspect of recent critical interest. There is also much interest in *sexuality*. These two terms – and the simpler seeming term 'sex' – have been generally distinguished in recent critical work. Elaine Showalter summarises the distinctions:

> within Anglo-American feminist discourse, the term 'gender' has been used for the past several years to stand for the social, cultural and psychological meaning imposed upon biological sexual identity … Thus 'gender' has a different meaning than the term 'sex', which refers to biological identity as female or male, or 'sexuality', which is the totality of an individual's sexual orientation, preference and behaviour. While a traditional view would hold that sex, gender and sexuality are the same – that a biological male, for example, 'naturally' acquires the masculine behavioural norms of his society, and that his sexuality 'naturally' evolves from his hormones – scholarship in a number of disciplines shows that concepts of masculinity vary widely within various societies and historical periods.[43]

Though the terms gender, sex and sexuality are thus distinct, ideas of binary opposition and of masculine/feminine identities are obviously important in all three areas. Indeed, Showalter's observation that in a traditional expectation 'sex, gender and sexuality are the same' is a key one for studying the differing relationships and interactions between these three categorisations of identity. It seems likely that representations of sexuality are precisely played out against 'normative' models of sex, gender and associated social roles and qualities.[44] □

> ◆ Read the two following passages. How do ideas of gender, sexuality and wider social roles interact in each? (I will provide a discussion of the first passage only.)

Oscar Wilde, 'Phrases and Philosophies for the Use of the Young'

The first duty in life is to be as artificial as possible. What the second duty is no one has as yet discovered.

Wickedness is a myth invented by good people to account for the curious attractiveness of others.

If the poor only had profiles there would be no difficulty in solving the problem of poverty.

Those who see any difference between soul and body have neither.

A really well-made buttonhole is the only link between Art and Nature.

Religions die when they are proved to be true. Science is the record of dead religions.

The well-bred contradict other people. The wise contradict themselves.

Nothing that actually occurs is of the smallest importance.

Dullness is the coming of age of seriousness.

In all unimportant matters, style, not sincerity, is the essential. In all important matters, style, not sincerity, is the essential.

If one tells the truth, one is sure, sooner or later, to be found out.

Pleasure is the only thing one should live for. Nothing ages like happiness.

It is only by not paying one's bills that one can hope to live in the memory of the commercial classes.

No crime is vulgar, but all vulgarity is crime. Vulgarity is the conduct of others.

Only the shallow know themselves.

Time is waste of money.

One should always be a little improbable.

There is a fatality about all good resolutions. They are invariably made too soon.

The only way to atone for being occasionally a little over-dressed is by being always absolutely over-educated.

To be premature is to be perfect.

Any preoccupation with ideas of what is right or wrong in conduct shows an arrested intellectual development.

Ambition is the last refuge of the failure.

A truth ceases to be true when more than one person believes in it.

In examinations the foolish ask questions that the wise cannot answer.

Greek dress was in its essence inartistic. Nothing should reveal the body but the body.

One should either be a work of art, or wear a work of art.

It is only the superficial qualities that last. Man's deeper nature is soon found out.

Industry is the root of all ugliness.

The ages live in history through their anachronisms.

It is only the gods who taste of death. Apollo has passed away, but Hyacinth, whom men say he slew, lives on. Nero and Narcissus are always with us.

The old believe everything: the middle-aged suspect everything: the young know everything.

The condition of perfection is idleness: the aim of perfection is youth.

Only the great masters of style ever succeed in being obscure.

There is something tragic about the enormous number of young men there are in England at the present moment who start life with perfect profiles, and end by adopting some useful profession.

To love oneself is the beginning of a life-long romance.

From *Chameleon* (December 1894); reprinted in *The Complete Works of Oscar Wilde* (London, 1992), pp. 1113–14.

Radclyffe Hall, *The Well of Loneliness*

To see Stephen Gordon's expression of horror if one so much as threw out a hint on the subject, was to feel that the thing must in some way be shameful, a kind of disgrace, a humiliation! And then she was odd about other things too; there were so many things that she didn't like mentioned.

In the end, they completely lost patience with her, and they left her alone with her fads and her fancies, disliking the check that her presence imposed, disliking to feel that they dare not allude to even the necessary functions of nature without being made to feel immodest.

But at times Stephen hated her own isolation, and then she would make little awkward advances, while her eyes would grow rather apologetic, like the eyes of a dog who has been out of favour. She would try to appear quite at ease with her companions, as she joined in their light-hearted conversation. Strolling up to a group of young girls at a party, she would grin as though their small jokes amused her, or else listen gravely while they talked about clothes or some popular actor who had visited Malvern. As long as they refrained from too intimate details, she would fondly imagine that her interest passed muster. There she would stand with her strong arms folded, and her face somewhat strained in an effort of attention. While despising these girls, she yet longed to be like them – yes, indeed, at such moments she longed to be like them. It would suddenly strike her that they seemed very happy, very sure of themselves as they gossiped together. There was something so secure in their feminine conclaves, a secure sense of oneness, of mutual understanding; each in turn understood the other's ambitions. They might have their jealousies, their quarrels even, but always she discerned underneath, that sense of oneness.

Poor Stephen! She could never impose upon them; they always saw through her as though she were a window. They knew well enough that she cared not so much as a jot about clothes and popular actors. Conversation would falter, then die down completely, her presence would dry up their springs of inspiration. She spoilt things while trying to make herself agreeable; they really liked her better when she was grumpy.

Could Stephen have met men on equal terms, she would always have chosen them as her companions; she preferred them because of their blunt, open outlook, and with men she had much in common – sport for instance. But men found her too clever if she ventured to expand, and too dull if she suddenly subsided into shyness. In addition to this there was something about her that antagonized slightly, an unconscious presumption. Shy though she might be, they sensed this presumption; it annoyed them, it made them feel on the defensive. She was handsome but much too large and unyielding both in body and mind, and they liked clinging women. They were oak-trees, preferring the feminine ivy. It might cling rather close, it might finally strangle, it frequently did, and yet they preferred it, and this being so, they resented Stephen, suspecting something of the acorn about her.

Stephen's worst ordeals at this time were the dinners given in turn by a hospitable county. They were long, these dinners, overloaded with courses; they were heavy, being weighted with polite conversation; they were stately, by reason of the family silver; above all they were firmly conservative in spirit, as conservative as the marriage service itself, and almost as insistent upon sex distinction.

'Captain Ramsay, will you take Miss Gordon in to dinner?'

A politely crooked arm: 'Delighted, Miss Gordon.'

Then the solemn and very ridiculous procession, animals marching into Noah's Ark two by two, very sure of divine protection – male and female created He them! Stephen's skirt would be long and her foot might get entangled, and she with but one free hand at her disposal – the procession would stop and she would have stopped it! Intolerable thought, she had stopped the procession!

'I'm sorry, Captain Ramsay!'

'I say, can I help you?'

'No – it's really – all right, I think I can manage –'

But oh, the utter confusion of spirit, the humiliating feeling that someone must be laughing, the resentment at having to cling to his arm for support, while Captain Ramsay looked patient.

'Not much damage, I think you've just torn the frill, but I often wonder how you women manage. Imagine a man in a dress like that, too awful to think of – imagine me in it!' Then a laugh, not unkindly but a trifle self-conscious, and rather more than a trifle complacent.

Safely steered to her seat at the long dinner-table, Stephen would struggle to smile and talk brightly, while her partner would think: 'Lord, she's heavy in hand; I wish I had the mother; now there's a lovely woman!'

And Stephen would think: 'I'm a bore, why is it?' Then, 'But if I were he I wouldn't be a bore, I could just be myself, I'd feel perfectly natural.'

Her face would grow splotched with resentment and worry; she would feel her neck flush and her hands become awkward. Embarrassed, she would sit staring down at her hands, which would seem to be growing more and more awkward. No escape! No escape! Captain Ramsay was kind-hearted, he would try very hard to be complimentary; his grey eyes would try to express admiration, polite admiration as they rested on Stephen. His voice would sound softer and more confidential, the voice that nice men reserve for good women, protective, respectful, yet a little sex-conscious, a little expectant of a tentative response. But Stephen would feel herself growing more rigid with every kind word and gallant allusion. Openly hostile she would be feeling, as poor Captain Ramsay or some other victim was manfully trying to do his duty.

In such a mood as this she had once drunk champagne, one glass only, the first she had ever tasted. She had gulped it all down in sheer desperation – the result had not been Dutch courage but hiccups. Violent, insistent, incorrigible hiccups had echoed along the whole length of the table. One of those weird conversational lulls had been filled, as it were, to the brim with her hiccups. Then Anna had started to talk very loudly; Mrs. Antrim had smiled and so had their hostess. Their hostess had finally beckoned to the butler: 'Give Miss Gordon a glass of water,' she had whispered. After that, Stephen shunned champagne like the plague – better hopeless depression, she decided, than hiccups!

It was strange how little her fine brain seemed able to help her when she was trying to be social; in spite of her confident boasting to Raftery, it did not seem able to help her at all. Perhaps it was the clothes, for she lost all conceit the moment she was dressed as Anna would have her; at this period clothes greatly influenced Stephen, giving her confidence or the reverse. But be that as it might, people thought her peculiar, and with them that was tantamount to disapproval.

And thus, it was being borne in upon Stephen, that for her there was no real abiding city beyond the strong, friendly old gates of Morton, and she clung more and more to her home and to her father. Perplexed and unhappy she would seek out her father on all social occasions and would sit down beside him. Like a very small child this large muscular creature would sit down beside him because she felt lonely, and because youth most rightly resents isolation, and because she had not yet learnt her hard lesson – she had not yet learnt that the loneliest place in this world is the no-man's-land of sex.

From *The Well of Loneliness* (1928). Extract from Virago edn (London, 1992), pp. 74–7.

▶ Discussion

I am undoubtedly influenced in my reading of these maxims by knowledge of Oscar Wilde's archetypal status – as the first writer in Britain to be publicly, and scandalously, known as homosexual, following his trial and imprisonment in 1896. Though readers in 1894 would not have been able to categorise him thus so clearly, it seems to me that this text is everywhere full of interlinked challenges to dominant ideas of gender roles, sexuality and social expectation.

Thus, two of the 'phrases' seem fairly directly to be about admiration for male attractiveness:

> If the poor only had profiles there would be no difficulty in solving the problem of poverty.

> There is something tragic about the enormous number of young men there are in England at the present moment who start life with perfect profiles, and end by adopting some useful career.

The viewpoint here is certainly not normative in several ways. The wisdom of the phrases is precisely not proverbial. Indeed, though the phrases seem immediately witty and elegantly turned, the logic needs some thought to unravel it – and can be quite resistant to elucidation. The following sequence of questions and answers helps us to unravel one of these phrases:

1.   If the poor only had profiles there would be no difficulty in solving the problem of poverty.
2.   Why? Because if the poor looked physically attractive, their poverty would be solved.
3.   Why? Because people would give them money.
4.   Why? Because it's easier to give attractive people money? Because money would be exchanged for sexual gratification?

I find it difficult to see what other meaning the phrase can have, or to account for it in more publicly acceptable 'Victorian' ways. If we stopped at the first 'because' of step 4, we could simply, if not really very satisfactorily, say that it is a stylistic judgement: the poor are unattractive. My assumption that the phrase refers to male attractiveness is, indeed, not clear from the 'phrase', since the label 'the poor' does not specify gender, though I feel that 'profile' might be a more masculine descriptor. If I am wrong to assume that the focus of the phrase is the male poor, there still seems to be the suggestion of sexual transgression, and indeed moral transgression: prostitution would abolish poverty if the poor were better looking.

Of course, prostitution was, indeed, a part of Victorian culture, but the reference to it here is wildly (Wildely?) unconventional. The genre of this text is that of a set of maxims, and maxims are brief rules or truths, especially concerned with 'good conduct'. As the title suggests, these maxims should be expected to provide moral guidance, particularly 'for the use of the young'. A recommendation of the potential social benefits of (probably male) prostitution sits surprisingly in this context. Moreover, the phrase's interest in aesthetics, in style over content or moral value is also odd in the contexts of moral guidance and of solutions to the moral evil of poverty. Like many of the other maxims in the set, this phrase refuses to take seriously a standard Victorian social and moral concern. It is particularly ironic that much Victorian anxiety about poverty was that it led the poor to moral ruin – yet here the solution is via what dominant morality would clearly consider moral ruin!

Each of these maxims has similar kinds of complexity. But the aestheticisation in particular is a key feature of them all and of the whole effect of Wilde's maxims (he published three different collections of these, as well as using similarly concise and witty apothegms in his comedy of 1895, *The Importance of Being Earnest*). The valuing of style, appearance over substance, runs counter to the period's dominant privileging of solidity and seriousness.

And these virtues themselves have strong implications for gender roles, sexuality and social roles. The Victorian manly man (the ideal husband) should indeed be solid and virtuous, the head of the household, a patriarch able to exercise rule and show activity in the world. The decorative graces of life are to be provided by women, who rule in the aesthetic realm – at least where it is private and unserious. Hence Ruskin in a well-known piece on ideal gender roles from his book *Sesame and Lilies* (1865) defines the feminine virtues:

> The man's power is active, progressive, defensive. He is eminently the doer, the creator, the discoverer ... But the woman's power is for rule, not for battle, – and her intellect is not for invention or creation, but for sweet ordering, arrangement and decision ...
>
> The man's duty, as a member of the commonwealth, is to assist in the maintenance, in the advance, in the defence of the state. The woman's duty, as a member of the commonwealth, is to assist in the ordering, in the comforting, and in the beautiful adornment of the state.[45]

Though there is nothing like an exact match between the implied viewpoint of the speaker of Wilde's phrases and the functions of woman according to Ruskin, there seems to be a closer match between womanly virtues than with the manly. In short, though the viewpoints of the maxims are not conventionally feminine, there does seem to be a style which is unmasculine and partly feminised in terms of contemporary expectations. The stress on the decorative, on surfaces rather than depths, on the illusory nature of depth, seriousness and activity are constant themes:

> Nothing that actually occurs is of the smallest importance.
> Dullness is the coming of age of seriousness.
> One should either be a work of art, or wear a work of art.
> Industry is the root of all ugliness.

The modern social role of men is undermined through complex and ironic manipulations of expectations about sexuality and gender. Indeed, part of the effect comes precisely from a playing with cultural classifications of all sorts, a refusal to let conventional definitions behave as expected. Thus these maxims undermine what should be their inherent claim to seriousness (but reassert it through some serious transgressions) – just as they flouted social conventions in the very act of providing fashionable society of the 1890s with just the outrageousness which was acceptable to it, because witty and daring. ☐

▶ Your Discussion of Passage 2

☐

◆ Finally, based on the work throughout this section and your general experience of using ideas about gender in critical discussion, consider the question which Elaine Showalter asks in *Speaking of Gender* (1989): 'What do we talk about when we talk about gender?'
◆ What do you think can usefully be achieved by thinking about gender and sexuality in literary studies?

5.4   Race and Nationality

Like gender and sexuality, issues of race and nationality are comparatively recent concerns of university 'English', but have similarly become focuses for a great deal of critical energy and exploration. 'Race' has a longer critical lineage, dating back to at least the theoretical developments of the 1980s, than 'nationality', which only became a common 'critical' topic during the 1990s. These developments are not, of course, simply an internal matter to the academy, but are influenced by/are part of wider social concerns. Thus in Britain in the nineteen eighties, it might be said that the spread of ideas – at various levels – about living in a multicultural society (as opposed to earlier ideas about 'assimilation'), the relatively better representation of some ethnic groups in higher education as students and staff, and new ideas about literature and identity, all interacted to make race a widespread (and, indeed, popular) topic. Likewise, it might be said that during the nineteen nineties, and especially after the break up of the former Soviet bloc, with the continuing impacts of colonialism, decolonisation and postcolonial statehood being lived out globally, and with more local developments in terms of shifts in British identity in the world and at home, it became clear that nationalism and national identity were still prime forces in the world and in every culture. More over, as a literary critical concern this could build on some of the work done on ideas of racial difference and identities. As with other forms of identity, much of this work has been concerned with critiques of stereotypes, representations, fictions and narratives of identity as well as with the rediscovery/invention/assertion/problematisation of more authentic conceptions of identity. In ways we have seen elsewhere in this book literature's traditional interest in narrative, stories, fictions, became in these contexts a vital concern with the nature of the 'real' identities which these devices construct, and not only in 'texts', inside books.

> ◆   Read the following passages from Shakespeare's plays *Othello* (1604), and *The Tempest* (1611). How are the identities of Othello and Caliban represented?
> ◆   What narratives of 'race' lie behind these representations?

* * * * * * * * * * *

Othello. Most potent, grave and reverend signiors,
   My very noble, and approv'd good masters,
   That I have ta'en away this old man's daughter,
   It is most true; true I have married her;
   The very Head and front of my offending
   Hath this extent, no more. Rude am I in my Speech   80
   ...
   ...   Yet (by your gracious patience)
   I will a round unvarnished Tale deliver
   Of my whole course of love: what drugs, what charms,   90
   What conjuration, and what mighty magic

(For such proceedings am I charged withal)
I won his daughter.

Brabantio.   A maiden never bold of spirit
So still, and quiet, that her motion
Blush'd at her self; and she, in spight of nature.
Of years, of country, credit, everything,
To fall in love with what she feared to look on?
It is a judgement maim'd, and most imperfect,
That will confess perfection so would err
Against all rules of nature, and must be driven   100
To find out practices of cunning Hell
Why this should be. I therefore vouch again
That with some mixtures powerful o'er the blood,
Or with some dram conjur'd to this effect
He wrought upon her.

Duke.   To vouch this is no proof
Without more wider and more overt test
Than these thin habits, and poor likelihoods
Of modern seemings, you prefer against him.

Senator.   – but Othello, speak:
Did you by indirect and forced courses   110
Subdue and poison this young maid's affections?
Or came it by request, and such fair question
As soul to soul affordeth?
              …

Othello. Her father lov'd me, oft invited me,
Still question'd me the story of my life,
From year to year; the battailles, sieges, fortunes
That I have pass'd.
I ran it through, even from my boyish days   130
To the very moment that he bade me tell it.
Wherein I spoke of most disastrous chances:
Of moving accidents by flood and field,
Of hair-breadth scapes I' th' imminent deadly breach,
Of being taken by the insolent foe
And sold to slavery; of my redemption thence,
And portance in my traveller's history;
Whereof of antres vast, and deserts idle,
Rough quarries, Rocks and Hills whose heads touch heaven,
It was my hint to speak. Such was my process,   140
And of the Cannibals that each other eat,
The Anthropophagi, and men whose heads
Do grow beneath their shoulders. These things to hear
Would Desdemona seriously incline;
But still the house affairs would draw her hence:
Which ever as she could with haste dispatch,
She'd come again and with a greedy ear
Devour up my discourse. Which I observing,
Took once a pliant hour, and found good means
To draw from her a prayer of honest heart   150

That I would all my pilgrimage dilate
Whereof by parcels she had something heard,
But not instinctively: I did consent,
And often did beguile of her tears
When I did speak of some distressful stroke
That my youth suffer'd. My story being done,
She gave me for my pains a world of kisses:
She swore in faith 'twas strange, 'twas passing strange,
'Twas pitiful, 'twas wondrous pitiful.
She wish'd she had not heard it, yet she wish'd   160
That heaven had made her such a man. She thank'd me,
And bad me, If I had a friend that lov'd her,
I should teach him how to tell my story,
And that would woo her. Upon this hint I spake:
She lov'd me for the dangers I had past,
And I lov'd her that she did pity them.
This onely is the witchcraft I have us'd.
Here comes the Lady: let her witness it.
                                        (Act I, scene iii, ll. 75–168)

Prospero. Thou poisonous slave, got by the devil himself
    Upon thy wicked dam, come forth!
    [*Enter Caliban*]
Caliban. As wicked dew as e'er my mother brush'd
    With raven's feather from unwholesome fen,
    Drop on you both! A south-west blow on ye,
    And blister you all o'er!
Prospero. For this, be sure, to-night thou shalt have cramps,
    Side-stitches that shall pen thy breath up; urchins
    Shall forth at vasts of night, that they may work,
    All exercise on thee; thou shalt be pinch'd
    As thick as honeycomb, each pinch more stinging
    Than bees that made 'em.
Caliban.   I must eat my dinner.
    This island's mine, by Sycorax my mother,
    Which thou tak'st from me. When thou camest first,
    Thou strok'dst me, and mad'st much of me; wouldst give
    Water with berries in 't; and teach me how
    To name the bigger light, and how the less,
    That burn by day and night; and then I loved thee,
    And show'd thee all the qualities o' th' isle
    The fresh springs, brine-pits, barren place, and fertile:
    Cursed be that I did so! All the charms
    Of Sycorax, toads, beetles, bats, light on you!
    For I am all the subjects that you have,
    Which first was mine own king: and here you sty me,
    In this hard rock, whiles you do keep from me
    The rest of the island.
Prospero.   Thou most lying slave,
    Whom stripes may move, not kindness! I have used thee

Filth as thou art, with human care; and lodged thee
In mine own cell, till thou didst seek to violate
The honour of my child.
Caliban.   O ho, O ho! Wouldst had been done!
Thou didst prevent me; I had peopled else
This isle with Calibans.
Miranda.[46]   Abhorr'd slave,
Which any print of goodness wilt not take.
Being capable of all ill! I pitied thee,
Took pains to make thee speak, taught thee each hour
One thing or other: when thou didst not, savage,
Know thy own meaning, but wouldst gabble like
A thing most brutish, I endow'd thy purposes
With words that made them known; but thy vile race,
Though thou didst learn, had that in 't which good natures
Could not abide to be with; therefore wast thou
Deservedly confined into this rock,
Who hadst deserved more than a prison.
Caliban. You taught me language; and my profit on 't
Is, I know how to curse. The red plague rid you
For learning me your language!
Prospero.   Hag-seed, hence!
Fetch us in fuel; and be quick, thou'rt best,
To answer other business. Shrug'st thou, malice?
If thou neglect'st, or dost unwillingly
What I command, I'll rack thee with old cramps;
Fill all thy bones with aches; make thee roar,
That beasts shall tremble at thy din.
Caliban.   No, 'pray thee!
[*Aside*] I must obey: his art is of such power,
It would control my dam's god, Setebos,
And make a vassal of him.
Prospero. So slave; hence!
[*Exit Caliban.*]
                         (Act I, scene ii)

▶ Discussion 1

Clearly, the representations of Othello and Caliban are very different from each other: they are not seen in terms of a single general seventeenth-century idea of African or black or 'savage' identity (something one might crudely have suspected). Thus Othello is represented as speaking a very different kind of language from Caliban.[47] At the same time, both seem to have distinctive modes of speech which differentiate them from the Europeans.

Othello, despite his claim to be 'Rude' in speech (but note the poetic inversion of the more normal word order), has, in fact, a markedly rhetorical and deliberate style of speech, which includes a careful use of sequence to create dramatic and impressive effects: For example, one might note the lines:

> That I have ta'en away this old man's daughter,
> It is most true; true I have married her.

Here the apparent admission of his role as a seducer is immediately contradicted (rescued for respectability) by the second admission of what is true. Both admissions turn on the phrase 'ta'en away' – but where one refers to an illicit taking, the other refers to a conventional, legal kind of removal from her father. The two different 'confessions' are linked together by a rhetorical figure in which the last word of one element becomes the first word in the second: 'It is most *true*; *true* I have married her'. This particular rhetorical patterning (known as *chiasmus* = a crossing over) would be recognisable to some at least of contemporary audiences as a common figure from classical rhetoric. There are many other examples in this passage of such deliberate rhetorical effects, and, indeed, of an elaborate and learned vocabulary: 'portance', 'antres', 'the Anthropophagi'. This seems somewhat contradictory in that Othello seems to share a common language with 'learned' Europeans. However, one might further note that the actual Europeans present here do not use anything like such a deliberate and rhetorical style: their speeches are decidedly plain and mundane compared to Othello's.

The difference between his speech and theirs is presumably a central device in distinguishing these culturally and racially opposed figures. But one might expect that Othello's speech would be represented as less sophisticated than that of the Venetians (especially since they were famed for this quality), given the identification made between him and the animal earlier on in the play ('the black ram is tupping your white ewe'). Even two of the Venetian officials – the Duke and the Senator – seem clear that Brabantio's speech is much less persuasive, much cruder than Othello's. Thus the Duke refers to the 'thin habits and poor likelihoods' of Brabantio's speech, while the Senator certainly envisages the possibility that Othello won Desdemona by 'request, and such fair question / As soul to soul affordeth'.

This effect might be explained in various ways. For example, it could be argued that since this must be a language Othello has learned, as an adult, it has a learnt rather than a natural quality – an artificiality of which Othello is always conscious – and the hypercorrectness of an acquired, but mastered language. Alternatively, it could be argued that Othello is seen in the play as having a natural nobility of speech, which is a sign of his difference. In this reading, the 'superiority' of the Europeans is not assured by their membership of the familiar; rather, this makes them mundane, inferior to the exotic otherness of Othello.

This might suggest that there is an element of the 'noble savage' in his conception – the idea that members of more 'primitive' communities may possess admirable qualities which the 'civilised' have lost. Thus, perhaps Othello speaks a naturally impressive language; what Europeans must learn and struggle to perfect, he can simply do. Certainly, we can see in the scene a conflict between Brabantio's narrative of what 'black men' are like, and Othello's presentation of himself. In his story of Othello and his daughter Desdemona, Brabantio assumes abduction, seduction, drugs, magic, and unnatural, hellish practices in general. Othello opposes this story with his own more sophisticated story of what has happened between Desdemona and himself. In a curious way, though, Othello's story does confirm Brabantio's suspicions, but with a twist. If Brabantio imagines Othello as completely outside the ordinary, Othello also seems to imagine himself as a highly exotic figure, whose lifestory is inextricably linked to battailles, sieges, deserts vast, the anthropophagi and other wonders. As Othello admits, he does use a kind of magic – but it is the magical conjurations of narrative, rather than the crude physical 'drugs' which Brabantio imagines. Indeed, Brabantio himself has fallen under the spell of Othello's military narratives – an experience which seems to have utterly disappeared from his memory now that Desdemona has found Othello's stories similarly irresistible. As we have already seen, Othello's stories are, unlike Brabantio's, compelling. The Duke and Senators believe Othello's stories to be true stories, just as Brabantio did, and Desdemona does. Othello's narratives seem to have the exotic quality of the most romantic adventure, while also possessing the quality of being 'unvarnished'. They have both a perfection – a faultlessness in the telling – and an immediate presentness.

If the narrator of autobiography 'tells the story of himself', then Othello is addicted to autobiography as a way of representing his own identity. One might ask how else a character is to tell their own story except through telling their own story, but, actually, Othello's self-presentation (and thus his presentation in the play) does not seem to follow the most obvious set of generic conventions. Whenever Othello is asked to account for himself, he does so through narrative of the past, rather than a statement of what he is or wishes in the *present*. Othello does not really engage in dialogue with other characters as a way of asserting or communicating his wishes or identity: rather he speaks grand monologues about himself. It is these stories which draw Desdemona in (noticeably in opposition to the gender role she is assigned by her household duties) rather than direct communication between her and Othello. Thus, it could be said that she falls in love with the Othello who is spoken about, as much as with the Othello who speaks. He in turn could be said to fall in love with the Desdemona who 'pities' the Othello in his stories. This would only suggest that selves are imagined through stories as much as through immediate presentation[48] (oddly, given that this is a play, through narrated forms, as much as through dramatic forms!).

Why is there this concentration on story-telling? Perhaps Othello – just as he uses the classical rhetoric of European traditions – does see himself from the perspective of a European narrative, as an exotic other? Perhaps this is a way of giving coherence to a life that has been radically fragmented ('most disastrous chances / Moving accidents': transitions from one status to another, one culture to another, African warrior, slave, Christian general...)? Perhaps, like the historical narratives of Hayden White's professional historians,[49] Othello's narratives of himself give Othello a perfection and wholeness, which he finds it difficult to feel more directly? Perhaps he thus partly resists – by making himself superior, whole – the demeaning racial narratives of the Europeans among whom he now lives, but partly also fulfils their own imaginary tales of black men who come from the land of the Anthropophagi and the men whose heads are set beneath their shoulders?

This may seem a somewhat indirect account of the representation of Othello's identity, but I would say that the indirection arises because the scene itself is so concerned with indirect representation, with representation through narrative, rather than through drama or action (Othello defends himself before the Duke by telling a story about a previous occasion when he had told a story). The representation of Caliban in *The Tempest* is relatively direct in that Caliban asserts his position and identity much more immediately: 'When thou camest first...'. Indeed, his position is apparently simpler than Othello's: he is enslaved by the European colonists, Prospero and Miranda.

Much of the exchange in the scene between Prospero and Caliban is taken up by naked demonstrations of power and resentment respectively (*Prospero*. So slave; hence! / *Caliban*. Cursed be that I did so!). Where Othello's relationship to the Europeans was complex, Caliban's is simple: he must do their will because they have the means to force him to do so. There is, however, a history to this relationship: it has not always been one of open power and resisted submission. After Prospero's initial outburst of vituperation in the scene, Caliban makes first a claim to possession of the island, and then gives an account of his earlier relationship to the colonists:

> This island's mine, by Sycorax my mother,
> Which thou tak'st from me. When thou camest first,
> Thou strok'dst me, and mad'st much of me ...

The claim is very much a legal one: he has priority since his mother left the island to him. The account is rather different. Instead of asserting Caliban's rights, it summarises his first reactions to Prospero and explains how he came to be in this dominated position. At first the new arrivals were kind (one notes the simple physical intimacy of 'strok'dst') and gave knowledge to Caliban – of alcohol (?), of the planets and how to name them. He, in exchange, gave them his learning about the island. Why does Caliban rehearse all this, which Prospero already knows? Presumably, Caliban wants to assert his resentment at the change and its injustice. What was at first an equal relationship of exchange has become one of subordination and exploitation. Caliban is well aware that, despite the initial wonders of the new arrivals, he has lost much and gained nothing. From being the ruler of himself, he is now a vassal: 'For I am all the subjects that you have, / Which first was mine own king' (it is notable that Caliban's subjection is bodily, rather than mental: he opposes Prospero freely in speech whenever he can).

From Caliban's point of view the first excitement of European knowledge (a mixed bag of the abstract science of astronomy, and the more immediate pleasures of alcohol) merely allows the new arrivals to gain entry easily; thereafter, it brings him nothing except a greater sense of his own loss of autonomy:

> You taught me language; and my profit on 't
> Is, I know how to curse. The red plague rid you
> For learning me your language!

Both Caliban and Prospero/Miranda's accounts concur that Caliban has no speech until Miranda teaches him language:

> I pitied thee,
> Took pains to make thee speak, taught thee each hour
> One thing or other: when thou didst not, savage,
> Know thy own meaning, but wouldst gabble like
> A thing most brutish, I endow'd thy purposes
> With words that made them known.

There is an assumption that Caliban before Prospero and Miranda is pre-linguistic, and hence has no consciousness ('thou didst not know thy own meaning') beyond the animal. It is also assumed that he is asocial – a solitary inhabitant of the island. This is to be expected in that he has had no chance to be or become social, but is more unexpected if he is to be seen as more widely representative of 'primitive' man, implying that living in social groups is unknown. However, this solitariness is a key part of Caliban's identity. Before the European's arrival, he has had no experience of other people – hence the extraordinary pleasure which he still remembers in their company and conversation. Hence also, his absolute trust in them, which now he sees betrayed him.

Prospero and Miranda feel equally betrayed by Caliban:

> *Prospero.*   Thou most lying slave,
>   Whom stripes may move, not kindness! I have used thee
>   Filth as thou art, with human care; and lodged thee
>   In mine own cell, till thou didst seek to violate
>   The honour of my child.

The attempted rape of Miranda is the turning point in the relations of Caliban and the colonists. For Prospero and Miranda it convinces them – or bears out their expectations? – that Caliban is irredeemably savage, lacking the sexual restraint of the civilised man (an accusation made by Brabantio against Othello, too). It is this assault which leads to Caliban's enslavement and his confinement to one part of the island. What is not clearly explained is what motivated Caliban's attack: Prospero and Miranda assume, afterwards at any rate, that it is always what was to be expected – the uncontrollable libidinousness, ineradicably antisocial behaviour and ingratitude which is inherent to Caliban's 'vile race'. The nineteenth-century editorial assignation of one of the speeches in the scene to Prospero, rather than to Miranda (see note 46 above) has tended to confirm this reading. However, if the speech is given to Miranda, as it is here, it might help us to see other possible explanations.

These arise from Caliban's status as solitary 'primitive' man. Since he has no knowledge of any human relationship, it may be no surprise that the intricacies of courtship and sexual behaviour are unknown to him. If it were Prospero who had taught him language, this would make the assault seem more opportunistic, and brutal. But since it is Miranda who has 'pitied' him, and 'took pains to make thee speak, taught thee each hour', there is a suggestion of a degree of intimacy between them, which Caliban could misunderstand. It is possible that what Miranda and Prospero interpret quite correctly as an assault from their perspectives is not so obviously that to Caliban – what does he know of any sexual behaviour if he is the primitive solitary which Prospero and Miranda describe? They know that he has to be taught speech, but they expect that he will know about the social rules which they, at least, associate with the faculty. It is possible that for Caliban his attempt was an innocent one, something which seemed to follow on naturally from his pleasure in learning. But having broken this rule, he must perforce learn of the other kinds of constraints which the Europeans command: the prison, the cramps and so on. Just as language allows him to divide up experience, to perform commentary on his actions, so too his life itself will now be divided into European categories, including those of good and evil. Indeed, the scene does suggest that in several ways it is about Caliban's Fall – at first the two other humans bring him from a state of unconsciousness into a state of paradisal pleasure (Miranda teaches him the names of things, just as Eve traditionally named the beasts and flowers in Eden). Then, he breaks the prohibition, attempts forbidden knowledge (he does not know it is forbidden) and enters a life of labour and punishment (the fate of Adam and Eve after Eden). This is the story of his fall from a European perspective, but Caliban has his own narrative of his fall too; one which takes him from utter, unconscious liberty ('mine own king') to a state where the only use of his new learning is the punishment of knowledge: 'You taught me language; and my profit on 't / Is, I know how to curse.' □

Discussion 2

As has probably become apparent in the discussion above, these two Shakespearean plays certainly refer to various narratives of racial and cultural difference – including ideas of primitive virtue, simplicity and nobility, libidinous savages, the speechless primitive, the natural man who has no consciousness. These narratives have strongly stereotyping tendencies, but these particular representations at least have great complexity, partly because there are multiple and conflicting ideas and narratives of identities and how they work. It is notable that the identification of characteristics in 'others' whose identities are perceived as different always implies an identification of features in the 'familiar' too. Thus civilisation is defined against savagery, simplicity against corruption, blackness against whiteness and so on. If there is complexity and ambiguity in the portrayal of racial others, it implies also complexities and contradictions in the identity of the 'known'. □

> ◆ Read the following passages: To what extent do they help you
> to understand the representation of Othello and Caliban in
> Shakespeare's plays? (I will provide my response to the first passage,
> but leave you to respond to the second.)

Ivan Hannaford, *Race – The History of An Idea in the West*

HAKLUYT

In 1589, two years after the publication of the second edition of the *Chronicles*, Richard Hakluyt (ca. 1552–1616) in his *Principal Navigations, Voyages, Traffiques, and Discoveries of the English Nation* more carefully observed Foxe's principle that history should rely not on descriptions of marvelous and fabulous origins but on authenticated records, acts, and monuments. Hakluyt's test of legitimacy and title to rule followed the familiar idea of a well-ordered civic arrangement acting publicly to combat the private excesses of barbarousness, brutishness, and incivility. For the most part Hakluyt's legitimate genealogy is maintained if the civil order and course of things are drawn from authoritative historical records prepared by those in the service of kings and bishops. What sets people apart – 'without' – is that, 'like the wild Irish,' they do not belong to a realm (*regna*) and, like the Lapps and Finns, 'they neither know God nor yet good order' and 'all studies and letters of humanitie they refuse'.

Hakluyt's judgments of what constituted good government would not have been unfamiliar to Vitoria, Las Casas, or Machiavelli. He reprinted early instructions given to John Cabot, which set out a right order for the proper conduct of a public enterprise of discovery. They prohibited the imposition of religion, laws, and rites upon the newly discovered peoples, who must be treated carefully, 'so as to induce their barbarous natures to a liking and mutuall societie with us', and with a view of learning about their natures and dispositions. This common recognition of the principles and procedures of what was thought to be the mark of good government characterized the reports in Hakluyt of Richard Cheinie's voyages passing through Russia to Persia from 1563 to 1565; Laurence Chapman's venture in Persia in 1568; Angrimus Jonas's powerful correction of the scurrilous reports brought back from Iceland by the German cosmographers Gamma Frisius, Sebastian Munster, and Albert Krantz (1448–1517); Sir George Peckham's account of Sir Humphrey Gilbert's visit to Newfoundland in 1583; and Walter Raleigh's account of the discovery of Guiana in 1595, which pleaded with the queen not to leave these territories to the 'spoile and sackage of common persons'. But as the enterprises encountered difficulties, including ambush, betrayal, and ransom, allusions to witchcraft, sorcery, and humoral disposition increased. And while in the early accounts captains conceded that drunkenness, idolatry, lust, and gambling were as common-place among their own men as among the people they encountered, after Sir Martin Frobisher's voyages, their comments were less cautious: 'What knowledge they have of God, or what Idoll they adore, we have no perfect intelligence, I thinke them rather Anthropophagi, or devourers of man's flesh than otherwize'.

This most striking departure from the early, ordered public framework is contained in George Best's *True Discourse of the Three Voyages of Discoverie: the Finding of a Passage to Cathaya, by the Northwest*, which was originally published in 1578 and is included in Hakluyt's compilation. In this account Best, who accompanied Frobisher in 1576, 1577, and 1578, sought to prove by experience and reason that natural causes accounted for the fundamental differences in men. Following comparative study of the peoples occupying these regions of the world, Best concluded that the Hippocratian hypothesis that people are black because of the parching heat of the sun, or because of their geographical position, was wrong. He cited abundant examples of different peoples living in similar latitudes with entirely different physical characteristics.

> I my selfe have seene an Ethiopian as blacke as a cole brought unto England, who taking a faire English wife, begat a sonne in all respects as blacke as the father was, although England was his native country, and an English woman his mother; whereby it seemeth this blacknes proceedeth rather of some natural infection of that man, which was so strong, that neither the nature of the Clime, neither the good complexion of the mother concurring, could any thing alter, and therefore, we cannot impute it to the nature of the Clime.

Blackness, Best concluded, must be due to some other hidden cause, which he identified as a natural infection that proceeds by lineal descent: 'and so all the progenie of them descended, are still polluted with the same blot of infection.' This infection does not proceed from a biological cause but from Berossus' account:

> It manifestly and plainely appeareth by holy Scripture, that after the generall inundation and the overflowing of the earth, there remained no moe men alive but Noe and his three sonees, SEM, CHAM, and JAPHET, who onely were left to possesse and inhabite the whole face of the earth: therefore all the sundry discents that until this present day have inhabited the whole earth, must neede come of the off-spring either of Sem, Cham, or Japhet, as the onely sonnes of Noe, who *all three being white*, and their wives also, by course of nature should have begotten and brought forth white children.

Best explained that the Devil caused Ham to transgress the laws of inheritance and to indulge in carnal copulation. Thus his sons were marked with a black badge to symbolize loathsomeness and banished to the cursed and degenerate voids of Africa, where they lived as idolators, witches, drunkards, sodomites, and enchanters.

From the time of Best, the African appeared in literature as someone outside the reach of classical Aristotelian politics. He was marked, not with an artificial badge and hideous raiment like the Jew, but with a natural badge of pigmentation understood to be caused by a natural infection brought about by an unnatural act encouraged by an evil spirit.

From *Race – The History of an Idea in the West* (Baltimore, MD, and London, 1996), pp. 164–7.

Edward Said, 'The Scope of Orientalism'

In *The Bacchae*, perhaps the most Asiatic of all the Attic dramas, Dionysus is explicitly connected with his Asian origins and with the strangely threatening excesses of Oriental mysteries. Pentheus, king of Thebes, is destroyed by his mother, Agave, and her fellow bacchantes. Having defied Dionysus by not recognizing either his power or his divinity, Pentheus is thus horribly punished, and the play ends with a general recognition of the eccentric god's terrible power. Modern commentators on *The Bacchae* have not failed to note the play's extraordinary range of intellectual and aesthetic effects; but there has been no escaping the additional historical detail that Euripides 'was surely affected by the new aspect that the Dionysiac cults must have assumed in the light of the foreign ecstatic religious of Bendis, Cybele, Sabazius, Adonis, and Isis, which were introduced from Asia Minor and the Levant and swept through Piraeus and Athens during the frustrating and increasingly irrational years of the Peloponnesian War.'

The two aspects of the Orient that set it off from the West in this pair of plays will remain essential motifs of European imaginative geography. A line is drawn between two continents. Europe is powerful and articulate; Asia is defeated and distant. Aeschylus *represents* Asia, makes her speak in the person of the aged Persian queen, Xerxes' mother. It is Europe that articulates the Orient; this articulation is the prerogative, not of a puppet master, but of a genuine creator, whose life-giving power represents, animates, constitutes the otherwise silent and dangerous space beyond familiar boundaries. There is an analogy between Aeschylus's orchestra, which contains the Asiatic world as the playwright conceives it, and the learned envelope of Orientalist scholarship, which also will hold in the vast, amorphous Asiatic sprawl for sometimes sympathetic but always dominating scrutiny. Secondly, there is the motif of the Orient as insinuating danger. Rationality is undermined by Eastern excesses, those mysteriously attractive opposites to what seem to be normal values. The difference separating East from West is symbolized by the sternness with which, at first, Pentheus rejects the hysterical bacchantes. When later he himself becomes a bacchant, he is destroyed not so much for having given in to Dionysus as for having incorrectly assessed Dionysus's menace in the first place. The lesson that Euripides intends is dramatized by the presence in the play of Cadmus and Tiresias, knowledgeable older men who realize that 'sovereignty' alone does not rule men; there is such a thing as judgment, they say, which means sizing up correctly the force of alien powers and expertly coming to terms with them. Hereafter Oriental mysteries will be taken seriously, not least because they challenge the rational Western mind to new exercises of its enduring ambition and power.

But one big division, as between West and Orient, leads to other smaller ones, especially as the normal enterprises of civilization provoke such outgoing activities as travel, conquest, new experiences. In classical Greece and Rome geographers, historians, public figures like Caesar, orators, and poets added to the fund of taxonomic lore separating races, regions, nations, and minds from each other; much of that was self-serving, and existed to prove that Romans and Greeks were superior to other kinds of people. But concern with the Orient had its own tradition of classification and hierarchy. From at least the second century B.C. on, it was lost on no traveler or eastward-looking and ambitious Western potentate that Herodotus – historian, traveler, inexhaustibly curious chronicler – and Alexander – king warrior, scientific conqueror – had been in the Orient before. The Orient was therefore subdivided into realms previously known, visited, conquered, by Herodotus and Alexander as well as their epigones, and those realms not previously known, visited, conquered. Christianity completed the setting up of main intra-Oriental spheres: there was a Near Orient and a Far Orient, a familiar Orient, which René Grousset calls 'l'empire du Levant,' and a novel Orient. The Orient therefore alternated in the mind's geography between being an Old World to which one returned, as to Eden or Paradise, there to set up a new version of the old, and being a wholly new place to which one came as Columbus came to America, in order to set up a New World (although, ironically, Columbus himself thought that he discovered a new part of the Old World). Certainly neither of these Orients was purely one thing or the other: it is their vacillations, their tempting suggestiveness, their capacity for entertaining and confusing the mind, that are interesting.

Consider how the Orient, and in particular the Near Orient, became known in the West as its great complementary opposite since antiquity. There were the Bible and the rise of Christianity; there were travelers like Marco Polo who charted the trade routes and patterned a regulated system of commercial exchange, and after him Lodovico di Varthema and Pietro della Valle; there were fabulists like Mandeville; there were the redoubtable conquering Eastern movements, principally Islam, of course; there were the militant pilgrims, chiefly the Crusaders. Altogether an internally structured archive is built up from the literature that belongs to these experiences. Out of this comes a restricted number of typical encapsulations: the journey, the history, the fable, the stereotype, the polemical confrontation. These are the lenses through which the Orient is experienced, and they shape the language, perception, and form of the encounter between East and West. What gives the immense number of encounters some unity, however, is the vacillation I was speaking about earlier. Something patently foreign and distant acquires, for one reason or another, a status more rather than less familiar. One tends to stop judging things either as completely novel or as completely well known; a new median category emerges, a category that allows one to see new things, things seen for the first time, as versions of a previously known thing. In essence such a category is not so much a way of receiving new information as it is a method of controlling what seems to be a threat to some established view of things. If the mind must suddenly deal with what it takes to be a radically new form of life – as Islam appeared to Europe in the early Middle Ages – the response on the whole is conservative and defensive. Islam is judged to be a fraudulent new version of some previous experience, in this case Christianity. The threat is muted, familiar values impose themselves, and in the end the mind reduces the pressure upon it by accommodating things to itself as either 'original' or 'repetitious.' Islam thereafter is 'handled': its novelty and its suggestiveness are brought under control so that relatively nuanced discriminations are now made that would have been impossible had the raw novelty of Islam been left unattended. The Orient at large, therefore, vacillates between the West's contempt for what is familiar and its shivers of delight in – or fear of – novelty.

Yet where Islam was concerned, European fear, if not always respect, was in order. After Mohammed's death in 632, the military and later the cultural and religious hegemony of Islam grew enormously. First Persia, Syria, and Egypt, then Turkey, then North Africa fell to the Muslim armies; in the eighth and ninth centuries Spain, Sicily, and parts of France were conquered. By the thirteenth and fourteenth centuries Islam ruled as far east as India, Indonesia, and China. And to this extraordinary assault Europe could respond with very little except fear and a kind of awe. Christian authors witnessing the Islamic conquests had scant interest in the learning, high culture, and frequent magnificence of the Muslims, who were, as Gibbon said, 'coeval with the darkest and most slothful period of European annals.' (But with some satisfaction he added, 'since the sum of science has risen in the West, it should seem that the Oriental studies have languished and declined.') What Christians typically felt about the Eastern armies was that they had 'all the appearance of a swarm of bees, but with a heavy hand ... they devastated everything': so wrote Erchembert, a cleric in Monte Cassino in the eleventh century.

Not for nothing did Islam come to symbolize terror, devastation, the demonic, hordes of hated barbarians. For Europe, Islam was a lasting trauma. Until the end of the seventeenth century the 'Ottoman peril' lurked alongside Europe to represent for the whole of Christian civilization a constant danger, and in time European civilization incorporated that peril and its lore, its great events, figures, virtues, and vices, as something woven into the fabric of life. In Renaissance England alone, as Samuel Chew recounts in his classic study *The Crescent and the Rose*, 'a man of average education and intelligence' had at his fingertips, and could watch on the London stage, a relatively large number of detailed events in the history of Ottoman Islam and its encroachments upon Christian Europe. The point is that what remained current about Islam was some necessarily diminished version of those great dangerous forces that it symbolized for Europe. Like Walter Scott's Saracens, the European representation of the Muslim, Ottoman, or Arab was always a way of controlling the redoubtable Orient, and to a certain extent the same is true of the methods of contemporary learned Orientalists, whose subject is not so much the East itself as the East made known, and therefore less fearsome, to the Western reading public.

From *Orientalism* (1978); extract from Penguin edn (1985), pp. 57–60.

 # Discussion

IVAN HANNAFORD

This material (from a history of ideas background) certainly often seems relevant to aspects of the representation of both Othello and Caliban. I note the potential relevance of the following:

Othello:

the marvellous and fabulous oppositions   Anthropophagi   black/white

blackness as 'unnaturalness'   Africans as enchanters   'witchcraft, sorcery and humoral disposition'

Caliban:

the marvellous and fabulous   blackness as 'blot', 'infection'

'they know neither God nor good order'   'all studies and letters of humanitie they refuse'

'so as to induce their barbarous natures to a liking and mutuall societie with us'

'witchcraft, sorcery and humoral disposition'   'an unnatural act encouraged by an evil spirit'.

However, though there seem to be these many promising links, their application requires considerable further work. I will try to summarise the shape of Hannaford's account and then to suggest some possible ways of using this knowledge.

Hannaford's project is evidently to trace the roots of Western ideas of race and to observe developments within those ideas. Just as *Othello* and *The Tempest* draw on knowledge and accounts of contemporary travellers, so too here travel narratives are selected as key sources for investigating how ideas of race were conceived.

The first part of the passage, with its discussion of what makes a society 'civilised', has points of contact with both Caliban and Othello. Sixteenth-century writers, it is said, conceived of civilised societies as having authentic histories, attested by particular kinds of sources. Peoples without these records could not be societies in any proper sense. Thus the Irish, the Lapps and the Finns are all classed by the travel writer Hakluyt as illiterate, godless and utterly unsocialised: 'they neither know God nor good order', 'all studies and letters of humanitie they refuse'. Hannaford also suggests that there is a parallel between the conditions for the legitimacy of states and the legitimacy of authentic narrative. Uncivil peoples have no true history, untrue history relies on 'descriptions of marvellous and fabulous origins'. This seems to lead to a curious contradiction at the heart of sixteenth-century categorisations of barbarous/uncivilised. The barbarous is that which has no true history – yet Europeans are strongly inclined always to explain 'barbarous' peoples precisely as 'marvellous and fabulous'. Hence while belief in magic was a sign of the uncivilised, travellers showed a great disposition to make 'allusions to witchcraft and sorcierie'.

Indeed, despite this apparent urge for 'natural' explanations, Hannaford moves on to say that a dominant way of accounting for racial difference had strong tinges of the fabulous in it; hence, according to Best's *True Discourse*, Africans were precisely banished to Africa to live as 'idolators, witches ... and enchanters'.

It strikes me that in the chart above of promising links, there are a number of potential similarities between the representation of Othello and Caliban which my earlier discussion of the two did not bring out. This in itself may suggest that despite the great differences in the representations of these two figures, there are also overarching assumptions about their racial identity. Both some Venetians (Brabantio) and Prospero and Miranda expect a link between blackness and witchcraft. And perhaps all of the Venetians as well as Prospero and Miranda do seem to operate on the basis of a distinction between legitimate and barbarous knowledge, between legitimate genealogies and fabulous and unnatural origins. Thus in *The Tempest* we can say that the European colonists worked in a textbook manner when they 'strok'dst, and mad'st much' of Caliban in order to 'induce' his barbarous nature 'to a liking a mutuall societie with us'. They try to change Caliban from his asocial, pre-linguistic state to that of a well-ordered subject, who knows his place in the cosmos and can express his purposes in language. Similarly, in *Othello*, the Senate precisely sees the case of Brabantio and Othello in terms of a distinction between marvellous and unnatural explanations and natural, rational ones; the Duke observes of Brabantio's stories of bewitchment: 'To vouch this is no proof', and the Senator invites Othello to provide a rational account: 'Othello, speak / ... Came it by request and such fair question / As soul to soul affordeth?' Perhaps Othello's powers of persuasion make his stories assume the status of 'legitimate histories', even though they refer to 'Anthrophaphagi, and men whose heads / Do grow beneath their shoulders'?[50] Indeed, perhaps *Othello* is centred on questions of what makes a narrative a legitimate or persuasive one. Othello can persuade his hearers that his accounts of his heroic past are true; Iago can persuade Roderigo that Desdemona may soon love him, and Othello that Cassio is a drunkard and Desdemona unfaithful. But what distinguishes a legitimate narrative from a fabulous one? As Hannaford's account of the underpinning assumptions about the civilised/uncivilised suggests, the distinction between the fabulous and the natural is not always easy to maintain.

I certainly found Hannaford's history of the idea of race illuminating for these two texts – it suggested interpretations which I would not otherwise have seen, and ways of seeing the two plays together in ways which would not have occurred to me. At the same time, knowledge of these sixteenth-century ideas certainly does not in one bold swoop explain those plays. On the contrary, Hannaford's account seems to me precisely to bring out a range of overlapping, contradictory narratives of race. Critical skills of interpretation allow us to use that knowledge to explore the ways in which those Shakespearean texts handle the complexity of relationships between the familiar and the exotic, that which is imagined as evident and that which is imagined as fabulous. □

▶️ Your Discussion of Edward Said

☐

> Read the following group of passages about slavery and
> Afro-American literature. How do they represent racial difference,
> 'blackness'; and 'whiteness'? (I will offer some discussion of the first
> passage, but leave you to work through your own responses to the
> remaining three passages.)

Narrative of the Life of George Frederick Douglass (1845)

CHAPTER I.

I was born in Tuckahoe, near Hillsborough, and about twelve miles from Easton,
in Talbot county, Maryland. I have no accurate knowledge of my age, never
having seen any authentic record containing it. By far the larger part of the
slaves know as little of their ages as horses know of theirs, and it is the wish of
most masters within my knowledge to keep their slaves thus ignorant. I do not
remember to have ever met a slave who could tell of his birthday. They seldom
come nearer to it than planting-time, harvest-time, cherry-time, spring-time, or
fall-time. A want of information concerning my own was a source of unhappi-
ness to me even during childhood. The white children could tell their ages. I
could not tell why I ought to be deprived of the same privilege. I was not
allowed to make any inquiries of my master concerning it. He deemed all such
inquiries on the part of a slave improper and impertinent, and evidence of a
restless spirit. The nearest estimate I can give makes me now between
twenty-seven and twenty-eight years of age. I come to this, from hearing my
master say, some time during 1835, I was about seventeen years old.

My mother was named Harriet Bailey. She was the daughter of Isaac and
Betsey Bailey, both colored, and quite dark. My mother was of a darker complexion than either my grandmother or grandfather.

My father was a white man. He was admitted to be such by all I ever heard
speak of my parentage. The opinion was also whispered that my master was my
father; but of the correctness of this opinion, I know nothing; the means of
knowing was withheld from me. My mother and I were separated when I was
but an infant – before I knew her as my mother. It is a common custom, in the
part of Maryland from which I ran away, to part children from their mothers at
a very early age. Frequently, before the child has reached its twelfth month, its
mother is taken from it, and hired out on some farm a considerable distance off,
and the child is placed under the care of an old woman, too old for field labor.
For what this separation is done, I do not know, unless it be to hinder the development of the child's affection toward its mother, and to blunt and destroy the
natural affection of the mother for the child. This is the inevitable result.

I never saw my mother, to know her as such, more than four or five times in my life; and each of those times was very short in duration, and at night. She was hired by a Mr. Stewart, who lived about twelve miles from my home. She made her journeys to see me in the night, travelling the whole distance on foot, after the performance of her day's work. She was a field hand, and a whipping is the penalty of not being in the field at sunrise, unless a slave has special permission from his or her master to the contrary – a permission which they seldom get, and one that gives to him that gives it the proud name of being a kind master. I do not recollect of ever seeing my mother by the light of day. She was with me in the night. She would lie down with me, and get me to sleep, but long before I waked she was gone. Very little communication ever took place between us. Death soon ended what little we could have while she lived, and with it her hardships and suffering. She died when I was about seven years old, on one of my master's farms, near Lee's Mill. I was not allowed to be present during her illness, at her death, or burial. She was gone long before I knew any thing about it. Never having enjoyed, to any considerable extent, her soothing presence, her tender and watchful care, I received the tidings of her death with much the same emotions I should have probably felt at the death of a stranger.

Called thus suddenly away, she left me without the slightest intimation of who my father was. The whisper that my master was my father, may or may not be true; and, true or false, it is of but little consequence to my purpose whilst the fact remains, in all its glaring odiousness, that slaveholders have ordained, and by law established, that the children of slave women shall in all cases follow the condition of their mothers; and this is done too obviously to administer to their own lusts, and make a gratification of their wicked desires profitable as well as pleasurable; for by this cunning arrangement, the slaveholder, in cases not a few, sustains to his slaves the double relation of master and father.

I know of such cases; and it is worthy of remark that such slaves invariably suffer greater hardships, and have more to contend with, than others. They are, in the first place, a constant offence to their mistress. She is ever disposed to find fault with them; they can seldom do any thing to please her; she is never better pleased than when she sees them under the lash, especially when she suspects her husband of showing to his mulatto children favors which he withholds from his black slaves. The master is frequently compelled to sell this class of his slaves, out of deference to the feelings of his white wife; and, cruel as the deed may strike any one to be, for a man to sell his own children to human flesh-mongers, it is often the dictate of humanity for him to do so; for, unless he does this, he must not only whip them himself, but must stand by and see one white son tie up his brother, of but few shades darker complexion than himself, and ply the gory lash to his naked back; and if he lisp one word of disapproval, it is set down to his parental partiality, and only makes a bad matter worse, both for himself and the slave whom he would protect and defend.

Every year brings with it multitudes of this class of slaves. It was doubtless in consequence of a knowledge of this fact, that one great statesman of the south predicted the downfall of slavery by the inevitable laws of population. Whether this prophecy is ever fulfilled or not, it is nevertheless plain that a very different-looking class of people are springing up at the south, and are now held in slavery, from those originally brought to this country from

Africa; and if their increase will do no other good, it will do away the force of the argument, that God cursed Ham, and therefore American slavery is right. If the lineal descendants of Ham are alone to be scripturally enslaved, it is certain that slavery at the south must soon become unscriptural; for thousands are ushered into the world, annually, who, like myself, owe their existence to white fathers, and those fathers most frequently their own masters.

From the Penguin edn (1986), ch. 1, pp. 47–51.[51]

Harriet Beecher Stowe, *Uncle Tom's Cabin* (1852)

CHAPTER I

In Which the Reader Is Introduced to a Man of Humanity

Late in the afternoon of a chilly day in February, two gentlemen were sitting alone over their wine, in a well-furnished dining parlor, in the town of P——, in Kentucky. There were no servants present, and the gentlemen, with chairs closely approaching, seemed to be discussing some subject with great earnestness.

For convenience sake, we have said, hitherto, two *gentlemen*. One of the parties, however, when critically examined, did not seem, strictly speaking, to come under the species. He was a short, thick-set man, with coarse, commonplace features, and that swaggering air of pretension which marks a low man who is trying to elbow his way upward in the world. He was much over-dressed, in a gaudy vest of many colors, a blue neckerchief, bedropped gayly with yellow spots, and arranged with a flaunting tie, quite in keeping with the general air of the man. His hands, large and coarse, were plentifully bedecked with rings; and he wore a heavy gold watch-chain, with a bundle of seals of portentous size, and a great variety of colors, attached to it, – which, in the ardor of conversation, he was in the habit of flourishing and jingling with evident satisfaction. His conversation was in free and easy defiance of Murray's Grammar, and was garnished at convenient intervals with various profane expressions, which not even the desire to be graphic in our account shall induce us to transcribe.

His companion, Mr. Shelby, had the appearance of a gentleman; and the arrangements of the house, and the general air of the housekeeping, indicated easy, and even opulent circumstances. As we before stated, the two were in the midst of an earnest conversation.

'That is the way I should arrange the matter,' said Mr. Shelby.

'I can't make trade that way – I positively can't, Mr. Shelby,' said the other, holding up a glass of wine between his eye and the light.

'Why, the fact is, Haley, Tom is an uncommon fellow; he is certainly worth that sum anywhere, – steady, honest, capable, manages my whole farm like a clock.'

'You mean honest, as niggers go,' said Haley, helping himself to a glass of brandy.

'No; I mean, really, Tom is a good, steady, sensible, pious fellow. He got religion at a camp-meeting, four years ago; and I believe he really *did* get it. I've trusted him, since then, with everything I have – money, house, horses, – and let him come and go round the country; and I always found him true and square in everything.'

'Some folks don't believe there is pious niggers Shelby,' said Haley, with a candid flourish of his hand, 'but *I do*. I had a fellow, now, in this yer last lot I took to Orleans – 't was as good as a meetin, now, really, to hear that critter pray; and he was quite gentle and quiet like. He fetched me a good sum, too, for I bought him cheap of a man that was 'bliged to sell out; so I realized six hundred on him. Yes, I consider religion a valeyable thing in a nigger, when it's the genuine article, and no mistake.'

'Well, Tom's got the real article, if ever a fellow had,' rejoined the other. 'Why, last fall, I let him go to Cincinnati alone, to do business for me, and bring home five hundred dollars. "Tom," says I to him, "I trust you, because I think you're a Christian – I know you wouldn't cheat." Tom comes back, sure enough; I knew he would. Some low fellows, they say, said to him – "Tom, why don't you make tracks for Canada?" "Ah, master trusted me, and I couldn't," – they told me about it. I am sorry to part with Tom, I must say. You ought to let him cover the whole balance of the debt; and you would, Haley, if you had any conscience.'

'Well, I've got just as much conscience as any man in business can afford to keep, – just a little, you know, to swear by, as 't were,' said the trader, jocularly; 'and, then, I'm ready to do anything in reason to 'blige friends; but this yer, you see, is a leetle too hard on a fellow – a leetle too hard.' The trader sighed contemplatively, and poured out some more brandy.

'Well, then, Haley, how will you trade?' said Mr. Shelby, after an uneasy interval of silence.

'Well, haven't you a boy or gal that you could throw in with Tom?'

'Hum! – none that I could well spare; to tell the truth, it's only hard necessity makes me willing to sell at all. I don't like parting with any of my hands, that's a fact.'

Here the door opened, and a small quadroon boy, between four and five years of age, entered the room. There was something in his appearance remarkably beautiful and engaging. His black hair, fine as floss silk, hung in glossy curls about his round, dimpled face, while a pair of large dark eyes, full of fire and softness, looked out from beneath the rich, long lashes, as he peered curiously into the apartment. A gay robe of scarlet and yellow plaid, carefully made and neatly fitted, set off to advantage the dark and rich style of his beauty; and a certain comic air of assurance, blended with bashfulness, showed that he had been not unused to being petted and noticed by his master.

'Hulloa, Jim Crow!' said Mr. Shelby, whistling, and snapping a bunch of raisins towards him, 'pick that up, now!'

The child scampered, with all his little strength, after the prize, while his master laughed.

'Come here, Jim Crow,' said he. The child came up, and the master patted the curly head, and chucked him under the chin.

'Now, Jim, show this gentleman how you can dance and sing.' The boy commenced one of those wild, grotesque songs common among the negroes, in a rich, clear voice, accompanying his singing with many comic evolutions of the hands, feet, and whole body, all in perfect time to the music.

'Bravo!' said Haley, throwing him a quarter of an orange.

'Now, Jim, walk like old Uncle Cudjoe, when he has the rheumatism,' said his master.

Instantly the flexible limbs of the child assumed the appearance of deformity and distortion, as, with his back humped up, and his master's stick in his hand, he hobbled about the room, his childish face drawn into a doleful pucker, and spitting from right to left, in imitation of an old man.

Both gentlemen laughed uproariously.

'Now, Jim,' said his master, 'show us how old Elder Robbins leads the psalm.' The boy drew his chubby face down to a formidable length, and commenced toning a psalm tune through his nose, with imperturbable gravity.

'Hurrah! bravo! what a young 'un!' said Haley; 'that chap's a case, I'll promise. Tell you what,' said he, suddenly clapping his hand on Mr. Shelby's shoulder, 'fling in that chap, and I'll settle the business – I will. Come, now, if that ain't doing the thing up about the rightest!'

At this moment, the door was pushed gently open, and a young quadroon woman, apparently about twenty-five, entered the room.

There needed only a glance from the child to her, to identify her as its mother. There was the same rich, full, dark eye, with its long lashes; the same ripples of silky black hair. The brown of her complexion gave way on the cheek to a perceptible flush, which deepened as she saw the gaze of the strange man fixed upon her in bold and undisguised admiration. Her dress was of the neatest possible fit, and set off to advantage her finely moulded shape; – a delicately formed hand and a trim foot and ankle were items of appearance that did not escape the quick eye of the trader, well used to run up at a glance the points of a fine female article.

'Well, Eliza?' said her master, as she stopped and looked hesitatingly at him.

'I was looking for Harry, please, sir;' and the boy bounded toward her, showing his spoils, which he had gathered in the skirt of his robe.

'Well, take him away then,' said Mr. Shelby; and hastily she withdrew, carrying the child on her arm.

'By Jupiter,' said the trader, turning to him in admiration, 'there's an article, now! You might make your fortune on that ar gal in Orleans, any day. I've seen over a thousand, in my day, paid down for gals not a bit handsomer.'

'I don't want to make my fortune on her,' said Mr. Shelby, dryly; and, seeking to turn the conversation, he uncorked a bottle of fresh wine, and asked his companion's opinion of it.

'Capital, sir, – first chop!' said the trader; then turning, and slapping his hand familiarly on Shelby's shoulder, he added – …

From the Penguin edn (1995), pp. 41–5.

Henry Louis Gates, Jr, 'Frederick Douglass and the Language of the Self'

I

By the end of 1894, Frederick Douglass had begun to prepare for his death. Unbowed and energetic even to the last, Douglass had, however, apparently reconciled himself to 'live and rejoice,' as he put it in 1881, to occupy with dignity and gravity that peculiar role conferred upon him by friend and foe, black countryman and white, contemporary and disciple alike: he was 'The Representative Colored Man of the United States.' Despite the unassailable respect he commanded throughout the country, one bit of common knowledge had never been Douglass's to possess, and, as Peter Walker movingly recounts it, the final entry in his *Diary* suggests that it haunted him to death.

On a March 1894 evening, just less than a year before he died, Frederick Douglass left his home at Anacostia and boarded a train for the brief ride from Washington to Baltimore. At Baltimore, Douglass went directly to the home of a physician, Dr. Thomas Edward Sears. After a carefully calculated but leisurely conversation, during which Douglass put to Dr. Sears a series of specifically formulated questions, Douglass returned by train to Washington and then by coach to Anacostia Heights. Early the next morning, he went to his study, took out his *Diary*, and wrote as that day's entry an account of his trip to Baltimore. This was to be the final entry in Douglass's *Diary*. In the final months remaining to him, no other event moved Douglass sufficiently to record another entry in his little *Diary*. Indeed, no other event had moved Douglass to make an entry since he had made an apparently hurried note in the *Diary* he was at London six years earlier. Douglass's visit with Dr. Sears can without hyperbole be called a mission. It was not that these two men bore so very much in common, nor that through their visit they sought to cement a friendship about to end. Rather, Sears, a descendant of Douglass's old master, would be the last contact Douglass was to have with the family that had once owned him. More important, Sears had some information about his slave past that Douglass wanted, and all his self-conscious life Douglass had pursued passionately all concrete information about his lost, or hidden, past.

Douglass's concern for his lost past, a past far beyond the reach of memory and recall, a concern that took him to the home of the Baltimore physician, is, as Walker demonstrates, one of the profoundly subtle yet fundamentally unifying themes in his life. His day's visit with Dr. Sears, in fact, was one of the most revealing and significant acts of Douglass's life. And that this pregnant event remains unmentioned by all of Douglass's biographers is significant in an analysis of the life of Frederick Douglass.

What sort of information about his own past had Douglass been seeking from Dr. Sears that day in March of 1894? What sort of private, compelling quest could have prevailed upon a great statesman, so honored and praised, to make such an odd pilgrimage so near to his own death? Surely it was not to reminisce with Sears about the good old days of slavery, back on Thomas and Lucretia Auld's plantation in Maryland. In Dr. Thomas Edward Sears, Douglass so painfully knew, resided his last opportunity to ascertain once and for all that crucial piece of data about his own origins which had been systematically denied to Douglass and the largest part of all other black slaves, the absence or presence of which marked the terrible terrain that separated the free person from the slave, and the possession of which alone could enable even a 'slave' of Douglass's bearing to recapture and master his own elusive past. Douglass had been in search of his birthdate, his lack of certainty about which he called in his *Diary* entry 'a serious trouble.'

A sense of self as we have defined it in the West since the Enlightenment turns in part upon written records. Most fundamentally, we mark a human being's existence by his or her birth and death dates, engraved in granite on every tombstone. Our idea of the self, it is fair to argue, is as inextricably interwoven with our ideas of time as it is with uses of language. In antebellum America, it was the deprivation of time in the life of the slave that first signaled his or her status as a piece of property. Slavery's time was delineated by memory and memory alone. One's sense of one's existence, therefore, depended upon memory. It was memory, above all else, that gave a shape to being itself. What a brilliant substructure of the system of slavery! For the dependence upon memory made the slave, first and foremost, a slave to himself or herself, a prisoner of his or her own power of recall. Within such a time machine, as it were, not only had the slave no fixed reference points, but also his or her own past could exist only as memory without support, as the text without footnotes, as the clock without two hands. Within such a tyrannical concept of time, the slave had no past beyond memory; the slave had lived at no time past the point of recollection.

...of such subtle yet poignant import is this imposed system of time that Douglass draws upon it in the first paragraph of the first of his three autobiographies as the very first evidence of his personal status as a slave. We recall that although Douglass knows where he was born (in Tuckahoe, near Hillsborough, about twelve miles from Easton, in Talbot County, Maryland), his date of birth is not for him to know. A 'slave' was he or she who, most literally, stood outside of time. To the end of his life, the mystery of his birth remained for Douglass what he called 'a serious trouble' and helps us to understand why a man in his seventy-sixth year took the trouble to mount one final attempt to obtain facts about his existence. The skeletal facts of Douglass's journal entry, as Peter Walker cites it, suggest the pathos of the unconsummated quest:

> I called yesterday while in Baltimore...upon Dr. Thomas Edward Sears, a grandson of Thomas and Lucretia Auld and learned the following facts:
>   Capt. Thomas Auld, was born 1795
>   Amanda Auld, his daughter was born Jan. 28, 1826
>   Thomas, son of Hugh and Sophia Auld was born Jan. 1824
>   Capt. Aaron Anthony, Died Nov. 14, 1823.

...Indeed, it is fair to say that Douglass, as he aged, increasingly subordinated a conception of self in his autobiographies to an embodiment of an ideology and a social ideal. As Paul Laurence Dunbar writes in 'Frederick Douglass,' it was 'For [Ethiopia] his voice, a fearless clarion, rung...'

> When men maligned him, and their torrent wrath
>   In furious imprecations o'er him broke,
> He kept his counsel as he kept his path;
>   'Twas for his race, not for himself he spoke.

But the writing of blacks had, since the European Renaissance and the Enlightenment, always assumed larger ideological and social implications than the mere rendering of a life. Perhaps the most remarkable aspect of the Enlightenment is that, by the middle of the eighteenth century, ethnocentrism and logocentrism had been forged together into one irresistible weapon drawn upon to justify the enslavement of the African. The absence and presence of writing, of a collective black voice that could in some sense be overheard, were drawn upon by European philosophers to deprive African slaves of their humanity.

For Hegel, as we have seen, cast into silence by their own loss or absence of voice, Africans could have no history, no meaningful text of blackness itself, since they had no true self-consciousness, no power to present or represent this black and terrible self. Being was here determined as presence, and presence in turn as consciousness. There could be no presence of Africans in history without this power of representation. Possessing no true self-consciousness, as signified by the absence of a voice, and therefore no history, for Hegel blacks lay veiled in a shroud of silence, invisible not because they had no face, but rather because they had no voice. Voice, after all, presupposes a face. That alone which separates the subject from the object is, for Hegel, the absence or presence of the voice, the phenomenological voice; the blackness of invisibility is the blackness of this silence. Without a voice, the African is absent, or defaced, from history. Literacy, in this grand sense, was a figure used to conjure with by the Enlightened philosophers of Europe, at the African's expense. 'The Dream of Reason,' Goya inscribed as a rubric on his *Caprichos*, 'breeds monsters.' As Diderot wrote of Samuel Richardson upon reading *Clarissa*, 'It is he [the writer] who carries the torch to the back of the cave.... He blows upon the glorious phantom who presents himself at the entrance of the cave; and the hideous Moor whom he was masking reveals himself.'

As a direct result of this curious, arbitrary critique, of which Hegel's and Diderot's are only emblems, abolitionists and ex-slaves conspired to break this resounding black silence by publishing the narratives of the ex-slaves. And this written language of the ex-slave, to borrow an idea from Jacques Lacan, 'signified for *someone*' even before it signified *something*. For, above all else, every public spoken and written utterance of the ex-slaves was written and published for an essentially hostile auditor or interlocutor, the white abolitionist or the white slaveholder, both of whom imposed a meaning upon the discourse of the black subject. Again to quote Lacan, what seems to be at work in this complex relationship between subject and interlocutor is that 'the subject progresses only by whatever integration he attains of his [particular] position in the universal: technically by the projection of his past into a discourse in the process of becoming.' To become subjects, as it were, black ex-slaves had to demonstrate their language-using capacity before they could become social and historical entities. In short, slaves could inscribe their selves only in language. Ironically, this selfsame notion of people as subjects and as language, which Europeans and Americans used to displace one sort of enslavement of the blacks for another sort of enslavement, is the very idea that lay at the core of the major innovations of post-structural analysis in contemporary literary theory....

Long after the issues for which he struggled so ardently have become primarily the concern of the historian, Frederick Douglass will continue to be read and reread. And surely this must be the literary critic's final judgment of Frederick Douglass: that he was Representative Man because he was Rhetorical Man, black master of the verbal arts. Douglass is our clearest example of the will to power as the will to write. The act of writing for the slave constituted the act of creating a public, historical self, not only the self of the individual author but also the self, as it were, of the race. Indeed, in part because of Douglass's literary successes, blacks in general compensated to Hegel and his less able disciples for the absence of a collective written history by writing a remarkable number of individual histories, which taken together begin to assume the features of a communal, collective tale. In literacy was power; as Ishamel Reed puts it in his satirical novel about slavery, *Flight to Canada*, the slave who was the first to read and the first to write was the first slave to run away. And as Stepto perceptively demonstrates, the correlation of freedom with literacy not only became the central trope of the slave narratives, but it also formed a mythical matrix out of which subsequent black narrative forms developed. For the critic, Frederick Douglass does not yet exist as a three-dimensional person; rather, he exists as a rhetorical strategy primarily, as an open-ended system of rhetorical figures and tropes.

From Henry Louis Gates, Jr, *Figures in Black*: *Words, Signs and the 'Racial' Self* (Oxford, 1987), pp. 90–100, 104–6, 108.

Amiri Barraka, 'It's Nation Time' (1970)

It's Nation Time

Time to get
together
time to be one strong fast black energy space
       one pulsating positive magnetism, rising
time to get up and
be
come
be
come, time to
     be come
     time to
     get up be come
     black genius rise in spirit muscle
     sun man get up rise heart of universes to be
future of the world
the black man is the future of the world
be come
rise up
future of the black genius spirit reality
     move
     from crushed roach back
     from dead snake head
     from wig funeral in slowmotion
     from dancing teeth and coward tip
     from jibberjabber patme boss patme smmich
when the brothers strike niggers come out

come out niggers
when the brothers take over the school
help niggers
come out niggers
all niggers negroes must change up
come together in unity unify
for nation time
it's nation time ...

        Boom
        Booom
        BOOOM
        Boom
        Dadadadadadadadadadad
        Boom
        Boom
        Boom
        Boom
        Dadadadad adadadad
                Hey aheee   (soft)
                Hey ahheee   (loud)
        Boom
        Boom
        Boom

sing a get up time to nationfy
singaa miracle fire light
sing a airplane invisibility for the jesus niggers come from the
   grave
for the jesus niggers dead in the cave, rose up, passt jewjuice
on shadow world
raise up christ nigger
Christ was black
kirishna was black shango was black
     black jesus nigger come out and strike
        come out and strike boom boom
             Heyahheeee come out
       strike close ford
         close prudentiatl burn the plicies
        tear glasses off dead stature puppets even thos
         they imitate life
            Shango budda black
          hermes rasis black
          moses krishna
                black
when the brothers wanna stop animals
come out niggers come out
come out niggers niggers niggers come out
help us stop the devil
help us build a new world

niggers come out, brothers are we
   with you and your sons your daughters are ours

and we are the same, all the blackness from one black allah
          when the world is clear you'll be with us
                 come out niggers come out
                   come out niggers come out
It's nation time eye ime
        it's nation ti eye ime
                          chant with bells and drum
                          its nation time

It's nation time, get up santa claus   (repeat)
   it's nation time, build it
      get up muffet dragger
        get up rastus for real to be rasta farari
          ras jua
            get up got here bow
                       It's Nation
                       Time!

From *The Norton Anthology of Poetry*, 3rd edn (New York and London (1983),
p. 1358.

▶ Discussion

George Frederick Douglass's autobiographical narrative opens with a contrast which arises, as he emphasises strongly, purely from a culture which
bases itself on an idea of racial inequality. Like any autobiography, this one
opens with an account of the narrator's birth. But Douglass's position as
(once) a slave is there even at that first moment of his life. He knows that
he was born, he knows where he was born, but he does not know when he
was born. His story can have no proper beginning, because the institutions
of slavery denied the simple knowledge of the year, month, and day of
his birth.

This is specifically a sign of racial identity in that culture: 'the white
children could tell their ages'. It is particularly disruptive to the story
Douglass can tell of himself, because he knows that the knowledge did
exist. It is not that it has been forgotten, but that his 'master' – and the
other slave-owners – deliberately suppressed that knowledge: 'he deemed
all such enquiries improper and impertinent'. While for the rest of the narrative of his life, Douglass can rely on his memory, he cannot, of course,
remember the time of his birth. For this first moment of his story he needs
a witness, a genealogy, someone else to rely upon. And since his mother is
taken away, and his 'master' deliberately will not tell him, the knowledge
is irrecoverable: 'the means of knowing was withheld from me'. This deliberate prevention of knowledge was presumably intended to reinforce the
inequality which the owners assert to be inevitable: an inequality between
levels of knowledge and the legitimacy of self-identity.

However, despite this vehemently policed gulf between what a
white child can know and what a black slave child can know, Douglass

immediately moves on to show that such 'racial' difference is, indeed, constructed rather than absolute: white and black are different only in the terms the owners assert through their positions of power. Thus, if he cannot know when he was born, and cannot know either his mother or his father with any intimacy, he can know for certain that his 'father was a white man'. This common occurrence of children of mixed race undermines in a whole range of ways the 'official' distinction between black/white, both literally and symbolically.

Firstly, Douglas can make the literal point that race is far from an unchanging characteristic, since, through imposed liaisons between owners and slaves, the racial character of American slaves has changed: it is 'plain that a very different looking class of people are springing up in the south'. It might be said, indeed, that racial difference is in this sense not a matter of race at all, but of brutal power. The owners will cross race lines as they wish, but can still forbid those on the other side of that line from doing likewise. As Douglass argues, if race really were an adequate reason for slavery, its force has been utterly undercut by the fact that many in the South are no longer the 'lineal descendants of Ham', but of the other sons of Noah.

Together with this literal, yet hypocritically denied, blurring of racial differences, comes a symbolic undermining. Clearly, the assertions of difference which the owners and their culture asserted do not sustain themselves in the light of this mixing of races; thus oppositions such as the following are implausible measured against the situation Douglass describes:

Christian/godless   civilised/barbarous   virtuous/libidinal
honest/dishonest   animal-like/supreme crown of creation.

Moreover, one further – and vital – distinction is caught up, and undermined by this narrative of a life. The importance which the 'masters' and Douglass himself place on the knowledge of one's own time of birth is part of a central distinction, which we have already met in a sixteenth-century form, when discussing Ivan Hannaford's applicability to the representation of Othello and Caliban. The owners will not let the slaves have access to this knowledge of their own origins because that would give them a 'legitimate genealogy', a personal point of origin unique to each, and based in a literate (and numerate) culture. The owners want slaves 'to know as little of their ages as horses know of theirs'. If slaves know their genealogy and can construct authentic, literate[52] knowledge of themselves, then they will have crossed into 'civilisation' from their 'natural' (enforced) state of barbarism.[53]

However, at the same time as Frederick Douglass records this loss, he also records that it can be – it has been – overcome. Despite this attempt to prevent the formation of 'proper' self-identity and bar access to literacy, he, a former slave, can write *The Life of George Frederick Douglass*, a book acknowledged in his lifetime as not only a supreme piece of personal testimony, but also a great literary achievement. The slave who could not be allowed his own birthdate has the victory of being able to write and

expose the ignorance and malice of the institution of slavery, the owners of
slaves and the assumptions of European ideas of racial difference through
a sophisticated and widely published narrative. □

▶ **Your Discussions**

□

> ◆ Read the following group of texts about British identities. What range
> of narratives of Britishness/Englishness do they represent? Is there any
> common core? (I will provide some discussion for the first text, but
> then leave you to work through the remainder and come to a general
> sense of the range of narratives.)

Rudyard Kipling, 'Puck's Song' (1907)

PUCK'S SONG

(Enlarged from 'Puck of Pook's Hill')

See you the ferny ride that steals
Into the oak-woods far?
O that was whence they hewed the keels
That rolled to Trafalgar.

And mark you where the ivy clings
To Bayham's mouldering walls?
O there we cast the stout railings
That stand around St. Paul's.

See you the dimpled track that runs
All hollow through the wheat?
O that was where they hauled the guns
That smote King Philip's fleet.

(Out of the Weald, the secret Weald,
Men sent in ancient years
The horse-shoes red at Flodden Field,
The arrows at Poitiers!)

See you our little mill that clacks,
So busy by the brook?
She has ground her corn and paid her tax
Ever since Domesday Book.

See you our stilly woods of oak,
And the dread ditch beside?

O that was where the Saxons broke
On the day that Harold died.

See you the windy levels spread
About the gates of Rye?
O that was where the Northmen fled,
When Alfred's ships came by.

See you our pastures wide and lone,
Where the red oxen browse?
O there was a City thronged and known,
Ere London boasted a house.

And see you, after rain, the trace
Of mound and ditch and wall?
O that was a Legion's camping-place,
When Cæsar sailed from Gaul.

And see you marks that show and fade,
Like shadows on the Downs?
O they are the lines the Flint Men made,
To guard their wondrous towns.

Trackway and Camp and City lost,
Salt Marsh where now is corn –
Old Wars, old Peace, old Arts that cease,
And so was England born!

She is not any common Earth,
Water or wood or air,
But Merlin's Isle of Gramarye,
Where you and I will fare!

From *Rudyard Kipling's Verse. Definitive Edition* (London, 1940), pp. 488–9.

'What is Britishness?', the *Guardian*, 20 January 1999

**Who do
we think
we are?**

Not so long ago, John Major told us we were a nation of 'long shadows on county cricket grounds' and 'old maids bicycling through the morning mist'. Yesterday, William Hague told his party the real Britain has more to do with Changing Rooms, the Notting Hill Carnival and 'Ricky and Bianca's ups and downs'. So what does Britain mean in 1999? We asked a selection of influential Britons (and a Canadian). **Ben Okri** found the question so intriguing he wrote us a poem

OF BEER, CRICKET AND JANE AUSTEN ... **John Major, former prime minister:** [Britain is a nation of] long shadows on county cricket grounds, warm beer, invincible green suburbs, dog lovers and – as George Orwell said – old maids bicycling to Holy Communion through the morning mist.

AS Byatt, novelist: We are a naturally pragmatic people. We know how to take the influence of the likes of Scott and Austen and turn them into new things. I am tired of the frontline of swinging Britain – it's false and artificial and has nothing to do with our inventive art, music and fashion. I don't think we care about cream teas and old maids on bikes, but we do love our landscape.

Terry Jones, film-maker: I suppose an essential aspect of being British is not liking each other very much. We are set apart as Britons by our lack of French-ness, German-ness or Italian-ness. Still, Britain is one of the few places left in the world that still has real beer.

A BOLD AND BRASSY PLACE ... **William Hague, Conservative leader:** [Conservatives must embrace] the Britain of big industrial cities and housing estates, the Britain proud of its world class designers and good restaurants, the Britain where hundreds of thousands go to the Notting Hill Carnival and the Eisteddfod, the Britain which watches MTV and Changing Rooms, and which is fascinated by Ricky and Bianca's ups and downs, the Britain which turns to the sports pages before the political news, where more people go on holiday to Florida than Butlins, the Britain, in other words, that has always been Britain too: urban, ambitious, sporty, fashion-conscious, multi-ethnic, brassy, self-confident and international.

Malcom McLaren, pop impressario: Being British is about singing Karaoke in bars, eating Chinese noodles and Japanese sushi, drinking French wine, wearing Prada and Nike, dancing to Italian house music, listening to Cher, using an Apple Mac, holidaying in Florida and Ibiza and buying a house in Spain. Shepherds pie and going on holiday to Hastings went out about 50 years ago and the only people you'll see wearing a Union Jack are French movie stars or Kate Moss.

Lisa I'Anson, Radio 1 DJ: Britain is about energy. We are a tiny little country and yet we exercise so much influence, particularly in the worlds of fashion and music. Britain for me is the designers – McQueen, Galliano, Ozbek – and the music. Someone like the band 4 Hero, an amazing fusion of jazz, soul and drum'n'bass.

Tracy Emin, artist: It's a good time to be British, especially for an artist. I wouldn't say I'm proud to be British, but for the first time, I'm not ashamed to be British. Britishness is looking out of a bus window, seeing sexy, stylish people laughing.

A COLD AND CURIOUS PEOPLE ... **UA Fanthorpe, poet:** This country is epitomised by surprise – nothing is as you expect it to be. Unlike a police state, there is a tradition of allowing eccentricity and variety in Britain. The language is terribly important. Of course they speak English elsewhere, but it does not have the same reverberations. That, for a writer, is one of the most important aspects.

Martin Bell MP: It's tolerance, decency and determination to talk about the weather on all occasions and a tendency, when a stranger stands on one's foot, to apologise.

Gillian Wearing, artist: The one thing that always strikes me is that people are pretty much reserved. Things take a long time to change. People are scared to let go of hundreds of years of history and keeping things in. It's partly to do with having so many people squeezed into such a small place. The overriding thing about Britain is that people are very reserved, the same attitudes prevail because of the way we are educated and our parents are educated.

Wayne Hemingway, designer: Typically British is not to pass comment for the sake of passing comment – long live British irony.

OF MARMITE, MARKS AND SPENCER AND A CENOTAPH … **Peter York, style commentator:** Britishness has to be about a quality of mind, a caste of sensibility and a sort of fun: Coronation Street as it was. I would also elect Alan Bennett for his combination of restraint, class sensitivity and the repression in his humour, Marks and Spencer for taking on the mantle of what Harrods used to be: organisation and absolute standards.

Julian Critchley, former MP for Aldershot: Britishness conjures up images of middle-aged men with their trousers rolled up paddling in Ramsgate. It's also drunken yobs following a football team. It's patriotism which verges upon nationalism if encouraged. It's a certain steadfastness under fire. We lack spirit and despise those of our fellow countrymen who possess it. We are not particularly artistic. We have a love for scenery which is a hangover from the romantic period.

Kirsty Wark, broadcaster: If I had to think of one thing to symbolise Britishness it would be the cenotaph in Glasgow – it represents the wars, which I see as a very British endeavour.

Carla Lane, writer and animal rights activist: The thing that comes to me immediately is the song of the thrush, which we have lost along with so many British things. Now Britain is the sound of guns on a Saturday and pheasants tumbling out of the sky.

Deborah Moggach, novelist: Britishness is newspapers, Marmite, pubs and the BBC – that is what people miss when they go abroad, and they must all be preserved and guarded jealously. It's also politeness – it's apologising, irony and self-mockery. It's speaking in codes and not saying what you mean, like telling someone 'We must have lunch' when you can't stand them – unlocking those codes is getting to know what it is like to be British.

PLAYING POLITICS WITH IDENTITY … **Melvyn Bragg, broadcaster:** I think that Hague seems to be criticising Tony Blair for things that he wants to do himself. I think Hague's view is a clichéd one of Britain. Britain has always benefited from having tensions and competing tribes inside it. The force of the country has come from that mix. To me, Britishness is a Saturday night in London, in Glasgow, in Cardiff, or in Belfast – it's the variety on offer for people aged 14 to 70, the vivid culture.

David Hare, playwright: The Conservative strategists have yet again grossly miscalculated if they imagine that an appeal to the 'British way of life' has any resonance. It is so childish. Most of us look with longing to the republican countries across the Channel. We associate 'Englishness' with everything that is most backward in this country.

Michael Ignatieff, writer and broadcaster: Every political party is in the identity business. Getting your mitts on the symbolism of identity is crucial to getting into power. The Labour party have successfully associated themselves with modernity. Hague is now playing catch-up. There is not a single image. When Major evoked images of maidens on bicycles, everyone disagreed. If Britishness is about anything it isn't about places or people, it's about institutions. Britishness is parliamentary democracy, rule of law, fairness and decency. It is the institutions that deliver this. It's not black, it's not white, it's not the shires, it's not London, it's not brassy and it's not old-fashioned.

A GREEN AND PLEASANT LAND ... **Shirley Williams, Liberal Democrat peer:** Britishness is the countryside, individual liberty, unbroken tradition, and no revolutions. For the British countryside I would pick out the West Highlands, the Lake District and the West Country. There is a strange mistiness alight, such as Turner picked up on so brilliantly. It is a country of poetry.

Derek Draper, radio presenter and former lobbyist: I increasingly think we should abandon the idea of Britishness and acknowledge that we're really talking about what it means to be English. Scotland has its own identity. To me the best things about English people are originality, tolerance and, most of all, understatedness. Sadly, I only manage two out of three. The place that best sums up England is the English countryside, particularly Oxfordshire and the Pennines.

WHAT BRITISHNESS? **Claire Rayner, writer and broadcaster:** For a lot of people, I suspect that Britain is epitomised more locally than William Hague's assertion. People define themselves as coming from Yorkshire or Lancaster, or as being cockney, like I am, rather than coming from Britain as a whole. There is a certain snottiness in trying to define 'Britishness'. If anybody asked, I would say I am a Londoner and a European.

Jon Snow, broadcaster: I think Britishness has died off in my lifetime and nothing has replaced it. When I was a child, it was Winston Churchill, beefeaters and lots of pink on the globe. Now it's an irrelevant concept. Personally, I'm a Londoner living in Europe.

Brian Sewell, art critic: What an idiotic Yorkshireman thinks is British is not what some cultured southerner thinks. There is no one type of Britishness.

David Cannadine, historian: Britishness is a complicated and enormous thing – what different people see as meaning different things. It can mean one island, a group of islands off the coast of Europe, or it can mean the British empire – at times it means all those things. Politicians, and the rest of us, define it in different ways at different times.

Linda Colley, historian: The concept of Britishness, or Frenchness, or Americanness is not that useful because everyone has different notions. The clichés – the English are reserved, the Scots are mean and the Welsh can sing – are very dubious generalisations. The debate about Britishness is promoted by the extent of our post-war decline. We are no longer kept together by the need to fight wars, we are no longer all Protestants and we do not have the self-interest of belonging to a massive global empire.

John Humphrys, broadcaster: I'm always slightly puzzled by any characterisation of a nation. Who exactly is 'bold and brassy'? The old-age pensioner struggling to get by? Or the mum with a couple of kids who's worried about how they're getting on in school? You simply cannot apply global definitions to an entire society for the obvious reason that we're all different. In the swinging sixties, I suspect it was about four per cent of London that was actually swinging, while the rest of the country wondered what 'swinging' meant.

Interviews by Hannah Pool, Emma Brockes and Claire Phipps. Research by R&I

Soul of the nation

A poem by Ben Okri

The souls of nations do not change; they merely stretch their hidden range.

Just as rivers do not sleep

the spirit of empire still runs deep.

Into a river many waters flow

the merging and conquest that's history's glow.

A gathering of homely and alien streams

a tumble of turbulent and tranquil dreams.

Classes overflow their rigid boundaries,

slowly stirring mighty quandaries; Accents diverse ring from the land's soul

a richer music revealing what is whole; new pulsings from abroad shake the shores,

troubling the sleep of the land's resonant bores.

But the gods of the nation do not change, their ways are deep and often strange.

History moves, and the surface quivers, but the gods are steadfast in the depth of rivers.

From the *Guardian*, G 2 (supplement), pp. 2–3.

David Dabydeen, 'On Not Being Milton: Nigger Talk in England Today'

One of the many ways in which young British blacks have resisted white domination is in the creation of a patois evolved from the West Indian creole of their parents. The poetry that has emerged from the black communities is expressed in the language of this patois, and one of its greatest exponents is Linton Kwesi Johnson:

Shock-black bubble-doun-beat bouncing
rock-wise tumble-doun soun music:
foot – drop find drum blood story;

bass history is a moving
is a hurting black story.

('Reggae Sounds')

Johnson's poetry is recited to music from a reggae band. The paraphernalia of sound-systems, amplifiers, speakers, microphones, electric guitars and the rest which dominate the stage and accompanies what one critic has dismissed as 'jungle-talk', is a deliberate 'misuse' of white technology. 'Sound-systems', essential to 'dub-poetry', are often home-made contraptions, cannibalized parts of diverse machines reordered for black expression. This de/reconstruction is in itself an assertive statement, a denial of the charge of black incapacity to understand technology. The mass-produced technology is re-made for self-use in the way that patois is a 'private' reordering of 'standard' English. The deliberate exploitation of high-tech to serve black 'jungle-talk' is a reversal of colonial history. Caliban is tearing up the pages of Prospero's magic books and repasting it in his own order, by his own method and for his own purpose.

A feature of Black British poetry is a sheer delight in the rhythm and sound of language that survives technology, and this joyousness is revealed in poems like Mikey Smith's 'R-ooTs' (the line 'lawwwwwwd', as Edward Brathwaite says, sounding like the exhaust roar of a motorcycle), or in the writings of Jimi Rand. There is a deliberate celebration of the 'primitive' consciousness of sound in:

> Me was fas asleep in me bed
> wen a nok come pun me door,
> bright and early, fore day morning
> before dawn bruk.
> Nock nock – nock nock,
> badoombadoom nock nock
> badoombadoom nock nock
> badoombadoom nock badoom nock.
> Who dat; a who dat nock?
>
>   ('Nock – Nock')

This deliberate wearing of the 'primitive' label is even more explicit in his 'Nigger Talk' poem:

> Funky talk
> Nitty gritty grass – root talk
> Dat's wha I da talk
> Cause de talk is togedder talk,
> Like right on, out-a-sight, kind-a-too-much.
> Ya hip to it yet?
> Ya dig de funky way to talk
> Talk talk?
> Dis na white talk;
> Na white talk dis.
> it is coon, nignog samba wog talk.

The use of language is inextricably bound up with a sense of being black. Hence John Agard's poem 'Listen Mr Oxford Don' is conscious of the way creole suffers from the charge of being surly and indecent ('Muggin de Queen's

English') and Agard links this literary indictment to attitudes in the wider society where blacks are accused of a host of criminal activities:

> Dem accuse me of assault
> on de Oxford dictionary /
> imagine a concise peaceful man like me /
> dem want me serve time for inciting rhyme to riot
> so mek dem send one big word after me
> i ent serving no jail sentence
> I slashing suffix in self-defence
> i bashing future wit present tense
> and if necessary
>
> I making de Queen's English accessory / to my offence

Johnson, Agard and others are reacting against the 'rational structure and comprehensible language' which Robert Conquest saw as a distinguishing feature of the Movement poets and which still afflicts contemporary English verse. The charge that Alvarez levelled against the Movement – the disease of gentility – is still relevant today. Andrew Motion for instance can visit Anne Frank's room and on emerging can conclude that all Anne Frank wanted was to

> leave as simply
> as I do, and walk at ease
> up dusty tree-lined avenues, or watch
> a silent barge come clear of bridge
> settling their reflections in the blue canal

There is glibness and gentility disguised as understatement but really amounting to a kind of obscenity. As Michael Hulse has commented, 'to go as a tourist to a house which, like many similar houses in Amsterdam, focused human hope and suffering, and then to parade the delicacy of one's response, savours somewhat of an opportunism that is slightly obscene'. The quiet understatement of Motion's response to human tragedy is as obscene as Conrad's heated, insistent rhetoric ('It was the stillness of an implacable force brooding over an inscrutable intention', etc.): both belong to a tradition of colonizing the experience of others for the gratification of their own literary sensibilities.

The pressure of the same racism that destroyed Anne Frank, and encounter with the thuggery that lurks beneath the polite surface of English life and letters, force black writers into poetry that is disturbing and passionate. The play of the light of memory upon pine furniture, touching vignettes of domestic life, elegiac recollections of dead relatives, wonderment at the zig-zag fall of an autumnal leaf, none of these typical English poetic concerns are of special relevance to them. They participate in a West Indian literary tradition which seeks to subvert English canons by the use of lived nigger themes in lived nigger language. Their strategies of 'rants, rudeness and rhymes' look back half a century to the West Indian struggle to establish 'black' expression. In March 1931, a new Trinidadian journal, *The Beacon*, attempted to instigate a movement for 'local' literature, encouraging writing that was authentic to the West

Indian landscape and to the daily speech of its inhabitants. 'We fail utterly to understand', an editorial of January/February 1932 commented on the quality of short stories received for publication, 'why anyone should want to see Trinidad as a miniature Paradiso, where grave-diggers speak like English M.P.s'. Emphasis was placed on the use of creole, and on a realistic description of West Indian life, for political and aesthetic reasons. To write in creole was to validate the experience of black people against the contempt and dehumanizing dismissal of white people. Celebration of blackness necessitated celebration of black language, for how could a black writer be true to his blackness using the language of his/her colonial master? The aesthetic argument was bound up with this political argument, and involved an appreciation of the energy, vitality and expressiveness of creole, an argument that Edward Brathwaite has rehearsed in his recent book, *The History of the Voice*. For Brathwaite the challenge to West Indian poets was how to shatter the frame of the iambic pentameter which had prevailed in English poetry from the time of Chaucer onwards. The form of the pentameter is not appropriate to a West Indian environment: 'The hurricane does not roar in pentameters. And that's the problem: how do you get a rhythm which approximates the natural experience, the environmental experience?' The use of creole, or Nation language, as he terms it, involves recognition of the vitality of the oral tradition surviving from Africa, the earthiness of proverbial folk speech, the energy and power of gestures which accompany oral delivery, and the insistence of the drumbeat to which the living voice responds.

England today is the third largest West Indian island – there are over half-a-million of us here, fewer only than Jamaica and Trinidad – and our generation is confronted by the same issues that Brathwaite and other writers faced in their time. The pressure then was to slavishly imitate the expressions of the Mother Country if a writer was to be recognised. Hence the vague Miltonic cadence of Walter MacA. Lawrence, one of our early Guyanese writers, in describing, quite inappropriately, the native thunder of the Kaiteur Falls:

> And falling in splendour sheer down from the heights
> that should gladden the heart of our eagle to scan,
> That lend to the towering forest beside thee the semblance
> of shrubs trimmed and tended by man –
> That viewed from the brink where the vast, amber volume
> that once was a stream cataracts into thee,
> Impart to the foothills surrounding the maelstrom beneath
> thee that rage as this troublous sea.

Brathwaite and others eventually rescued us from this cascade of nonsense sounds. The pressure now is also towards mimicry. Either you drop the epithet 'black' and think of yourself as a 'writer' (a few of us foolishly embrace this position, desirous of the status of 'writing' and knowing that 'black' is blighted with negative connotations), meaning cease dwelling on the nigger/tribal/nationalistic theme, cease *folking* up the literature, and become 'universal' – or else you perish in the backwater of small presses, you don't get published by the 'quality' presses and don't receive the corresponding patronage of media-hype. Put bluntly, this is how the threat against us is presented.

Alfred Ford, summarizing these issues, puts them in a historical context: the pressure is to become a mulatto and house-nigger (Ariel) rather than stay a field-nigger (Caliban).

I cannot however feel or write poetry like a white man, much less serve him. And to become mulattos, black people literally have to be fucked (and fucked up) first. Which brings us back to the pornography of Empire. I feel that I am different, not wholly, but sufficient for me to want to contemplate that which is other in me, that which owes its life to particular rituals of ancestry. I know that the concept of 'otherness' is the fuel of white racism and dominates current political discourse, from Enoch Powell's 'In these great numbers blacks are, and remain, alien here. With the growth of concentrated numbers, their alienness grows not by choice but by necessity', to Margaret Thatcher's 'swamped by people of a different culture'. I also know that the concept of 'otherness' pervades English literature, from Desdemona's fatal attraction to the body of alien culture, to Marlow's obsession with the thought that Africans are in one sense alien but in a more terrible sense they are the very capacities within Europeans for the gratification of indecent pleasures. But these are not my problem. I'm glad to be peculiar, to modify the phrase. I'd prefer to be simply peculiar, and to get on with it, to live and write accordingly, but gladness is a forced response against the weight of insults, a throwing off of white men's burdens.

As to 'universality', let Achebe have the last word, even if in the most stylish of English:

> In the nature of things the work of a Western writer is automatically informed by universality. It is only others who must strain to achieve it. So-and-so's work is universal; he has truly arrived! As though universality were some distant bend in the road which you must take if you travel out far enough in the direction of Europe or America, if you put adequate distance between yourself and your home. I should like to see the word 'universal' banned altogether from discussion of African literature until such time as people cease to use it as a synonym for the narrow, self-serving parochialism of Europe, until their horizon extends to include all the world.

From the 1989 essay reprinted in *The Routledge Reader in Caribbean Literature*, ed. Alison Donnell and Sarah Lawson Welsh (London, 1996), pp. 410–15.[54]

▶ Discussion

Kipling's story here is of a nation which is special: 'She is not any common Earth'. Indeed, it is a magical land, 'Merlin's Isle of Gramarye' ('Gramarye' = magic, wizardcraft). Perhaps, in fact, nation is the wrong word – since the poem concentrates on England as a *country* – a pastoral place of various countryside landscapes. There is little direct representation of any contemporary *people* who might form a nation. Rather England is represented as made up of *places*, each of which contains a historical memory for those who know. The narrative form of the poem springs from this: the narrator points out the hidden special meanings in the English countryside, over which he and the addressee (the reader) have a particular kind of panoptic vision.

This seems a version of a traditional kind of patriotism – love for country springing from close local attachments. Hence the panoptic vision is not an elevated or grand one, but presented as if taking place from on a level with each scene. It is not a grand overview, but a reminder of the ordinary local scenes which really matter to an English person (or is it an English*man?*). There is, underneath the pastoral ground, a notably military aspect to the hidden qualities of England: seven out of the twelve stanzas refer to a battle or battles or another military context. And all the battles mentioned are victories for England over her enemies – in Scotland, over Viking invaders or against France – with the exception of Hastings.[55] Thus beneath – or even *because of* – the pastoral appearance of England there is a military edge. The present overlays the past, but there is a continuity between the two, which can always be recovered: 'And see you the marks that show and fade, / Like shadows on the Downs?' In fact, England is born out of the losses of the past: out of long development: 'Trackway and Camp and City lost, / ... / Old Wars, old peace, Old Arts that cease'.

The narrative of England conjured by the poem is one where past and present are entwined, where modest appearances conceal and reveal past glories, where rural scenes underpin military successes, and where a sense of local bonds to the land is at the root of patriotic feeling. It is a 'blessed isle' whose magic ordinary people can feel – where the ordinary English speaker of the poem and its ordinary English hearer(s) can feel the unique ties of Englishness: 'Where you and I will fare!' (Were one cynical, one could observe that all countries have long histories, that battles and conquests mark many lands – but perhaps the point is that the poem fits into a widespread feeling that England has a special destiny.) ☐

▶◁ **Your Discussions**

   ☐

◆ Finally in this section, read the following two texts about nationalism. How does each see the relation between individual identity and national identity?
◆ In a literary studies context, how often are ideas about national identity relevant? Do they need to be invoked for interpreting all texts, or only specialised kinds of literary text?

Ernest Renan, *What is a Nation?* (1882)

(Translated and annotated by Martin Thom)

What I propose to do today is to analyse with you an idea which, though seemingly clear, lends itself to the most dangerous misunderstandings. [Consider] the vast agglomerations of men found in China, Egypt or ancient Babylonia, the tribes of the Hebrews and the Arabs, the city as it existed in Athens or Sparta, the assemblies of the various territories in the Carolingian Empire, those communities which are without a *patrie* and are maintained by a religious bond alone, as is the case with the Israelites and the Parsees, nations, such as France, England and the majority of the modern European sovereign states, confederations, such as exist in Switzerland or in America, and ties, such as those that race, or rather language, establishes between the different branches of the German or Slav peoples. Each of these groupings exist, or have existed, and there would be the direst of consequences if one were to confuse any one of them with any other. At the time of the French Revolution, it was commonly believed that the institutions proper to small, independent cities, such as Sparta and Rome, might be applied to our large nations, which number some thirty or forty million souls. Nowadays, a far graver mistake is made: race is confused with nation and a sovereignty analogous to that of really existing peoples is attributed to ethnographic or, rather, linguistic groups.

I want now to try and make these difficult questions somewhat more precise, for the slightest confusion regarding the meaning of words, at the start of an argument, may in the end lead to the most fatal of errors. It is a delicate thing that I propose to do here, somewhat akin to vivisection; I am going to treat the living much as one ordinarily treats the dead. I shall adopt an absolutely cool and impartial attitude.

[...]

Geography, or what are known as natural frontiers, undoubtedly plays a considerable part in the division of nations. Geography is one of the crucial factors in history. Rivers have led races on; mountains have brought them to a halt. The former have favoured movement in history, whereas the latter have restricted it. Can one say, however, that as some parties believe, a nation's frontiers are written on the map and that this nation has the right to judge what is necessary to round off certain contours, in order to reach such and such a mountain and such and such a river, which are thereby accorded a kind of *a priori* limiting faculty? I know of no doctrine which is more arbitrary or more fatal, for it allows one to justify any or every violence. First of all, is it the mountains or the rivers that we should regard as forming these so-called natural frontiers? It is indisputable that the mountains separate, but the rivers tend rather to unify. Moreover, all mountains cannot divide up states. Which serve to separate and which do not? From Biarritz to Tornea, there is no one estuary which is more suited than any other to serving as a boundary marker. Had history so decreed it, the Loire, the Seine, the Meuse, the Elbe, or the Oder could, just as easily as the Rhine, have had this quality of being a natural frontier, such as has caused so many infractions of the most fundamental right, which is men's will. People talk of strategic grounds. Nothing, however, is absolute; it is quite clear than many concessions should be made to necessity. But these concessions should not be taken too far. Otherwise, everybody would lay claim to their military conveniences, and one would have unceasing war. No, it is no more soil than it is race which makes a nation. The soil furnishes the substratum, the field of struggle and of labour; man furnishes the soul. Man is everything in the formation of this sacred thing which is called a people. Nothing [purely] material suffices for it. A nation is a spiritual principle, the outcome of the profound complications of history; it is a spiritual family not a group determined by the shape of the earth. We have now seen what things are not adequate for the creation of such a spiritual principle, namely, race, language, material interest, religious affinities, geography, and military necessity. What more then is required? As a consequence of what was said previously, I will not have to detain you very much longer.

A nation is a soul, a spiritual principle. Two things, which in truth are but one, constitute this soul or spiritual principle. One lies in the past, one in the present. One is the possession in common of a rich legacy of memories; the other is present-day consent, the desire to live together, the will to perpetuate the value of the heritage that one has received in an undivided form. Man, Gentlemen, does not improvise. The nation, like the individual, is the culmination of a long past of endeavours, sacrifice, and devotion. Of all cults, that of the ancestors is the most legitimate, for the ancestors have made us what we are. A heroic past, great men, glory (by which I understand genuine glory), this is the social capital upon which one bases a national idea. To have common glories in the past and to have a common will in the present; to have performed great deeds together, to wish to perform still more – these are the essential conditions for being a people. One loves in proportion to the sacrifices to which one has consented, and in proportion to the ills that one has suffered. One loves the house that one has built and that one has handed down. The Spartan song – 'We are what you were; we will be what you are' – is, in its simplicity, the abridged hymn of every *patrie*.

More valuable by far than common customs posts and frontiers conforming to strategic ideas is the fact of sharing, in the past, a glorious heritage and regrets, and of having, in the future, [a shared] programme to put into effect, or the fact of having suffered, enjoyed, and hoped together. These are the kinds of things that can be understood in spite of differences of race and language. I spoke just now of 'having suffered together' and, indeed, suffering in common unifies more than joy does. Where national memories are concerned, griefs are of more value than triumphs, for they impose duties, and require a common effort.

A nation is therefore a large-scale solidarity, constituted by the feeling of the sacrifices that one has made in the past and of those that one is prepared to make in the future. It presupposes a past; it is summarized, however, in the present by a tangible fact, namely, consent, the clearly expressed desire to continue a common life. A nation's existence is, if you will pardon the metaphor, a daily plebiscite, just as an individual's existence is a perpetual affirmation of life. That, I know full well, is less metaphysical than divine right and less brutal than so-called historical right. According to the ideas that I am outlining to you, a nation has no more right than a king does to say to a province: 'You belong to me, I am seizing you.' A province, as far as I am concerned, is its inhabitants; if anyone has the right to be consulted in such an affair, it is the inhabitant. A nation never has any real interest in annexing or holding on to a country against its will. The wish of nations is, all in all, the sole legitimate criterion, the one to which one must always return.

We have driven metaphysical and theological abstractions out of politics. What then remains? Man, with his desires and his needs. The secession, you will say to me, and, in the long term, the disintegration of nations will be the outcome of a system which places these old organisms at the mercy of wills which are often none too enlightened. It is clear that, in such matters, no principle must be pushed too far. Truths of this order are only applicable as a whole in a very general fashion. Human wills change, but what is there here below that does not change? The nations are not something eternal. They had their beginnings and they will end. A European confederation will very probably replace them. But such is not the law of the century in which we are living. At the present time, the existence of nations is a good thing, a necessity even. Their existence is the guarantee of liberty, which would be lost if the world had only one law and only one master.

Through their various and often opposed powers, nations participate in the common work of civilization; each sounds a note in the great concert of humanity, which, after all, is the highest ideal reality that we are capable of attaining. Isolated, each has its weak point. I often tell myself that an individual who had those faults which in nations are taken for good qualities, who fed off vainglory, who was to that degree jealous, egotistical, and quarrelsome, and who would draw his sword on the smallest pretext, would be the most intolerable of men. Yet all these discordant details disappear in the overall context. Poor humanity, how you have suffered! How many trials still await you! May the spirit of wisdom guide you, in order to preserve you from the countless dangers with which your path is strewn!

Let me sum up, Gentlemen. Man is a slave neither of his race nor his language, nor of his religion, nor of the course of rivers nor of the direction taken by mountain chains. A large aggregate of men, healthy in mind and warm of heart, creates the kind of moral conscience which we call a nation. So long as this moral consciousness gives proof of its strength by the sacrifices which demand the abdication of the individual to the advantage of the community, it is legitimate and has the right to exist. If doubts arise regarding its frontiers, consult the populations in the areas under dispute. They undoubtedly have the right to a say in the matter. This recommendation will bring a smile to the lips of the transcendants of politics, these infallible beings who spend their lives deceiving themselves and who, from the height of their superior principles, take pity upon our mundane concerns. 'Consult the populations, for heaven's sake! How naïve! A fine example of those wretched French ideas which claim to replace diplomacy and war by childishly simple methods.' Wait a while, Gentlemen; let the reign of the transcendants pass; bear the scorn of the powerful with patience. It may be that, after many fruitless gropings, people will revert to our more modest empirical solutions. The best way of being right in the future is, in certain periods, to know how to resign oneself to being out of fashion.

From essay reprinted in *Nation and Narration*, ed. Homi K. Bhabha (London, 1990), pp. 8–22; extract is from pp. 8, 18–21.

George Orwell, *Notes on Nationalism*

Notes on Nationalism

By 'nationalism' I mean first of all the habit of assuming that human beings can be classified like insects and that whole blocks of millions or tens of millions of people can be confidently labelled 'good' or 'bad'.* But secondly – and this is much more important – I mean the habit of identifying oneself with a single nation or other unit, placing it beyond good and evil and recognizing no other duty than that of advancing its interests. Nationalism is not to be confused with patriotism. Both words are normally used in so vague a way that any definition is liable to be challenged, but one must draw a distinction between them, since two different and even opposing ideas are involved. By 'patriotism' I mean devotion to a particular place and a particular way of life, which one believes to be the best in the world but has no wish to force upon other people. Patriotism is of its nature defensive, both militarily and culturally. Nationalism, on the other hand, is inseparable from the desire for power. The abiding purpose of every nationalist is to secure more power and more prestige, *not* for himself but for the nation or other unit in which he has chosen to sink his own individuality.

So long as it is applied merely to the more notorious and identifiable nationalist movements in Germany, Japan, and other countries, all this is obvious enough. Confronted with a phenomenon like Nazism, which we can observe from the outside, nearly all of us would say much the same things about it. But here I must repeat what I said above, that I am only using the word 'nationalism' for lack of a better. Nationalism, in the extended sense in which I am using the word, includes such movements and tendencies as Communism, political Catholicism, Zionism, anti-Semitism, Trotskyism, and Pacifism. It does not necessarily mean loyalty to a government or a country, still less to *one's own* country, and it is not even strictly necessary that the units in which it deals should actually exist. To name a few obvious examples, Jewry, Islam, Christendom, the Proletariat, and the White Race are all of them the objects of passionate nationalistic feeling: but their existence can be seriously questioned, and there is no definition of any one of them that would be universally accepted.

It is also worth emphasizing once again that nationalist feeling can be purely negative. There are, for example, Trotskyists who have become simply the enemies of the U.S.S.R. without developing a corresponding loyalty to any other unit. When one grasps the implications of this, the nature of what I mean by nationalism becomes a good deal clearer. A nationalist is one who thinks solely, or mainly, in terms of competitive prestige. He may be a positive or a negative nationalist – that is, he may use his mental energy either in

---

* Nations, and even vaguer entities such as the Catholic Church or the proletariat, are commonly thought of as individuals and often referred to as 'she'. Patently absurd remarks such as 'Germany is naturally headstrong,' are to be found in any newspaper one opens, and reckless generalizations about national character ('The Spaniard is a natural aristocrat' or 'Every Englishman is a hypocrite') are uttered by almost everyone. Intermittently these generalizations are seen to be unfounded, but the habit of making them persists, and people of professedly international outlook, e.g., Tolstoy or Bernard Shaw, are often guilty of them.

boosting or in denigrating – but at any rate his thoughts always turn on victories, defeats, triumphs, and humiliations. He sees history, especially contemporary history, as the endless rise and decline of great power units, and every event that happens seems to him a demonstration that his own side is on the up grade and some hated rival on the down grade. But finally, it is important not to confuse nationalism with mere worship of success. The nationalist does not go on the principle of simply ganging up with the strongest side. On the contrary, having picked his side, he persuades himself that it *is* the strongest, and is able to stick to his belief even when the facts are overwhelmingly against him. Nationalism is power-hunger tempered by self-deception. Every nationalist is capable of the most flagrant dishonesty, but he is also – since he is conscious of serving something bigger than himself – unshakably certain of being in the right.

From essay first published in *Polemic* (October 1945); reprinted in *Decline of the English Murder* (Harmondsworth, 1965), pp. 155–79; extract is from pp. 155–7.

Your Discussions

☐

Further Reading

Belsey, Catherine and Jane Moore, *The Feminist Reader: Essays in Gender and the Politics of Literary Criticism* (London, Macmillan, 1989).

Bennet, Tony, *Formalism and Marxism* (London, Methuen, 1980).

Bhabha, Homi (ed.), *National and Narration* (London, Routledge, 1990).

Caplan, Pat (ed.), *The Cultural Construction of Sexuality* (London, Routledge, 1989).

Easthope, Anthony, *Englishness and National Culture* (London, Routledge, 1998).

Gates, Jr, Henry Louis (ed.), *Black Literature and Literary Theory* (London, Routledge, 1984).

Marwick, Arthur, *Class – Image and Reality in Britain, France and the USA Since 1930* (London, Collins, 1980).

Morris, Pam, *Literature and Feminism: An Introduction* (Oxford, Blackwell, 1993).

Neale, R. S., *Class and Ideology in the Nineteenth Century* (London, Routledge, 1972).

Said, Edward W., *Culture and Imperialism* (London, Chatto & Windus, 1993).

Showalter, Elaine, *Speaking of Gender* (London, Routledge, 1989).

Williams, Raymond, *Culture and Society 1780–1950* (Harmondsworth, Penguin, 1963).

Conclusion: What Next? Thinking About Texts

This is the conclusion of a book called *Thinking About Texts: An Introduction to English Studies*; I would like to end by giving some sense of where I hope the book will have got you, and where you might go next. The book is very much an *introduction* – a text to be studied early on in degree-level English. It cannot hope to have covered everything currently studied under the name 'English' and, indeed, it has made no attempt at exhaustive coverage. Instead it has attempted to support you in the accomplishment of the following aims:

1. To develop your ability to read a wide variety of texts – literary, critical, theoretical – in a sophisticated and flexible way.
2. To develop a complex awareness of how we (might/can/do) think about texts.
3. To develop capacities of reflection: of analysis of every stage of reading texts, not just analysis of the 'text itself'/not just accepting other people's explanations, other people's assumptions.
4. To introduce some central issues in reading the subject of English.

I hope that working towards these aims will allow you to develop further towards advanced skills and knowledge of the kinds required for the most enjoyable, creative and professional study of all aspects of English. Thus, I hope that you will feel able to read any text of any kind, since, if you have worked through this book, you will already have met a representative variety of 'English' texts, from Aristotle to Atwood, from *Widsith* to Orwell, from Derrida to Theocritus, from Barthes to F. R. Leavis, from Eliot (George and T. S.) to Markham, from Marianne Moore to Elizabeth Barrett Browning, from Sally Goodman to Paul St Vincent, from Saintsbury to Shakespeare ... and so on. I hope also that you will feel no automatic aversion from texts which are not self-evidently 'literature', that the borders between literature/non-literature, literature/history, literature/popular, literature/critical, literature/theory are not uncrossable or even always well-marked out. Most of all I hope that *thinking* about *texts* has become instinctive (in a reflective sort of way), so that you know what you are doing, can think new things, can analyse theories and practices in every text, so that *you* can continue the development of English, feel your own capacities for English. English in all its varieties – the varieties with long lineages, the new varieties, the expansions and inventions, the debates about variety – is what, I hope, comes next.

Notes

Introduction

1. Though you will have read parts of texts by writers – Barthes and Derrida – working in those modes (and in many others).
2. In other books, on other courses or units of study. See 'Conclusion: What Next? Thinking About Texts'.

1   The Study of Literature

1. Of course, these historical definitions are invaluable for understanding the terms in older contexts, as well as for understanding how their meaning has changed.
2. There are, of course, several answers to this, including the 'authority' of the (relatively) established status of English and lack of knowledge of newer degree subjects.
3. As the passage examined in the next exercise suggests.
4. Raymond Williams devoted much thought to understanding the complexities of the relationships between culture and social and economic organisation. My definition here does not attempt to record the subtlety of his understanding – but simply makes the point that it is a belief in these relationships which makes him a Marxist critic.
5. Leon Edel wrote the article in the *Guardian* on Keynes.
6. This may be a peculiarly modern notion of the literary which has arisen only since the nineteenth century, and which exists despite the persistent use of generic elements and terms in both literary texts and in critical writing about literary texts. 'It is even considered a sign of authentic modernity in a writer if he ceases to respect the separation of genres', observes Tzvetan Todorov in *Genres in Discourse*, p. 13. See also the whole of the essay in that book from which this quotation comes, 'The Origin of Genres', and the discussion of part of that essay in section 1.3 below.
7. See section 5.1 for discussion of ideas about the boundaries of individuals.
8. See the definition in the *Oxford English Dictionary* or a dictionary of literary terms, to get a sense of this history.
9. See the 1915 Methuen cover illustration for *The Rainbow*, reproduced on the cover of the Longman critical reader, *D. H. Lawrence*, edited by Peter Widdowson (London, 1992). The cover shows an illustration of a kneeling man supporting a woman, who also kneels, probably on straw in a barn. She rests her head on his shoulder, whilst clasping one of his hands on his knee. The two gaze into each other's eyes. The illustration seems to fulfil the kinds of function which I suggest above for a contemporary 'Romance' novel cover.
10. *Textual Practice*, vol. 3, number 2 (1989); also reprinted in *New Historicism and Cultural Materialism – A Reader*, ed. Kiernan Ryan (London, 1996), pp. 82–91. Quotation is from p. 83.

11. p. 85 in Ryan, *New Historicism*.
12. A historian might perhaps ask which class, classes or class formation this was exactly; and how consciously and uniformly 'English' was promoted as a (or the?) solution to religious decline; see also sections 4.1, 5.1 and 5.2 for material about the practices of both historians and critics in generalising and narrativising ideas of both history and class. Other factors, including the introduction of compulsory schooling, the subsequent growth in literacy and the invention of new forms of popular printed culture within a society where social cohesion was valued and where there was an urge to 'educate' might also play a part in the rise of English. Some Victorian sources suggest that English is as much focused on the middle as on the working classes: 'it is, however, in connection with what is called "middle-class education" that the claims of English literature may be most effectively urged. In that literature, properly handled, we have a most valuable agency for the moral and intellectual culture of the professional classes ... And such a lesson the middle classes of this country greatly need. They are generally *honest* in their opinions, but in many cases they are *narrow*' (Rev. H. G. Robinson, 'On The Use of English Classical Literature', *Macmillan's Magazine*, II (October 1860), 425–33, quoted in D. J. Palmer's *The Rise of English Studies* (Oxford, 1965), p. 45.
13. On the other hand, Eagleton's account can be said to be less abstract in its linking of 'English' to a wider set of national concerns, such as class antagonisms and religious decline, and in giving a particular history of the rise of English which is not very well known to English students.
14. You do not, of course, have to accept this as canonically true – as elsewhere in this book, disagreement is possible. For the moment, the aim is to be clear about Eagleton and Easthope's arguments; at the end of the section there is an opportunity to argue for other – perhaps more positive – possibilities in literary study, or to argue that these versions of English are themselves 'abstracted'. Or to see where the critique carried out by Eagleton and Easthope might be extended to contemporary English. While *Thinking About Texts* inevitably does construct its reader – the person/function I address as you at times – in a certain way, my conscious aim, at least, is to offer that reader room for manoeuvre.
15. There are numerous connections between the issues raised by Easthope's chapter and topics discussed elsewhere in this book. It would be valuable in particular to refer back and forth between the discussions here and those in sections 1.1, 1.2, 1.4, 2.2, 5.1, 5.2, 5.3 and 5.4.
16. See sections 5.2, 5.3 and 5.4 for more on this.
17. Not everything about Cultural Studies was entirely new at this period, though the term and its wider impact was. Raymond Williams had been working with a wideningly inclusive sense of culture since he published his two books about the definitions of culture, *Culture and Society* (1958) and *The Long Revolution* (1961). The breadth of interest of Williams's work and of later cultural studies work can be traced back in some respects to the interests of Marxist and other leftist critics in the nineteen thirties. Though they often disapproved of much (contemporary) popular culture, critics such as Christopher Caudwell and George Orwell took it as a serious focus for discussion.

2   Texts, Authors, Critics

1. There are, of course, other approaches to literary criticism (such as studying culture and history *through* texts, studying histories of reader response or reception). Many critics would deny that they are looking for a meaning which is simply contained *in* a text. Nevertheless, I think my rather simple account is still generally true of how English as a discipline sets up its teaching. The text is still at the centre of English studies.

2. In his New Cambridge Shakespeare edition of *Hamlet* (Cambridge, 1934). See Harold Jenkins's discussion in the Arden *Hamlet* (London and New York, 1982), pp. 74–5.

3. Holderness and Loughrey specifically condemn the kind of close comparison I suggested you carry out on the grounds that it already accepted the superiority of the written text before the exercise is even started: 'to enter into a detailed defence of *The Tragicall Historie of Hamlet Prince of Denmarke* (1603) against this tradition of comparative condemnation cannot be done without complicity in the established parameters of this bibliographical problematic – piracy, memorial reconstruction, the self-evident inferiority of "a stolen, and surreptitious cop[y]". In a hierarchical configuration of texts separated by principles of moral discrimination, priority is automatically given to the readings of the text judged "good". On a level playing-field of textual plurality, variant readings can be objectively compared and apprehended as different from one another, without any establishing of discursive hierarchy' (Introduction, p. 22). The task on 'To be or not to be' below tries to adopt this second approach. One does not, though, have to accept that there are no criteria other than 'moral discrimination' for judging Q1 as a garbled version of an original resembling Q2. This may still be the best explanation of how Q1 came to exist in its particular form. Accepting the idea that Q1 was pirated does not necessarily mean that we must refuse to accept it as *a* valid text of *Hamlet* in the terms suggested by Holderness and Loughrey.

4. See discussion of the texts in *The Division of the Kingdoms: Shakespeare's two Versions of King Lear*, ed. Gary Taylor and Michael Warren (1986) and in *King Lear – A Parallel Text Edition*, ed. René Weiss (London, 1993). The somewhat earlier Arden Shakespeare *King Lear* argues that 'it is generally accepted that Q is substantially inferior to F, and that the latter must therefore serve as the basis of a modern edition' (Introduction, p. xiv). Much textual work has been done on *King Lear* since that edition, and Weiss argues that 'it is unlikely that a Platonic (i.e. ideal, single) *Lear*-Text will emerge from the mists of the past' (Introduction, p. 39).

5. *Twelfth Night*, II. iv. 116–17 in the Arden Edition. Holderness and Loughrey discuss the lines in their Introduction, p. 22.

6. See Arden Introduction to *Hamlet*, p. 30.

7. This concise summary of Kristeva's argument is quoted from K. Wales's *A Dictionary of Stylistics* (London, 1989), p. 259, under the entry 'Intertextuality'.

8. Katie Wales, *A Dictionary of Stylistics* (London, 1989), p. 460. See entry for 'Text'.

9. Q1 has its own version of this speech, which has additional interesting material on the acting practices of clowns and fools. Harold Jenkins in the Arden *Hamlet* has a note for the last line of the speech quoted above, saying that 'In Q1 an addition of 10 lines at this point provides, ironically enough, an instance of the thing complained of' (i.e. ad libbing), p. 289. This note, of course, assumes in a particularly clear way the authenticity of Q2 – and even of the character Hamlet's views on acting and authorship!

10. Arden edition of *Hamlet*, Act III, sc. ii, line 1, ll. 38–45.

11. The first professional performance of the play was at the Old Vic, London, by the National Theatre Company, 11 April 1967.

12. Clare was a 'peasant poet'. His early poetry was well received, but his later volumes sold less well. He wrote a number of poems which refer to being deserted by poetic inspiration. In 1837 he was certified mad, and confined in asylums, first in Essex and then in Northamptonshire, till his death in 1864. The surgeons who certified him noted that he had for many years been 'addicted to poetical musings'. This poem was written while in the asylum. These few comments on this complex figure – inevitably written in the context of the question asked above – may, of course, be used in your consideration if you feel they are useful.

13. Though ideas from further on in this section about biography and authorship might not support this move.

14. A poem that may have been in circulation as early as the seventh century, but which is known in written form from the collection of manuscripts known as *The Exeter Book*, usually dated to the second half of the tenth century.

15. *Anglo-Saxon Poetry*, ed. and trans. S. A. J. Bradley (London, 1982), headnote to *Widsith*, p. 336. See Sainstbury's comment on *Widsith* in section 4.1 below.

16. Authorship may well be an anachronistic word for the function of the *scop*, but I use it to indicate some potential continuity.

17. This presence of an author in the narrative was interestingly made explicit in the BBC's TV adaptation (1997) of *Tom Jones*, where an actor played Fielding as a narrator bodily present during the story (rather than as a voice-over, implying a narrating voice rather than a present character).

18. Perhaps the *scop* in *Deor* can be thought of as this kind of narrator? See discussion above.

19. The essay is reprinted in *The Foucault Reader*, ed. Paul Rabinow (Harmondsworth, 1990), p. 111.

20. You might like to compare this poem – and 'Sojourn in a Second Language' with some of the texts in section 5.4.

21. Contributors' Notes, *Panjandrum 6 & 7*, ed. Dennis Koran (San Francisco, 1978), p. 140.

22. Notes on Authors, *Bluefoot Traveller – An Anthology of Westindian Poets in Britain*, ed. James Berry (1976), p. 52.

23. Notes on Authors, *Bluefoot Traveller – An Anthology of Westindian Poets in Britain*, ed. James Berry (1976), p. 52.

24. After leading their separate publishing careers for some years, the three poets were finally brought together in the book, *Living in Disguise* (Anvil Press, 1986). Their poems were published in distinct sections under their own names, but the book's author was 'unmasked' (back cover) as 'E. A. Markham'.

25. Various arguments already met with above in sections 2.1 and 2.2 might well suggest that there are potential problems with this distinction – but that does not mean that it is not commonly assumed to be true.

26. Moore's own footnote: '*Diary of Tolstoy* (Dutton), p. 84. "Where the boundary between prose and poetry lies, I shall never be able to understand. The question is raised in manuals of style, yet the answer to it lies beyond me. Poetry is verse: prose is not verse. Or else poetry is everything with the exception of business documents and school-books".'

27. Moore's own footnote: '*Yeats: Ideas of Good and Evil* (A. H. Bullen), p. 182. "The limitation of [Blake's] view was from the very intensity of his vision; he was a too literal realist of imagination, as others are of nature; and because he believed that the figures seen by the mind's eye, when exalted by inspiration, were 'eternal existences', symbols of divine essences, he hated every grace of style that might obscure their lineaments".'

28. This kind of interpretation is also undoubtedly the one suggested by the nature of this exercise – which focuses on a single text, and provides no other contexts in which to read it.

29. It is the three-line version which is printed in *The Complete Poems of Marianne Moore* (1953), p. 36. Does this make the shorter version the definitive text? One might note also Moore's epigraph to that volume: 'Omissions are not accidents'.

30. *The Norton Anthology of Poetry* (3rd edn), Biographical Sketches, p. 1919.

31. The opening of this chapter is discussed in section 1.2, above.

3 Genre

1. Both starting and end dates are approximate. Medieval mystery plays developed from religious drama originally performed in churches from as early as the tenth

century; versions played in European cities and towns developed later. Mystery plays stopped being performed after Henry VIII's reformation in the 1540s, but not immediately in all places. Mystery plays were still being performed in York in the 1560s, and it is often assumed that Shakespeare saw such plays being performed during his childhood in the 1580s, since there is reference in *Hamlet* to King Herod and the particular acting style associated with him in the mystery tradition ('it out-Herods Herod', Act III, scene ii, l. 14, The Arden Shakespeare, 1982).

2. The term 'discursive properties' is one coined by Todorov to indicate the features or rules about what is to be included and excluded which are specific to a particular 'discourse': 'we find that any aspect of discourse can be made obligatory'.

3. Unless that is a non-generic category – but if it is to be distinguished from another genre through 'discursive properties' that seems unlikely.

4. A kind of 'discourse on genres' which Todorov calls 'metadiscursive' in contrast to the 'discursive' form manifested in examples of texts which display markers of genre. See 'the Origin of Genres', p. 17 in *The Genres of Discourse* (1978, 1990).

5. Sidney was probably on fairly unsafe political ground here. A tragedy might make a tyrant manifest himself by causing him to openly seize powers beyond those properly belonging to a king – an idea of a check to royal power which it might not be risk-free to assert. All plays, and theoretically all books, in sixteenth- and seventeenth-century England were subject to censorship by the monarch's appointed censor, and plays certainly did provoke direct royal intervention on occasion. It has been suggested that Sidney had republican leanings; certainly the power of tragedy seems a radical one here.

6. There has been an assumption so far in this section that genre labelling does correspond to the empirical occurrence of genre and genre markers in texts. It is, of course, possible that things are not so straightforward, and that assigning texts, or at least some texts, to a genre category is an interpretative as much as a 'factual' decision. If this is so, then it is possible that the reader's or critic's expectations about genre – even if manifestly mistaken or unusual – can contribute considerably to how a text constructs its meanings for them. To put this another way, there is not necessarily an exact match between a discourse of genre in a text, and the metadiscursive 'discourses of genre' which are used to describe or analyse it.

7. This is, of course, the kind of reading we carried out for the poem 'Poetry' in section 2.3 and which Anthony Easthope suggests is a specific kind of reading practice: 'the modernist reading' in section 1.3.

8. This particular opening to a novel also seems to show us collapsed into one both the ancestor and the descendant of the self-narration/novel genre Todorov discusses earlier in this section: the first person speaker here is indeed telling us a story about himself and is also the central character of a novel.

9. I am undoubtedly influenced in my reading by a further piece of knowledge – or conditioning – which could be called generic. This poem is famously one which is used to exemplify Pound's imagist ideas about poetry, in which the image was meant to have precisely the effect I have just described. The distinction between what we expect to happen and what actually happens is not an easy one, since our starting points in reading a text are very influential.

10. I hope it is needless to say that you do not have to be convinced by this or any other of my 'sample' interpretations! It might be equally interesting to argue that this poem really has done things which cannot be done in the pastoral genre, and has thus broken out of the genre to which it seems to belong.

11. Like the poet's feelings in 'Iago Prytherch'.

12. The second half of the essay, which is omitted here, discusses the particular example of a story called 'The Madness of the Day' by Maurice Blanchot – the same writer whose proclamation of the death of genre is referred to by Todorov in section 3.1.

13. Though I am nervous of the phrase 'an internal pocket larger than the whole'. I have drawn a diagram based on the assumption that 'whole' means larger than the 'genre

"itself" ' set – by drawing an enveloping boundary round the central set. It is possible that the phrase could be read differently to mean that there is a set actually within 'genre "itself" ', which is nevertheless of larger extent than that set. This would be more paradoxical and difficult to represent within a Venn diagram, since the 'genre boundary set' would have two differently sized inside/outside spacial representations – which would presumably undermine the normal assumptions of 'the codes of set theory'. This does not rule the interpretation out though, since Derrida specifically says that his use of ideas of set is figurative. It may be that the paradoxical set constituted by the 'law of the law of genre' is not representable in terms of this kind of diagram which, for those with subdegree maths, at least, seems to be based on sets of a single and finite size.

14. The 'codification of discursive properties' discussed in section 3.1.

15. T. S. Eliot argues that this kind of space for manoeuvre is what allows genre to be more than a dead, static order through allowing both tradition and the individual talent' to interact. See the end of this section.

16. A country festivity to celebrate Whitsun.

17. See R. S. Thomas's 'Iago Prytherch' in section 3.2, who is also without art, though to somewhat different effect.

18. See Todorov's discussion of this view in section 3.1.

19. Quotation from *Chekhov: The Critical Heritage*, ed. Victor Emeljanow (London, 1981), p. 103.

20. *Reliques of Ancient English Poetry: Consisting of old Heroic Ballads, Songs and other pieces of our earlier poets, together with some few of later date* [compiled] by Thomas Percy; ed., with a general introduction, additional prefaces, notes, glossary etc., by Henry B. Wheatley, 3 vols (1886). (Reprinted New York, 1966.) Includes 'Titus Andronicus' Complaint', 'The Merchant of Venice (the Bond story)' and a version of John Ford's play *The Broken Heart*. See vol. I, pp. 224–9, 211.

21. Both comments are quoted in Wayne McKenna's 'Lamb as Critic of Shakespeare', *Charles Lamb and the Theatre*, ch. V (Gerrards Cross, 1978), p. 97. The chapter also includes, of course, discussion of Lamb's essay on Shakespeare.

22. It is notable how much Lamb's essay is preoccupied with *Hamlet* in particular. Indeed, his comments on the merely physical gestures of actors seem closely related to Hamlet's lecture about acting and his concerns about the relation of acting to the 'passions' within: 'What's he to Hecuba and Hecuba to him?' See discussion of *Hamlet* in section 2.1.

23. See the discussion of interpretation in section 2.3.

4   History

1. Sidney is, of course comparing literature itself with history, rather than literary criticism with history – which is the focus of this section. Nevertheless, the contrast between fact and fiction is still relevant in contrasting the broad interests of the two disciplines and the ways in which they have been thought about.

2. No actual degree may look quite like this archetype, but many share this general organisation.

3. Genre is often another criterion (usually, as here, within a generally periodic grouping).

4. I don't think it was April 1.

5. The issues are particularly complicated for works which began in an oral tradition and which were therefore in circulation for a long period before being recorded as written texts. In effect, such texts might be said to carry their own history of frequent rewritings within themselves, and to have a *number* of different periods of origin. A related effect could be said to have an impact on all works which occur in more than one text or edition, since there will be material from different periods associated with the text, which bear on its interpretation.

6. There will be more to say about history and stories – but for the present, this is a reasonable assumption to start from.

7. Though as the Marianne Moore 'Poetry' exercise in section 2.3 showed, some kinds of critical enquiry invoke history more than others.

8. Though presumably some of the texts involved would be of an unfamiliar kind to literary critics – particularly ones with mainly numerical contents, such as statistical tables, financial accounts and so on.

9. Though students on joint History/English degrees can claim expertise in both disciplines.

10. Membership of a dissenting church, such as the Methodist or Baptist, rather than of the established Anglican Church.

11. Reflecting what I take to be real historical practice; I suspect that any instruction to produce an interpretation of this passage without any particular line of enquiry would make little sense to a historian.

12. It is notable that history has not been much interested in the *genre* of its primary sources (though a distinction is sometimes drawn between public and private documents), whereas literary critics regard genre as a major determinant of meaning. It could be argued that 'real' documents are genreless – but this is not self-evident (see section 3.1).

13. So too would some literary critics, but critics, as you will have gathered from reading earlier sections of this book, tend to be less happy with any simple assignation of a text's meaning to the author. However, such a complication does not necessarily make the author an irrelevant figure in the interpretation of a text for either historian or critic.

14. And he died in 1892 anyway – so he may not tell us that much about the whole decade of the 1890s!

15. But as discussed in section 2.1, the question of where texts end is not a simple one either.

16. Just as we looked in section 2.3 at a range of actual examples of what critics do.

17. See the approach made to this feature of the poem in section 2.1.

18. This question seems similar in its supposition of an actuality behind the textual evidence to that posed as a historical enquiry in section 4.1: 'What does this primary source tell us about unity in the period 1850–1880?'

19. There is detailed discussion of the plays in the whole article, but the focus of the argument is not one which suggests interests too close to the literary end of the line.

20. See section 4.1 for this as a definition of history's inclusive field of study.

21. As discussed in the Introduction II, there are no ultimate definitions which answer all questions – yet we must continually act and speak with the range of definitions which we (variably) understand.

22. A phrase borrowed from the American thinker Frances Fukuyama's book, *The End of History and the Last Man* (1992). Fukuyama argues that with the collapse of Soviet Communism, the dynamic of history as a struggle between opposed forms of politics has ended. I am adapting the phrase to suggest that if certain accepted assumptions about the discipline of history collapse, then there will be a different kind of end to 'History'. Both senses may well be related to aspects of postmodernity.

23. Annals are a form of history, or at least a record of the past, in which events are briefly and simply listed in chronological order. Chronicles also list events, usually year by year, but give more detail and description of events. Both forms were often used in the early middle ages in particular. Hayden White observes that historians usually rank chronicles above annals as being closer to 'proper' history – on the grounds, he suggests, that chronicles in their reporting of details have a higher element of narrativity than is found in annals, though they do not obviously have a full plot structure and narrative closure.

24. This would make the 'plotting' performed so clearly by Arthur Pollard on the history of Victorian England (discussed in section 4.1) – where he divided the period into what we can now call a 'story-shaped' beginning, middle and end – less 'unhistorical' than if being compared to a model where history was seen as 'nonnarrative'.

25. This is not the first time that we have seen literary devices crossing the boundary (if that is what it is) between the textual and the real. The new historicist Stephen Greenblatt's piece on *Henry V* also suggested that textual relations operated in reality – though in that case they were reported as actually occurring in Elizabethan society, rather than involving them only at the stage of writing about those events in historical study. We might also recall Todorov in section 3.1 arguing that generic models were not confined to literary texts, but common to all utterance.

26. The scientific 'nomological-deductive mode' is distinguished in Hayden White's Preface from narrative modes, but, while some would argue for the objective basis of science, probably not all thinkers would accept that scientific reasoning is outside narrativity or the discursive construction of meaning. Jean-François Lyotard, for instance, notes that science frequently does justify itself through narrative forms, at least, even though its formal procedures are often regarded as 'nonnarrative': 'This return of the narrative in the nonnarrative...should not be thought of as having been superseded once and for all. A crude proof of this: what do scientists do when they appear on television or are interviewed in the newspapers after making a "discovery?" they recount an epic of knowledge that is in fact wholly unepic. They play by the rules of the narrative game...' (from 'The Narrative Function and the Legitimation of Knowledge', in *The Postmodern Condition: A Report on Knowledge* (1984; first published in French, 1979), pp. 27–8.

27. We have already met this idea in the context of literary history in section 4.1, with Frank Kermode's argument that periodisation always constructs the past in terms of the values of the present.

5   Identities

1. That is, ideas about the function and nature of authors and texts.

2. Just as, perhaps, the texts in this book are as much functions in a system as autonomous wholes with clear borders. See section 2.1 – and, of course, the whole procedure of *Thinking About Texts*. At the same time, the specificity and particularity of individual instances is still important: texts are not simply interchangeable.

3. Though we also met a number of different models of originality and authorship – some older, some newer.

4. A state which the phrase 'expatiate in common' nevertheless seems to imagine as a gentleman's club.

5. These are all vast areas in which much work has been done: these sections can only hope to be introductory; they are intended to trace some possibilities, not to give an exhaustive account of current approaches, let alone of the enormous primary or secondary literature.

6. *Chambers Twentieth Century Dictionary* (1979 edn).

7. Ibid.

8. A distinction that some would deny – see for example the discussion of the passage from Margaret Atwood's *The Handmaid's Tale* in section 3.3, as well as the remainder of this discussion.

9. You do not simply have to accept this idea – the death of the person – of course. The material which follows may suggest some ways of resisting these ideas, if you wish.

10. Or, anyway, Barthes as Author of the essay refuses to allow the reader to be an Author. See the discussion which follows.

11. A phrase from John Clare's poem, 'An Invite to Eternity', l. 14, in *Clare: Selected Poems and Prose*, ed. Eric Robinson and Geoffrey Summerfield (Oxford, Oxford University Press, 1966), p. 223.
12. Or would 'explore' be a better word?
13. From Edward E. Sampson's 'Foundations for a Textual Analysis of Selfhood', cited above.
14. Quoted by Edward E. Sampson, see p. 278 above.
15. See section 4.1 for the work there on Victorian social cohesion and class unity.
16. And it is important to be aware of other factors: was there not a notion of 'literature' needed for middle-class Victorians too? Perhaps this might be motivated by a different set of class viewpoints. Moreover, I suspect that many historians would see literature as playing a relatively small part in this process of diffusing class conflict, so that to see its most immediate role as an agent in this should perhaps not be taken as self-evident. See section 1.3.
17. That is the Walter Raleigh who was Professor of Literature at Oxford from 1904 until his death in 1922.
18. Eagleton, *Literary Theory – An Introduction* (1983), p. 35.
19. Recent introductions to literary theory or English studies for undergraduates rarely give class any prominence, but do tend to discuss gender, sexuality and race extensively.
20. A hybrid genre, presumably using features of a novel with the underlying function of allowing the author to 'tell his own story', as Todorov puts it (see section 3.1). Isherwood points out in a note 'To the Reader' that 'I have used a novelist's licence,… and given … fictitious names'.
21. It is said that it was considered impolite amongst certain classes in England between the wars to mention class terms too explicitly. Arthur Marwick in *Class: Image and Reality* (London, 1980), quotes in his epigraph an observation made by the British historian A. H. Tawney in 1931: 'the word "class" is fraught with unpleasing associations, so that to linger upon it is apt to be interpreted as the symptom of a perverted mind and a jaundiced spirit'.
22. Note the pun linking shared education and class identity.
23. Though one should note Engel's footnote, which points out that – according to then recent archaeological/anthropological work – class struggle was not necessarily the key theme of pre-history, since that period was dominated by primitive communism.
24. Though one might note that their multiple-term terminology and their two-term terminology are not perhaps of quite the same kind: while class labels like 'vassals, guild masters, journeymen', etc. are terms which they suggest were actually used in medieval society, it is not mentioned that the terms 'bourgeiosie' and 'proletariat' are not necessarily taken verbatim from the language use of nineteenth-century European society. Victorian class terminologies in Britain, for example, often deploy a three-term scheme: labouring, middle and upper classes. The terms 'bourgeoisie' and 'proletariat' could be said to be analytic terms developed by Marx and Engels from existing but already rarer and more technical terms than the more colloquial terms in use. Marx and Engels' sense of the two terms is not necessarily one found in any usage before their own. See Arthur Marwick's comments in Passage 2 on both class terminology and on two- or three-term class divisions, and the *Oxford English Dictionary* entries for 'bourgeoisie' and 'proletariat'.
25. Marx and Engels' ideas were, of course, developed through many different texts written at different stages of their thought, contain cruxes and are variously interpretable. But these basic ideas from the Manifesto are central and basic ideas which underpin their – and subsequent classic – Marxist thought.
26. Roger Webster, *Studying Literary Theory: An Introduction*, 2nd edn (London, 1997), p. 58.
27. Unless, those descriptions refer to a middle period – and she has now died of grief?

28. I suspect the poem is influenced at some level by the popular Victorian genre of painting called narrative painting; these paintings implied a narrative by showing one (inevitably) static moment, but from which the preceding and succeeding elements of the story could be more or less clearly deduced. Not only something of the technique of Christina Rossetti's poem, but perhaps even the subject matter might be influenced by creative response to this genre, since one strand of the genre often did depict moments of marital harmony or breakdown, and another strand quite often took scenes in artists' studios for their subject.

29. Though 'art' in Victorian Britain was also sometimes seen as belonging to a feminised, aesthetic sphere – outside the more properly masculine industrial sphere of making 'real things', of transforming the actual world, rather than of making images. This feminised view of art – and literature – may play a part in Christina Rossetti's artist whose obsession with the image removes him from 'reality'.

30. A very well known essay in which Woolf discussed what she sees as the failings of the previous generation of 'Georgian' novelists and suggests some ways forward for the novel.

31. Reprinted in the appendix to Lyn Pykett's *Engendering Fictions: The English Novel in the Early Twentieth Century* (1995), pp. 160–1.

32. The eponymous heroine of Arnold Bennett's novel *Hilda Lessways* (1911).

33. I note, for example, that sometimes gender oppositions are complicated: thus the male author is compared to a hostess at one point, and that which passes for literature seems feminised rather than masculine.

34. They are terms particularly associated with Cixous, and with Jacques Derrida, but have been quite widely used in feminist criticism since the 1970s. The two terms – which suggest related conceptions – are also run together in the term 'phallogocentrism' = a centring on the phallos/logos.

35. The phallus both in its Greek origins and in the thought of Cixous is not necessarily a literal penis, but the – allegedly – masculine generative principle in general.

36. This perception of an end point for (Western?) logocentrism might be related to several other perceptions of major shifts of culture towards the end of the twentieth century: see Barthes on the death of the Author in section 2.2 and Hayden White's sense of the collapse of narratives in section 4.3.

37. This is a genre question, of course: can the genre 'critical essay' contain the departures undertaken here?

38. *Thinking About Texts* should ideally, for instance, be a model of this kind of step-by-step explicitness, so that every move and every assumption in an argument is clear.

39. I take it that the point is that these couples are never really couples, but always victor and victim, twinned always to be immediately separated, with one term reduced to ruin and death.

40. Laura Kipnis's summary of the association between *écriture féminine* and postmodernism in *Modernism/Postmodernism*, ed. Peter Brooker (1992), pp. 207–8.

41. There are possible responses to this, of course. One could say that the majority of human experience is textual, and that shifts in one kind of textual representation or reading establish the possibility of shifts in other kinds of text. Indeed, the postmodern is notably said to be not only a form of avant-garde art, but also to have become the dominant popular mode. But then not all commentators see postmodernism as inherently radical, liberating or necessarily a mode with any single deterministic meaning.

42. As Peter Brooker observes in his introduction to the essay, in *Modernism/Postmodernism*, p. 197.

43. From 'Introduction: the Rise of Gender' in *Speaking of Gender* (Routledge, London and New York, 1989), pp. 1–2.

44. We have already seen striking examples of these kinds of interactions in the passage by Christopher Isherwood in section 5.1.

45. Paragraphs 1 and 7; the piece is reprinted in J. M. Golby (ed.), *Culture & Society in Britain 1850–1890* (Oxford, Oxford University Press, 1986), pp. 118–22.

46. This speech was, and in some editions still is, given to Prospero, rather than Miranda (and similarly in some performances). However, there is no textual evidence for this: in the Folio, the speech is Miranda's. The text of *The Tempest* is a good one, with little sign of problems in transmission, so there is no warrant for the alteration. It was first made in the nineteenth century – on the grounds that Miranda could not speak such 'masculine' lines. The speech was felt to be immodest in its anger, and also in its direct reference to her own sexual assault, particularly in speaking to the 'black man', Caliban. I take it that the speech makes most sense if it is Miranda's: indeed, if it is taken away from her, a vital part of what happens between Caliban, Miranda and Prospero is lost, and elements of the play are obscured. Thus assumptions about gender and race can alter 'the' text (see section 2.1 for discussion of textual stability in general).

47. There has been much critical discussion of the distinctiveness of Othello's speech, slightly less of Caliban's.

48. As discussion in section 5.1 may have suggested, some recent thinkers have begun to think that it is *only* narrative which can attempt to bind the multiple experiences of a 'subject' into 'identity', but nevertheless, Othello's emphasis on narrating himself is not what we would expect, since we would be generally more inclined to believe that identity – a continuity between a self and its past selves, between its different experiences and aspects – does not need to be stressed.

49. That is: 'What I have sought to suggest is that this value attached to narrativity in the representation of real events arises out of a desire to have real events display the coherence, integrity, fullness, and closure of an image of life that is and can only be imaginary. The notion that sequences of real events possess the formal attributes of the stories we tell about imaginary events could only have its origins in wishes, day-dreams, reveries.' See section 5.1. This narrative perfection is reminiscent of Othello's frequent use of figures of unalterable perfection, for example: 'content so absolute' (Act II, scene i), 'another world / Of one entire and perfect chrysolite' (Act V, scene ii).

50. But perhaps in the light of sixteenth-century travellers' inclination to report the fabulous, despite the doctrine of natural explanations, this reporting of the Anthropophagi actually asserts his status as European traveller, rather than his own membership of the marvellous/barbarous?

51. This text, edited with an Introduction by Houston A. Baker, is reprinted from the 1845 edition published by 'the Anti-Slavery Office', Boston; there were two later editions with authorial revisions published as *My Bondage and My Freedom* and *The Life and Times of Frederick Douglass*. As ever, the choice of text may have considerable impact on how 'the' text is read. See the Introduction to the Penguin edition for some further detail.

52. This knowledge need not even be written – merely having oral possession of exact dates is regarded by the owners, and by the slaves, as a kind of entry into literacy. Some of the reasons for this emphasis are much clarified by one of Henry Louis Gates's well-known essays on Douglass, an extract from which is the third passage in this group.

53. This, of course, is the owners' formulation of the situation.

54. You may find it useful to compare its references to Caliban to the discussion earlier in this section.

55. The exception perhaps arises from a sense that actually that was a unique defeat for England – that with the death of Harold Godwinson, a certain authentic tradition of Englishness (anglishness, as it were) was lost. The general development of the poem suggests that conquests – Roman and Norman – are part of English history, but it is

notable that while one of the stanzas which refer to the Norman invasion is concerned with continuity ('Ever since Domesday Book'), this other one suggests a break in the continuity of England. Perhaps this loss is one of the things 'lost' referred to in stanza 11, whose 'cease' nevertheless contributes to the birth of England, its long tradition.

Index